A Robert Coles Omnibus

A Robert Coles Omnibus

BY ROBERT COLES

UNIVERSITY OF IOWA PRESS

IOWA CITY

University of Iowa Press, Iowa City 52242

Essays, 1987–1992 copyright © 1993 by the University of Iowa Press

That Red Wheelbarrow: Selected Literary Essays and *Times of Surrender: Selected Essays*

copyright © 1988 by the University of Iowa

Printed on acid-free paper

Library of Congress Cataloging-in-Publication Data

Coles, Robert.

  A Robert Coles omnibus / by Robert Coles.

    p.   cm.

  Contents: Essays, 1987–1992—That red wheelbarrow—Times of surrender.

  ISBN 0-87745-411-6 (pbk.)

  I. Title.

PS3553.O47456A6 1993

814'.54—dc20   92-38346

                                        CIP

97 96 95 94 93 P 5 4 3 2 1

Contents

Essays, 1987–1992

To Jane

Contents

Introduction

As I looked at something called a bibliography of mine, and at the two books which are now to become this one, and at the additional, recent articles now added to the ones already collected in those books, I worry that I may have taken too seriously a self-directed injunction I once heard William Carlos Williams speak: "I've had my low spells, when I wonder about the point of it all, writing included; but the words keep arriving as I sit and think about things, and there's a lot in the world for a writer to see, and try to put into words, so others will see—if you've done a good job!—and that puts an obligation on the one sitting at the typewriter, fingers ready to go: keep trying to do the best you can!" He knew, of course, that we all stumble more than occasionally—yet, he was addressing something other than the matter of success or failure. He was telling himself that the writer's pride (or egoism) notwithstanding, there is, as he pointed out so insistently and powerfully in *Paterson*, much to be seen, documented, contemplated, handed over to others for their notice and reflection: "Outside / outside myself / there is a world, / he rumbled, subject to my incursions / —a world / (to me) at rest, / which I approach / concretely—."

Simply to recall those lines is to return to my college days, when Dr. Williams' writing meant so much to me, and when I met him— a big moment in my life. I still remember him, of course—find myself, at times, looking at a picture of him on a wall of my study; and I still carry in me so many remarks I heard him make, not to mention the poems and stories and novels he gave to all of us readers. As I looked at the essays that follow, including a new batch that takes anyone interested up to the early 1990s, which will coincide, year for year, with my sixties, I thought back to Williams, to the various sides of him I came to know, to admire so much. So doing, I realized, yet again, how much he has meant to me—and, too, how hard I've tried, in my small way, to follow his giant lead.

He was a writer who never stopped being a physician, until illness and old age intervened. Back then I sometimes wondered why—there were so many literary projects inside him, craving expression. But now I think I understand the reason he kept wanting to be with his patients—all they taught him, all they meant to him, and now I think I know how they informed his thinking, his writing, not only in the obvious ways, as his teachers of sorts, but in an indirect manner as well. Once, after we'd left a tenement house where he'd made a doctor's house call, he turned to me and said, tersely: "I think of all this later, and I wish I could do more, so their *life* would be better, not just the illnesses they're struggling to overcome."

He said no more on that subject—we had another visit to make, another child to see. But I read between the lines I'd heard; I realized that a doctor, much engaged with his patients' world—their hopes and worries, their (mostly) hard circumstances—was also a writer who was trying to do with words what justice he could to those people, among others, as he had indicated to be the case in the lines from *Paterson* just cited. Even now, over forty years later, I can remember him working hard to figure out the nature of his various commitments, loyalties, passions, and, too, the way in which he ought to respond to them, given the limits this life sets on all of us.

I think the reader will see, after a glance at the essays I have added and at those that already have a book life in *Times of Surrender* and *That Red Wheelbarrow*, a certain continuity in a writer's concerns—as Williams once put it, laughing, "the same voice trying, still trying, to make itself intelligible and worth attending." The subject matter of these essays of the past six years, in a sense, shadows my current life. I enjoy teaching college students, medical students, very much. I still see a few patients. I have loved bringing stories and novels and poems to business school and law school students at Harvard. I have done some volunteer teaching in ghetto schools in Cambridge and Boston and have learned much from the children I've thereby met. I continue to be my parents' son—my interest in novels and stories surely reflects their great passion for them. More than an "interest," actually: a conviction that a Nadine Gordimer, a Graham Greene (to mention two wonderful novelists about whom I have recently written) have much to tell us, far more, indeed, than the many secular "experts" of various kinds (all too many of them social scientists) whose voices we have in recent decades heeded rather more closely than perhaps we ought to have. But there I go picking a familiar chord, as I suspect the reader will soon enough realize!

I will be most pleased if those who choose to spend time with this book will move from it to others—will make or renew acquaintance with some of the wise, wise souls I've met through the novels, short stories, and poems mentioned in the pages that follow. Even as I was gathering the new essays for this rather large collection and preparing these introductory comments, I had a conversation with theologian Martin Marty of Chicago. At one point he asked me to try to pinpoint, in a sentence, what I felt to be the heart of my work. With little hesitation I heard myself making mention of my favorite writers, from Dr. Williams and James Agee to George Eliot and Tolstoy—thoughtful storytellers and poets whom I've tried to hold up high for myself and for anyone I happen to meet, in person or through the mediation of the printed word. The essays that follow, collected now in one place, give me yet another chance to applaud a sensibility such as George Eliot's and Tolstoy's—a sensibility wide-eyed in its responses to the world's complexities, ironies, ambiguities—and, alas, to remark one more time upon the failure of many of us in today's world to appreciate how much we lose when we ignore or turn away from such a way of seeing things, in favor of the kind pressed upon us daily, it seems, in the name of secular authority.

From the beginning of my work in pediatrics and child psychiatry and psychoanalysis I saw the hunger for certainty, for conclusive and categorical definitions, generalizations with respect to who we are and how we ought to live and for what reasons—a hunger by no means confined to patients and their families. We ourselves, the doctors, were all too easily caught up in one or another enthusiasm, if not cultural or professional obsession. In my own profession of psychiatry I have watched, in a generation's time, an almost unquestioning adherence to psychoanalytic orthodoxy yield to an almost unquestioning expectation regarding so-called social and community psychiatry—and now it is psychobiology, with its proliferating chemical substances that will solve this problem and that one if not, in time (so I hear), all problems that were once "psychological," and soon will be in the domain of biochemistry and neurophysiology.

A mind as subtle and knowing as George Eliot's or Tolstoy's has quite another sense of who we human beings are and what is in store for us. For all we discover (and one doesn't at all intend to demean the accomplishments of recent decades, centuries) we are still very much creatures of language, anxious (as an aspect of our very being, not our psychopathology) to try to understand not only what we are (our material nature) but where, if anyplace, we might be or ought to be headed. Put differently, we are seekers, pilgrims, travelers in search of a moral destination—a way to look at this life, and ourselves as part of it—as well as "psycho-socio-biological entities," a phrase I saw the other day in a journal of social science. A few pages of such a journal and I'm certainly ready to return to Tolstoy's ethical quandaries, as he worked them into his novels, or to Chekhov's wry and poignant evocations of our humanity, embedded in story after story—and I suspect the reader who is interested in traveling a distance with me will not be disappointed by the encouragement, in that regard, I seem to keep giving myself and those who pick up this book.

Why, though, the need for such repeated insistence of a point? My answer, I suppose, is again that of W. C. Williams. In 1955, after I finished medical school, I met him in Chicago; he was reading his poems on a national tour, ailing though he was. He asked me how I was doing, and before I had a chance to go into the details of my exhausted state as an intern he fired another question at me: "What are you reading, when you have some time to read?" I was about to start in with a familiar, self-pitying lament—the little time I had to pick up any printed matter at all. Suddenly, he saw full well, in my face, what was crossing my battle-fatigued mind, so he put another inquiry to me: "Alright, what *would* you want to read, if you had half a chance?"

I hemmed and hawed, said I'd fallen out of touch, mentioned a book or two of nonfiction that dominated the public's interest at the time (and how quickly those books come and go!), only to hear this: "What happened to your old friends?" I looked bewildered: what did he mean? He didn't take long to remind me of conversations we'd had, a few years before, about Dickens and Hardy and Eliot, my English born and reared dad's great favorites, and Tolstoy, whom my Iowa born and reared mother loved all her long life. (She died with *Anna Karenina* and a collection of Tolstoy stories at her bedside.)

Alas, I'd forgotten those novelists, amidst the stresses and strains, the daily tumult of a hectic year. Dr. Williams was there, though, not to listen to my "problems"; not to suggest (God save us, these days) that I find a "support group"; not to give me some reassurance—yes, this will pass, and you'll be much more relaxed and easy-going soon—but rather, to grasp me by the collar, as it were, and bring me to my senses, remind me of those wonderful friends, those companions, those wise folk; those novelists and poets. I left that meeting with Dr. Williams brought up short a bit—newly aware, actually, of what ought to matter. I would be most happy, I would be thrilled, if I were to know that even a little of what he had done for me with his questions, his comments, that time long ago, might also happen to some of those who come upon this book.

New Miscellaneous Essays

Caught in the Undertow

Less than an hour into Thursday, June 13, 1985, a seventeen-year-old black youth, Edmund Perry, of 265 West 114th Street, died in a nearby hospital. He had been shot by a white plainclothesman, Lee Van Houten, who claimed self-defense: two black men had assaulted and beaten him in a robbery attempt, and he had fired at one of them; meanwhile, the other had escaped. It was another brutal encounter, but one that might well have gone unnoticed by the world at large were it not for Perry's educational background. He had graduated with honors eleven days earlier from Phillips Exeter Academy in Exeter, N.H., one of the nation's leading private schools, and had received a full scholarship to the college of his choice, Stanford University.

Soon enough newspapers across the country, radio announcers and television reporters were telling Americans Perry's story—his brief, successful life and his quick, violent death. One of those who learned of the tragedy was Robert Sam Anson, a freelance magazine writer and the author of *McGovern: A Biography* and other books, whose son also attended Exeter and knew the Harlem youth. Mr. Anson's son spoke for many when he doubted the policeman's assertion that he had reacted to an attempted mugging and severe beating—that he feared for his life: "Couldn't be true. Eddie was too smart for that. The cop musta' just killed him."

The author makes clear that the Exeter connection "was, as reporters say, a hook"—the distinctive aspect of a life that made its end a national news event (a front-page story in the *Times*) and, eventually, the subject of *Best Intentions*. Perhaps the most stunning facts the author provides are not about Perry, but about his neighborhood, his people: "In a city like New York, where there are nearly three hundred thousand serious crimes every year, such events are a relative commonplace, particularly in areas like Harlem and especially among young black males, one in ten of whom, the statistics say, will either meet or cause an unnatural end." Such appalling information has somehow disappeared from our nation's consciousness—a fact of everyday life that surfaces occasionally in a parenthetical way, only to recede quickly as we other Americans go about our daily business. For Perry, however, it would not be possible to escape what threatened him, no matter his excellent secondary-school education, and continues to threaten so many others like him.

For a few days the editorialists, black and white, were indignant. The police were bitterly condemned, the young man proclaimed by journalists "a future Moses for his people" and "a prized symbol of hope." Yet less than two weeks later a Manhattan grand jury refused to charge the police officer and described the killing as justifiable homicide—at which point, for many, moral outrage gave way to embarrassed silence and a gnawing perplexity. Moreover, Perry's older brother, Jonah, then nineteen years old and a sophomore at Cornell University, was indicted as an accomplice in the aborted mugging. The policeman's record and testimony no doubt influenced the grand jury. He was young, well educated, anything but gun-happy, a decent person who obviously had been assaulted and beaten before he used his gun—and he was devastated by what had happened, what he had done, had felt he had to do, lest he be killed.

Mr. Anson is interested in exploring Edmund Perry's short life, and especially his education—the irony that someone who had already traveled so far would end up lying on a sidewalk so close to where he had grown up, a cop's bullet in his belly. Perry had not only attended Exeter, he had done well there, and he had also studied in Spain for a year. He had become friendly with a wide circle of white and black students and with a number of teachers in that distinguished northern New England setting—a national high school of sorts that for generations has attracted bright, able young people who want a particularly strenuous, demanding education. How could it happen that someone who spent years in such an environment had come to such an end?

The book is meant to address that question. The author sought out Perry's mother and father, his friends and former teachers, in Harlem and at Exeter. Their comments are the heart of this well-told, melancholy story—so much praise for such a promising life, so much bewilderment and outrage over its outcome.

Without question Edmund Perry was a gifted young man to

whom the white world of private schools extended an earnest, benevolent hand. At Exeter he no doubt struggled hard academically and psychologically, as so many other students do, no matter their racial or social background. He was, like his classmates, away from home, and he was especially close to his mother, a strong and sensitive woman who had obviously inspired her two sons to try to swim free of the ghetto's powerful undertow.

But unlike most of his classmates, Perry was among a relatively small cadre of black students in an aristocratic, white preparatory school, and what can happen under such circumstances was compellingly described to the author by a woman who had filmed Perry one day—while doing a project for A Better Chance, the organization that had recruited him for Exeter. The black film maker's unsparing words tell of her own experiences in a boarding school, and by implication are meant to help all of us realize what it was like, what it can still be like, for the Edmund Perrys who live in such a privileged, yet also difficult, frightening (and confusing and confused) world:

"A white girl can look spacey and people will say, 'Oh, she's being creative.' But if you walk around campus with anything but a big smile on your face, they'll wonder, 'Why is she being hostile?' You always have the sense of being examined. When your mama works for 'em, works for 'em, she can at least go home at night. But when you're at prep school, you're always on—like a twenty-four-hour-a-day cultural attraction. . . .

"Kids would always be asking me about my hair. 'How do you keep it up? What happens when it gets wet? Can I touch it?' It never dawned on them that I found these questions offensive. Why would it? If you are a kid born with a silver spoon in your mouth and grew up on a big estate with servants, then no one has ever said no to you in your life. That's the problem with the white wealthy in this country: they don't know any limits. If you are black, you are there for their pleasure. To provide them with 'an experience.' Sometimes I think that's how these scholarships are sold to white parents. *By God, their kids are going to be well-rounded. They're going to have Rossignol skis and Lange boots and a black roommate for 'an experience.'*"

There was much more said, a good deal of it harsh, unforgiving, heatedly rhetorical. Edmund Perry is described at one point as becoming "schizophrenic," as going "crazy." "That's what they had taught him," the film maker asks, "wasn't it?" But no one, not Perry's family, not his friends or Exeter teachers, had any reason to believe he had lost his mind; quite the contrary, he was a tough, disciplined person who seemed more solidly grounded than many other students—white, from well-to-do and prominent families— some of whom might well have been on their way to schizophrenia, a mental illness that by no means spares white youths of the haute bourgeoisie.

Mr. Anson discovered, eventually, that Perry was a drug dealer at Exeter, that he peddled high-grade pot to some of his classmates, no doubt fueling their laid-back, snotty, solipsistic insouciance. But those Exonians, who lived in a particular dormitory, were not utterly dependent on him for drugs (there were other, white drug dealers around), nor did they turn Perry into a pothead or worse. In them and others all too full of themselves, Perry saw the worst side of a supposedly charmed and erudite world—and he survived it handily. His death took place on the Upper West Side, not at Exeter, but one doubts whether the film maker is right when she calls it a suicide.

Such talk, of schizophrenia or suicide, is perhaps meant indirectly to address the issue of a continuing racism in our society, in our suburbs, our schools, our colleges—the effect of such prejudice on the minds of its victims. The reported incidents, substantial in number (never mind those that go unrecorded), offer their own grim, telltale evidence—of a nation still split by fear, distrust, hate. Nor are the Exeters (or Harvards) of this country entirely blameless—as Exeter's decent and thoughtful headmaster, Stephen Kurtz, was quick to acknowledge when he spoke with Mr. Anson. Indeed, after Edmund Perry's death, the school moved quickly to increase the number of black students there, to increase its scholarship funds, to keep closer watch on its pupils, especially its drug-prone ones, to develop as best it could an atmosphere of understanding and concern for one another among its students and teachers.

Nevertheless, if the grand jury was right, the bottom-line truth is that a youth who had a lot going for himself, no matter the difficult moments in a New Hampshire school, ended up a tough street thief, beating someone up badly because he refused to hand over his wallet. The bottom line for the rest of us is our comprehension of that awful, final moment in a hitherto promising life. Do we reflexively summon those explanatory staples of the liberal, secular pantheon, sociology or psychiatry—even though thousands of youths of all races have overcome terrible personal and social hardships and become eminently decent, law-abiding, and successful people? Do we seize on this life's story as a convenient excuse for racist innuendo or worse—ignoring the gratuitous stealing, the vandalism, the drug dealing, the cheating that take place (but often go unreported) in our finest boarding schools or suburban high schools—well-to-do white youths, smart but of flawed character, who can be mean and crooked in their own sly or not-so-sly ways?

Nor should we forget that policeman—out there on the line, taking it on the chin for many others. He was dispatched to Morningside Heights and Harlem, Mr. Anson tells us, because thieves had been "ripping the radios from the BMWs belonging to the doctors at nearby St. Luke's Hospital." We will never know for sure what exactly transpired. Jonah Perry was acquitted. But Harlem's world persists, and so do the racial incidents on our campuses. And so do the social and political priorities that in their sum have made Edmund Perry, the policeman who killed him (I wish we were told more of his life, his thoughts) and even the students and teachers of the rich and influential and geographically remote Exeter Academy, not to mention all the rest of us Americans, witnesses to a continuing national tragedy.

New York Times Book Review, May 17, 1987

The Death of a Child

*I*n early November 1987, a six-year-old girl, Lisa Steinberg, brought to a New York City hospital comatose, was pronounced dead—a victim of severe and repeated beatings. In the melancholy and wrenching *What Lisa Knew*, Joyce Johnson, a novelist and a contributing editor to *Vanity Fair*, has tried hard and long to understand what such a brief life was like—those few years of agony that culminated in the violent death of a child of supposed privilege: the ostensible mother, Hedda Nussbaum, a onetime editor of children's books at Random House, the ostensible father, Joel Steinberg, a well-off lawyer.

Not that Lisa's death was unique. Ms. Johnson has given much time and energy in an effort to understand what happened to this one child, but reminds us, right off, that "in 1987, an estimated four thousand children died in America as a direct result of abuse." A number of these children, born to humble and impoverished parents, go to their graves with no attendant notice or outcry from the news media. In comparison, we are reminded, "Lisa was one of those children to whom we assign high value." Such "value" prompted close and extended journalistic attention when the story broke, and later, when the father stood trial as responsible for the death. (He was ultimately convicted of first-degree manslaughter and is now in jail.)

Not much detective work was necessary at the hospital before Lisa's experience could be surmised: "Elizabeth Steinberg's small body was a map of pain," Ms. Johnson writes. "The marks were different colors, different vintages. Red, purple, yellowish-brown. It seemed as if she had been hit just about everywhere—on her arms and the calves of her legs, on her chest, her buttocks. One of the biggest bruises was in the center of her lower back—not a place where a child would be likely to injure herself. There were fresh scratches on her elbows, as if someone had grabbed her there. Her parents had just let her go dirty—her feet and ankles had a crust of black grime. The hair and the feet shocked everyone almost as much as the bruises." As for the mother, she had "two black eyes, a split lip, a nose that no longer had a bridge."

Understandably, the world (and later, the criminal justice system) turned on Joel Steinberg. He became known, soon enough, for what he was—a crook, a liar, an accomplice of underworld figures, a spiteful, tricky, brutish man whose professional life is yet another reminder that virtue is not by any means a prerequisite for financial success. Many began to call him a monster, someone whose life in one way or another warrants setting him apart. Yet Ms. Johnson keeps reminding us that this man lived gregariously in a comfortable Manhattan world, had many business associates and friends who had plenty of opportunities to take his moral measure—and see what he was doing to the woman with whom he was living, to his daughter—but who raised no voice of concern, let alone alarm.

The author does her best to try to understand this man, as well as the woman he kept beating for years, even as she refused to leave him—remained stubbornly, even fiercely, attached to him. If Mr. Steinberg inhabited a legal and business demimonde, Ms. Nussbaum achieved a substantial professional respectability. Mr. Steinberg's mean, manipulative, manic manner, his crude personality, his upstart ways and half-crazy palaver came as no surprise to his shyster companions and associates and earned him no reprimands or warnings. But Ms. Nussbaum's fellow workers at Random House became increasingly worried and then horrified by her bruised and battered appearance. The more her women friends tried to advise or warn or help her, the more she angrily detached herself from them and the cultured, refined world in which they had all, as colleagues, hitherto worked. Eventually, Ms. Nussbaum lost her job, became Mr. Steinberg's full-time, constant object of derision and assault. She also became a drug addict—a sometime zombie, people began to notice. Cocaine was her obsession, and she had no trouble stashing away large amounts of it for her daily consumption.

These two not very attractive or stable unmarried individuals refused to settle for their own harsh, coarse madness. They had no problem in illegally procuring two children—Lisa, whose death made her so-called parents all too well known, and Mitchell, who was seventeen months old in 1987 when the public side of this tragedy first began to unfold. Mr. Steinberg was a criminal lawyer in several senses of that phrase. He defended many a lowlife, and he knew how to cut corners, to put it mildly. He and Ms. Nussbaum manipulated the New York State adoption laws to secure a girl and a boy from two frightened young single women. Of help, in that regard, was a network of unscrupulous doctor friends—another riff-raff professional world Mr. Steinberg knew well. In the months that preceded Lisa's death, she and her baby brother—living in New York City's Greenwich Village, on West 10th Street, in the very building Mark Twain once claimed as a residence—had become part of what was supposed to be an upper-middle-class family, but was in fact a living arrangement run amok: a man jabbing and punching at a woman; she, in turn, all drugged up day and night; a little girl increasingly knocked about; a baby boy ignored, left to lie for hours in a urine-soaked crib.

Inevitably, a substantial part of this book is given over to exercises in speculative psychology. The author does her best with that discipline's overwrought, portentous phrases (a secular lingua franca of our time) as she introduces us to Mr. Steinberg's family and Ms. Nussbaum's. But the most careful psychiatric scrutiny doesn't quite explain how these two college-educated, well-to-do, late twentieth-century Americans turned into such a debased, callous, utterly self-preoccupied couple, to whom the lives of two young children meant next to nothing.

No question, Mr. Steinberg's mother comes across as shallow, egotistical, stingy; Ms. Nussbaum's parents as no paragons of emotional strength. But so what? The world is full of vulnerable people who have had difficult childhoods, who have known all sorts of psychological strain and pain—and who have not turned into malign emotional partners or parents. The author, a sensitive and skilled novelist whose work has received quite favorable critical attention, knows to call it quits at a certain point. "In a way," she points out, "it would be a relief to learn that Hedda Nussbaum had been beaten by her parents, that her relationship with her father had been incestuous. That would both explain her and distance her from those of us who consider ourselves more normal than she is. In fact, it appears she was not an abused child at all, that her upbringing was truly as average and uneventful as she said it was." Not that child abuse or family violence is exclusively a matter of "upbringing" come home to roost. Social and economic upheaval or vulnerability prompts an increase in such violence, as emergency ward physicians

and pediatricians living in certain neighborhoods or entire cities that
have been hit hard by rising unemployment well know. Family violence also increases in response to alcohol and drug abuse—and
those problems also rise in frequency among jobless people.

Needless to say, partisans of psychological determinism will insist
on some formulation that accounts for the behavior of Mr. Steinberg
and Ms. Nussbaum, both individually and together. The author
tries her best to address this issue: quotes at length, for example,
from Rollo May's *Love and Will*, even imagines Ms. Nussbaum,
"with her appetite for literature on sex and psychology," reading that
1969 book, and offers us such startling and original cultural profun-
dities from it as this: "It is always true that love and will become
more difficult in a transitional age, and ours is an era of radical
transition. The old myths and symbols by which we oriented ourselves are gone, anxiety is rampant; we cling to each other and try
to persuade ourselves that what we feel is love." As for Ms. Nussbaum's way of getting on with her so-called lover, Rollo May has
this dramatic pronouncement for his readers: "When inward life
dries up, when feeling decreases and apathy increases, when one
cannot affect or even genuinely *touch* another person, violence
flares up as a daimonic necessity for contact, a mad drive forcing
touch in the most direct way possible. This is one aspect of the
well-known relationship between sexual feelings and crimes of violence: to inflict pain and torture at least proves that one can affect
somebody."

Such a way of seeing things was quite familiar to Ms. Nussbaum,
whether she had read Rollo May's book or not. She knew phrases
such as "sadomasochistic relationship," or "folie à deux"—phrases
that one day would fill the air as people tried to put a fast fix on her
psychological life. She had been in and out of "treatment" for years
before she took up with Mr. Steinberg, was seeing a therapist three
times a week as she cemented that fateful friendship. She had visited
doctors alone and in "group sessions." She had "tried Biofeedback."
She had been "Rolfed for a few months." She had gone to "Dr.
Albert Ellis, a best-selling authority on sexual responsiveness." The
author dryly observes that "none of these therapies succeeded in
liberating the real Hedda." Meanwhile, naturally, Mr. Steinberg
talked with no one about himself—only looked for people whom (at
work or at play) he might con.

As this patient, shrewd storyteller worked her way through what she calls the "blanks and blind alleys" of an attempted biographical study, the weight of psychological banality obviously became oppressive and stifling to her. One by one certain words start making a credible appearance in her text—"choice," "will," "evil," "responsibility." At such moments, as with George Eliot's authorial voice in *Middlemarch*, Ms. Johnson becomes the aroused chronicler of a moral tale. At what point is any of us responsible for our actions—no matter the trials and tribulations (evident or hidden) of our early or later years? (Hitler was a victim of what we now call child abuse—he and his mother constantly tyrannized by an alcoholic man whose raging fists surely marked a stepson for life.) Put differently, when ought psychological analysis to give way to moral judgment? The author makes clear, finally, her own position.

It is not hard, Ms. Johnson knows, for many of us to condemn Mr. Steinberg, his putatively unhappy childhood notwithstanding. Ms. Nussbaum, in contrast, received from many enormous sympathy. She was quickly wrapped in a thick psychiatric cloak, was flanked by her lawyer and doctor, neither of them especially camera-shy, and was not put on trial, even though many of the jurors felt that she was partially responsible for Lisa Steinberg's death (she testified that after the child was severely injured, she smoked cocaine with Mr. Steinberg for hours before calling 911). By the end of the book, the author is also quite willing to emphasize the significant "role" that Ms. Nussbaum "played in Lisa Steinberg's life and death." In an interesting afterthought, Ms. Johnson declares: "Clearly she has no understanding of what she did that was so wrong—of how she sinned, if one dares to use such an old-fashioned term."

Some will charge the author with blaming the victim, but she argues, in her own way, for a kind of old-fashioned respect for Hedda Nussbaum that is moral rather than psychological—her right to be judged ethically rather than exculpated through the dreary, trite phrases of contemporary psychology, a dubious ally, anyway, because what can be given (the masochist as a onetime hurt child) can also be taken away (the masochist as a sly, insistent, clinging aggressor, feeding off and provoking constantly a tormentor's rage).

Ms. Johnson is neither a Diana Trilling nor an Elizabeth Hardwick, either of whom, I suspect, would have written with more sardonic bite and would have risked a grander impatience with the cast of seedy, self-absorbed, nasty characters who populate this story—

their actions, finally, the essence of "what Lisa knew" in her all too brief life. But Ms. Johnson, constrained by factuality as Henry James was not when he gave us *What Maisie Knew*, does eventually develop a fine narrative momentum. Her novelist's eye for detail and character portrayal serve her and us well—nowhere better than during those moments when she reminds us that some New Yorkers possessed both moral intuition and moral energy in response to their fleeting encounters with young Lisa. Even though the girl's teachers apparently (and incredibly) noticed nothing alarming in their day-to-day work with her, hours and hours of presumably close contact, a frightened neighbor repeatedly contacted city agencies and warned of the violence she suspected was taking place in the Steinberg apartment. And a New York State Thruway toll collector (unlike those teachers, she had no fancy university degrees, had taken no courses in something called educational psychology), on the basis of a second's look at Lisa and her father in a car, immediately suspected that the child was in grave jeopardy and got the highway police called—in vain, though. The lawyer Joel Steinberg, ever the wily, truculent blabbermouth, knew well how to keep secure guard over his particular realm—until death carried off one of its young inhabitants.

New York Times Book Review, April 8, 1990

Teaching Our Children to See

I first started asking children to draw or paint pictures—of themselves, their friends, parents, teachers, the schools they attended—when I was learning to be a pediatrician and, then, a child psychiatrist. Boston experienced in the mid 1950s a polio epidemic, one of the last before the Salk vaccine came into use. At the Children's Hospital, we young doctors had a lot to do, struggling with a disease that could not only paralyze limbs but take lives. As the condition of the children improved, I heard Job's questions and doubts surface in all sorts of ways. Here were boys and girls, suddenly frightened, anxious, moody, asking what this life means and why they, so young, had been hit so hard by fate, by bad luck.

It was at such moments, when a particular child would become silently sad—uninterested, even, in talking about his or her worries—that I called upon crayons and paintbrushes. I asked whether we might draw or paint together, explaining that I was interested in what young people choose to depict. Soon enough I had a portfolio of pictures—the visual testimony of boys and girls wondering long and hard about their present circumstances, their future lives. One girl drew herself standing, with a pair of crutches leaning against a nearby tree. She was not sure she'd ever be able to walk without those crutches, but she was expressing a hope—and indicating an apprehension. Only after she'd completed her drawing would she begin putting into words some of what she felt.

A few years later, when I was working with black and white children caught up in the school desegregation struggles of the 1960s, I would ask the children of eight or nine to draw or paint. These students were delighted to portray themselves or their school buildings as a way of conversing with me, telling me what was on their minds. As Anna Freud once told me, "For many children a drawing is a serious, heartfelt statement." I would often think of those words as I saw black children taking pains to let me know, through the use of crayons and paints, how vulnerable they felt, how endangered—

or white children declare, also through a drawing or painting, how important they felt (in contrast to blacks) or, yes, how sorry they felt for "them," the black classmates, whom they depicted as smaller or more disjointed. The more I studied those drawings and paintings, the more I realized how adversely racial conflict bears down on everyone, the weak and the powerful alike.

Recently I have introduced a modest "art history" course in certain third- and fourth-grade classrooms. We look at Renoir's paintings, some of van Gogh's, including his prison and hospital scenes, Käthe Kollwitz's lithographs, Picasso's early works and *Guernica*, and pictures by others, including Max Beckmann, Edvard Munch, N. C. Wyeth, Camille Pissarro. The children, many from ghetto families, are quick to respond to the thematic side of the works, but also note arrangements of color, or the shapes and sizes of objects. Then the children do their own drawings—not merely copying but showing their originality and capacity for social and moral reflection. Our discussions reveal how affected they are by what they see.

Yet, in a year or two, those same children will have absolutely no contact at school with crayons and paints, with slides, with art books. I have worked in every part of this country, visited junior high schools and high schools, and noticed with dismay and sadness how abruptly the visual education of the children is terminated once they leave elementary school. Not that art education is always so well taught in the lower grades. Too often the "subject" called art is regarded as a "minor" one. But at least it offers some recognition of the possibilities that painting and drawing can present to students— a chance to take reflective stock of the world, size it up, render it, and of course, construct one's own world, first in the imagination, then on paper. In high school such occasions are denied young people—at just the moment when they might use them to significant intellectual, aesthetic, and ethical effect.

Drawing or painting or the contemplation of art history can be a way of coming to terms with the world. I have been able to talk with children about matters of race and class, about a whole range of moral, social, and political questions, as we sat looking at Rembrandt and Gauguin, Hopper and El Greco—crossing at will centuries and continents in pursuit of moments of meditation. A pity such moments are denied our youths as they grow and become even more open to the world in all its variousness.

Especially for ghetto youth, but for all high schoolers as well, art and music can be more immediately accessible than academic language. I have brought Charlie Parker's music to classrooms where children sit gazing at Gauguin's Tahiti scenes, and the result is a room full of excited minds, intensely responsive to sights, to sounds. These days as I hear talk of "cultural literacy," I think of visual literacy—how it might be taught in our schools and colleges. Need we let children become visually illiterate, when so much might be done for them, for all of us, to connect their eyes and what they see to their mind's reflective power, their heart's motions? In giving up painting and drawing, children are losing a native language.

Children of Poverty Making
Do with Ease and Zest

An observer's assumptions, interests, social outlook, and political viewpoint can give telling shape to what is seen, learned, and later recorded through words or pictures for others to know. So it has gone with many of us who have tried to understand the thinking of children, their hopes and worries; and so it has gone, too, with photographers who have tried to document the everyday lives of children.

For more than a century, children have figured in photographic explorations of social reality. In 1877 John Thompson, a well-known English photographer, collaborated with a reporter, Adolphe Smith, in a study published as "Street Life in London." The effort was supposed to show as well as tell how ordinary people spent time in the streets of one of the world's great capital cities. The reader meets children examining wares, shining shoes, peering into restaurants, ogling or eating "halfpenny ices," looking at locksmiths at work. Attention is not directed specifically toward the children, however; they appear, mostly, with adults—as part of the complex, bustling neighborhood activity we are meant to observe at a remove through pictures.

A few decades later, in America, Lewis Hine used the camera to approach children quite differently: they stand before cotton mills, inside factories, down mine shafts, already young workers. Thompson wanted to inform viewers, satisfy their curiosity; Hine wanted to awaken their conscience, stir them to social concern, if not moral outrage. His children are much like those in Dickens' novels: they are victims, and the privileged readers and viewers, now newly informed, have a chance to try to rescue other children—presumably by the way they vote or the causes they rush to endorse.

Much of Hine's best documentary work with children was done around 1910. More than a generation later, during the middle 1930s, Farm Security Administration photographers roamed the American land, though, unlike Thompson or Hine, they weren't inclined to look with any special interest at children. The young people who appear in some of the photographs that make up that tradition are usually (in the case of Dorothea Lange or Walker Evans or Ben Shahn) members of families that are down and out, even dispossessed, and so on the road. Viewers are again asked to be aroused, to make known their compassion, their political sympathy, but the major thrust of the FSA work was directed at rural America, then a more significant part of the country's population than it is now. Roy Stryker, who headed the FSA, knew that the destitute children of white farm workers were the ones to enlist the pity of millions of bourgeois Americans, for whom the yeomanry class had special meaning.

Helen Levitt, whose photographs have recently been on display at the Metropolitan Museum of Art, came to photography a little later, toward the end of the 1930s, when the Great Depression would soon give way to a recovery much boosted by World War II. She never worked for the FSA, and her interests were urban. She took to the streets of her native New York in search of images—rather than in the interest of muckraking journalism or at the behest of a social conscience.

To be sure, the streets whose life she recorded were in Spanish Harlem; the children whose lives she especially wanted to know and document were by and large poor; and the neighborhood in which they lived forms a quite visible background to her various pictures of them—rows of old brownstones, other tenement houses with less interesting architectural properties, the old El, casting its darkness on people, on stores, on half-abandoned buildings or the empty lots beside or behind them.

But taking center stage are the children, who most emphatically do not strike us as victims, as sick, beaten down, exploited. They play games intently, smile, boast, strut, tease, and taunt. They make do with ease, even zest—dipping in the water that hydrants can be made to give, finding hideaways, climbing walls, even a lone city tree, and always keeping on the move, their legs taking them every-where, it seems, and their arms ever ready to play tag, their hands to grasp a toy.

Their faces often wear smiles; their eyes are open, eager to take in the world. Sometimes they are seen as artists; they have used chalk to draw on the sidewalks and the street. These chalk drawings

(Levitt did more than a hundred photographs of them) show boys and girls full of fun, ingenuity, joy: birds and fish and animals and boats and bicycles and people keep company with all sorts of wonderfully appealing or provocative comments, exhortations, questions. "F. Mintz owes Henrie 35 cents," we are told. "Lardy is conceited," a young moralist has concluded. A child asks: "Have you got a jolly face?" We learn that: "Bill Jones mother is a Hore" and "Brother Loves His Mother" and, more discursively, "May and Junior Wet out to the store and spent 10 cents: A Trew Story."

Helen Levitt's children are sporty, canny, constantly ready to find a good time. They build their forts, sort themselves in accordance with their psychological chemistry, declare their loves and hates quite openly, but seem altogether lively, funny—not at all despairing. Even in the presence of urban decay, the young people call us away—toward themselves, their natural rhythms, their spontaneous gestures, the winks and nods and smirks and grimaces of childhood. They take a broken-down building and make it a club. They convert empty, garbage-strewn city acreage into a makeshift playground, and are seen living it up there. Viewers are given a visual urban sociology in accord with the deep store of moral, intellectual, and psychological energy in essentially solid, sturdy youngsters.

A generation later, in 1972, and virtually on the same territory, Bruce Davidson offered (in his book *East 100th Street*) *his* Spanish Harlem, *his* children, now a quite different scene to contemplate. The children witness forlornly, grimly, and in obvious jeopardy, a bleak, deteriorating, even squalid world. A girl, her head bent, her face enveloped in a shadow, is virtually impaled on a fire escape wall, a late twentieth-century crucifixion. The viewer's eye is directed at litter and debris, at utterly desolate streets, at drunks and derelicts and the deranged. Helen Levitt's children know that there may be hardship hereabouts, yet their humanity in all its complexity somehow transcends it; Davidson's children are melancholy, indeed. His is a more recent version of the FSA documentary tradition, though the landscape is unrelievedly focused on one ghetto street.

Even closer to our time, Sally Mann, a Virginia photographer, has an altogether different slant on children. Hers are well-to-do rather than poor, and they tend to be self-absorbed—no gangs, no messages for or about others, only gazes that bespeak a host of worries or anxieties or lusts within young bodies that are often as exposed as the assorted feelings within them: visual accompaniments to or artifacts of what Christopher Lasch has so precisely and shrewdly called the "culture of narcissism." Those photographs, and of course Bruce Davidson's, suggest that we are all doomed to loneliness or misunderstanding, or God knows what hang-ups, be it by virtue of sociology or psychology.

In contrast, Helen Levitt's pictures remind viewers of the redemptive possibilities within a community, even one down on its luck: boys and girls who don't have much nevertheless have one another, and with great exuberance seize each day for all it is worth. The viewer is asked for no sorrow, no act of condescending pity, no highfalutin "policy paper" with various social and political recommendations—only to marvel at and enjoy, in Flannery O'Connor's phrase, the "mystery and manners" of childhood.

Community Service Work

W hen I was a college student I did "volunteer work," as we then called it. I tutored some boys and girls who were having trouble with reading, writing, arithmetic. I left one part of Cambridge, Massachusetts, for another—often on foot, so that I could enjoy what my father had taught me to call a good hike. When I came back to "school," certain scenes I had witnessed and certain statements I had heard would stay with me—come to mind now and then as I pursued various courses, lived a certain late-adolescent life.

Often, when I went home to visit my parents, they inquired after my extracurricular teaching life. My mother was inclined to be religiously sentimental: it was good that I was helping out some youngsters in trouble. For her the sin of pride was around any corner; hence our need to escape that constant pull of egoism—to work with others on behalf of their lives, with our own, for a change, taking a back seat. My father, a probing scientist, commonly took a different tack and asked me many times the same question, "What did you learn?"

I was never quite sure how to answer my father, and often I had no need to do so. My mother was quick to reply, emphasizing her notion of the education such tutoring can afford a college student: "the lesson of humility," a favorite phrase of hers. If any amplification was necessary, she could be forthcoming with another well-worn piety: "There but for the grace of God. . . ."

My father's question often came back to haunt me, no matter my mother's hasty, biblical interventions. What *did* I learn? What was I *supposed* to learn? I was, after all, the teacher, not the student. Anyway, these were elementary school children, and there was nothing new in the ground I was covering with them every week. But I had listened to my father too often, on long walks through various cities, to let the matter rest there. He was born and grew up in Yorkshire, England, and was a great walker, a great observer as he kept his legs moving fast. He was also an admirer of George Orwell long before *Animal Farm* and 1984 were published—the early Orwell who wrote *Down and Out in London and Paris, The Road to Wigan Pier,* and *Homage to Catalonia;* the Orwell, that is, who explored relentlessly the world around him and described carefully yet with dramatic intensity the nature of that world.

My father had introduced me to those books before I went to college, and they returned to me as I did volunteer work—a scene, some words, or, more generally, Orwell's social and moral inquiry as both are conveyed in his several narrative efforts. I was beginning to realize that Orwell was a "big brother" for me in a manner far at variance to the already widespread meaning of that phrase. He was helping me make sense of a continuing experience I was having— sharing his wisdom with me, giving me pause, prompting in me scrutiny not only of others (the children I met, and occasionally their parents) but my own mind as it came up with its various opinions, conclusions, attitudes.

Later, at college, I would read the poetry and prose of William Carlos Williams—his long poem *Paterson,* his Stecher trilogy, *White Mule, In the Money, The Buildup.* Williams tried hard to evoke the rhythms of working-class life in America—the struggle of ordinary people to make their way in the world, to find a satisfactory manner of living, of regarding themselves. He knew how hard it is for people like himself (well-educated, well-to-do) to make contact in any substantial way with others, who work in factories or stores or on farms, or, indeed, who do not work at all or are lucky to be intermittently employed.

When he emphasized his search for an American "language," Williams was getting at the fractured nature of our nation's life— the divisions by race, class, region, culture which keep so many of us unaware of one another, unable to comprehend one another. Often as I went to do my tutoring, and heard words I never before knew—or heard words used in new and arresting ways—and as I learned about the memories and hopes and habits and interests of people in a neighborhood rather unlike the one where I lived, I thought of Williams' poems and stories and realized how much he owed to the humble people of northern, industrial New Jersey. As he once put it to me, years after I graduated from college, "Those house calls [to attend his patients] are giving me an education. Every day I learn something new—a sight, a phrase—and I'm made to stop and think about my world, the world I've left behind." He was reminding both of us that the "education" he had in mind was no one-way affair.

I fear it took some of us doing our volunteer work a good deal of time to learn the lesson Williams was putting to word. At my worst, I must admit, a sense of noblesse oblige was at work—a conviction that I would share certain (intellectual) riches with "them." Only when I went with Williams on some of his house calls—observed him paying close heed to various men, women, and children—did I begin to realize how much his mind grew in response to the everyday experiences he was having.

Now, many years later, I find myself a teacher at a university, offering courses for undergraduates and for students in professional schools (law, medicine, business, education). I work with many young people who are anxious to do community service of one kind or another—teach in urban schools, offer medical or legal assistance to needy families. At times I stand in awe of some of those youths— their determination, their decency, their good-heartedness, their savvy. I also notice in many of them a need for discussion and reflection: a time to stop and consider what they would like to be doing, what they are doing, what they are having difficulty doing. A college senior put the matter to me this way one afternoon: "I started this work [volunteer work in a school near a large urban low-rent housing project] as something apart from my courses, my life here as a student. I wanted to be of use to someone other than myself—and in a really honest moment, I'd probably add that I was also being selfish: It would beef up my brag sheet when I apply to a graduate school. But hell, I'd been doing this kind of [volunteer] work since high school—a part of our church's activities, so I shouldn't be too cynical about my motives! But the last thing I expected was that I'd come back here [to his dormitory] and want to read books to help me figure out what's happening [in the neighborhood where he does volunteer work]. I've designed my own private course—and it helps; I can anticipate certain troubles, because I've learned from the reading I do, and I get less discouraged, because I've seen a bigger view, courtesy of those writers."

He said much more, but the gist of his remarks made me realize that there are social scientists and novelists and poets and essayists who have offered that student so very much—their knowledge, their experience, their sense of what matters, and not least, their companionship—as fellow human beings whose concerns are similar to those of the youths now sweating things out in various student volunteer programs. Put differently, those writers (or film makers or photographers) are teachers, and their subject matter is an important one for many of our country's students, engaged as they are in acts of public service.

Our institutions of higher learning might certainly take heed—not only encourage students to do such service, but help them stop and mull over what they have heard and seen by means of books to be read, discussions to be had. This is the very purpose, after all, of colleges and universities—to help one generation after another grow intellectually and morally through study and the self-scrutiny such study can sometimes prompt.

Liberal Education, September/October 1988

Sinner Swaggart and Our Smugness

When my wife and I read of preacher Jimmy Swaggart's abrupt decline into the role of a public sinner, we remembered the hold he has had on so many people we have known, not only in our country's South, but the South that stretches from the Rio Grande valley way down to the Strait of Magellan. So many families we have met over the years have found Swaggart's performing skills irresistible. He has a way of collaring his listeners and viewers, insinuating his hyped-up alarm and foreboding into their nervous systems. He has a way of hitting a home run with his hysteria, evoking it in others, proving what Freud learned in the Vienna of 1900—that passions denied at home or in the workplace can suddenly burst forth, inexplicably or in response to something . . . or someone. It is all too easy for someone like me to pursue the above line of psychoanalytic thinking, to render a discourse on the contagious power of religious emotionality on certain kinds of psychologically vulnerable people. It's rather easy, as well, to join the ranks of those who prefer a more sociological or economic or cultural mode of analysis—the ignorance and impotence, the near desperation, the edge of despair in so many men and women who can take little, indeed, for granted, who live in constant debt or with no hope of any real security, any sense of achievement. To pursue such inquiry is to risk the cool, confident self-importance of the quite privileged intellectual—one more "them" to comprehend, maybe pity, maybe keep at a distance as a negative drag on the kind of enlightened politics my kind proudly tries to favor and practice.

As I tried to discuss the foregoing with a few friends "up here" (in New England), as opposed to "down there" (in Louisiana)—ah, the occasional symmetry of language and egotism—I was met with a barrage of skepticism, if not scorn. Swaggart is a phony, a manipulative fraud, an exploiter of sorts. He rakes in millions, lives high off the hog, exudes contrived bombast, offers hurt and ailing people—

well, the list is familiar: an opiate; false consciousness; illusions; a crutch; or as a friend of mine, a decent, hardworking psychoanalyst whose liberal politics and sane rationality I admire, put it in his quiet, understated Jamesian way, "some dubious satisfactions, indeed." Yes, yes, I want to say, and do say—but. I stop with that small qualifying word, have trouble spelling out what "but" is meant to announce.

I am tempted, maybe, by my own condescensions, but certainly by my own memories—all those fervent people I've met, hard praying and hard working and poor as can be, with few prospects. I especially remember the rural folk I've met in Nicaragua, or the *favelados* in Brazil—for whom Swaggart is the messenger of the existential Christ, as opposed to the sacramental or ecclesiastical Christ, not to mention the Christ endlessly examined by smart theologians: "I hear him [Swaggart] and I see Him, our Jesus—sweating and crying and trying to do right by God, Who sent Him here to suffer, the way we do. In his voice [Swaggart's] you can hear Jesus getting upset, and getting ready to fight all His enemies. I will look up at Him [the well-known statue of Jesus, arms outstretched, atop a Rio de Janeiro mountain] when I hear this man from the North [Swaggart] telling us to watch out, because God will soon come here and straighten everything out."

She dearly wishes for that day to come, when a leveling will take place, when a topsy-turvy change will happen, when "the last shall be first, the first last." So it goes—an excited populism in the mind of this impoverished mother of seven who has lost other children to miscarriages and to the deaths that go with hunger and malnutrition. She lives in a hillside shack which lacks adequate sanitation or clean drinking water. For her, Swaggart offers a direct, energetic encounter with biblical emotion—unmediated by institutional coolness or arrogance. She explained her response to me once—after I had taken pains to tell her, in a soft-spoken but pointed aside, that this big-shot television evangelist, who pressed Jesus on half a billion people, lives like a king on the proceeds of all the humble families who pour out what little they have into his coffers: "Maybe he does live big. I don't mind. Look at all the people who live big, and they don't care about Jesus, or about us, either. They only care about themselves. I'm sure he [Swaggart] is a sinner, like you and me. But he speaks to us. We're sinners, too. The others [she pointed toward Ipanema and Copacabana, the affluent, educated secular world] don't give us a glance. They only call us their names—think bad of us. I'll take Swaggart the sinner to them."

I had my rejoinder, perhaps the same one many readers of these words would immediately summon. I reminded this woman of no schooling and no work and no money that Swaggart was not only rich, he was a hypocrite—pretending righteousness, yet shrewdly a self-promoter who drives fancy cars, lives in a mansion, wields plenty of power on his own behalf. I was not harsh, simply factual and a bit melancholy in the tone I used, as was the translator who gave her the thoughts and observations in Portuguese. She was not to be educated (or patronized), however. She told me that she assumed Swaggart did not live like her. A silence, as I digested that brief moment of wry understatement. Then, her outburst again—at the Catholic church, and all *its* wealth, splendor, power; at some university sociologists and government officials who keep coming to the *favela* and keep making various suggestions but who deliver nothing tangible to her and others she knows; most of all, once again, at the well-to-do people who live in the fancy neighborhoods of Rio de Janeiro, and who (she knows) would love to have the *favela* where she lives "cleared"—out of sight, out of mind.

My mind went back several years to those talks with her and others like her as I thought of Jimmy Swaggart prowling the seedy motels of the old Airline Highway outside of New Orleans, the "city that care forgot," the city of so many sinners—and like those who sin in other cities, they are not just strippers or errant, hypocritical preachers. I remembered how "respectable" people, even those who ran newspapers and universities, didn't stand up to the mobs that heckled black children going into the once all-white schools of New Orleans, even as in my native Boston all sorts of respectable folks keep an arm's distance between themselves and the hard-pressed life of the city's white and black people alike. In our comfortable parlors, with our educated tongues, we deplore so many people, not only the Swaggarts of this world, but all who attend them, and all who aren't quite "up" to us—a pride, a sinful pride. Was my mother wrong when she admonished us children that of all sins, pride is the worst? Exactly how does one weigh the various sins: sinner

Swaggart's sexual transgressions, as against the smugness and self-satisfaction of some of us liberals who think we know what is best for everyone, who judge without worrying about being judged, and who call everyone to account, with no forgiveness in our vocabulary—except, of course, for ourselves?

New Oxford Review, June 1988

Thomas Merton the Healer

In the spring of 1955 I was an intern at the University of Chicago clinics. I had put in months of hard work in medicine and surgery. In February and March I had seen one patient after another die of leukemia and cancers that had eaten away their lungs, stomachs, and livers. I had worked day and night, trying to be of help to those patients, to the hospital's residents, to the attending physicians, to the medical students. A rough internship, all we interns consoled ourselves, but one that would last only a year. A particularly rough internship, we reminded ourselves with a touch of pride, as we mentioned the undeniable fact that, save a week's vacation, we never really could take for granted any time off. We could sign out, of course, but only if we were satisfied that we were not leaving any patients in jeopardy; that we'd done all the work that had to be done; and, not least, that we were covered, meaning that another intern had agreed to take on our responsibilities, actual or potential, no matter his or her own evening or weekend obligations.

In my case such a request of another doctor was made difficult by my strenuous if not overwrought New England conscience. I was always afraid something terrible would take place in the middle of the night or on a Saturday or Sunday afternoon and that my absence would make a grim turn for the worse even grimmer: all those cards I carried, with all their medical information, would not be as readily usable in someone else's hands as they occasionally were in mine. Moreover, I wasn't then married, and so it was natural that those who were husbands or wives (one of us was the latter, among two women interns) would turn to a bachelor like me with a conviction, a willfulness I didn't seem able to muster with that question, Will you cover for me? Even if I knew how anxiously we all whistled in the dark, knew I'd likely as not be stuck with not one but two (or three or four) emergencies, perhaps a four-bell page (a patient dying then and there or, not rarely, found dead by a nurse) I still relented, thinking maybe, just maybe, the night would be quiet—four hours' sleep as opposed to none at all.

I summon those old days, those tough as hell days of a demanding internship because I want to describe an interlude which occurred in the midst of that year. My vacation took place in late March of 1955, and it followed a week of severe flu that had robbed me of energy and made me feel weak, tired, depressed, and, I regret to say, self-pitying. I kept wondering what I was doing, why I was where I was. I had stumbled into medicine, as it were. I got to know William Carlos Williams as a consequence of writing my undergraduate thesis on the first two books of *Paterson*, his long, lyrical evocation of America's complex social and cultural traditions; and then I became so enamored of him and his life (he was a hardworking physician as well as a writer) that I resolved to imitate his life, knowing full well I couldn't imitate his art. The result was a hasty (and not very successful) attempt to master premedical subjects and a lucky admission to Columbia University's College of Physicians and Surgeons, I suspect because the biochemist who interviewed me, Philip Miller (how well I remember that kindly man and the hour we spent together!) had read Williams' poems and short stories and novels and essays and didn't think me completely loony for trying to follow (partially at least) an admired other's lead. I had not done well at all in the first two years of medical school, and though I liked the last two years much better, I never did (as one doctor urged and warned me I must do) "get my act together." I was lucky, yet again, to get the relatively good university-connected internship I'd wanted—one in a hospital located wonderfully close to a college setting, I thought to myself so innocently as I left upon completion of a quick preliminary visit a few months before the end of medical school.

Now I was nearing the end of that internship hurdle, too, and I felt sadly lost as well as weary. I had no idea what I'd do next; I'd eliminated as possibilities most of the specialties because of my sense of inadequacy in relation to their requirements. Moreover, my body seemed ready to give out—not just a flu attack, but a cumulative exhaustion that seemed to be, at least, fearfully consuming. "You'd better *really* rest," I was told by Robert Ebert, then my "attending" (on the "medical chest service").

I knew my malaise wasn't only physical; I knew I was at loose ends about a career and I knew I had to do something to alter those circumstances. It never occurred to me to go see a psychiatrist nor had it then occurred to me to try to be one! I had read *The Seven Storey Mountain* by Thomas Merton in college at the urging of Perry Miller, my advisor at Harvard College, and for some reason had taken the book with me both to medical school and then to the hospital where I interned. As I struggled with the flu that spring and wondered what to do with or on my week of vacation, I found myself picking up Merton's book again and again. I even found myself realizing that Kentucky wasn't all that far from Illinois, and that Chicago wasn't a million miles from the spot where the Trappist monastery Gethsemani was located. (In it, as a day-to-day monk, lived Thomas Merton.)

The long and short of it was that I got into my car on the first morning of my week's respite, still coughing, throat sore, a fever of a hundred degrees, and headed south and then east. The next day, after a night in Louisville visiting a college friend, I headed nowhere in particular, as I'd told him, one minute thinking I'd end up in Cincinnati visiting another college friend, the next minute thinking I'd just bum around—do a minor version of Kerouac, whose effort to comprehend and experience America Dr. W. C. Williams, himself quite old and ailing by then, had noted with interest and discussed with me several times in our phone conversations that past year.

But there were those other, odd moments; they had me looking intently at the map of Kentucky, remembering Merton's address. Eventually I showed up one late afternoon at the monastery he'd done so much, through his writing, to place in the consciousness of many fellow human beings. I drove through the adjoining farmland, past the wooded terrain, stopped my car in front of a modest (but to me, all of a sudden, fearfully imposing) building, reached for the door, turned the knob, noticed that there was no lock at work, and, soon enough, to condense things yet again, found myself a welcomed guest: I could stay, it seemed, as long as I wanted, though I had to understand the daily (and nightly) rhythms of those who had chosen to stay as long as life remained in their bodies.

Immediately upon entering the room given me and sitting on the bed to gather my thoughts, I realized that I both did, indeed, very much want to see, meet, and talk with Thomas Merton—yet I had no right to be where I was with such egotistic presumptions on my bedeviled mind. I decided to leave the next day, but I also wanted to stay, to drink up a particular haunting, unnerving atmosphere. This tourist's self-indulgence, this self-serving thoughtlessness and arrogance, protected me, I fear, all too well and in no way seemed to trouble those wise and shrewdly observant monks, who had learned well to put up with the likes of me, I later realized. By the time I had left that place in Kentucky for good, two days later, I could say to myself that I'd met Thomas Merton, that he had given me a warm smile, had made the sign of the cross, had touched me in ways I didn't then understand and which, later, when I'd become a psychiatrist and was in the middle of a prolonged psychoanalysis, I'd try hard to figure out.

My analyst was not himself uninterested in religious matters, and as we discussed that brief, increasingly clouded, obscure moment in my all too lengthening life, I heard the word "healer" used: Merton as a healing writer, a healing presence. I wasn't sure what my analyst meant when he used that descriptive category, but I knew I agreed with him, with his use of it. More recently, I thought of that word "healer" as I read Michael Mott's splendid biography of Merton and a recent volume of selected letters Merton addressed to his many (oh, so many, and he a cloistered monk) friends scattered all over the world. The biography tells what Merton himself told in his celebrated autobiography and in the many articles and books that followed it, an outpouring of passionate eloquence rendered readers throughout the world, in God's name, but also, one dares say, and in no way to cast any skeptical shadows, out of Merton's particular human calling as a healer. For he was one who began knowing pain and watching suffering as an infant. His artist mother, who austerely observed him when he was an infant and recorded her daily impressions in a diary, became ill with cancer when he was scarcely four years old, and when he was sixteen his father, also an artist, also died of cancer. Lucky because he was born to parents of some standing (talented, educated, not at all poor), he was thus unlucky, too. Even his younger and only brother died young—killed in the Second World War while fighting the Nazis. Merton lived a lonely if privileged youth, attended private schools in England and then Columbia University in the 1930s, that "low dishonest decade," W. H. Auden called it, and all the while tried to find his bearings: with the help of Freud and Marx; through efforts to write journalism, poetry, fiction; by recourse to bouts of drinking, sexual liaisons, intense spells of moody self-scrutiny; by seeking lots of camaraderie and good food; and always by giving devoted attention to verse, to the stories of writers who had preceded him.

Finally there was the conversion to Catholicism and shortly thereafter the dedicated search for sanctity—the decision to give a lifetime to priestly contemplation and prayer as a Trappist. The irony is obvious—a man of letters, a man obsessed with words and their possibilities, chooses a monkhood which emphasizes silence and the strongest kind of self-abnegation. But there are additional ironies. Merton withdrew from the world when he entered the monastery, and yet he kept writing, pouring out his essays, poems, journal entries—one article after another, one book after another. The result was a worldwide following which included the famous and the utterly unknown. To all of his readers he gave consolation, advice, sympathy, understanding; he also offered ideas to consider, values to uphold. He was, of course, a Christian moralist, but he was also a bravely self-critical and confessional monk who dared to share his worries and hurts, his doubts and misgivings and fears with his correspondents, his readers. The power of *The Seven Storey Mountain*, of course, had to do with just that psychological candor, that willingness to be forthcoming on the part of a remarkably gifted lyrical writer. He was an artist of the English language who harnessed his literary skills to the task of an intense and continuing self-scrutiny and, yes, self-exposure. The result was a human being's suffering become redemptive—contagiously affecting others, prompting them to stop, think, wonder, ask questions, even take various moral or spiritual steps to follow Merton's healing lead, it may be said.

Dorothy Day and Daniel Berrigan and Walker Percy and so many others sought Merton out. I especially remember Dorothy Day's remarks about him: "He had known much pain, and he knew how to lift pain from others." She was content to state those two aspects of Merton without connecting the one to the other in what people like me call a psychodynamic way. Nevertheless, she knew that an essential and important part of Merton's life was his passionate desire to minister unto others, to hear from them, learn of their tensions and turmoils, and tell them of his, too. Once Dorothy Day said this about Merton as we talked of his voluminous writing: "He cured with words—all the time he did! I know! I can remember those letters, the good medicine that they were to me. And I always knew that with Merton it was the doctor healing himself as well as the rest of us who were his patients."

She was no stranger herself to such a healing effort, and her words about Merton echoed in my ears as I read the recent biography of him—a thoughtful inquiry aimed at comprehending an important life. The biographer is especially challenged by an anguished involvement Merton experienced late in life, one which stunned him, among others: the middle-aged monk, sick in the hospital, falls in love with his attending nurse. I have no desire here (or elsewhere) to probe psychologically or morally that time of passion and great apprehension and soul searching. I simply want to point out that Merton had become a patient, and that a kind and generous nurse had surely reminded him of what he'd at least partially missed receiving as a child—the devoted, caring regard, the everyday healing of another person. But Merton the monk had found a way of redeeming his childhood losses. He followed the advice of St. Francis, he gave, and thereby received; he healed with poems and essays and letters and thereby himself was healed. But the healer suddenly vulnerable is the healer in great jeopardy, because exposed to the deepest sources of his or her calling, hence tempted yet again to try to redeem them, as that sick, bed-ridden monk endeavored to do: feel a deep and grateful love for the one attending him.

Not long afterward Merton would venture to Asia, ever anxious to be connected with wisdom and with healing other than the kind he knew. Yet while there he died suddenly, the victim of an accidental electrocution. A person present at the conference he had gone halfway across the world (Bangkok) to attend remarked upon his kindly manner, the gentleness he radiated and its calming effect on her: to the very last that humane touch of grace offered without guile or pretense to others.

From *In Search of the Modern Hippocrates*,
edited by Roger J. Bulger, 1987

A *Last* Conversation
with Anna Freud

Several times in these columns I have mentioned Anna Freud, who did so much to connect psychoanalytic knowledge *about* children (learned from the memories of adults) to psychoanalytic work *with* children. Much of the understanding today's child psychiatrists possess was enabled by the work she did for over half a century with boys and girls troubled by virtue of their experiences in particular families, or as a consequence of the Nazi air assaults on London during World War II, or, horror of horrors, as a result of living in concentration camps during that same war. To such children Miss Freud, as she was called by so many of us for so long, gave all she had: a brilliant, knowing mind; enormous, unflagging patience; and the consummate skill she had as a clinician—able, I often noted, to get to the heart of the matter with a child, with his or her parents, in what struck the rest of us as no time at all. Toward the end of her life (as happens with some of those men and women who have not only learned a discipline inside out, but come to realize how much they still don't know, how much is yet to be discovered), she had about her a real wisdom—not the feigned or pretentious wisdom of yet another late twentieth-century secular guru, but a quiet, humble, wry, though still passionate, interest in the world that got translated, at times, into remarkable observations, which she made unselfconsciously, with no eye to who might be ready to venerate and celebrate what had been spoken.

My last visit with her was in late 1980. She would be dead in less than two years and was already in failing health. I had known her, by then, almost fifteen years, and had much treasured our times together, our correspondence. The latter could be edifying beyond expectation—long letters, sometimes, or brief ones with candid, occasionally brisk and sharp observations, not to mention constant reference to her work as a child psychoanalyst, all delivered in the clearest of narrative prose. During our last meeting (and I knew then

35

it would be fatuous to expect there would be any more) she was quite willing to review some of the past discussions we'd had—about the ways children come to personal terms with those "variables" called "race" and "class," and about the lives of two individuals who meant a lot to me, and about whom I told her a lot: Simone Weil and Dorothy Day.

At one point, as I was talking about those two women, yet again, and more broadly about the way all of us (including children) formulate our religious or spiritual yearnings (or, for that matter, most emphatically formulate a lack of such yearnings), she had this to say: "It comes as no surprise to many parents that a child is for them an opportunity: to discover themselves, their own childhood, once again; to find the only 'immortality' most of us can ever hope to see, in the children we see before us, as I heard a mother once say, 'carrying on, where I'll leave off'—a very tactful way of talking. I am getting around to saying that we can find in children what we are looking for (within limits, yes); and the reason is, we have put there [in them] what we're later so surprised (sometimes) to notice! I'm afraid this [formulation of sorts] applies to us, too [child psychiatrists and psychoanalysts]. We have found in children what we suspected—an endlessly complex psychology. When you started your own work, you found what you suspected: sociology, race, the circumstances in which a family lives—all that has a life in a child's mind. Before any of us [psychoanalysts] appeared on the world scene, others knew what they were looking for: a capacity to *believe*—and they certainly found that capacity in children and learned themselves to work with that capacity! Now, more and more, I hear about biology and the brain, and surely children will help out those [biologically oriented investigators] who are looking at them from that angle!"

She paused long enough to see on my face a mix of consternation and anxiety—as if I were hearing an indictment of all of us who spend time with children: We impose on them, so I feared she was implying, our own agendas—the child as a mirror of us observers, if not an instrument of our ideological passions, maybe even our ambitions. But no, she had something quite else in mind—and she had a way, I'd noted for years, of quietly seeing through someone else's confusions, and without mentioning them, or in any manner putting the person in question on the spot, clarifying her own remarks in such a way that the one she was with, suddenly, was with her, so to speak: "It is natural, all this [that she had described]. What is sad is—when we don't quite realize what we're all doing. Maybe *that* is what my father did for us, after all—give us a way of being more aware of what we do, so we're not so surprised when we finally understand not only what others are doing, but what *we're* doing!"

She was not at all interested in reserving for herself the privileged position of the one who is beyond the limitations and blind spots to which everyone else is heir. Rather, she was reminding herself, never mind me, toward the end of her life, that psychoanalysts (and social scientists, and all sorts of other theory-bent individuals) can single out and explore what is there in the world, but also miss what's there or, alas, dismiss what others notice and regard with great interest as not being worthy of much notice, hence to be put aside with one or another pejorative description: religion as a neurosis, for instance.

During that same meeting, a short one (by our standards) of less than an hour, she came as close to a full and sympathetic interest in spiritual questions as I'd ever heard her manage to do: "The longer you live, the more you realize how little time there is—and how little we really know about this universe! It is impressive—the way some people can put distance between themselves as believers and themselves as human beings, with all the passions we have as human beings. I suppose that is the soul [in them] at work: their ability, at times, to be bigger morally than they usually are. It's a struggle— but they have moral passion, working in the interest of certain ideals. I am not interested in *explaining* those people—only saluting them, some of them, who are such good men and women, and have found for themselves a faith that inspires them. I am not sure there are too many [such people]—I think there are plenty of churchgoers, but maybe far fewer people who really take to heart what those churches were once meant to be!"

Silence, then her signal to me that she was tired: an offer of a refill of coffee. I said I had to go. She said she too "had to go." As I left, I heard myself saying (a free association!): Yes, so do we all, in time, "have to go." As I left, too, I saw, still, her face after she had spoken those last words, made that last observation—a certain wist-

fulness, an ironic detachment, but also, I thought, a kind of yearning: the great joys of honorable and decent spiritual transcendence
(a commitment to the beyond) that some can find, but among them
not her.

New Oxford Review, April 1992

Senses and Sensibility

Alabama's Institute for the Deaf and the Blind was founded two years before the Civil War began. It is now a nationally known and respected institution located in Talladega, about fifty miles east of Birmingham. I remember Anna Freud mentioning AIDB, as it is known, during a discussion of the special challenges that fate puts to blind and deaf children as they grow up. She and her colleagues in child psychoanalysis were much interested in such children and had done some substantial work with them, especially blind boys and girls. Miss Freud asked about AIDB in the way foreigners often do when they come to a country with only a finite amount of knowledge about its geography. She came regularly to New Haven and New York, was no stranger to certain other cosmopolitan cities, but the South was not her regular beat. With a certain wistfulness she looked around the Yale dormitory room where we had been sitting and then made a comment I can still hear: "I'd like to go visit that school [AIDB] one day."

She never realized that wish, but she would certainly be enthralled by the results of someone else's visit. Frederick Wiseman's four film documentaries run nine hours: an effort to show how the blind, the deaf, or those both blind and deaf (and impaired in other ways, too) manage at a residential school, and while there become reasonably educated, even begin to make their way in the outside world. With his films, Wiseman has been directing a school, of sorts, for two decades: he has wanted to help us overcome our own versions of blindness and deafness. He started his documentary career with the still controversial *Titicut Follies*, a film about a Massachusetts hospital for the criminally insane. (I still cannot show that film to my medical students without obtaining their signatures—a collective declaration that they are an educational audience rather than mere film buffs.) Some Massachusetts officials worried that the "privacy" of certain inmates was violated—though the utterly outrageous and degrading circumstances shown in the film seem to have troubled those officials rather less. To this day, the hospital earns consistently negative ratings, and is a recurrent subject of journalistic muckraking.

After he had completed *Titicut Follies*—despite his troubles with Bay State bureaucrats—Wiseman turned his attention to one institution after another: a high school, a court, a department store, a hospital, a racetrack, a seminary, a city's welfare system, a place where young military recruits are indoctrinated, a slaughterhouse that enables us to have meat on our tables. Each film is meant to place us who watch in the midst of a particular social and institutional scene, in the hope that as we view people going about their chores, doing what they are paid to do or are required by law or custom to do, and hear what is said (or shouted or whispered), we will know rather more about our large and complex nation.

These four documentaries amount to Wiseman's most ambitious project yet. "Before I made these films my experience and knowledge of deaf and/or blind people was limited, practically nonexistent," Wiseman explained. "When I began to think about it I realized that I had never gone to school with anyone who was deaf or blind, nor did I have any contact in my work or social life with anyone who was without one or both of these basic senses." Of the four films, *Blind* and *Deaf* are the two basic texts. They aim to show how children made do without sight or hearing—learn to take care of themselves, to read and write, to get on successfully with others, to negotiate their way in a world where vision is taken for granted, as is the capacity to understand the spoken word. *Multi-Handicapped* and *Adjustment and Work* take us further along: to the more strenuous difficulties of those who are both deaf and dumb (or have, for instance, cerebral palsy as an additional disability); and to the adulthood of those who have attended AIDB, and now hope to find work, achieve a significant degree of personal and financial independence.

Each of the four films invites us, first, to the South, to Talladega, Alabama: the country roads, the fields with their crops, the Winn Dixie market, the homes, modern and Victorian, the courthouse, and inevitably, a strip, with its gas stations, honky-tonk stores, fast-food restaurants. All four present a southern city's social life—the genteel white neighborhoods, the modest homes of working-class white or black families, the streets where impoverished blacks struggle for survival. All four also offer sights and sounds many of the children who attend AIDB have missed—the well-known Talladega stock-car racetrack, with its zooming machines and boisterous crowds, the predictably mock-elegant world of mall shopping, and most affecting, the simple but powerful noise of the railroad engine—Willa Cather's "cold, vibrant scream."

Deaf and *Blind* essentially chronicle the way children in two quite unusual residential school settings spend their time. Early in *Blind*, we notice one form of affluence—the sunglasses of those who can afford to dim their vision. Minutes later we meet boys and girls who are learning to feel their way along corridors, who follow voices, who brave their own kind of adventures. The students are black and white, boy and girl, quite bright and average in intelligence and retarded. No matter, they hold hands; they seem thoroughly at ease with one another—blind in a different sense of the word to differences the rest of us are quick to regard as important, even when quite young.

Not able to notice skin color or the kind of clothes worn, they attend to the texture of cement or wood or glass—what it feels like when a cane (or one's hand) moves from one part of a building to another. They learn with the cane to sight an approaching door or set of stairs. They learn not so much to rely on the cane as to master it. With no embarrassment or sense of irony they and their teachers talk of going to "see" what is out there awaiting them—paths to trod, directions to pursue, choices to make. They "keep looking." They "watch for" landmarks. They listen hard. They find a water fountain and feel the obvious satisfactions of an important discovery.

They play sports. They learn braille. They let their fingers feel their way to a control of a needle, some thread: knitting, sewing. They talk with their teachers about family troubles—a drunken father, a broken marriage, a disappointment experienced on a home visit. They feel low and hesitant at times. But they are constantly encouraged, complimented—in soft, southern drawls that seem especially fitting for such occasions. Throughout the film the camera is kept constantly busy—moving from room to room, activity to activity: children playing, cooking, learning to make change, creating messes, cleaning up after themselves, dancing, and finally, getting ready for bed. As they pray before falling asleep—a particularly poignant moment—the film begins to conclude. The moon is out.

The lights of the city are turned on. Soon, though, all will be darkness—though for these children there is, alas, no such transition.

Deaf (2 hours, 43 minutes) is half an hour longer than *Blind*. The structure of *Deaf* is similar to that of *Blind*—the camera's constant attention to a school day's events. Children learn to sign, to read lips as well, and not least to use their vocal chords, to talk—no easy task for someone who has not heard himself or herself speak, never mind anyone else. Gradually Wiseman's camera informs us of the special technology a contemporary school for deaf children requires—lights for a phone or a clock alarm, closed-caption television, a "minicom" typewriter that enables telephone conversation. But teachers matter more than those devices—what happens between them and their students as they try to comprehend each other. Some of the teachers are deaf themselves, and their earnest professional devotion obviously draws on reservoirs of personal experience.

The centerpiece of *Deaf* offers a family squabble (one by no means peculiar to AIDB children and their parents). A fourteen-year-old boy has threatened suicide several times, declared his mother indifferent to him. She has driven to the school from Mobile, and for three-quarters of an hour we watch her, her son, a wise and empathic counselor, and the school's principal talk about what is happening to a family. The biological father has spurned Peter because of his deafness, yet even though a stepfather likes him, pays him favorable attention, he yearns for his "first daddy." The estrangement between mother and son is obvious—the aloofness each uses for self-protection, the hurt pride each displays.

All over the world youths and parents struggle with one another in similar ways for similar reasons. What distinguishes this confrontation is the obvious difficulty a mother and a son have in speaking to each other. The mother's signing is inadequate, and the youth is ready at a glance to use such a failure as an indictment of her. Not that, of course, parents and children who have excellent hearing are spared such family impasses. Wiseman dwells on this scene not to show a special psychopathology, but to remind us of universals that transcend difficulties such as deafness—the failures of trust and of love that mark the lives of so many of us.

In all four of Wiseman's documentaries, teachers are heard at some length discussing the progress of various students, their small victories and persisting troubles. Often the talk becomes psychological—the dreary jargon one hears everywhere in this country today. Several times the viewer is transported from a concrete, arresting teaching situation to an abstract psychological discussion, with banal words such as "individuation" and "adjustment" filling, if not fouling, the air. So it goes, the bemused film maker seems to be telling us. At such moments I kept wishing Anna Freud had visited AIDB before she died. She had little use for psychological pretentiousness, and enormous respect for the daily fortitude and intelligence of the many teachers she knew in the course of her life. She never patronized them with overblown psychoanalytic language. Often enough, I remember, she presented herself as the one who needed to learn— and she would have learned a lot had she gone to Alabama, or for that matter, seen Wiseman's films. She put in a considerable number of clinical hours observing and working with blind children, and in volume 5 of her *Writings* ("Research at the Hampstead Child-Therapy Clinic and Other Papers") she several times takes note of the stumbling blocks and quandaries blindness and deafness (or bodily impairments of various kinds) can present to children. The young take in the world—including the image of a mother, a father, and needless to say, themselves—through the use of the eyes: the sight of others, the sight of oneself in a mirror or a picture taken. The young also hear the words "yes" and "no" every day—the encouragement and the disapproval that go to make a conscience that works effectively (but not imperiously, crazily) in later life.

It is probably no accident that *Deaf* is a noisier film than *Blind*, and has more truculence in it. In the former the teachers at times— no matter the camera's presence—seem sorely tested, even on the verge of an outburst or two. The deaf children are more combative, the blind more self-effacing. In psychoanalytic language, the deaf sometimes experience special hurdles in "super-ego formation"; the blind may be particularly tested by the vicissitudes of "narcissism." For years, however, Anna Freud urged on her psychoanalytic colleagues restraint in such formulations, common sense in their application to individuals or groups of people, and most insistently, the research initiative she called "direct observation"—with theoretical conjecture kept to a minimum until, as she once put it, "we have something to contemplate." Wiseman's films would have held her close attention, prompted her, I suspect, to want to look at the entire footage he secured in Talladega.

Even as the psychoanalyst must struggle with his or her subjectivity, a film maker such as Wiseman presents us with a mix of objective reportage and a particular artist's attitude. He is at pains to let us hear the school officials talk about budgets and political lobbying in the state capital, Montgomery, because he wants to make the point that lots of the sensitivity and compassion we have witnessed is enabled by tough, shrewd behind-the-scenes bargaining sessions. He asks us to listen to A. D. Gaston, the ninety-two-year-old black Birmingham entrepreneur, talking of "dream power," of his "handicapped" (segregated) earlier life as a grandson of slaves, who lived in turn-of-the-century poverty, because the speech is animated and entertaining, but also, one suspects, because yet another big shot comes across as occasionally full of himself and full of hot air, and we had best remember that neither blindness nor deafness (Gaston's words are translated beautifully into sign language) need deny anyone an exposure to life's funny or absurd moments. Wiseman the film maker and editor is Wiseman the visual poet, the social critic, the ironist—someone probing social reality, yes, but also arranging it, composing it, as artists or writers always do.

During the days I watched these four powerful films, I kept reading reviews of them, and biographical accounts of the man who had to fight hard, against considerable odds, to make them, to have them shown uncut. He is on record as taking on the very people whose power can stand between his work and thousands of viewers, the Corporation for Public Broadcasting, where an endemic anglophilia often threatens, and where, in Wiseman's words, "personal politics, the buddy system, jealousy, and pop ideology dominate the panel discussions."

One way his critics get back at him is by calling his work boring or repetitive or too demanding. I kept seeing such comments, even from those who in general admire his work. My wife, a schoolteacher, suggested we show the films to some children the age of many who appear in *Deaf* and *Blind*, ten to thirteen, and we did. They were utterly taken by what they saw. They scarcely moved. They remained silent. At moments they gasped in admiration or disbelief. All right, they were suburban children going to fine schools, and no strangers to serious assignments pushed by their elders. We gave the films to one of our sons, who has been working this summer with troubled ghetto children. They, too, sat still and were held spellbound throughout *Blind* and *Deaf* both. Afterward they voiced a flurry of questions, offered a range of lively comments.

Exactly who is bored by these films? Perhaps some of us are offended because as experts or announcers we have been denied employment, refused permission to do what we otherwise do so commonly on television and elsewhere in our national life: make pronouncements, assert our authority, get seen and heard. His are not the neatly packaged, carefully timed productions that feature smooth-speaking narrators and pundits always sure of themselves. For years Wiseman has kept the experts at bay. He has had no trouble finding so-called "average" men, women, and children who have a lot to say about this life, about their fate.

Throughout his career Frederick Wiseman has dared explore directly the fullest range of human experience. In film after film he has rendered us as we are—the complexities, ambiguities, ironies, inconsistencies, contradictions that inform our life. He is, really, kin to some of our writers of short fiction, anxious to comprehend through a particular angle of vision our contingent lives: the way we are shaped by institutions, certainly, but the way we may stand up to them, take only so much from them, or find our own ways of breaking free of them. His careful, respectful, persistent regard for plain, ordinary people puts him in the company of writers such as Raymond Carver, Richard Ford, Bobbie Ann Mason, Toni Morrison, James Alan McPherson: storytellers, not social scientists. While sociologists increasingly play with banks of computers and spew an impenetrably mannered, opaque, highfalutin language, and most anthropologists stay resolutely in the Third World, he and his camera attend the contours of our daily life, and in the end, as with fiction, help us better see and hear ourselves—what such films as *Blind* and *Deaf* do so very well, indeed.

New Republic, August 29, 1988

A Doctor's Odyssey

Side by side, at the very beginning of her new book, Sara Lawrence Lightfoot, a sociologist and professor of education at Harvard, chooses to offer the reader more than a hint of what is to come—with words from a lamentation of Jeremiah and from an old Negro spiritual. Both make reference to "balm in Gilead," which is her book's title. (That balm was an ancient aromatic resin used for medicinal purposes in biblical times.) In a touching way, before a word of her own is offered the reader, the author connects the longtime suffering of the Jews and the blacks, and their similar search for healing. *Balm in Gilead* is about such healing; it is a personal portrait (a word the author favors in her teaching and research) of one of the world's first psychoanalytically trained black child psychiatrists, Margaret Lawrence, who also happens to be the mother of the author.

It is not rare for psychiatrists to have vivid memories of pain and suffering. Dr. Margaret Lawrence's life may take its place in that tradition. She grew up an only child in a family that E. Franklin Frazier would have firmly labeled a part of the "black bourgeoisie." Her father was an Episcopal minister, her mother a schoolteacher. An older brother, known as Candy Man, died at the age of one; and a picture of him, with his "white skin and blond curls," haunted his family: "Each time they moved, Candy Man's picture would be hung in the central spot in the living room over the couch." Eventually his darker-skinned younger sister would connect her medical aspirations and her interest in children to that tragedy—a resolve to struggle on behalf of others like Candy Man, and a desire to help those who have lost children, and, so doing, have lost themselves beyond the power of time and talk and tears to heal. Hence the need of Gilead's special substance, the equivalent in this modern day of a career in pediatrics and psychiatry.

Sara Lightfoot is an exceedingly graceful narrative writer, and this is a delightfully affectionate rendering of a woman of great personal poise and professional achievement. But no effort is made to spare the reader the most demanding possible moments—a tough, candid analysis of what has happened to black people who have tried to better themselves during the twentieth century. Lawrence grew up with "painful memories of family struggles." Her mother was subject to prolonged spells of melancholy. For days she withdrew to her room. The girl's father was a minister who moved the family from town to town—eventually to Vicksburg, Mississippi, where a certain stability descended upon this threesome. But always there was the fear and the anxiety that went with being black in the rural South during the 1920s and 1930s. Lawrence, reminiscing for her daughter, reminds us of our country's recent past: "I can remember walking back from town with my mother on Jackson Street near First North [in Vicksburg]. Suddenly she grabbed me and shoved me off the sidewalk and onto the grass because a white man was approaching from the other direction. She was frightened of staying on the sidewalk."

Even more confusing and degrading, perhaps, was an intense color consciousness among black people—a constant kind of self-scrutiny based on the degree to which one did or did not resemble white people. The pride and the arrogance of light-skinned blacks, and the disdain they showed others who were darker, has been noted by any number of writers and social scientists. This book conveys the sad consequences of our nation's prolonged racial strife in an especially gripping manner: through the recalled experiences, the stories, of one family as they have been relayed from mother to daughter, and now to us. As I read these accounts of self-hatred, I remembered the words of a black woman in Georgia who had no education at all, yet knew enough to tell my wife that "as bad as the whites are with us, we're worse with each other." When my wife asked why it is that victims become their own persecutors, the thirty-year-old scrubwoman and mother answered tersely: "You be scared, you copycat the ones who scare you, and try to do them one better, and that way you can catch a taste of the boss man's life!" The subtleties of such a psychological inclination are each family's secret, of course, as the future psychoanalyst Margaret Lawrence well knew by the time she ventured north (at only fourteen) to fulfill her dream of becoming a physician.

Even as we know the facts of southern segregation—it was a caste system that obtained for generations and only began to end a quarter century ago—we also know that the North for a long time was only a relatively better place for black people. The chapters that tell of Lawrence's situation as "the only black undergraduate on the arts and sciences campus" of Cornell, of her similar experience as a medical student at Columbia's College of Physicians and Surgeons, and of her lonely, tense, even tearful time as the sole black psycho-analytic candidate at one of New York City's institutes provide a devastating glimpse of an aspect of upper-class intellectual life that all too frequently goes unnoticed. "I listen, disbelieving," Lightfoot remarks, as she compares her mother's "solitary arrival at Cornell in the fall of 1932" with her own Swarthmore life of three decades later.

The great virtue of this book is its preference for storytelling rather than abstract argument or theoretical assertion. The reader is en-raged, surely, at the injustices that took place in Ithaca or New York City, in those high-and-mighty university settings. But he or she is also immersed in the details of particular incidents, and so, soon enough, made to feel as Margaret Lawrence did, utterly and arbi-trarily and relentlessly wronged. Put differently, before we learn that the Cornell student Margaret Lawrence could not even live on cam-pus ("No blacks were allowed in the dormitory, of course"), we hear her asking, upon arrival at the Ithaca train station, "My Lord, where is this?" We also see her: "Margaret was wearing a suit that had been made for the occasion by her mother's seamstress in Vicksburg: steel gray, with shoulder pads and a fitted waist. She carried a black purse, with matching shoes, but did not wear the gray gloves that would have completed the outfit. Her thick black braids, gleaming almost blue in the bright afternoon sun, were wrapped into buns on either side of her head, a concession to the adult image she was try-ing out."

At moments the author-daughter finds it hard to comprehend the responses of her mother, who is also the "subject" of her presenta-tion. She has just been told by Lawrence that "if I walked across the campus, people would stop talking, turn their heads, and ask 'Who is that?'" She has also been told this: "One Sunday a white woman from one of the local churches invited Margaret to come and speak about her experiences in Mississippi. The Vicksburg girl responded with style and grace as she told the Ithaca folks about her life in the

Deep South. We can only imagine it was not the exotic tale or the rags-to-riches story that they had anticipated. Perhaps disappointed by the girl's sophistication, or perhaps unknowingly resenting it, the woman who had invited Margaret approached her after her talk. Her smile was sugary sweet as she took Margaret's hand. 'I am so pleased you came,' she gushed thankfully. Then, without skipping a beat: 'You remind me so much of a maid I had. The only problem she had was that she would steal.'" Such a memory is told with lightness and humor—and the author remarks upon her "shock and anger at the humiliation that my mother does not seem to be feeling."

The reader begins to realize that Lawrence's life was constantly visited with outrages, small and large. She was rejected by Cornell Medical School for no reason but her race. She became an excellent medical student, but for similar reasons was turned down for a pediatric residency at New York's Babies Hospital. Even her psychiatric and psychoanalytic training was marred by rebuffs, insults, brush-offs. Black patients were remanded for "supportive therapy," she heard, "because they can't use anything deeper." Similarly with black doctors interested in psychiatry and psychoanalysis. This book presents a discouraging yet revealing glimpse of a little known matter—the condescensions and worse, the outright racism that blacks experienced in the course of their postgraduate medical and psychiatric education. Just before her certificate of psychoanalytic training was to be awarded, Dr. Lawrence was suddenly told she needed a further evaluation. She had dared express reservations about the ways some of her psychoanalytic teachers regarded black people—their problems and burdens. She had dared have misgivings about Abram Kardiner's *The Mark of Oppression*, a book that many social scientists, black and white alike, have come to regard as inadequate in its portrayal of black life in America—all too preoccupied with psychopathology.

She is still, obviously, offended by such past memories: even today "for Margaret, the feeling of being in the elevator of the Columbia Presbyterian Hospital opens up the old wound of self-consciousness." Yet she never really wavered. She had acquired a necessary forbearance and a determination to prevail. She married a strong, decent, bright, and able man, Charles Lawrence, a sociologist. She became a distinguished clinician, researcher, educator, writer. She worked for years in Harlem with troubled children, and with the distinguished psychologists Kenneth and Mamie Phipps Clark tried to help hard-pressed parents to do better by their sons and daughters. In a sense, she was redeeming her own childhood difficulties—doing an about-face on her mother's legacy of dejection and episodic withdrawal from life. In her interviews with her daughter, she comes across as her own mother's opposite, as a lively, outgoing, delightfully engaging person and doctor. Most of all, Margaret Lawrence's career has been in the pastoral tradition of doctoring—years and years spent with her patients, black and white, adults and children, the well-to-do and the poor.

I first heard of Margaret Lawrence from a number of civil rights activists whom she had taught or treated. I heard of her, too, from her white colleagues, who by the 1960s were beginning to make her concerns theirs. This book, in that regard, is especially interesting for the complex professional issues it raises. During her psychiatric and psychoanalytic training a talented, energetic, empathic, and resourceful trainee learned to keep silent about certain matters dear to her, to wait until she graduated. In a fascinating comment, Lightfoot tells this about her mother's way of holding on to her religious convictions during a trying period: "Her faith endured even the inhospitable environment of the Psychoanalytic Clinic. Throughout her analytic training, she simply kept her contrary theology quiet, continued to go to church every Sunday at St. Martin's in Harlem, continued to 'be in touch with the Spirit,' and continued to rehearse the words of her father's favorite psalm, 'The Lord is my light and salvation.'" Such quiet spells have not only been the habit of black candidates of religious sensibility in psychiatric or psychoanalytic training, as any number of us will testify. There can be an unfortunately ideological quality to such training; vulnerable young doctors learn to keep their mouths shut with respect to certain matters, to bide their time.

Balm in Gilead is a daughter's loving witness to a mother's important healing life. Margaret Lawrence is obviously Sara Lightfoot's heroine—and black or white, we need such heroines. But *Balm in Gilead* is something else, too: an attempt to demonstrate by example what a humane and clearheaded kind of social science might offer us, were it more a presence in our social and intellectual life.

New Republic, March 27, 1989

New Literary
and Art Essays

Bringing Poems to
Medical School Teaching

Early in 1974 I had just returned to New England after living in New Mexico for several years, studying the ways American Indian children and Spanish-speaking children of the Southwest grow and think about the world that is theirs. Shortly after we'd settled in, I received a call from a friend, the poet L. E. Sissman—Ed to everyone who knew him. He wanted to meet and have a talk. I could tell by his voice that this was no casual request. I was about to suggest a place and time, when he made it clear to me that he wanted to come see me in my study at home, and sooner rather than later.

The next day when we met I heard a reserved, soft-spoken man in his forties beg my forgiveness, initially, for the "self-indulgence" to follow—the talk about himself. I was struck by the memorable quaintness of this formality—such a contrast with the assumption so many of us have (and not only with respect to the doctors we go visit) that the subject of oneself is an ideal one for the ears of others. Ed was, anyway, polite, considerate, and eminently interested in other people—their ways of speaking, of course, but also their habits, interests, values. He seemed out of sorts, sitting opposite me, slipping into a patient's posture—yet he wanted leave to concentrate on what was happening in his life, and to do so with someone else, and as a citizen of late twentieth-century bourgeois America, to do so with such as me.

He was dying, he reminded me. We all are, I observed with the genuine weariness of someone who had just battled a viral pneumonia—though I was also aware of a patronizing, awkward, foolhardy effort at reassurance on my part. Ed received my statement without apparent animus. He smiled. He nodded, even. But the silence that fell was, I realized, either a measure of second thoughts on his part ("Can I trust this guy to get it?") or a gesture of tactfulness: best to let an interlude separate us from what was to follow.

In a second or two he was on his way, telling me in a fluent narrative about his recent life—as a businessman (he worked for a Boston advertising agency), as a writer (the poems he'd done in recent years, the book reviews for the *New Yorker*), and as a husband (he and his wife lived in a town not far from the town that is home to my family and me). When he'd apparently finished, he looked right at me, his eyes meeting mine—and as if to head off any comment I might feel compelled to make, he added another, more terse comment, "I also have a life as a patient, and it gets busier and busier these days." I knew, then, why we were there.

Soon we were getting together weekly. Ed had been having more and more medical troubles with a Hodgkin's disease that was not (as some are, today) curable. He was also at that time having trouble writing poems. Lines would come to him, especially in the morning, upon awakening, but he couldn't seem to pull them together into a poem. Sometimes, he had no "energy. or desire" even to write down the words, the images, the analogies, the metaphors. Yet, he had energy, he reminded me, for enjoying his sports car, for good food, for a laugh with friends. He had desire, too—at home, and on the streets or at work: an eye for the beautiful in people, places, things. His prose was as fluent and pungent as ever—and as shrewdly intelligent. His essays for the *New Yorker* were a valuable part of that magazine's middle-1970s life. Why, then, the end of making poems?

A smug fool (and that is what lots of us can be, on occasion, in the kingdom of shrinkdom) might have supplied an answer; and I'll have to admit to the temptation to say something that sounded smart and knowing—therapy for me, I suppose. Once, taking absolutely precise aim at me, my quandary, and himself as the provocateur, if not agent of truth, he wryly observed, "You're going to use words now, I guess, to explain my inability with them." I had not one word to say at that point. I sat nervously, sadly, wondering how to get us elsewhere—a car ride, an ice cream cone together, some looking at birds and plants while walking near a stretch of woods: all the actions that silenced talk on the occasion of our meetings. He did not prod me. He took charge of me and himself both, saying, "The muse has departed the body—looking back upon its quickening decline." A line, I thought—a Latin line, maybe. His smile assured me he was not that serious. I think he had guessed by then that he had on his hands an anxious doctor, who needed to receive rather than give guidance—as is so often the case, some wise older clinicians had told us in medical school, with the dying and their doctors. As Yale Kneeland, a wonderful physician and teacher, put it to us one afternoon, "Wait for your cues, and give them your full attention." He was referring to the manner in which someone approaching death can help the doctor to a reconciliation with the inevitable, as opposed to that last-ditch fury of distracted busywork which can mask an attending physician's despair as he or she sees the battle to be nearing the end.

After the smile came more words, evidence of a shift: at a minimum, his desire to have done with himself as our subject matter of the day, or more likely, I felt both at the moment and later, his wish to help out a doctor who looked frustrated and forlorn as he wondered what to say, how to say it. The words were given the form of a question, "Why don't you bring some poems to those medical students of yours?" I had felt useless—nothing to do in the face of what was happening to him. He had responded with an agenda. He knew I was just starting a course with the title "Literature and Medicine" at Harvard Medical School; he had helped me construct a reading list—novels and stories by such writer-physicians as William Carlos Williams, Chekhov, Walker Percy, and by others: Tolstoy, George Eliot, Flannery O'Connor. I knew of poems, lots of them, that described the subjectivity of madness, a lesser number devoted to the evocation of illness, or to a description of a hospital scene, some odes to doctors, and a few lines that rightly put them in their place for various sins of omission or commission. I knew, too, that certain poets who have fallen ill during the course of the centuries have been prompted by their experience not only to look inward, but backward, and yes, forward—to ask Gauguin's questions, inscribed on the great Tahiti canvas of 1897, finished a short time before his death: "Where do we come from? Where are we? Where are we going?" Indeed, when Ed suggested that I take a poem or two with me to class, I thought not of a particular poem or two, but those words of the great French painter-in-exile, because they belonged very much to my childhood: my mother looking at the triptych, explaining it to me, translating from the French those three questions, the biggest we can ask of ourselves or one another. A few minutes later, as we talked about which poems might be suitable for my class, I told Ed what was ringing in my ears: those questions—Gauguin's, as enunciated by my mother. He smiled. They were his, too—very much so these days, he emphasized. Then, a further comment: "I ask them [those three questions] so often, they crowd out other questions, and I haven't come up with any answers I'd like to share."

As good an explanation as any, I thought, for a dying poet's stretch of silence. What he neglected to say, of course, was that he had already, in a major way, addressed those questions—in his poem "Dying: An Introduction," and in other poems, too, with titles such as "Negatives," "Homage to Clotho: A Hospital Suite," and "Cancer: A Dream." He did not have a writer's block, as some had told him—suggesting he get help. He had already done his inquiry with words, and was still doing it as we lapped our coffee ice cream or drove through the countryside, smiling at sights and responding to sounds (a car radio's jazz). The posthumous title of his collected poems, *Hello, Darkness,* says so much about this tall, dignified gentleman whose sheer brilliance and erudition had been humbled by an illness which, yet, gave him cause for powerful, terribly unnerving lyrics—ones which medical students today, over a decade since he left us, find "exactly to the point," as I heard it put in class recently. Ed Sissman's hello to darkness was quietly thoughtful. He was waiting to see. He was watching for signs. He was coming to no conclusions, and leaving a few doors wide open. He called me shortly before he died to tell me he'd not be keeping our next "appointment." He'd used that word, no matter my efforts to rid both of us of it. I hastened to offer another one. "No need for that," he told me. Stupidly, fearfully unaware (not only patients "deny"), I pressed the matter with an announcement of my open schedule—so that he had to do it, finally, say a firm good-bye, "I hope I'll see you anon." That last word succeeded—its slight awkwardness, its timelessness, its rendering of the now and the future, its capacity to break through the conventional, temporal statements: I'd been told what he had long known better than some of us doctors—that death had no intention of waiting very long for him. That word *anon* was the next to the last one I heard from Ed. He said good-bye after I promised, too wordily, an imminent visit. He soon took leave of us, and the next thing I knew, I was sitting in a church, listening to his friends sing of him, and sitting in a class, talking with future doctors about the singing he did during his stay here.

Each year they come, those students—full of their decency and earnest goodness. We read prose, mostly, but every once in a while I tuck in a poem; and with those who get serious about writers and writing (a few do every year) the poems become a mainstay. Many of them are well known, the obvious ones to call upon: Robert Lowell or Sylvia Plath telling us of madness; William Carlos Williams of his various patients; Peter Davison (Ed's friend, editor, and literary executor) of alarm and grief as the shadows fall upon the several victims of any, particular, approaching death; Auden doing one of his requiems—reminders that the end of life can move us back reflectively toward the splendors of its middle. Even a twentieth-century collection of poems which tell of pain or a fatal illness, of melancholy or craziness, of losing a wife, a husband, a child or a patient, with all the attendant sorrow and bitterness and anger, would be a substantial one to assemble. I draw upon the doctor-poets (Williams, of course, and Dannie Abse and John Stone and Jon Mukand), upon the patient-poets as they have given us their moments of worry or apprehension, things slipping badly, with no good end in sight, or things only temporarily awry, with just enough of the jitters to jog the mind loose of words—Philip Levine's "The Doctor of Starlight," Theodore Roethke's "Infirmity," Karl Shapiro's "The Leg," Richard Eberhart's "The Cancer Cells." But mostly, there is Ed's voice in me, his words, the "invitation to the dance" he had to accept when he went to the doctor, told his story, submitted to the poking, the peering, the gadgetry, the trays of instruments, the encounters:

> Like hummingbirds syringes tap
> The novocaine and sting my thigh
> To sleep, the sword play begins.
> The stainless modern knife digs in—
> Meticulous trencherman—and twongs
> A tendon faintly. Coward, I groan.

He did more than groan timidly. He gave us words not only with respect to a finite life's last act, but also words for those high moments of consciousness that philosophers keep saying make us what we are, the creature of language, the creature of Gauguin's questions, the creature who can joust bravely with Clotho, dig (from the sands suddenly let loose to pour so fast by a trickster fate) the phrases

that render not only himself but the larger scene of hospitals everywhere: the I clinging to itself, the M.D. standing in for all of us,
who know that our turn, too, will come:

> Today. Tonight. Through my
> Invisible new veil
> Of infinity, I see
> November's world—
> Low scud, slick street, three giggling girls—
> As, oddly, not as sombre
> As December
> But as green
> As anything:
> As spring.

Each year, when I bring Ed's music, the "spring" of his "Dying"
to young men and women readying for their own swordplay, soon
enough to start, I remember him, and try to share him with these
fighters-in-training. I tell them of his mind's liveliness, and show
them his beloved Hopper with a slide or two. So often we ended our
times together looking silently at Hopper's stillness—though Ed always knew to remind me, as he did in a poem, that "a shaft of
morning sun / Peoples the vacuum with American light." His
poems, as he remembered them being born, came with pictures,
early in the mornings, out of dreams. ("Don't 'free associate,'" my
analyst would sometimes say, feeling derisive toward the wordy banality of my posture and his; and then the plea: "Try to describe
what you saw last night before you woke up and remembered to
cover it with words.") Like Jorie Graham, Ed saw erosion; and like
her, he thought a lot about life's meaning. I think he'd admire her
"At the Long Island Jewish Geriatric Home," as my students do:

> This is the sugar
> you're stealing
> from the nurses, filling
> your pillow
> with something
> for nothing,
> filling my pockets
> till I'm some kind

of sandman
you can send away. As for
dreams,
your head rustling in
white ash,
who needs them?

Dying when he did, he was spared that erosion—a kind that gets observed but goes unexpressed. When I read that poem of Jorie Graham's, I think I realized why Ed stopped writing verse a couple of years before he died. He'd "had a few stark nightmares recently," he once told me, but they'd eluded him on waking. I think they had told him that it was best for someone in his shoes to stop fighting for such memories, and let others step forward—those whose unblinking vision by day didn't have to reckon with the immediate reality of a night with nightmares. Meanwhile, "today, tonight" we doctors can be grateful to him, to Jorie Graham, to lots of poets who help us stop and listen, hear ourselves walking toward those ward beds, toward our own, final bed, too.

Meanwhile, my medical students try to make sense of their stage of that journey—make sense of the long struggle they will soon enough be having with death. Already, in school, they know the burdens and obstacles: so much factuality to master; so various the professional possibilities to consider; so many diseases that are yet to be understood. Time had already become their adversary in the premedical years, and will never let go of their lives—all the things to know and do, the tests that follow tests, and even in middle age, when every possible certificate covers every available office wall, the test that any disease can offer the person who takes it on seriously. Time is a battlefield of sorts—the doctor trying to obtain it for someone, and death anxious to take it away, the sooner the better. With such a combative future, no wonder a poem or two can have such a powerful meaning for an apprentice in a profession not known for the leisure it affords serious practitioners.

With certain medical students, poems have been a psychological if not spiritual mainstay throughout the years of their educations. I have known them as undergraduates, introduced them in my college courses to William Carlos Williams, Howard Nemerov, Elizabeth Bishop, W. S. Merwin, Robert Lowell, Philip Levine, Denise Lev-

ertov, Peter Davison, and of course, Ed Sissman; then, in my medical school course, continued the encounter with poets, even as we
meet doctors such as Lydgate (in *Middlemarch*) and Dick Diver (in
Tender Is the Night). In some instances, we have continued our
informal reading right through the so-called postgraduate period,
the hurry and foreboding of the internship and residency years—an
hour here and there for a discussion of a story, a poem. "I carry
around that book [a thin anthology of poems] in my pocket," one
resident in internal medicine told me, "but on most days I have no
time to read even one poem." Then he added, "Maybe I'll reach for
the book, read a couple of lines and try to remember them. In a
week, I'll have a poem under my belt." He had done so, in that
fashion, with Ed Sissman's "A Death Place"—and sometimes, when
we sat and had coffee, he joked with me about the poem: "That
opening, those first lines—'Very few people know where they will
die, / But I do: in a brick-faced hospital . . .'—they are lines written
for me, I sometimes think! There are days I never leave the hospital,
and I find myself thinking I never will. I'll live here and die here!
I'll be walking down one of the corridors—I know them all so well
I could be blindfolded, yet get where I need to be—and the lines
from 'A Death Place' will come to me again: 'Very few people know
where they will die, / But I do: in a brick-faced hospital.' I'll begin
to think I'm crazy, hearing the words over and over, but no, we do
that with lines from songs, and those are lines from a 'song,' and I'm
singing it along with the poet! I've been living out the doctor's side
of that poem—seeing people who are staring at death. I've wished I
could share some poems with those patients, but you can't put words
in someone else's mouth! Each of my patients finds a way of thinking of what's ahead. Some will read the Bible—there's plenty of
poetry there. Others will find a poem in the newspaper, or in a
religious card that's been sent them. Or in the words of a relative. A
patient of mine was reading Robert Frost. One morning he asked
me what I thought Robert Frost was reading when he lay dying. I
drew a blank. I wasn't sure how Frost died—suddenly, or from a
lingering illness.

"I don't think we give our patients credit enough for the meditation they do when they're very sick. Even when I was a medical
student, and just 'let loose' on the wards, I noticed that some of my
patients (people who had no education beyond high school, and

some of them not even that much) would keep repeating the lyrics of a song, or they would repeat a phrase they'd heard in church—holding on for dear life to some words. That's why poems have meant so much to me in medical school and since then [during his residency years]. Like patients, poets are probably holding on for dear life to some words!"

He stopped abruptly and looked into the distance—beyond a dusty window toward a cloudy sky. A shrug and a sigh reminded both of us how tiring his work can be; but a faint smile on his face asserted something else—a thoughtful young doctor's realization that he'd heard something significant, maybe even memorable, come out of his mouth. Earlier that day he'd told me how dissatisfied he was with his various responses to his patients, how inadequate his words sounded as he recalled them during those few minutes of respite he secured for himself. Now, he felt as if a gift had been given him, "There's a terrible poetry to suffering. Your friend Ed Sissman experienced it and gave it to us in his poems; and I think some of us doctors experience it, too, and we try to say what we're experiencing, and sometimes we can't find the words, and other times, we're lucky we run into a poet who gives us the words!"

All the time medical students are learning to concentrate their minds sharply, get to the very heart of this or that matter. All the time those students are struggling to tame life itself, in its excesses, its madness, its fateful moments. All the time those students are being stopped in their tracks by moments of high drama, terrible tragedy, exceeding bad luck. No wonder, as some of them tell me, their minds ache to give sharp, pointed expression to what has been seen, heard, felt, comprehended. Poets are always attempting to sharpen their sight, to harken closely, to attend language carefully in hope of calling upon it shrewdly, wisely—a boost to an understanding of what is happening or can happen. Poets distill the mind's thoughts to a point that—well, a young doctor can hear a couple of lines and know what Ed Sissman and all other people in each "brick-faced hospital" are trying both to remember and forget. Poets give us images and metaphors, even as doctors feel at times overwhelmed by what they witness, and so long for someone's help in making sense of it all. Poets offer the epiphanies doctors and patients alike crave—even if in the silent form of a slant of late afternoon light: "I was standing in the corridor outside that patient's room. I knew she would be dead soon. The blind was down. It was so damn dark. I looked at my watch. It was four-fifteen—a mid-January four-fifteen. Suddenly I saw a line of light—the sun peeking in from the side of the window, sneaking along the floor, climbing up the side of the bed, falling into a patient's hand. I stood there gazing: I was in a dream. Then I heard the patient move a little. I looked at her. *She* was looking at the light on her hand. She was moving her hand—into the light, out of it. She was smiling a little, playing with light—before the darkness took her. I thought of Sissman; I thought of my sister [who had died of leukemia when he was in college]. A doctor is someone who knows lots of moments like that—if we'd only let them happen!"

Perhaps one way of looking at poets is to think of them as akin to that doctor—willing and able to catch light, have fun with it, mourn its disappearance, render it for the rest of us. I think Ed Sissman knew how akin his sensibility was to that young doctor's— hence his desire to give word to the hospital scenes he had joined as a protagonist, yes, but also as a willful, watching presence, eager to shine upon us, bring us out of the shadows always ready to claim us. When a medical student tells me that, finally, an entire course called "Medical Humanities" comes down to a remembered line or two (with luck, a whole stanza) amid the rush and chaos of hospital duties, clinic emergencies, I think of Ed singing to the death that dogged him so early on, so hard and long; and I think of that young doctor, poised at a room's entrance, watching a patient make light of light, and thinking of Ed Sissman and his poetry—a poet become a doctor's light.

Poetry, August 1988

A Different Set of Rules

Throughout her career, the South African novelist Nadine Gordimer has wanted to explore the terrain where personal interests, desires, and ambitions encounter (and, not rarely, contend with) the demands and trials of a politically active life. She has had a keen eye for the exceedingly precarious moral situation of her own kind—the privileged white intelligentsia that abhors apartheid, detests the exploitation of 25 million unfranchised, economically vulnerable citizens at the hands of 5 million people who, so far, have had a powerful modern army at their disposal, not to mention the wealth of a vigorous, advanced capitalist society.

To oppose the assumptions and everyday reality of a particular world, yet be among the men and women who enjoy its benefits—those accorded to the substantial upper bourgeoisie of, say, Johannesburg and Cape Town—is at the very least to know and live uneasily, maybe at times shamefacedly, with irony as a central aspect of one's introspective world. At what point is one's thoroughly comfortable, highly rewarded life as it is lived from year to year the issue—no matter the hoped-for extenuation that goes with a progressive voting record, an espousal of liberal pieties? Put differently, when ought one to break decisively with a social and political order, put on the line one's way of living (one's job, the welfare of one's family)?

In past novels, notably *Burger's Daughter*, Ms. Gordimer has asked such questions relentlessly of her own kind and, by extension, of all those readers who share her color and status in other countries less dramatically split and conflicted. Now, in *My Son's Story*, a bold, unnerving tour de force, she offers a story centered around the other side of both the racial line and the railroad tracks—yet the dilemmas that confront her characters are at heart very much like those that plague affluent whites, insofar as they allow themselves to oppose the entrenched authority of the South African government: how to measure up in one's daily, personal life to one's avowed ethical and political principles, one's activist sentiments and commitments.

The father who figures as the central character in this "son's story" is Sonny, a once obscure, humble schoolteacher whose political radicalization and prominence have been achieved at the start of the novel, which is told by the traditional, anonymous narrative voice of the author and by another, equally significant interpretive voice, that of Sonny's son, Will. Right off, the major psychological themes of disenchantment and betrayal are struck. The adolescent Will, telling a lie ("I would say I was going to work with a friend at a friend's house, and then I'd slip off to a cinema"), encounters his father in that very movie theater living a lie—there with a white woman, his lover. This is contemporary urban, cosmopolitan South Africa—movies desegregated, interracial sex no longer outlawed, but the heart of apartheid (its economic and political basis) still very much alive. The son's surprise, anger, disappointment are expressed with great passion and vehemence—he, in fact, becomes the novelist's alter ego, an interesting split and one that enables a complex, many-sided, even contrapuntal presentation of what is at once a story of domestic manners (those all too familiar triangles of two women and a man, or of father, mother, and son) and a tough-minded, fearlessly candid political novel in which any number of psychological and racial clichés are subject to a novelist's searching scrutiny.

In the early sections of *My Son's Story* we learn about the transformation of a "coloured" schoolteacher, his father an upholsterer, into a revolutionary leader and orator. An autodidact, he had read Shakespeare and Kafka over and over, obtained from them the ultimate secular wisdom of Western letters—a wry, stoic sense of life's tragic and comic (sometimes absurdly comic) aspects. From his people, family and neighbors alike, and out of his own soul's decency and kindness, he found the daily strength needed by anyone who wants to be an honorable, loving husband and father. For Aila, his wife, for Baby, their daughter and first child, for Will, named after Shakespeare (how do some of us jaded folk, schooled for years, ever recapture the innocence and heartfelt sincerity of such a parental decision?), Sonny, the low-paid, earnest, hardworking civil servant and educator, once had an almost infinite supply of concern and affection. He attended them in every way—a sturdy house-holder, no matter the constant, terrible shadow of apartheid. But gradually Sonny got connected to his people's political struggle, an exceedingly dangerous one in a country whose ruling class for decades ruthlessly punished any and all activist dissent: a democracy for a white minority, a harsh totalitarian regime for a black majority. Gradually, too, he found less and less time for his family. He shows up now and then, but hurriedly leaves. To call upon a well-known biblical polarity, he is trying to gain a whole new world for others, yet his own family's world, maybe his soul, too, are in grave jeopardy.

Sonny's political ascent is a major topic for the novel's one narrator (who is obviously horrified by apartheid and anxious to see it ended, and is struggling to find the self-respect that goes with a principled observer's persistent dissent). It is this narrator who gives us a rather conventional, well-told account of a family's ups and downs, its transition from social and emotional ordinariness to a life of both marginality and prominence. Sonny goes to jail, and with that experience comes a spiritual transfiguration of sorts—the emergence of the political leader whose worth and integrity have been tested in the oppressor's bestial dungeons. Soon enough, he is privy to the exceptional life of the freedom-fighter—the hardship during and after imprisonment of relentless state surveillance, but also the respect and even worship that come his way from certain whites as well as his own people. One of the former, Hannah Plowman (she has a last name, none of the "coloured" people do), visits Sonny (talk about names!) in prison as a representative of an international human rights organization, and upon his release they become intimate.

This love affair is treated by Ms. Gordimer in her regular authorial presence with great tenderness, compassion, good will. Indeed, much of the novel's power and interest derive from her almost uncanny ability to portray each of the novel's characters with sympathy and subtlety. Sonny's gentle goodness, his immense personal dignity, his courage are emblematic of the best we have come to know over the past decades in Nelson Mandela and Martin Luther King, Jr., and in those lesser known but no less brave, resourceful, idealistic men and women who have worked alongside them. Aila's endurance, her carefully maintained emotional stability, her generosity of spirit bring to mind any number of wives who have tried with all their might to hold things together at home while their husbands took on social and racial evils in the public arena.

Hannah Plowman is no fatuous or self-indulgent or arrogantly patronizing white liberal activist, a stereotype the author obviously wants strenuously to avoid giving to the legions waiting for just such satisfactions from her. Hannah's good will and intelligence are obvious, and so is her essential uprightness and honesty. She is the proverbial Other Woman, without the protection that racial victimization and political heroism afford. Yet the author who tells us of her wants us to understand, sympathize with, admire her; and in similar fashion, we are nudged toward a compassionate understanding of Baby, who is, however, the least satisfactorily examined of the major characters. Her youthful, rebellious self-centeredness is all too readily redeemed by an abrupt marriage, exile, and a turn toward her own kind of radical activism against South Africa, though from the relative safety of Tanzania.

There is, however, another way of looking at Sonny and, more broadly, at those who in public exhort others with respect to all sorts of virtues, even fight gallantly on behalf of them, yet who abandon their families for the heavy demand of political activism, though also for personal pleasures—not only sex, the easiest one for many of today's novelists to describe, but arguably more problematic (if not perverse) thrills and addictions such as celebrity and power. This alternative view is given expression by Will; the story, as the title tells us, is his take on yet another of our great men, our heroic figures whose courage and values we gladly applaud.

A novelist's brilliant decision works wonders, ever so slowly yet decisively. A boy stumbles into his august father's secret life, is stunned by the casual, relaxed manner in which the father is living that life, is confused at the seeming expectation that he, too, an adolescent belonging to a once tight-knit family, will take in stride such circumstances. His perplexity and frustration give way to a sustained, withering scorn—a sardonic voice that keeps at the reader, reminds us that this is a novel meant to look closely and with nuanced force at moral complexity, moral ambiguity, but most pointedly at moral hypocrisy, which is in no short supply among many of us, no matter our nation, our race, our class, and, not least, our educational attainment. One more leader, a larger-than-life figure, is found to have clay feet—by his son, who has occasions aplenty to witness the human consequences of such a disparity between a public and a private person.

To the end, Will won't let up—his sharp, unsentimental vision contrasts tellingly with the lofty aspirations of the others. Even Aila gets drawn into revolutionary politics and, eventually, a trial that threatens to end in her imprisonment, too. (Like her daughter, she chooses exile.) Only Will stands apart—saddened, hurt, alarmed, disgusted. A fearful, cynical youth, he slowly becomes a discerning, thoughtful observer of his own family, not to mention, by implication, all those who talk up a good storm (in their books and articles, their lectures, their graduation talks, their political speeches) but live by rules other than those they choose to enunciate for their readers, listeners. In a stunning conclusion, a mix of prose and poetry, Ms. Gordimer tells us that her Will has lived up to his name: "What he did—my father—made me a writer. Do I have to thank him for that? Why couldn't I have been something else? I am a writer and this is my first book—that I can never publish."

She is suggesting that with respect to our moral and political leaders many important biographical facts may go unmentioned, even by those who know exactly the nature and significance of those facts. The sons of our idols (or the husbands, the wives, the daughters) keep quiet; friends and colleagues, even journalists and historians, speak tactfully, if at all, about certain matters, and justify their silence, their discretion, their apologias, with clever rationalizations.

The idol must not fall—consequently, a public deception persists, and with it a kind of public blindness. It is left to playwrights and novelists, our Shakespeares and Tolstoys and their descendants today (they who have no claim upon factuality or realpolitik) to render the many and often disparate truths of human experience, the inconsistencies and contradictions, the troubling paradoxes. The heart and soul of this brilliantly suggestive and knowing novel is its courageous exploration of such matters, of the conceits and deceits that inform the lives not only of ordinary people but those whom the rest of us invest with such majesty and awe.

New York Times Book Review, October 21, 1990

On Moral Conduct

So often, recently, when I try to grapple with moral matters, alone or with my wife and children, or with students in lectures or in formal discussions, my mind goes back to earlier days: the college years, when I worked hard to fathom William Carlos Williams' *Paterson* (the first two books), and the medical school years, when I visited him fairly often and heard his own explication de texte, and more: a wise man's ethical intensity put to strong, unaffected and often colloquial word. In the early parts of *Paterson* he is quick to scorn the abstract mind at work, whether in the construction of verse, religious ideas, moral philosophy. He will make a "reply to Greek and Latin with the barehands." Unlike J. Alfred Prufrock, he will, indeed, be found daring. He deplores a contentedly aesthetic poetry. "The rest have run out— / after the rabbits"; but he will stay, and provoke all the well-to-do ones, not to mention a few of the well-educated ("The knowledgeable idiots, the university"). He dares assert himself as "Sniffing the trees, / just another dog / among a lot of dogs." He quotes from the past, draws from John Addington Symonds' *Studies of the Greek Poets*, but not as so many others have, to applaud the established, the traditional. He will reach for the ordinary, the local, will hope to connect in both mind and heart with the energies of this century's ordinary American working men and women.

Williams issued warnings to himself in *Paterson*, and they were moral as well as aesthetic. He worries about his craft becoming "subverted by thought"; worries that he will end up writing "stale poems." But he is ready to take on more than the aridity of pedants. His repeated call to arms, the well-known phrase "no ideas but in things," is a prelude to distinctions he keeps making throughout *Paterson* (and he had made them elsewhere in his writing career): between poetry and life, between ideas and action, between the abstract and the concrete, between theory and practice, and, not least, between art and conduct. As he keeps stressing the importance of testing thought, whether the poet's or the moralist's, with the measurement of conduct, he keeps submitting himself as an instance, if not a case history: the doctor who attends patients regularly, and who writes poems such as *Paterson*—and who is, thereby, in double jeopardy, because like others he may well fail to practice what he preaches to patients and readers alike.

Williams uses the device of a nameless woman correspondent to confront himself—a powerful Augustian arraignment by a writer and physician of his prideful side, his unreflecting egoism, to use a phrase of George Eliot's in *Middlemarch*. Those prose segments interrupt the poetry—as if the author is reminding himself and the reader both lest an aesthetic achievement, however graceful and persuasive, fail to get translated into the ordinary life of the world. "My feelings about you now," says the letter writer, "are those of anger and indignation, and they enable me to tell you a lot of things straight from the shoulder, with my usual tongue-tied round-aboutness." She amplifies: "You might as well take all your own literature and everyone else's and toss it into one of those big garbage trucks of the Sanitation Department, so long as the people with the top-cream minds and the 'finer' sensibilities use those minds and sensibilities not to make themselves more humane beings than the average person, but merely as a means of ducking responsibility toward a better understanding of their fellow men, except theoretically—which doesn't mean a God damned thing."

This pointed outburst of scorn for certain academic habits, if not values, this strain of anti-intellectualism, is not unusual in Williams' work. True, he distances himself from the remarks by attributing them to an anonymous, made-up character. But he is the one, after all, who has fashioned this statement, even as he is the one who, in his own prose remarks about himself, almost as if part of a diary, dares confide this in *Paterson*: "He was more concerned, much more concerned with detaching the label from a discarded mayonnaise jar, the glass jar in which some patient had brought a specimen for examination, than to examine and treat the twenty and more infants taking their turn from the outer office, their mothers tormented and jabbering. He'd stand in the alcove pretending to wash, the jar at the bottom of the sink well out of sight and, as the rod of the water came down, work with his fingernail in the splash at the edge of the colored label striving to loose the tightly glued paper. It must have been varnished over, he argued, to have it stick that way. One corner of it he'd got loose in spite of all and would get the rest presently: talking pleasantly the while and with great skill to the anxious parent."

With a novelist's eye for the precise details of an apparently meaningless moment in a busy doctor's life, Williams announces yet again a challenge that is both psychological and moral: our preoccupations and obsessions, however innocuous and transient in nature, indicate how hard it is for any of us, no matter our good intentions, to break out from what elsewhere in *Paterson* is called "the regularly ordered plateglass of his thoughts." When Williams speaks in this mode he approaches those daily, small conceits that keep many of us all too self-centered—and particularly confine us when the needs of strangers are at stake. For him "plateglass" is a contemporary medium—our version of that water into which Narcissus peered so eagerly and fixedly. I remember the old doctor, waving his hands angrily, as he looked at some of that postwar "plateglass" in New York City—its capacity to separate people from others, while promoting the illusion of transparency. Once, a bit enigmatically, he blurted out: "That glass is always painfully cold—the air-conditioning hits it in summer and the winter slaps it hard." He was letting me know cryptically how aloof and icy our solipsism can be—some of it our very own, some of it socially and culturally sanctioned. At times, as he waxed indignant, I thought of young Emerson, writing his essays, such as "Self-Reliance": an earlier assault on the rigidities and smugness and arrogance of the universities—in Williams' phrase, "the whole din of fracturing thought." But he knew to include himself in those at times overwrought or all too unqualified generalizations, if not denunciations. Like Emerson (in "The American Scholar" essay, and elsewhere) he was interested in the distinction between character and intellect, and knew painfully that the former by no means necessarily correlates with the latter, and indeed, in some instances one finds a reverse (a perverse) correlation. As Williams once reminded me about the Nazi Goebbels, and yes, his own friend Ezra Pound: "Look at the two of them, one a Ph.D. and smart as they come, and the other one of the twentieth century's most original poets, also as brilliant as they come in certain ways—and they both end up peddling hate, front men for the worst scum the world has ever seen."

If an impediment to moral conduct is the tug of our vain selves, as it may affect our thinking, our choices in life, our daily actions, one more obstacle has been presented to us for consideration by another writing physician, Anton Chekhov. In the story "Gooseberries" the reader comes across this remarkable, discursive statement uttered by the character Ivan Ivanych—something Chekhov clearly and unnervingly wants us all to contemplate:

> I saw a happy man, one whose cherished dream had so obviously come true, who had attained his goal in life, who had got what he wanted, who was satisfied with his lot and with himself. For some reason an element of sadness had always mingled with my thoughts of human happiness, and now at the sight of a happy man I was assailed by an oppressive feeling bordering on despair. It weighed on me particularly at night. A bed was made up for me in a room next to my brother's bedroom, and I could hear that he was wakeful, and that he would get up again and again, go to the plate of gooseberries and eat one after another. I said to myself: how many contented, happy people there really are! What an overwhelming force they are! Look at life: the insolence and idleness of the strong, the ignorance and brutishness of the weak, horrible poverty everywhere, overcrowding, degeneration, drunkenness, hypocrisy, lying—yet in all the houses and on all the streets there is peace and quiet; of the fifty thousand people who live in our town there is not one who would cry out, who would vent his indignation aloud. We see the people who go to market, eat by day, sleep by night, who babble nonsense, marry, grow old, good-naturedly drag their dead to the cemetery, but we do not see or hear those who suffer, and what is terrible in life goes on somewhere behind the scenes. Everything is peaceful and quiet and only mute statistics protest: so many people gone out of their minds, so many gallons of vodka drunk, so many children dead from malnutrition—and

such a state of things is evidently necessary; obviously the happy man is at ease only because the unhappy ones bear their burdens in silence, and if there were not this silence, happiness would be impossible. It is a general hypnosis. Behind the door of every contented, happy man there ought to be someone standing with a little hammer and continually reminding him with a knock that there are unhappy people, that however happy he may be, life will sooner or later show him its claws, and trouble will come to him—illness, poverty, losses, and then no one will see or hear him, just as now he neither sees nor hears others. But there is no man with a hammer. The happy man lives at his ease, faintly fluttered by small daily cares, like an aspen in the wind—and all is well.

How do we find that "hammer" for ourselves—for surely our neighbor's hammer, even our wife's or husband's, our mother's or father's will get us nowhere in the long run. To be sure, we do, indeed, acquire our assumptions and values from others to a considerable extent. When those whom we love or respect (for example, our teachers) assert certain principles, urge them on us, hammer them home, we are likely to agree, to try going along. Our espousal can be deeply felt—no mere intellectual agreement. The gut, the heart register agreement: this is how I see things, too. But Chekhov is getting at something else—not so much our enthusiastic nod to his observation as our inclination, even when prodded, to respond only so far. His use of an adverb is singularly important—the suggestion that outside anyone's door someone with a hammer ought be standing, "continually reminding" the person of the message Chekhov has put to his readers. The implication of the word "continually" is obvious: that a knock on the head occasionally (whether a sermon, or a lecture, or a whole course, or the reading of a story such as "Gooseberries," or this statement, or any book) will not quite do. We shrug off, shake off, walk away from, close our eyes to the world of unhappiness—even to our own, never mind that of others. Chekhov insists upon the commonness of this maneuver— to keep under wraps any inclination the conscience has not only to prompt one's awareness, but one's conduct.

Not that we don't pay a price for our seeming happiness. In a devastating moral judgment, rendered almost like a whispered afterthought to a long, blunt address, Chekhov describes his happy man as "faintly fluttered" by the "daily cares" of a particular life, and summons the image of an aspen in the wind. Whereas Emerson might have hectored those in his audience with the exhortation to nourish the acorn of their conscience so that it might become, one day, a mighty oak, Chekhov compares many of us who think of ourselves as reasonably content in life with the aspen, a nimble piece of nature, indeed. They can be arresting and lovely, banks and banks of aspens, especially in the early autumn, when they catch fire wonderfully before dying. But they assert themselves en masse, rather than individually—an all too appropriate reminder to some of us how significantly we rely upon social and cultural approval for the enjoyment of the pleasantly lived life. Chekhov knows to steer clear, here, of an image that would suggest sturdy, willful independence—a willingness, even, to go it alone, and at any cost, to the point of ending up permanently bent or broken, hence unhappy. Aspens are a delight, but hardly the defiant loner. They blanket the land, and give us a sense of familiar security. I do not picture William Tell standing in front of an aspen.

Chekhov's wry commentary can, at best, prick the conscience. We remember for a while that misery exists but, made uncomfortable, we soon enough want to forget what we have just had called to our attention—and alas, soon enough we succeed in going about our business, those daily cares mentioned. Of course, Chekhov is ready to hammer us with a big threat—that eventually all of us fall from the (secular) grace that has luckily been ours, to face illness and death, if not the poverty to which he makes reference. One would think, then, that a certain self-interest would caution us to be a bit more vulnerable to that hammer, pay it heed on behalf of others, so that one's own eventual jeopardy, in the evening of one's time here, won't be all that unhappy: it would be done unto us as we have done unto others, or so we'd hope, were a lot of folks being similarly foresighted, at a minimum, if not, eventually, persuaded that their good deeds were satisfying in themselves as well as a moral down payment, as it were, on old age.

Yet, we don't think that way for long, most of us. Perhaps (a gloomy thought) the best of us are in the tradition of Dr. Williams and Dr. Chekhov: we are seized by spasms of genuine moral awareness, but we are as pliant as aspens in our capacity to accommodate to the prevailing rhythms of the haute bourgeoisie world we inhabit, an accommodation made by Williams, who knew (a painful recognition, he often said) that the poor and working-class people, his "ordinary folks," didn't read *Paterson*, even though he tried so hard to give them an important voice in it; and an accommodation also made by Chekhov, who knew well which people went to see his plays, read his stories—certainly not those jailed on the Sakhalin Island he visited and described so painstakingly. The irony persists— a gnawing if not galling one—that powerful poems and poignant prose can affect us, excite us, cause us to see more clearly, yet not be that daily hammer Chekhov prescribes, and Williams seemed to require, hence his confessional spells in *Paterson*, meant to say loud and clear that at least one moralist was trying strenuously not to point his finger at others, such a great temptation and opportunity for writers, not to mention those who teach what has been written.

Are we left, then, to savor irony, such a delicious part, anyway, of the academic menu? Both Williams and Chekhov have their time with irony, the former in his fiery or truculent manner, the latter wryly, wistfully. The ironies of *Paterson*, or those mentioned by Chekhov in "Gooseberries," are unsettling, though not exactly new discoveries. That one can be well-educated and not especially decent or kind-hearted is a recognition not denied over the generations to all sorts of people, the highly literate (looking inward, perhaps, or casting a glance at a neighbor or two) and the relatively uneducated (some of whom may, in their "menial" work, perhaps on one or another campus, see ample evidence that big-shot intellectuals can also be as petty and mischievous as their so-called lessers). That one's happiness depends to a degree on a willful or unselfconscious disregard of the misery others all over constantly experience has also been evident over the generations to many of us who have counted ourselves as fortunate. Nor are advanced degrees in philosophy, theology, or psychology the necessary conditions for such knowledge. Indeed, even the most brilliant and self-aware of men and women, highly educated and psychoanalyzed to boot, can still be fitting subjects for the kind of moral observations those two literary doctors made. Put differently, I can take courses in literature (reading Williams and Chekhov), and courses in moral reasoning and courses in social ethics, and I can have my head examined, so that I am less and less prone to use certain "mechanisms of defense," such as denial, hence more and more aware of what is happening to me, and presumably, to others in the world, through a growing capacity for identification—and yet, in important respects still be all too smug and self-preoccupied: a moral failure in those brief, small everyday moments that have a way not only of accumulating, but working their way into the texture of one's being, one's character.

I remember my father talking about character, telling us when young, around the dinner table, that "character is how you behave when no one is looking." I also remember having a similar discussion with my psychoanalyst—and won't, I hope, forget his interesting response to my mention of my father's shrewd way of putting the matter: "He [my dad] told you something that applies here, too [the psychoanalytic situation]. For all the 'honesty' about emotions we encourage, there is a performer at work in all of us when we're analysands. We have to reckon with the analyst—and it's not all a question of transference." I wrote those words down long ago, and have mulled them over many times since then. Are we ever in a situation when "no one is looking"? In analysis we obviously will account for ourselves with the doctor whom we are "seeing," and who, presumably, sees through our all dodges and deceits, and needs to help us to do likewise, since many of them are done unwittingly. But the billions of people who don't go through psychoanalysis (or read *Paterson*, or "Gooseberries") nevertheless carry inside themselves company of sorts, those eyes which either watch us resolutely, attend us closely, or in varying degrees don't pay us much heed. In a sense, then, my father's wise remark has to be amplified: crooks and thieves are such because in their heads "no one is looking," apart from whether the police or anyone else happen to be nearby; and for some of us, who try to be conscientious, someone is always "looking," even if we are as solitary as Thoreau was at Walden during those years he spent there—with the whole of Western civilization, one begins to realize, assembled at his side in the Concord woods near the lake.

I suppose I would have my father's aphorism assert that character is how you behave in response to the company you keep, seen and unseen. As is often the case, the extremes are the easiest to discuss or comprehend. The so-called psychopath or sociopath, the amoral one, is a person who has no such company or, maybe, pretty bad company at best—the terrible silences of an emotionally abandoned early life or the demonic voices of a tormented childhood. In contrast, an overly conscientious person who hems and haws endlessly, if not crazily, about every possible matter is plagued by all too much company—the strident and insistent commands that won't for a moment let go of someone. Most of us, however, are not criminals, and not caught in the minute-by-minute tyranny of obsessions and compulsions. We live our lives in what gets called a reasonably "normal" way. Dr. Williams tells of us in his long, lyrical examination of America—the ordinary people who go about our business, don't get into trouble with the law, have our blind spots, and, too, our reasonably good moments, when we are kind and thoughtful toward others. Dr. Chekhov tells of us, as well—we whose happiness, he makes clear, is not necessarily misguided or a mean-spirited kind of selfishness, but rather often a matter of fate, chance, circumstance: the busy motions of the cheerful heart which leave little time or energy even for a consideration of the world's widespread wretchedness, let alone a concerted effort to take up arms against it.

Certain students of mine have taken to heart the moral analysis Williams and Chekhov put to themselves first, then the rest of us. They have come to talk, having done a good deal of quiet reflection on their own, and the result sometimes has been lively exchanges which prove hard to forget. Particularly memorable for me were the comments of one student who was always trying to ask a lot of himself—though he made it clear to me that if he had gone through some kind of moral transformation, the reasons for it were not entirely elusive. Here are some of his observations and self-observations, as taped and then edited—several segments of our various and rambling conversations pulled together for the sake of an essay's requirements:

> I'm only 21, so what do I know—I mean, about "life." I've been about as lucky as you can be. I've never really been in any trouble. All four of my grandparents are alive and healthy. My parents are happily married, and we've got plenty of money. All my friends used to say—when I was in high school—that I came from the "ideal family." I'm not saying everything was perfect. My dad has had a drinking problem; he's not an alcoholic, but when he gets depressed, once or twice a year, he

binges out. He'll go at it for a few days, then level off—and we're fine for months. My mother gets very upset when that [drinking] happens; she'll be real "down" afterwards. She goes to church a lot. When things are normal, they don't go too much, except for Christmas and Easter. My mother has a bit of a "money problem," I guess. She goes on binges herself, buying binges—like dad, about twice a year. She builds up for one, and then—well, the bills start coming in. She went to see a doctor—I don't know if he was a psychiatrist [I'd asked]— and he said she needed "treatment." But she said she'd stop on her own. For two years she was fine. Then she had a buying spree, and she was going to start therapy, but she and my father talked, and they figured she'd spend more money seeing a doctor than she spent with all that plastic [the credit cards].

But they're good people, and they've always tried to *be* good. My dad gives a lot of money to charities, and so does mom. She inherited $40,000 from an aunt of hers, and she gave the whole thing to CARE. I remember when that happened. I was twelve or thirteen. I could tell that she had some second thoughts, and so did dad, but they had one of their talks, and I was allowed to sit and listen, and I could speak up, if I wanted. I did! I suggested they give half to charity, and keep half. My mom asked me why. I said—oh, I said "because," and I clammed up. My dad drew me out; he asked me what "we" should do with the half we'd keep, if we stuck to my plan. I didn't know, at first. Then I remembered what he'd been discussing with mom—that they buy a Boston Whaler [motorboat]. So, I said we could do that, get the boat. Dad lowered his head, and then he said, yes, we could. Mom said yes, we could, too. Then she gave her lecture on her [maiden] aunt, and how she had been a volunteer at a hospital for twenty years, and she had raised a lot of money for the hospital, and she had given money to all those other "causes," and we had to do what she wanted us to do. But she gave *us* the money, not the hospital—I said that. My father nodded; and I thought I was speaking for him then. His eyes and mine met, I could tell! But my mother shook her head, and that's when dad told her *she* should make the decision, and she did. All the money went to the hospital.

I now realize that it was only a little while later that she went on another of her spending sprees. I mean, I now think there was a connection. I remember dad saying to me and my little sister that he wished mom had decided *not* to give that forty thousand away: he could use it "now." I still remember the look on his face. He seemed "low." He *was* "low"; he said so—I heard him talking to his brother on the phone. That was my first lesson in "psychology" and in "ethics." I had seen a real moral struggle taking place in my parents, and I began to realize that you can be high-minded and selfish at the same time, and sensitive to the needs of others and worried about your own needs at the same time. It was then that I realized my mother's buying wasn't totally a mystery; and it was around then that my father's drinking began to make a little sense to me—the way he'd come home from work and tell us that "the company" (that's all I heard for years: "the company") was putting "pressure" on him and others, but he'd "proven" himself and got his "bonus." The next day or so, he'd be coming home with slurred speech, and stumbling all over, or we'd find him in the morning sleeping in his car, parked in front of the house. My mother would be upset with him; but I began to notice back then that she worried as much, maybe more, about the neighbors. What would they think?

When I got here [to college] I thought I'd major in economics and maybe go on to business school. But I got bored with the numbers and the theories. I liked reading history, and I liked reading novels. I like working with computers, too. I'm my dad's son! [His father was a whiz at computers.] At first I majored in history and literature, and then I switched to English. But I never liked the way the professors used the books—zeroing in on "the text," raking and raking, sifting and sifting it through narrower and narrower filters. I'm not against learning about symbols and images and metaphors, but there was something missing in those tutorials. Maybe I just had bad luck. There are some great people teaching here, but I didn't get them. All I knew—well, lots of snobby, "literary" talk, lots of pretension and *phoniness*: that word Salinger used so much in *Catcher in the Rye*. They'd be so obscure about *Jude the Obscure* that you lost sight of the big picture—Hardy taking on Oxford and Cambridge and all the arrogance and privilege; Hardy taking on *us*, if you stop and think! You can read those "texts" in [such] a way that they're not stories anymore with big moral issues and questions and challenges; and the characters in them aren't people anymore, like you and me, all caught up in contradictions, and fighting to stay above water morally. But I'd better stop blaming "them." It was me; I don't have an abstract interest in "literature." I love to read stories and get lost in them, and some of the characters—they become buddies of mine: friends, people I think of. I hate to see a movie of a novel. The movie always disappoints me. I imagine the characters looking and talking one way; and suddenly it's different—there's Robert Redford playing Jay Gatsby. Robert Redford! I walked out after half an hour.

I went back to computers. I ended up majoring in computer science, and that was when I started working in PBH [Phillips Brooks House, a student volunteer organization whose activities include tutoring in poor neighborhoods, work with the elderly, efforts in prisons, attention to the problems of the homeless]. I went to Roosevelt Towers [a low rent housing "project"] and I got to know some kids there, and they "made my day." I'd play basketball with them, and help them with their schoolwork, and take them places in Boston and Cambridge they'd never seen; and I'd get them reading—not a lot, just enough so they could begin to get "turned on." I'd read a story to them—one of Williams' about his patients, or even a Cheever story about the "fancy richos," one of the kids called them. I'd try to explain what was happening, but while I was doing it I'd suddenly remember some of those hotshot graduate students with all their put-on airs. I'd cringe and hope I wasn't being patronizing. I hope I'm not turning those kids off. I don't think so. At first, they just put up with me. That's him, his thing—those books! But I think I got a few of them hooked. I love Salinger. I used some of his stories. His wonderful, electric anger—his contempt for people who think they're big shots and lord it over others—rang a bell with those kids. They listened. They asked me questions. We're on our way, I think, I hope, I pray.

No, I don't go to church much. Lots of "phoniness" there.

Maybe I'm too hard on those ministers—and the professors.
All I know is that you can go to church, or you can take a
course in "ethics" and get high marks, and you can still be a
pretty "low-life" person—the way you behave. I learned that
before I ever came here. My dad used to point out the churches,
and he'd say they don't "work." He went because my mother
wanted him to go. Once we drove by when people were coming out on Sunday, and he was pretty cynical. He used words
like "hypocrites" and "two-timers," getting a "Sunday wash-
job." I think he'd started drinking. But you know, he wasn't
saying anything different than Cheever says in some of his stories—for instance, "The Housebreaker of Shady Hill."

When I have some big moral issue, some question to tackle,
I think I try to remember what my folks have said, or I imagine them in my situation—or even more, these days, I think
of Jude Fawley or Dr. Lydgate or Binx Bolling, or Levin in
Anna Karenina, or Johnny Hake. Those folks: they're *people*
for me. Nick Carraway or Jack Burden, they really speak to
me—there's a lot of me in them, or vice versa. I don't know
how to put it, but they're voices, and they help me make
choices. I hope when I decide "the big ones" they'll be in
there pitching.

His struggles are not all that unique. So many of us grow up in
homes with obvious virtues and secret flaws, or all too visible weaknesses and less apparent strengths. So many of us try to reconcile
our vain, ambitious, grasping side with inclinations we have to be
thoughtful toward others, considerate toward them. The moral contradictions and inconsistencies in our personal lives more than reso-
nate with those in our social order, our nation's politics, our culture.
As my students keep reminding me, one can go to the Bible itself
and find plenty of those same incongruities, those clashes of different or opposing values, ideals. Nor have our universities been all
that successful in figuring out for themselves what their obligations
are with respect to the moral questions many students put to themselves. In that regard, the young man just quoted at some length
could be quite unsettling:

I've tried to take courses in moral philosophy. I read the
books. I become smarter in the analysis I do. But I leave the

lecture hall and I can see myself as the same—the way I'll think of certain people, the way I'll behave. I guess this place is where your *intellect* changes. I guess it's no behavior modification place. But a history tutor said that Harvard used to be a place where they worried as much about the students' morality, their character, as they did about how well they memorized books and wrote exams. That was in the eighteenth and nineteenth century. Not now: we're way "beyond" that here. It's each person to himself on a lot of these moral issues, so long as you don't break any laws or rules. One day that's fine with me, but the next I wonder whether that kind of attitude will be enough for me when I get married and have a family.

Meanwhile, he tries each day to live his particular life, to get those "good" grades that will advance him along, give him one or another boost; and he tries, rather often, to *be* "good," to live up to the notions of what that "good" is that he brought with him to college, and to modify or expand (or weed out, hone down) some of those notions in accordance with the courses he's taken, the experiences he's had—with his roommates, his friends, his teammates (lacrosse) and, not least, his volunteer activities as a tutor. He keeps telling himself (even as he said so during our talks) that he counts among his "friends" certain characters in certain novels. So doing, he denies any distinctiveness or originality: many of his "high school buddies," he reminds me, "would talk about Holden [Caulfield] as if he was one of us." Having said that, he asked a rhetorical question of me, well worth a pedagogical conference or two, I think: "Why don't you guys [college professors] teach that way?" What way, I wanted to know. "As if Holden was—I mean *is*—as real as you or me." I fear my response was all too defensively, protectively, ingratiatingly self-serving. But he wasn't really interested in an ad hominem discussion, or in an argument. He was reminding me, really, of the wonderful mimetic power a novel, a story can have—its capacity to work its way well into one's thinking life, yes, but also one's reveries, idle thoughts, even one's moods and dreams. When one is also "out there," having certain kinds of daily or weekly experiences as, say, the kind of tutor he had become, one has yet further thoughts, memories, daydreams, maybe a nightmare of two—a doubling effect, it might be said, it *has* been said: "I come back from working with those kids and I think of what Chekhov wrote [quoted earlier in 'Gooseberries']. What he wrote isn't just another paragraph in a story; it's what's happening to you, right here, right now."

So it goes, the immediacy that a story can possess, as it connects so persuasively with human experience of a certain kind. Lord save us from the "behavior modification" my young friend mentioned, or from any number of self-righteous moralists who have little doubt about anything and all too many pushy agendas for everyone. But Dr. Williams and Dr. Chekhov and the needy children whom that student got to know as his "tutees" can offer their own kind of moral instruction. Dr. Williams urges intense, searching self-scrutiny. Dr. Chekhov urges a close look not only at ourselves, but at others—the terrible contrasts of this world. The tutees urge—well, themselves as fellow human beings who have something to give (their neediness becomes our opportunity to be generous) as well as receive (the instruction they get). All in all not a bad start for someone trying to find a good way to live this life: a person's moral conduct as his or her response to the moral imagination of writers and the moral imperative of fellow human beings in distress.

American Poetry Review, November/December 1988

The Gloom and the Glory

Graham Greene's many masterly fictions have entertained and inspired readers the world over for half a century. (One can only speculate on the politics that have denied him a Nobel Prize in literature.) His personal story brings to mind a number of the stories he has written—a tireless ever-watchful wanderer, an ironist, a materialist, a rationalist, eager always for new experiences but deep down hoping against hope for the promised calm and rest that comes with the gift of faith.

The author of this first volume of the authorized biography of Mr. Greene has previously done "a ten-year stint on Joseph Conrad." In his preface to this foray into a life still being lived, Norman Sherry tells us that he "vacated the library" when studying Conrad, in order to find his "subject in the countries in which he had lived and travelled." Mr. Greene, who has long admired Conrad, also admired Mr. Sherry's way of stalking him, and by the middle 1970s an extraordinarily patient and resourceful biographer had new reasons to visit distant continents. When Mr. Sherry is finished doing on-site work in the many countries and continents where Mr. Greene has spent various lengths of time, he may well decide to pick carefully the direction of his next biographical passion.

Many years ago Mr. Sherry published a biography of Jane Austen, and as I read the pages of *The Life of Graham Greene* (only thirty-five years chronicled, with at least fifty more to be covered), I wondered whether he hasn't recently thought of her quiet, contained existence with some nostalgia. On the other hand, this literary effort has surely provided special satisfactions. Graham Greene's years have been full of high adventure, great achievement, much drama, no small amount of romance; and he has been continually available to his chosen biographer, as have been his wife, Vivien, and various relatives and friends. As for those who might not be friends, we are told of this early exchange: "What stands out particularly in my meetings with Greene was his charging me, as we walked across Berkhamsted Common, that I had asked his friends for the names of his enemies. I replied that no one could succeed in life without making enemies—it was in the nature of the human condition." Mr. Greene's delightful response? "He countered that he did not live and work in an academic institution."

He did, however, spend his childhood in an "academic institution." His father was a teacher at Berkhamsted School, and eventually would become its headmaster—a stern, outspoken, decent man in the long tradition of the English public (that is, private) schools. Mr. Greene's mother was a first cousin to Robert Louis Stevenson, and comes across as distant, hardly preoccupied with her children, who had a nanny to attend their daily needs. In an instructive comment, Mr. Greene has remembered his mother's "occasional state visits to the nursery." The family is of some distinction—an upper-bourgeois lineage "which included banking, brewing and trading with offshoots into education, literature and the arts" (Christopher Isherwood was among Graham Greene's cousins).

The first chapters of this book establish painstakingly the comfortable if reserved family life that was Mr. Greene's from the time of his birth in 1904 to his early adolescent years, which partially coincided with World War I. Nearly a million Englishmen died in that war and arguably Britain never recovered; it was the beginning of the end of its worldwide imperial power. Several years after the war was over, Mr. Greene, in a letter to his mother, remembered "the endless memorial services" at the school, the "death feeling" that had pervaded the atmosphere—the intense bleeding of a nation's ruling class, a stiff price to pay for the continuation of its privileges. As a student, Mr. Greene witnessed firsthand his father's conflicts: a compassionate, liberal-minded man who worried about the poor at home and abroad, he was also a staunch patriot, and of course the boys to whom he taught history were the sons of barristers and financiers. How deeply did he dare delve into contemporary history—the plots and counterplots, the greed, envy, and malice that were ultimately responsible for the bloodsoaked fields of Ypres and Verdun? How much easier it was for all those teachers to go back to ancient Athens and Rome, or to look passionately among their students for misdeeds, which were surely far less embarrassing to comprehend than those committed by the Foreign Secretary's office.

Not that those boys—so lucky in the wealth and social standing of their families—didn't bear close watching. Schools such as Berkhamsted, which Mr. Greene attended, were rife with small-minded conspiracies, with cliques, with all sorts of petty conceits and deceits. In middle age the author Graham Greene looked back with no great joy at a childhood spent at boarding school (from fourteen on he lived away from his parents); and Mr. Sherry, through many interviews, lets us know that his subject suffered both mentally and physically—scorned by some, physically abused by others. He was the son of the headmaster and a shy, unathletic youth, an easy target for those who had need of anyone available for their frustrations and resentments. Finally, at the age of sixteen, Mr. Greene precipitated a family crisis: he ran away. The biographer as sleuth helps us understand what actually happened: "A letter has survived, unknown to Graham, written in 1948 by his mother to his wife and kept secretly by her for forty years. In it, Graham's mother recalls the day he disappeared and his peace-destroying note." At one point in the letter she mentions that her son "had tried to poison himself with eye-drops." He let it be known in the note, she recalled, that "we should not see him again." He was actually wandering about nearby, and soon (a comic anticlimax) his older sister ran into him, persuading him without difficulty to return home.

Mr. Greene has himself described the consequences of that family crisis. In a chapter titled "Psychoanalysed" his memories from the distance of middle age are offered: "Raymond (his older brother, eventually to be a physician) was hastily summoned home for consultation; my father found the situation beyond him. . . . My brother . . . suggested psycho-analysis as a possible solution, and my father—an astonishing thing in 1920—agreed." In no time he was in London, seeing a Jungian analyst daily, exploring dream after dream, going to the movies and the theater—a far cry from the uptight meanness that had driven him to near despair. His analyst, Kenneth Richmond, had gained a reputation for the successful treatment of disturbed schoolboys. He was "utterly opposed to boarding schools, seeing them as artificial orphanages." Significantly, when Mr. Greene returned to finish school he did not board. His mother described him as "a different person after that treatment." He had learned that his moody moments could provide a transformative momentum—the effect of prompting in him action as an alternative to an acquiescence to the emotional status quo.

By 1922, at eighteen, he was a freshman at Oxford's Balliol College, where he began to flourish. He wrote both fiction and poems; at the end of his university career, when he was twenty-one, a volume of his poetry was published under the title *Babbling April*. Around that time (1925) he met Vivien Dayrell-Browning, whom he would marry two years later. She was a Roman Catholic convert, a poet, a young woman of great beauty. Mr. Greene courted her relentlessly, wrote to her day after day, dreamed of her constantly. Their intense, complex friendship (sexually chaste until marriage, emotionally passionate) is deftly conveyed by Mr. Sherry's use of the surviving letters Mr. Greene wrote. Through this love affair he made a second departure; his future wife's moral and religious preoccupations became very much his. Early in 1926, at the age of twenty-two, he was received into the Roman Catholic church.

While pursuing Vivien and taking religious instruction, he gradually developed as a most versatile and productive writer—doing so even as he made a living as an editor on a Nottingham newspaper, then on the *Times* of London, where he worked for four years. At the same time he began to fashion his career. He reviewed books for various papers and magazines. He wrote novels (later repudiating two of the early ones). He became a film critic. By 1935 he had published five novels (among them *The Man Within, Stamboul Train, It's a Battlefield*) with a sixth one on the way (*England Made Me*). He and Vivien were the parents of a young daughter. He was a regular reviewer for the *Spectator*. He had written, too, a biography of John Wilmot, the second Earl of Rochester, a man whom Norman Sherry describes as a "dissolute courtier at the Restoration court of Charles II, a lecher and a drunk, but also a poet who could treat himself and his world with satiric coolness and who helped to establish the tradition of English satiric verse and assisted Dryden in the writing of *Marriage-à-la-Mode*." Not least, Mr. Greene was very much a part of London's literary world, as the pages of this book attest: lunches and high teas and dinners, introductions to this person and that one, new and more coveted reviewing assignments, negotiations with publishers. He was a writer trying hard to be known, to be received favorably and to rise in the world's ranks.

Mr. Greene displayed enormous energy. He also continued to experience spells of gloom. Even after his experience with Dr. Richmond, he was intermittently melancholic and had thoughts of suicide. He has described much of this in his autobiographical writing (*The Lost Childhood and Other Essays* and *A Sort of Life*), and at times Mr. Sherry, trying to figure out the relationship between depression and a writer's work, summons outside help in the form of portentous quotations, such as an all too unqualified remark of Proust: "Without nervous disorder there can be no great artist." Proust was, no doubt, modest enough to omit mention of another element in the life of the "great artist," talent. The world is full of people with "nervous disorders," but graced with only a handful of Prousts and Greenes.

How did Mr. Greene manage to keep being so productive, given the distress his letters and essays have conveyed? In fact, he was ambitious, determined and a repeated winner in the psychological contests his mind waged with itself. Mr. Sherry occasionally connects the constant traveling, the trips to near and distant countries, to an agitated, down-in-the-dumps state of mind, to the need for "escape"—from the pressures of a life, "the tasks of fatherhood." But this image of Mr. Greene, now and then cultivated by him and so, inevitably, an important element in an account of his life, begs a biographer's skeptical scrutiny. Unfortunately, by now we in the West have given psychodynamic speculation an ex cathedra status. So when a writer who has looked inward with the help of a psychoanalyst tells us ever so candidly that he has felt seriously at loose ends, that he has taken a pistol to his head repeatedly, we nod knowingly, gratefully—though a few doubters have refused to go along, have questioned those personal accounts and asked whether to some extent they provide a kind of self-presentation calculated to appeal to an audience all too eager for psychiatric confessions.

Mr. Greene's letters to his wife and others leave no doubt of the sway miserableness (the word he once used to describe his state of mind) had over him periodically. Yet, as I read this long, exhaustive book—with so much of Greene's spirited, wry correspondence nicely

worked into its various chapters—I kept wondering whether his accusatory self-arraignments ought not be regarded as carefully weighed
moral and spiritual reflections, and as descriptions in retrospect of
moody spells. He had, after all, joined a church whose saints for
centuries have not shirked the toughest kind of self-scrutiny.

Put differently, Graham Greene was well on his way, even in his
twenties, to a modest literary success. He was clever with words. He
was savvy, indeed, about the London world of magazines and newspapers and fiercely anxious to climb the heights of that world—to
eat and drink with people of influence, win their interest, secure
commissions from them. He had a caustic tongue, nowhere displayed more openly than in his film criticism for the *Spectator* and
the short-lived magazine *Night and Day*. But he had also become a
serious, introspective Catholic—aware, quite likely, of the spiritual
risks posed by an urbane, grasping, snobbish life.

There were other risks, too. One of his reviews for *Night and Day*
prompted libel action by Twentieth Century–Fox on behalf of the
nine-year-old Shirley Temple, whose role in the movie *Wee Willie
Winkie* Mr. Greene had described this way: "Already two years ago
she was a fancy little piece (real childhood, I think, went out after
The Littlest Rebel). In *Captain January* she wore trousers with the
mature suggestiveness of a Dietrich: her neat and well-developed
rump twisted in the tap-dance: her eyes had a sidelong searching
coquetry. Now in *Wee Willie Winkie*, wearing short kilts, she is a
complete totsy." He had written a funny, smart-aleck essay full of
sly or bold provocations. In response the lord chief justice in London was all wrought up—ready to slam him with a major adverse
judgment. But he was in Mexico by then (1938), trekking the obscure roads of Chiapas, even as a few years earlier he had gone to
Liberia on Africa's west coast.

His readers and admirers would eventually marvel at the travel
essays ("Journey without Maps" and "The Lawless Roads") that
came out of those first two of many excursions. The chapters that
narrate those excursions are compelling and touching, the best in
the book. Norman Sherry's own restless inquiries carefully mirror
those of his subject (he followed Mr. Greene's tracks, interviewed
everyone he could find connected to those expeditions) and show a
side of the novelist far more interesting and convincing than the

familiar one of the bored or disheartened and troubled upper-class twentieth-century existentialist.

Mr. Greene suddenly becomes a character out of the Conrad stories he admired. He exposes himself to all sorts of pain and jeopardy. He explores hitherto unpenetrated jungles. He climbs mountains, crosses wild and unbridged rivers, endures the pain and vulnerability of tropical sicknesses. He looks everywhere, it seems, listens with respect to the most obscure of his fellow human beings and thereby not only learns about and from others but finds the direction of his own life's compass. In the midst of those daring and extremely dangerous trips—what a survivor he is, about to turn eighty-five—psychological distress and the artist's hunger for experience were turned into quite something else: a pitch of soul-searching. During such urgently pursued, far-flung travel came the intense Catholic sensibility, the moral seriousness that would begin to appear in *Brighton Rock* (1938) and would really take shape in the whisky priest of his magnificent novel, *The Power and the Glory*, a vigorous discussion of which ends this first book of the biography.

The Graham Greene who feverishly explored Mexico in 1938 surely was in flight from big-shot England: "I want to get out of this bloody country." For years he had been trying to figure out what to do with his considerable gifts as a writer. His conversion to Catholicism enabled him to walk away from the cool, smug life he had inherited and that he had sought in his twenties and thirties to advance. It was to be a conversion that haunted him, that gave him the strength to face down demons more scary, even, than those he describes in his essays of psychological examination and disclosure: self-centeredness and self-importance, the endless circus of self-promotion, the cynicism and callousness and pretentiousness that not rarely accompany the secular success he so ardently sought. Like the rest of us he had his fair share of "nervous disorders," but during an important part of his life he also was spiritually obsessed, and blessed with the genius to turn to good account such a state of mind. The man who might have been one more clever British satirist became, instead, the person who well merits Norman Sherry's long Boswellian venture.

The words Graham Greene chose as a title for his Mexican story, *The Power and the Glory*, are of telltale, personal importance:

"*Thine* is the Kingdom, the Power and the Glory." The author, one suspects, is not only describing his whisky priest's renunciatory philosophy, but talking to himself as well as to his readers. Thus to try humbling oneself as a matter of deep religious principle, while at the same time offering oneself with inevitable pride to the world of Caesar and Mammon through one fiction after another, cannot have been an easy task, as we will no doubt discover in great and revealing detail when the next volume of this major biographical study emerges.

New York Times Book Review, June 18, 1989

Two Tolstoy Stories

Tolstoy's admirers and critics have many times pointed out the significance of his religious crisis for his fiction. Nothing he wrote afterward would approach the grandeur of *War and Peace* and *Anna Karenina*. Some push the matter further, telling us that novels written by moralists such as Tolstoy in the last three decades of his life never really work because their didactic intentions (the wish to convert the reader to one or another point of view) inevitably undermine art.

Of course Tolstoy is being held, in this regard, to the highest standards. Those two novels, arguably, in their sum, offer fiction of a quality never before or after equaled. Even had Tolstoy's later life been calm and untouched by moral and psychological tempest, he might not have been able to give us a third story that would be a fit companion in stature to those giant novels. Moreover, what we love about them is the visionary side, as it connects with the particulars of various incidents and events. That is, Tolstoy's religious sensibility was at work long before he had his well-known "crisis," and that sensibility informs both *War and Peace* and *Anna Karenina*. In any event, as we think of the religiously agitated Tolstoy, who even dismissed his earlier work (those two novels!), we understandably feel art a victim of a writer's life—thereby heightening yet again a certain distance demanded between the two by any number of literary essayists. To be sure, art will naturally draw upon or respond to the life, we acknowledge—but it has to have its own protected territory.

Yet, Tolstoy's *the Death of Ivan Ilych* was written in his late fifties, in the midst of his religious crisis and *Master and Man* appeared in 1895, when he was in his late sixties and, by his own inflammatory statements in the essay "What Is Art," at a passionate remove from the aesthetic point of view with respect to literature which any number of his critics uphold as a matter of course. In that essay he insists that art ought to provide a moral life—become, functionally, rhetoric or propaganda, some readers understandably conclude. Still,

from a turbulent and aging mind and from a pen explicitly dedicated
to ethical instruction came two stories which are themselves full of
turbulence, and do indeed instruct—and yet, also, possess in abundance the traditional requirements of art: the beauty and guile and
indirection and openness to interpretation which a more aesthetic
criticism demands.

When I was an intern I worked with a distinguished cardiologist whose patients, not rarely, were similarly prominent men and
women. I recall even now one such individual, a lawyer who had
been a judge, then had resigned to return to the law. He was dying
of an especially painful and fast-moving cancer, lodged in his
esophagus and moving assertively to other parts of his body. One
morning, taking his blood for tests I knew to be of no real use to him
or any of us (doctors and their need to show their continuing effec-
tiveness and authority, if not magical powers!), I heard him say what
I was thinking: "I will soon be dead, so why bother?" I was grabbing
hard for responsive words, with no success, when he changed the
subject abruptly with another question: "Have you ever read that?"
His head pointed in the direction of his bedside table, on which,
beside a box of Kleenex and a dish meant to receive his spit and
vomitus (there was plenty of the latter), I spotted a book: a selection
of Tolstoy's stories. I said yes, I'd read some. He asked if I'd read *The
Death of Ivan Ilych*. Yes, I had. What did I think of it? Oh, it was a
great story—the usual banal words meant to signal a willingness to
tarry only so long over an essentially passing moment or short-lived
exchange. But the patient had another intention in mind—or maybe,
had surrendered to other demands at work in this universe. When I
had finished with the tourniquet and syringe and needle, he leaned
over, picked up the book, opened it to the Ivan Ilych story, read me
a few lines, and then, all of a sudden, burst into tears.

This was a tough, self-possessed, taciturn lawyer whose cool,
somewhat haughty, and even arrogant manner had up until then
put me off considerably—another big-shot patient of my big-shot
"attending," as we interns called one or another of our bosses. Now
I was really speechless, and in a way, confronted with myself as well
as with him and his changed behavior. What to think not only of
him, but of my confident and unqualified estimate of him? Within
moments he had pulled himself together—excused himself, but also
given me a terse explanation: "You read a story like this and you

can't help identifying with what you're reading." Yes, I said quickly—and soon enough had excused myself, left the room.

Now I teach the story at a medical school, and am always impressed by its power to take hold of young, would-be physicians. It is a story that turns things around—examines a sequence, not of life, then death, the sequence we assume is everyone's fate—but rather of death, then life. For Ivan Ilych is presented to us not only as dead when the story opens (his physical death is announced right off) but as a cold, austere, ambitious, calculating lawyer and judge who has been "dead" all his life, or maybe, has never been "born." It is this person who falls ill, and will endure a slow, painful demise, in the course of which we see how sadly isolated and constricted his so-called life, with all its successes, has really turned out to be. As a human being, as a husband and father, as a professional man, he has lacked the virtues which in their day-to-day expression make for real life: thoughtfulness toward others, a willingness to give of oneself, considerateness—all the words and phrases we use to describe aspects of the love which had so obviously not informed Ivan Ilych's days and nights.

In the last moment of his life, however, he is wondrously born—is able to open up his mind and heart to others, accept them as he never had before; thereby he becomes alive, finally. Such a transformation is achieved by a writer who takes all the risks of sentimentality and banality, and instead, offers a story that is original, lively, arresting, and not in the least maudlin or dramatically forced—a story that shows the best of Tolstoy's narrative skill at work. A dying man who has pushed everyone away from himself emotionally becomes close to his young servant Gerasim, close to him physically as he is attended by the youth, but in time responsive to him, aware of him as a fellow human being, with his own worth and dignity—a comrade in life, so to speak. It is such an awareness that Ilych all along has lacked, and it is such an awareness that brings life to this man about to die. His son and wife come into his eyes—for the first time, really; they reach him, touch him. His heart has opened, even as it is ready to stop. A "light" descends upon him—and newly alive, he leaves the death of a life.

Even as Gerasim has been the instrument of this moment of salvation, the "man" in another Tolstoy story, *Master and Man*, is also a servant, Nikita, whose businessman boss, Vasilii Brekhunov, has all sorts of plans and schemes and strategies. What Brekhunov wants is money, more and more of it, and influence. He swaggers. He is impatient with everyone, including those close to him. In a provincial nineteenth-century Russian setting, Tolstoy gives us a man in search of mammon, at all (personal) costs. The story reaches its climax in a terrible winter storm, as the master and his servant, through the exertions of a horse named Dapple, are taken on a trip that is supposed to result in a successful and rewarding business deal. Brekhunov's greed prompted the trip, and as it unfolds, the servant begins to realize what has happened—these two and their horse are prisoners of a fierce, unrelenting, blinding blizzard which shows no sign of ever loosening its grip. Brekhunov has a chance to escape; they can spend the night in warmth and safety at an intermediate place; but no, he wants to get to his proposed assignation as quickly as possible. He has lost all his judgment as he dreams of the money he expects to make.

The outcome is predictable: the master is in a winter's hell, and as lost as any character in Dante's *Inferno*. They go in circles, get nowhere—or rather, get closer and closer to death. The stoic endurance of the horse is tenderly, knowingly evoked—yet another animal who suffers the stupidities of his master, a so-called civilized creature known as a human being. Nikita, the servant, also complies—aware that he is caught between the devil, as it were, and the deep sea of snow and a driving, tireless wind and sub-zero temperatures. Soon the three are stopped altogether. The horse stands there, dignity intact, awaits the end. The servant is similarly acquiescent, and touchingly reflective: so it goes in this hard life. The master has been wild with his determination to keep going and save himself at all costs—and to the devil with anyone else. But he can't save himself—the point of the story: he can't do so either literally or in the metaphoric sense. He is "saved" by what happens to him in relation to his servant near him. Vasilii realizes that the one thing he can do before he dies is to put his body, still warm, on that of his servant Nikita. It is this gesture of concern for, appreciation of another which is Tolstoy's moral point, and which he works into a story indescribably compelling, poignant, touching. As in *The Death of Ivan Ilych*, a greedy egoist just barely escapes a lifelong death—is born right before he dies—through circumstances that enable a last-ditch moral rescue.

These two Tolstoy stories tell us of life's redemptive possibilities; remind us that those who by secular standards have a lot can be in terrible spiritual jeopardy, and indeed, can be spared hell only through the mediation of a humble one, even as Jesus himself lived a humble life; and finally, insist that the time we have here is never over until the very end, no matter the various (psychological and sociological) determinisms, the stages and phases and complexes of various theorists who would have us marching like automatons through life. The book of our lives is open—even until the last breath. With these haunting tales Tolstoy admonishes us—but also invites us—to risk the saving grace of human love, an opportunity for which may fall upon us out of nowhere, it seems, and enliven us in preparation for that last and most important journey to meet our maker.

New Oxford Review, July/August 1987

On Edward Hopper, Loneliness, and Children

Three years ago I began teaching a fourth-grade class in a Cambridge, Massachusetts, elementary school. I noticed, right off, that on the playground or in the halls, or even in the classroom itself, the children were often marvelously forceful and vigorous storytellers. But when they were asked to write, they commonly became inarticulate, even fearfully so. "I can't write," was their refrain, and I decided not to take them up directly on that claim.

Instead, I turned the English class into an informal art seminar. I brought in slides, fed them into a projector, and we all looked at Picassos and Pissarros, Remingtons and Renoirs, and nearer home, John Sloans and Edward Hoppers. I noticed that Hopper's paintings, especially, both excited and puzzled the children. I also noticed that they wanted to connect what they saw to stories, which they constructed as I flashed one Hopper slide after another against the wall. It was almost as if this twentieth-century American realist painter (who died only twenty-three years ago) somehow addressed these children, prompted in them a desire to respond to his pictures by telling of their various experiences.

I remember, especially, some personal tales told by those children in response to the more familiar Hopper paintings. I remember the girl who said of the "folks" who figure in *Nighthawks* (three customers at a food counter in the middle of the night, being served by a waiter): "They have a different day—I mean, night. Night is their day. Maybe something is on their minds, and they can't sleep—but maybe they just work at night, like my mom does." Her mother runs a Dunkin' Donuts shop on the eleven-to-seven shift. "She says she has a good time talking with some of the people, and they have a good time talking with her. She says people talk more at night—or maybe it's that night people talk more. It's easier then."

Other Hopper paintings prompted an almost universal chorus of perplexity or apprehension. Pictures like *Sunday*, in which a man sits, arms folded, in front of stores that seem empty, abandoned, or *Approaching a City*, in which tenement buildings hover over subway tracks that head underground, stirred the children to anxious questions, to gloomy statements about not only the content of the slides but their own lives as well. "That's a funny one," said one girl. "It's weird—it's *spooky*." The emphasis on that last word said it all for the whole class—nods, several "yeahs," and the fidgeting that is more telling, at times, than any words. In their own way, these children may have been circling around the thoughts I was entertaining—the grim, sinister, dangerous side of urban life, maybe even that aspect of our psychological life: the electric third rail, the dark underground that looms before the viewer.

In *Approaching a City*, a mood of stark stillness dominates; in the better-known *Early Sunday Morning*, with its storefronts, and above them, tenement apartments, with its street hydrant and old-fashioned barber pole, a serene stillness is offered—the city sleeps, as it should on the morning of the week's seventh day. Such pictures prompt the children to ask about people: where are they or, better, why are they left out?

At that point, I was ready with some pictures in which human beings are given a more intimate kind of attention: *Office at Night*, or *Hotel Room*, or *Hotel by a Railroad*, or *Sunlight in a Cafeteria*, or *Automat*, or *The Barber Shop*. The result, however, is often further unease. A boy tells me: "The people don't seem happy. Their heads seem bent. Either they're alone, or if they're with someone, they don't look at each other. No one is smiling." A chorus of agreement—though a girl demurs: "Just because they're not smiling doesn't mean they're unhappy. I think they're *thinking*."

That line of reasoning evoked much discussion. Some children pointed out that in several pictures Hopper's women look sexy but his men seem cold, buttoned up, self-preoccupied—or, as in the dramatic *Excursion into Philosophy*, of a man seated on a bed, introspectively tied to reading matter rather than connected to a woman who is lying nearby, her back (with its exposed bottom) to him. Others expressed indirectly their sense of the confinement of those urban rooms and offices, the frustrations of the people who

inhabit them, through urgently stated therapeutic recommendations: "Those people should get out and go take a long walk in the
country; then they could unwind."

·This high-strung, tense, self-preoccupied side to certain of Hopper's American city dwellers, office workers, travelers, doesn't yield,
unfortunately, to the remedy suggested by that nine-year-old child.
I follow her advice, in a way—we move to Hopper's suburban and
rural world.

If anything, things get worse away from the downtown streets. In
East Wind over Weehawken, no one is in sight, but a large For Sale
sign tells of a collapsed economy. (The picture was painted in 1934.)
In *Ryder House*, a field of grass is overgrown near a house whose
windows are boarded up—a forlorn, abandoned farm.

In *Cape Cod Evening*, overgrown grass again surrounds a house
whose two occupants, a man and a woman, are outside, grimly
stoic, their dog turned away from them. Even more threatening, a
dark cluster of nearby trees seems on the march, ready to overwhelm
a rural scene already stifled, uncompromising. The woman's crossed
arms, her dark blue dress, the man's T-shirt—this is a bedraggled,
woebegone couple, as the children recognize.

Again, rather than analyzing and explicating, they suggest action:
"Let's go back to the city—that restaurant, where there was the food,
or to the movie one." The boy who said that was referring to *Tables
for Ladies*, which features a couple eating, a cashier, and a worker
arranging a display of fruit, and to *New York Movie*, which emphasizes not a film or its audience, but a pensive usher who stands aside
under some light.

In the former, however, the viewer is outside the restaurant,
maybe hungry (the picture was painted in 1930, as the Great Depression deepened), and in the latter the viewer is asked to think of
someone who is, literally, outside a particular mainstream: others
lose themselves in a few hours of film distraction, while the one who
has helped them get to their seats, who has been, in a way, an instrument of their subsequent pleasure, is left to stand apart—left to
her own, isolated, personal resources.

To return to the city, we need gas, I remind the children by showing them Hopper's *Four Lane Road* and *Gas*—but again, a couple
in the former, running a gas station, seem out of touch with each
other, and without customers, big as the road is, whereas the latter

poses yet another of those dark, encroaching forests next to a Mobil station tended by a man who is alone as evening settles upon a carless road, this one narrow and headed obliquely into the dark. No wonder these children have become restless—and, finally, have resigned themselves to the realization that all does not go well in Hopper's America: an alienation of individuals, one from the other, and, too, a good deal of social and economic dislocation, distress. When I use Hopper's slides with Harvard college students, only a few blocks away, a different emphasis can often be heard. I teach a seminar titled "American Light," named after a wonderful poem written by L. E. Sissman. It is meant to honor Hopper's shrewd eye for much of what takes place in our country, as well as his extraordinary way with light and darkness—a cold, even supernatural glow, often given intensity and prominence by a nearby stretch of darkness in the form of shadows cast by buildings or by trees.

We look at the same slides the elementary school children do, but we also read and discuss Raymond Carver's fiction, his brilliantly constructed, emotionally piercing stories, in so many of which a failure of communication, of human understanding, figures so prominently. The loneliness of his characters, their down-and-out state becomes transfigured by the genius of this writer into the greatness of one compelling, dramatic moment after another. The students respond with feeling as well as intellectually to Carver—they examine his texts, but also let themselves personally enter and walk their way, open-eyed, through his narratives.

Yet, with respect to Hopper, they are wont to favor analysis of his pictures: shapes, sizes, forms, arrangements of objects, nature of pigment, contrasts of color—all noted with big-deal words like chiaroscuro coming up now and then. Yes, I think, this is important, to learn critical skills, but we sometimes go further, hasten to question common truths entertained outside the academy: "Too much is made of the loneliness and alienation in Hopper," a student announced. Maybe so, I think.

In Hopper, we begin to realize, there is a twentieth-century sensibility at work: his often explicit interest in a documentary art that tells of a nation not at ease with itself, and individuals not at ease with one another.

To be sure, Hopper's paintings lend themselves especially well to the viewer's inclinations—in the tradition of Rorschach cards or, better, Henry Murray's "Thematic Apperception" pictures, they tell about us viewers, as opposed to an American "them." The elusive ambiguities of those paintings are fodder for our conflicts and worries, for the constant complexities of feeling within us that struggle for expression and find it in our dreams (our own private, nightly art) as well as in the pictures to which we become attached, and to which we make our various personal attributions.

Still, Hopper remarked, in connection with *Nighthawks*, that he "simplified the scene a great deal and made the restaurant bigger" than the one in Greenwich Village in New York City that he used as a model of sorts. He went on to say: "Unconsciously, probably, I was painting the loneliness of a large city."

In our university sanctuary, we read those words, look again at his various railroad tracks slicing through the land, his empty drugstores and bleak bridges, his eerie country houses or massive tenement blocks, his hotel lobbies and roadside gas pumps, and begin to realize that this was an artist whose unconscious knew well not only how to supply energy to a wonderfully gifted talent, but also knew well how many Americans, at least some of the time, both live and feel.

New York Times, March 3, 1991

Whose Museums?

*I*n 1981 I heard an earnest, conscientious official of the Boston Museum of Fine Arts tell a group of schoolchildren, "This museum belongs to you," and he obviously felt in his heart and believed in his mind what he said. As if to make clear his sincerity, he offered an explanation of his assertion—he told his listeners, a mix of black and white girls and boys around ten years old, that the museum where they then sat, seemingly attentive, was "open to everyone" and, playing on that phrase to escalate its significance, "meant for everyone." The children weren't about to question that declaration; in fact, I had begun to notice, they had their own shrewd ways of paying more attention to one another than to any well-intentioned adult who addressed them. They winked, or smiled, or frowned—facial maneuvers meant to tell their seated friends and neighbors, rather than the few standing adults, what was crossing their minds. When the above remarks were spoken, I noted a number of raised eyebrows and a grimace or two. I wondered what those youngsters meant through such signaling.

A few days later, as I talked with some of those children (whom I was getting to know in the course of a study I was doing on school desegregation and its impact on those taking part in it), I asked about that visit to the museum—what various children experienced, chose to remember, and had to say. A sturdy, athletic black boy, from whom I did not expect any great flowering of fond memories about that museum visit, was at pains to let me know that he had, in fact, had a most memorable time:

> I've never been to such a place. I never knew there was such a place. They had all those pictures, and they showed them to us. Then they brought us to a room and they said we could come back—anytime. I thought to myself, sure thing, tomorrow! They kept saying we should make the place our home, and I thought, wow, one room in this place is bigger than anyone's home I've seen.

The pictures were nice. We saw so many, you forget a lot. There was one I remember—of George Washington, because George is my name, too, and my daddy was born in Washington, and my mom, too, and we go there a lot. When we got back to school, the teacher asked us what we saw, and I told her, and she said there's a lot of museums in Washington, too, and I should go see them. I didn't tell her, but that's not high on my list. When I go, I go to see my cousins, and there's usually a basketball game they're in at their high school.

I'm not a guy who ever was very good in art. I used to like to draw the sky and the sun, I remember that—mainly because it was easy, to tell you the truth. I had trouble drawing people. I couldn't get it straight, how to do that. I'd always mess up. We had this teacher in the third grade, and she was a nut about detail. She always used that word and said that we should put lots of "detail" into what we were drawing. I never could figure out what she meant, until one day she came to my desk and sat down with me, and she showed me how I could put in clouds, all different kinds of them, and I could give the sun some "character," and sure enough, she showed me how. She gave the sun a face, and she used orange and red, as well as yellow, for the rays, and then she put these black marks there, on the sky, the blue, and I remember I didn't know what she was doing, so I told her she was ruining it, my picture, and she said, "No son, I'm not," and then she explained it was birds—she was putting all those birds in the sky. That was a great idea! I liked that because I could draw birds—that's easier. So, I drew a lot of skies, and once, in class, the teacher had me show a few of them. She tacked them up on a board, and the kids laughed, and they clapped, and you know what? One guy said I'd drawn "us," and the blue, that's "them," and no one knew what he was talking about, but the teacher figured it out real fast, and she said, "Yes, in a way," but we couldn't follow her, so she had to back up and explain it to us—that we're the blackbirds, you see, and the white folks, a lot of them have blue eyes, and that's what the guy meant. I don't know what happened to him. His father was "fancy." He was aiming to teach in some college, I recall someone told me. They moved away a year or so later.

I'll bet *they*, they're the kind who go to those museums a lot. You listen to the people there, and you get the feeling that if one of us folks, a black dude, walked into their place, they'd pin a medal on him and clap their hands off, and they'd be real proud of themselves. But you know what? They'd be nervous, I know they would.

He was not anxious to expand on that last matter. Trying not to appear overly curious, I casually asked him why such nervousness might occur if a young black visited the Boston Museum of Fine Arts—which is, in fact, only a few blocks from a substantial ghetto. He shrugged his shoulders, feigning ignorance. I hesitated to pursue the question any further for fear of offending him. We were no strangers to each other, but I worried that he might feel I was trying to get him to say the obvious. On the other hand, I sensed that he wanted to tell me something, to address the subject more fully, or else he wouldn't have gone as far as he did. So, a bit nervous myself, I asked about the nervousness he had evoked in the scene he had just described. His answer was longer and more wide-ranging than I had anticipated:

It's window dressing they want, that's what I think. You can tell, they're wanting to convince themselves that they're not stuck-up, so they invite all of us kids. It's not just the black folks they try to get to come. They get others, white kids, and those kids aren't going to come back either. They want every school to come visit, and maybe they'll have us there a few times, but if I went alone, I'll tell you, they'd worry I'd be intending to steal their pictures, I'm sure of it! It's their museum, not ours!

I saw those guards watching over us as if they thought any second we'd pull out our knives or our guns! If we were white kids, they still would be ready to tackle us! They size you up! They have these ideas about you before you even get by the entrance and pay your money, if you're going to pay. We got in free, I think, but they were afraid we might try to take something, and if we'd paid the admission, they'd still be afraid, I'm sure of it. It makes you want to go away and not come back! That's how it goes, if you're from a family like mine and there's no money, people will look down on you, and no matter how nice one of the teachers is, they'll keep looking down their noses at you, those guards. My daddy says someone who has just a little, he'll be the one to find folks that have less just so he can dump on them!

By then, needless to say, I was all ears as we both carried the discussion along, he bearing most of the weight in the form of a mighty incisive and clearheaded inquiry into the sociological issues often summarized by such single words as *race* and *class*. A youth not doing well in school, though obviously bright, was letting me know how observant he could be and, beyond that, how analytically perceptive. He had by no means been a mere sheep, taking a prescribed walk through those museum corridors. Perhaps he had been unfair to the intent of his hosts—too quick to condemn them and sadly unwilling to give them credit for comprehending some of the same difficulties he had noticed. When I tried to make that point by acknowledging the truth of his comments while expressing some faith in the favorable possibilities that might arise if he were to make a return visit to the museum by himself, he hesitated, then went along: "I guess it's true. They might be suspicious. They'd follow me around, but they wouldn't try to throw me out, and if I just kept looking at the pictures, then left, they'd probably ask me to come back *again*, and pretty soon, I'd be a regular customer!"

A charming scenario, I thought, and he could tell by the look on my face that I was pleased. A personal breakthrough, I believed, for him—an enlargement, really, of his social imagination, as well as his moral imagination. Not that he was totally convinced that things would work out that way, and not that I had any right, then or now, to be clapping my hands with the barely concealed, smug satisfaction of noblesse oblige, as experienced by yet another practitioner of "social activism," of "mentoring." (I was working as a volunteer fourth- and fifth-grade teacher in the school he attended.) Still, a lad with plenty of reason for skepticism was able to let his mind wander and wonder, to summon a scene less of harmony and reconciliation than of shared doubt, like breaths mutually held in some hope—a truce of sorts.

I often think of the educational moment that student offered me as I walk in one or another museum and take note not only of who is there or who is not there, but of those who are obviously there for the first time (or, maybe, through a school program, the second or third) as was the case for my young friend and teacher. Often enough, we who watch such events are intrigued and pleased. We have known our moments of self-accusation—a dissatisfaction based on the knowledge that we have the run of a place while others, equally entitled to its opportunities and pleasures, are oblivious to what might be theirs, too. Or they stay away from, even shun, what they know to exist, having been "taken through," as the expression goes, in the manner my young student experienced: "a cultural experiment program," the museum's officials called it. On the other hand, many of us, like him, can see all too clearly the limits of such well-intentioned efforts and even fathom for ourselves—standing there in those grand halls and those beautifully appointed rooms, with, say, a Renoir or a Gauguin nearby and "lots of furniture from way back" (my student's nice way of telling a friend about a big bunch of French antiques he'd seen)—how indelibly we all get marked by the very dividing elements in our society he had mentioned to me, at first indirectly, and then with a vivid power that finally brought me up short. No wonder, then, at *our* nervousness, never mind the kind he had experienced for half a day, then shrugged off. I could easily imagine him saying, "Hey, man, I'll never go back to that scene again!"

Later, more than a little frustrated by the aforementioned swirl of conflicting attitudes or realizations, I turned to a group of children (the youngster quoted here among them) and asked them for their advice. I described the dilemma one of their classmates had posed and noticed that no one was surprised or inclined to take issue with the analysis he had made—no one, that is, except me. *I* was the one who initially felt confronted by that child's unduly harsh and unforgiving, even strident, point of view, hence my hemming and hawing, my anxious inability to know quite what to think or say. As I watched the universal assent in the room, the savvy that greeted my recapitulation not only of an event but of a boy's interpretation of an event, I felt, yet again, that earlier combination of perplexity, melancholy, even shame spawned by an awareness of all that has contributed to such a separation of citizens and the impasse that gets spelled out as racial, social, and cultural—those modifiers that, each one, have so many stories to haunt and bedevil us, despite the victories and achievements of recent decades in a country still the envy of so many the world over.

As all that ran across my mind, I threw the class open to the children and awaited their comments and suggestions, for which I'd directly asked. But they were not at all forthcoming during what seemed like an eternity to their teacher. Once they had registered, through lifted eyebrows, tilted heads, knowing smiles, and grim frowns, their street-smart knowledge, they fell into an unyielding silence. I poked at it and prodded it with my questions and remarks to no avail. Finally, I was ready to call it quits, apologizing for bringing the entire matter up, and then trying to explain why I had done so. I told the class of my own childhood, of my mother's trips to the Boston Museum of Fine Arts with my brother and me, of the pictures she'd taught us to love, of the moments I, too, had had with those guards, and of my dad's memorable response to my complaint about the guards "following" us around: "They're probably bored, don't you see." The last phrase in that comment was one he had brought with him from his native England and was now poignantly used—an effort to get me to *see* (as opposed to the offer of a didactic explanation). He went on to ask me to put myself in the shoes of those guards, to think of myself as having to don a uniform, stand all day, look at people with some skepticism, and keep them under scrutiny, all for rather low wages. By the time he'd finished, I wasn't exactly ready to feel sorry for those guards, but I sure knew that I didn't want to be one of them. My dad, seeing that knowledge cross my mind and reveal itself in my lowered eyes, then asked for a bit more—some sense, some understanding, some realization on my part of who those guards might be and why they made their living that way. When he was through and though with me, I was even able to remember the one guard who had been not only courteous (most of them were that) but also instructive to my mother: he'd told her things to tell us and done so, I would later realize, with tact as well as his own kind of intelligent self-assurance.

I guess I had lapsed into more of an extended apologia on behalf of those guards than I had realized, because a voice suddenly interrupted my anxious soliloquy: "You're trying to make us feel sorry for the guards in those places!" I was taken aback and then about to apologize (all too quickly) when another voice was heard: "My dad has a night job. He guards a store, and what your dad said, it's right, it's true." Then, in summation, he stated simply, "That's how it is," responding to the desperate nostalgia of a teacher trying to get something going, himself trying to learn as he got others to learn. Soon, there were plenty of opinions expressed, none more telling, I thought, than that of my first informant: "Well, you see, we've got a long way to go before it's better, but it's nice they have all those pictures hanging there, and maybe they should guard them all the time, *all* the time, or else someone would steal them, and then no one would see them, except the robber, and that wouldn't be fair."

Justice and equality had made an entry into the classroom, even as the guards had become, after a fashion, defenders of that justice rather than gratuitous, condescending agents of privilege, power, and the status quo. These children weren't about to go rushing back to the museum now that we had all made it a successful subject for classroom discussion. But they had used an experience and their memory of that experience in such a way that enabled them to connect one of their parents and his job to what they had seen, not on the walls of a museum but in the flesh, so to speak: a warehouse guard and a museum guard, a black man on the night shift and a white man on the day shift—a connection, I had begun to understand, that was a kind of art all its own, born of all the mixed and sometimes turbulent emotions a visit to the museum could prompt.

Still, those children had given their attention not only to a museum's guards or even to its pictures. I can, even now, remember the description I heard of the enormous rooms, the marble floors, the hushed silence that threatened to envelop the children, so they felt, and dared in them the urge to make noise as a statement of self-assertion: "It was the hugest place I've ever been in," a girl said, adding, "It was like—well, everyone was holding his breath, and so we were whispering at first, and then we giggled, and then we really spoke up, and then people would stare at us, and they didn't stop, but we wouldn't stop talking either. A friend of mine—she said she wanted to scream so everything would be more 'real,' like it is where we live."

This sense of disparity between the world of museums and that of the ghetto is not, of course, utterly different from a similar sense of incongruity that even young people from well-to-do families might experience. The enormity and splendor of many museums bears down on the eyes and ears, strained to see and hear so much under such awesome and, yes, constrained or regulated circumstances. But for many children from poor neighborhoods, there has been no introduction to such a world, and so a museum visit can prompt a surprised, even stunned reaction: "The steps going upstairs are huge, and they put wood around those pictures, fancy wood frames, and there's a store, and they have big books, lots of them, and the guards, they're nervous. Not just about us, but about their bosses. They must own the pictures, and the guards would lose their jobs if anything bad happens."

That last observation, a child's intuition, touches on so much— that the guards (easily criticized or scapegoated by a new young visitor, because they are *there*, constantly watching and, if necessary, speaking up) are really at the very bottom of a ladder that becomes increasingly invisible, yet powerful, as one climbs the rungs. Needless to say, it is the curators and the trustees who are the bosses the boy mentioned—"rich white folks," he later called them when asked to be more specific. Perhaps the guards' fierce, fearful possessiveness, which some of the children made a point of citing in their descriptions of museum trips, is not all that unique. Rather, it has to do with those on the top of a hierarchy who convey a particular attitude and set of assumptions, which are most certainly understood by others who work, as the expression goes, down the line.

American Art, Winter 1992

Illiteracy and Loneliness

We are the creature of consciousness; and we are the creature upon whom language descends, as if a gift from on high, in the first years of life—the words of a baby an inauguration of sorts into his or her humanity. It is words that enable us not only to reach out, learn from others and teach them, but also learn from ourselves—the constant conversations we have as we go through the days of our journey here. I well remember the matter of language being discussed by a girl I treated at the children's hospital in Boston, one of the first patients I had when I was learning to be a child psychiatrist. She was only seven, was in the second grade of a not-so-good elementary school. She came to our clinic because she was a rebellious tyke who constantly provoked her teacher, a rather charming and kindly woman of about fifty who couldn't at all understand why a child from a solid and sensible family was so given to what her mother rather quaintly called "excess," and her teacher described more reprovingly as "really obnoxious behavior." I recall our clinic's social worker reporting, in that regard, on her interviews with the girl's mother and her teacher—and, in fact, both the mother and the teacher feared that something was troubling a youngster who seemed not able to stop talking for very long. The girl constantly volunteered words: comments and questions; unrequested critical remarks about others; declarations of apprehension, worry, concern; or statements of what was felt to be right or wrong. Often the young student failed to raise her hand and ask for permission to speak. She blurted out what was on her mind, to the point that, finally, her teacher and her parents began wondering whether she wasn't in significant psychological distress since, clearly, she lacked the control her classmates had, and seemed, in contrast, all too driven to talk—and talk and talk. Not that she spoke in a crazy manner—as the social worker reported to us: "This girl isn't saying wild or incomprehensible things; she is saying much that people find interesting. But she speaks off the top of her head a lot of the time, and her teacher is losing her patience!"

When I met the girl, I decided right off to tell her what I'd heard about her, not as an accusation but as an exploration. She had, after all, wanted to know why "everyone" wanted her to come talk with us at the hospital, so when I asked her what she thought, only to hear her puzzlement, I offered what I'd heard from our conversations with her family and with those who knew her on the teaching staff of the elementary school she attended. Her response was one I'll never forget—as frank and outspoken, I later realized, as other observations she'd been making: "I speak my mind! If I didn't, then no one would know I had one!"

I was a bit taken aback—a girl who appeared to be a bit prim, rather guarded in the way she stood or sat, anything but easygoing in her way of presenting herself, could all of a sudden become provocative, unsettling, challenging. I decided to respond vigorously to her, take on her statement. I pointed out to her that we have other ways than speaking of indicating our possession of a mind. She wondered what ways I meant. I told her that when we sat quietly and listened and read and did our arithmetic and wrote our papers and followed the teachers' orders, we were surely indicating ourselves to be in possession of a mind. She paused only briefly, before saying this to me: "Yes, but if you don't tell people what you're thinking, they won't know, and then you're not you, you're just someone in the class—you could be anyone!"

Now I thought I knew a bit more about what troubled her—a strong, even fierce desire to distinguish herself from others. Now, needless to say my own mind could go through its fancy, learned (psychoanalytic) assumptions, and begin to contemplate the kinds of questions I'd soon enough be asking her—inquiries aimed at ascertaining how she got along with her younger sister and younger brother, and how she felt about an older brother who was the apple of her father's eye, because he was so smart in school and already, at ten, headed for a career in science, or so he told his family and friends (another outspoken child!). Still, the girl's somewhat terse, dramatic responses stuck in my head, and possessed, I began to feel, a decisive, emphatic, intellectual worth, no matter their psychological significance. She was struggling in her own way with a larger, philosophical question—the sources of human distinctiveness. She felt strongly that who she was had a lot to do with whether (and how) she spoke—a verbal literacy that she felt impelled to put on the record, so to speak. Yes, the impulsive manner in which she did so had gotten her into obvious difficulty. Still, she defended her point of view with a mix of tenacity and eloquence that I found impressive, and she certainly had me thinking about larger—so-called existential—issues as I talked with her.

Gradually, we got to know each other, and gradually she quieted down in my office, and in school, too, as she began to realize how competitive she felt with her older brother. When she asked me, one day, about my "hobbies," I took pains to tell her that one of them was reading—that I loved to read novels and poems, that I'd majored in English and American literature, that I still remembered certain books I'd read as a college student, that those books were to me "companions." My use of that word caught her attention. She asked me what I meant, and I tried to explain myself simply and forthrightly: a good book as a good friend—the words, the message, someone else's gesture or offering. She was beginning to learn how to read herself and hadn't really been excited by anything she read, but she did like to hear her parents (and her teacher) read aloud from books they liked, and she slowly began to realize (and eventually, let me realize with respect to her) that she could keep utterly silent, yet very much feel herself to be in possession of a mind with its own authority, dignity, character. Indeed, on one visit to my office, she announced: "The teacher read to us, a long story. It was *Robin Hood* [a shortened version of the old-fashioned tale]. Then, she asked what we thought. No one said anything. I was going to say something, but I thought I'd fool her and keep quiet! She wanted us to say something, I could tell—so she asked us for a show of hands: who thought Robin Hood was right to steal (and give stuff to the poor), and who thought he was wrong? I raised my hand both times. The teacher told me she saw me doing it, and why [was she doing so]? I said I could see why it was right, and I could see why it was wrong! That's why I raised my hand both times. She smiled." After a pause, the girl added this: "I guess that just by raising my arm up, I was talking without saying a word!"

This bright, introspective girl was pulling both of us nearer to a discussion of the essentials of human communication: how we let others know what is on our minds, and thereby who we are—

meaning what we think and value and hold dear, or find objectionable and worse. She had already, at seven, grasped the essentials of literacy: to know how to understand a language; to know how to read it and listen to it and absorb it and make it one's own; to offer it to others as a part of oneself. She would eventually put in many an hour in her local branch library, eagerly meeting others—authors who had written books—and just as eagerly deciding she liked those authors or disliked them. In that last regard she remained true to the original "self" I met when she was seven (she stopped seeing me at eight): she was then still, if more quietly, the assertive person, the one who made clear her opinion, albeit now to herself more commonly than to a classroom, a schoolteacher.

Whenever I hear the subject of "literacy" being discussed I think of that child—and of the many children I have come to know in America and abroad who come from hard-pressed, down-and-out families, who live with few advantages, and who seem destined never to be able to read and write, to enjoy the pleasures of companionship a book offers, to enjoy the opportunity to find and to affirm oneself that reading a book or thinking about a book offer. In a sense, children who lack literacy are apt to be lonelier than many of us grown-ups realize, cut off from many worlds (thoughts, facts, ideas, speculations, suggestions, stories) available to us who, after all, can walk to a shelf and meet the wisest and most interesting and informative men and women who have ever lived, who are immortal by virtue of the words they have set down, the words generation after generation can try to comprehend. Without literacy, those writers and thinkers, those tragedians and humorists, those storytellers and historians and versifiers and scientists and reporters and commentators are lost to a person—and in that sense my young patient was right, a kind of existence is lost, a fear she had with respect to herself that prompted her class outcries, but a fear she could begin to assuage not only with psychotherapy but with the achievement of literacy: once a reader, she could more confidently develop her own opinions, her own point of view, and, so, more self-assured, she could afford the luxury of silence, of quiet contemplation of others.

It is true, a child without literacy is a child destined to be at an economic disadvantage later in life; and we are right in this practical-minded nation to emphasize that point. But a child without literacy is also someone sadly isolated and bereft—deprived of friendship with Tolstoy and Dickens, but also deprived of his or her own mind's capacity to venture forth, to explore through others all sorts of intellectual, moral, and spiritual terrain. Without question, we must remind ourselves, some people of great goodness and decency and honor lack literacy—even as some of us who are learned, never mind literate, have shown ourselves capable of being moral idiots, vain and smug and loudmouthed and callous. (The Nazis had no trouble, alas, attracting to their infamous and murderous ways all sorts of big-shot intellectuals: Hitler's right-hand man, Joseph Goebbels, for instance, had a Ph.D. in comparative literature from Germany's preeminent university!) Even so, literacy can be a most useful vehicle, at the very least—can help us range widely across the continents and the centuries, help us discover what others have to say, and help us discover (as that young girl I have called in witness knew) what we ourselves have to think and say in response to the meetings, of sorts, we have with those others when we sit down and read their words. Such an opportunity—ours through the achievement of literacy—won't take away from us our human limitations and frailties, our darker or sinful side. But at least we have one less excuse for ourselves, because there are potential advisers and mentors and moral guides out there, in all those books, those libraries, and so we have reason to hold ourselves more responsible for our actions—we who can read and write: literacy as a path toward a fuller human accountability for each of us to render with respect to ourselves.

From *Proceedings*, United States Board on Books
for Young People, 1991

That Red Wheelbarrow

To Alex Harris

Contents

The Red Wheelbarrow

so much depends
upon

a red wheel
barrow

glazed with rain
water

beside the white
chickens.

From Paterson, *Book One*

                                    The sun
winding the yellow bindweed about a
bush; worms and gnats, life under a stone.
The pitiful snake with its mosaic skin
and frantic tongue. The horse, the bull
the whole din of fracturing thought
as it falls tinnily to nothing upon the streets
and the absurd dignity of a locomotive
hauling freight—

                            Pithy philosophies of
daily exits and entrances, with books
propping up one end of the shaky table—
The vague accuracies of events dancing two
and two with language which they
forever surpass—and dawns
tangled in darkness—

                            —William Carlos Williams

Introduction

When I started applying to medical schools, I slipped into a black mood of considerable tenacity. I had not intended to be a physician, never mind a psychiatrist. I had majored in English and had written what for me was a major essay on William Carlos Williams. He (poor soul) got to see what I had done, and kindly as he was, he wrote and said I should "drop by." I did, pronto. He immediately took me to Paterson, the city where he did much of his work: making medical visits, mostly to poor families. I became taken not only with him—for his wonderful vitality, his eager embrace of America's working people and *their* vitality—but also with the work he did with his stethoscope during the day before he tried the typewriter at night. Soon enough, I was taking premedical courses, looking at the catalogs of medical schools, and finally seeking entry into a batch of them.

I was turned down by most, though, for not very good grades in "organic chemistry" and such; hence I felt a growing despair. But Dr. Williams and I had become friends, and he was tough in his insistence that I stay hopeful about my medical school prospects and also, as he kept saying, about life. He could be terse and blunt in that regard: "Don't confuse what you are with what some chemistry professor says about your grades in his damn tests." Such common sense, obviously, does not always arrive at one's doorstep, nor does it stay. I kept expressing my doubts and worries, and Dr. Williams kept telling me to persevere—and to read novels and think about what I had read. Once he handed me a list of four or five written on one of his prescriptions slips—books by George Eliot, Hawthorne, Melville, and Tolstoy. He was usually interested in recommending young, relatively unknown poets, but he must have known I needed the moral perspective those four novelists have by now provided many generations of readers. A week later, he asked how I was doing with respect to his recommendations and suggested I write down some of my responses to the reading I'd begun to do: "Better to pour yourself into a novel, and then come up with some thoughts about it, than letting yourself go to ruin over a few college courses, or anything else." I still remember him, tapping his neurological hammer on his knee as he spoke those words. Now, decades later, I realize I've never wanted to forget his advice.

I did manage to get into a medical school—and out (just barely.) I started in pediatrics, still in mindful awe of Doc Williams, who by then was ailing but still a wonderful friend to me. I would go to see him, from time to time, to hear his blunt, tough talk and to feel the sweetness, the kindness he was reluctant to acknowledge directly. When I moved over to psychiatry and child psychiatry, when I became all taken with psychoanalytic training, he was more than a little skeptical but still a great one to visit—warm, gracious, robustly amused by the jargon I was picking up: "Hey, you're talking about *folks*, so come down from that abstract high horse and walk with us, talk with us, be with us!"

When I found myself in the South, first running an Air Force psychiatric hospital in Mississippi (under the old doctor's draft, which mandated two years of military service for all of us physicians) and then (after discharge) studying school desegregation and working with the Civil Rights movement, I tried to stay in touch with a phone call, a Northern visit. But he was getting sicker and sicker, and soon he was eighty, and soon, in 1963, he was dead. The last time I spoke to him, in 1962, he listened intently as I talked of certain black children I was getting to know in New Orleans and Atlanta and of some white people who were going through their own crisis, as the region that had steadfastly been saying *never* to integration now began to yield. I was beginning to pick up a new vocabulary—the talk of sociologists and "race relations specialists," as some in the South then called themselves. Dr. Williams was, yet again, unimpressed: "Lord, that's heavy, heavy talk." I realized later that I had used certain phrases in order to hear them dismissed, mocked by someone who could spot cant and double-talk, pretense and self-importance, a mile away. As I left I got another warning, if not a reprimand: "Watch your words—and every once in a while pick up a novel or read a poem and see what others are doing with words and with people!"

I tried hard to do as told—even back then, with all the excitement of rapid social change in the region I was trying hard to understand. I began, upon his urging, to write in "plain, unaffected, ordinary language" about the children I was meeting; and I began trying to figure out what their parents and teachers were thinking and to render their sentiments, also, in everyday words as opposed to social science phrases. As I did so, I found myself thinking of his poems, his short stories, his novels, his literary criticism, and his personal remarks, made in letters and, of course, in his autobiography. I remembered, too, his enthusiasms—the novels and poems he liked; and often I'd return to them or to some of my own favorites from college days. Nor was such recourse to American, English, or Russian novelists or poets unconnected to my work, I gradually began to realize. It was a novelist, after all, Margaret Long, then editor of *New South*, who in 1962 first got me to write about my work through the telling of stories—what I'd seen and heard, what the children had to say about their lives and, indeed, about life itself. Moreover, when I met the extraordinarily accomplished Southern historian, C. Vann Woodward, in the early 1960s, he made clear, right off, not only his enjoyment of novelists such as Flannery O'Connor or Walker Percy but also their importance to someone like me—and *not* as interpreters of a region but rather as keen observers of the world-at-large, the human scene.

The more I had to write, then, with respect to the children I was coming to know, the more reading of novels and poems I did; and soon enough, I was beginning to write about that reading, to respond to particular novelists or poets with the comments that an essayist or reviewer makes. Eventually, I began to realize that this aspect of my writing life was no mere diversion; I very much needed the help of certain novelists as I tried to figure out what I was observing and hearing in the course of my so-called fieldwork, all those visits to homes and schools. Moreover, my wife, an English teacher, only strengthened that growing reliance. Together we read James Agee's *Let Us Now Praise Famous Men* and George Orwell's *Down and Out in London and Paris*, *The Road to Wigan Pier*, and *Homage to Catalonia*. We began to think of such books as a "literary-documentary" tradition, one we found helpful and instructive, indeed, as we did our wandering work. Together we read and read again not only Flannery O'Connor but also younger writers we'd met, such as Cormac McCarthy; and, of course, we returned to

William Carlos Williams. We also tried to teach those writers and others in the classrooms we kept visiting.

No wonder I gradually wrote more and more so-called literary essays—though for us they were, I must emphasize, efforts at establishing a lifeline for ourselves, lest we drown in a torrent of all too contemporary journalism, not to mention the kind of social and psychological analysis people like me are so quick to offer a public not especially interested in *Middlemarch* or *Bleak House* but endlessly entranced with the theories of psychiatrists or sociologists. Dr. Williams knew how much I loved some of his poems, not least of which the brief, well-known yet still compelling "The Red Wheelbarrow." Once I joked with him: now that I was beginning to do writing about my work in the South, I would toss the results in "your wheelbarrow." He laughed and responded: "You can have it, you know. I'm sorting out everything, before I leave." I never imagined then that twenty-five years later I would be thinking of him, of that moment between us, of that wheelbarrow, as I pulled together some essays, sought a title for them, and wrote a few words to explain their origin.

My debt to Dr. Williams is by now obvious. I hope the substantial portion of this book devoted to him and his work does at least some justice to the regard I still feel toward him, to the gratitude, acknowledged elsewhere in a couple of books and a dedication or two, for all he has come to mean to me. He was always urging me to explore, to "poke around," a phrase he favored—to see the world as keenly as possible and then describe it as carefully as possible, but with "liveliness," a word he used repeatedly. He admired James Agee's and Walker Evans' efforts to "poke around," as given us in *Let Us Now Praise Famous Men*. I think he would admire, too, the documentary efforts of my friend Alex Harris, who as a matter of fact studied with Evans at Yale. Alex is a talented photographer; he is also a fine writer and has a great affinity with novelists, some of whom have responded to his respect by offering their own personal, childhood memories, which Alex edited and gathered into an extraordinarily compelling volume, *A World Unsuspected*. The title words are from Dr. Williams' *Paterson*. I dedicate this book to Alex with admiration and with thanks and more thanks for all the help during all these past years. I also thank Jay Woodruff for his recent considerable help to me, a great source of strength. As always, speaking of sources of strength, I mention my wife, Jane, whose literary interests have, over the years, become mine, and our three sons, Bob, Danny, and Mike, avid readers of some of the novelists and poets whom I so admire and try to praise for reasons I hope this book makes clear. The reasons make up my central theme, actually: they tell why the humanities ought matter to so many of us, still, no matter the contemporary preference of a secular society for science and social science.

Victorian Writers
and Viewpoints

Charles Dickens
and the Law

Some of the important details of the life of Charles Dickens are as familiar to many of us as the various qualities of mind and heart that we have come to associate with such memorable characters as David Copperfield and Philip Pirrip, otherwise known as Pip; or Esther Summerson and Little Dorrit; or yes, Vholes, Jaggers, and Stryver, three lawyers whose names suggest no strong authorial admiration. As a boy, Dickens knew poverty. His father was a clerk in England's Navy Pay Office; he was, as well, all too relaxed when it came to spending the modest salary he earned. When Dickens was twelve years old (in 1824), his father was sent to prison because he had accumulated debts and lacked the means of paying them. This prison, Marshalsea, figures prominently in *Little Dorrit*, even as it did in the life of the young Dickens, who spent time behind bars in accordance with prevailing custom: a debtor's family often accompanied him when he was locked up. As a child, Dickens also worked for extremely low wages in a shoe-blacking factory: he pasted labels on bottles. In his spare time he wandered the streets of London, a penniless lad curious to understand the teeming confusion of a great port city. It was only the death of his paternal grandmother that enabled his father to be released from prison. She left a small legacy to her son. The lesson would never be forgotten by the novelist, who was forever reminding his readers through the workings of one or another plot how arbitrary fate can be and how good can come of bad—or, of course, vice versa.

At fifteen Dickens was studying law as an attorney's apprentice. He mastered shorthand. He read legal texts long and hard. He also, in a matter of months, became bored. He loved the English language and dreamed of using it in one way or another. In 1829 he became a court reporter for the Court of Chancery, whose majestic inscrutability would, decades later, dominate *Bleak House*. By 1832 he was bored with that job, too. He tried journalism: first the *True Sun*, then the *Mirror of Parliament*, then the *Morning Chronicle*. His specialty was parliamentary reportage. He had a keen eye for nineteenth-century English politics—its moral postures, its moments (and longer) of theater, both high and low, its possibilities, and its sad limitations. He also had developed a compelling manner of narrative presentation—strong, suggestive prose. He worked quickly. He observed exactly. He rendered accurately. Moreover, he was astonishingly energetic—a quality he'd never stop possessing. He traveled anywhere and everywhere in search of a good political story. All London became his routine beat; all England easily tempted him if he felt the story demanded that extra effort.

Inside him burned, even then, a writer's desire to expand upon incidents, to convey a given atmosphere, to give moral shape to a particular factuality. In December 1833, the *Monthly Magazine* published Dickens' first sketch of London street life. In August 1834, he began using the name Boz, and by February of 1836, at the age of twenty-four, he had published *Sketches by Boz*—with the additional explanatory title *Illustrative of Everyday Life and Everyday People*. Shortly thereafter he began the first of his Pickwick pieces—"The Posthumous Papers of the Pickwick Club." By then he was ready to marry and to shift course as a writer. He abandoned the writing of conventional journalism, though he worked for a while (two years) as an editor. At the same time he immersed himself in his own world and reported on the workings of his imagination, its exceedingly vigorous life.

Soon enough a substantial segment of the English reading public, rich and poor and many, many in between, became familiar with the antic and sometimes soberly edifying carryings-on of Samuel Pickwick and his fellow clubsmen Nathaniel Winkle, Tracy Tupman, and Augustus Snodgrass—and those they met: Alfred Jingle, Dr. Slammer, Mr. Wardle, his daughters Bella and Emily, his spinster sister Rachael, Samuel Weller, Job Trotter, and the landlady Mrs. Bardell, not to mention those two shady lawyers Dodson and Fogg, and that shrewd master of realpolitik, the lawyer Perker. Samuel Pickwick, we all know, survives crooked lawyers and even, it seems, the temptations of love. He retires to the country with his servant Sam Weller for a long and restful life. Dickens, on the other hand, with the publication of *Pickwick Papers* in book form (1838), had ahead of him more than thirty years of demanding labor. No matter the success those years brought, there was in this greatest of storytellers an unyielding attachment of sorts to his early social and moral experiences; he worked them over repeatedly in the later novels—*Bleak House, Hard Times, Great Expectations, A Tale of Two Cities, Little Dorrit*: down-and-out English life, the exploitation, and not least, the miscarriages of justice. No acclaim, no money, no amount of achieved influence seemed enough to stop him from looking closely at a nation he loved and yet found urgently in need of reform. Nor did his success as a writer and an eager public speaker, if not performer, prevent him from going back, time and again, to the memories generated by an earlier life: the child in a debtor's prison, the youth struggling with a harsh and mean life, the young man observing lawmakers at their shilly-shallying or corrupt worst, and above all, the apprentice writer taking note of lawyers— who, of course, are right there when men and women go to prison, or lose whatever rights or privileges they may have had, or find themselves in severe straits because the laws work this way rather than that way or on behalf of these people rather than those. Charles Dickens in his fifties, the most celebrated writer in Britain, still scanned hungrily London's lowlife, a substantial population indeed; and doing so, he gave us not only memorable characters (Jo of *Bleak House*, the Dorrits of Marshalsea Prison, the prisoner Magwitch) but also terribly searching moral issues to consider and (he would surely have hoped) to connect in their continuing significance to our own considerably later lives.

Again and again lawyers figure in the penetrating enactments of ethical conflict that Dickens insisted on making a central element of his most important novels. In *Bleak House*, of course, the issue is not just lawyers but the law itself—its awesome, pervasive, perplexing, unnerving presence. Even in Dickens' lifetime, some of the tedious, if not outrageous, aspects of London's Chancery Court had succumbed to reform. And, too, Dickens knew when he wrote *Little Dorrit* that the very Marshalsea Prison he described (and knew as a young inmate) no longer was the giant debtors' world of old, filled with entire families whose crime was an inability to pay their bills. For all his urgent responsiveness to Victorian dilemmas, Dickens was a moral visionary who wrote *sub specie aeternitatis;* hence the continuing provocation and edifying satisfaction of his novels, not to mention the still mighty power of his caricatures. The fog of *Bleak House,* after all, still obtains. The law still offers many of those caught in its exertions any number of frustrations, confusions, delays. Men, women, and children still find themselves irritated, then confounded, then outraged, and finally maddened by cases that affect them deeply and seem to go on and on and on—maybe not for generations, as happened in *Jarndyce v. Jarndyce,* but long enough for particular children to suffer in extended custodial fights, and for particular workers and families to suffer while the responsibility for, say, dangerous environmental pollution is argued in court for months that become years.

Yet *Bleak House* is much more than a novel that portrays the outcome of a legal impasse. Too much is made, one can argue, about the protracted nature of the celebrated Jarndyce litigation. In one enumeration, made in the well-known first chapter, Dickens does indeed mention "procrastination," but he also mentions "trickery," "evasion," and "spoliation." He even makes reference to "botheration," surely of interest to this proudly self-conscious age wherein the social sciences, especially psychology and psychiatry, are thought to explain so much to us. Nor is that list, certainly applicable to our contemporary scene, intended as a précis of a novelist's coming preoccupations. *Bleak House* is ultimately about character—even as, occasionally, professions such as the law or medicine come down (or up!) to that: how so-called practitioners skirt various temptations (or fail to do so); and how a certain lawyer or doctor justifies his work, comes to terms with his perceived obligations, responds in mind and heart to the hurt, the vulnerability, the alarm if not panic of his clients, his patients. Even as in *Middlemarch* we see George Eliot trying to comprehend the fate of Dr. Lydgate—the transformation of an avowedly idealistic young doctor into an all too (by his own early and high standards) compromised and self-serving one—the many chapters of *Bleak House* offer their own chronicle of a profession variously practiced, its supposed purposes variously interpreted, and, alas, not always to the good.

Of all Dickens' lawyers, Tulkinghorn of *Bleak House* is surely the highest in rank—that is, the one who has achieved the most professional success. He is a distinguished lawyer and advisor to one of England's most powerful families. True, Dickens tips his hand (as he so often does) with the name of Dedlock: Sir Leicester is indeed a baronet who (with others in England's nineteenth-century nobility) is headed nowhere. The social foolishness, the moribund paralysis, intellectual and moral, of a particular upper class is more than indicated in the early chapters of *Bleak House*. But Sir Leicester is, nevertheless, rich and influential, and, we eventually learn, more decent than many of his ilk; and to be his lawyer is, well, to be a notable success. Tulkinghorn is no Lawyer Tangle, arguing his way to no apparent purpose in the obscure, dreary, muddy, fogenshrouded trenches of the law:

> "Mr. Tangle," says the Lord High Chancellor, latterly something restless under the eloquence of that learned gentleman.
> "Mlud," says Mr. Tangle. Mr. Tangle knows more of Jarndyce and Jarndyce than anybody. He is famous for it—supposed never to have read anything else since he left school.
> "Have you concluded your argument?"
> "Mlud, no—variety of points—feel it my duty tsubmit—ludship," is the reply that slides out of Mr. Tangle.
> "Several members of the bar are still to be heard, I believe?" says the Chancellor with a slight smile.
> Eighteen of Mr. Tangle's friends, each armed with a little summary of eighteen hundred sheets, bob up like eighteen hammers in a pianoforte, make eighteen bows, and drop into their eighteen places of obscurity.

For Tulkinghorn, such "duty tsubmit," such ingratiating bowing and scraping, such "obscurity," is hardly the point of a legal career. He holds his own with the best. He even manages to have the high and mighty watch their step with him around; indeed, they cower before his acquired legal knowledge of the facts of their personal lives, knowledge that inevitably becomes his property. Here is a description by no less than the wife of Sir Leicester Dedlock. She has just told her daughter that she dreads a certain person. The daughter asks: "An enemy?" The mother replies: "Not a friend. One who is too passionless to be either. He is Sir Leicester Dedlock's lawyer; mechanically faithful without attachment, and very jealous of the profit, privilege and reputation of being master of the mysteries of great houses." A bit further on the lady expands: "He is indifferent to everything but his calling. His calling is the acquisition of secrets, and the holding possession of such power as they give him, with no sharer or opponent in it." Still further on her husband adds this: "He is, of course, handsomely paid, and he associates almost on a footing of equality with the highest society."

That is about as far as Dickens really wants to go in explicit psychological analysis. He does let Lady Dedlock's apprehensiveness, elsewhere in the novel, turn into an occasion for psychological speculation rather than diagnosis:

> Whether he be cold and cruel, whether immovable in what
> he has made his duty, whether absorbed in love of power,
> whether determined to have nothing hidden from him in
> ground where he has burrowed among secrets all his life,
> whether he in his heart despises the splendour of which he is a
> distant beam, whether he is always treasuring up slights and
> offences in the affability of his gorgeous clients—whether he
> be any of this, or all of this, it may be that my Lady had better
> have five thousand pairs of fashionable eyes upon her, in dis-
> trustful vigilance, than the two eyes of this rusty lawyer, with
> his wisp of neck cloth and his dull black breeches tied with
> ribbons at the knees.

Still, a mood of suspicion and fear and guilt is not to be confused with a clear, precise moment of apprehended truth. Tulkinghorn, we know, listens and stalks and prompts respect if not outright alarm. But his exact purposes are not evident—as if Dickens believed that we are, really, what we manage to present of ourselves to the world around us. Put differently, the depiction of a given social and professional reality is for one nineteenth-century novelist a sufficiently complex psychological evocation. For many of today's readers, however, the more Tulkinghorn's enigmatic but exceptionally significant involvement in this long and darkly suggestive story is chronicled, the more we search for motives, a ruling mode of comprehension for us of the twentieth century. And the less satisfactory, I suppose, Dickens' stubborn refusal becomes—as in this tantalizing moment, wherein a chance for "depth analysis," as we call it, is once more forsaken:

He passes out into the streets, and walks on, with his hands behind him, under the shadow of the lofty houses, many of whose mysteries, difficulties, mortgages, delicate affairs of all kinds, are treasured up within his old black satin waistcoat. He is in the confidence of the very bricks and mortar. The high chimney-stacks telegraph family secrets to him. Yet there is not a voice in a mile of them to whisper "Don't go home!"

Here we are granted drama, even melodrama; certainly we note a touch of irony, even poignant irony—though, to be sure, no sympathy. Perhaps at this moment, in frustration if not annoyed condescension, we begin to remind ourselves that Dickens is not George Eliot, after all, or Tolstoy. He was, that is to say, not notably enchanted by the possibilities offered by the novel for the analysis of personality—our moral life as it is prompted by the various emotional reasons each of us finds compelling. Yet that observation is all too categorical—and unsatisfying. In fact, Dickens was a direct predecessor of Kafka, of Flannery O'Connor. He believed in the literal truth that exaggeration aims to apprehend. He believed in the down-home, concrete reality that inspired his flights of fancy called caricatures. What were they, those caricatures, but emphatic statements with respect to especially salient personal qualities, whose moral import, often enough, the author believed to be well worth a particular literary effort?

Moreover, when Dickens wants to explore rather distinctly a certain character's mind, he does so without hesitation or awkwardness. Here is Bucket presented to us; Bucket, the first detective to enter English literature; Bucket, whose activities also connected with the legal system Dickens wanted to portray; Bucket, who was as much an urban walking man as Tulkinghorn:

> Otherwise mildly studious in his observation of human nature, on the whole a benignant philosopher not disposed to be severe upon the follies of mankind, Mr. Bucket pervades a vast number of houses, and strolls about an infinity of streets: to outward appearances rather languishing for want of an object. He is in the friendliest condition towards his species, and will drink with most of them. He is free with his money, affable in his manners, innocent in his conversation—but, through the

placid stream of his life, there glides an undercurrent of fore-finger.

That last phrase may not be the kind of abstract declaration we have, alas, found so congenial: the superego as a factor in our mental activity. But "forefinger" will do—as a means of reminding us that this fellow Bucket, like others (let us pray!) who hunt down criminals, supposed or actual, is impelled by voices that worry about what is right and what is wrong; voices that urge, too, that such worries not be altogether abstract but rather worked into the fabric of a given occupational life. If Bucket is a covert moralist, then what is Tulkinghorn? He is not immoral, one gathers. He seems to be without moral anguish of any kind—a lofty one who prompts alarm, even panic, in others, while he goes about his weighty business. In Tulkinghorn, Dickens may have all too uncannily anticipated our contemporary scene: as in a supposedly value-free social science, or in the proclaimed worth of professional neutrality, or in the dispassionate claims of the adversarial system, not to mention the carefully cultivated, circumspect anonymity of our psychiatrists. Tulkinghorn is contained, cool; oh, so cool—as the saying goes: a real professional! Such a person is best probed, perhaps, by a psychological observer keenly attentive to the powerful influence social and cultural norms exert on human motivation, not to mention behavior. Dickens was such a psychological observer.

As for Bucket, it is not just a latent moralism that attracts our interest in him. He is one of those relatively minor characters in a Dickens novel who comes to attract our strongest scrutiny, if not perplexity, because his various activities and attitudes remind us, needless to say, of our own continuing social and ethical dilemmas. Bucket is the one who initially goes after such good and decent people as Gridley and George, and, lo and behold, our dear and defenseless Jo, the incarnation in *Bleak House* of all that is vulnerable and innocently injured in this high-powered life we call "civilized." Why such a pursuit? Why, of all people, hound Jo? What Dickens thought about Jo is contained in one of the most memorable passages he ever wrote:

> And there he sits munching, and gnawing, and looking up at the great Cross on the summit of St. Paul's Cathedral, glitter-

ing above a red and violet-tinted cloud of smoke. From the boy's face one might suppose that sacred emblem to be, in his eyes, the crowning confusion of the great, confused city;—so golden, so high up, so far out of his reach. There he sits, the sun going down, the river running fast, the crows flying by him in two streams—everything moving on to some purpose and to one end—until he is stirred up, and told to "move on" too.

What kind of "inspector" hunts down such a child? Why, a man who has a job to do! Is Jo guilty of a crime, or is he not? Never mind urban problems and problems of class and caste; never mind a child's hurt life, a city's rampant evil as it bears down on those least able to protect themselves, to assert their claim to citizenship. After a while this harsh, moralistic Bucket begins to win us over: he is decent and fair as he does his duty. We know that this is one agent of the law who will not be gratuitously mean spirited. He has driven Jo out of the city (to his death!) because he believes him (wrongly) to have been a criminal. But Dickens is unwilling to push this matter as far as he might—the personally good worker who obeys his superiors and hurts others, no matter their decency, their merit. Rather quickly we see Bucket befriending all the people we've come to love: he wards off the Smallweeds from Sir Leicester, helps preserve a marriage (that of the Snagsbys), works hard (if in vain) to rescue Lady Dedlock, and discovers who it is (Hortense) who really killed Tulkinghorn. Now we are pleased: this is a professional man who clearly acts in the service of "good." Again one poses the issue, now in the form of a question: why didn't Dickens push matters in quite another direction—explore the matter of the loyal, efficient, hard-working professional man (avowedly well intentioned and honorable) whose loyalty to a given job, to a given social and economic system, persuades him that (for instance) the Jos of this world would have to be put in their place, made to stop loitering and begging, and prevented from distracting and disturbing the rest of us?

Perhaps the answer is that Dickens (and indeed, the entire nineteenth century) had yet to feel as desperate as we have come to feel—hopelessly caught, so often, in the grips of one or another totalitarian system. The utter evil, the everyday evil, worked into the daily lives of millions of law-abiding citizens of this or that state, the evil of the Holocaust and the Gulag, were surely beyond his exuberantly reformist, Christian sensibility. But his moral intuition is as broad and deep as his moral yearning—and so Bucket, for more than a few pages, deeply troubles us, for we have heard one self-proclaimed totalitarian functionary after another (doctors and lawyers among them) assert his loyalty to duty as an excuse for what he ended up doing to others.

In the Victorian legal system—its workings, its possibilities for some, its constraints and worse on others—Dickens keeps managing to embody our century's moral dilemmas; in the novelistic tradition, they have been considered by Conrad and Solzhenitsyn, and in the tradition of the political and philosophical essay, by Camus and Hannah Arendt. "The one great principle of the English law," Dickens tells us, "is to make business for itself." No wonder, then, that one attorney in *Bleak House* gets called Vholes: a "vole" in a card game is a situation in which the dealer gets all the winning cards. Over and over Dickens emphasizes the ordinary in Vholes, the regular and conventional:

> Mr. Vholes is a very respectable man. He has not a very large business, but he is a very respectable man. He is allowed by the greater attorneys who have made good fortunes, or are making them, to be a most respectable man. He never misses a chance in his practice, which is a mark of respectability; he is reserved and serious, which is also a mark of respectability; his digestion is impaired, which is *highly* respectable; he is making hay of the grass which is flesh, for his three daughters and his father are dependent on him in the Vale of Taunton.

Therein is, I fear, an account all too contemporary—we earnest, hardworking, thoroughly loyal, occasionally (but discreetly) troubled citizens, always at a ready for Alka-Seltzers (maybe, if necessary, a visit to the psychiatrist for our psychosomatic ailments), and prepared as well with our psychological or moral justifications: I do it for my wife, my children; I do it for my family, my very well deserving family; so, hands off, you with the forefinger, you preachy cultural essayists or social critics, you thinly disguised moral rhetoricians masked as lecturers who come to one or another university!

In *Great Expectations* Dickens continues to explore this theme—the relationship between the practice of a profession (the law) and the moral life as it (one hopes) presents its predicaments, if not out-right demands, to all of us. The lawyer Jaggers is surely one of Dickens' best-known characters. He is a tough, hugely successful (and just plain huge) barrister who strides the legal netherworld of London to the accompaniment of everyone's awe. Dickens knew how hard-pressed life was for thousands of English families in mid-nineteenth-century England, and he knew the legal side of such des-peration—a jungle of suspicion and fear and hate. He was especially attentive to the meanness and spitefulness, the crazy outbursts of anger, the trickery and cunning, the resort to lies and more lies that characterized the so-called lowlife; hungry, jobless men, women, and children, with few if any prospects, become reduced to a fate not only marginal with respect to its socioeconomic character but also with respect to its very humanity. True, as Dickens reminded us in *Bleak House* with Esther Summerson and in *Little Dorrit* with the character whose name titles the novel, human dignity is not really ever extinguished, only put in severe jeopardy. But there was plenty of that jeopardy for the people Jaggers knew so well, and to this day the problem remains: what can an earnest, competent law-yer do, given the hard facts of a continual and severe exploitation of men and women by their fellow creatures?

The very name Jaggers, needless to say, suggests the cutthroat quality of a particular existential situation. One is a bit indirect, un-easy, and evasive here: Jaggers himself is not so easy to write off as yet another of Dickens' villainous lawyers. He is imperious and gruff; he is as manipulative as, well, an attorney of his caliber and practice would naturally be. He trades in secrets, skirts the edges of the law, bullies strangers and associates, keeps all sorts of tricks up his sleeve—and yet is by no means a moral monster. He is oddly com-pelling, even touching, in his blunt poses of neutrality, aloofness, and skepticism. The more we get to know him (and Dickens wants us to do so, thereby rescuing a character from the limitations of the caricature) the more we wonder at his purpose—and at that of Dickens as well in making him so arresting and complex. He is, after all, the instrument of the boy Pip's moral and spiritual journey. He is also capable of saving a soul or two amid the hellish life he ob-served and, within limits, dominated. And he shows evidence of an-guish—the constant handwashing that bespoke a keen recognition of just how sordid a given job was.

In a sense, then, Jaggers is the lawyer who has to work in a world exceptionally flawed by sin and suffering—and somehow not himself slip hopelessly into that world. No question, he profits from that world—as a person who wields his influence and receives the urgent entreaties of a bewildered and impoverished population of Londoners and as a lawyer who can pick and choose among would-be clients. His very credibility as a character attests to Dickens' moral seriousness at this point in his literary career: we don't laugh at Jaggers or with him either at the various people with whom he works. Nor do we simply enjoy his brusque power, his moments of mocking arrogance, his clever instincts for survival. He is, we begin to feel, a lonely and driven figure himself. He belongs with those who wait on him—Molly, for instance, his servant, whom he defended on a murder charge. She was a tramp, wild and crude. Upon her acquittal she went to work for him. She is, we learn, Estella's mother, the father being the convict Magwitch, Pip's benefactor. Dickens unashamedly wove such a tightknit plot—a reminder to all of us how intimately we are connected to one another as members of a particular society. Molly is an animal barely under control, we are persuaded; and Jaggers, her keeper, is himself a predator one minute (not hesitating to push aside the law, even violate it, while fighting as someone's courtroom advocate) and the proverbial dumb beast another minute—lost and mute and confused when not at work, hence not able to show his swagger, his cunning, his crude and relentless appetite.

His legal associate Wemmick also tells us something about ourselves, I fear. This lovely, genial, generous, thoughtful, and considerate man (at home) becomes a willing agent of greed and brute force at work. Dickens once again wants to emphasize the duality of our natures, the capacity we have to split ourselves in half, to live without shame our contradictory lives—acquisitive and coldly impersonal under one set of circumstances, tactful and sensitive and utterly humane in another setting. John Wemmick's Walworth Castle is necessarily just that—a refuge, a bastion, a place that offers protection against the marauding, normally bankrupt demands of the covetous world outside. There is in him, at home, an element of the self-reliant yeoman, once England's proudest claim. He builds. He plants. He fixes things. He dreams of yet further projects to make life in the country more relaxed and enjoyable. But even in the castle, he's always storing things, calculating how much property he's been able to accumulate. He's not a lavish party-giver, someone bent on self-advertising consumption. But he knows the reassuring comfort that accumulated property can bring, and he is willing to be, day after day in a law office, the strong-faced sidekick of a big-deal criminal lawyer—to do his various errands, collect cash for him, and, one gathers, help work up his cases. In today's (English) terms, Jaggers was a flamboyant, sly, not always unkind, and some-times socially discerning and compassionate barrister; Wemmick, on the other hand, was his firm's chief solicitor—someone who didn't need to wash his hands after seeing each client, as was Jaggers' wont. Rather, a trip to the outer precincts worked right well—as it does, perhaps, for some of us today.

Dickens was not, however, beyond imagining redeeming possibil-ities in the lives of the individuals he created and, too, in the work they did. In *A Tale of Two Cities*, Sydney Carton—a well-known character indeed (especially to high school students!) in the world Dickens created—is (we sometimes forget) a lawyer. He drinks too much. He seems aimless, sad, troubled. He helps the lawyer Stryver free Charles Darnay, who has been accused of committing treason as a spy for France. Unlike *Bleak House* or *Great Expecta-tions*, this novel does not directly approach the law as a profession. Sydney Carton's work as a lawyer is shown to be clever, even bril-liant; but our interest in him has to do with his human qualities per se rather than with a professional predicament that tests the moral strength of those qualities. His moral strength is, to be sure, tested—but by an international crisis, by a social revolution, and, not insig-nificantly, by the constraints and turmoil of love. It is as if Dickens were saying to us: I have shown you, in *Bleak House*, how terribly perplexing and crippling the law itself can be; and I have shown you in *Great Expectations* how terribly insinuating the law can be, mor-ally and psychologically, as its practitioners struggle with the hypoc-risies and worse of an industrial order (one not totally unlike our own); now let me take a lawyer and put him in the midst of a tu-multuous political scene, a time of drastic upheaval, and see not what happens to his profession or what he does with his profession but what happens to him as a human being. In *Bleak House* the law is fog; in *Great Expectations*, at times, the law is a snake, an aspect of man's post-Eden fate; in *A Tale of Two Cities* the law is a given person's trade, a footnote—as so much we do can end up being—to an ongoing spiritual struggle, one all too commonly masked, as a matter of fact, by the seeming excellence of our professional and even personal adjustment.

Not that such was the case with attorney Carton. He comes to us dissolute, if nothing else. His crony Stryver is not *quite* dissolute—though the difference between the two, Dickens wants us to realize right off, is more apparent than real. They drink together and offer evidence of a mutual cynicism, an essential boredom with life. Stryver is what his name suggests, still pushing for money and influence. But he is in many respects burned out—morally for sure and psychologically as well. Carton is smarter by far but also less self-protective. He is our professional man who has a good head on his shoulders and might go far but seems curiously paralyzed, hence headed for alcoholism, suicide, or (is it our fate to hope?) a psychiatrist's office where, presumably, he will be enough helped to—what? Resume work with the Stryvers of this world? Abandon one sort of practice for another? Seek another occupation?

No, we are likely to declare: the problem is not Carton's profession; the problem is Carton himself. He needs to see a doctor. But is that the case? Do we find ourselves wanting Stryver to have *his* head examined? Stryver, whom Dickens describes as "a man of little more than thirty, but looking twenty years older than he was, stout, loud, red, bluff, and free from any drawback of delicacy"? Stryver, who "had a pushing way of shouldering himself (morally and physically) onto companies and conversations"? Once more Dickens is our late twentieth-century social observer, quite ready to confound us with the ongoing riddle of this psychological era: why is it that some who seem quite obnoxious in every way are not usually regarded as candidates for psychiatric scrutiny, while others, in comparison exceedingly refined and decent, are quickly considered in serious difficulty and quite in need of "help," as we choose to call it?

For Dickens, the law and the prison that awaits those who violate the law were not only recurrent subjects to be explained in novel after novel. Nor was the interest in those subjects a mere consequence of an early personal experience. Like other nineteenth-century social critics and moralists who had not once been in trouble with the law or inside a prison, Dickens took close stock of an emerging industrial order and was truly aghast. In *Hard Times* he lets us know how much so—how vicious he deemed not only the treatment accorded the poor but also the burden put upon those who were not at all poor. Again and again we are reminded that exploitation cuts both ways—that those who coldly manipulate others or bring up their children to do so will pay a stiff price indeed: the fear, the suspiciousness, the nervous, self-justifying smugness, the isolating arrogance that, in sum, amount to a vision of the blind leading the blind, the meanly powerful worrying over the sadly hurt. In *A Tale of Two Cities* Dickens dares suggest that all London is a prison of sorts, and all Paris is too. The streets are narrow and confusing. Even Tellson's bank, which has offices in both cities and to which the affluent come to tap their resources, is dark and dingy and has its "own iron bars proper." The Paris bank has a "high wall and a strong gate." Mention is made of "depositors rusted in prison." Jerry Cruncher, the bank's odd-jobber, is an "inmate of a menagerie"; he has rust on his fingers and is at the beck and call of anyone and everyone. As with France's royalty and, eventually, with its murderous revolutionaries, England's rich and powerful know constant apprehension, can take little for granted, and keep a wary eye on friends and all too numerous enemies. And in *Little Dorrit*, needless to say, that theme of pervasive confinement, of jails as the lot of people badly isolated from one another, reaches a climax with Marshalsea Prison, the Circumlocution Office, and Bleeding Heart Yard: England's bureaucratic and legal and commercial and moral confusions, duplicities, and aberrancies are, in sum, a heavy, collective constraint upon the nation's people.

But Dickens not only regarded closely a nation and criticized it with earnest passion (through humor, gentle or biting; through sentiment, gentle or mawkish or extremely touching; through caricatures, heroic portraits, sustained imagery, shrewdly engaging character portrayal, and plots that have a way of holding the reader, no matter their lapses into the all too expectable); he was, as mentioned, his own kind of moral visionary. In an essay on Dickens, a fine one, a trenchant one, and maybe an autobiographical one, George Orwell emphasizes this side of Dickens, his strong interest in seeing justice done. Orwell stresses the presence in Dickens of a "native generosity of mind" and reminds us how continually, in those many novels, we are reminded of the twin importance of "freedom and equality." Dickens hated all who lord it over others, as Orwell did. Let any onetime victim rise up far enough, they both knew, and the danger of yet additional wrongdoing immediately arises. Our century, alas, has made such an observation (stressed throughout *A Tale of Two Cities*) a huge and awful banality—and the result, of course, has been the untimely deaths of millions and prisons whose size and nature even a prophetic novelist with the imagination of a Dickens could never possibly have foreseen.

In a memorable phrase Orwell calls Dickens a Christian out of a "quasi-instinctive siding with the oppressed against the oppressors"; and one can scarcely disagree. Dickens took careful, calculated aim at those oppressors and, like Orwell, knew that they can appear, out of nowhere it seems, in every possible location—among the poor as well as the rich, among people of all races and backgrounds, among professional men and intellectuals as well as men of commerce, and among women as well as men. Madame Defarge in *A Tale of Two Cities* need only be mentioned, along with Skimpole in *Bleak House*, whose clever, self-enhancing egoism bears an astonishing resemblance to what can be found in various centers of literary and artistic activity. Dickens knew well what we have called "the culture of narcissism," the seductive power of the mirror. His prisons have mirrors in them—a double jeopardy! So does the London courtroom where the prisoner Charles Darnay fights for his life with the help of the lawyers Stryver and Carton. Even the members of the crowd watching the trial become "mirrors reflecting the witness." There is, of course, and necessarily so, a last-ditch narcissism at stake in many courtrooms: a life itself will be saved or lost, not to mention the personal reputation (and sense of self-worth) of this or that lawyer. But for Dickens any particular trial is emblematic, as in Kafka's *The Trial*: we reveal our desperate situation as human beings by not recognizing just how trapped we are in our own world of eager pretentiousness and by pursuing endless circularities as if they were a straight road to an absolutely certain destination.

Dickens himself, despite the gloom so many of his stories contain (and the gratuitous quality to their happy endings), was not without hope. He found decency in ordinary, unassuming people, the humble of this earth who (we are promised, we were solemnly warned) would inherit the world. He saw plenty of evil and saw children, always, as victims, as born prisoners who never seem to get their sentences fully commuted. Yes, Pip marries Estella, one ending of *Great Expectations* tells us. Yes, Esther Summerson marries Dr. Allen Woodcourt, *Bleak House* informs us. Yes, Arthur Clennam finds Little Dorrit, and Sydney Carton finds Lucie Manette, and through those two women each man is affirmed—all the pain and suffering of their early lives somehow recede in personal significance. But in all Dickens' novels the meanness and brutishness of this life are made abundantly clear. Pip's famous moment of searching introspections, his trenchant statement about himself and his life, turns into an authorial comment on justice and its vicissitudes, on our fate as human beings, born into an arbitrary and imperfect world and soon enough to depart:

> In the little world in which children have their existence whosoever brings them up, there is nothing so finely perceived and so finely felt, as injustice. It may be only small injustice that the child can be exposed to; but the child is small, and its world is small, and its rocking-horse stands as many hands high, according to scale, as a big-boned Irish hunter. Within myself, I had sustained, from my babyhood, a perpetual conflict with injustice. I had known, from the time when I could speak, that my sister, in her capricious and violent coercion, was unjust to me. I had cherished a profound conviction that her bringing me up by hand, gave her no right to bring me up by jerks. Through all my punishments, disgraces, fasts and vigils, and other penitential performances, I had nursed this assurance; and to my communing so much with it, in a solitary and unprotected way, I in great part refer the fact that I was morally timid and very sensitive.

But there is, the same author knew, a chance to reverse things, to render a kind of fitting if finite justice—a redemption here on earth that must precede any further redemption to be gained elsewhere in the universe. Dickens' interest in practical, everyday charity (of the kind Jesus offered again and again as he walked Galilee nearly two thousand years ago) is well underscored in this extraordinary passage in *Little Dorrit*, as another one of his hurt souls looks back and looks ahead:

> As the fierce dark teaching of his childhood had never sunk into his heart, so that first article in his code of morals was, that he must begin, in practical humility, with looking well to

his feet on Earth, and that he could never mount on wings of words to Heaven. Duty on earth, restitution on earth, action on earth; these first, as the first steep steps upward. Strait was the gate and narrow was the way; far straiter and narrower than the broad high road paved with vain professions and vain repetitions, motes from other men's eyes and liberal delivery of others to the judgement—all cheap materials costing absolutely nothing.

So it goes, or so we hope it will go, for ourselves—a chance to do the Lord's will in the way he showed, through daily tasks, obligations, and possibilities of charity. Sometimes I hear Dickens faulted: he saw wrongs, but he failed to give us an overall scheme to right them. In view of the various all-encompassing ideologies we have seen at work in this century—ones offering personal and social rehabilitation on the grandest scale—we can be grateful, maybe, for Dickens' restrained reformism, for his humane egalitarian liberalism, and one also insists, for his down-to-earth Christianity, so beholden to Jesus of Nazareth rather than to the various "principalities and powers" that have come to speak so confidently, if not imperiously, in his name. In that last regard, Orwell does well to quote from a letter Dickens wrote to his youngest son in 1868:

> You will remember that you have never at home been harassed about religious observances, or mere formalities. I have always been anxious not to weary my children with such things, before they are old enough to form opinions respecting them. You will therefore understand the better that I now most solemnly impress upon you the truth and beauty of the Christian Religion, as it came from Christ Himself, and the impossibility of your going far wrong if you humbly but heartily respect it. . . . Never abandon the wholesome practice of saying your own private prayers, night and morning. I have never abandoned it myself, and I know the comfort of it.

What is the law but a necessarily finite effort on our part to find some earthly vision that at least partakes in a small way of that larger biblical vision offered us by the Hebrew prophets Jeremiah, Isaiah, and Amos, and by the one who followed them, Jesus Christ? A vision of what? A moral vision, surely. A vision put negatively at first of what must *not* be done—so that over time we will edge nearer to a more honorable and decent world, where "equal justice" will not only be a phrase cut in the marble of a particular Washington, D.C. building but something known and felt to be a daily given the world over. Meanwhile, we all struggle with this life's hardships, its terrible lack of justice, a curse for so many; and we struggle also to figure out how to change that state of affairs—through (among other ways) laws written, through laws challenged, through laws argued and argued, through interventions here and there on behalf of one person, then another.

In the midst of those struggles a moral visionary such as Charles Dickens is no small ally. He takes in his hands the abstract matters of a subject, legal ethics, and gives them the complex, provocative life of a story. He gives us character as fate shapes it. He gives us chance and circumstance, good luck and bad luck, humor and melancholy—an opportunity not to figure out the world theoretically but to put ourselves in it correctly. As a moral visionary, he left us situations to heed, people to know, a whole range of ethical matters to attend in a very special way—the personal immersion enabled by a novel. One can, he knew (to use the phrase of our contemporary, American novelist, the Southerner Walker Percy) "get all A's and flunk life." One can, he knew, do well in a course called Legal Ethics or Moral Reasoning and go on to be a not so honorable and straightforward and compassionate human being. The novels of Dickens offer reminders enough of people who preach a good tune to others and fail to heed it in the everyday particulars of their lives—the Mrs. Jellybys of this world. The novels of Dickens offer us *ourselves*, plenty of us flawed, all too many of us thoroughly wretched, yet more than a few of us sometimes graced by moments and longer of honor.

Recently I came across this observation, made by Viktor Frankl, a physician who only barely survived years of Hitler's hell: "We who lived in concentration camps can remember the men who walked through the huts comforting others, giving away their last piece of bread. They may have been few in number, but they offer sufficient proof that everything can be taken from a man but one thing: the last of the human freedoms—to choose one's attitude in any given set of circumstances, to choose one's own way." As one goes over those words again and again, surely it is not inappropriate to think of Charles Dickens and his enormous, hard-earned moral quarry, which he dug and dug, a lifetime's effort. He knew how constrained we all are, how hard it is for us to break free, to achieve a measure of continuing dignity. His exhortation of a particular profession, the law, was meant to honor its possible role in our lives—at its best a bulwark against anarchy and a pointer in the direction of fairness. Still, there are awful lapses, as he knew, and as we in this century have also come to know—to the point that the often isolated and lonely good folk of the world of Charles Dickens seem to reach out to join hands with those Dr. Frankl describes: orphans all amid the terrible human disasters of our history, yet also heroes whom each of us needs to remember with a certain tenacity, perhaps, as we go about our daily lives, our daily business, including that of the law.

Virginia Quarterly Review, Autumn 1983

Dickens and Little Dorrit

For several years I have been teaching a course at Harvard Law School titled "Dickens and the Law." We read three novels in which lawyers figure prominently: *Bleak House,* obviously, with its evocation of the nineteenth-century English law's procedural eternity; *Great Expectations,* wherein a lawyer, Jaggers, is an important agent in a child's transformation from rural rudeness (in the sense of a humble life) to urban sophistication (that of London) with all the attendant moral risks; and *A Tale of Two Cities,* with its not unknown lawyer, Sydney Carton, whose purposes and acts troubled and enthralled us in high school and, I've noticed, still do in this particular graduate school setting. We also read *Little Dorrit,* even though its purview is not as directly legal, because in it the author resists the explicit caricature or scolding of the law he had hitherto practiced through presenting such lawyer-characters as Tulkinghorn and Vholes in *Bleak House* or, besides Jaggers, the interesting Mr. Wemmick in *Great Expectations,* and of course, the lawyer with the not easily forgotten name Stryver in *A Tale of Two Cities.*

In *Little Dorrit* the reader is urged to take the largest possible look at the world—to consider its seemingly endless constraints. Long before the French philosopher Michel Foucault reminded us that there are prisons and prisons, so to speak—that what we do with the various "others" of our society tells a lot about us—Dickens had come to an even more revealing conclusion: we are all (writers and social theorists included) in one or another degree of bondage or confinement, whereas only some of us realize that such is the case and hence are at least not deluded or unknowing with respect to the nature of our lives.

Perhaps we are not surprised, today, at such an insight—we, who can take for granted Freud and Kafka, Samuel Beckett and Solzhenitsyn. Even Dostoevski's major novels, such as *Crime and Pun-*

ishment, The Possessed, and *The Brothers Karamazov,* all so similar to *Little Dorrit* in certain psychological respects, appeared well after *Little Dorrit's* publication in 1857, the result of several years' strenuous effort by Dickens. True, Jane Austen had by then left a psychological legacy that no novelist would ever be able to surpass: her characters, in their domestic confinement and exceedingly limited social world, reveal as clear an authorial comprehension of the so-called mechanisms of defense as any possessed by today's psychoanalytic practitioners. But Dickens is a more ambitious social realist than Austen—or is, maybe, less interested in exploring exclusively the restrictions and escapes available to any one segment of society. He aims to wander; his social realism is ever ready to encompass new territory—but at no sacrifice of what we would call "depth psychology." Dickens, alas, did not understand that sociology and psychology, not to mention moral philosophy, are separate disciplines.

Yet, for many of us, this master observer of human nature in various settings is known still as a comic, a satirist, a nineteenth-century documentary storyteller—someone who made, and who still makes, people laugh, who made them notice the poor, the oppressed, the odd, the rather loony, those who populate all places and times in one or another disguise (as we may remind ourselves when we try to "update" Dickens or grant him that necessary and high distinction of ours known as "relevance"). His best-known novels continue to be the earlier ones: the Pickwick saga, *Oliver Twist,* and (needless to say) *Nicholas Nickleby.* The later novels, *Bleak House, Little Dorrit,* and *Our Mutual Friend,* are, as one undergraduate student of mine put it tactfully, "quite long." When I suggested that he read *Hard Times,* the shortest of the novels, he said he would, and he did; whereupon I heard his "amazement" that Dickens had anticipated so well today's faddish excesses in the realms of child-rearing and education—as if utopian fantasies about what we can do with and for our children (and get out of them, so to speak, through this or that technique) is a special conceit of the later twentieth century rather than a general aspect of our continuing egoism. When the same student was ready to tackle *Little Dorrit* I was pleased—only to hear this when a given project had been completed: "He [Dickens] was instructive about psychology. In his own way he knew about the Oedipus complex—what Freud discussed."

I fear it is too easy (talking about a teacher's egoism) for a listener to turn on such a comment, to ridicule both the speaker and the general intellectual climate that has, surely, helped prompt a particular line of thought. The student, in fact, was responding correctly to a central theme in *Little Dorrit*, the complex, edifying relationship between Arthur Clennam and his mother. A grown man, already well into a Victorian bourgeois middle age, is made deeply anxious and afraid in the presence of a stern, reproving, distant parent, a woman whose obvious rejection of her son causes no one who reads Ann Landers' daily column any surprise. For that matter, Dickens evokes with great shrewdness not simply what we call a "disordered mother-son relationship" but also an interesting range of psychiatric and somatic responses to that relationship—including Clennam's early aging, a most intriguing recognition by a man who had never studied medicine and was writing over a century ago that mental distress can influence the body in important and diverse ways.

As critics have pointed out for generations, *Little Dorrit* is essentially a long rendering of imprisonment in its many forms, a forceful reminder to the reader that a more or less democratic, capitalist society can nevertheless turn out to be—for almost everyone, it seems—one giant penal colony. Clennam is in a psychological jail, and so is his mother. Her servants are indentured by their economic vulnerability, true, but also by its consequences—the conniving and suspicion and self-loathing so many of us demonstrate in a situation of dependency. But the novel moves even further and wider—from character portrayal to insistent and penetrating social analysis. This is a book that offers us Marshalsea Prison, the Circumlocution Office, Bleeding Heart Yard—the muddled, self-serving, smug, absurd world of public and private bureaucracy. Dickens, we are told, was as perplexed and enraged as many others of the English intelligentsia by the Crimean War debacle—the reckless and callous nature of the British government's involvement in a far-off military conflict that would cause a severe loss of life, and to no purpose whatsoever. He probed deeper than others, though. He began to think about the larger follies to which we seem heir as human beings: the way we con one another with words and phrases; the way we similarly con ourselves; the way our pretenses and postures become institutionalized so that enormous bureaucracies become monuments to human conceit, deceit, and plain foolishness.

Long before *The Trial* and *The Castle* of Kafka, Western readers were given a chance to ponder the weird, maddening inscrutability of the modern office—the empty administrative pronouncements, the interminable evasions and endless duplications, not to mention duplicities. A Harvard professor tells his class a couple of decades before the year 2000 that "Max Weber showed us how institutions have a life of their own." So the student quoted above wrote in his notebook. Are we to be surprised when he begins to scratch his head as he reads *Little Dorrit*, when he experiences a twinge or two of recognition and so now links Dickens not only to Freud but to Weber: "It's amazing how smart Dickens was about public bureaucracies—the way they function." It's amazing, too, how difficult it is for all of us to obtain an accurate *chronology* of our intellectual history, so that we might know accurately who saw what when, and so that we will comprehend the *range* of prophetic voices that have preceded us. Of course, this is a subject worthy of its own special and long examination—why we prefer (or have been taught) to acknowledge a Weber, say, over a Dickens when analyzing institutional rigidity and bureaucratic arrogance or stupidity.

Little Dorrit is filled with moments that, in their sum, tell us that Dickens was no *naïf*, momentarily and by psychological accident the beneficiary of a correct, telling hunch. The novel's prominent socialite, for instance—a person others emulate and try to meet, a person whose high status earns him the ingratiation and self-abasement of just about everyone—turns out to be a fraud, yet another business schemer who has used his connections to trick the gullible, the fawning. He commits suicide. His name is Merdle, as in the French word *merde*. Then, there is the young woman who is fiercely interested in another woman. In a chapter titled "The History of a Self-tormentor," the author has the possessed woman, Miss Wade, tell us of her early life: "My childhood was passed with a grandmother. . . ." We get to know the formative years of a person who could take very little for granted, whose considerable intelligence was constantly ignored, insulted, demeaned. Here is how she describes a later, significant attachment in her life: "In that company I found a girl, in various circumstances of whose position there was a singular likeness to my own, and in whose character I was interested and pleased to see much of the rising against swollen patronage and selfishness, calling themselves kindness, protection, benevolence, and other fine names, which I have described as inherent in my nature."

Dickens knew quite clearly and exactly, quite consciously and thoroughly, the sources of our egoistic discontent—the way early injuries to our sense of self-worth become lifelong sources of bitterness, become the fuel of rages and grudges, become the incitement to so many attachments (if not liaisons) we think of ourselves as making out of the blue. We are right, too, when we use such a phrase—it is the "blue" of our lives, the melancholy hurt, that Dickens knew to have his forceful, defiant Miss Wade chronicle for us. We see the solace of others, we try to repair our wounds, and often enough the ones to whom we turn remind us of—who else?—ourselves. I suppose the present-day (and all too faddish) terms are "narcissistic injury" and "narcissistic [love] object choice." The trouble with such phrases, of course, is that they apply to so many of us. Who hasn't endured some assault to his or her sense of self-respect? Who hasn't tried to find in another a friendly mirror of his or her own despair, to find therein a redemptive experience of self-recognition, not to mention the company in suffering that banishes a conviction of utter uniqueness? What Dickens knew, however, is that there are wounds and wounds; that one's social and economic situation can amplify terribly and indeed fatally one's psychological experiences; that private passion sometimes conceals a persisting social resentment, even as so much that we do and say as citizens—in the public arena of work and involvement with neighbors and friends—gets its energy from rebuffs or entanglements long since put aside as part of a particular past life. None of this is all that surprising, we may say—thinking of the Vienna of 1910 or 1920, no doubt, rather than the London of the 1850s. Yet, I wish my own profession, in the 1980s of America, relying properly on that Vienna, would be able to regard subjects such as narcissism or homosexuality with the kind of wide-eyed subtlety managed by the author of *Little Dorrit.*

Not the least of the challenges posed by *Little Dorrit* is Little Dorrit herself. This younger daughter of a man jailed in a debtor prison, this child of a father suddenly (later on) become rich and privy to a world of high society, this girl and then woman whose sister has become a snob, whose father has become a snob, whose life is filled with fancy lunches and big-deal evening banquets and luxurious travel and great social events, this family member who is always being patronized, manipulated, and addressed rudely, peremptorily, and meanly by her self-absorbed relatives—who is she meant to be? A long-suffering heroine, a continually decent, straightforward, honorable, kindly, compassionate soul, a woman who reaches out to heal so many others, and not always with any acknowledgement of thanks on their part—shall we call her "masochistic," or a "Christ figure," or maybe even say that the one is the other and both are "unreal," because Little Dorrit's kind of sensibility is mythic rather than representative of what we see and hear in our everyday lives? The question is obviously rhetorical. This creation of Dickens is, perhaps, the best reproof to those who see him as a writer endlessly on the prowl for social malaise, for any and all evidence of human absurdity, human folly—all to be given the teasing, taunting, comically satisfying, expression of a parade of wryly named characters. Little Dorrit is the patient one in several senses; she suffers, she endures suffering, she persists, she lasts. Little Dorrit, I suppose, is an aspect of the sensibility of the Dickens who wrote this to his youngest son in 1868: "You will therefore understand the better that I now solemnly impress upon you the truth and beauty of the Christian Religion, as it came from Christ Himself, and the impossibility of your going far wrong if you heartily respect it."

Such a summons, such an effort, actually, of self-description, surely omits other aspects of the given letterwriter's life—his pride, his relentless desire to mix with important people, his eagerly sought, lavish income, his failures of loyalty and affection. He was no Little Dorrit. At times he was her father—and maybe some of the other snobs and upstarts and social climbers he offers his readers. But he could not shake off a strong, even importunate moral imagination. Nor could he avoid noticing in the greatest detail how the mind works, how society does. Nor could he fail to see what was happening to us of the industrial West—the ways we have become so cut off, one from the other, so bedeviled by rules and regulations, social customs, and habits, so (literally) faithless and hence (for lack of Anyone, Anything better) so self-obsessed. We are prisoners of our own great progress, of our own important lives, he knew—and consequently we wander in a moral wasteland. Hence the commanding presence of the innocent and humble Little Dorrit—a reminder of what was (in ancient Galilee) and might yet be again, were we somehow able to catch secure hold of our better instincts and give them the ultimate leeway this one character gets in this long, rambling, suggestive, utterly affecting fiction. The Dickens of *Little Dorrit* is, finally, anyone East of Eden, so to speak, who has had the wits to look back with sadness, to be sure, but also with hope and determination that the past can at least somewhat inspire the present and the future. If we are all prisoners, we are at least able, a good many of us, to dream of freedom, to rise to its demands, as Arthur Clennam finally begins to realize with the help of not only what Little Dorrit is but, just as important, what she became for him, what she ended up being in his mind.

American Poetry Review, January/February 1985

The Virtues of Middlemarch

*I*n the last few decades of this century, our American culture has been preoccupied with the social sciences, and especially psychology, as if their increasing prominence is a particularly important achievement: we are the ones who have dared investigate the mind, who have insisted upon studying every aspect of the social system. True, Freud and many other distinguished psychological and sociological theorists have not been American, but Hitler's rise gave a substantial number of them to us. They emigrated to this country and received a wholehearted welcome here.

Yet for all our interest in therapy, in the various psychiatric schools, and in group dynamics, there is another side of the American cultural tradition: a vigorous skepticism about the limits of knowledge, including the psychological kind, and a pragmatic insistence that if concepts meant to explain behavior or society are to have any significance, they must be tested by the direct observation of ongoing lives. William Carlos Williams argued "no ideas but in things" and kept reminding his readers (reminding himself, he willingly acknowledged) that smart is not necessarily wise or good. Walker Percy in *The Second Coming* has one of his characters say: "I made straight A's and flunked ordinary living."

Such cautionary voices (twentieth-century intellectuals casting a sharp eye on themselves and their kind) have their predecessors, of course, such as Emerson, with his famous distinction between intellect and character, and William James, with his effort to tether metaphysical speculation to the constraints of empirical verification. But no one struggled longer and harder with these twin aspects of our present-day American cultural life (a faith in and a doubt about the value of the various kinds of proclaimed knowledge that come before us) than the nineteenth-century English novelist George Eliot, and especially so in her masterpiece *Middlemarch*, which proves in many ways to be the most contemporary of books—full of even our prized virtue, psychological "relevance."

All through *Middlemarch*, various aspects of the intellectual life assert themselves. Each of the book's central characters has a strong, actively observing intelligence. The mind of Dorothea Brooke, the ardent idealist and would-be social reformer, is described as "theoretic." She possesses an "eagerness to know the truths of this life." Casaubon, whom she marries, is in pursuit of "the key to all mythologies"; he has given his life to that search, driven by a conviction that the many, early explanatory accounts of man's earthly fate have a singular origin. His scholarly purposes immediately impress Dorothea, not one to settle for an ordinary, village, domestic life. She is especially taken with the comprehensive boldness of his idea: everything will be connected to a particular something.

As for the physician Lydgate, he is "young, poor, ambitious," but—very important—he "has lots of ideas." He is foresighted—already, in the early nineteenth century, aware of the role of "ventilation and diet" in the health of his patients. In chapter fifteen George Eliot is at pains to establish this doctor's interest in "the pursuit of a great idea," his hopes for his own scientific success: "He was ambitious of a wider effect: he was fired with the possibility that he might work out the proof of an anatomical conception and make a link in the chain of discovery." Not for him "the showy worldly successes" of London. He was after "careful observation and inference." Moreover, "that was a more cheerful time for observers and theorizers than the present," the narrator tells us, looking back from a later point in the nineteenth century to its first decades.

What this young doctor, who despises the self-enhancing and often crooked ways of many of his colleagues, wanted more than anything else was to broaden "the scientific, rational basis of his profession." His contempt for greed was more than equalled by his horror of ignorance, of superstition. Knowledge, he was sure, would make a big difference to medicine in his lifetime, and the consequences would spread to other realms. People would become more rational and would behave more thoughtfully and sensitively toward one another.

Even the banker Bulstrode (another important figure in this historical study of England on the brink of the age of political reform,

the late 1820s) is not characterized exclusively as the craven phony
he certainly is at certain points in the novel. The author spends a lot
of time developing the personality of this *nouveau arriviste*—aware,
surely, that in a rapidly expanding capitalist society his qualities were
becoming increasingly representative. She emphasizes his canniness, his quick-witted ability to take accurate, detailed account of
the world's social reality—indeed, to penetrate beneath its avowals
and protestations, and hence to capture its secrets. In the great moral
struggle that overtakes him in chapter seventy, he is rescued by his
creator from mere caricature. (Eliot hated religious hypocrites,
whom she boldly calls "Christian carnivora," and had initially set
him up as one in this novel.) When she says that "his mind was
intensely at work" she lets us know that this was not only an exceptionally endowed one but that it belonged to someone who, like
others whose lives she wants to explore, was not without a certain
decency of intent: "Strange, piteous conflict in the soul of this unhappy man, who had longed for years to be better than he was . . ."

Yet each of these major figures, however bright or learned, comes
to naught in ways remarkably similar. What their minds have done
most to assert, to build strong, somehow turns to rubble. Dorothea
wants to save the whole world by marrying and associating herself
with someone who will reveal its essential mysteries. Her husband,
Casaubon, turns out to be the arid pedant—one more reminder that
the brainy can fool themselves and end up with little to show for all
their library exertions. In the marriage of Dorothea to Casaubon, a
novelist herself anxious to see the world change socially and politically, herself deeply erudite, herself long interested in religious and
philosophical study, brings to a kind of ruin two individuals who
might have been used quite otherwise, of course, in a different storyteller's scheme of things. Moreover, Bulstrode's steep decline—the
only one we expect from the beginning—is matched by that of Lydgate, whose medical idealism yields ever so gradually (as in real life,
alas) to, well, this: "He had gained an excellent practice, alternat-
ing, according to the season, between London and a Continental
bathing-place; having written a treatise on Gout, a disease which has
a good deal of wealth on its side."

In one startling moment, at the very start of chapter twenty-nine,
George Eliot seems to be chastising not all those characters, not the
sensibility of her readers, but herself, her own temptations and

flaws, her own mistakes: "One morning, some weeks after her arrival at Lowick, Dorothea—but why always Dorothea? Was her point of view the only possible one with regard to this marriage?" The narrator (who in this novel, more than most, is a constant, assertive presence) has suddenly called a line of reasoning into serious question—as if to signal something rather important. We have, by now, become quite accustomed to *her* intellectuality—an omniscient observer, if ever there was one. She weighs and balances, interprets and qualifies; not rarely, she remonstrates. Dante, Shakespeare, and Pascal are summoned, as well as others whose names are not acknowledged in the quotes she sets before each chapter; and inside those chapters similes and metaphors tell of a formidable intellect intensely at work. But she wants our doubts to extend even to such brilliance—lest we forget her overall skepticism of anyone's abstractions that go unconnected to the concrete particulars of experience.

She is anxious to offer us a body of practical wisdom—thereby, perhaps, to redeem our trust of her and maybe her own trust of herself. Pithy, hard-to-forget warnings or exhortations are in evidence throughout *Middlemarch*. We are told that "one must be poor to know the luxury of giving." We are reminded that "it always remains true that if we had been greater, circumstance would have been less strong against us." We are instructed in this way: "Character is not cut in marble—it is not something solid and unalterable. It is something living and changing and may become diseased as our bodies do." We are given notice that "people glorify all sorts of bravery except the bravery they might show on behalf of their nearest neighbor."

Such comments tell of a mind at ease with irony, unafraid of uncertainty, ambiguity, and complexity. They also indicate an author's interest in the way her main characters and just about everyone, it seems, responded to a given world. *Middlemarch* is, after all, a novelist's retrospective look (like Tolstoy's *War and Peace*) at a moment of historical change. The title refers to a particular landscape both geographic and social. The range of classes, occupations, attitudes, and opinions represented is all-encompassing, yet evoked always with an acknowledgement of the intricate connections that hold any community together. But the author is interested not only in social knowledge; she gives close attention to the interior life of her fictional creatures. In fact, George Eliot's nineteenth-century comprehension of mental life requires no update from today's psychiatrists or social scientists. She was quite aware of the unconscious and its workings and of childhood as an important source of later personal troubles. She has her Dr. Lydgate desiring "to pierce the obscurity of those minute processes which prepare human misery and joy, those invisible thoroughfares which are the first lurking places of anguish, mania, and crime, that delicate poise and transition which determine the growth of happy or unhappy consciousness."

This breathtaking vision of so much we have claimed as our very own discovery is quickly followed, a few paragraphs later, with an authorial warning whose import is as necessary for us to remember as it apparently was for those alive over a century ago: "Our passions do not live in locked chambers, but, dressed in their small wardrobe, bring their provisions to a common table and mess together, feeding out of the common store according to their appetite." As some of us in our conceptual zeal fix *our* passions on *this* explanation or *that* formulation, it is helpful to be reminded of the relatedness of things—of the many aspects of ourselves that variously assert themselves. Nor will the condescension of the word *intuitive* quite banish the prophetic George Eliot from membership in any accurate pantheon of psychological luminaries. She knew what we know in the exact same way we know it, and she used our favorite buzzwords, such as identity or guilt or repression, in ways many of us consider to be original with us—as when a certain vicar's elderly aunt is characterized as "conscious of being tempted to steal from those who had much that she might give to those who had nothing, and [as having] carried in her conscience the guilt of that repressed desire."

But I suspect George Eliot would be impatient, indeed, with any effort to applaud her special gifts of social analysis and psychological prophecy—even as Jane Austen would not feel especially honored to be told that her fictions show masterly apprehension of (as we call it) the "ego" and its "mechanisms of defense," the elucidation of which, in recent decades, has enabled psychoanalysis to abandon a preoccupation with "drives" in favor of an awareness of the significance of "adaptation." What these two storytellers really understood, above all, is the timeless workings of pride, a word one of them used in a book's title and the other showed to be a central force in *Middle-*

march—and by extension, a central force in all history, whether writ large or small.

"Unreflecting egoism" was Eliot's way of putting it in the novel. It is a narcissism that is quite unanalyzed, we'd say, and (since irony abounds in all places and times) a narcissism that may be found ("countertransference") in the most experienced of analysts, including even those who might well end up narcissistically propounding theories of narcissism. For her, what mattered finally was the perspective we develop on such matters. In her letters she referred to "egoism" as her "besetting sin," meaning that she wanted to regard her psychology from a moral vantage point. (In this regard are we who announce the importance of a "value-free" social science ahead of her or way behind her, or are we simply deluded by pride, again, in our very insistence on what is an utter impossibility?) Not that she was a scold, of herself or others, certainly including those she constructed out of her great originality. There is in all her writer's pride (and in the size and detail of the canvas she presents) an astonishing charity continually at work, starting with the famous prelude when Saint Theresa and, yes, all women are judged by a subtle and knowing historical sensibility that contrasts instructively with some of today's reductionist social science, not to mention our overheated political rhetoric: "Many Theresas have been born who found for themselves no epic life wherein there was a constant unfolding of far-resonant action; perhaps only a life of mistakes, the offspring of a certain spiritual grandeur ill-matched with the meanness of opportunity; perhaps a tragic failure which found no sacred poet and sank corrupt into oblivion." So much for what now gets called the "relationship" between "the individual and society," not to mention the "methodology" of "psycho-biography."

As for the novel's "finale," it offers a ringing exhortation of human complexity and unpredictability that certainly shuns the "stages" and "phases," the "periods" and "complexes" that we use to march people, automaton-like, from birth to their last moments on this earth: "Every limit is a beginning as well as an ending. . . . For the fragment of a life, however typical, is not the sample of an even web: promises may not be kept, and an ardent outset may be followed by declension; latent powers may find their long-waited opportunity; a past error may urge a good retrieval." And always, as she had said much earlier, "destiny stands by sarcastic with our *dramatis personae* folded in her hand.*"*

Those are the words of a Victorian moralist who knew when to smile wryly at herself and her own conceptual efforts, however impressive—who had learned the aching lesson of humility, no doubt after many bruising battles with the "vanity" she keeps attributing to one or another character in *Middlemarch*. The implicit self-criticism one encounters in this novel, Augustinian in its severity, is leavened by such a worldly, knowing candor—and it is brought up for discussion, I have noticed, by both college students and medical students. Often in our discussions they contrast Eliot's Dr. Lydgate with F. Scott Fitzgerald's Dr. Diver, noting the lack of sentimentality in *Middlemarch* and the forthright appraisal its author makes of the progressive shift in a physician's professional life. The reader is denied all the alibis, the sources of secular absolution we have learned to take for granted, to demand. Lydgate is not "troubled" or "sick." Lydgate doesn't succumb to a "marital problem" or to a series of "social pressures."

Eliot has scant patience with either psychology or sociology as glorious excuses for a lapse of ethical resolve. She refers, rather, to the doctor's "commonness," to his "slackening resolution," just as the students and their teacher are set to reach for his wife as his "problem" and an unwise marriage as the cause of an abandonment of lofty medical ideals. There are many virtues to *Middlemarch*, and they have been justly celebrated over the generations, but this particular righteousness, utterly indifferent to the modern usurpation of the social sciences as a means of moral extenuation, deserves mention, as does the novel's rendering of life's thickly textured quality without recourse to formulaic simplifications.

The author of *Middlemarch* wants us to consider the question of will—how much energy we dare to give our professed values, never mind the cost of convenience. More than occasionally the intelligent, well-meaning reader may feel brought up short by an author who constantly reminds him or her (and herself) that to be smart is not necessarily to be good, and that anyone's claim to knowledge (say, in ethics or its application to medical or legal matters) is a hollow one indeed unless tested by conduct in this life. If there is a utopian strain in the novel it is in the presentation of the ordinary, not especially successful, working people. Their decency is a constant, unqualified presence, perhaps intended as a reproach to the others, who have so much more (materially, at least) going for them. George Eliot can't seem to stop pressing the strange notion that the only kind of moral imagination that matters is the kind given expression by our daily lives, and that such a moral imagination is by no means the exclusive property of those who have acquired university degrees, reputation, money, or power.

American Poetry Review, July/August 1985

Thomas Hardy, the Populist

*I*n 1895, when Thomas Hardy's *Jude the Obscure* was published, Victorian England was hardly ready to accept that novel's story of a love affair between cousins—Jude, married and estranged from his wife, and Sue, married and estranged from her husband. Moreover, Sue is a woman whose mind is restless and inquiring; her frustrations with the age's conventions and ideals are obvious. To make matters worse, the unmarried couple has three children, one of them "Little Father Time," Jude's by his earlier marriage. Toward the end of the novel Hardy has that boy kill his two half-siblings; he leaves behind a note that says, "Done because we are too menny."

The reception to the novel was stormy. Church officials were especially shocked, and one Anglican bishop ordered the novel publicly burned. Hardy fought back; he insisted that he was not trying to undermine the institution of marriage but rather to indicate, as had novelists before him, the hold sexuality can claim on us, no matter a society's demands. (Freud was then a young Viennese physician who had yet to write his first book.) However independent a thinker and writer Hardy was, he never wrote another novel, though of course over the years *Jude the Obscure* did become for readers of the twentieth century a powerfully suggestive statement, a means by which they could look critically at recent social and religious history.

These days, of course, few readers would blink at the sexuality of Hardy's last novel. By our standards, alas, the story is quaint and is narrated with a delicate primness. The instance of a child killing other children still surprises and upsets readers, I am sure, but we who live almost a century after the appearance of *Jude the Obscure* will be touched simply by a story of yearning love and unrequited love, love impaired or thwarted by the conscience of lovers, never mind the customs of the world around them.

In certain respects, however, this novel continues to challenge its readers, who are surely among the more comfortable and better educated of this earth's population. Jude Fawley is a stonemason of humble origin who has a strong desire to educate himself. He dreams of mastering Latin and Greek, of becoming a thoroughly civilized, erudite man of letters. He studies at every possible turn and aims to emulate a local teacher, Mr. Phillotson. His eager, conscientious mind is not unlike that of the melancholy heroes D. H. Lawrence would later offer us; he too is a decent English working-class youth who dares hope (and work) for a much better life, and who soon enough discovers the costs of such ambition.

Young Jude wants desperately to leave his country life and live and study in Christminster, a thinly disguised Oxford, with its emphasis on classical education as well as philosophical and religious learning. Hardy sends him there, and what he sees and hears, what he experiences day by day, is in a way the heart of this novel—a major statement about the significance of class in important institutions of higher learning and, too, in church life. In a heartbreaking series of scenes, Jude soon enough learns his "place." He encounters the smugness and self-importance and arrogance that live all too comfortably with academic excellence and, yes, with spiritual contemplation. All the Latin and Greek Jude had hungrily studied, all the natural religious piety of his decent and honorable soul, are not much help to him as he tries to make sense of a world-renowned center of intellectual and spiritual inquiry.

Hardy is relentless in his rendering of Jude's emergent class consciousness. Moreover, the moral corruption that afflicts a snobbish academy (and snobbish religious community) is sharply observed by an authorial presence obviously much identified with the impoverished and snubbed stonemason. "It was not till now, when he found himself actually on the spot of his enthusiasm, that Jude perceived how far away from the object of that enthusiasm he really was," Hardy tells us—and then he spells out a harsh fate indeed:

> Only a wall divided him from those happy young contemporaries of his with whom he shared a common mental life; men who had nothing to do from morning till night but to read, work, learn, and inwardly digest. Only a wall—but what a wall!

It is not just the presence of such divisions that Hardy wants us to notice but their consequences. He develops the theme of the invisibility of the poor and vulnerable, an anticipation of such twentieth-century novels as *Invisible Man*:

> He was a young workman in a white blouse and with stone-dust in the creases of his clothes; and in passing by him they did not even see him, or hear him, rather saw through him as through a pane of glass at their familiars beyond.

Lonely, saddened, he yet dreams that somehow, someday he will be granted entry to those "palaces of light." But he also starts exploring the other side of Christminster:

> He began to see that the town life was a book of humanity infinitely more palpitating, varied, and compendious than the gown life. These struggling men and women before him were the reality of Christminster, though they knew little of Christ or Minster.

Still, he burned with frustration and indignation:

> The gates [of Christminster, of Oxford] were shut, and by an impulse he took from his pocket a lump of chalk which, as a workman, he usually carried there, and wrote along the wall: "I have understanding as well as you; I am not inferior to you: yea, who knoweth not such things as these?—Job xii, 3."

With that quotation from the Bible, Hardy connects his powerful populist critique of a particular intellectual and religious world to the Bible itself, a grim reminder to his readers that Jude is but one in a long tradition of unfairly injured men and women, the "rebuked and scorned" upon whom so many educated and self-righteous ones have managed to turn their backs. The novel's populism is meant to address the comfortable and literate reader, all of us who are proud of our understanding but may well be as blind as Hardy describes so many Oxonians as being. Nor is it only academic walls that enforce a certain parochialism, a coldness of heart, a pitiable haughtiness. Hardy meant to take aim at institutional religion too, at those fancy church walls that can also become the smug, complacent sanctuaries of an all too privileged membership. There were lots of ministers and priests, Hardy knew, at Oxford with its long past of knowledge wedded to high-minded espousals of Christianity and with scarcely a thought given, it seems, to the likes of this world's Judes: such a contrast with the kind of life Jesus lived, he who gave so generously of his time and energy to fishermen, to peasants, to laboring people, he who never did show up at any big-deal educational institution.

New Oxford Review, July/August 1986

Pen Browning
"The Child is father of the Man"

At one point, as Maisie Ward valiantly tries to comprehend the relationship between the Brownings and their beloved son, she reminds us that "child psychiatry was an unknown science in those days," meaning it was unknown all through the nineteenth century and the first years of this century. I am not at all sure that any one of today's various "experts," who claim to know so very much about children, can be of any real help to the author or the readers of this book; in fact, I wonder whether the Brownings would have felt the need to avail themselves of those "experts" had they been available in England or Italy over a hundred years ago. Even more to the point, I am not so sure that the Brownings, all *three* of them, would have emerged any the better had there been child psychiatrists like me in Rome, Siena, or London and had Mr. and Mrs. Browning been willing to take themselves and their growing child Pen for one or more consultations.

I hesitate to start an introduction on such a skeptical note; I am in a sense undercutting my own credentials before I venture upon a particular interpretation of that extraordinary household Maisie Ward has sketched for us. Still, these days psychiatrists have much too much say in far too many matters and are given an authority—as secular priests of sorts—that does not always serve them well, not to mention how it serves their uncritical and often enough desperate admirers. Nor is it fair to blame only what one hears described as the lay public for such a state of affairs. All one need do is go through the so-called psychiatric literature to understand why any number of people (I hope their number is growing) feel moved to smile or frown, if not scream in indignation, because of this or that article, monograph, or book. And God save the writers studied—it can be a scandal, what happens to their novels and plays and poems, the characters they have constructed out of their mind's sensibility, the ideas and passions, the subtleties of temperament and nuances of social life, the ironies and ambiguities and contradictions and inconsistencies that reveal themselves so constantly in the course of our lives. I have in mind those gross simplifications that, in this instance, would have Elizabeth Barrett Browning an overprotective mother, among many other bad (here substitute "neurotic") things, and Robert Browning a passive or overly dependent father.

I dislike going even this far—making mention of the way some of us in this psychological-minded age handle (and devour) the lives of particular men and women and children. But I had better go even further and as quickly as possible set down for the reader one train of thought I sadly know all too well—so that I can then show what is inadequate about any exceedingly influential contemporary manner of looking at people and their behavior. The story goes something like this: Pen was the only child of relatively old parents, who doted on him, paid him far too much attention, and not only spoiled him but set up in him certain unconscious resentments that are less easily discerned than his various loyalties, attachments, or involvements, whether with people or ideas or projects. The result was a life propelled by powerful energies never acknowledged. And if to a certain extent that is how we all live, many of us (psychiatrists would argue) have not been so watched over, so indulged, so held up in virtual awe; hence we have no cause to feel as bitter, angry, and fiercely defiant, as self-pitying and self-defeating as Pen did, unknown to himself of course.

I don't like that kind of schematic and persistently negative view of Pen's childhood. I don't like the overly theoretical literature of child psychology and psychiatry that passes itself off as science yet offers all of us, in one way or another troubled and confused, a new set of moralistic pieties. Still, one has to take wisdom, or at the very least a bit of help, where one can get it—and I do think someone who does the kind of clinical work I do ought to ask the reader to stop and wonder about the lifelong burden created by overzealous parents, too insistently preoccupied with a child.

As I went through Maisie Ward's manuscript, I first was struck by the joy Pen inspired in not only the Brownings but their staff, their friends and relatives, and even their correspondents, who apparently over and over again read those letters, all taken up with the child's everyday life, his words, his comings and goings, his efforts to assert himself, or his moments of hesitation. Now, one might suppose that a child who by his very arrival caused so much happiness would himself be, in the main, happy—and would continue to be so later on in life. What is more, since we live in an age filled with talk of sibling rivalry, we have to remember that young Pen had no competitors, and just as important, his parents were not devoted to him because they had fallen away from each other. One can feel the great love those two poets (and extraordinary human beings) felt for each other in so much of what they wrote and what was written about them. Nor is it likely that their boy had any bad luck so far as genes go. Most geniuses are not born but made (I believe), but neither do geniuses defy certain biological laws. The Brownings were neither retarded nor dull-average in intelligence. They were easily able to offer both themselves and the world a healthy, well-developed child, who showed every evidence at ages one, two, and three (and on and on) of being thoroughly well endowed with native intelligence and in addition a good, strong body.

Why, then, the cumulative sense of sadness that at least this reader felt as he read about Pen? I mean sadness for the child Pen, let alone the grown man we end up *also* feeling a little troubled by, if not pity for. Is it that we want Pen to follow his parents, to become a *third* Browning of the kind schoolchildren read, and then as college students meet up with again, and finally pore over when and if they become scholars? Was the child, and afterwards the man, rather disturbed—something we sense, even if we can't quite put our fingers on exactly what was wrong? Do we quite simply take annoyance at the spectacle of a child being so flagrantly (wantonly, I fear) spoiled? And does it offend our present-day psychological sensibilities (successors to but not wholly unlike both Puritan and Victorian sensibilities) that the grown man Pen should vacillate so and never quite commit himself to a way of life, a job, a wife? I suppose we are somewhat disappointed with the older Pen, and maybe we do recognize that something in him went awry—even if we do not want (I would hope) to saddle him with all those grim psychiatric labels that can be misleading and even at times insulting, though upon occasion clarifying.

I fear, however, that something else gets in our way as we read about Pen, and I again have to be evasive as I begin to describe what

I have in mind—for the simple reason that both Browning parents were equally evasive about the same thing, as was their son all through his life. Here was a child, after all, about whom practically nothing bad or complaining was said for years and years by a mother and father who were thoroughly sensitive, perceptive, and psychologically astute. (If they lived before our kind of psychological sophistication arrived on the scene, then maybe they were both lucky and all the more astute because less encumbered with jargon and that mixture of self-consciousness and self-importance that our social sciences often bequeath to those who pursue them.) I know that parents don't like to complain about their children, find fault with them, or advertise their difficulties in letters or by the spoken word. I know that there is a long tradition of sentiment that protects babies and even older children from sharp-eyed, gloomy, skeptical observers, who are always on the lookout for what *doesn't* work, for what is wrong behind all the pleasant and appealing faces of children. Nevertheless, one wonders whether young Pen was *ever* really disciplined, and if so, by whom. And I suspect that some of the hysteria his mother conveys as she virtually sings the child's praises has to do with her own struggle to push out of mind the darker side of childhood—*anyone's* childhood—however kind and thoughtful and considerate and understanding (or psychologically sophisticated) be the parents. What is more, if I were asked to guess at what went wrong with Pen as he grew up (I suppose something goes wrong with each of us, inasmuch as we rarely measure up as adults to *all* the possibilities we demonstrate as children), I would have to say that throughout Pen's life the issue of self-restraint was especially important and never resolved.

When a child is given just about everything his or her heart craves at this or that moment, something is thereby both learned and not learned: desire is followed by satisfaction with impressive regularity, and so there is no need to hold on and wait and maybe experience a little hardship, sweat a little, persist in the fact of one or another complex and somewhat frustrating obstacle—because it is unheard of to meet them, those obstacles that prepare so many of us for life's inevitably troublesome moments. Put differently, Pen as a baby and child lived in a world whose exhilarating joy was purchased at a very definite price: the young prince, and he was indeed that in many respects, was not prepared to deal with the confinements, rigidities, and restrictions that the world places upon most people. No wonder, then, that he had trouble in college and never really settled into the long haul of a conventional career. And it must have been especially hard for such a young man to face the rigors of a strict classical education—accompanied by the demands of a social life that was not meant to be fun but rather to reflect the stern, self-justifying ethic of England's ruling classes and those who felt the need to follow their lead. Given so much, disciplined so little, Pen all of a sudden had to submit, submit, submit—to demanding teachers, to a difficult course of study, to the arbitrary but carefully regulated impositions of an intensely class-conscious society. Even artists and writers have to suffer and systematically come to terms with various conventions and orthodoxies—such as the arbitrariness of their particular guilds, not to mention those inner or psychological rules and edicts that can cramp the mind hard but also evoke in it spirited resistance. At best the result of such tension is a compromise that we call art—the product, that is, of a person's fight to express himself or herself within the confines of a particular craft or art form, and to do so in a manner that both frees the reader or viewer or listener but also ties him or her to a given tradition, however challenged by the artist.

Of course, Pen was not brought up to be a wild man or a confidence-man who has been taught nothing about the ethical restraints we all require of ourselves and others around us. Obviously the child was disciplined, told no as well as yes, and frowned upon as well as cheered and praised extravagantly. The question is how much, with what consistency, and yes, with what devotion, for after all discipline is also an art, requiring the same care and good judgment and sense of balance that a poet or composer or sculptor tries to mobilize. And speaking of balance, those who describe children as *only* full of love and joy and spontaneity and the desire to learn and express themselves are ever so often not those who must spend the long, long hours that bringing up a child requires: hours spent coming to terms with the darker, more impulsive side of childhood; hours spent stopping the child, telling the child no, keeping the child from going here (lest he or she be immediately killed) or there (lest there be trouble or danger or disappointment or pain); and yes, hours spent teaching the child that anyone's willfulness or "spontaneity" has to be accommodated to the fact that millions and millions of us share space and time on this planet, and hence are at one another's mercy in more ways than we often think about—no doubt because, thank God, we have indeed learned some minimum amount of self-control.

I am sorry if in this modern, proudly sophisticated age I come forth with the old Puritan notion that self-control is very important; yet I do, in fact I *must*, and not because pieties are in order but because anyone who has worked with troubled children (let alone those brought up to be reasonably normal and happy) cannot for long escape noticing how much a growing child needs what the term self-control literally implies: a sense of self and a sense of control over oneself. And it is in precisely this respect that little Pen Browning may well have suffered: his parents loved him so very much that they never for a minute could really think of him as living his own life, growing up to become someone other than their child—someone with control over his own destiny. If Elizabeth Barrett Browning died when Pen was not yet fully grown, Robert Browning lived on, an exceedingly concerned and devoted father, sadder than he could perhaps bear to acknowledge, bereft in a final way, it seems—except for the boy whose life offered a reason to persist, a connection with what otherwise seemed irretrievable, and except perhaps for those moments and longer when the mind flexes itself and through reveries and daydreams (and nightmares) fashions a semblance of the past. So the boy probably had to fight harder than most to become a man, and he may well have remained more a child than most of us do all his life—though by no means do I want to turn the man into a nothing, a case history of sorts, a bundle of neuroses such as psychiatrists all too often dwell upon in such a way that they see little else and manage to miss rather a lot.

Maisie Ward gives us a lively and well-rounded account of Pen Browning, even if necessarily an incomplete account, inevitably limited by time's ability to erase memories and further hindered by a certain elusiveness or inscrutability in the subject himself. Pen had his faults but he was obviously a man of talent and imagination. He reached out to people and in turn obtained from them affection and upon occasion sustained friendship. (In this regard I am much inclined to accept Mabel Dodge Luhan's account, in which the man's overall integrity and discretion come across—and in addition, his impressive willingness to turn the other cheek in the face of gossip, insults, and slander. Maybe it is only a much-loved child who later on can ignore or be puzzled by such provocations.) Pen could also be energetic and resourceful, a shrewd observer, a competent and upon occasion inspired artist. He was no isolated, paralyzed man; if he had what we today call his "problems," he repeatedly sent off sparks of warmth and humor, nor was intelligent activity beyond his reach. But he foundered, and finally one does begin to feel sorry for him as this biographical sketch draws to a close: his marriage was unsuccessful; his work never became fully realized; he loved and was loved (as a man, never mind as a child) but he seems to have been a lonely man, and there are moments when one even feels like calling him pitiable. And pity may stand as an ultimate low in the ladder of emotions that people direct at one another. I have no use for those who *explain* lives or wrap them up tidily with one or another formulation, but again, I can't help feeling that at least one important issue in Pen's life—one persisting, unyielding, and in the end unsurmountable issue—may be his struggle for discipline: as a child he seems to have had not very much of it; and as a man he may well have felt at loose ends, unable to pull himself together and in fact *be*—be himself in a quiet, unassuming way that is not to be confused with the showy, endlessly self-conscious, proudly psychological and existential postures we in this century have adopted or found ourselves compelled to sanction.

Before I stop and let the reader go on to Maisie Ward's observations, I would like to make one more conjecture, and it is only that because I will be speaking of what *might* have been—if. If only Pen and his wife had been able to have a child, especially a son—then I rather suspect the couple would have stayed together, and maybe Pen would even have found himself driven as an artist in ways he never actually could be in the course of the life he did live. Rather obviously, his wife was in love with more than Pen; she loved the Brownings and loved their poetry, their intellectual and social prominence, their achievements. No doubt she too would have doted on a Browning infant, on *another* possible poet, on yet one more chance to make Robert and Elizabeth immortal in flesh as well as spirit. But for her husband I believe a child would have meant something else: an opportunity to assert himself, at last, as a father rather than a man who otherwise seemed unable to shake off being the dearly cherished personification of the love two famous poets had for one another. And when a man starts being a father in earnest, his larger life can change: he can put aside, can solve in an apparent flash, so very much that has bogged him down, distracted, or enervated him; he can look to the future, his own as well as his child's, and feel driven now to provide, to build up, to consolidate—rather than to live out the past again and again. A son might have enabled Pen to stop being *the* son—and though I am sure Pen's wife would have paid such a child no less attention than Pen himself received as a baby, I would also be willing to hazard the guess that Pen as a father would have been less desperate than either of his parents was.

I say such things not, I hope, as a professional exuding authority but as a reader responding to a particular person's rather interesting and unusual life, as portrayed in these pages. The longer I live and the more I try to do my work as a psychiatrist, the less impressed I am by all those psychological theories that try to tell us what causes what, what leads to this, or what precludes that. Lives do indeed move along in response to various psychological urges, "drives," and necessities; but at every moment in our lives we are open to new possibilities and are capable of turning in surprising directions. Accidents, unexpected incidents, fateful encounters—all of those developments and much else that is mysterious or elusive or hard to pin down in words make up what in the end (and only then) any of us gets to call his or her "life."

If as we read this account of Pen's life he seems at the end still very much in the grips of the unusual and fascinating (and at times unsettling) childhood that Maisie Ward evokes for us, then we are obliged to remind ourselves that it didn't have to happen like that; and what is more, in certain respects the grown Pen did indeed come forth as his very own person—so it wasn't *all* like that anyway.

Introduction to *The Tragi-Comedy of Pen Browning, 1849–1912*
by Maisie Ward, 1972

*Twentieth-Century
European Writers*

To Break the Shell
of Self

I n past centuries, philosophers and theologians, playwrights
and novelists were the major voices of social and cultural criticism. These days, the social sciences bear down hard even on
literary critics and historians, never mind the rest of us. They are
ever glad, it seems, to show enthusiastic appreciation for any available psychological or sociological statement. Christopher Lasch, for
instance, is an exceptionally intelligent social historian and a powerful, clearheaded writer as well. His book *The Culture of Narcissism*
used psychoanalytic theory tactfully, cautiously, as a help in understanding what is happening to us; we live, after all, in an advanced
capitalist society so dependent on consumerism that the cultivation
of the self has become a major industry as well as a pagan religion
of sorts. Lasch did not, however, write *The Narcissistic Personality of
Our Time*. No doubt such a title would have attracted hordes of
readers and maybe reached the best-seller list. In fact, his chosen
title accurately suggests that a kind of psychology (self-centeredness)
has come to dominate a particular society's cultural life. The title
probably boosted sales a good bit too, ironically confirming that the
public is eager for any news of itself, even in the form of a devastating critique of its shallow self-preoccupations. However, had Lasch
chosen to make his important points through the interpretive help
of, say, contemporary American fiction, would his book have been
so successful? In different ways Saul Bellow, Walker Percy, and John
Updike have been making a reading of our culture similar to Lasch's,
focusing on the peculiar spiritual dislocation of people who have so
very much and yet seem to feel empty, confused, even panicky. But
we prefer abstractions, even banal, jargon-filled ones, to dramatic
evocation. Lasch's social analysis, the best kind, is not without resemblance to a morality play, yet one suspects that his use of the

psychoanalytic speculations of Heinz Kohut and Otto Kernberg gave many readers a false sense of assurance (the supposed voice of science), when both those theorists and Lasch well know how precarious the leap is from a theory of individual narcissism to a generalization about its dominant presence in the life of a particular nation.

Unfortunately, many readers of Lasch's book will not find their way to Robert Kiely's *Beyond Egotism*, though (as the title suggests) it also tries to comprehend what has been happening to us psychologically and spiritually in this century. The agents of that understanding, however, are three novelists who used the English language—James Joyce, D. H. Lawrence, and Virginia Woolf. The mode of analysis is that of reflective literary criticism offered as a group of carefully presented essays, in which textual analysis keeps relaxed company with social comment and moral reasoning. Kiely knows that Joyce and Lawrence had no great admiration for each other, that critics often have sided with one or the other (thereby gaining for themselves an object of contempt as well as veneration), and that although Virginia Woolf spoke well of both men, she is not associated with either by many who teach the twentieth-century novel. But they were contemporaries, and the three shared a common struggle:

> In the very innovations—stylistic and structural—that have made their books difficult and have discouraged some readers, they have extended the domestic bourgeois historical conventions of the old novel to a breaking point that opens the way to a wider range of experience.

As Kiely mentions, Joyce, Lawrence, and Woolf were strong-minded, stubbornly ambitious writers; hence "in their pride in the power of the imagination, they were undoubtedly egotists." But, as with the psychiatric term *narcissism*, there is a danger in such attribution. We all struggle with narcissism; it is an inevitable aspect of each person's life. The issue is one of degree and, very important, the use made of a particular mental inclination. Some of us boast endlessly, drearily about ourselves or use ourselves mischievously or brutishly to badger and trick anyone available; some of us use ourselves to edify others—as writers, as teachers, or, for that matter, as psychiatrists, even as theorists interested (narcissistically) in the vicissitudes of narcissism. Kiely is wise to emphasize that "the underlying sense that human nature possesses certain common and generalizable traits does not necessarily restrict the artist." Quite the contrary, writers delight in showing variations in the universe, whereas all too many social scientists forget the fact of that (psychological) universality. Kiely refers to "the burden of personal history" and then, in a fine, qualifying phrase, observes "the artist's need to transform it, since he can never hope to avoid it."

Lasch reminds us that a seriously faltering economy and its close companion, a rudely, cynically materialist culture, have settled on the self with a vengeance. Kiely offers us a contrast; he shows that for three influential novelists of this confused, tormented century, egotism turned out to be no final barrier but rather a prelude to a fiercely insistent effort "to break the isolating shell of personality." The artist as an individual may be yet another of this world's many egotists. The artist's work, however, constructed with paint or through words, and set down on canvases or in published arrangements of description, imagery, analysis, and so on, manages to take all of us beyond ourselves. Kiely quotes Virginia Woolf on so many influential people of her time: "They afflict us because they have ceased to believe. The most sincere of them will only tell us what it is that happens to himself. They cannot make a world." The specially talented do that—build a world quite convincingly; and doing so, they help not only themselves but the rest of us, their readers, transcend for a while the continual tug of self-regard. Thereby, strenuous exertions on behalf of a muse represent a moral act—even as the struggle of an analysand (and analyst) to escape the mean and aggrandizing aspects of narcissism is not to be confused with the exertions of the many self-displaying hucksters who infest our commercial, political, and cultural life.

Kiely reminds us of a common sensibility in his three chosen writers—"the impulse to strain against categories." Good novelists, God bless them, make that kind of effort all the time; they try to approach this life through particulars and try to avoid generalizations (in William Carlos Williams' phrase, "no ideas but in things"). Not that fiction can't help us understand the biggest issues. Joyce wanted to examine, no less, the effect of time on cross-cultural imagery. Lawrence assaulted accepted opinion with his analysis of sexuality and class. Woolf had a keen sense of what "personality" is—for her, something quite other than the stages and psychodynamics that textbooks of human development offer us.

Kiely roams the writings of the three writers in an interesting and rather unusual manner: he uses plots and character portrayal to show not only what they have told us but what we, their readers, have come to learn. Put differently, a literary critic embraces a kind of social history—hence the inclusion of essays on marriage and the family and on friendship. The point is to connect our consciousness with our lives, to understand that the way we see things affects the way we live. Nature, once a repository of hope, became for these writers one more unruly, unpredictable, and often threatening aspect of a mixed-up, if not completely loony, world. Kiely shows that the sea, for Byron the "unchangeable" and "glorious mirror where the almighty form glasses itself," presented itself to Joyce as "fitful music," to Lawrence as a symbol of all too tentative human opportunity, and to Woolf, of course, as an intensely dangerous place, a reminder to the people of all continents that death is both near and ready. Those writers were struggling for all of us. Kiely makes a statement with a question: "How does one look at the natural universe without being blinded by convention, or overwhelmed by nothingness?" Egoistically, rather than egotistically, we all may want to wonder in that vein. Egotistically, some press answers upon us. The novelists Kiely celebrates in this book move beyond themselves and their ambition, beyond showy brilliance, to reveal the centrality, these days, of human doubt and apprehension, with the artist as chronicler, even exemplar, rather than as patronizing, fatuous therapist or ideologue.

It is a pleasure to be brought back to *Dubliners, A Portrait of the Artist as a Young Man,* and *Ulysses;* to *Sons and Lovers, Women in Love, The Rainbow,* and that powerful story of English mining life, "Daughter of the Vicar"; to *The Waves, The Years, Mrs. Dalloway,* and *Between the Acts,* as well as, inevitably, *To the Lighthouse.* In all that writing and more, Kiely finds a modern kind of thinking struggling to exert itself, to come to terms with what it means to be a child, to marry, to be a friend; in short, the universals of human experience as they have been shaped into the lives of us who live in the late capitalist, significantly secular West.

After all that has been said about mothers in these recent decades, a sentence such as the following seems either impossibly naive and romantic or (I think) an elixir of subtlety and shrewdness: "The mother's gift is two fold: Individuality and the consoling, but also humbling, reminder of the presence of life outside the self." Kiely has been taught the breadth of psychological responses available to us by Joyce, Lawrence, and Woolf; he has seen how their authorial self-centeredness or arrogance can yield to character portrayals meant to offer a redeeming moral integrity. Here is another of Kiely's telling, original summaries—an alternative, indeed, to the latest articles or textbooks on "oedipal fixation," some of them, in recent years, written by critics of literature:

> The novels of Woolf, Joyce, and Lawrence teach us that the ghostly mother will not be denied by daughters or sons. She haunts her artist-offspring by a too palpable presence or a disabling absence. Either way, she keeps the artist honest. She abhors egotists and aesthetes. She will not be banished, buried without reverence, shattered like a lamp, turned into a girl or an enchantress or even into an exquisite ideal of beauty without finding a way to chide the dreaming child and call him back to earth.

That "child" soon enough grows up, contemplates his or her own family, seeks the consolations of friendship, or nervously avoids them. Kiely reminds us that until the late nineteenth century (up to Hardy, really) novelists presented marriage as an ideal state, to which all couples, however floundering for a while, eventually repair. Joyce, Lawrence, and Woolf have certainly followed Hardy's lead and regarded marriage as an institution to be explored rather than exalted; they have, that is, looked hard at the distances that modern couples commonly accept as well as struggle to overcome, at the textures of emotional ambiguity characteristic of modern family life. These novelists have needed none of our contemporary social or psychological theorists to remind them of the effect on marriage of sexual tension, or the problems of class and race, or the personal difficulties that arise from an awareness that life is all too brief, and often enough, arbitrary, terribly unfair, if not close to meaningless. What the novel has enabled for Joyce and Lawrence and Woolf is an exploration of human experience that does justice to its complexity. At one point Kiely tells us that "the novel comforts with local history." Yes, and discomforts plenty, too.

The temptation is to escape localism, particularity, the instances of this life—not to mention the differentials of personality, so mysterious and persisting—for the immediate satisfactions of a general, inclusive statement. Even these three novelists craved a moment of the universal, intent though they were on dwelling intimately with those elements of human individuality—luck, chance, circumstance, the accidental. The nature of friendship, as Kiely points out, attracted them for precisely that reason, the relative variability and subjectivity of that form of human involvement. But if we stumble into people and become friends in accordance with private tastes and preferences—no contracts to sign, laws to obey, public announcements to make—we also lapse, occasionally, into musings on the grand scale: what is this life phenomenologically all about? And we get swept up by larger social currents, even historical tides. Kiely shows us how each of his favored trio accommodates to such internal demands, not to mention the requirements of many readers that a philosophical novelist deliver a few ideas. Through the incorporation of drama (as in the Circe episode in *Ulysses*, as in the Covent Garden opera scene in *Jacob's Room*) these canny, ambitious, and wonderfully agile storytellers took advantage of the leeway offered by crowds, performers, and the staged activity of ritual, the rhetoric of roles. Social rhythms are voiced in set, fixed, assertive lines, no matter the personal history of the actor or the actress.

The novel always has been a wonderful means of character analysis—so responsive to our own, strange human diversity and inconsistency. But the novel, too, has aimed for social observation and analysis of the ways individuals connect with each other in one or another setting. The novel, finally, has been an instrument of grace, a book of wisdom wherein a writer tells something interesting or instructive about this uncertain journey we all take. Such grace is evident in Kiely's book too; it brings three souls together, shows us their common search, and makes their exceptional skills comparatively evident. Readers are meant to take an important, responsive part in the fiction of these three novelists; one reader now shows us compellingly and brilliantly how to do so. If *Beyond Egotism* generates among us a similar contagious response, we will have arrived (by some miracle?) at a point described precisely by the title Robert Kiely chose for this welcome gift of literary and social essays.

New Republic, January 17, 1981

Kafka's Metamorphosis

O f all Kafka's stories, *Metamorphosis* is certainly the best known; perhaps more people have read it than his three novels—*The Trial, The Castle,* and *Amerika.* Certainly this story reveals a particular author well on the way to achieving a masterly style; its direct lucidity of presentation unnerves readers as, disarmed and eager, they struggle with provocative, if not overwhelming, mysteries. Though Kafka died at forty-one in 1924, his writing—at once plain and earthy, yet quite suggestively metaphysical, even religious—has become a major literary presence throughout the twentieth century. Long before existentialism became a faddish way of indicating a concern with some of this century's widespread and dangerous moral, cultural, or psychological conflicts, Franz Kafka, who made no claim to being a philosopher, a psychiatrist, or a social critic, had taken the measure of many of our contemporary lives and figured out a way of rendering what ails and torments us.

There is no point trying to figure out *the* explanation for this startling, elusive, powerfully affecting story. Numerous scholars have studied *Metamorphosis* and tried to get at its heart and soul, only to be followed by others, similarly dedicated and agile, yet anxious to recommend a quite different angle of approach. The story is a Rorschach card of sorts. As the reader thinks about Gregor Samsa, who "found himself transformed in his bed into a gigantic insect," a moment or two of self-recognition may ensue. The story opens with a *fait accompli* (the sentence just quoted), and nowhere in the pages that follow are we told what in the character's life prompted this impossible (though, thanks to Kafka, quite imaginable) transformation. Nor, for that matter, is the exact nature of the transformation specified. Gregor Samsa, we do learn, has become a kind of insect, a bug or a beetle, but by no means are we told how such an event took place, and for that matter, with what authorial purpose in mind.

Our surmise about these matters, even our carefully argued analytic interpretations of them, may well bring us closer to ourselves (to our way of seeing the world) than to Kafka's intent as a shrewdly evasive storyteller.

We do know, however, on the author's say, that Gregor—as he is called throughout the story, no matter what his strange fate— "awoke one morning from a troubled dream" and immediately realized what had befallen him. That information is the one piece of evidence (a clue?) granted us. We may choose to ignore it and deal with *Metamorphosis* as a description of what happens to someone who is somehow, and for some impossible-to-know reason, stripped of his humanity; or we may characterize that restless sleep, that nightmare, as portentous in the extreme—a psychological prefiguration. In the latter instance we approach *Metamorphosis* as a brilliant psychiatric parable—an evocation of severe mental illness and, too, a reminder that when such a tragedy takes place, not only does the patient suffer (and change) but so also do those who belong to his or her family. For instance, Gregor's sister Grete (the similarity of their names is no accident, surely, even as Samsa is not all that unlike Kafka in form) becomes deeply affected by this bizarre visitation upon the household; and some readers have wondered whether the story's title doesn't describe marked alterations in her character as much as in that of her brother.

It can be argued that in Gregor's tragedy Kafka has tried to portray what gets called "dehumanization" by people in my profession of psychoanalytic psychiatry. Not rarely, in fact, clinicians hear seriously disturbed patients describe themselves as utterly lost, to the point that they feel themselves to be animal-like rather than men or women. Alas, in mental hospitals an occasional patient can be heard barking or trying to imitate the purring or the wild cry of a cat, a wolf, or a coyote. A colleague of mine once told me of an especially eerie experience in his hospital work—a young patient, recently graduated from college, had declared himself to be a cockroach. Moreover, he gave himself a curious sanction for so doing: he had read *Metamorphosis*, written a paper on it, and concluded (as a biology major) that "the monstrous kind of vermin" Kafka describes is, in fact, the cockroach, and that the story is about the hallucinatory experience of psychosis.

The young man had gone through a schizophrenic episode while in college, and now, as a would-be graduate student in biochemistry, he had become agitated, withdrawn, depressed, and severely anxious. To his doctor he kept repeating incoherent phrases. Alternatively, there were spells of unyielding silence and bodily contortions. Eventually, the patient told a nurse to go find and read every book of Kafka's so that she would then be able to understand him! The nurse rather astutely asked the patient to narrow the selection of Kafka down a bit and was told that *Metamorphosis* would suffice. She and the doctor working with the young man felt that they had, indeed, been given a message—a statement of pain and radical isolation made through resort to a literary reference. Kafka, a master ironist, would no doubt appreciate such a moment—a strange story's strange usefulness!

Of course, in our century dehumanization and even madness have been declared social commonplaces—everyone's problems in the so-called civilized world, where people by the millions feel useless and isolated from one another, or where they die in wars that so often are as senseless as they are (on a grand scale) life-consuming. Dorothy Day and Peter Maurin, cofounders of the Catholic Worker movement, a religious and social effort, were each steeped in the existentialist tradition; both could be heard saying, years ago, how harsh this twentieth-century urban, industrial life can be—to the point, Miss Day once observed, that "we become ants."

She would not then have claimed any originality for such a comparison. She knew how bewildered and vulnerable many people feel, and indeed she once described that condition in words Kafka might have appreciated: "We are lonely and hurt, millions of us, and we wonder what we are meant to do, to *be*. We are cut off from one another. Is there any difference between us and the creatures we stare at when we go to the zoo?" I heard her make those remarks, ask that question, as an introduction to a personal statement of faith, of Catholic conviction, but she knew that many conclude their contemporary expressions of perplexity, if not despair, with no such devotional assurance. On the contrary, like Gregor in *Metamorphosis* they feel themselves to be in a limbo; they are morally drifting, spiritually and psychologically at loose ends.

Kafka does not hesitate to give us a good deal of information, social and economic, about Gregor and his family. Gregor, we learn, is a commercial traveler, a salesman, though the exact nature of his wares is not disclosed. His job kept him on the move "day in, day out." He was far from independent. His parents had taken a loan from his company's boss, and his work was helping pay off that loan. When he fails to appear for work, the boss sends his subordinate, the General Manager, to visit the Samsa home to find out what is wrong. The General Manager is solicitous but also ominously pointed in a skepticism that he attributes to another: "The chief did hint to me early this morning a possible explanation for your disappearance—with reference to the cash payments that were entrusted to you recently—but I almost pledged my solemn word of honor that this could not be so."

With the word *almost* the author conveys an entire subjective world: the fear and doubt so many working men and women must endure, the personal jeopardy that goes hand in hand with one's all too uncertain economic situation, the dog-eat-dog atmosphere of our twentieth-century industrial society. Kafka makes much of Gregor's time-consciousness, the alarm he feels as he watches the clock move and yet cannot leap from bed to get to the office at the usual early hour. Such punctuality is no mere idiosyncrasy but rather a measure of what we become if we are to survive (just barely, often enough) in a given social order. "Sometimes I think I'm an animal completely owned and run by a clock inside by head," I was once told by a factory worker who had never heard of Kafka, never mind his stories or novels. I think we can safely assume that Kafka was substantially aware of how such a man's sensibility had developed—through the nervously prompt exertions so many of us feel to be utterly necessary lest we become penniless, homeless.

Not that psychosis and social malaise exhaust the interpretative possibilities *Metamorphosis* can prompt in us. Gregor may well have awakened from his "troubled dream" only to fall back asleep and have another one—the story. Kafka needed no psychiatrist to inform him of the workings of the unconscious. His fable is well stocked with the kind of psychological conflict our age takes for granted and maybe dotes on excessively. Gregor's attachment to his sister is obvious, as are his frustrated longing for his mother and his abiding fear, distrust, and dislike of his father. The scene that has the father running after the son in circles, throwing apples at him, trying to kill him once and for all, is at the same time sad and hilarious—as if Kafka was already (twelve years after Freud's *The Interpretation of*

Dreams was published) able to appreciate our present-day psycho-analytic mentality, and even to mock its future banality.

Moreover, the story shows a remarkable integration of psychology and sociology: the author is aware that a twentieth-century Oedipus, namely each of us, has to work—and so is confronted with emotional conflicts not confined to the family. Gregor's travail with his boss is as powerfully compelling in its impact as his resentment of his father. Kafka, like one of our family therapists, insists that we carry home the tensions generated at work, even as we bring to work the worries and fears of our childhood years. Gregor, after all, upon finding himself so drastically altered, has to come to terms with his employer, his sister, his parents, their lodgers, and not least, himself—an entire social spectrum.

Kafka had a strong and subtle religious side. Both *The Trial* and *The Castle* lend themselves to theological and philosophical analysis. So does *Metamorphosis*, with its references to both the "Heavenly Father" and the devil, not to mention the apple that figures prominently in Genesis. Gregor may appear to be an insect, but the reader never fails to regard him as a *person*—someone who thinks, observes, and struggles long and hard to understand the world, to be understood by others in it. A mind and soul lose a given body and yet persist (for a while, at least) in their earthly journey.

Kafka is not intent on anthropomorphism; he has no interest in attributing human qualities to the natural world. Rather, through a marvelously ambiguous story, he invites an examination of this life's purposes. Ought we surrender and be conventional burghers—harassed, intimidated, obliging with respect to the status quo? Ought we try to break free, to take on various "principalities and powers," and hence become feared outcasts, soon enough killed? Gregor is hardly an Old Testament prophet, or a redeemer for pre–World War I Prague, but his metamorphosis turns him into a hurt, suffering, intently observant outsider, who experiences the callous rebuff, and worse, of just about everyone. Both the emotional and moral suggestiveness are surely biblical in nature.

The story ends not with Gregor's demise but with his sister Grete's eerie ascendance; she is lovely, flowering. A bizarre, dislocating event, carefully portrayed in its impact upon a series of individuals, yields to an idyllic termination. A brother's death is followed by a sister's birth—her sexual emergence. Were they all too close, those two? Has one, accordingly, had to pay the price, to be punished as severely as possible? Dare any of us reach out to others, except fearfully, as children with demanding parents or workers with overbearing bosses? The psychological implications are obvious, and so the reassurance at the end is, as always with Kafka, minimal.

This Samsa family as a whole is meant to remind us that not only workers but their kin suffer the alienation that Marx, Jaspers, and Gabriel Marcel (or in literature, Camus and Walker Percy) have evoked in various ways. Gregor's sacrifice oddly nourishes (redeems?) others in the Samsa family—a statement of the costs alienation can exact. This story is, after all, an early and profound assertion of a theme now familiar—"the death of a salesman." Gregor's fierce solipsism, erotic and intellectual, is a consequence, one suspects, of more than a particular family's private disorders. Kafka saw how wretchedly some of us treat others (parents and bosses as against children and employees). He saw the result in the betrayal of life, the strong feeding upon the weak. His *Metamorphosis* asks us to consider not only Gregor's deadly transformation but our own continuing experience as survivors. Do we profit handily from the human degradation of others? Is our comfort earned at the expense of a terrible suffering? If so, what happens to us, what metamorphosis falls upon us? Kafka's story is of immense and continuing moral significance, a means by which each of us can take a demanding look at what we are and, yes, what we might become.

Introduction to *Metamorphosis* by Franz Kafka,
Limited Editions Club, 1984

George Orwell's Sensibility

ven as Eric Blair became the prophetic voice George Orwell, that pseudonym has in turn become, since January of 1950 when it was stilled forever, an almost mythic presence among many who live in the Western world. The advantages for countless numbers of reflective men and women have been considerable. An intellectual and moral figure of the first rank in English letters (in both the general and the more limited sense of that word) has become a familiar and readily available companion: the books, long essays, and shorter, journalistic pieces are much used in schools and colleges and commonly summoned, still, in the public discourse of the day, certainly in England and America. On the other hand, there are inevitably costs to a writer's posthumous celebrity when that writer was so evidently anxious to address controversial social and political matters in a manner that was not petty or frivolous. We have, for instance, recently watched the author of *Nineteen Eighty-Four* claimed by self-avowed conservatives and, in reply, claimed yet again by vigorous socialists or skeptical liberals of leftist inclination. The occasion, of course, was the arrival of that year of years, 1984—and the self-consciousness so many of us felt about that particular year was, needless to say, a measure of the powerful impact one writer's moral and political imagination has had upon millions of readers.

I have for years taught Orwell to college freshmen in a seminar that couples his literary documentary work (*Down and Out in Paris and London, The Road to Wigan Pier, Homage to Catalonia,* and some of his briefer efforts at social observation, such as "Hop-Picking," or the two quite compelling essays published in 1931 under the name Eric A. Blair, "The Spike" and "A Hanging") with the altogether different writing in a similar genre of James Agee (*Let Us Now Praise Famous Men,* obviously, and a number of pieces written for *Fortune* magazine). There is an obvious coherence and continuity to this side of Orwell—the man of Wigan and the two capital cities and the Spain of the first half of 1937, torn apart not only by right and left but also within the left by fateful schisms, the nature of which at least one writer immediately knew had enormous significance for all of us in the following decades of the twentieth century. This is the Orwell who wants to wonder and look hard, who has an appetite for factuality and a pen able to render human and social complexity lucidly yet with no sacrifice of narrative subtlety or interpretive depth. This is the Orwell who was an eagerly adventurous hobo or tramp or waiter or reporter on assignment; or yes, a soldier fighting on behalf of a worthwhile cause. This is the Orwell who seemed to notice everything and forget nothing. No tape recorder for him, or other assorted scraps of audiovisual equipment! His eyes and his ears, his scrutinizing intelligence, and his developing writer's craft were quite enough. With persistence and tenacity he watched his fellow creatures and always, through them, learned about himself as well. With a wry skepticism, interrupted on memorable occasions by compelling outbursts of sympathy for certain people, places, or, more generally, human predicaments, he constructed his reports—news from other worlds to the more conventional one of the upper-middle-class intelligentsia he knew so well. In those reports one does not miss his attentiveness to the accidental, the irregular, the unexpected, and the quite odd; and one does not miss a strong mindfulness of the ironies of everyday existence—as in Hardy's phrase, "life's little ironies."

Of course some of them were not so minor in impact, Orwell noticed. Those who have lots of money and enjoy their leisure with a meal in a fine restaurant may be more vulnerable than they ever realize—because waiters scolded or pushily confronted with demands can always, unobserved, desecrate food with a mouthful of spit and then enjoy the satisfaction of seeing it downed with everything else on the plate. I mention that not very pleasing discovery relayed in *Down and Out in Paris and London* because it possesses an instructive suggestiveness with respect to the man who chose to set it down in his first book. All through his life Orwell wanted to uncover the conceits and deceits of a given social and economic order. He had little use for things as they were in the England of the 1930s, the time he did his major documentary writing; he was determined as well to expose the failings (or worse) of individuals and institutions as he came across them. But he was not given to the broad social statements or economic interpretations some of his intellectual friends favored—or at least not until he earned such generalizations as he saw fit to earn through the illumination of particularity. Put differently, he brought to bear upon social reality and the individual psychology of workaday English life (vintage 1930 to 1937, especially) the talents and inclinations usually and correctly associated with the novelist: an eye for detail; an interest in dramatic progression; a knowledge of how willfulness (or the absence thereof) can affect a given life; a fascination with rendering the puzzling mysteries of humankind, not the least of which is the at times ineffable yet absolutely determining influence a person's character has upon his or her life. Armed with such a stock of perceptual gifts, prompted as well by an obvious yet not greedy or, with respect to others, competitive ambitiousness, and aided upon occasion by that quiet web of privilege that can often be counted on to respond readily and with modest generosity to the temporarily fallen members of the British ruling class, even its "lower-upper-middle class" segment (his social self-definition offered in *Wigan Pier*), Orwell took to the road, quite literally in instances such as those he related in *Down and Out*.

The result was not only the nonfiction we all know so well but moments of sharp, piercing drama that almost stand on their own—as if the text that surrounds them is, for all its considerable virtues, a mere ornament, or a prelude and then a postlude. One suspects Orwell knew his own literary and sociological might; in his last summary paragraph of *Down and Out* he reminds the reader of not only what the author has "learned" but what the reader, a stranger of time and space, will surely remember: at least one graduate of Eton, no less, will never "enjoy a meal at a smart restaurant." The appearance yet again of this vivid moment is a powerful writer's urgent goodbye to his reader—an embrace of sorts that is meant to last.

There is, of course, an intrusiveness to such a concluding autobiographical remark. Why need the rest of us, who have already learned pages earlier what revenge can be taken, say, in "Hôtel X" of Paris, find ourselves confronted with *that* scene? This has been a book full of interesting, humorous, and sad events. Without question any number of them might have been used as suitable moral jogs, as parting suggestions that money and power cannot control all events, large or small, and indeed can generate their own considerable or at least personal impasses in the course of a day, a week, and longer. But Orwell had Conrad's willingness to link apparent, even gross, success to the seedy destructiveness that both enables it, often enough, and lingers on, commonly without letup, as an echo of the past that won't go away. Even as the fate of Kurtz in *Heart of Darkness* is very much connected, we are told, to the drawing rooms of Europe's bourgeoisie, the young Orwell has come to realize something far more revealing than his witness of one flaw in one Paris hotel: that some resentments are not only abstract attitudes described by the writers of textbooks, to be digested by hungry intellectuals in search of a political position or a social view, but rather are evidence of a personal bitterness generated by flagrant and demeaning inequality and vented upon the very people who seem the luckiest, the most secure, so that they too are daily tricked, if not demeaned.

Not that, again, there aren't (there weren't) other ways to make that point stick. But to eat is what all of us who are intent on staying alive must do, and so a seemingly incidental vignette manages to get at our jugular via our palate, our stomach. Orwell is graphic, lest we miss his point. "Everywhere in the service quarters," he says toward the end of chapter 14, "dirt festered—a secret vein of dirt, running through the great garish hotel like the intestines through a man's body." And, alas, it is "mostly Americans" who frequent this place, the saviors of the capitalist order. It is we who are exposing ourselves, at high cost and with great and ostentatious pride to—well, this state of affairs:

> When a steak, for instance, is brought up for the head cook's inspection, he does not handle it with a fork. He picks it up in his fingers and slaps it down, runs his thumb around this dish and licks it to taste the gravy, runs it round and licks again, then steps back and contemplates the piece of meat like an artist judging a picture, then presses it lovingly into place with his fat, pink fingers, every one of which he has licked a hundred times that morning. When he is satisfied, he takes a cloth and wipes his fingerprints from the dish, and hands it to the waiter. And the waiter, of course dips *his* fingers into the gravy—his nasty, greasy fingers which he is forever running through his brilliantined hair.

This is by no means the most unnerving of Orwell's offerings in the book, but it contains a representative capacity for causing disgust that won't, one guesses, easily be banished to convenient forgetfulness. Not only is the writing blunt, vivid, and obviously self-assured (this man knows whereof he speaks, *we* know!) but the symbolic language, well executed, clinches the purposes of the narrator's portrait. The themes bring us face to face with ourselves, with our situations as the ones who go to Hôtel X's here and there, and with ourselves as the ones who are smart as can be yet utterly unaware of an entire social reality, a reality that one person intends to know well and to evoke with precision and liveliness. Moreover, even that small section, a part of one paragraph, tells us a lot not only about the cook, the waiter, and soon enough, the paying customer, but about the kind of observer Orwell was. He was ever disgusted by the dirt and filth he was constantly noticing and, later, keeping in mind as he wrote.

One recalls the Brookers, who ran a lodging house in Wigan, and the disgust their daily rhythms inspired in Orwell, culminating in "the day when there was a full chamber-pot under the breakfast table." It was then, we immediately learn, that he left, and this dramatic departure, so explained, is purposely made to warn us about the seedy life of minor burghers. It contrasts, of course, to the one lived by badly exploited miners, whose own dirt—all over their bodies and worked into cracks and pores in such a fashion that no soap can possibly manage to do its intended job—Orwell finds not at all offensive, quite the contrary: "It is impossible to watch the 'fillers' at work without feeling a pang of envy for their toughness," he tells us. A bit further on he describes their "most noble bodies," observing too that "when they are black and naked they all look alike."

The contrast with Hôtel X or the home of the Brookers is edifying and tells us a lot about Orwell's political convictions as well as his moral and literary sensibility. That "great garish hotel" is obviously meant to represent the industrial West, whose rot Orwell, like Dickens, intends to survey. In such a place "gravy" gets turned into soiled water, and in such a place the various surfaces (as in "brilliantined hair") lie badly. In *Wigan Pier* the reader is asked to descend from the sick pretensions of the top French places to the foul habits of the English burghers. From haute-bourgeoisie to petite-bourgeoisie, it is all unedifying, tainted, contaminated, defiled—except for the bracing condition of the miners; those who are ostensibly the very dirtiest of creatures are, for Orwell at least, "noble" not only in body, as he specifically says, but in the direct, vigorous dignity of their working lives.

There was in Orwell a romantic side that he only occasionally indulges in his tough, documentary writing. Where more intellectual socialists would herald all too theoretically the coming ascent of the proletariat, he would select miners, even some tramps, and certainly some ordinary Spanish people, and find in their daily toil, in their cheerful persistence against great odds, whatever encouragement there is to be found on this earth. So doing, he abandoned consistency and even, one suspects, accuracy of observation. Lord knows how many full chamber-pots he might have found in the homes of Wigan's miners, had he been inclined to poke and pry and chronicle his discoveries. Lord knows what those miners' wives served in the way of food and what their hands looked like as they did the cooking. *Wigan Pier* is indeed about miners and mining. Orwell even descended into the mines. But the book has, too, the ambitious intent of a general statement about twentieth-century capitalism, an intent disclosed even in the first section, which was meant to set down direct observations, never mind the well-known argumentative second section, so full of cranky and blistering assaults on so many aspects of socialist intellectual life.

The writer's tough critical mind spares a few and damns many others, to quite dramatic effect. The reader is, after all, likely to be uncomfortably akin to the people roundly denounced. The book, one gathers, so pained those in the Left Book Club (which commissioned the effort in the first place) that Victor Gollancz, acknowledging "well over a hundred passages" with which he took issue, wrote a preface both appreciative and shrewdly admonishing. What had been meant to enlighten a readership ended up also offending a sponsor. Such a result, perhaps, serves to show how original-minded and fussy and feisty and truculently suggestive Orwell was but also how successful as a writer: no one would be bored or put off self-protectively by this book; and for decades after its topicality was no longer a mainstay of its interest, readers would keep returning to its manner of exposition, reasoning, and contention. That is to say, Orwell the writer and the polemical moralist had triumphed over one moment's political issue.

Orwell the political prophet made his first major appearance in *Wigan Pier*, and this side of his intellect also emerged triumphant— a mix of autobiographical candor and a bold willingness to examine carefully and censure vigorously the assumptions of his own kind, the socialist reformers of England in the 1930s. At times, of course, the prophet's self-criticism and the roasting given his ostensible colleagues or fellow partisans sound remarkably similar. "When I was fourteen or fifteen I was an odious little snob," we are told in the intensely confessional ninth chapter of *Wigan Pier.* We learn a bit further on that "at the age of seventeen or eighteen" the author was "both a snob and a revolutionary." Still further on, that word *snob* once again is used, now to describe the "typical socialist," who is "either a youthful snob-bolshevik who in five years' time will quite probably have made a wealthy marriage and have been converted to Roman Catholicism; or, still more typically, a prim little man with a white collar job, usually a secret teetotaller and often with vegetarian leanings, with a history of Nonconformity behind him, and, above all, with a social position which he has no intention of forfeiting."

There is, no doubt, an Augustinian self-scrutiny at work here; an intellectual anti-intellectualism too, as Victor Gollancz insists in his introduction, which also gives every indication of the offense taken by many who belonged to the Left Book Club. Orwell was able to see his own situation and that of his fellow writers and political activists as one of privilege, with all the attendant risks of self-importance, smugness, arrogance, hypocrisy, and pettiness. The "literary world" was for him a "poisonous jungle," and he could be outspoken, to put it mildly: "In the highbrow world you 'get on,' if you 'get on' at all, not so much by your literary ability as by being the life and soul of cocktail parties and kissing the bums of verminous little loins." Such rage, self-directed by implication, was of course a warning to others, lower in station, toward whom Orwell had more affection that he could easily express. Time and again he reaches out to England's working-class people, whose hard work and simple life and unpretentiousness and decency he admires—and may see to the exclusion of those warts possessed by all human beings, and all classes of them. After he launches his tirade against the English literati, he turns directly to that working class. He worries about the fate of its bright lads, who might well end up, he is sure, in his terrible world. Orwell is split not so much in opinion as in loyalty. The strenuousness of his assault, when compared with the flimsiness and pettiness of its object, makes one wonder whether he has not cast himself unwittingly in the position of a rather impoverished working man, bright and aspiring but proud as can be and unwilling or unable to make the necessary social gestures that ensure success.

The author is in his early thirties at this point, and he is by no means the world-famous writer he became in the last years of his life and, of course, after he died. He is fighting his way up and yet is constitutionally (a matter of character and principles dearly held) unable to ingratiate himself as he has seen others do. He is tempted enough to turn sour, testy, sardonic; the spleen vented measures the vicissitudes of a promising career. As for the working class, its distance from the intelligentsia had always been a haven of sorts: a population without one's felt vices, temptations, or self-serving aspirations, and hence a population to contrast with one's own social or occupational kinsmen, to be defended and protected and upheld passionately as a means, really, of holding on to one's own self-respect.

Even as Eric Blair, the reserved but determined writer, had to make his accommodation to others, to friends who did him favors and arranged for him to get assignments or to receive a loan or two, the writer George Orwell was to the end of his life an uncanny mixture of the idealist and the realist. His idealism obviously accounts for many of his lasting sympathies—for the underdog, for the exiled or hurt or suffering people whose experiences he has rendered to perfection. Nor was this idealism merely abstract. Anti-intellectualism worked against such a development. Orwell's insistence on a concrete knowledge of how others live, how they endure pain, even how they die (in a hospital, in the field of battle, or when hung until dead under the auspices of England's glorious empire) is one of his notable achievements. Moreover, it is all the more remarkable that he could convey such a response—a sense of the individual's burdens in one or another difficult or dangerous set of circumstances— within the constraints of the documentary essays that he wrote. Not that he didn't have the space to discuss the particular men and women he'd met; rather, he himself had a sensibility that loved negotiating those two polarities, the concrete and the theoretical, and one wonders that he never lost his balance and never succumbed to the temptations of large-scale, ever so confident generalizations about, say, the poor, or the Spanish people he met in 1937.

He was, of course, a novelist, which must have helped keep under wraps any overwrought theoretical ambition. But I suspect he was assisted by an interesting writing split he made: the socialists he aimed to parody receive the brunt of his conjectural instincts, and often their excesses; the humble folk were thereby spared, and as a consequence their vulnerability·was not exploited. Given the number of social scientists who have turned this or that kind of impoverished or tyrannical human being into cannon fodder for one or another all-embracing, ideological analysis, one can only marvel at Orwell's abstinence.

His larger gift of allegorical prophecy, an aspect of his sensibility, has become worked into our Western culture's sensibility; hence these lecture-essays, among others surely to be spoken and written in this year, 1984. But in his documentary writings, literary pieces, and strongly personal essays, Orwell could demonstrate, in retrospect, a stunning foresight, usually stated so casually the contemporary reader may well miss what he or she has, in fact, happened just to read. For example, in the last chapter of *Homage to Catalonia* Orwell is expressing his affection for the Spanish people and says this:

> I have the most evil memories of Spain, but I have very few bad memories of Spaniards. I only twice remember even being seriously angry with a Spaniard, and on each occasion, when I look back, I believe I was in the wrong myself. They have, there is no doubt, a generosity, a species of nobility, that do not really belong to the twentieth century. It is this that makes one hope that in Spain even Fascism may take a comparatively loose and bearable form. Few Spaniards possess the damnable efficiency and consistency that a modern totalitarian state needs.

Here was Orwell the offhand observer, with no academic pretenses, no anthropological caution, no worry that a given remark lacks the justification of proper methodological research. At the time his companions on the left were fighting to the death against Franco but, Orwell had learned, against one another as well. Those companions, and the writers who were on their side, had scant time for the niceties of cultural reflection about how the people of nations differ and, accordingly, how the fates of particular social and political and economic ideologies vary across the world. Orwell was also a volunteer combatant. Still, he found time for the above passage, and it is in my opinion as shrewd and knowing a presentiment of what would obtain in a generation or two as Orwell or anyone else has made during this century. Spain, as all know, has now become a country whose prime minister is a socialist; and even during the Second World War Franco managed to stay clear of fighting, and yes, "comparatively," the brutish excesses of fascism. There are two others whose good judgment matched that of Orwell with respect to the Spanish Civil War, Georges Bernanos on the right and Simone Weil on the left, both of whom spotted the serious misdeeds of even their own side. But Orwell, characteristically, went even further and allowed an almost anecdotal remark to carry within it a sweeping historical prediction.

In the same final chapter, Orwell offers his well-known tribute to the essential "decency of human beings," a hymn of praise not as biblical and lyrical in nature as the one James Agee offers in *Let Us Now Praise Famous Men* but perhaps all the more affecting in its quiet understatement. It is interesting, too, that the remark about decency in others is followed immediately by an astonishingly candid and sober moment of self-appraisal:

> And I hope the account I have given is not too misleading.
> I believe that on such an issue as this no one is or can be
> completely truthful. It is difficult to be certain about anything
> except what you have seen with your own eyes, and con-
> sciously or unconsciously everyone writes as a partisan. In
> case I have not said this somewhere earlier in the book I will
> say it now: beware of my partisanship, my mistakes of fact and
> the distortion inevitably caused by my having seen only one
> corner of events.

How many others who were writing about the Spanish Civil War at that time were prepared to issue such a cautionary warning? How many social scientists who have returned from their various and sundry field trips have felt the requirement for such a modest disclaimer? Orwell could be cranky, irritating, exaggerated in his scorn of one group or admiration of another, but he was never the man of answers for all about everything—nor did he fail to spot that vice in others, especially the social and political theorists of earlier decades of this century who claimed to know so much about so many matters, including the workings of history itself. For Orwell, a chance to visit Wigan, or to get to know a tramp like Paddy (what a fine job is done in presenting this fellow to the readers of *Down and Out!*), or to fight against fascism in Spain was a chance (as he remarked

in many ways and on many occasions) to get to know oneself:
one's blind spots, animosities, wayward tendencies, limitations of
empathy, charity, and not least, one's vision. Again and again students of mine who have read *Wigan Pier* or *Down and Out* or *Catalonia* (I've been using *their* common abbreviations in this essay)
remark upon the refreshing bluntness in Orwell and the lack of self-
importance, not to mention the down-to-earth honesty. They compare him with an assortment of intellectual authorities or celebrities—and interestingly enough, remark upon the injustice that
history has done him, to be in such company! Why? He is, they
reply, far too "ordinary" in his approach (meaning without affectation or pretense) with a surprising modesty of self-presentation,
while at the same time, they note, he takes the considerable risks
that go with the use of the first person in documentary narration.

For Americans in the 1940s, Orwell was a recurring source of exemplary edification. He put his clean, straightforward prose in the
service of one essay after another for the *Partisan Review;* each
"London Letter" he sent tells of England's wartime struggles and its
postwar social and political transformation. Those dispatches were a
prize for a quarterly then congenial to a given English correspondent—socialist in spirit, literary in sensibility, a touch anarchist in
politics for fear of yet again becoming trapped in the monstrous evil
of commitment to an ideology. The *Partisan Review* letters are to
this day of great interest; they show a familiar Orwell—spotting the
reasons why many of the British disliked American soldiers stationed
in England during the war (for their enviable salary and provisions
and for their great self-confidence) or explaining what the prospects
of the Labour party were, and why. Orwell is outgoing and friendly,
perceptive, even at times didactic, yet able to disarm himself of
any preachiness or highhanded assertiveness, both of which, Lord
knows, are the besetting hazards of the genre of social comment,
especially the kind that aims to facilitate transnational (in this case,
transatlantic) understanding.

At moments the brilliant polemicist becomes quite the stolid and
tolerant educator, anxious to remind Americans why this terribly destructive Second World War is being fought and why they, along
with all other democratic nations, have such a high stake in its outcome. At other times Orwell is, quite simply, the marvelously earthy
man who is at pains to remind himself how earthy, in fact, his

American readers are; they, he tells his readers in one essay, could long ago read the word *bullshit* without abbreviation, while their English counterparts had to keep reading "b——." Nor should one fail to observe, in connection with America, that Orwell's last notes, meant to help him write a story or two and some literary pieces, reveal him—dying though he was, and so with every excuse for self-absorption or withdrawal of interest—still solidly intrigued with matters American, with the enormous complexity of our nation, and indeed, the several nations within a nation that we are in several important respects. One also comes across this striking phrase, obviously one of the last he would write: "The big cannibal critics that lurk in the deeper waters of American quarterly reviews." There seems, really, no limit to the spaciousness of his knowledge, nor to the range of his eye for pinpointing exactly the various kinds of meanness and spite that so-called educated people can visit upon others.

Orwell was not to be a captive of his own shrewdness with respect to shrewd people. Put differently, he wanted "out" from the world of fashionable slander, rather than "in" as the one, say, who mocks it, detests it, or merely stresses its tawdry nature. His heart was always with victims of one sort or another; and there he was, in his final days, an eminently successful writer who took care to worry about how certain writers treat other writers in the name of something called a "critical tradition." Moreover, he was able, in the face of an extremely serious illness, yet again to reach out, to take notice of those in London who easily went unnoticed—both the comparatively obscure American critics and the quarterlies they favored.

There is in Orwell's sensibility more than a touch of the anger those "cannibal critics" demonstrate to this day among us English-speaking readers. At his worst Orwell can be almost irrationally (certainly inconsistently) belligerent—as in portions of *Wigan Pier*, when his rage at England's socialists becomes not argumentative, or even partisan, but simply spiteful, and only understandable as the response of someone who takes for granted in his readers (those of the Left Book Club, after all) a robust dislike of the kind of brutish and callous capitalism that ruled in the England of the 1930s. If that real enemy of Orwell's is spared—perhaps because there was little hope then of budging it, no matter the pitch of one's passionately espoused invective—then a scapegoat of sorts becomes rather tempting, and given Orwell's satirical gifts and his self-imposed limitations with respect to targets for their exercise (the poor, the infirm, and the defenseless must be given sanctuary at all costs), the upper-class socialists were, really, his only possible choice.

On the opposite side of the coin, Orwell can also be as hopeful and uncritically adoring, in brief spells, as he was mostly thoughtful and careful, scrutinizing and sensibly balanced. The love he felt for his ordinary, working-class English countrymen was, as I've mentioned, considerable, and upon occasion turned wonderfully blinding. I use that last adverb out of delight, I suppose, and pleasure in an honorable, sensitive writer's obvious demonstration of his humanity: his strong patriotism preceded the Second World War, was gloriously heightened by it (and given the enemy, why not!), and was, too, not subdued by the terribly short period of postwar time he was to experience. Indeed, Orwell's love for his country can be considered the greatest source of his writing energy. His novels are, so significantly, efforts at evoking English life. His best essays are similar efforts, as in the marvelous approach to Charles Dickens, an approach that unintentionally (one dares say) becomes quite autobiographical. Dickens the moralist, the one who disliked much of organized religion but deeply loved Jesus and his disciples, those radical egalitarians and communitarians, becomes so dear to us in the critical piece because Orwell's own anarchic political compassion, social generosity, and yes, spiritual vigor also become eminently clear.

Orwell's sensibility was, to the end, a thickly textured mix of the political, the literary, the moral, and the social. His was a mind constantly taking notice of how people live, under what constraints, and with which degree of uprightness; a mind utterly persuaded that words can make a difference in this life and, very important, that the writing of words bears with it a substantial responsibility. He was with all those words—so many in such a foreshortened life—an exceptionally able craftsman, a wide-ranging commentator, a spirited instructor, an occasional scold, an honorable and lovable author whose message has touched the minds, the hearts, the souls of millions with a simultaneity extraordinary in this God-forsaken century of ours. Watchful of this strange life, wary of absolutes wielded to explain away its mysteries, George Orwell has become himself someone all of us watch, himself a source of outstanding mystery—

that one man, and for so long a man fighting death, could leave us with so much lasting good sense. He himself, one feels, would tolerate poorly the acclaim that has been his since his departure and the possessiveness toward him of certain writers (indeed, he would have quickly questioned their motives). And maybe that is the highest honor we can pay this singularly literate spiritual wanderer—a determination on our part to strive always for his clear-headed integrity, his big-hearted, open, and above-board nature, his frank and powerful manner of expression. One searches in vain for his successor; hence the special necessity of remembering him as someone especially dear and important to us who live in 1984.

In Robert Mulvihill, ed., *Reflections on America, 1984:*
An Orwell Symposium, 1985

Knut Hamsun
The Beginning and the End

On February 19, 1952 a man of ninety-three died near Grimstad, Norway. He was a writer, indeed one who had won the Nobel Prize for Literature in 1920. He was also at the time of his death an officially recognized traitor, allowed by his nation to live out his last years at home only because of the "permanently impaired faculties" that advanced age was supposed to have caused. Now, fifteen years later, Knut Hamsun's first novel, *Hunger*, has been translated into English by the American poet Robert Bly. At the same time we are offered a translation by Carl Anderson of *On Overgrown Paths*; it is the last writing Hamsun did, completed while he was a prisoner and forced inmate of a mental hospital between 1945 and 1948.

Some lives are themselves epics, and Hamsun's was an epic life, as long and rich and defiantly unique as anything he wrote. He was born Knut Petersen, the son of a faintly aristocratic mother and a father who farmed for a living but loved to recite legends and walk endlessly in the woods. When the boy was four, his parents took him north from a valley in central Norway to the region near Bodö, way up the coast, in *true* Nordland, where a growing child must come to terms with nights that last a month and summers that must seem like much more than a prize, or even a form of reparation and reconciliation—perhaps like a passionate act of atonement by a God who can stay sullen and aloof only so long. Hamsun's family settled on another farm called Hamsund, hence the name that Knut Petersen later assumed. Neither the mother nor the father was eager to send their son to school. Instead, he worked on the land, worked with a shoemaker, and began to write.

At twenty Hamsun had finished a short novel called *Frida*. He took it to Oslo—then called Christiana—but failed to secure a publisher. He returned to a rooming house in the capital city and nearly starved to death. Eventually he left for the countryside. He spent what seemed like his last bit of energy looking for anything physical to do. He had had enough of thinking and putting ideas into words. He worked as a farm hand and he worked on the roads. At twenty-three he left for America, where like many of his countrymen he sought out the plains of the Middle West. He lived in Wisconsin and in Minnesota, worked in lumberyards, and became an auctioneer. He was always on the move and never with much money. In time he became desperately ill with tuberculosis, and he returned to Norway, supposedly to die. He recovered, though, and resumed his marginal existence in Oslo.

Still thinking of himself as a writer, still unable to write, still a proud, eccentric, willfully isolated young man, he returned to America in 1886 at twenty-seven. I suppose it can be said that his mind was unsettled; certainly his body was incredibly restless. He made for Chicago, where he worked as a streetcar conductor. He went to North Dakota and harvested wheat. For a while he was a barber. In 1888 he thought of working as a fisherman on the Newfoundland Banks, something he had once before done for three years; but he was homesick at last and that year returned to Europe—first to Copenhagen, then to Oslo. In Denmark he began working on *Hunger*. In Norway he wrote—apparently in a frenzy— a book called *The Cultural Life of Modern America*. In some respects it is like Kafka's *Amerika*, full of sly, humorous irony, and at heart a fanciful, extravagant work of the imagination rather than a literal description of anything American that Hamsun had experienced. He had lived close to our soil and had came to know our late nineteenth century life very intimately and concretely; yet the New World seemed to stir his mind in the direction of private imagery and extraordinary metaphor.

In 1890, when Hamsun was thirty-one, *Hunger* was published. He would never again be unknown. Robert Bly tells us that Hamsun's style in his first novel was somewhat similar to Hemingway's— curt, almost severe, and to the point. Others have claimed that America's raw, nervous, and informal life comes across almost miraculously in Hamsun's Norwegian prose. Yet the novel's plot and its central character also manage to evoke Russians like Gogol and Dostoevski and contemporary European existentialist writers like Camus and Sartre. Hamsun seems to have drawn upon the best of two continents, and the result is a work of art that is still forceful, still provocative, and not in the slightest out of date. In point of fact, *Hunger* is a "fashionable" novel, all taken up with our current concerns and discoveries—the world's injustice as it affects the individual, the unconscious and its various workings, the question of what is psychologically normal and what is socially permissible.

Hunger is one nameless man's narrative, his description of what it is like to live on the extreme edge of life, without a supply of food that can be taken for granted and without the friendship or love of anyone. Right off, the suffering man announces that "all of this happened while I was walking around starving in Christiana"; and much later, when he has had enough of both starvation and the city, he takes a job on a ship and describes himself as he "straightened up, wet from fever and exertion, looked in toward land and said goodbye for now to the city, to Christiana, where the windows of the homes all shone with such brightness." The hero is apart at the beginning. He continues to keep people at arm's length, no matter how closely he watches them. At the end he goes away, out of the way, a long way off.

Hamsun was always an uncompromising outsider. In *Hunger* he showed he could even stand outside himself. If the city is full of the comic, the preposterous, and the fake, the mind of its half-wretched, half-indulgent observer emerges as no less ridiculous and pitiable. Though the narrator of *Hunger* reminds one of Raskolnikov or even of Kafka's K, Hamsun is neither as strict and serious as Dostoevski nor as incurably forlorn as Kafka. He does seem to have a pilgrimage in mind for his hero, or at the very least some serious traveling. Perhaps it is a mistake to try to find in *Hunger* the quests *we* have made. The Hamsun who wrote *Hunger* might have had *Piers Plowman* in mind or the strange and bizarre events that can be found in almost any medieval chronicle of a soul's "way."

In 1893 Hamsun published *Mysteries*, in many respects a sequel to *Hunger*. (Farrar, Straus and Giroux have announced that an English translation of *Mysteries* is on the way.) Again there is a stranger, now given the name of Nagel. Again he observes everything, particularly himself. Again the reader is forcibly confronted with a character's resourceful capacity to deceive both himself and the outside world. Before Pirandello, before Freud, before the self-conscious twentieth century began, Hamsun was obsessed—and systematically so—with the nature of illusion. He did not take man's psychological life for granted, nor did he simply allude to the terror, the vagaries, and the caprices of the mind's daily life. Deliberately and carefully—as if he were one of today's psychologists or psychiatrists—Hamsun examines (through Nagel and the people he manages to confuse, puzzle, and torment) all sorts of familiar subjects: the child in man; the motive that hides other motives; the power of a shrewd and willing observer both to anger a person and to lay bare his most ingrained and self-sustaining conceits.

In 1894 the Norwegian public had to deal with an avalanche of Hamsun. *New Ground* and *Editor Lynge* were published, neither of them great books and both of them totally unlike the two novels that had previously appeared. From portraits of very particular, very unusual, and very inward individuals, Hamsun turned to devastating and scornful descriptions of social cliques. In *Editor Lynge*, Oslo's politicians are relentlessly exposed as mean, calculating, and dishonest. In *New Ground*, the city's literary set is subject to withering ridicule. Hamsun fixes upon the so-called artists and thinkers every stereotype that they so often use to brand businessmen or members of the petit bourgeoisie. Fake, pretentious, calculating, and self-serving "intellectuals" are contrasted with mere workers, mere shopkeepers. Let other authors turn their biting satire on the greedy, hypocritical mercantile class and the aspirants who serve it; Hamsun scorns the scornful, the nervously "aware" and the proudly "enlightened," those who score points on one another rather than make money, and who can be as showy and snobbish and fiercely competitive as the most successful of burghers. These two books ordinarily might be ignored in any account of Hamsun's significant artistic successes, yet they give an important clue to his way of looking at politics and society. And if they do not explain his later pro-Nazi statements, they at least show how uncongenial his mind was to a rising liberal or progressive intellectual and political tradition—and therefore how susceptible he might have logically become in later years to the powerful military alternative of Nazi fascism. A man who at thirty-five saw rot and scandal in the "best" of the Western world, and who even then was living his own, proud and intensely private life, could much later flinch not at all when Hitler called for more purges and bloodbaths.

Also published in 1894 was *Pan*, a contrast to Hamsun's twin effort at social criticism. (An excellent English translation by James McFarlane was made available ten years ago.) *Pan* is a love story in the Nordic tradition, full of sadness and tenderness, passion and disappointment—and finally, that threesome of separation, search, and death. Hamsun is done with Oslo. He places his heroes in the North, in a fishing village. The sea, the forest, and the weather figure prominently. The movement is away from the inward, the private, and toward Nature. At the same time there is an ironic new interest in groups of people, in contrast to *a* person. I suppose one can say the hero of *Pan* is a repressed Victorian; he takes women for granted and seems to want to use them rather than to respect their particular desires and needs. They are "objects," a term still used by some psychiatrists to describe a person who is wanted and sought.

In *Victoria*, his next novel and a companion piece to *Pan*, Hamsun also describes a youthful love affair. Johannes, the suitor, is again brusque, uncouth, and distant—but poetic. He desires a rich man's daughter—perhaps to marry his native poetry to some firmly established way of life. What Johannes wanted, Hamsun himself achieved. He gradually became a well-to-do, insistently private man whose lyric inspiration was to be shared with the world only out of a writer's need. No longer was he hungry or jobless, and if he remembered the wild sea and the inviting forests of his youth, he largely forgot the social and economic injustice he had occasion to see firsthand for so long. Now the odd spirit moved and the cloistered pen obliged. Hamsun ignored causes and with them all of Norway's intellectuals. He wrote plays and a number of short stories and poems. He traveled all over the world and described what he saw and felt while living in various places. He wrote several gentle and witty novels, and it has to be noted that their characters are no longer poor, hungry, desperate, or even very young and uncertain about life. Indeed, by 1915 he had completed a two-volume portrayal of a rich and powerful family whose rural, aristocratic ways can no longer survive modern, technological society. Hamsun feared what would happen when the various "classes" of people are less firmly ordered

and separated. With *Growth of the Soil* (1917) he even gave up trying to understand that kind of social change. His concern is now
with the land, with man the tiller and lonely pioneer who lives in an
essentially timeless and constant world. Factories, political upheavals, scientific achievements for the good and the bad—none of them
has anything to do with the bleak, inhospitable, and unpeopled terrain described by the increasingly patrician man of letters.

Hamsun's chief public was in Germany. He was relatively ignored
in England and America. Unlike Strindberg he payed little attention
to contemporary events, and unlike Munch he lost his early interest
in the mind's hard and sometimes terrible struggle for day-to-day
coherence and sanity—though Munch's barren landscapes are perhaps parallels to Hamsun's later works. Germans responded to his
unashamed romanticism more than his own countrymen did. In
Norway he was admired and respected as a world-famous writer; but
he made no effort to be loved by his fellow citizens, who reportedly
found him personally austere and in a flash capable of being piti-
lessly derisive.

Like Ezra Pound he became a traitor, though for different reasons
and in a very different way. He committed himself briefly and severely to "the new order." There was none of Pound's furious, apocalyptic writing. Certainly he did not share Pound's economic and
ideological justifications of fascism. He welcomed Hitler, but he
constantly interceded with him for captured members of the Norwegian resistance. He was over eighty when the Nazis came—and a
famous man quietly living out his last few years. To many Norwe-
gians his words of support for the Germans were but a final proof of
his "reactionary" style of life and his "irrelevant" books. When the
war ended, he was arrested, jailed, and in keeping with our century's
enlightenment, sent off to be queried and observed by a collection of
nurses, social workers, and of course psychiatrists.

All the while—from 1945 to 1948—he wrote down his thoughts
and experiences. He was nearing ninety; eventually the doctors
would tell a court that he should be let go because he was a "person
with permanently impaired faculties." He was found guilty, heavily
fined, and sent home to die. He lived on, though, and in 1949 published what he modestly called "trifles," all of them written by a man
under the constant examination of doctors. We now have those tri-

fles in English; they are a series of vivid, keen reflections, and they have been translated with real tenderness by Carl Anderson. Hamsun's title for this last book is *On Overgrown Paths*, and its haunting self-scrutiny justifies the author's right to claim that he was not only always sane but also considerably more intelligent and subtle of mind than his observers. Of course Hamsun never cares to argue with his jailers or doctors. He lets his words show his moods, his sadness, his detachment, his occasional wry humor, his open conversational intimacy with Death. One sees again how stupid, vulgar, or evasive it is possible for doctors and lawyers and judges to be. Hamsun wants justice, and he certainly preferred explicit condemnation to the humiliating and absurd treatment he received at the hands of his psychiatrists, who took "four months to affix learned labels to every conceivable state of mind I might have been in." In this, his last testament, he resumes a long-abandoned self; once again he is pointing out how insulting and humiliating people can be to other people. No one has done a better job of documenting the simple-minded, abusive, and condescending questions a breed of psychiatrists can ask and inflict on their patients.

To the very end, Hamsun could recognize banality, and he described it effortlessly but pointedly: "The professor required me to explain my 'two marriages' as he put it." Well, eventually the doctors "explained" more than his marriages. They brushed aside with medical and psychiatric jargon a complicated, defiant man who right under their eyes wrote mournful, cheerful, and loving words. At all times he comes across clear and unafraid. He does not deny his past or even try to excuse it. The paths he took were overgrown— certainly not as clear-cut as those who evaluated and judged him. Long before the Nazis arrived to make murder a "civilized" nation's chief purpose, Hamsun had withdrawn from the world out of choice, not because his mind was impaired. He lived long enough to see his personal prejudices and social fears become accessories to a much larger enterprise—the Nazi armies and crematoria. He died late enough to know that even the valleys and fjords he sought in sanctuary were of no avail. The inner and near-mad world that he first described in *Hunger* came back to plague him in the late evening of his life. Now madness was fantastically institutionalized; it was everywhere and into everything. Yet the Hamsun who as a youth virtually made a study of madness, of all that is weird and bizarre, was destined to be unprepared for what happened to Norway and to the world from 1940 to 1945. By the end of the war even Quisling and the Nazis ridiculed him. He was a tragic, broken, and discredited man who had not an ounce of dignity left. It seems that it was his accusers and his keepers who gave him back his dignity.

New Republic, September 23, 1967

The Song of the Painted Bird

I suppose in fifty years or so some sensitive social historian will pick up *Centuries of Childhood* by Philippe Ariès and realize how urgently it needs an epilogue—a long and frank account of what the most recent of centuries has seen fit to do with children. It will be a sad moment for us all, because the "progress" we have made has not kept us from unprecedented murder, of children among others. Germany, whose citizens believed strongly in science and contributed significantly to medicine, emerged as the Anti-Christ, ready to take the world to hell and laugh as we all burned. To the east we saw further irony. A socialist revolution committed to economic justice fell into the hands of a vulgar, suspicious tyrant who ordered people (and associates) killed for the most gratuitous and arbitrary reasons.

If Germany and Russia have furnished us naked totalitarianism at its worst, I need not remind anyone who has lived through these past few decades how persistently we have had to face the presence of war. There was Spain and the innocent families killed by both sides. There was Korea, only a few years after the *second* World War was over. Today there is Vietnam. Not for long in this century have we been spared the faces of terrorized children, made homeless or orphans by bombs, injured by fires and bullets, hungry and cold because soldiers have orders to kill one another and destroy whatever cannot be killed. For those of us in America, it is and has been far off. We may be asked to give a few dollars to "save the children" or to this or that rescue committee, but the boys and girls have belonged to other people.

A year or two ago a book appeared with the inviting but mysterious title *The Painted Bird*. From the literary viewpoint alone it was of interest: the author, Jerzy Kosinski, was a young Polish emigré who seemed in surprising control of the English language, and though we have had that kind of thing happen once before, the likelihood of a recurrence has always been considered small. Moreover, the form of the book was as unusual as its content. In it a boy narrates his experiences from age five or six to age twelve—though not the way it is done in a children's book. The book concerns itself with what must be one of the most sordid moments in man's entire history, and the child who lived through those moments—now to tell us about them—presumably is not talking to his age-mates but to *us*, who still murder and otherwise torment children.

In any event, *The Painted Bird* startled its reviewers, who could only say again and again how awful and terrifying yet haunting its pages turn out to be. They didn't have to give the plot much of a summary; we have learned to be unsurprised when mention is made of the Nazis and, in general, the Europe of a few years ago. One point was unusual though: the child is described as living in eastern Europe, and his experiences are not those inflicted upon inmates of concentration camps or prisoners of the German or Russian armies; rather, the boy moves from village to village, presumably in Poland, or Hungary, or thereabouts, so that the disasters he experiences could only indirectly be called the result of Hitler's war.

The sad facts of history make Hitler and Stalin mere successors to a long line of tyrants and exploiters whose benighted rule has kept countries like Poland incredibly backward for centuries. In 1782, a French nobleman and priest, Hubert Vautrin, came back to Lorraine after five years in Poland and Lithuania, full of somber and disheartening experiences and observations. In 1807, he published *L'Observateur en Pologne*, a book very much like de Tocqueville's *Democratie en Amérique*. Much of what the boy in *The Painted Bird* comes to experience is described by Vautrin: the coarse, violent men; the fearful, superstitious women; the extreme poverty, the extreme ignorance, the extreme suspiciousness; and side by side, the isolated centers of wealth and privilege shared by the nobility and, of all people, the bishops of the Church.

It is safe to say that the Eastern Europe of *The Painted Bird* would not surprise Vautrin. The nameless boy in Kosinski's novel—if that is the word for the book—takes us from village to village amid that squalid backwater of European civilization. At six he learns of war, and thereafter there is nothing to face but hate, punishment, hunger, fear, and death. He is dark but not Jewish. Because they have been anti-Fascists, his parents, city people, fear he will be killed on sight by the Nazis. Thus they surrender him to a man who promises to find foster parents for him in a distant village. As the Germans approach, the parents themselves flee. Within two months of his arrival, the boy's foster mother dies; and from then on, for years and years, the boy has to wander from village to village, as if hounded by God himself.

What is one to say about this book? When I first started reading it, I thought I would find a tender and gentle story, suited for a certain kind of high-school student who was near enough the age of the book's narrator to feel very much a part of his mind, if not of his experiences. That is one of the book's most brilliant and unnerving characteristics: it only gradually confronts the reader with the full dimensions of the evil it means to describe. In so doing, the author is true to life and perhaps enables us to understand how this boy—and others like him—kept alive in the face of what emerges finally as hell itself.

What else, after all, can people like us do but speculate intellectually on the implications—psychological, educational, moral, and theological—of such a book? As the pages became increasingly impossible to face—the brutality and violence, the monstrous, horrible injustice—I found myself more and more thoughtful, to the point that the book became rather stimulating by the end. That is, I had a dozen things to dwell on, all of them large and weighty issues.

In contrast, the boy's survival clearly had very little to do with his inability to speculate and analyze. Humiliated and degraded again and again, he becomes like his brutish oppressors and stubbornly holds on, even as they have for centuries. He does not fight them—that would mean certain death—but learns to crawl, to cling tenaciously to whatever miserable, wretched half-promise is available. Home is where you find it, and survival does not require mental health.

What, in fact, does happen to the boy's mind as he sees the darkest side of any moon that ever was? As do other exiles and outcasts, he develops a shrewd knowledge of the moods and susceptibilities of the powerful. If they are crudely sensual people, perverse and deceitful, he can be shrewdly disarming, cooperative, or evasive. Desperate fear and paralytic anxiety are perhaps luxuries of the comfortable or expressions of some last-ditch, impossible situation. The long, slow grind of most suffering and persecution exacts quite another order of adaptation from the victim. It is to this book's credit that the boy rather briskly sets about his business: accommodation in the interests of life. Let the middle-class American intellectuals fight over the morality of such behavior—when a Hannah Arendt exposes its banality, as she did in Eichmann in Jerusalem. Nor should the reader fall back upon the child's age. The author rather obviously sees him as a representative of all refugees, all outcasts, all suffering and debased people. His desire to persist, to live no matter what, can be found unbelievable or wrong—but only by those who cannot know how absurd it is for them even to try to comprehend the kind of choices that so-called civilized Europe presented to millions in our time.

The worst part of this book, this story that tells a million stories, comes at the end, when miraculously the child is found by his parents. For years he has escaped the instant death the Germans threatened and somehow had lived through a succession of inhuman and savage experiences: torture and hunger; sexual perversions of one sort or another, including the bestiality that Kraft-Ebbing attributed to "rustic" people; assault and, worse, comfort offered, then withdrawn; bizarre, mystifying encounters with an assortment of witches, idiots, and mad people. All this becomes if not second nature then life itself, world without end; until, that is, the world catches up with its own lunacy and confronts its bewildered prisoners with the fact that now all is well. To your feet—Jews, Negroes, gypsies, indeed poor people everywhere! We are through for a while. Thirty million died, and rest assured that in a few years there will be more bombs; but for a moment pause—and go back to your old ways. We will stop the firing squads, end the hangings, empty the prisons, and give orders that no more ovens be stoked. You, all of you, return to one another. Accept our retribution. Receive your rights, your vote, if that is what you want, and some bread. And be sensible, be mature. Forget the past, the broken twisted past—that some of you persist in seeing still at work, still around to exploit and murder in the name, always, of God and country. Look to the future, to what you can have, can be—that is, some of you. (Don't ask how many; that is something we shall have to learn in time.)

I suppose we too will have to wait and see how this boy and all the others manage. Fortunately, the author at least allows him the dignity of his own past, his own circumstances. He does not need guidance or "treatment." It is not a neurosis or psychosis that threatens him. Words like *rehabilitation* or *help*—with all their gratuitous, naive, and sometimes absurd implications—are not summoned. The boy had become mute, and his parents, whatever their love, cannot draw him out. He is back with them, but he prefers the company of night people, those who for a variety of reasons live on the edge of the law. His parents are worried and hurt, but the suffering they have in common with him prevents them from becoming moralistic. They do not find him full of "problems"; they see him naturally and appropriately reluctant to deal with any world except the brutal one he has learned to deal with and indeed now possesses.

Eventually he talks. He has gone off to ski, sent by his parents in the hope that hills and snow would be neutral territory. In a fierce blizzard, he again struggles for life, for action and yet another victory. Again the direction is downward; but now the struggle is different and weighted in his favor. In a hospital room, after sustaining injuries on the ski slopes, he hears a telephone and can answer it. That is the end of the book.

I note that in the original hardcover edition the author adds something more. The boy will find eastern Europe under the Communists as hard and oppressive as the life he experienced in the villages during the war. In point of fact, Jerzy Kosinski is a pen name for Joseph Novak, who wrote *The Future is Ours, Comrade,* and *No Third Path* before *The Painted Bird* was published. Fortunately, the paperback edition eliminates the author's desire to harness the power and originality of this story with a political sermon. Nothing in the book has prepared the reader for propaganda, and if Joseph Novak had to intrude on Jerzy Kosinski, he did it in the right way, with an obvious and expendable afterthought.

As for the world that presumably now has that boy as one of its men, the evil, hate, and murder continue. The title of *The Painted Bird* comes from an incident in the book. The boy meets up with Lekh, a birdcatcher who sadly and grimly paints birds and then releases them to be killed by their own kind. The boy is, of course, a painted bird, different in one or another respect from the majority. Yet I fear things are even worse these days. So many birds are hunting down so many other birds that the individual tragedies created by one birdcatcher seem almost exceptional. In our world, majorities not only persecute minorities; the strong not only persecute the weak; but the powerful set themselves against the powerful, and the earth itself must live in fear.

Harvard Educational Review, Summer 1967

Twentieth-Century
American Writers

An American Tragedy

Moralists wear many disguises, perhaps none more intriguing than the particular concealment practiced for so long by F. Scott Fitzgerald: his alcoholic, moneyed self-indulgence fueled a relentless self-examination, not to mention the stories and novels whose social scrutiny of America's values over a half century ago still works rather well when applied to our contemporary life. Fitzgerald has not lacked for the attention of critics or biographers. In a concluding section of *F. Scott Fitzgerald: A Biography* (the latest effort to comprehend as gifted and intriguing a literary personality as this country has produced in this century), André LeVot, a professor of American literature at the Sorbonne, offers a bibliographical essay titled "Fitzgerald's Posthumous Glory." We learn about hundreds and hundreds of reviews and critical essays and theses and memoirs written by friends and acquaintances. By now some two hundred books have been given over entirely or in major part to Fitzgerald and his work—and surely none of them offers the interested reader a better sense of who this complex writer was and what he was trying to do with his short, hectic, driven, persistently and fiercely expressive life than this new biography.

LeVot's biography is in the tradition of storytelling; a given life is an occasion for clear narrative presentation rather than an excuse for the assertion of one or another ideological claim. This century has been so dominated by sociological and psychological speculations and by materialist convictions with respect to the nature of our personal lives or our historical past that one is almost shocked by Professor LeVot's manner of approach to his subject. Moreover, F. Scott Fitzgerald was hardly a writer who managed to live a quiet, stable, uneventful life, reserving high drama, not to mention emotional turmoil, for his various fictions. I remember, as a matter of fact, a spirited panel discussion on Fitzgerald's work at Harvard in the late 1950s. I was all full of psychiatry then, taking my training in it. "Poor Scott," one elder statesman of the English department whispered to another, "they're devouring him." The "they" were critics rather uncritically infatuated with the blandishments of psychoanalytic psychiatry, and I fear I was one of their enthusiastic listeners. Lest a pair of elderly gentlemen get in our way, even through a barely audible comment, I took upon myself the obligation of defense—and the best kind, we know, is an attack. In my mind it went like this: poor old creatures—they are blind to the truths of psychoanalytic formulations and hence fearfully willing to identify themselves with a very, very sick man.

Nor is such self-protective idiocy only the property of naive young "trainees," as we were called. (We were, alas, the same age then as the author of *The Great Gatsby* was when it was published!) I expected Professor LeVot to remind us that alcoholism is a serious psychiatric disorder and to show us how Fitzgerald's literary work reflected his mind's disorder, revealing those preoccupations we've learned to connect to this or that kind of psychopathology. I also expected to hear more of what I'd heard back then at Harvard about the well-known *folie à deux*—mad Zelda and her wild-living husband, Scott. Yet Professor LeVot is French, and not once does that term get used. But then we'd learned more than twenty years ago that the French had never really taken to psychoanalysis the way Americans had—a certain national or cultural "resistance," perhaps. Of course these days, with Lacan and his school so evident, one remembers that all "resistances" aren't bad—and as a matter of fact one is saddened, in this instance, at the inroads made upon a particular nation's posture of skepticism.

For a particular French intellectual, however, the old-fashioned psychology of F. Scott Fitzgerald (who knew a thing or two about how the mind works) is still suggestive and compelling enough to require no faddish additives—nor the reductionist schemes so many of us find necessary. LeVot's biography is intensely loyal to the particulars of a given time spent on this earth. He has immersed himself in factuality so that he can chronicle not only the big, important moments but the illuminating details of everyday life—and, of course, Fitzgerald was never one to get lost in boredom. For instance, in June of 1925 Fitzgerald sent *The Great Gatsby* to Edith Wharton, whose writing he had long admired. She was impressed, and replied with a "detached analysis" of the book's strengths. She also invited Fitzgerald to lunch, and eventually he would go. LeVot interviewed Esther Murphy, who drove the young American to the much older American's home. Here is the way LeVot describes the trip:

> Zelda, not very interested in being judged by a woman of the world known for her caustic wit, refused to go along, and Fitzgerald, full of apprehension, went without her. He stopped frequently in cafes along the way for quick drinks to calm his nerves. According to Miss Murphy, this took so much time that she had to phone Saint-Brice [Mrs. Wharton's home] to warn that they would be late for lunch.

We learn more, naturally—that the Claudels and Bourgets were also guests at that lunch, that Mrs. Wharton was austere, that Fitzgerald tried to hold himself together, tight as he was, but ended up telling a rambling story about some friends of his who had taken a room in a supposedly quiet Paris hotel that was, they finally realized, a brothel. Mrs. Wharton wanted to know more, much more: who were these people, and how did they respond to this situation? A novelist's questions all right, to which Fitzgerald had no answers. He was silent thereafter, to the point of everyone's obvious, continuing embarrassment. Mrs. Wharton put down a single word, "Horrible!" to describe her sense of that event.

The above was no major, dramatic crisis (and there were plenty of these) in Fitzgerald's life. But this was a revealing episode, worthy of note not only for its biographical significance but as a moment of sorts in the history of American letters. Moreover, the rhythm of a day in Fitzgerald's life is persuasively conveyed—not merely as an illustrative point but as a story that needs telling; the day shows Fitzgerald's alcoholism gaining momentum, shows writers of distinctively different generations unable to accept each other, and shows the influence of French life on American expatriates who tried ever so hard to lose a supposed innocence and gain access to a cosmopolitan culture's ostensible self-assurance. For LeVot, the ascertained details possess their own cumulative, edifying lesson, at once psychological and moral, as in a well-told story. We see Fitzgerald at the top of his reputation and *still* apprehensive, earnestly anxious for approval, and willing to sing for his supper, so to speak. Any conclusions—again, as in a story—depend upon the reader's sensibility: one feels an inclination toward the younger writer, with his fragile pride, his fearful innocence, or toward the older one, with her vulnerability and her apprehension of the quite definite limits of mortality—that of a body of work as well as of a particular body. For this biographer, Fitzgerald lived an exceptionally instructive life. Let others stress the waste, the scandal, the self-indulgence, the impetuous, or the plain stupid; LeVot responds to the moral, even puritanical rhythms of a man whom others choose to view in terms of the theatrical—the comic and the tragic, the farcical and the stagy. Zelda is not allowed to take over this story, nor is her own decline turned into a melodramatic, catchall explanation of another decline, that of her writing husband. Fitzgerald was not only (upon occasion) drinking heavily but blacking out upon doing so before he ever met her. Anyway, she inspired him mightily and, it can be said, sobered him up—that is, she brought him face to face with the terrible implications of his own wild, hurt, fractious egoism. At the same time, her long-standing, incurable insanity revealed conclusively the intricate and unyielding ethical side of her husband's life. He was a loyal, decent, generous man—and the contrast, say, with Hemingway (a comparison so many have made in a literary or man-to-man vein) is significant with respect to their natures as husbands. Here LeVot is, again, quite detailed, anxious to show us two giants in all their rather evident, flawed humanity. He is, of course, similarly enriching when he renders the expatriate years, all that time the Fitzgeralds spent in France.

Youth, success, fame, money—all of that was unable to protect Fitzgerald from the unnerving demands of his eyes, his ears, his raw intelligence, and his passion for telling, telling. He was always at work. At one point LeVot puts the matter this way: "The basic alternative appeared in almost allegorical terms after he came to know the Murphys and Hemingway: to expend his talent in living or in writing." But living for Fitzgerald *was* writing; nothing in his life escaped the notice of his feverishly alert, knowing mind, and everything was grist for his literary workings. Put differently, LeVot has written a biography of a writer for whom the short story and the novel were a means of autobiographical comprehension, of performance, and not least, of moral reflection and moral exorcism.

Fitzgerald knew how all of us struggle with vanity, with the pride that the upper intelligentsia is not, in this century, inclined to regard as the sin of sins. In the character of Gatsby (whose evil was no match, really, for ours) and in that of Dick Diver (whose descent into purgatory or hell is almost emblematic for many students—and not only those in medical school—who wonder what will become of them and why), a bold and shrewd writer gave us ourselves, all too covetously enamored of what is all too readily available "this side of paradise." Dr. Diver, like Dr. Lydgate before him, begs our interpretation but also our shuddering mercy, we who in significant numbers aim to pick and choose our way through the wares (personal and professional both) of this life. Fitzgerald's moral assumptions were very much like those of Dr. Lydgate's creator, George Eliot. Eliot and Fitzgerald were two writers who tried hard but in vain to shake off their Christian scrupulosity, two writers for whom psychology was not a bundle of ponderous terms and self-important pronouncements but the earned wisdom life presents to those who attend closely its various aspects. With this book André LeVot brings us (and himself, of course) closer, as have some of Eliot's biographers, to the two writers' urgently scrutinizing and essentially righteous company.

Virginia Quarterly Review, Spring 1984

Shadowing Binx

In late 1956 I was a psychiatric resident at the Massachusetts General Hospital in Boston—and wondering why, not to mention whither. I had stumbled into psychiatry out of frustration, innocence, and inadequacy. Indeed, I'd stumbled into medical school for somewhat confused if not inappropriate reasons. As an undergraduate I'd become much taken with the poems, short stories, and novels of William Carlos Williams. My advisor (and hero) at Harvard, Perry Miller, had encouraged me to write my thesis on the first book of Williams' *Paterson*; I had thereby come to correspond with and then get to know Dr. Williams, who was at the time in good health but who would soon enough be struggling with several illnesses. His writing life was my intellectual concern, but I became interested in the uncanny and (I thought then, and still do) exemplary intensity of his personal commitment to his medical practice—to his working-class patients, actually—despite all the headaches involved. Such passionate attentiveness to hurt and ailing men, women, and children struck me as an edifying contrast to, well, my own late-adolescent self-centeredness. Moreover, I was beginning to wonder what the devil I'd be doing with this uncertain stretch of time given each of us called a life to live. In that regard, I seemed by my junior year badly adrift. Others I knew were headed in one or another direction—and their determination was often, in those years after the Second World War, a reasonable response to their past experiences as veterans. But I was younger, and my battles were, it seemed, taking place in my head.

Once, while seeing Dr. Williams work with his patients (he was an old-fashioned doc who regularly visited the tenements of northern New Jersey and made no fortune doing so), I told him I was at loose ends and wished there were a doctor like him to attend my dreary ills. He laughed, even as I was half-joking. We then got a bit serious, and when he asked me my "interests," I answered theology and moral philosophy and American literature, all of which, in a way, I was studying with the brilliant and inspiring Perry Miller. Perhaps I could pursue that line of study, connect literature and history with theology in some fashion; but to do so meant going to graduate school, and I had no real inclination in that direction. Instead, I talked of finding a job, any job, and in my spare time reading and thinking about what gets called one's "future."

Dr. Williams's response was characteristically quick, sharp, concrete, specific, and yes, impatient: "Try medicine, why don't you! Lots to keep you busy, and lots to make you think. The great thing is—you get to forget yourself a lot of the time."

I was properly reprimanded and prompted to get going—somehow—down some road. And I did. I took chemistry, biology, and physics and applied to some schools; and with the help of one very patient, kindly (and, I now realize, properly puzzled) interviewer at Columbia's College of Physicians and Surgeons, the biochemist Philip Miller, I got into medical school.

Once there I continued to flounder badly. I had trouble working in the labs; I had trouble dissecting the cadaver. I would go visit old Doc Williams and tell him I was wasting my time. He said no; he said "stick it out"; he said in the long run I'd be glad I ended up knowing how to use a stethoscope and a neurological hammer and an ophthalmoscope. I argued with him but was convinced. I got by—but I read lots of novels, took courses at Union Theological Seminary, and got myself signed up to work in a small hospital in rural India. I was searching for ascetic indulgence, an obligation nurtured in my head by my idealistic mother, who would always tell me how I must "give unto others," and so on and so on, until at times, as a child hearing that talk, I would want to run and buy a Cadillac or a gold watch—anything to show how independent or immune I was.

I tried pediatrics after medical school and had trouble with the children: they'd cry bloody murder when I approached them with a syringe needle or an otoscope. I'd say soothing things; and correctly, they'd not believe me, and I began to realize I hadn't the iron in me to be the best friend a sick child needs—an effective, able physician who gets done what has to be done so that a diagnosis is set and treatment begun. It was at this point (in 1955) that my friend Dr. Williams suggested psychiatry—a proffered solution that meant, I feared, his complete loss of respect for me. So I signed up for the psychiatric residency, and I kept reading: more and more novels, lots of poetry, and magazines, all sorts of them—for example, the fall issue (1956) of the *Partisan Review*, in which I found a piece called "The Man on the Train."

I was drawn to the title, and at one point in reading the essay, I remember checking to see who the author was: someone named Walker Percy. I remember saving that issue, then throwing it away, having cut out the Percy essay. I showed it to my friends. One of them, a Catholic doctor training in surgery, returned the favor a year or so later with two issues of *Commonweal* featuring articles by the same Walker Percy, who carefully identified himself as a physician but *not* a psychiatrist, even though he had titled those articles "The Coming Crisis of Psychiatry." The essays were a tonic, and I glowed: they pointedly exposed all the dreary, smug tautological reasoning of the social sciences—all the secular, agnostic obsessions of self-preoccupied people for whom the mind was the latest fad, if not the last refuge and hope. The essays also offered a knowing, appreciative critique: Percy respected Freud's contributions to human knowledge, yet he saw in the reductionist labeling, in the arrogant, condescending postures, both the overwrought generalizations and the messianic promises of a certain species of experts, a certain category of American doctors. And these doctors represented what we had all become in mid-twentieth-century America, namely, a people terribly afraid and alone, dangerously adrift, cut loose from our spiritual moorings.

In 1958 I found myself in the United States Air Force under the auspices of the doctors' draft, which fingered all of us physicians at that time. I was sent to Keesler Air Force Base in Biloxi, Mississippi, and put in charge of a large military neuropsychiatric unit—forty beds, and a substantial out-patient evaluation service. I was now, at twenty-seven, a psychiatrist; I had even taken my further specialty training in child psychiatry. I had a sports car. I was a captain, and with the help of my uniform, which turned potentially hostile Mississippi policemen into smiling onlookers, I could speed along on Route 90, along the beaches of the Gulf of Mexico, past the lovely ocean-front homes of Pass Christian, over the Bay St. Louis Bridge, over smaller bridges, traversing bayous, then along Gentilly through the suburban outskirts of New Orleans, "The City That Care Forgot." Finally the sign: Elysian Fields Avenue, which can connect with Desire; and then the low-slung buildings, columned or with elaborate grillwork and high, high windows; and bars open all day and all night, and jukeboxes with lots of Louis Armstrong, and restaurants with fine, fine food, and soon, Preservation Hall and its jazz; and The River, and its levees, and those enormous tropical plants, and tall, wide (and enveloping) trees and azaleas everywhere; and plenty of attractive women, who even in January or February wore no coats to hide or mar the lines of their bodies; and after a while a doctor to visit, one of those shrinks (we were calling them shrinks then, too) who examines heads gone awry.

"Captain Coles," said the colonel in charge of the big Biloxi hospital, "why do you need to go see a psychiatrist in New Orleans when *you're* one, and in charge of four others? Are you looking for excuses to visit that city?"

The charming innocence, I thought—but he was a tough, cynical man: No, the captain avers: depression, that's it, low spirits, down in the dumps, moodiness that won't go away.

"Hell," says the boss, "we all get like that sometimes, and it's not a 'problem,' it's part of life!"

I remember looking at him closely at that minute, saying to myself: the smart old bastard, he may be right, and I might save a few dollars and lots of time if I dared give his way of seeing things a chance. But no, I was in trouble, I definitely was—all those movies!

The movies: I'd been going to them more and more—so much that I couldn't find enough to see for the first time on any given day. (This was not New York, or Cambridge, where in fact I'd not gone much at all, but "La.–Miss.," as the combined two-state abbreviation was often rendered on advertisements.) I'd go to see my analyst every afternoon, and I'd go to a movie afterwards, then there'd be a girl-friend, a long ride in the car, a jazz bar—and, too commonly, memories of the movie intruding in my mind as I talked with the young lady, or as I made hospital rounds the next morning and talked with all those tough, strong, brave SAC pilots who were defending us against anyone and everyone and flying incredible speeds in incredible planes—and were also breaking down in fear and in tears, unaccountably it always seemed.

"Doc, what in hell does this life mean?" one hot-shot jet pilot kept asking me, and some scene out of some movie would come to mind—*Purple Noon*, for example, which I saw five times, and wherein the hero (Alain Delon) gets away with everything (money, love, adventure) and sails into the warm, Mediterranean sun: *that's the meaning of life!*

"Why do you keep seeing *Purple Noon?*" my Prytania Street doctor asked. "Why do you see those James Dean movies over and over—what do they, what does he, *mean* to you?"

"Dunno." Then, on my back, my face turned toward the wall, I would see a scene in *East of Eden* or *Rebel without a Cause*, or one or another John Wayne movie, or Billy Holden in *Sunset Boulevard*, a movie I'd not seen when it came out (1950, I believe) but saw three times in three days in New Orleans in 1960.

The Moviegoer was published on May 15, 1961. I read it in the fall of that year—an obscure novel, headed for extinction, a few hundred copies sold, mostly in New Orleans.

"He lives here, in Covington, across the Lake" (Pontchartrain) I was told by the clerk in Doubleday's bookstore on Canal Street, when I seemed to be clutching at the book, afraid to let it go, so he could (all he wanted!) see the price.

I missed my movie that afternoon and evening. I phoned "a certain someone," as the author of *The Moviegoer* puts it, to claim illness. I finished the novel around midnight. I took a slug or two of bourbon: who *is* this Walker Percy?

"But the real question," said the Prytania Street analyst the next day, "is who are you?"

"What do you mean?"

"You're always asking questions in response to my questions."

"What do you mean?"

"There you go again."

"Well, I'm now seeing that movie *Purple Noon* again—the sky, the water, the boat speeding away."

"You are?"

"Yes." Long silence.

It is, I fear, a psychological banality of our time that biographers have their personal reasons when they happen upon their subject, someone's life and work. For me Walker Percy's writing has offered a continuing intensity of awareness and, I suppose, self-recognition. His writing has made me feel less lonely and more in touch with this world: his has been a voice in the wilderness, to use a phrase, and a voice that makes one's own high-pitched raspy drone seem less peculiar and, yes, not quite so loony. To my mind Binx was, for all too long I fear, myself writ large—put into a book, rendered for others. "You seem to be shadowing Binx," the New Orleans doctor said. I was delighted: Binx had become real enough for *him* so that he had stopped addressing him (disdainfully, I thought) as "this fictional character in *The Moviegoer*, Binx Bolling." But doctor, thinks the snotty analysand, of course a character in a novel is "fictional"! (Best not to tell him what just came into the head; he'll be offended.) "Are you thinking of something now?" asks the doctor, aware of a restless pause.

"Oh hell, I was just being a jerk in my mind again."

Then I had, well, not a vision of *Purple Noon* but this question, and I wondered aloud to the listening alienist: did Walker Percy ever see a psychoanalyst?

"How would I know?"

Yet another long lull. Years later I would get to ask the question in person.

I found out in 1973 that the answer is yes. In 1966, actually, I had begun to suspect so, having read *The Last Gentleman*. Will Barrett was Binx up North, Binx moving across America, Binx still on "the search," which was mentioned in *The Moviegoer* and enacted in *The Last Gentleman*. And "the search" is what the *New Yorker* editors called the profile I did of Dr. Percy, published in 1978.

For me, the act of asking the *New Yorker* whether I might write about Walker Percy's essays and novels and the act of getting in touch with him to say that such a project was feasible were—I suppose the characterizing word is *existential*. Percy's essays and novels are efforts to explore the moral and spiritual dimensions of the twentieth-century middle-class life so many of us live in America, with our god Mammon, our materialist culture and its artifacts, and with the mind and the promise of science, including the so-called social sciences. Percy is in the tradition of novelists such as Dostoevski, Kafka, Sartre, and Camus—a contemporary American mind at work connecting European existentialist reflections to storytelling and essay writing. For me, a magazine profile about him and his writing and a later book about the same were chances to address some preoccupations I'd long possessed (been possessed by!). Moreover, Percy's humor is obvious, highly developed, and important to his work—and I found it from the first especially intriguing and powerful. That wry, modest, pointedly ironic humor is very much a hovering presence, with the eyes ever aware, the faint smile, the head slightly tilted: hey, what's next to see and to hear, as the clock ticks and the human parade continues?

In person, Percy is intelligent, hospitable, gracious, informative, alert, willing to be friendly, and generous with information about his life, his ideas, his questions, and the answers he's tried to find for himself. Existentialism emphasizes the meeting of people, the so-called encounter, the fidelity (Gabriel Marcel's term) that we seek of each other—of ourselves as would-be spiritual kin of others. For me, Percy has been that, a spiritual kinsman—if I dare presume a substantial moral and intellectual connection to him as a physician, a writer, a person anxious to ask lots of questions about the nature of things, and willing, also, to be unhappy with lots of all too readily accepted, influential answers.

I never had any intention of trying to bring my psychiatric training into this personal effort—this friendship with an interesting, thoughtful, enjoyable, and relaxing friend. I was doing an *intellectual* biography, to be somewhat self-important about the task. The result was a lot of reading, some of it damn difficult for me: Heidegger and Merleau-Ponty and Husserl, not to mention the relatively more accessible, if no less weighty and suggestive philosophers Buber, Marcel, and Jaspers. Percy himself is a learned man indeed. His humor and his storytelling gifts mask a penetrating, wide-ranging, eager intellect. For years before he wrote his essays, never mind his novels, he studied philosophy, ethics, and theology, and he read and read in the New Orleans home he occupied with his wife, Bunt, in the early years of their marriage. His deep knowledge of Kierkegaard is a real challenge to those of us who want to know what he is really about. I've read *The Moviegoer* four times, and each time I see more of that difficult, provocative, unnerving Danish essayist and theologian in the story of Binx and his struggle to figure out how (and with whom) to live a life. Since I've continued to teach Percy's writing, fiction and nonfiction, both to college students and medical students, I sometimes find myself rather disappointed with my own interpretations, as rendered in the profile I did and the book I wrote. A particular student does much better; and when prodded by the requirements of leading a seminar, giving a lecture, or responding to students' questions during office hours, I find myself a much better reader and critic of, say, "The Message in the Bottle" (an essay of his I especially love) or *Love in the Ruins* (a novel my medical students find compelling) than I'd once been as the anxiously knowing and assertive writer intent on examining a particular philosophical novelist's work.

My own lack of interest in applying psychoanalytic metaphors to the lives of men and women such as Walker Percy and Flannery O'Connor (did not Freud himself give us permission to abandon the idea when he tried to confront the genius of Dostoevski?) may have, at times, been an unnecessary obstacle in comprehending Percy's literary life. He himself observed, after reading an early version of my profile, that his father's suicide was a given and not by any means a secret. He had no objection to the mention of that important event in his life and those of his two younger brothers. I had not wanted to conceal the fact, yet I feared not so much the busybodies of the world as the fools. Among whom, these days, are those obsessed by psychology, as we see in the "Living" pages of all our newspapers and, regrettably, in a substantial segment of our intellectual life: the terms *psychosocial* and *psychohistorical* and *psychopolitical* appear world without end, it seems. To be sure, a father's self-imposed death and a mother's accidental death two years later can be, *were*, an enormous ordeal for a young teenager, and surely for his even younger brothers. They were adopted by their cousin, the distinguished lawyer and poet and essayist William Alexander Percy, and he was a wonderfully thoughtful, kind, decent, and generous person. But pain there was, sadness and disappointment—and yet Walker Percy the novelist is not at all to be *explained* by such unlucky personal circumstances; else we'd have hundreds of thousands of others, remarkably gifted because remarkably injured by all sorts of tragedies that children all over the world suffer.

True, one can argue, the issue is *themes*—the relationship between a kind of suffering and a topical continuity in a given writer's life. But do one scene in *The Last Gentleman* (the recollected suicide of Will Barrett's father) and one scene in *The Second Coming* (Will's potentially suicidal descent into a cave) constitute a preoccupation? And even if existentialism itself, arguably, can be deemed a mode of philosophical inquiry characterized by speculation as to the meaning of life and the meaning of death—with despair a constant threat and challenge—we still must wonder whether each of those men and women taken by that line of reflection is to be declared morbid, neurotic, or endlessly compelled by obscure or all too apparent childhood injuries to ruminative speculation.

Needless to say, a knowing summons of psychoanalytic theory as an instrument of biographical inquiry requires the constant reminder that conflict is in everyone, that we are all neurotics, that even craziness lurks in each mind, though most of us fight it back successfully, and that (very important) there is no straight line between any particular trauma any of us experiences and any future interest, capacity, predilection, or antipathy we happen to end up having. How we love the *this-equals-that* way of thinking, as if the salt of our lives is a constant matter of adding Na to Cl, and voilà! The texture of any life is, in the end, a mystery—or if that word scares or embarrasses the twentieth-century reader, then at the least he or she has to settle for an astonishing degree of complexity, the result of irony and contingency and paradox and inconsistency and chance or luck (good and bad) all doing their exceedingly intricate work, so that one's fate, so often regarded as linear by us in the convenience (and ambition) of retrospect, has in actuality been a matter of personal circumstances gradually emerging, with a turn here, a setback there, a leap forward now, a stretch of consolidation then. The correct model, of course, is George Eliot's vision in *Middlemarch*, or Tolstoy's in *War and Peace*, wherein even those large-scale events, war and political reform, exert their chief encouraging or disabling influences on the particular lives of human beings. Hence history both public and private has been an intensely shaping force on the development of personality, character, and talent. I wonder whether Percy's essays, or indeed his novels, especially *Love in the Ruins* and *Lancelot*, can be illuminated by reference not only to Percy the existentialist, or the physician, or indeed the physician whose parents died when he was relatively young and who fell dangerously sick himself with tuberculosis when in his twenties, but to Percy the American who watched the world go utterly mad, murderously so, in the late 1930s and early 1940s.

For me, writing about Percy's work was a way of learning what I believed—how I saw and comprehended this world. I had, long ago it now seems, "shadowed Binx," as many of us have—lucky and comfortable heirs of Western civilization who nevertheless are quizzical, at loose ends often enough, and not sure what really matters, even as we go about our appointed rounds, accumulating certifications and cash and nods and having our "relationships." Now older, I see Binx still, in my students and my patients, in my sons growing up, and still in myself as I catch myself up to his (my) old tricks; and I think of Binx while walking and noticing, driving and forgetting, stopping and all of a sudden—yes, feeling that one, by god, *is*: that elusive *being* of those high-and-mighty existential philosophers. In a sense, then, doing a certain kind of biography of Percy has in this instance meant not so much dealing with this or that challenge, so far as the subject goes, as coming to terms with one's subjectivity.

To repeat the old question: who is this Walker Percy? He is, a biographer finds out, not only a doctor, an essayist, a novelist, but a rather thoughtful and humorous and unpretentious human being. I think of him, again, as a friend, a person of wisdom, still there—with whom to correspond, to whom one turns for a now-and-then conversation or a drink or two of bourbon. Is friendship fair game as a variable, to be discussed as an aspect of the relationship that develops between biographer and subject? Is a "good and decent example" another variable? Ought we mention the pleasure we've obtained—the fortunate and delightful encounter with a wry, quiet, but strong and lively intelligence? We are all (in one or another way or moment) lonely, as those existentialists Walker Percy knows so well have insisted again and again. Still, their own tradition is sturdy and growing and, not least, a real and mighty help to us. Each of them is a presence for many of us (and a book can be a persuasive companion), and so we may often feel less lonely. Sometimes I will look at my Percy shelf and think of statements I've heard him make, of time spent chewing the fat with him (and dissolving it in a good, strong amber fluid), and incline, just then at least, a little more toward *yes* in respect to this life rather than toward *no* or *maybe*; a consequence, for one soul, not of "doing work on" or "doing a biography of" but *getting to know* another soul.

In Peter Graham, ed., *Literature and Medicine*, vol. 4, 1985

Frank Conroy
Manchild in the Promised Land

I recently went through the heartache of committing a young man to a mental institution in Boston. He is twenty-two and last year graduated from Harvard. I had known him as a student, not as a patient. Once, in a paper, he scorned psychiatrists and the clichés they peddle to America's middle class: "Psychiatrists offer people with diplomas, but no real education, a pleasant, good-tasting stew—a dash of medicine, a little bit of philosophy, some 'art,' some 'science,' some 'depth.' We eat it and for a moment we don't feel hungry any more."

He went on to demonstrate how easily and outrageously "the psychiatric world-view" (as he called a particular profession's ideological tendencies) takes care of life's ironies and riddles. There are all those labels, all those ways of giving a name to a person or calling a person a name. There is "mental health," which sounds as if it can be determined by a thermometer or a stethoscope. And there are the doctors themselves, urging on their patients "adaptation," or "adjustment," or "group experience." Still, his concluding remarks were charitable—and full of yet another set of images:

> The blind lead the blind. Psychiatrists are not the idiots or monsters that some critics would have them be. They are trying to keep the traffic on our new highways moving. They are the good cop, and we are grateful to them. They tell us where we're supposed to go, the best way to get there. If we get stalled, they help us out—with a push or a ride. If a car doesn't belong on the road they take care of that, too. They know where all the junk yards are, all the repair shops and service stations. They know the land, the larger picture. With their special radios and telephones and sirens and whirling lights they can "communicate" better than the rest of us.

Now he has had to take cover, and I was the cop who told him how. A gifted, sensitive youth, he does not have a good prognosis. His past and all his early sorrows and later confusions are pressing on him with a vengeance. I suppose I could go back and read his various themes or papers and find in them the signs, the foreboding evidence that all was not and would not be well. We're good at that, looking back at a life and making sense of it. We're good at explaining things, at making statements about what happened or what *is*. We're not falsely modest either. Here, for example, is how a psychoanalyst comes to terms with the issue of creativity: "The problem is not one of organic inferiority per se, but rather one of body image formation, permanently distorted self-representation, cathectic imbalance, irreversible ego impairment and ego restitution."

So you see, it's not so mysterious after all. One man's "irreversible ego impairment" contrasts with another's "ego restitution." Writers like Frank Conroy may have had a bad time of it, but they don't go under. They swim, or rather, they "restitute." Now I don't know why you restitute and I go mad with megalomania and have to enter a hospital, or become a psychiatrist, or an astronaut in love with the wild blue yonder, or a president of the United States. But "we don't have all the answers," as I hear it put occasionally at clinical staff conferences. Unfortunately, Gertrude Stein never got around to asking psychiatrists to ask themselves what *questions* they have (or should have) in mind.

All of this comes to my mind as I think about Frank Conroy's autobiography, *Stop-time*, an unnerving, beautifully wrought book whose influence becomes at times hypnotic. The author summons his childhood so insistently, so shrewdly, so provocatively that the reader has no choice but to submit. A novelist takes advantage of an agreed-upon tradition that provides the writer and the audience with the common ground of the mind's willingness to read and *imagine*. The ordinary biographer (or the "great man" who writes his own biography) calls upon something else. We all recognize glory; and if we can't achieve it, we can at least learn of (and immerse ourselves in) its rise and fall. But what of the "ordinary" men and women who have only their own unspectacular stories to tell? They refuse us the free reign of fantasy. They give us no example to follow, no clues about how to win, about onetime or seeming losers somehow coming out on top. All we have, in this instance, is Frank Conroy. He is upon us because he is a writer, but he appears to have very little consideration for us. Who is he, after all, and why should we care what happened to him when he was a small boy? As a writer, of course, Frank Conroy's task is to make us care. He must exercise the power and skill of his writing hand in such a way that we forgive him for the explicitly factual or real content of his book, that we forgive him, indeed, for being a young, unknown person just beginning his career. Nor can he really fall back on the admittedly strange or unusual features of his past—no doubt full of "distorted self-representations" and even a few serious "cathectic imbalances." Yes, his parents were an offbeat pair, the mother, Dagmar, from a bourgeois Danish family, the father a rather well-to-do man with a ruinous capacity for alcohol and a turn of mind that could be variously called bizarre, gothic, unconventional, or pathological. And yes, not all children lose their fathers when young and then acquire a stepfather like Jean, who isn't really a Southerner, a fading aristocrat from the region's "old-order," but an un-American gentleman, literally a soft, delicate, useless man cut off from the worldly and cynical French nobility. America's schemes and chances tempt Jean; he wants to graft them on to himself. He spends his life trying to do so, but the transplant won't take. Though he behaves like a buccaneer or an entrepreneur who someday will make it—and prove everyone conventionally wrong—he is at heart a very sad man, given to foolish ideas that lead nowhere. For his stepson, though, he is a decent and reasonably tolerant man—something, if not enough.

Jean and Dagmar lived wandering, pointless lives. They moved from New York to Florida and back. For a while they settled in a home for retarded children where they worked as caretakers or aides on the night shift. They gained and then lost an assortment of jobs, and were it not for a substantial income from Dagmar's first husband, from Frank Conroy's father, they might well have lived classically poor and shiftless lives. With money guaranteed every month they could be eccentric, marginal, foolish—but well fed, well clothed, and even at times rather indulgent. In fact, money has a critical role in their activities and in their son's survival and emergence as an intelligent, observant, well-educated person. They have to have some purpose, and the vain pursuit of a fortune is a convenient one, along with sex or escapist travel.

Whatever their hang-ups or problems, they do not emerge in their son's eyes as particularly awful or cruel people. They are each self-centered and in a way bound to one another by that shared trait. They gave Frank Conroy a kind of distant attention, which in turn enabled him to become a detached, knowing, stubbornly independent person. They have eyes only for themselves, and he develops an almost frightening "cool": what is there is seen, but quietly and exactly rather than excitedly. There are lapses, when he runs away and the whole world seems ready to cave in. He is someone about to give up, perhaps fatally so. For a moment things appear blurred, confused, and dangerous, but recovery comes quickly and soon the wayward youth is back in a comfortable New York apartment. His mother is in Europe, his stepfather is hopelessly caught up in an affair with a madwoman. He is left with the consolations of comfortable privacy and a chance to forge his own way, his own world.

It is, of course, foolish to speculate about what might have become of Frank Conroy had he not been left a substantial and carefully controlled income by his father. He himself comes to the end of his story on a distinctly hopeful note: "My trustee had paid my tuition and agreed to an allowance of a hundred dollars a month. I was rich and I was free."

He had been admitted to Haverford College, and somehow he knew even then that his future was not as bleak and foundering as his parents' lives were. If they had done nothing else they had provided him with an example *not* to follow—no mean gift for an otherwise capable and determined young man. Had there been no Haverford for him, no trip to Paris, no Jaguar to drive, might he have become one more drifter, one more sad or desperate man whose struggles lead to nothing remotely like the book *Stop-time?*

To be sure, the rich produce more than their fair share of tormented souls, but Frank Conroy's book is among other things an additional reminder—if any is needed—that money, plain old money, crass and vulgar money, helps a lot and can even be called redemptive now and then. When a brilliant and sensitive young man is moody and on the run, it is handy to have the range of possibilities and opportunities that a steady income enables. In fact, one feels that all along the loneliness and confusion of Frank Conroy's early life were no match for what he could see and do as an intelligent person whose parents could give him, in place of love, a certain easy and ironic confidence that luck is a real thing and that fate is generous if not kind. He quite obviously knows all this because he avoids self-pity, demonstrates his capacity for humor, and in general emerges as a man who has had his troubles but is well on his way to making them much less significant than his power and competence as a writer.

Partisan Review, Winter 1969

J. D. Salinger
Coming Full Circle

By now J. D. Salinger's Holden Caulfield would be approaching forty, and perhaps (with him one can't be certain) he would have fathered one or two of those children he dreamed of catching, in case their frolic in the rye led them dangerously astray. By no means have readers wearied of Holden. As of April 1972 his youthful preoccupations had gone into their thirty-third paperback printing. It is hard to estimate the influence of a widely read book, but surely few writers have affected certain young people of a generation as strongly as Salinger did in the 1950s and into the early 1960s. And by some fateful irony, his stories stopped appearing at just the point that some of his longtime admirers began to turn to other writers and thinkers for sanction—as if he sensed that he had gone as far as he could in a particular direction: so, better silence than repetition, or worse, the scorn of the young idealists whose sense of the world he had made such a keen effort to understand.

Over and over again Salinger's name crossed the lips of the white, middle-class Civil Rights activists who a decade ago began to leave Ivy League colleges for work in the South. I was living in the South then, working with SNCC (the Student Nonviolent Coordinating Committee) and with the black and white youths who pioneered school desegregation. Scarcely a day went by that Salinger's name wasn't mentioned. For the high-school students, including a number of black ones we were talking with, Holden Caulfield was very much a saint of sorts. Others were fooled by all the "phonies" who run and work in schools, but Holden knew better, and perhaps (the hope was repeatedly expressed) some of those who read about him would gain enough toughness and imaginativeness of spirit to follow his example. Of course those youths often failed to mention what happened to Holden; in the last chapter he is in a psychiatric hospital, and one guesses it is a private one. In contrast, that outcome certainly was not ignored by the somewhat older youths who had interrupted those blissful years at Harvard, Yale, the University of Chicago, or Berkeley for a stint of by no means easy political protest in obscure counties of Mississippi, Alabama, or Louisiana. To them Salinger had become a temporary enemy of sorts—the lot of any fallen hero, I suppose.

As I returned to *The Catcher in the Rye* and *Franny and Zooey*, I thought of what I had heard in the South ten years ago—it seems like a century has intervened; and so at my wife's suggestion I also went through again some of my old working notes and reports. Here, for instance, is what I heard one evening in a Freedom House, set up in the Mississippi Delta during the summer of 1964:

> There was a time I thought Salinger was God Almighty—he saw so much, and he made *me* see so much. I read *Catcher in the Rye* in high school, and it was the most important thing I read then. It's strange to think back, but for a long time I *was* Holden Caulfield. I remember thinking that Salinger must have disguised himself in my hometown and taken notes on all of us my age; he knew how we spoke, what we thought. I even wrote him a letter—the only time I've ever done that. I told him he'd written a ghost story; Holden Caulfield was my ghost, haunting me. My girlfriend said the same thing: Holden was her and her brother and me—and, well, everyone in our school, it seemed, or at least the people we liked. It made no difference that Holden was a boy; he spoke for her—they were soul mates, she used to say. But I'll tell you, that's all a thing of the past. Who can spend his life calling people phonies? The Negroes here in the Delta aren't phonies. Even the redneck segregationists aren't; they say what they believe. (In a way they're more honest than my liberal parents and my liberal professors.) And lately Salinger has really flipped; all that mystical business. Here you meet people who can't vote and don't know where their next meal is coming from, and he's giving us that screwy Glass family and their endless obsessions. That just has to be the most self-centered family in all literature!

There was more, much more. I remember how angry I became as I listened, for I had been almost as haunted by the Glass family as he had once been by Holden Caulfield. When I remarked that I thought it wasn't exactly fair to connect Mississippi's serious and awful racial problems with Salinger's stories this young radical—I will call him Jim—let me know how fair he believed it was to do precisely that:

> I don't deny Salinger's skill as a writer. I'm not even opposed to the subject matter. If he wants to keep examining the minds of those upper-middle-class misfits, then let him. He's got the Madison-Park-Lexington Avenue scene down cold. He knows every nook and cranny. I still respect him as a writer; he can seduce you like mad. But I can't take his philosophy: sit back and contemplate the universe; say your prayers, day and night; look for the Fat Lady like Seymour Glass did. The Fat Lady was Jesus Christ. Well, are these Klan guys down here Jesus Christ? If so, we have plenty of ugly Fat Ladies down here, and we're out to take a stand against them, win a war against them, not contemplate our navels.

That was the end of that; I was by then even angrier at Jim but also rather critical of myself. I was not taking the risks he was, and I was expecting of him a degree of detachment and literary objectivity that was unreasonable given his circumstances. Worse, I was plain condescending: *he* could forsake Salinger, but certainly I would never outlive the need to keep in mind what an important writer was trying to expose and satirize, or on the other hand indicate to be significant.

It has turned out that Jim has perhaps forgotten a good deal less of his Salinger than I have. He stayed in Mississippi for the rest of that summer and was once almost killed by an explosion of dynamite planted by someone. A year later he was back. Two years later he was back again. Three years later he was demonstrating against the Vietnam War and teaching English in a high school. The book he found most useful: *The Catcher in the Rye.* The self-important phonies Salinger bears down upon so hard and relentlessly were all around him, and he was glad for the help of a writer who could be satirical without bitterness or nastiness. Anyway, many of the students he taught had already read the book on their own—one of the few they actively sought out.

By 1968 he was disenchanted as never before and increasingly without interest in politics. Mississippi was becoming a fading memory. The war in Vietnam outraged him, but he wanted more and more to fit that particular horror into a much larger "frame of reference," to use his words. "Why do people behave so meanly and think so narrowly and worry themselves endlessly over things that are of little if any consequence?" Jim asked that question when I saw him in 1970. I remember thinking (with the inadequacy, if not the idiocy, of those adjectives we call upon to type a person or his mood) that he was becoming very philosophical. And a year later I was less casual with my adjectives and maybe a little vexed: he was indeed philosophical, to the point that he had used some strong drugs, was "into" yoga, and spoke of Eastern religious ideas that I knew little or nothing about—only that Salinger had referred to them once obliquely in *Catcher in the Rye,* and again, with more emphasis, in "Zooey." It had come about that the young teacher was urging Salinger on me, and I was holding back.

Yet as I returned to Salinger's novel and stories recently, I began to appreciate what that no longer so youthful but still idealistic, gentle, and thoughtful Jim was trying to tell me a few years ago. "Don't you see," he had said, "J. D. saw it all; he saw it all ten years ago, twenty." I didn't like the way he referred to Salinger—folksy informality can irritate—but found it hard to argue with him; Salinger long ago went beyond spotting phonies in private schools (or among psychiatrists). Unlike some satirists, he came up with a remarkably compelling (and, it has turned out, contemporary) analysis of what might be a better way for us to live with each other, not to mention with ourselves.

Holden Caulfield is yet another quizzical adolescent, scornful of what he does see and quite sure there is even more to unearth and condemn. He is kin to Maisie in Henry James' *What Maisie Knew* and to Portia in Elizabeth Bowen's *Death of the Heart*; like them, he serves the author's purpose: to scrutinize the banalities and cruelties that the rest of us, grownup and so sure of our right to preach to children, often make a point of ignoring or justifying. But Salinger is not only a shrewd and winning observer or critic; he is also a rather active proponent of certain values—and, it turns out, a man of considerable vision. In the late 1940s, when Holden first began to appear (in *Collier's,* December 1945, and in *The New Yorker,* December 1946) men wore their hair short; the nation was hopeful that its industrial productivity, so accelerated by World War II, would continue to increase by leaps and bounds; psychoanalysis was becoming a virtual religion among the agnostic haute bourgeoisie of cities like New York, Chicago, and San Francisco; and certainly the idea of being a soldier and fighting a war was not looked down upon—the worst tyrant in history having just been defeated through the efforts of millions of American, British, and Russian troops. Nevertheless Holden differed strongly with those and other habits or assumptions of postwar America. If his differences were destined to be overlooked or unduly taken in stride by his admirers, then one has to ask whether *any* criticism could really unnerve Eisenhower's America.

Much of the criticism of *The Catcher in the Rye* (thoughtfully and diligently assembled a decade ago by Henry Anatole Grunwald in *Salinger: A Critical and Personal Portrait*) centers on Holden Caulfield as the *enfant terrible*, or the mixed-up, if not seriously disturbed, adolescent. He is praised for his social commentary or condemned as a snotty kid who sees the obvious, all from the vantage point of obvious money and power. (His father is a corporation lawyer.) But the emphasis is always on the private schools he attended, one after the other, or the New York scene that keeps coming up: the Hotel Biltmore, Central Park, the museums, the theater, the skating rink, a movie, a cafeteria, a train terminal, a swanky apartment building or two. That is, either Holden is given credit for getting the number of all the phonies he meets in those places, or he is called a self-indulgent brat who has no real depth, only a kind of smart-aleck, superficial shrewdness.

In fact, Holden long ago addressed himself to the most serious of concerns; and they are ones that still hold our attention. He can't imagine himself fighting in a war. He is aghast at the tawdriness of urban life; he yearns for a place that is quiet, that is "nice and peaceful"—not surrounded by defaced buildings and noisemaking machines and air that one can't enjoy breathing. His girlfriend wonders why people have to wear crewcuts. And he extends his criticism of a particular culture a lot further than that: to the dreariness and rigidity of the "best" education; to the smugness and narrowness that a certain kind of psychoanalytic ideologue can demonstrate, and for doing so be worshipped as a virtual messiah; and not least, to the subtle nature of that social and psychological adjustment most of us make to the various "powers and principalities" we recognize both dimly and quite clearly (depending upon which moment it is) as our ultimate masters—always to be taken into consideration and appeased, if not followed blindly.

Today there are words, names, and phrases for developments that

Holden Caulfield, Franny and Zooey, and their creator had no idea they would anticipate: ecology, the counterculture, the educational reform movement, and the insistence of doctors like R. D. Laing that psychoanalysis amount to something more than a clever means of enforcing the "politics of adjustment." Holden ends up being questioned by doctors who might have profited from what he saw. If he is a wise guy, one wants to use the expression in the literal sense. Besides, what are we to call the people who run or teach in Pencey Prep and Saxon Hall and all the other places he attended? What are we to make of that psychiatrist he mentions, so eager to push a youth of bothersome intelligence and candor into various straitjackets— after which he can be called normal or mature? In "Franny" briefly, in "Zooey" at greater length, such ironical issues again get probed rather well, and in addition a few others are brought into focus. The arrogant and priggish Lane Coutell, at lunch with an extraordinarily spiritual yet enraged and offended Franny, soon enough was to be exposed by thousands of women as a pretentious male egotist. As for the minister, Dr. Homer Vincent Claude Pierson, Jr. (author of "God is My Hobby"), he and his kind have ready access to cozy Sunday services at the White House—"little informal visits with God" is Salinger's all too prophetic description.

I have no idea why Salinger has not in recent years graced us with more stories. It is no one's business, really. He has already given us enough, maybe too much: we so far have not shown ourselves able to absorb and use the wisdom he has offered us. Today the man I have quoted, Jim, finds Salinger "as important as any writer" he has read; in a sense he has come full circle—from Salinger to Salinger. A dedicated if somewhat offbeat school teacher, his mind and spirit are not unlike Zooey's: sarcastic at times, tender and vulnerable at other times; now indignant, now resigned and intensely prayerful. A while back one could read Salinger and feel him to be not only an original and gifted writer, a marvelous entertainer, a man free of the slogans and clichés the rest of us fall prey to (or welcome as salvation itself) but also a terribly lonely man. Perhaps he still feels lonely; but he is, I think, not so alone these days. The worst in American life he anticipated and portrayed to us a generation ago. The best side of us—Holden and the Glasses—still survives, and more can be heard reaching for expression in various ways and places, however serious the present-day assaults from various authorities. I put down *Catcher in the Rye* and *Franny and Zooey* this year again grateful to their author. I wondered once more how to do justice to Salinger's sensibility, to his wide and generous responsiveness to religious and philosophical ideas, to his capacity to evoke the most poignant of human circumstances vividly and honestly and with a rare kind of humor, both gentle and teasing. No doubt that sensibility continues to attract the many young men and women who read him; it can be said that they read him out of a special and occasionally desperate kind of thirst and hunger that he has all along appreciated and, "a certain Samaritan" that he is, tried both to comprehend and assuage.

New Republic, April 28, 1973

Tillie Olsen
The Iron and the Riddle

The prelude to *Middlemarch* is only three paragraphs long, but in them George Eliot makes one of the most powerful and satisfactory statements about the predicament of women: she refers to "blundering lives," to "a life of mistakes," to "a tragic failure which found no sacred poet and sank unwept into oblivion." She had in mind both masses of women and particular women, all of whom have suffered by virtue of what she describes as "meanness of opportunity," both the general kind so many men and women alike faced in the nineteenth century and the special kind women had to endure then, and still now. The novel is a masterful psychological presentation and analysis of rural, middle-class, early nineteenth century England but also, for the most part, a chronicle of loss, sadness, disappointment, and failure. Characters endowed with intelligence and ambition, one after the other, fall upon bad times—not poverty but rather the consequences of fate, the sum of the world's accidents, incidents, and circumstances that exert their enormous, tellingly destructive influence. The novel falls just short of tragedy; a village, a county, all of England's rising bourgeoisie had at least another half-century or so to go, yet the story is littered with unfulfilled dreams.

So with Tillie Olsen's *Tell Me a Riddle*; her four short stories lack Eliot's extended, intricate dedication to character portrayal or the workings of historical change but their sensibility, point of view, and mood are spiritually akin to those aspects of *Middlemarch*. The first and briefest, "I Stand Here Ironing," introduces the reader to a woman who has known and suffered from the "meanness of opportunity" George Eliot mentions, a twentieth-century American version of it. The title reveals the scene and tells of all the action to come—a mother reflects upon the hard, curbed, sad life of her nineteen-year-old daughter, born in the Great Depression of the early 1930s. A social worker or guidance counselor or psychologist or psychiatrist (who knows which, and who cares—a substantial number of them all sound drearily alike) has told the mother that the young woman, her oldest child, "needs help." The mother is skeptical and quietly, thoughtfully scornful, but not defensive or guilty, not lacking in a capacity for psychological introspection either—as might be said of her by the person who wants her to come in for one of those self-conscious talks that have become so much a part of so many lives in recent years. She is determined to hold on to her dignity, to her right as an intelligent woman, however hardpressed by life, to comprehend what has happened to herself and her children, and just as important, to resist the interfering, gratuitous, self-serving, or wrong-headed interpretations of others. "Let her be," the mother says to herself—a remark meant also for the one who, with the barely concealed arrogance and condescension of the clinic, had called and said, "I wish you would manage the time to come in and talk with me about your daughter." The story is a mother's effort to understand for herself how her daughter came to be the person she is, and to do so by taking account of the overwhelming social, economic, and cultural reality of a certain kind of life—a reality that generates rather than merely influences currents in the mind's life. Put differently, the story is an interior monologue devoted to the exterior—the insistent, enduring, molding press of the things of this world upon our dreams, nightmares, hesitations, and aspirations.

"She was a miracle to me," the mother remembers. When the baby was eight months old there was a sudden change: "I had to leave her daytimes with the woman downstairs for whom she was no miracle at all, for I worked or looked for work." The father, desperate for lack of a job, humiliated and beaten, said good-bye. The mother was only nineteen, as old as the daughter she is now thinking about as she does her ironing. The story moves on from there—a chronicle, related in one heartbreaking incident after another, of a girl's growing up under the adversity of the depression years. A chronicle, too, of a mother's attempt to keep her own head above water (she remarried, had more children, pursued work to the best of her ability, and tried to do right by her children and new husband). And a chronicle of a particular child's suffering: nurseries where she was ignored at best; schools where the teachers were callous or mean;

clinics where arbitrariness and bureaucratic self-importance determined the way she was treated and the recommendations made to
her mother; a convalescent home whose horrors were covered by a
veneer of sugary sentiment Charles Dickens would have known how
to document. And in her family, a fight for herself, for her rights and
her terrain, in the face of the children born later to her mother—an
especially hard and bitter fight because there were so few victories
possible in a family so impoverished and vulnerable.

But the child did not grow to be a mere victim of the kind so many
of us these days are rather eager to recognize—a hopeless tangle of
psychopathology. The growing child, even in her troubled moments, revealed herself to be persistent, demanding, and observant.
In the complaints we make, in the "symptoms" we develop, we reveal our strengths as well as our weaknesses. The hurt child could
summon her intelligence, exercise her will, smile and make others
smile: "The control, the command, the convulsing and deadly
clowning, the spell, then the roaring, stamping audience, unwilling
to let this rare and precious laughter out of their lives." At times her
mother could observe, "She is so lovely"; and then immediately
wonder why they in the clinic were so anxious to talk about the
daughter's "problems."

"Let her be," the mother says, not defiantly and not out of escapist ignorance. "So all that is in her will not bloom," she continues,
"but in how many does it? There is still enough left to live by." And
in case the people at the unnamed clinic already have in response
their various "interpretations," their "insights," the mother has a
quiet request to make—that the young lady be accorded respect, be
allowed her dignity, be regarded as and told she is "more than this
dress on the ironing board, helpless before the iron."

That is all; the last words of the story bring the reader back to the
first words, but not in a forced or contrived way—not the all too
clever and tidy work of a "literary" writer of short stories who has
learned in school about rising action and falling action, and structure, and the need for impact or coherence. A working woman is
making the best of *her* situation, even as she expects her daughter to
do so. A mother shakes her fist at the universe, not excitedly, and
with no great expectation of triumph, but out of a determination to
assert her worth, her capabilities, however injured or curbed, her
ability to see, to comprehend, and to imagine—and to assert too her
daughter's—everyone's.

The other stories reveal the same struggle for personal dignity against the same high, almost impossible odds. They are each sad stories, yet leavened with humor and made compelling, even entertaining (despite the subject matter), by the writer's wonderful, eye-opening ability. She makes her fine social awareness, her strongly felt political passions, her abiding interest in and her fighter's anger at the condition of her sex here and in other countries mere instruments in a commitment to the integrity of the private psychological reverie. She uses it to show the idiosyncratic as well as the representative ideas and emotions of the men, women, and children she chooses to portray and wants desperately (the heart of her effort, the basis perhaps of her special appeal) to uphold and make the rest of us also uphold as, thereby, her companions.

The last story, whose title the author has given to the collection as a whole, is the longest and is again all too easily given a summary— an aging couple, once poor and active in radical politics but now reasonably well-off, comes to terms with death. The author allows herself a bit more leeway than she has before; the story has sustained, compelling dialogue, a more relaxed pace of development, and a thread of humor and sarcasm that offset the grief and heartache. The husband and wife, married forty-seven years, have developed their own ways with each other. He is alternately teasing and encouraging. Most of all he wants to forget the past and make the best of everything. She is suspicious, silent, and quite unwilling to gloss over a lifetime's trials and sorrows. There are marvelous exchanges as he coaxes her and, in the course of the story, calls her a succession of bittersweet names that provide the story's continuity: Mrs. Word-Miser, Mrs. Take It Easy, Mrs. Telepathy, Mrs. In a Hurry, Mrs. Excited Over Nothing. She parries his thrusts and lets him plan, involving her in his hopes for a new life. They will move to one of those "havens" for the elderly. But in the clutch she says no; she is tired, and she will not go along with him. She seems to know that she is sick and will soon die. She has a critical detachment with respect to him, their children, and grandchildren (never mind the world at large) that contrasts with the immediacy and warmth of his response to people, places, and things. A husband and wife in America—old, full of memories, scarred by a life that was not easy either materially or psychologically, and now compelled to face their last challenge together. Tell me a riddle, the grandchildren ask; the grandmother cannot, will not. How can she when she has learned, decade after decade, that life itself, hers and maybe everyone's, is a bundle of riddles? The grandmother can only have silent reveries, occasions for the author to turn into a haunting, brooding poet. And the grandfather's bravado soon enough gives way, as he struggles to face death, his wife's and his own—the final riddle that no one, of whatever disposition or station in life, manages to avoid or figure out.

Since the collection *Tell Me a Riddle* was published fifteen years ago, Tillie Olsen has not come out with more short stories. She was forty-seven then and is now in her sixties. Her own life is well worth knowing. She was the Nebraska-born daughter of a Socialist organizer and worked for years in factories. She married a union man, a printer, and fought alongside him in a long series of working-class struggles during the 1930s and 1940s. She also brought up four children, and being poor and a conscientious political activist, she had little or no spare time for the writing she yet craved to do. She has written about herself and much more in two essays, "Silences: When Writers Don't Write," and "Women Who Are Writers in Our Century: One Out of Twelve." She is (and has been for decades) a feminist—unyielding and strong-minded but never hysterical or shrill. Her essays reveal her to be brilliant, forceful and broadly educated, if without degrees to wave around. She also published in 1974 the novel *Yonnondio* about working-class life in the 1930s—its terrible, lacerating reality. And she has written a long biographical interpretation to accompany a reissue by the Feminist Press of Rebecca Harding Davis's *Life in the Iron Mills*, originally issued in 1861.

At times, in a confessional vein not unlike that of "I Stand Here Ironing," she has allowed herself a moment of regret, if not self-pity: if only there had been more time, an easier life, and hence more stories, novels, and essays written. Proud and stoic, though, she pulls back immediately: that is how it goes—and besides, for others, for the overwhelming majority of the world's people, in the past and now too, there has been *no* spare time, no chance for anything like writing or constructing stories and in them giving expression to ideas and ideals. She need not, however, have one moment of regret. Others have produced more, but she has never once faltered. It is as if she had no time for failure either. Everything she has written has become almost immediately a classic—the short stories especially, but also her two essays, her comment on the life and writing of Rebecca Harding Davis, and her novel. She has been spared celebrity, but hers is a singular talent that will not let go of one, a talent that prompts tears. She offers an artist's compassion and forgiveness but makes plain how fierce the various struggles must continue to be.

New Republic, December 6, 1975

Painfully Human

Ann Cornelisen, a gifted social observer and novelist, has lived in the southern provinces of Italy, on and off, for twenty years and has done her best to understand the region's poor but proud people. In *Torregreca*, a beautifully wrought social document, she told of her efforts to set up a nursery for the children of the area. She has also given us a novel, *Vendetta of Silence*, that draws heavily upon local legend and truth. Now, in *Women of the Shadows*, she returns to nonfiction with a strong and lyrical account of how the women of these provinces—Lucania, in particular—manage, barely, to keep themselves above despair, despite the constant threat of hunger and the other hardships that beset them.

Miss Cornelisen, an American, describes her relationship to southern Italy, right off, as one of "voluntary bondage." In a few words she provides a textbook's worth of comment on the psychology of social observation; she says that her "allegiance" to the region is "a chronic, even pernicious affinity which familiarity and disappointment have not cured and which neither absence nor bitterness can weaken." She suffers what she calls "an inconvenient malaise"— one that "imposes its own quarantine," even though she has always realized that she can, if need be, leave the place and stay away as long as she wants. When she is there, however, she takes up a quite special and limited life. In a matter-of-fact way, neither self-serving nor martyrish, she tells us how it went in Lucania: "I shared what there was, including food of poor quality at high prices, capricious utilities, a wretched climate and the disdain of every outsider. Money could not buy comfort, much less delicacies or amusements."

The men of the southern provinces have their cliques, the women theirs. They are all hardworking. There are few illusions. The only solace is gossip—the satisfaction that comes from voicing doubts or misgivings about others. All are victims of one kind or another, even those who belong to the petite bourgeoisie. And so the apparently quiet, forbearing, enduring people crave occasions to release tension: "Those same women who used weeding hoes with infinite care and patience lunged at their buttons and darns as though seeking revenge for the day's frustrations." Miss Cornelisen does not seem especially interested in rendering the more dramatic moments of the life in which she has immersed herself, convenient as they probably would be for narrative purposes; nor is she a polemicist, interested in making points and assembling them into lectures. At times, as she introduces the reader to a village or to a particular person, she writes like the curé in Georges Bernanos's *Diary of a Country Priest*; she is very much entangled, as a neighbor, with certain hard-pressed women, yet she also watches them somewhat dispassionately:

> When I lived there I did not have to think each day, This is all of life, there is nothing more. I doubt that I could fight as they fight in enduring their days, or that whatever is human in me, that sets me apart from an animal, could survive their lives. They say "life brutalizes." That they recognize it explains why, for all that has been said to the contrary, they remain painfully human. They are women of tremendous strengths, these women of the shadows. One of their strengths, and not the least, is their silence, which outsiders have understood as submission.

Women of the Shadows is primarily an effort to bring us closer to some of these remarkable women, whose resourcefulness and liveliness flourish in spite of their brutish social circumstances. It offers, in a quiet, understated way, a demonstration that even extreme poverty does not necessarily make for equality between the sexes. The men of Lucania strut, play cards, pontificate, and sit and sip wine in cafés; the women are more wary—they stay nearer home and confine their talk to the concrete particulars of village life. There is mutual distrust as well as an abiding loyalty. Men and women size one another up cannily, sometimes scornfully, but they also fall passionately in love and never for a moment think of betraying one another. There are exceptions to this rule of fidelity, however—couples doomed by personal incompatibilities or victims of an economic order that forces men by the thousand to leave the countryside and look for work in Milan, Rome, and Florence, or even farther away, in Germany, France, and Scandinavia.

Six women are portrayed here in detail. They are farm workers and peasants, as are about eighty percent of the people who live in southern Italy. They work a reluctant, exhausted land and are glad if they manage to survive. Many don't. There is meager medical care, and children often die young. The people are always "one step behind disaster," Miss Cornelisen tells us, and are always "trying in their desperation to lay it low with the blunt instruments of superstition." The author is sensitive, delicate, and at times admittedly perplexed when she writes about Catholicism. As she says, "it is hard to know whether the practices of the Catholic Church in Southern Italy are the result of a domestic evolution of theology or simply versatile adaptation to the mores of the parish," but she does seem to believe that the Church should not become a scapegoat, to be held entirely responsible for its flock's abject condition. In fact, the Church is to some degree responsive to its adherents: they are able to exert a certain amount of influence on it by choosing among symbols, rituals, and traditions. The women Miss Cornelisen knows carry enormous burdens, and for all the braggadocio of their husbands, they are the ones who really exercise power and command respect. The religious beliefs of the peasants reflect that state of affairs: there is a strong Marian cult, and by the author's estimate it has turned into "the core of local belief."

The author's approach to the women she describes is refreshing. They are never excuses for ambitious generalizations, nor are they romanticized and made into accusers of the rest of us—the noble, suffering poor versus the wicked wealthy. "These are not lovable women," we are told at one point. "They are blunt, often crude and at times unable to control their grotesque ferocity. Their minds are not cluttered by theories; they know no extenuating circumstances; almost any means, except murder, can be justified." Having presented that candid portrait, the author turns around and says, in the same paragraph, "I know them as Teresa who solves problems this way, Maria that way, and Carmela, with whom everyone can work because no matter what the tension she has a remark ready to ease it. They have a certain wit and resourcefulness and a kind of bludgeoning courage." Like the women she writes about, Miss Cornelisen is of two minds. She knows that consistency, whatever its proclaimed virtues, is an illusion.

The peasant women of southern Italy not only are in many respects unknown to their more comfortable countrymen and to us but also too often lack the time or energy to be in touch with themselves. Yet even this formulation has to be qualified, as the author tells us:

> Odd that we insist that "simple" people, poor people, do not feel deep, continuous emotion. We allow them animal explosions of rage or passion or illogical exuberance and then dismiss them as too insensitive to suffer from the more subtle miseries, the psychological peas that we, the princes and princesses of a more intellectual world, must endure. We have a lot of time for rambles through our psyches. We tell each other about them—in excruciating detail—or we pretend we would not give ourselves away for the world, while we long for the relief of boring someone. In the end I suspect is is not a matter of our feeling more, but rather that we have more verbal facility and more time to kill, for we have to do less to stay alive.

This final attempt to distinguish one group of people from another also founders, for the women show in their speech a great deal of vitality, spontaneity, and shrewdness. They can be meditative and unnervingly observant. Speaking of the anguish she has experienced in the course of bearing her many children, one woman remarks:

> The men used to say, "She's a brave one, she is." But I'll never forget the pain. I remember all nine times, just how they felt—and every one is different, I can tell you—and you just lay there and bite the towel and never let out a sound. Not once. So many times it was all for nothing too. Six of mine died. I could have wailed then—that's all right—but there are some hurts that stay inside.

The woman who says this reveals herself to be quite adequate with words and as reflective as many of us who are better educated and have an easier life. She may even be better-spoken than some of those who are all too anxious to study her and her neighbors. Italy's social scientists and bureaucrats, with their reports and conclusions, get a bad time of it in this book. The author has watched them come and go, has read their analyses, and, alas, has seen what comes of them: nothing, except maybe a conviction on the part of those who profit from the status quo that there is little to be done with the peasants because they have certain "traits." Miss Cornelisen is devastating in her exposure of the arrogance and dishonesty that characterized the "reforms" set in motion after the Second World War in order to prevent communism from taking hold in southern Italy. She documents the tragedies that were caused by new laws, edicts, and programs developed by outsiders who, however well-intentioned, had no real knowledge of the people they wanted to help. And she asks us not to forget that the blunders she has seen have their parallels outside Italy:

> It has all happened before in other countries. Wineries were built where no grapes grew. Every town has a slaughterhouse, though it may see only one aged cow a month. Tuberculosis sanatoriums were built but never opened for lack of patients (one was finally adapted to the care of children with ringworm). Entire agricultural villages were constructed *ex nuovo* and then inaugurated by the local Minister-protector, flanked by the obligatory potted palms and unknown Powers in black suits. Still no one has ever lived in those villages.

In spite of their moments of bitterness, the author's women of the shadows have not lost their sense of humor. They are wryly fatalistic; they know that when all is said and done they have only themselves to fall back upon. That knowledge has given them self-respect as well as suffering. They turn out to be not only stronger and more intelligent than we might have thought (and than their husbands may want to know) but privileged in a way some of us are not, for they realize what their situation is—which shadows fall on them, and why.

New Yorker, April 12, 1976

James Agee's Search

In his senior year at Harvard, James Agee and some of his *Advocate* friends did a brilliant parody of *Time*, then only a few years old. One of Agee's best friends, Dwight Macdonald, was working on another Luce magazine, *Fortune*. Agee did not exactly have the best prospects at graduation in 1932, with the depression in full sway. The *Time* parody probably helped Macdonald get him a job at *Fortune*, thereby launching a journalistic career of almost two decades. In 1933 Agee was a New Yorker—in the borough of Manhattan, that is. He worked in a new skyscraper, the Chrysler Building, on the fifty-second floor. His habits as a *Fortune* essayist have become a part of the awesome reputation that clings to him still, a quarter of a century after his death. Agee and his Beethoven symphonies blasting away through the night, with the lighted streets of the world's greatest city far below. Agee and coffee, Agee and booze, Agee and the typewriter, Agee and cigarettes, and most important, Agee and deadlines—which seemed with him to take on a literal meaning. He drove himself ruthlessly and experienced terrible spells of apprehension and despair as he contested time and his superiors, not to mention his own exacting conscience, in a (usually) desperate effort to turn in finished copy before it was too late.

But for all the drama, if not histrionics, the articles by and large got done; invariably they were brilliantly constructed, witty, informative, entertaining. Here was a poet harnessed to the things of this commercial world and somehow able to sing well indeed for his supper. He wrote of rugs and roads and railroads. He wrote of flowers and towns and quinine cartels and commodities speculators. He was able to mobilize within himself the dispassionate curiosity of the reporter, and when linked to the storyteller's eye for detail the result was superb journalistic narrative. Just below the surface, though, was a strong moral sensibility, held in check by the constraints of the Luce empire, but never banished outright—even when the subject was as innocuous as strawberries: "In England, behind walls of a respectable age, strawberries are still served at Solemn High Tea. In England this June the school tuckshop will be clamorous with hard-hatted little Harrovians absorbing 'dringers,' a somewhat lily-gilding mixture of fresh strawberries and strawberry ice cream."

This and more was served to us in an English course I took at college, when Agee was a name I was yet to know. We were told, as Agee may have told himself, that any crop, fruit or vegetable or cereal or so-called raw material, can open up whatever doors the writer wishes. Strawberries took Agee to the privileged realms of England's so-called public schools—an indirect reminder to *Fortune*'s wealthy that while millions could take no meal, however meager, for granted, a small group of kids, not especially prone to modesty or self-criticism, were making an innocent strawberry an object of scandal. Soon, in 1936, there would be cotton, the staple crop of the American South's sharecropper and tenant farm agriculture. It was this assignment that took Agee to Alabama, and the result would be a long, memorable personal and moral struggle, as well as a book, *Let Us Now Praise Famous Men*, which is Agee's single most significant piece of writing—the only book of his, arguably, that will continue to be connected with those banal adjectives *great* and *classic* over the generations.

Agee went to Alabama to a small farming community between Montgomery and Birmingham during the summer of 1936, an election year. The depression was becoming a way of life. Strong federal efforts by the Roosevelt administration softened considerably many of the edges of extreme poverty and unemployment, but the country's economic system, everyone agreed, was still quite sick. Few were harder off than the South's farmers, black and white. At the time *Fortune* was not about to do an article on the region's rural black people. For that matter, Agee and Evans were not sent down to do a searching documentary even of the wretched circumstances bedeviling white yeomen in rural Alabama, among other parts of Dixie. Cotton was king, still, and an economic analysis of that particular royal condition, colorfully written, was what Agee's bosses had in mind.

For him, however, this was an opportunity of the greatest import: a way of drawing upon interests he came by as a Southern boy; a way, too, of exploring not only an economic problem but the moral aspects of a nation's life; a way of escaping Manhattan's cosmopolitan culture to pursue that elusive honesty, purity, and integrity so many of us keep looking for, around corner after corner of our lives. And he was to work with Walker Evans, a friend of similarly conflicted temperament: anxious to pursue Art, willing to break rules to do so, stubbornly independent, of broad sensibility, and not beyond the inclination to call upon bourbon as a dear, helpful friend.

They stayed in Alabama over a month, July and into August. They lived with three families and tried to understand, deeply and respectfully, their everyday existence. They failed in their assigned mission; *Fortune* would never show its readers, through Agee's words and Evans' photographs, the human aspect, so to speak, of cotton production. The photographs that appear in *Let Us Now Praise Famous Men* are not really meant to be a part of work done at the behest of the Farm Security Administration, which employed Evans during the 1930s. Evans' pictures show not only terribly hurt, perplexed, and vulnerable people but scenes, interior and exterior, worthy of an artist's careful and controlled recognition. For Evans, an old pair of country shoes, a chair and broom, or a linoleum-covered kitchen table were opportunities not for the muckraking or polemical mind but for the unashamedly observing eye of a particular kind of artist.

Evans and Agee in the South were two well-bred and well-educated young men, each in search of a career in one of the arts. There was not much time for them to figure out in detail, never mind argumentatively, what their ultimate purposes were. They were guests. They were obliged to follow the rhythms of others—extremely harassed people, living under a hot sun, moneyless, and with no great expectation of doing very well in the world.

Agee was as hungry in his own way, as confused and uncertain and apprehensive, as his hosts. They were up at dawn and ready for bed shortly after sundown, tired from hard, demanding agricultural labor. He was up with them, trying to learn the details of their days and their ways—but driven, one realizes, by a strong conscience determined this time to have its say and then some. The seething, anarchic rebelliousness that had hitherto (at Exeter and Harvard and in Manhattan) taken an erratic course—now apparent in sarcasm or satire or parody, now buried under layers of religious sentiment or literary analysis—began at last to emerge as a full-fledged moral force. It was as if Agee heard a voice within saying something like this, loud and clear: here you are, close to the proud and hurt Appalachian people of your childhood, close to the people your Lord Jesus Christ kept mentioning, kept keeping near at hand, kept attempting to heal and feed and comfort; so you had best take exceeding care, you who are good with words, you who have been quick to turn on others, the hypocrites and pretenders and sycophants, the self-absorbed tastemakers of a world very far, socially and culturally, from north-central Alabama.

Under such personal circumstances, it is small wonder that an apparently routine *Fortune* assignment turned out to be the most challenging and frustrating task Agee would ever have to confront. When he got back he went with his second wife, Alma, to a small town in New Jersey, where he took on, it seemed, not only Alabama's injustices but the whole world's. And his efforts to describe what he saw were similarly monumental—as if the college student who admired James Joyce hoped to make out of a Southern scene what Joyce had made of Dublin. Nor was this effort one Agee would ever feel satisfied with. It is safe to say that he ultimately surrendered and reluctantly allowed a portion of his labored, intense, tormented prose to emerge as the book we know as *Let Us Now Praise Famous Men.* Even to call it that, a book, is to tread on the writer's infinitely (it seems) sensitive toes: "This is a *book* only by necessity," he insisted. More seriously, "it is an effort in human actuality, in which the reader is no less centrally involved than the authors and those of whom they tell."

Agee was himself a great performer—a mimic, a scold, a man capable of large, defiant, and self-wounding gestures. He had the dramatist's interest in the great audience of others, and he wanted from them a kind of engagement worthy of his own high theatricality. *Let Us Now Praise Famous Men* can in fact be regarded as a moral drama, a long prose poem structured as a dramatic presentation. We begin with "persons and places," a dramatis personae of sorts. There are "verses," a "preamble," a quotation from *King Lear*, a section called "Intermission: Conversation in the Lobby," and a section described as "Inductions." The author wants to tell us about essentials, things like money and shelter and clothing and education and work, but he is constantly searching for ways to turn such topics into an edifying spectacle, with protagonists, confrontations, rising action, and a compelling denouement or two. Agee's chief enemy was that of every ambitious moral writer—the potential boredom of the proudly well-intentioned reader, for whom *Let Us Now Praise Famous Men* would provide merely a vivid account of a problem, namely, 1930s Southern tenantry.

Before Agee begins his book he offers a footnote to explain his reasons for putting on page 1 some lines from *King Lear* ("Poor naked wretches, whereso'er you are, / That bide the pelting of this pitiless storm") and, on the opposite page, the well-known political exhortation that begins with "Workers of the world, unite and fight." Agee's explanation for these two quotations tells a lot about what he has in mind for his book and about the many (and seemingly conflicting) sides of his writing personality. He begins provocatively, if not with condescending resignation: "These words are quoted here to mislead those who will be misled by them. They mean, not what the reader may come to think they mean, but what they say." This is an author fighting hard against the inclination in all of us (including himself) to forget the terribly demanding urgency in what, ironically, is already familiar to us.

"Expose thyself to feel what wretches feel." This is *Lear*, we nod, and recall the scene, the act. This is a Communist rallying cry, we nod, and think of Marx and Engels, of Leninism-Stalinism, of revolutions won, then badly betrayed. Agee had, in his own fashion, read *Lear* carefully, and he had risked his own kind of exposure. Now he wondered, in the words of Lenin: "What is to be done?" Agee knew, too, that Lenin himself ought to have begun asking that question a second time around, so to speak, from within the walls of his Kremlin office soon to be occupied by Stalin. Agee's dilemma was that of the revolutionary postrevolutionary who has seen a decent hope crushed by traitors and by blind submission to arrogant dogma, not only in this century but, as Agee the Christian (in spirit) well knew, in the travesties of historical Christianity.

He had plenty of doubt and sarcasm to hand out, and one gets the impression that no political party, no idea become a "movement" would achieve immunity from the skeptical part of his mind. The danger, needless to say, is captiousness—a chronic insistence, all-or-none fashion, that various political leaders or social movements, or writers for that matter, either pass full muster or submit to withering, continual criticism. At times, Agee falls victim to his own scruples—turning ironic bitterness or snide contempt or outright scorn on a wide spectrum of individuals: on Franklin D. Roosevelt and his New Deal for instance, on the teachers of the rural South, black and white alike, on New York intellectuals, even on the reader. The *reader*, a catchall designation if ever there was one, gets swiped at by, of all people, a writer who worries about "the average reader's tendency to label." But Agee was nothing if not self-critical. He knew the reader and labeler in himself, working in conjunction with the reactively humble writer, still unable to overcome pride, the sin of sins.

It seems to me curious, not to say obscene and thoroughly terrifying, that it could occur to an association of human beings drawn together through need and chance and for profit into a company, an organ of journalism, to pry intimately into the lives of an undefended and appallingly damaged group of human beings, an ignorant and helpless rural family, for the purpose of parading the nakedness, disadvantage and humiliation of these lives before another group of human beings, in the name of science, of 'honest journalism' (whatever that paradox may mean), of humanity, of social fearlessness, for money, and for a reputation for crusading and for unbias which, when skillfully enough qualified, is exchangeable at any bank for money (and in politics, for votes, job patronage, abelincolnism, etc.); and that these people could be capable of meditating this prospect without the slightest doubt of their qualification to do an 'honest' piece of work, and with a conscience better than clear, and in the virtual certitude of almost unanimous public approval.

Little is left, one begins to feel. We are all suspect after such an assault, all the readers and editors of all the magazines and publishing houses—all of us who are human beings with our blind spots, our self-centeredness, our wish to live in comfort and with some approval from others. Yes, we do write out of egoism and vanity, but our outcry of preachiness is meant, sometimes desperately, for our own ears more than anyone else's, and while we are indulgent with ourselves in dozens of ways, we nonetheless struggle with ironies and paradoxes, including the terrible humiliation of discovering that the more we expose and denounce the blatant evils of this world, the more we become a prominent part of the very world in which that evil seems to flourish. We get rewarded, if that is the word, and become "famous men" because we have highlighted the lives of some of "them" (even if called "famous men"). So it goes, as a writer who once went to St. Andrews School in Tennessee would not be averse to putting it, "world without end."

Moreover, such self-criticism is scarcely a guarantee of absolution. Mea culpa can be a sly form of arrogance or a canny means of currying favor, enlisting the reader's sympathy on behalf of an earnestly disarming breast-beater who turns out to be, in the clutch, quite capable of a cleverly effective self-defense. But Agee wasn't only taking on himself in the old monkish tradition of endless, excoriating introspection. He spells out what he has called "curious, obscene, terrifying and unfathomly mysterious" in a sentence that bears repeating here—an example of his thinking, surely, but also an example of the kind of sonorous, suggestive, baffling, cranky prose he could mobilize and put in the "average reader's" way:

So does the whole subsequent course and fate of the work: the causes for its non-publication, the details of its later acceptance elsewhere, and of its design; the problems which confronted the maker of the photographs; and those which confront me as I try to write of it: the question, Who are you who will read these words and study these photographs, and through what cause, by what chance, and for what purpose, and by what right do you qualify to, and what will you do about it; and the question, Why we make this book, and set it at large, and by what right, and for what purpose, and to what good end, or none: the whole memory of the South in its six-thousand-mile parade and flowering outlay of the facades of cities, and of the eyes in the streets of towns, and of hotels, and of the trembling heat, and of the wide wild opening of the tragic land, wearing the trapped frail flowers of its garden of faces; the fleet flush and flower and fainting of the human crop it raises; the virulent, insolent, deceitful, pitying, infinitesimal and frenzied running and searching, on this colossal peasant map, of two angry, futile and bottomless, botched and overcomplicated youthful intelligences in the service of an anger and of a love and of an undiscernible truth, and in the frightening vanity of their would-be purity; the sustaining,

even now, and forward moving, lifted on the lifting of this day
as ships on a wave, above whom, in a few hours, night once
more will stand up in his stars, and they decline through
lamplight and be dreaming statues, of those, each, whose lives
we knew and whom we love and intend well toward, and of
whose living we know little in some while now, save that quite
steadily, in not much possible change for better or much
worse, mute, innocent, helpless and incorporate among that
small-moted and inestimable swarm and pollen stream and
fleet of single, irreparable, unrepeatable existences, they are
led, gently, quite steadily, quite without mercy, each a little
farther toward the washing and the wailing, the sunday suit
and the prettiest dress, the pine box, and the closed clay room
whose fraily decorated roof, until rain has taken it flat into
oblivion, wears the shape of a ritual scar and of an inverted
boat: curious, obscene, terrifying, beyond all search of dream
unanswerable, those problems which stand thickly forth like
light from all matter, triviality, chance, intention, and record
in the body, of being, of truth, of conscience, of hope, of
hatred, of beauty, of indignation, of guilt, of betrayal, of innocence, of forgiveness, of vengeance, of guardianship, of an
indenominable fate, predicament, destination, and God.

It is no small relief, after that paragraph of a sentence, to come,
immediately afterwards, on the following: "Thereby it is in some
fear that I approach those matters at all, and in much confusion."
The "average reader" sighs and nods affirmatively. But what is Agee
doing here? Trying, perhaps, to make his confusion as contagious as
it turns out to be anyway? I have used this book of his in my courses,
and I have heard the confusion expressed vigorously: sincere annoyance, plaintive cries for interpretive assistance, angry shrugs, or
straightforward contempt. Nor is the teacher always grateful for the
student who becomes ecstatic about Agee's writing and its various
postures. While his writing has a kind of transcendence, a great, dramatic, daring lift upward—away from all the petty, self-serving, uncritical ones who live on campuses or in various commercial offices—
and while he can disarm one utterly with the sweetness of his talk
and his compelling evocation of a complex kind of compassion, he
is at the same time a very angry writer who wants an engagement

with the rest of us, a joint willingness to say no, to say wait, to say stop, to say, even, enough!

His inconsistencies, near to contradictions, are worthy of the novelist, resulting in marvelous descriptions of people, places, and events. His lyrical gifts show themselves over and over again in touching, even stunning, moments in which the ordinary (earth, flowers, furniture, buildings) is rendered miraculous. "Behind the house," we are told, "the dirt is blond and bare, except a little fledgling of grass-leaves at the roots of structures, and walked-out rags of grass thickening along the sides." As for the pinewood of those tenant farmer cabins: "In some of this wood, the grain is broad and distinct: in some of it the grain has almost disappeared, and the wood has a texture and look like that of weathered bone." And of other buildings: "The henroost is about seven feet square and five high, roofed with rotted shingles. It is built rather at random of planks varying in width between a foot and four inches, nailed on horizontally with narrow spaces between their edges." We learn more than this about that henroost, about its structure and function, including the marvelous, wry observation that "most of the eggs are found by the children in places which are of the hens' own selection."

On the other hand, Agee has by no means contented himself with close, pastoral cataloguing or even with good storytelling, as when he turns a sleepless night into the hellish experience it was, with a hot, sweaty, city-spoiled visitor struggling desperately to deal with bugs and ticks and flies and mosquitoes. We get to know some Alabama people of the 1930s "right well," as they might have put it. But there are other more confounded pages, like a section titled "Education," in which the author is a social critic with, literally, a vengeance. His anger is boundless in that chapter, and it spills from Alabama to just about everywhere. And shaking his fists hard and often, he naturally risks losing his grip on logic.

He makes clear, for instance, the deficiencies of a particular Alabama county's school system. He quotes scornfully from the books used in class: "Personally I see enough there [in the various educational matters he has examined] to furnish me with bile for a month." Alert to the banality, if not stupidity, that passes for instructional materials in many schools, he anticipates Paul Goodman by some decades. He even goes after the school buildings, "a recently quiet, windowy, 'healthful' red brick and white-trim new structure which perfectly exemplifies the American gusto for sterility, unimagination, and general gentleness. . . ." That was a *white* school, one hastens to add. As for the *other* school: "The Negro children, meanwhile, continue to sardine themselves, a hundred and a hundred and twenty strong, into stove-heated one-room pine shacks which might comfortably accommodate a fifth of their number if the walls, roof, and windows were tight." What, precisely, would Agee have wanted for such children, in the way of books, teaching, and buildings? In the course of a criticism of Alabama education, he blasts *all* education—including his own: "I could not wish of any one of them [the children he has met down South] that they should have had the 'advantages' I have had: a Harvard education is by no means an unqualified advantage." What are such bold pronouncements supposed to mean? It is all right for James Agee, Harvard '31, well-paid writer, and Alabama visitor, to decry universities, those who teach in them ("few doctors of philosophy are literate"), and one or another educational establishment. But what is this to mean to the Alabama children he met? Would he really tell one of *them* to stay clear of scholarships offered by Harvard or some other college on the grounds that a good deal of hypocrisy and pretense go on in such places, among others?

Nowhere is Agee's rock-bottom philosophical and psychological romanticism more evident than in *Let Us Now Praise Famous Men*, and especially in his analysis of education. He anticipates not only Paul Goodman but R. D. Laing: "As a whole part of 'psychological education' it needs to be remembered that a neurosis can be valuable; also that 'adjustment' to a sick and insane environment is of itself not 'health' but sickness and insanity." By now, when there are more than enough individuals willing to celebrate various kinds of eccentric behavior, if not madness itself, this is perhaps a familiar stricture, but when Agee wrote it, psychoanalysis was just making itself felt as a strong presence in the relatively well to do intellectual circles to which he and Evans belonged. The point at that time was to conquer neurosis through analytic treatment. There was a good deal of hopefulness and even fatuous conviction among such analysands, not to mention among their doctors, that a new kind of person would emerge, no longer heir to the various conflicts others keep having. Anna Freud, in *Normality and Pathology* (1965), has documented rather compellingly what came to be a sectarian, messianic ("prophylactic") movement of sorts. For Agee to have resisted such a line of thinking, even to have seen that there is a social and cultural aspect to psychiatric nomenclature (it can be used to put people down, and alas, as a justification for locking them up in order to silence unpopular voices) was to indicate a certain stubborn independence of mind, as well as a shrewd capacity to puncture a given kind of faddish illusion.

Yet at other moments he can spin his own illusions, however earnestly well-intentioned: "I don't know whether negroes or whites teach in the negro schools; I presume negroes. If they are negroes, I would presume for several reasons that many of them, or most, are far superior to the white teachers." The man who shuns categorical approximations and gratuitous labeling proves himself for such reasons easy prey to the practice. To be sure, he indicates his reasons: whites can get better jobs, whereas for a black to be a schoolteacher is to be at the top, and hence "many of the most serious and intelligent negroes become teachers." But apart from the fact that in the 1930s it wasn't so easy for whites, no matter their abilities, to get very good jobs in Alabama or elsewhere, some of us who have worked in schools, in the rural South or in the North, have not found race to be so definitively correlated with teaching excellence. Agee knows about and even refers to "the Uncle Tom attitude" that was certainly in the 1930s the terrible choice of fates, it seemed, for blacks working under segregationist authorities. Yet I have seen black teachers in Alabama show other unfortunate attitudes also, those very attributes, in fact, that Agee seems ready to lay exclusively at the door of white teachers, maybe even a few who teach at Ivy League colleges—meanness and narrowness.

I suppose I am circling a particular bush—that of liberal *and* radical sentimentality. Agee tells us at one point that "'Education' as it stands is tied in with every bondage" he can think of; he goes on to say that it "is the chief cause of these bondages." Mere rhetoric one suspects, or a bloated version of what education is, and does, and is able to do. Agee himself claimed to have learned rather a lot at St. Andrews, at Exeter, and at Harvard, from teachers whom he mentions with considerable thankfulness and praise in *Permit Me Voyage*. He came to Alabama a thoroughly educated young man, no matter the flaws in the schools he attended. The families he visited in the South didn't quite need the kind of burden he places on them of being virtuous innocents, who ought to be protected from the corruptions of something called "Education." Nor need their human dignity be used as a foil by one of a relative handful lucky enough during the depression to be able to obtain an Exeter and Harvard education.

When that college graduate, so literate himself, takes up the subject of literacy, he makes it hard for anyone to figure out what should be done about it in Alabama or in the rest of the United States. He declares scornfully that literacy is "a pleasing word." Why shouldn't it be? Well, the supposedly educated aren't very smart. As for the tenant farmers we've been learning about, they may have a lot of trouble reading or spelling or writing, never mind "critically examining any 'ideas,' whether true or false." But know this: "That they are, by virtue of these limitations, among the only 'honest' and 'beautiful' users of language, is true, perhaps, but it is not enough." As if that paradox weren't itself enough, we are reminded immediately that such people are "at an immeasurable disadvantage in a world which is run, and in which they are hurt, and in which they might be used, by 'knowledge' and by 'ideas.'" And as if *that* weren't hard enough to digest, we are offered the quite categorical assertion that "to 'consciousness' or 'knowledge' and its uses in personal conduct and in human relationships, and to those unlimited worlds of the senses, the remembrance, the mind and the heart which, beyond that of their own existence, are the only human hope, dignity, solace, increasement, and joy, they are all but totally blinded."

How to sort out the various lines of reasoning, the various assumptions that prompt such statements (and there are dozens of a similarly stunning nature)? Agee loved the people he met. He also felt, and acknowledged feeling, terribly guilty while with them; he was, after all, the lucky, privileged outsider, soon enough back in Manhattan, playing Beethoven's Ninth Symphony in a room with a majestic view of, well, New York City's ghettos, as a matter of fact, among other neighborhoods. He wanted to hold up his new (temporary) friends as honorable and decent people. But he was with them rather briefly, and there must have been an element of restraint on all sides, as hosts and guests fumbled toward some reasonable trust. Still, one doubts Agee saw and heard all there was to see and hear— and he knew, of course, that such was the case. In a year, in two years, there still might have been secrets not discovered, though as a rule the more time people spend together, the better they get to know one another. The point is that Agee spent much less time than he knew would be reasonably adequate—and that fact only added to self-recrimination already bordering on self-flagellation. Going through *Let Us Now Praise Famous Men,* one begins to notice, not surprisingly, that such responses and conclusions lead the writer to the edge of despair, if not to its very center. I do not mean to get into a clinical psychological analysis of James Agee's complex mental life and its bearing upon his work. Quite frankly, I believe such an effort, directed at any writer's life, produces a low yield of fairly banal information. Everyone's mental life, plumbed deep and wide, turns out to be complex. Millions of us have been hurt or made to feel vulnerable or especially sensitive, yet we don't find ourselves able or willing to wrestle with words as Agee did, and did with such conspicuous success. The point is not Agee's childhood as a putative source of later literary productivity, nor Agee's psychopathology (which we all have, in one form or another) as an explanation of later interests, attitudes, or involvements; rather, the point is that Agee's sort of mission is bound to push the mind hard. If we are, that is, to follow the advice of Shakespeare or of those nineteenth-century political revolutionaries who wanted to overthrow various despots (leaving aside what history would give us as the consequence), then we had best be prepared to deal with the moral anger that goes along with such moral analysis, namely, the kind meant to prompt social change. And anger craves objects.

Agee is continually self-lacerating, but he rouses himself at critical times to a fierce, sometimes surprising assault on a wide range of others. In the section "Money," he begins with a remark of Franklin Delano Roosevelt's during one of his campaigns: "You are farmers; I am a farmer myself." We are then yanked down to Alabama, to learn about the finances of some impossibly poor farmers, with whom the squire of New York State's Hyde Park, overlooking the Hudson River, has declared his occupational solidarity. The effect, of course, is achieved: devastating irony. The reader is brought up short, confronted through the disarming use of a quotation with all sorts of uncomfortable facts and thoughts, not least the glibness of liberal rhetoric viewed from a certain vantage point. What is one to say? Did not Roosevelt try hard, extremely hard, all during the 1930s, and against great opposition, to alleviate the distress of America's poor farm people? If the mental and moral life of tenant farmers is worth painstaking consideration, as in *Let Us Now Praise Famous Men*, are we to dismiss the political struggle of the 1930s waged by Franklin Delano Roosevelt, among others, and all because of a cleverly placed quotation taken out of the context of a given speech, never mind a campaign? What can be said in defense of what seems like a blatantly cheap shot?

He would, no doubt, laugh if not sneer at such a series of questions. He was a writer responding to a given set of circumstances and making all sorts of connections so as to agitate other minds to thought, even as his own had been awakened and moved to cry, sing, perform. If while he contemplated rural Alabama, a line or two spoken by an American President in the 1930s struck Agee's fancy, then so be it. His job, as a poet, novelist, and literary essayist, was not detailed political analysis (either with respect to farm labor or reformist national politics), nor for that matter psychiatric analysis; it was not even cool, documentary exposition or logical argument. I had the privilege of knowing, when in medical school, William Carlos Williams, like Agee a poet and novelist with a strong interest in social and political matters from which he couldn't keep away, despite the strong intuition on his part that his judgments, spoken subjectively, often went awry. "I sound off, sometimes—and strike out," he once said to me. "But even so, I think I strike out making a lot of noise, and catching the attention of some people, and if it's an issue that's important, and they stop and think what *they* think, I'm glad." Perhaps Agee wouldn't mind associating himself with Dr. Williams' candid self-assessment.

Not that Agee didn't come up with his own rather vigorous apology of sorts for an occasional misstep:

> I am not at all trying to lay out a thesis, far less to substantiate or solve. I do not consider myself qualified. I know only that murder is being done, against nearly every individual on the planet, and that there are dimensions and correlations of cure which not only are not being used but appear to be scarcely considered or suspected. I know there is cure, even now available, if only it were available, in science and in the fear and joy of God. This is only a brief personal statement of these convictions: and my self-disgust is less in my ignorance, and

far less in my 'failure' to 'defend' or 'support' the statement, than in my inability to state it even so far as I see it, and in my inability to blow out the brains with it of you who take what it is talking of lightly, or not seriously enough.

He is writing, then, in a nonacademic tradition, even an anti-academic one. He does not advertise himself as a field-worker, and certainly not as a social scientist. Nor is he a journalist reporting in the factual or muckraking traditions—or, at least, not *only* such a writer. There are, definitely, reportorial aspects to the book. But this is the book, mainly, of an unashamed moralist, who happens also to be a man often marvelously exact and discerning in his use of words. It is the book, too, of a mind reared in twentieth-century technological hope, edged by a lingering Christian vision, not at all triumphant yet not acknowledged with mere lip service either. There are, once again, the strenuous assaults on the author's own worth, a bit startling, given his membership in an intelligentsia more apt to turn its criticism on others or to define the tendency to self-criticism as evidence of psychological illness. For Agee, the self-disgust mentioned in his confessional outcry connects, one keeps feeling, with St. Augustine, and St. John of the Cross, and Pascal; it is a tradition of Christian critical self-scrutiny that will not yield its dignity even today to the claims of those who use words such as *masochism* or *depression*.

As for his regret that he hasn't quite been able to "blow out the brains" of various readers with the truculent assertions he has worked into a deliberately discordant and unwieldly book, it would be unwise to ignore the remark as a foolish and regrettable instance of hyperbole. Agee's rebellion, Walker Evans insisted from the retrospective vantage point of 1960, was "unquenchable, self-damaging, deeply principled, infinitely costly, and ultimately priceless." The principled voice of Agee's was not easily shed; it sets the tone for a lot of his writing, and the rebellion Evans mentions was part of a particular religious tradition. The Judeo-Christian principles, after all, which prompted such dedicated rage in Agee were stated first by an angry Jeremiah, an angry Isaiah, and in the New Testament by a Jesus suddenly not meek and accepting but full of scorn and disgust as he confronts the arid pietism of the Temple.

When Agee talks of "murder," he is once again flirting with hyperbole, or so we might think, and when he says that this murder is being committed "against nearly every individual on the planet," we may well want to know precisely what he means. Who is doing the killing, and with what in mind? And when we are told that a *cure* is available but is not being "considered or suspected," we have reached a logical impasse. The verb *consider* leads down one road, the verb *suspect* down quite another. Issues of will, availability, responsibility, and possibility—all are thrown into a boiling, moralistic stew. Can what is not "suspected" be "considered"? Or is the author referring to the workings of the unconscious—the ability not to consider, not even to suspect, when the mind wants to blot certain matters from awareness?

There is, further, the enigmatic statement of Agee's that he knows "there is a cure." Or is there? The qualifying expression ("if only it were available"), rendered as a conditional clause of hope, makes one wonder yet again what Agee is really thinking. But soon enough he summons the phrase "personal statement," as if any of his readers had, by page 307 of his book, any substantial doubts that his statements are personal. The final thrust about wanting to "blow out the brains" of the reader anticipates again the R. D. Laing who used a similar phrase with respect to *his* readers in the 1960s, thereby breaking as much new ground as some of his followers wanted to believe.

We must go another mile, critically, and contend with the preacher who demands that his audience not take a given message or problem lightly or with insufficient seriousness. But who is to make these calibrations, and by what criteria? What does the author want—empathy, sympathy, understanding shouted from all available rooftops? A stint of time in Alabama in an effort to help others with their various problems? How long a spell, as a matter of fact, since Agee himself was gone in August of 1936, having arrived in July? And doing what: teaching in schools the author condemns so bitterly, helping in the fields when no help is really required? Cash: is that the answer, a philanthropic inundation? The people Agee knew might have generously responded to that last question, with undisguised, unmodified enthusiasm. But one wonders what pitch of skeptical scorn might then have been forthcoming from a writer so contemptuous of the material side of American capitalism, even while he lived off it as a writer and before that as a student at a wealthy school and an even wealthier college.

The question persists, therefore: what kind of seriousness did the author have in mind for us, if he is not to shoot us through the head? I fear there is no clear answer to this question. There remains, inevitably, the reader's sense that he or she is being hit hard with rhetoric and that maybe the best thing to do is proceed, turn the page, and hope for some further acquaintance with Alabama's people or even for a few more jabs at the reader's assumed complacency. Or is this to be unnecessarily or gratuitously tough, crabbed and mean spirited about the book? Maybe so. I have tried to read a paragraph of Agee's fairly closely, assuming that someone who spent three or four years working on the writing, each sentence a struggle, we are told, ought to be attended to rather faithfully; but I have done so without the blanket approval of a fellow traveler, to use that expression in a more literal rather than symbolic or idiomatic sense, since I have talked, as Agee did, with families and worked with them for a number of years in the rural South, Alabama included. Nor have I been consistent over the years in my own sentiments about Agee's book. There was a time when it was scripture to me, every word and idea a heavenly gift.

Let Us Now Praise Famous Men was reissued in 1960, a generation's time after its first publication in 1941, at which point it received a decidedly mixed critical response and a singularly poor one with respect to buyers. In 1941, the Great Depression was finally receding; the prospect of America's involvement in a second World War was accomplishing what no federal recovery program had been able to do. By 1960, however, an altogether different climate of opinion was fast developing. A war had been fought and won; a cold war had begun. America, or at least a segment of it, was prospering. But by the late 1950s there were, as they say, a few problems; one of them turned out to be an entire region of the country—the South. With its racial conflict, with its severe, unremitting rural poverty, the South had scarcely been affected by the social and economic improvements many other Americans had come to take for granted. In 1954, the Supreme Court sent a strong signal to the South; in 1956, an extremely reluctant President Eisenhower had to send federal troops there; by 1957, Rosa Parks had taken her stand in Montgomery, Alabama, saying *enough!* to segregationist laws that told the people of that state and its neighbors where to sit, stand, eat, and learn. A hitherto unknown minister, Dr. Martin Luther King, Jr., leader of a Montgomery, Alabama, Baptist Church, was quickly at Rosa Parks's side and would soon become an important national leader. The election of 1960 gave us the youngest president in American history, ready and willing to bring new energy to political life— though possibly no more prepared than most other Americans to deal with the sudden tide of social change that was given dramatic impetus in early February of 1960 when four black students asked to be served at the food counter of a Woolworth store in Greensboro, North Carolina. It was therefore an especially opportune time for Houghton Mifflin to give the public, a whole new generation of Americans, a chance to meet James Agee and Walker Evans and the fellow citizens the two of them had met a quarter of a century earlier in that part of the South that had been left for too long with a peculiar obsession with its mythic past, left to indulge a terrible reluctance to relent on laws and social habits that were increasingly seen by the rest of the country as a national disgrace.

I remember not only buying *Let Us Now Praise Famous Men* at that time but seeing many others do so. I remember finding copies of the book, in hard cover no less, all over the South. And I especially remember copies of the book in Freedom Houses, as we called them in the summer of 1964, during the Mississippi Summer Project, an effort by young Americans of both races to bring voter registration to the steadfastly segregationist Delta. In Canton, Mississippi; in Greenwood, Mississippi; in Yazoo City, Mississippi; on a table, on the floor, on a bed, on a chair; read by white, well-to-do students from Ivy League colleges but read as well by black students from the North and from the South—it was a bible of sorts, at least for a while, a sign, a symbol, a reminder, an eloquent testimony that others had cared, had gone forth to look and hear, and had come back to stand up and address their friends and neighbors and those beyond personal knowing.

I often wondered why some of the blacks I knew in SNCC (the Student Nonviolent Coordinating Committee, a major organization involved in the Civil Rights struggle of the early 1960s) had such favorable words for Agee's books, along with strong reservations, which grew stronger as those same blacks withdrew increasingly from a cooperative effort with whites into the insistent position of "black power." Here, for example, is a black youth from Tuscaloosa (not all that far from the Alabama territory Agee stalked) reflecting on "*the* book," as he kept calling it:

> There's no book like it, at least that I've seen. It's *the* book— the one book where a white man lets it all hang out, and he's not trying to kid himself, and he doesn't let you and me, reading him, pull all kinds of tricks. I mean, this guy is honest! He may be troubled, but that's the truth of his life and everyone else's, that we've got a lot of trouble. Like he says, if you're *not* troubled by all the trouble, big trouble, we have in this country—well, then, you're *really* in trouble, big trouble.
>
> To me, the proof of the truth in Agee's writing is that he makes mistakes, big ones. I mean, for a black, the big moment is in that small section called "Near a Church," where he's with his buddy Walker Evans, I believe, and they're getting the camera set up, and they see a Negro couple, and I guess Evans wants to photograph them, but whatever the couple has on their minds, Agee is walking behind them, and he disturbs them. They hear him and look, and he gets closer, and they freeze, they just freeze: who is this white guy, and what in hell is he going to do to us? Pretty fast, Agee sees the whole lousy situation: the young Negro couple, scared to death, and he wanting to be nice and friendly, but knowing there was no way, no way, not even for him, big and easy with words, to dissolve the crazy, terrible stuff that was going on between them and him and his buddy. The two young Negroes stare at him. They just stare. I guess he stared back. Talk about fear!
>
> We see that same fear today here, doing our organizing. I'm black, and *I* scare the people here, because I'm an outsider. They don't know what I want. They can't get a fix on me. Anyway, Agee saw the whole horrible story of "race relations" in the South in those few seconds, and he tells you how he felt—as rotten and no good as can be. Do you remember— how he says he wanted to get down on his knees and kiss the feet of the Negroes? That's the image in the book I think of most. It's powerful, man! I told my kid sister about it, and she said Agee must have been a pretty crazy white man to think

like that. I asked her what she meant. She said no "normal
white man" thinks like that! She's eleven! She's pretty smart!

Agee's own description of the scene goes like this: "They just kept
looking at me. There was no more for them to say than for me. The
least I could have done was to throw myself flat on my face and embrace and kiss their feet. That impulse took hold of me so powerfully, from my whole body, not by thought, that I caught myself
from doing it exactly and as scarcely as you snatch yourself from
jumping from a sheer height. . . ." He knew he would, indeed, be
thought loony, or a sinister confidence man, up to some mischief.
Blacks, back then, had to put up with all sorts of white craziness in
terror-struck or bitter or mocking silence. But what are we to make
of the somewhat overwrought impulse of self-abasement that drives
Agee so close to its active expression? Is he, with a good storyteller's
narrative impulse, exaggerating for dramatic purposes? Is he pushing
us, morally and psychologically both, and educating us as well—
here is what goes on down South, and here is how we ought to feel?
Might he be dismissed as the archetypal bleeding-heart liberal? Why
did he bother that couple, who only wanted their privacy? *That*
question might, of course, be applied to the entire expedition, a kind
of raid on the vulnerability of the poor white folk interviewed and
photographed and portrayed as down-and-out objects of pity for
countless others rich enough to buy books.

Agee's book *Let Us Now Praise Famous Men* is a great one precisely because it prompts such moral and social questions about the
responsibilities of the various observers, investigators, and writers
who make their way into this or that community in hopes of discovering something, doing documentary work, finding material for
an article, story, or book. How much can one get to know about
people in a few days, a week or two, or a month, as a "guest" of
theirs, a visitor with a deadline in mind? What matters are *not* discussed, even looked into, by those of us who do fieldwork, learning
as we go from home to home certain limits of conversation? How
ought one to behave in that field, with what degree of tact, reticence, and respect for the privacy of others? Is it exploitive to enter a
neighborhood, learn certain facts, get a sense of certain attitudes,
and then make a living by writing about it? Ought the writer then, at
the very least, offer to split financial payment for an article or book

with the people who have, after all, given their time and energy and been one's patient teachers? Or if they are not to be reimbursed personally, should something be given to a cause or organization that works with and is of help to their particular neighborhood, town, or region?

On the other hand, isn't it possible to wonder at all this fuss, this self-accusation, these declarations of personal confusion if not outright wrongdoing? James Agee was an intelligent, careful, considerate writer. He went South at the behest of an important national magazine in hopes of doing a good reporter's job and, presumably, of reaching and significantly touching a host of readers. It is hard to imagine him being rude or crude in any way; it is hard to imagine any harm he did as a visitor. Why then his nearly hysterical self-recriminations? And are the people Agee visited well served by the various literary, philosophical, and political asides—which, it can be argued, turn the situation of particular families into an occasion for James Agee's various ruminations, reflections, and diatribes?

Agee worries about *himself* a lot; he regrets the terrible discrepancies between his kind of life and the lives of others. But what were his *hosts'* worries, not to mention their wishes? Maybe one or two of them might have said something like this: look, mister Jim, take it easy and stop working yourself up into such a lather. We're not having an easy time of it, no question we're not. But we're not wringing our hands and crying and feeling sorry for ourselves, and we don't need anyone else crying for us. Sure, we'd like a better deal. Some of the things that upset you don't happen to upset us. We just want to do a little better as farmers, get better prices. We don't want you going around saying that we're sorry ones, that we're the sorriest people ever, and all we deserve is everyone's tears. We're working hard, and we'll keep working hard, and we're proud of that, not sitting around feeling glum, waiting for someone to pat us on the back and tell us they really do sympathize, you know!

I have to mention still another matter I have previously discussed (in an issue of the *Harvard Advocate* devoted to James Agee, February of 1972). Agee does make relatively brief but pointed mention of segregationist sentiment among some people he met in the course of his travels through Alabama, but he doesn't spell out what, if anything, his hosts had to think and say about black people. We learn a lot about what *he* feels, and after awhile begin to wonder at his reticence about such an obviously significant subject—the black people, their proper situation—much discussed in the South during its long history by white people of all classes. One wonders whether Agee couldn't bear to hear, or having heard, to relay to others some of the racial attitudes of the people he got to know. Is it an outrageous generalization to assume, back in 1936, a substantial amount of racial prejudice among just about all of Alabama's white tenant farmers, not to mention its lawyers and doctors and college professors, and wouldn't the same go for plenty of the people of Illinois and New York and Massachusetts?

I remember in the march from Selma to Montgomery during the early 1960s that many ordinary white tenant farmers came and stood, and alas, had their say. I worked in three mostly rural counties of Alabama during that decade and have elsewhere (in *Migrants, Sharecroppers, Mountaineers*, which is Volume Three of *Children of Crisis*) tried to describe some of the fears and hatreds any number of men, women, and children were quite willing and indeed determined to express. When I first read *Let Us Now Praise Famous Men* in college during the early 1950s, I never stopped to ask myself about the question of race or how it had or hadn't been handled by the author. When I read the book again in the early 1960s, I couldn't stop noticing what seemed to be the disproportionate assumptions of guilt and innocence. Agee as the one who ought to feel shame, if not guilt, and the New York (or Harvard) intellectuals whose limitations were plentiful enough: here were the terrible crooks and frauds and bigots who run things in the South or the North—the schools and colleges and public institutions. And then, in sharp contrast, the hurt families Agee and Evans met, and the young black couple they met, and the badly exploited blacks they did not meet but do mention—all of these people seemingly without blemish, or relatively so. I suppose there is a degree of idealization in all of us when we leave home to see the world in the hope of rendering it justice in words. So that if we readers wonder how silly, self-important, and egotistical some of Agee's intellectual colleagues are made to appear, perhaps we ought to remember how wonderfully gentle and kind (is the word forgiving?) Agee is toward others less like himself in certain respects. He forgives some to the point where there is little forgiveness left for others.

My questions and criticism show the great strength of Agee's literary-journalistic writing, with its mixture of accurate, suggestive description, compassionate portraiture, skeptical cultural observation, and pungent social analysis, all rendered in a prose distinguished, when compared to that of other writers of documentary nonfiction, by a caring, lyrical intensity. And there is also an uncanny and quite special mix of individualism and communitarianism. Agee's anarchism is rooted in his Christian sense of life as precious and as a gift from above. He is, I suspect, nearest in spirit to Dorothy Day and the Catholic Worker movement, to Emmanuel Mounier and his "personalism," to George Orwell and Ignazio Silone—members of Irving Howe's "homeless left," men and women unable to live comfortably either in a capitalism that seems unwilling to address itself to the worldwide matter of equity, or in a communism that has become, again and again, arrogant, despotic, and murderous. If there is any writing of Agee's that places him, tells us what he believes deep down, it is to be found in this paragraph, one that rescues the clichés of twentieth-century existentialist literature and philosophy, as they certainly must be rescued, from the banality of faddishness:

> All that each person is, and experiences, and shall never experience, in body and in mind, all these things are differing expressions of himself and of one root, and are identical: and not one of these things nor one of these persons is ever quite to be duplicated, nor replaced, nor has it ever quite had precedent: but each is a new and incommunicably tender life, wounded in every breath, and almost as hardly killed as easily wounded: sustaining, for a while, without defense, the enormous assaults of the universe.

Those "assaults" did not spare his personal life. His first marriage, to Olivia Saunders, was followed in 1939 by a second one, to Alma Mailman, that did not last long. Their son, Joel, is now a writer in his own right. A third marriage, to Mia Fritsch, began in 1946 and would, in the less than ten years left to Agee, result in two daughters and one son. He had a rough time in the late 1930s while writing *Let Us Now Praise Famous Men*. Besides being constantly short of cash, he wasn't at all sure how to cope with the families he'd met or with himself, the one who saw and heard, who came and left, who writes and is read. The book was written in Frenchtown, New Jersey, and was originally called *Three Tenant Farmers*. The decision, with respect to the title, to use words from the Apocrypha—Ecclesiasticus, chapter 44—was an extremely significant one. The reader is told right from the start to contend with a moral narrative, with a literary sensibility intent on an ironic rather than a predominantly sociological angle of vision. And not surprisingly, the author's critical response to his own book is severely moral, if not moralistic. He wrote to Father Flye in 1941 that "what you write of the book needless to say is good to hear to the point of shaming me—for it is a sinful book at least in all degrees of 'falling short of the mark' and I think in more corrupt ways as well."

Year after year, as I use Agee's writing in my courses and read student papers about him, I ask myself, as do they, why we bother with him and what he means to us, who are alive more than a generation after his untimely death. In my lectures I try to stress his singular gifts as a writer of English, a voice of brave and candid dissatisfaction with the way things are—the inhumanity, the injustice, the meanness and callousness, the smugness and arrogance. He was a giant of a man, with a wide-ranging, restless, hungry mind that crossed all sorts of boundaries, borders, and established limits; he was a teacher, who through poems and stories and essays made people morally uncomfortable, morally alert, more morally searching. He was not least a pilgrim. A student once sent me a note after the course was over. Only twenty, dying of leukemia, he went to lectures, read books, and wrote papers, feeling it his duty, his responsibility, as the particular person he was, to "keep going as before." In his note he had this to say about James Agee:

> I expect to die in a few months. I'll be less than half as old as he was when he died. I've been reading everything of his I can get my hands on. I feel that he's the one who has the most to say to me, before I die. The reason is this: he seemed to have lived each day as if it was a gift, and as if it was his last, and he wrote that way. He makes me feel that there's reason to be proud that I'm a human being, that I can sit and read James Agee and understand what he wrote and respond to his language and his ideas. A lot of the time, after I read the newspapers or the weekly newsmagazines, or watch the news on television, I'm ashamed to be a human being, because of all the terrible things we do to one another. We make animals seem so civilized!

But with Agee, your faith is restored. He was such a good person; and he was such a wonderful writer. I'm sure he had his faults, like the rest of us. But he gets through to you. He reaches your heart, and he reaches your mind. A lot of people reach your heart, and a lot of intellectuals reach your mind, but to do both, to make you feel and make you think—and even to make you try to be a better person, that's a lot! To me, Agee is someone who knew what it meant to live in this crazy century. He only lived 45 years, but he saw it all, the wars, the nuclear madness, the depression, Hitler and Stalin. Even so, he kept his sense of humor, and he wrote those beautiful books. They tell you about yourself, because they tell you what a human being is, whether a child or a teenager, whether a poor person or a guy who tries to understand poor people, those way below him on the social ladder, and with no money at all.

There was more, including a self-deprecatory apologia worthy of Agee himself. I have kept that letter tucked in a copy of *Let Us Now Praise Famous Men*—a decent, thoughtful, dying youth's homage to a writer with a keen and abiding sense of how fragile and tentative things are and, for that reason, how precious is this existence allowed us. James Agee was a promising poet who never became more than that. He was shrewd and knowing, a marvelously poignant storyteller who never became the self-assured narrator of fiction he might have been. He never got enough beyond himself and his given world, never attained the distance of a great novelist. He was a sharp, powerful critic of books and films, though he never lived to become a more substantial analyst of them. He was an utterly unique and brilliant social observer; his effort to do justice to the Alabama world of 1936 stands apart from the entire field of documentary writing as an example that makes the rest of us pause with extreme modesty. He was a movie scriptwriter just beginning, though already the enormous talent and great good humor and magical dramatic sense were more than apparent. He was, not least, a letter writer, not only to Father Flye but to other quite remarkable people, like Dwight Macdonald and Robert Fitzgerald—someone who could combine friendship with continuing, contained, highly intelligent discourse, though a less harassed, more relaxedly meditative correspondence might have been possible in a life longer than Agee's was to be. And finally, he was a person thoroughly, completely, in every sense *sui generis*. Those like myself, who never knew him, bow in respect, wince a bit with sadness, and admit quietly and regretfully the inevitable twinge of envy.

So if we mourn his premature death, we have to declare our gratitude for what was given us—a rich talent, brightly displayed, to an enduring effect. The testimony of that dying youth is one of thousands from those who have known James Agee as readers, as men and women grappling with the moral issues of our world and trying to figure out what truly matters, as against what comes and goes, the silly, stupid, and all too flashy diversions that tempt many of us, no matter the region or the neighborhood, to betray ourselves.

Raritan, Summer 1983

Camera on James Agee

We are months short of a quarter of a century since James Agee slumped dead of a coronary seizure in a New York City taxi on his way to a doctor. He was forty-five and had been suffering anginal pain for several years. The intensity of his gifted life had already become a legend; and no doubt his obituary prompted some who knew him to shake their heads and lament the waste or to nod knowingly as they asked rhetorically: how could anyone expect to live into old age at his pace? And there were, always, the comments about his work—the failure to follow through as an artist in any of the various directions he took, each with such promise: poet, story writer, essayist, novelist, film scriptwriter.

In his memoir of Agee, at once personally giving and sharply analytical of the writer's considerable assets and wounding handicaps, Robert Fitzgerald took pains to question the notion of journalism as a spoiler—and of course, as a cover for ruinous mental propensities. "Was it weakness," he asks, "that kept James Agee at *Fortune*, or was it strategy and will, for the sake of the great use he would make of it?" Certainly Agee might have written poems or a novel in the years that he gave to Alabama's tenant farmers—the exalted gropings toward human actuality, and not least, the self-probings and presentations that collectively became *Let Us Now Praise Famous Men*. But who is to judge what is required of a writer such as Agee?

Especially prominent these days, as Fitzgerald knew (hence the reference to "weakness") is the marriage of psychological reductionism to literary criticism. It is convenient for some of us to be rid of Agee's powerful assault on many social and scholarly conventions by demonstrating his failure to achieve what we presume to say he ought to have had in mind for himself. That way, we don't have to look not only at what he did accomplish but also at what he well may have wanted to do with all his mind and soul. As for his neurotic conflicts, they were unquestionably substantial, persistent, and harmful. But Agee was enormously talented, and he was crafty at finding expressions for the various ideas and visions that pressed upon him. Anna Freud has reminded us that "creative energy" is a "universally envied gift." Envy can work its way into our lives through a certain kind of moralistic psychological scrutiny that confuses a writer's sensibility with his worries or fears—as if the hundreds of people who have worked for Henry Luce, or the millions who have drunk and smoked to excess, have ever been in serious danger of possessing the lyrical and narrative skills that James Agee lived with, drew upon, and embodied in the writing left us. And that writing, the magic of his words, is the only reason we read about him and argue over the kind of life he lived.

Now we have a chance to think about Agee while watching a film devoted to his life, his work, and his relatively brief but still unforgotten presence among us. Ross Spears is a young filmmaker from Johnson City, Tennessee; his *Agee*, released last spring, makes the documentary camera a powerful instrument of literary biography—a hitherto neglected use of a medium that has not hesitated to connect itself to sociology, contemporary history, politics, and anthropology.

Spears brings us to Agee initially through Father Flye, the Episcopal minister who was the writer's lifelong older friend and sometime correspondent. Now in his middle nineties, and in ways fragile, Father Flye still has a lively, touching voice. He knew Agee most of his life and loved him; he tells the viewer right off that this is a special, difficult man, yet someone with a significant artistic and intellectual struggle to his credit—nowhere more evident than in the vexing, demanding, eye-opening, tortured, immensely rewarding *Let Us Now Praise Famous Men*.

We next receive the image and the words of our present-day leader, and we all have a right to be on guard—against not only him but also the filmmaker's purposes. But President Carter knows his Agee; he speaks out of his own south Georgia memories of the 1930s. He insists that *Let Us Now Praise Famous Men* is something more than another exposé of rural poverty, and he connects the book, quietly and intelligently, to Thoreau's nineteenth-century scrutiny of Concord's terrain in its use of the sights and sounds of the countryside (north-central Alabama) as a means of moral reflection.

Agee takes many sideswipes (some, arguably, gratuitous and demeaning to his own aspirations) in the course of his execution of *Let Us Now Praise Famous Men*—including the ironic one he directs at himself when he confronts the reader, in possession of a rather large volume of complicated, arresting prose, with this announcement of failed self-denial: "If I could do it, I'd do no writing at all here." The President of the United States, who may be conned by other individuals and their intentions, gets through exactly to Agee: the writer is taking huge personal risks in this book, and he has every right to whatever emotions happen to confront him, such as the nervous self-criticism of his strong Christian conscience, ever wary of that sin of sins, pride.

Young Agee learned of that sin and became a child of Christian awareness in east Tennessee, first in Knoxville, where he was born in 1909, and later (from the age of ten) at an Episcopal boarding school, St. Andrews, situated near the Cumberland mountains, a two-hour drive west of Chattanooga. Agee's father was of mountain stock; the name is familiar to Appalachian people but prompts consternation, as far as pronunciation goes, for many in other parts of the country. Agee described his childhood, its special textures and strains, in the novel *A Death in the Family*, published posthumously. When he was six, his father was killed in an automobile accident; we are shown the newspaper clipping, "Found Dead on Clinton Pike." We are shown a lot more too: pictures of the gentle, hilly region of the upper South that Agee grew up knowing; an enactment of the middle-class family life he experienced as a child; a further, less charming and nostalgic enactment of the visitation of death upon a mother and child; a glimpse of the St. Andrews School and a suggestion, through Father Flye's narration, of the lean, unpretentious, humbly reverent religious and educational ministry that to this day obtains there.

Ross Spears is a young filmmaker, and he might have been forgiven for succumbing to the sentimental seductions of Agee's first years, an intensely dramatic third of a life never destined to be without worthy excitements. But these enactments are brief, pointed, instructive, and entirely without melodrama. We meet the child who will appear in *A Death in the Family*, the youth whose moody turmoil, at once religious and personal, figures in the novella *Morning Watch*. We meet, really, what Agee sought to evoke when he wrote

"Knoxville: Summer 1915"—an earlier America that one American writer never shook off, not after a couple of years at Phillips Exeter, and not after four years at Harvard, or even two decades in and out of midtown Manhattan, Greenwich Village, and Hollywood. An America with a climate of moral earnestness and social innocence, qualities hard to come by these days anywhere in the nation, though in certain Appalachian villages, as Mr. Spears knows, one can skip back a good distance in time and feel culturally, spiritually close to the young Agee's kin. A marvelously rich, mellow, ever so delicately accented voice, that of Earl McCarroll, reads to us from Agee during this visual acquaintance with Agee's background. No didactic burdens are put upon us, but we grow thoroughly alert to the world a particular writer mined so stubbornly and ingeniously, if at great personal cost.

Agee's life and work, so difficult to separate, anyway, lend themselves very well to spoken commentary, and we get plenty of it in this ninety-minute film. Jimmy Carter and the acted vignettes, done in color, give way to skillfully edited and assembled black-and-white statements from the television producer Robert Saudek, Agee's college roommate, from the poet and translator Robert Fitzgerald, also a friend acquired in Agee's college years, and from the critic Dwight MacDonald. And Agee's three wives tell us of their respective times with him—each with obvious affection, each with her own subdued suggestion of the difficulties this feverish, sometimes ungovernable man posed for those close to him. The film orders a disorderly life—one at times seemingly made to defy any number of psychological and cultural categorizations.

Olivia, Alma, and Mia are the wives, and one worries at first that these women will get lost in the winding, twisting pathways of a man's emotions, a man's writing, a man's rainbow of interests and involvements. But a strange chemistry affects these human beings. Each holds on to herself; and more, each claims sure yet tactful possession of a certain element of Agee's almost boundless psychological complexity. Olivia's outgoing innocence, her perplexity in the face of the shadowy, the demonic; Alma's poise, her sharpness of intellect, her compassionate integrity; Mia's worldliness, her intensity of observation, her mixture of openness, emotional immediacy, and skeptical distance—these are not the residual traits of extortionate sexual and personal associations. Three women speak lovingly but differently about a man who, as with so many of us, was a different man at different times in his life, who even, no doubt, at any given moment had different sides of himself to share with one or another individual. These women show what *they* were. They lent of themselves to Agee, but alas, we are not going to hear about them in one of the best ways possible—that is, from him.

With Agee's friends, the men he worked with, drank with, talked and talked and talked with, a similar, compelling, edifying diversity comes across: Saudek's dramatic eye, quick to notice someone's force of personality—a presence alternately enchanting and saddening; Fitzgerald's wonderfully knowing and precise eloquence about a dear comrade in the never-ending struggle with words; MacDonald's urbane, shrewd, broadly educated critical intelligence, missing few tricks but tolerant of this life's unyielding mysteries; John Huston's warm yet tough estimate of a brilliant, irregular companion in the jungle trek of movie-making; Walker Evans' brief but pointed distinction between his chosen task as a somewhat austere observer and Agee's deep dive into the currents of subjectivity; and yet again in the film, the kind and alert Father Flye, *there*—as Agee, even in his most doubtful and fearful moments, must have hoped and prayed an almighty God would prove to be. These women and men seem drawn together, seem to be addressing each other—through the skillful use of documentary film footage. We hear a solemn yet lively conversation about a writer's achievements and failures: the film allows a friend's, a husband's, a colleague's continuing contact with us of this world through retained, and now declared, shared memories.

An important contribution, worthy of Agee's own best journalistic instincts, is quietly worked into this running exegesis; we meet Alabama country people, survivors of the fearful, desperate 1930s—notably the two women who were, in fact, hosts in July 1936 to the writer and a young photographer on their *Fortune* magazine assignment. They are presented to us (under "Persons and Places") in *Let Us Now Praise Famous Men* as Margaret Ricketts, "aged twenty," and Annie Mae (Woods) Gudger, "aged twenty-seven"; and now, forty-three years later, they are introduced as Elizabeth Tingle and Mae Burroughs, who remember the two guests from far away—with their "Northern talk," their earnest friendliness, their humor, and their persistent desire to experience, to understand. The rural women remember "mixing" with Agee; they remember his eyes:

"He watched, he watched." Mae Burroughs says that she "hated to see them go," that she and others "got attached to them." The camera moves from color shots of these two elderly Alabama citizens, and from color footage of a landscape that has not changed all that much these past years, to Robert Fitzgerald's brief reminder: "Jim Agee was a Christian"; he had gone South to try to be with "the least of the Lord's people."

The side of Agee connected to the Bible, to the Old Testament prophets, and to Jesus and His disciples knew the special fate reserved by God for the poor, "the least." The secular side of Agee, the New York intellectual he was despite the contempt he felt for the collective breed, could only be hurt, discouraged, and enraged by the evidence all around Bibb and Perry and Hale Counties, Alabama (and elsewhere in America), of hunger, malnutrition, and flagrant inequality. Hence one of the persisting tensions in *Let Us Now Praise Famous Men*: the tenant farmers are ironically awesome figures, noble by virtue of a divine choice, but the same men, women, and children are the humiliated ones of this earth—objects, for all too many, of easy, privileged pity. Agee knew the ethical torment of sensitive social observers: they come, leave, and cover themselves with the glory of written or photographic compassion; those they visited stay, and soon enough fade into obscurity. True, muckraking can facilitate social or political change. Nevertheless.

The last part of the film *Agee* is devoted to his short, luminous, still influential career as a reviewer, a scriptwriter, even (once) a bit actor. He is starting a new life for himself, yet (we know) there is little time left. John Huston gives a chilling account of Agee writing all night, writing more by day, playing tennis, drinking, and smoking—and then boom: the coronary vessels at last say no. We see Agee as the town drunk in *The Bride Comes to Yellow Sky*, one of the films for which he wrote the script, and originally a Stephen Crane short story. We listen to readings of his penetrating remarks about various movies. We watch an excerpt from another of his creations, *The African Queen*—the wonderful moment when Hepburn empties bottle after bottle of Bogart's gin. We are given Agee sitting beside a friend and hero of sorts to him, Chaplin. And we learn of his last months—frequent chest pain and a losing battle with abstinence (cigarettes, liquor). A clipping tells of his death on May 16, 1955, the same day (thirty-nine years later) his father died; both died in cars.

A man who saw early on, the special province of the camera and did his fair share to connect the world of ideas to that of celluloid, has inspired a thoughtful, imaginative response from a young filmmaker, and a Tennesseean at that. The voices, the sound track full of Beethoven, so loved by Agee, the quiet visual procession supplying witness and analysis of him, affection for him—it all amounts to a fine tribute to a hectic, pained, buoyant, decent, exceptionally radiant life, which, in its limited tenure, managed to offer us songs of real distinction and power. A moment of sentiment would permit us to imagine that somewhere in the universe the smile of James Agee, so large and winning, covering up bravely some of a given destiny's heartache, must surely be registering its pleased reaction to this film, a particular message from one of us still on this side of things.

New Republic, November 3, 1979

Joel Agee
Growing up East German

J ames Agee was a writer of strong talent and many interests, but when he died at forty-five he was by no means the master of his discerning, anguished intellect, not to mention his tempestuous emotions. Even at Harvard he had called attention to himself by the way he lived as well as by his abilities. Until heart disease slowed him down (and eventually killed him), he was much talked about as an insomniac, hard-drinking poet, novelist, and critic, and he was also well known as a film scriptwriter and essayist. An iconoclast, a rule-breaker, a performer, he was a visionary barely able to keep ahead of his own demons. Many of those who admired his prose viewed his life with pity or outright disapproval, thinking of the waste, the promise only partially fulfilled.

When James Agee died in 1955, he was living with his third wife, Mia, and their three small children. By Alma, his second wife, he had become the father of a son, Joel, born in 1940, when the long struggle with the writing of his book *Let Us Now Praise Famous Men* was finally being put aside rather than won. By 1944 Alma had left him—angry, she told an interviewer in the recent documentary film *Agee*, because of her husband's unwillingness to settle into a stable family life. She took their son to Mexico, and there she met and married Bodo Uhse, a writer and longtime Communist who had fled his native Germany when Hitler came to power. In 1948 the Uhses (including a baby son, Stefan) returned to East Germany on a Soviet freighter. Joel took his stepfather's name and became a resident of Gross-Glienicke, a town near Berlin at the outermost edge of the Soviet zone. He already spoke English and Spanish; he now began mastering German. He became, ostensibly, a German child whose family belonged to the privileged Communist intelligentsia.

Joel Agee is now over forty. He describes his autobiographical memoir, *Twelve Years*, in its subtitle, as *An American Boyhood in East Germany*. He apparently wants to connect his own childhood with conflicts of recent decades: Western capitalism and democracy as against Eastern socialism, with its ever-present bureaucratic centralism. Before we read of his life, however, we are told this:

> Everything in this book is true, but not everything is precisely factual. While none of the events described are fictitious, I have taken liberties of fiction to disguise the identity of most characters outside my immediate family: I have changed names, I have transposed heads, bodies, attitudes. Place names have occasionally been altered for the same reason. Here and there, I chose to imagine the nuance of a gesture or look or utterance rather than bore the reader with repeated complaints about my spotty recollection. By far the greater part of my story, though, is faithful to the facts and their chronology. Foremost among my intentions, throughout the book, was finding the right word, the right phrase and image, to render as honestly as I could the essential atmosphere, conflicts, and hopes of those twelve years as I remember them.

An interesting avowal. One understands the need to shield certain people from totalitarian revenge and to protect the privacy of those one has watched and learned from. But why the distinction between truth and factuality? Mr. Agee is not a journalist and has no intention of documenting the facts of a given news story. He is relying upon a kind of witness—his memory, as it has been shaped by a moral intelligence. Ought we now ask our children to keep tape recorders handy, lest in future years they stumble into the terrible trap of fiction as they try to recall a conversation or a moment of action? Subjectivity and imagination have yet to be declared enemies of what is "true." The oddly apologetic tone in Mr. Agee's preliminary note reminds us how hard it is, these days, to take anything for granted—even the right of a well-intentioned writer to turn his own childhood recollections into an interesting story.

Agee evidently feels he must explain the way his mind works. When he draws on an early image of his stepfather, he points out that it is "probably the composite of many nearly identical moments." At another point he remarks upon how "strange" it is—"the way memories cluster and illuminate one another, or even blend, as if whatever agency handles the punctilious business of storing up the past had at some point lapsed into reverie and become more mindful of meaning than accuracy." *Twelve Years* contains a great deal of such "reverie." The risk, of course, is self-indulgence—especially so when the essential story of the autobiography is one of youthful searching. There aren't any chapters in the book, only three sections whose titles are certain years: 1948–1955, 1955–1958, and finally, 1959–1960. But Agee immediately holds the reader's attention, maintaining a wry distance from his story of how he became aware of himself and his odd situation between the ages of eight and twenty. He has no interest in sentiment or in showing himself to be a genius in the making. His book is in the American tradition of the distinctly unpromising hero, the slightly sad, perplexed youth who doesn't quite know where he belongs and what he ought to do; the sort of child who once prompted heads to shake because he didn't quite fit and who now would provoke his parents to call up the local child-guidance clinic.

He mentions his "pushy superiority"; he observes that his jealousy of his brother "materialized as physical disgust." He wants to win over the reader by showing himself as a ne'er-do-well who had some funny and not so funny adventures and emerged successfully after all—by being cool and knowing at just the right moments.

Nowhere is Agee's writing better than in his account of a Mexican scene before he went to Germany:

> The rat swam in slow circles, drawing a line in the water with its long, pink tail. The boys threw stones at it, big stones and little stones. Some stones splashed into the water, and some hit the rat with a thud, and often the rat would squeal when it was hit. The boys kept running off to collect stones and stuff their pockets with them, but there were always enough boys around the puddle to keep the rat inside. One of the richer boys had a slingshot, and he was a smart shot and got a lot of applause. He was using marbles, an impressive gesture because they were worth something, and he hit the rat with terrible accuracy and force, you could see its little head snap back, and for a moment it seemed, and I hoped, that it was dead. But then it started swimming again. It was bleeding from the mouth and one eye was smashed, everyone pointed

that out. The rat came up to the sidewalk where I was standing, rose on its hind legs, and curled its incredibly delicate pink fingers around the edge of the curb; its mouth was open, I could see its pink tongue, its whiskers, the smashed eye; and the other, myopically blinking eye seemed to be looking up at our faces. Someone took me firmly by the elbow, and only then did I realize that I had bent over a little and started reaching out to the rat.

The death of a verminous creature somehow is intended to remind us of how vile and murderous human beings can be—how quickly we grab at excuses that will help us do needless harm to others while justifying ourselves. All through his book Agee circles around that theme, though never didactically. The birds in Germany replace the Mexican rats as victims. The boy shudders as he learns of Nazi death camps and, soon enough, of Stalinist murders. The East German government, he tells us, made a strong effort to wipe out the Nazi legacy of anti-Semitism and to promote a conviction of equality among school children. But he notices how lucky, how privileged his parents are, not to mention the parents of his friends:

> Ulla was spoiled, incidentally, because the state spoiled her parents: they owned a Mercedes, their back yard was a small park, their villa could have housed two families twice their size, and they had another house near the Baltic Sea, and a sailboat. How else to keep an eminent brain surgeon from going to the West to get rich?

Agee tells how earnestly he tried to defend the validity of Communist slogans against his own growing realization that much was askew in a proclaimed socialist republic. He belonged to the Young Pioneers, to the Free German Youth. When doubts arose, when glaring social mischief or political duplicity appeared, there were always official rationalizations and excuses. Look, he would be told, at what the Germans had done to Russia—any continuing Soviet appropriation of East German wealth was therefore unquestionably defensible. As for Khrushchev's stunning revelations of Stalinist terror in 1956, "What capitalist government could boast of such candid, courageous self-criticism?"

In time, though, the author became fed up with all the talk of *Selbstkritik*. He had watched too many people ingratiate themselves with his parents, groveling before them and others of their class. "In my opinion," he blurted out one day, "self-criticism is just hypocrisy." But he shows how he was himself smug and self-important—hard on the weaknesses and flaws of others and taking some satisfaction in passing judgments on himself. He judged his own adolescent journal to be "arrogant"; he was quite prepared to issue "pompous pronouncements." The ideological self-criticism that Communist officials have forced upon their opponents and their victims had its counterpart in Agee's private ruminations, as he tried to make ethical sense of evidence his eyes and ears couldn't stop accumulating. Agee was an independent spirit. He trusted his own aspirations and urges more than the conventional promises of the social order. He wanted, early on, to be a writer, and he did not surrender that hope, notwithstanding the insistence of the authorities that he settle down and learn mathematics, chemistry, or biology. He thought a great deal about sex, allowing erotic adventures and fantasies to consume the energies that many of his classmates (especially the scholars and the athletes) learned to tame. Inevitably, he became a problem to his teachers, to his parents. He tried to appear aloof, ironic, a boy intellectual; on the other hand, he was forever trying to hug and kiss, to get laid.

His brother had severe asthma, and his parents increasingly quarreled. When their marriage fell apart in 1960, his mother, who had been born in America, showed up with her son, who had also been born in America, at the U.S. consulate in West Berlin. The infamous wall had yet to be built, and they were issued passports. Agee had by then dropped out of school, become a shipyard worker, and finally gone to bed with a woman. All the while he kept making entries in his journals—ideas and observations he hoped later to redeem in some literary form. Of course, others had different expectations of him: "In a few years," he was told by a friend's mother, "you will have gotten to know capitalism at first hand, not just theoretically. And with your experience of life in a socialist country, you'll be in a position to become a very fine Marxist indeed."

Before the author left East Germany, he had already become a better Marxist than that nation's officialdom would have thought desirable. For all his protestations of boredom or aimless self-regard, for all his dreams of personal glory (as opposed to collectivist self-submergence), he had developed a robust conscience, a reflective political intelligence. The journal reveals a morally serious young mind that can't let go of its own continuing perception of the various ways people deceive and bully themselves and others. This is what is "true" in *Twelve Years*—a kind of sidelong knowledge modestly offered.

As a result Agee helps us to comprehend not only East Germany's life but our own when he describes the constant pressure of Western clothes and music, the popular culture that no wall can withstand. He has a muscular humor. He plays off English and German wonderfully, to the point that the fumbling, nondescript Tom Sawyer starts resembling the shrewd, self-assured Mark Twain whose essay on "The Awful German Language" offered a hilarious examination of the conceits of one tongue as observed by someone who is not native to it. Joel Agee has learned to parody himself as well as others and turn to good advantage his stumbling youth.

New York Review of Books, July 16, 1981

The Regional Vision

Mood and Revelation
in the South

Just a few weeks ago in Baton Rouge, Louisiana, I was sitting in a courtroom with a young man who had once been charged by that state with the "criminal anarchy" of trying to alert his people to the possibility of the vote—not that those who *do* vote in Louisiana, and in other states too, always shun the criminal anarchy of some of their elected officials. Two years of litigation still found this college student facing undaunted segregationist justice—and in this case a kind that had once driven the youth near insane and could likely do so again.

In such a state Shirley Ann Grau lives, and of such matters she writes—of black and white caught in the tension between their private lives and a society commonly less than just or charitable to all its blacks and to enough of its whites who are unimpressed by the validity of its racial conventions.

The story of her latest novel, *The Keepers of the House*, is simple: Abigail sets out to tell about her family's long and fairly aristocratic history, including the most recent moments that have resulted in her lonely but defiant position. We learn about her grandfather, Will Howland, a wealthy farmer descended from generations of similarly established and prosperous people. He is the comfortable man in the midst of relative poverty and occasional desperation. As a young man he lives in Atlanta for two years studying law, and while there he meets his wife. They return home to his town in Alabama, though the town can clearly be located allusively anywhere in the Gulf Coast states, the heart muscle of the Confederacy. His wife bears him two children but dies shortly after delivering the second one, and that one dies a year later.

Will Howland spends his major energies thereafter at his work, growing crops, developing a dairy farm, and sitting on the slow realization that his land is worth a fortune for its wood alone, wood for pulp for paper. His daughter, Abigail, marries and shortly afterwards he meets a young black woman and takes her as his mistress. They have three children. In the midst of this, his daughter, Abigail, separated from her husband, returns home with her daughter, also Abigail. The younger Abigail lives and plays with her mother's half-brother and two half-sisters. All three of these children are eventually sent north to school to avoid the fate of the Southern black. Abigail also leaves home for college, and in time she marries an ambitious law student who hopes to be governor of the state; they have four children. He works hard at politics, and soon he has the governorship in his apparent grasp with a victory in the Democratic primary.

During the campaign he makes the required racist remarks and one of them makes its way north to Robert, his wife's mulatto half-uncle and Will Howland's only son by his black mistress. Robert returns enraged and looking for vengeance. He reveals that his father had secretly married his mother in Cleveland, thus making their children legitimate. A segregationist thus becomes kin by his wife to a black, and of course, even a Republican is preferable. (Sperm have always been allowed their willful racial abandon, but the courthouses with their license bureaus are an entirely different affair.) The book ends darkly: the politician leaves his wife and children, thus clearing himself of the devil's work in the hope that a few years' forgetfulness will allow him another political try. His wife is left to face an angry mob bent on destroying their home, and she is only narrowly saved by her own ingenuity and steadfastness. She confronts Robert with his outsider's thoughtless, ill-informed, presumptuous behavior and her town with the penalty they must expect for theirs, economic ruin at her wealthy hands.

Plot aside, it is a Southern novel all right, and one often beautifully written: the flowers and trees in all their semitropical variety and abundance; the kin that connect and connect until you think everyone is related to everyone else; the swamps and rivers and bayous—much of the region is graced with water enough to make its rich and black or copper-red land seem fresher than the rest of American soil; the birds, grateful in their wide assortments for the temperate climate—herons rising out of a bleak patch of wet, wild grassland and ranging near moss-dripping oaks are an unforgettable sight; the special food and the names for the food; and everywhere the special relationship, grounded in history, buttressed by customs (insisted upon by laws) of blacks and whites, so close to one another, so dependent upon one another, so mutually frightened.

I read this novel on my way to present a paper on the psychiatric roots of prejudice. I felt like throwing away my reports and reading passages from this almost haunting book, stunning passages, offering descriptions of how a black child of mixed blood grows, sees the world, and learns its severe lessons on skin color and human worth. (Most black children in the segregated South *are* of mixed blood, and I have seen pictures of their white forbears on flimsy cabin walls, a startling experience for a naive if earnest field-worker.)

Shirley Ann Grau has been demonstrating her gifts as a sensitive observer of human development and growth for some time now. With a few words she can establish a mood, mixing man's emotions with appropriate reflections of them in landscape. She knows her heavy, low Southern moon, her Southern turtles and snakes and herb gardens. She knows the old houses with their long windows and the nodding breezes that come upon thankful, clammy skin. She knows the people and knows the ambiguities of race relations, the devices, pretenses, ironies, absurdities, and incredible frustrations, all of them constant reminders of the mind's capacity for illusion, rationalization, and even delusion under an irrational but powerfully coercive social and economic system. She knows the black culture as an emotional alternative for the white man's personal loneliness or isolation. She knows the white culture as an awesome, enviable attraction for many blacks. She knows how a black mistress must silently and discreetly grieve at her white man's death; and she knows the rising warmth and fear that struggle in a white man when he begins to respect a black person rather than to use one.

Most significantly, she writes at a time when she can know some answers too. For this is a novel that in its own sudden and firm way has a statement to make. Robert is, after all, the composite Northerner, the outsider, black and white, and the South has its reasons to fear and hate him. The author does not shirk the complicated nature of the problem. Her segregationist is not a demon but any region's ambitious, aggressive politician. He can be tender with blacks, affectionate with his family, and can even disbelieve his own racist talk. How many Americans can really get very smug with him about his adjustment to his society? And who can deny his wife her anger at what this "outside agitator" has done?

The South's blacks and liberal whites have a real need for national help in their struggle for freedom. Yet I have seen dedicated black and white students of the sit-in movement horrified by some of the ignorance, recklessness, and self-righteousness displayed by certain distant or only passingly nearby supporters. Some of them have had to be asked for silence or a return north, leaving the hard battle to those tough and wise enough, and especially flexible enough, to know the power of the enemy, the supple strength of its social and economic institutions and the many chances, as well, of undermining them as well as assaulting them.

Still, the author does not back and fill between a story crying out for change in the ways blacks and whites get along with one another and a justifiable criticism of those whose efforts to change merely lead to worsened strife in the future. She gathers herself together and ends her story by insisting that deceptions exposed are ultimately if painfully better than compromises and falsehoods endured. Robert may have been gratuitous and ignorant in his intervention, but his action reveals to the white community and to the wife of its segregationist politician the reality they have so long dodged. The town learns that economic ruin follows violence. A wife learns what she had really sensed all along, her husband's faulty, compromised nature.

It is said that people are tired of the South and the Southern novel. Yet I wonder where else in this country our past history and present social conflict conspire to bring forth so much of the evil in people, so much of the dignity possible in people, so much of the "pity and terror" in the human condition. Looking at people living elsewhere, in bureaucratized passivity and efficiency, in faceless bustle, in cliché-riddled "progressive" comfort or sophisticated but paralyzed bewilderment, we can turn to the South in horror and fascination, and on those counts alone, in some hope.

New Republic, April 18, 1964

The Manners, the Manners

*U*ntil the nineteenth century, those who made it their business to observe the way people get along with one another had to rely in their reports upon the printed word. The best of them—such as Arthur Young, the English author of *Travels in France,* a carefully detailed description of French society in the eighteenth century—were called "vivid writers"; they were observers who evoked such clear and lifelike mental images that they made their readers practically see things. By the middle of the nineteenth century, "vivid" was not quite enough; when Frederick Law Olmsted's first-hand accounts of the South were published in the 1850s, James Russell Lowell and Edwin Lawrence Godkin applauded Olmsted's writing not only for its "vividness of description" but for its "photographic minuteness." The camera had already opened up new possibilities, and writers were beginning to worry: Could they demonstrate not only "minuteness" but the peculiar power of a photograph—of being at once thoroughly accurate and powerfully suggestive?

In this century, photographers have joined hands with writers, and to particularly good effect when the subject has been an urgent social problem. In the 1930s, Roy E. Stryker, Chief of the Historical Section of the Agriculture Department's Farm Security Administration, inspired a remarkable group of photographers to wander over the bewildered, impoverished American land. He had in mind the work of Jacob Riis and Lewis Hine, who around 1900 moved a nation with photographs of slums and sweatshops, and he urged Walker Evans, Carl Mydans, Ben Shahn, Arthur Rothstein, and Dorothea Lange, among others, to spare the viewer nothing in their recording of a decade's hurt and sadness and misery. Eventually, Walker Evans collaborated with James Agee to produce *Let Us Now Praise Famous Men,* and in *An American Exodus* Dorothea Lange joined her pictures to a text by Paul S. Taylor. Both books document

179

the fierce struggle of our small, independent farmers, our tenant farmers and migrant farmers, for work and a little money and bare survival; both try to summon words and pictures to a psychological analysis of man's responses to social stress—stubborn defiance, disappointment, forbearance, and resignation; both writers appear hard-pressed, worried, even galled or desperate. How can James Agee's four hundred pages of lyrical, biblical prose possibly match the faces and shoes and chairs and tables and cabins Walker Evans manages to present so starkly? There are times when Agee seems in honest, unenvious awe of the power another kind of artist can command. With words he tries to make a picture, but it is hopeless: "This is why the camera seems to me, next to unassisted and weaponless consciousness, the central instrument of our time." This is not to say that photographs without words are sufficient. Dorothea Lange knew that when she exhibited some of her most unforgettable pictures: their titles—"On the Great Plains, Near Winner, South Dakota," "One Nation Indivisible, San Francisco," and "Funeral Cortege, End of an Era in a Small Valley Town, California"—had their own impact. When Robert Flaherty covered the same ground, he too found the camera—even a motion-picture one—not quite enough. "The Land" is considered by many his least successful documentary, and he himself labored hard over the script in an effort to give his always brilliant film footage coherence and plausibility.

Wright Morris, writer and photographer, combines in his one person the spirit of artists like James Agee, Dorothea Lange, and Robert Flaherty, who tried to make those who read see, and those who see well informed and humanely literate. *God's Country and My People* is his third and, I believe, his most effective attempt to walk back and forth between words and pictures in such a way that his readers will feel themselves on a voyage of their own—to the American past he tries to recapture and in particular to our midcontinental Nebraska farm country. Wright Morris was born in Central City, Nebraska, in 1910, and though at the age of nine he started wandering the earth, the scenes of his first nine years appear and reappear in his novels and essays. In the mid-forties, he returned to those scenes, with not only his mind's eye but his camera. In 1946, the first of his three volumes of "photo-texts" appeared. Titled *The Inhabitants*, it contains fifty-two full-page photographs facing passages of text—statements, poems, bits of dialogue, descriptions, exclamations, and lamentations (it is hard to classify them all). The author wants to know, as have others before him and others now, what it means to be an American, to inhabit this great big nation of regions, states, peoples, and races. He has a highly developed sense of history, his own and his country's, and the two match: he left the family farm and the small town that caters to men who work the land; and in his lifetime hordes of Americans have also said goodbye to all that and sought the cities, where they have been redeemed at last or betrayed rather sooner but are still mindful of the old days— the past we neither forget completely nor remember accurately. The nation's pulse may be in its cities, but its soul is, or should be, elsewhere. Morris may not believe this, but he recognizes that it is a sentiment shared by millions of Americans whose ancestors not so long ago left farms here and abroad for tenement flats and factories and crowds of people who ignore and suspect and resent one another. The past is gone, the statistics say, but statistics don't quite tell the whole story. We yearn for other days and ways. We have reveries. We have heard tales that are perhaps merely the wistful stuff of nostalgia, yet they live on in us, ready to respond to a slogan, a candidate, or a turn of events, as American history continues to demonstrate.

In 1948, Mr. Morris resumed his look backward and inward with *The Home Place*. Again he offers photographs, but now they accompany fiction. Nebraskans who long ago moved east return home and are enchanted and made sad and brought up short and in the end left (by their experiences as well as the author) neither here nor there, unable to decide where they ought to or want to belong. The farm boy become city slicker glares at his aunt:

> I looked right straight at Clara's good eye, which is blurred and a little faded—not so good, really, as the strain has worn it out. This is the kind of nerve, the kind of calm, the mean in heart have. You get it after ten or twelve years in the city— it's the kind of spunk that makes good alley rats, Golden Gloves champions, and successful used-car salesmen. It doesn't take much nerve to sell used cars, but I always like to bring in used-car salesmen, all of them, when I have reference to something pretty low. With this kind of nerve I stared at Aunt Clara, and after a moment it occurred to me that I—we, that

is—had her buffaloed. She had never seen the like of us before. She had never seen a woman, with two children, throw
a well-rehearsed hanky-tantrum while her husband looked on,
admiringly. Simple folk don't know how to deal with vulgarity. They're puzzled by it, as real vulgarity is pretty refined.
You don't come by it naturally. Maybe you can tell me why it
is that simple folk are seldom indelicate, while it's something
of a trial for sophisticated people not to be.

So we leave in search of a destiny, find it in business offices and law
offices, and eventually we stop thinking about ourselves because it is
too painful. We have sold out to The Coming Thing; let us forget
our Aunt Claras.

But in *God's Country and My People*, Wright Morris seems to
have concluded, twenty years after *The Home Place*, that forgetting
is impossible: the more we push things out of our minds the more
they gnaw at us. It is best, then, to go back—not simply to conduct a
survey, and so to be done with a whole problem, not to cull another
novel out of the effort, but to say yes, I know about all that, I lived in
it, and I will rejoice at the chance of a homecoming. Along with
that "yes," though, comes the feeling that one just can't take the
scene for granted anymore. Nor, for that matter, can one try to deny
its presence in one's mind. So the situation is tense, a mixed bag,
and maybe good on that account, because sympathy won't become
sticky with sentiment.

Nebraska is the God's Country of Wright Morris—the Nebraska
that Willa Cather first saw at age nine, that Morris left at age nine,
and that both wrote and wrote about and fled from and never could
quite shake off. Morris uses his camera, as Ansel Adams does, to
look closely at the texture of things we see so often but never really
notice; at the same time, he is after the larger look that goes under
the name of social comment or social analysis. He wants us to see
the contours of the land, the quality of the soil, and the details of
man's artifacts. He wants us to know what man and his works and
the prairie and its God-given possibilities have amounted to in the
years since 1843, when John Fremont took the Indian word *nebraska*
(flat water) and applied it not only to the Platte River but to the broad
territory that river dominates, feeds, and drains. The Platte Valley *is*
Nebraska; well over half the state's eighty thousand square miles are

in the drainage basin of the river and its tributaries. During the nineteenth century, Easterners followed the Platte across the plains, sure that it would lead to mountain passes. Traders and trappers, missionaries and fugitives, Mormons and gold seekers passed through or stopped for good, challenged by the rich land that seemed to have no bounds. Nebraska, Morris constantly emphasizes, is a great, gently undulating land that slopes gradually from the northwest to the southeast. To the west are the high plains, the tablelands, broken by deep canyons. Eastward come sandhills and finally the plains. The land grows abundant crops and furnishes fine grazing, for it is rich and fertile. Yet it can suddenly seem old, weathered, and abandoned; to the west, buttes almost without vegetation rise hundreds of feet above the countryside, and the slopes of the sandhills are wind-raked, pitted, and creviced. All this Morris shows in his photographs.

God's Country is divided by its concerns: with God's Country as Nebraska, a land of valleys, lakes, rivers, and farms that only happen to be of human significance (or so it seems when the photographs are viewed apart from the text) and with My People—the kin that still live in the minds of Morris and many others, rather than the men, women, and children who are living today as citizens of the God's Country that persists. (Not all Nebraska's sons and daughters leave.) Morris has us see old clapboard houses whose angular roofs point toward the vastness of the prairie's sky. One house is newly painted; another is about to collapse; a third is little more than a cabin in the endless snow; others are alone and a touch eerie, or alone and merely drab, or part of a settlement, a small town. And there are churches flourishing and decrepit, stores open and abandoned, water towers and windmills, barns and outhouses, and a marble-like bank and a huge grain elevator, and a grandstand and a railroad station, still waiting for Willa Cather's train whistle—"that cold, vibrant scream, the worldwide call for men." There are things that bring the viewer closer to the everyday habits of people: chairs patched but still sat upon, porches and windows and doors and mailboxes, mirrors and pictures on flowered wallpaper; trees that stretch their arms toward a chimney or raise fingers at a power line but also support a swing, or rim a road, or shelter a waiting place; pieces of wood joined together, spoked wagon wheels, a saddle and stirrups, a barber's chair, a barber's sign—without those flashy lights, just a red-and-white column beside a hydrant.

So it goes in God's Country. Wright Morris assigns no captions to his photographs, but many of them speak—to the point at which one can almost hear voices pointing out things as the pages turn. An egg is waiting to be gathered. The water pump still works. Half the chimney is painted white, but there's just no reason to paint the other half. The old clock in the barbershop will still do, and so will the mug and the brush. Letters from way back deserve keeping, and the same goes for those old receipts and stubs. And those kerosene lamps—well, it's a foolish man who relies on electricity. The old city hall is fine with us; a bigger one will only encourage more officials who don't work for a living themselves and want to interfere with those who do. Telephones and Western Union are fine, but not in a bad winter storm. That's our stove, and I'm just as happy with coal as with the new kind of fuel. There's nothing like a clean, nicely made-up bed. I know where every bucket in this house is, and I never misplace my hat. Do you remember those old cars? Well, we have them still. Sit and be comfortable. I want my children to read a lot, and I have the books for them here, and they're good books. Kids, kids—they're always marking things up. Oh, in there they have the big new record machine—the latest kind, I hear.

Wright Morris's camera just about says all that; his text is reserved for more personal comment on the people he knew when he was growing up. Each page brings us closer to the way they were—to the boy who later would write and take pictures, and to his mother and his father and his uncles Harry and Verne, and to his friends. Who are all these people, and what have they to tell us? It depends, Morris seems to conclude. They may seem quaint and stubborn and mistrustful and secretive and provincial, but they are also patient, clever, strong-hearted, strong-willed, sensible, decent, and kind. They live in Holdrege or Sidney or Beatrice, and a lot of their kinfolk are gone to the cities—to Chicago, or to Milwaukee. And as for the smart young ones, there's Harry in Washington, D.C., and Calvin in New York, even if their brother Jim is happy teaching back home in Lincoln. Morris names the people he knew, but he wants readers to experience on their own a spate of recollection, which this book, if any book can, will certainly inspire. Nor does a hard look back toward childhood have to be a strictly psychological (or therapeutic) effort. A mind set upon recall, upon fresh intimacy with its origins, ought to seek out not solely the doctors who study free associations (which lead back to only one part of the past) but social historians and writers and photographers like Wright Morris, who is merely literate and merely a sensitive observer of people.

The words in *God's Country and My People* struggle to convey irony and seriousness and complexity, yet they come across as direct, natural, clear, and even playful. In *The Territory Ahead*, his book of literary criticism published ten years ago, Morris never gets far away from the question he is still asking: What do neighborhoods do to people over a span of time, and people to neighborhoods? Space, place, and time are abstractions whose concrete expressions surround our lives and make them what they are, and the titles of his novels show how much these abstractions concern Morris: *One Day, In Orbit, The Field of Vision, The Huge Season, The World in the Attic, The Man Who Was There.* More than once, to be sure, Morris has wanted to be done with all of that—with the Nebraska in him, in us, and in the entire world. He admires D. H. Lawrence, who had the courage and brilliance to break with the past and strike out for "the territory ahead." He sees the writer constantly threatened by both the past and the present, his own and his country's. He sees little room in our time for more T. S. Eliots (can there possibly be a *Fifth* Quartet?). The great exception, for Morris, is Henry James. Writers like Mark Twain and Thomas Wolfe and Hemingway got caught in the traps of nostalgia; they allowed the past to define the present, to narrow their vision of what is in store for us, and ultimately they paid the price as writers. Henry James certainly sought out the past and even left his native land to find it, but, says Morris, "We have had hundreds of exiles, and many of them talented. . . . Among all of these exiles, he alone is not a captive of the past."

James knew that a person's character and temperament, even his "deepest" thoughts (as we put it these days), can only be *approached*, not defined and labeled and—in the case of a novelist—dramatically submitted to the turn of a phrase or to a particular plot. The job of analysis and portrayal is a lifelong one for those who want to try. Freud knew that—that anything he saw in people was only part of the story. (If he has now been turned into a caricature of himself, a man with all the answers, that is another matter.) For James, too, there could only be the attempt, with each approximation a beginning, with each of his "impressions" an endless challenge to him as both observer and writer. "On the evidence, and on nothing else,"

Morris declares, "it is possible to say that no other book contains so much of the American scene, since no other book has so much to give out." (He is referring, of course, to *The American Scene*.) Of James, the expatriate come home, Morris remarks, "He is consciously self-conscious; the impressions he records are not those of a traveller but those of a native who is finally aware of what it is he feels. In James, the American scene becomes articulate." The great, proud, discreet man would no doubt smile appreciatively at such praise, but he might be even more grateful for *God's Country and My People*. "The manners, the manners: where and what are they, and what have they to tell?" Wright Morris, paying heed to those words of Henry James, has done a fine job of giving us yet another answer to that demanding, exhausting question.

New Yorker, October 18, 1969

The Empty Road

Loneliness can seize anyone, but some of us are peculiarly susceptible because we live almost alone in out-of-the-way places—places whose very appearance suggests mystery, grief, and suffering. In parts of the South, the trees weep with moss, and a bayou can be wholly the property of a single heron at the water's edge, unconscious of time, its long neck arched and motionless, its long bill pointing to something miles away, its long, fragile legs planted in sand or muck, or seemingly on the water's surface. North of moss and bayous come the foothills of the Appalachians—and fear. The roads wind dangerously. The driver feels dizzy; the trees hover; and rocks can come tumbling down at any moment upon the highway. Finally, one catches sight of the Cumberlands—high, misty, many a mountain still untouched: "Hereabouts, it's just you and what you're doing each day, and you don't have much time for talk and visits and like that. In the morning you hope you'll be here to go to bed, and at night you're glad you're still around up here. So you close your eyes and look at one of the hills and say, thank you God for sparing me this far. Tomorrow He might not be so kind."

As I read Cormac McCarthy's second novel, *Outer Dark*, I kept thinking of the man who said this to me. He lives in Needmore, a North Carolina town near the Great Smoky Mountains. McCarthy's people could be from Needmore. They talk and act like Appalachian highlanders or yeoman farmers, but they seem meant to represent something else, something that stretches beyond the limits of space and time. What matters is not the where and when of McCarthy's story, for all the intricate and lyrical descriptions of rural life, but the feeling that he wants to make his stories suggestive, allegorical, even apocalyptic. Plot means little, even this mixture of the sublime and the grotesque, the religious, the rude, and the barbaric. The ground rules are clear: We will be told a story that will frighten and alarm us, but as in a nightmare the mood evoked will matter more than details—the mood of darkness and hopelessness that no technological progress, no refinement of psychological analysis, can explain away or (that cool, slippery word of our times) resolve.

Cormac McCarthy's outer dark is not that by now cozy unconscious whose wild and irreverent and banal tricks continue to amuse our fashionable novelists. Nor is he interested in becoming a gilded version of the American social scientist, who has a name or a label for everything and wants at all costs to be *concerned* and *involved*. McCarthy's dark is not the mind's interior or the world's exterior; it does not deal with the conceits and deceits that are always at work everywhere—even, say, in the White House and the Kremlin. One begins by wondering what McCarthy's psychological and political purposes are. (Everyone, we have discovered, must have such purposes and be knowingly or unwittingly at their mercy.) Soon, though, we are asked by the author to stay in the presence of this outer darkness and suffer what Conrad called "the horror, the horror" or else to dismiss his novel as dense and out-of-date and so muddled with biblical and Attic overtones that it is the worst of all possible things today—*irrelevant*.

Culla and Rinthy Holme, brother and sister, are lovers and the parents of a son. Culla delivers his son in a shack no visitor has entered in months and immediately abandons him to the woods. A tinker whom Culla, shamed, has rebuffed outside the cabin because Rinthy, inside, is obviously pregnant, discovers the child, gives it to a wet nurse, and goes his way. Rinthy sets out to find her child, because she does not believe Culla's assertion that he is dead. She senses that the tinker may have come upon her child; she may have heard his wagon pass by. Then Culla sets out to find Rinthy. So they pick their way through woods and hills and across swamps and rivers, resting under trees, in houses, and in towns that seem deserted. Mostly, because they are wary and haunted, they stalk the land. Who are they and what do they intend, the country folk along the way ask. "I'm a-huntin this here tinker." And why the tinker? Did he steal something? "Well. Somethin belonged to me." What? "It was just somethin." Culla is often assumed to be an outlaw, a rascal on the run, and therefore easily exploited by law-abiding citizens, who can have it both ways—the profit from a desperate man's plight and the pride and power that go with hospitality. Hungry, frightened, and driven, Culla and Rinthy never stop anywhere for long. They meet all sorts of obstacles, human and natural, as they move relentlessly on:

> She slept through the first wan auguries of dawn, gently washed with river fog while martins came and went among the arches. Slept into the first heat of the day and woke to see toy birds with sesame eyes regarding her from their clay nests overhead. She rose and went to the river and washed her face and dried it with her hair. When she had gathered up the bundle of her belongings she emerged from beneath the bridge and set forth along the road again. Emaciate and blinking and with the wind among her rags she looked like something replevied by grim miracle from the ground and sent with tattered windings and halt corporeality into the agony of sunlight.

It is a hard book to read—a book written with fervor and intensity and concentration, an urgent and at times an inscrutable book. As if to assert timelessness and universality, McCarthy moves from the clear, concrete words of the mountaineer to a soaring, Faulknerian rhetoric of old, stately words, unused words, medieval words. Here is the baby, left to die: "It howled execration upon the dim camarine world of its nativity wail on wail while he lay there gibbering with palsied jawhasps, his hands putting back the night like some witless paraclete beleaguered with all limbo's clamor." Yet a few pages later, the mother, on a road that will never end, can stop at a store and ask for water and remark simply that it's "been a little warmer" and say "I thank ye" and comment that she "ain't eat two pones of lightbread in my life." The brother and sister are forever alone: "They ain't a soul in this world but what is a stranger to me." The author uses nature to establish an ironic tone, to comment indirectly on mankind, and to entrance his readers with his flowing and at times stunning descriptions of rats and turtles and spiders and snakes and birds and trees and flowers:

> When he came out on the creek a colony of small boys erupted from a limestone ledge like basking seals alarmed and pitched white and naked into the water. They watched him with wide eyes, heads bobbing. He crossed at the shallows above them with undiminished speed, enclosed in a huge fan

of water, and plunged into a canebrake on the far side. Crakes, plovers, small birds clattered up out of the dusty bracken into the heat of the day and cane rats fled away before him with thin squeals. He crashed on blindly.

That he does—crashes on blind to his fate, blind the way fugitives and vagabonds become, blind the way Cain was when God said to him, "Now art thou cursed from the earth."

Cormac McCarthy's first novel, *The Orchard Keeper*, won him the William Faulkner Foundation Award and a grant from the Rockefeller Foundation. Faulkner's *Light in August* comes to mind as *Outer Dark* unfolds: the poor white people, the harsh puritanism, the disastrous collision of instinct with piety and custom, and the imagery—of the exiles, the wanderers, the outcasts, all dressed up, though, in rural American habit. "I et polite . . . like a lady I et. Like a lady travelling," says Faulkner's Lena Grove, and then, "So she seems to muse upon the mounting road while the slowspitting and squatting men watch her covertly." In *Outer Dark*, as in Faulkner's novel, we are required to pay close attention. But McCarthy directs our attention to very few people, nor are we allowed to sit back and relax and just laugh, though there are lovely, tender moments and a few eerily comic scenes. McCarthy's handful of characters move from place to place, always going downhill. Their curse is explicit, and the futility of their lives is spelled out: Rinthy finds the bones of the tinker and her child, and Culla meets a blind man on a road toward a swamp, "a spectral waste out of which reared only the naked trees in attitudes of agony and dimly hominoid like figures in a landscape of the damned." In *Outer Dark*, characters touch, collide, and then go on rather than get to know one another; they hurt and are hurt in accordance with unfathomable necessities. They don't analyze themselves or others. They don't have to earn their distinction, their significance. Their origins don't have to be expressed and related to society or to the culture. They are immediately presented as people larger than life, important for reasons everyone can sense. The action—again there is the contrast with Faulkner—is swift and unequivocal. One person commits a crime against the gods, then others are drawn into a series of accidents, misfortunes, and finally disasters, all of which make for a tragedy whose meaning every reader had better comprehend.

Not for a long time has an American writer—a young one, at that—attempted to struggle with the Fates and with what Plato called their mother: Ananke, or Necessity. On our way to another planet or layer of the unconscious or new social structure, we of this century don't worry about the dread every man is heir to, nor do we consider envy, passion, and hate things that will always plague man, however lovingly and scientifically he is reared, and in whatever social, political, or economic system. Always it is the next bit of progress, the next device, the next body of knowledge, the next deal or plan that will—what? Make man superman? Free man of himself, of his nature as someone who is born, lives, and dies, and in between, for a second of eternity, tries to flex his muscles, clench his fists, and say "It is me, me amid the outer dark"? Necessarily, said Plato, the Fates can never be thwarted, and they cannot be thwarted today, even by a million computers and consulting rooms. Necessarily, says McCarthy, the dark is out there, waiting for each of us. Necessarily, our lot is assigned; we have to contend with our flaws, live with them, and all too often be destroyed by them.

We do not learn what Rinthy and Culla Holme were like when they were young and perhaps smiled and laughed from time to time. We meet them in hell, and we keep wondering what they could have done to earn their desperation. At worst, they are a little too stubborn, thickheaded, and unwilling to share themselves with others, to share their vision, their secrets, their temptations, their humanity. When questioned, they demur, they flee. A touch of self-righteousness comes through—brilliantly and subtly arranged by a writer who can bring about emotions in both his characters and his readers without making a whole showy business out of the effort. Then all is scrambling and grumbling; the road turns and one desperately makes the turn, and no fire, no roof, no blanket will work. McCarthy's outer dark is austere and bleak and blue and cold and ultimately impassable; his mountains open up only to reveal a foul swamp, a wild river, and yet another mountain. If exiles and fugitives have fascinated writers—who themselves often keep their distance—so have men like McCarthy's tinker. V. K. Ratliff, Faulkner's sewing-machine agent, is a reminder that we the readers are there, with advice and ideas and *our* stories to tell. *Outer Dark*'s tinker, who not only sells or repairs kettles and pots but offers everything from food and soap and liquor to gadgets of all kinds, is something else. It is a measure of McCarthy's seriousness that we are allowed no letup. The tinker provides us no alternative, no vision of a better world. What hope and encouragement we do get can come only from a rural landscape that is rich with life, variety, spontaneity, endless possibilities, and an unselfconsciousness that Culla and Rinthy Holme will never possess.

The only diversion granted us is in the best sense unintentional; it is the commanding diversion a writer's skill provides. McCarthy works hard to write well and ingeniously, but there are moments in this sad, bitter, literally awesome book when only an exceptionally gifted and lyrical writer could take his audience's continuing attention for granted. To say that a book is hard to put down is no compliment these days, when books pour upon us from all quarters and when the reader impatiently wants to hold on simply because he wants to be done, to go on to the next experience. *Outer Dark* is arresting and puzzling enough to drive one to distraction, but always to the next surge of reading. It is as if the reader too becomes a traveler and for doing so is rewarded with an astonishing range of language—slow-paced and heavy or delightfully light, relaxed or intense, perfectly plain or thoroughly intricate. Eternal principles mix company with the details of everyday, pastoral life—always under some apocalyptic cloud, though. Errors will be punished and retribution exacted. The blind lead the blind, though some think of themselves as seekers rather than driven, as knowing rather than compelled. And we all must face that final reckoning. Three horsemen ride through *Outer Dark*, looking for someone, covering the brooding countryside with their dark and fierce presence. Cormac McCarthy knows the Revelation of St. John the Divine, who announced that he would set down "all things that he saw" and the "bare record of the word of God." I suppose good writers also come dangerously close to doing that, seeing so much and putting so much down on paper that the universe itself is spread out before us and the words come near to being the Word—to haunt us and make us pause and wonder for a moment, even though, alas, we keep moving on our particular roads.

New Yorker, March 22, 1969

The Stranger

Nothing about man's psychological nature amazes us these days, for our novels explore ruthlessly or gleefully all the passions, ordinary or peculiar. We take pride in being liberated; we bear down hard on matters people once shunned examining or had no knowledge of. Centuries ago, a few writers may have examined incest, fratricide, sexual perversions, or violence, but not with our own fearless attentiveness. Sophocles is almost casual in his presentation of Oedipus, an outcast whose very name is a source of horror but whose actions (we would now say "behavior") were not dismissed due to understandable causes. What was once awesome or inexplicable is now ours to call grotesque, bizarre, clinically significant, and then to analyze.

Cormac McCarthy is a forty-year-old American novelist who lives in the high country of Tennessee. His first and second novels, *The Orchard Keeper* and *Outer Dark*, earned him awards and fellowships. His *Child of God* will further enhance his reputation. The "Child" is Lester Ballard, aged twenty-seven, "small, unclean, unshaven," a stranger to everyone, including himself, and of "Saxon and Celtic bloods." His activities will surprise no one interested in contemporary fiction: he lusts, he hates, and he has voyeuristic and necrophilic tendencies; he is capable of violence; he is, in fact, a mass murderer. Mr. McCarthy might easily have obtained a fortune with this novel, but he was not intent upon a psychiatrist's bestseller. Indeed, one begins to wonder whether he must reach many Americans through the long, circuitous route Faulkner took—a limited recognition here, increasing response from Europeans to his strange and brooding novels, and only later a broader acknowledgment in his own country.

McCarthy's territory is the hill country of Appalachia; this novel is set in solidly Republican, somewhat impoverished eastern Tennessee, and it chronicles Lester Ballard's descent into isolation, loneliness, and a craven, frenzied self-sufficiency that is extraordinary even for the region's country people, who believe in fending for oneself. He has been living in an abandoned farmhouse, apparently content to keep his own grouchy, suspicious company. But the place is being auctioned. Ballard, ignorant of law, confused by the assault upon his privacy and stability, and resentful of those who would dispossess him, raises his rifle toward the auctioneer and is clubbed down:

> Lester Ballard never could hold his head right after that. It must of throwed his neck out someway or another. I didn't see Buster hit him but I seen him layin on the ground. I was with the sheriff. He was layin flat on the ground lookin up at everbody with his eyes crossed and this awful pumpknot on his head. He just laid there and he was bleedin at the ears. Buster was still standin there holdin the axe.

But the author is not beginning yet another novel about the corruption of society; Ballard is not an innocent whom "the system" ultimately drives to madness. He was on his own by the time he was nine; his father had committed suicide and his mother abandoned him. "I don't know," a schoolmate remarks. "They say he never was right after his daddy killed hisself. . . . He come in the store and told it like you'd tell it was rainin out." And McCarthy has little more than that to say about his principal character's childhood. The author seems not to wish our twentieth-century psychological sensibility to influence his work. Ballard's madness is simply acknowledged, and he ends up in a mental hospital. But his state of mind is not the subject of inquiry. His motives are not examined, nor is his behavior sorted out and labeled. Ballard comes upon a parked car, two lovers within, and remains to watch. Later, he comes upon other cars, other lovers, and each time suffers the loneliness and despair of a man who can taste life only at a remove: "On buckling knees the watcher watched. The mockingbird began." Then, on a hunting expedition, he encounters a car with two dead lovers in it. He pulls the girl out, so that he can take her back to his cabin. Birds sing. A wind rises, then falls. The squirrels he has shot weigh heavily on his belt. He is "a crazed gymnast laboring over a cold corpse." But we never learn why he is "crazed," nor are we asked to feel compassion or contempt.

The author is not indifferent to our curiosity; he simply cannot, for reasons of his own as a novelist, oblige us. When he tries to (maybe one should say when he is tempted to), the result is a fleeting moment of sentiment that discomforts the reader. Falsely accused of rape, Ballard spends nine days in jail, talks with a black man in the opposite cell, and prodded by this neighbor's unashamed introspection, tries to be good company. Nigger John admits to being "a fugitive from the ways of this world. I'd be a fugitive from my mind if I had me some snow." He swears and rails against the white world. He is trying to explain his life, its trials and misdeeds. Ballard finally tries to account for *his* life: "All the trouble I ever was in," he begins, "was caused by whiskey or women or both." The author quickly adds, "He'd often heard men say as much."

The storyteller seemingly has gone as far as he wants to go. Ballard isn't really of a mind to talk about himself, and he has no very original insight into his condition. He is alone but not really lonely. He is attentive to himself; he makes do, in spite of poverty and the suspiciousness or outright hostility his eccentric manner generates. But he does not wonder who he is and why he has come to live as he does. He drifts. The author moves him relentlessly through the Appalachian countryside, offering us the language and habits of fiercely proud people who still struggle against the influence of the industrial life beyond their hills. A country fair is held. Men and women come to a store and exchange news. When Ballard is with them there, he is alternately surly and compliant, clever and disarmingly innocent, and then vulnerable. His meanness and eccentric manner diminish as others reveal themselves to be cranky, narrow, and calculating. Yet we are not persuaded to feel any special pity for him. He moves toward his fate, and others have theirs to contend with.

Ballard has no relationship with any of these people, who, though they demonstrate briefly a capacity for humor, are mostly self-preoccupied. So it is with animals:

> The hounds crossed the snow on the slope of the ridge in a
> thin dark line. Far below them the boar they trailed was
> tilting along with his curious stifflegged lope, highbacked and
> very black against the winter's landscape. The hounds' voices
> in that vast and pale blue void echoed like the cries of de-
> mon yodelers.

And so it is with him:

> Ballard has come in from the dark dragging sheaves of snow-
> clogged bracken and he has fallen to crushing up handfuls of
> this dried or frozen stuff and cramming it into the fireplace.
> The lamp in the floor gutters in the wind and wind moans in
> the flue. The cracks in the wall lie printed slantwise over the
> floorboards in threads of drifted snow and wind is shucking
> the cardboard windowpanes. And Ballard has come with an
> armload of beanpoles purloined from the barnloft and he is at
> breaking them and laying them on.

Lester Ballard destroys and is destroyed, but we have not a clue as
to why. It is as if the author thinks his character is beyond scrutiny—
possessed of a nature and a destiny that lead to the impersonal colli-
sions of the Oresteia rather than the exchanges and confrontations of
our contemporary theatre; it is as if only when we learn to accept the
mysterious and the terrible judgment of the gods do we come close
to what wisdom is allowed us. Ballard is the child of only one God;
he is a desperate man set down among professed Christians who
claim to know more about life than he does: that it is a pilgrimage
toward a destination, heaven, rather than a brief span of time filled
with absurd moments and events. The high sheriff who keeps Ballard
under surveillance for a long time and then arrests him has not only
the law but a larger moral vision to uphold.

Cormac McCarthy resembles, in a strange, incompatible mixture, both the ancient Greek dramatists and the medieval moralists:
Ballard is blind to himself and driven by forces outside his control,
and Ballard is also the desperately wayward vagrant whose life is one
day to be judged by God. Strangers like Ballard, errant outsiders who
bewilder and sometimes brutally assault a community, remind those
who shun them that a "child of God" can inexplicably become, in
the imagery of ancient Greece, an instrument of the gods. Cormac
McCarthy does not know why some men are haunted Ballards while
others live easily with kin and neighbors. He simply writes novels
that tell us we cannot comprehend the riddles of human idiosyncrasy, the influence of the merely contingent or incidental upon our
lives. He is a novelist of religious feeling who appears to subscribe to
no creed but who cannot stop wondering in the most passionate and
honest way what gives life meaning. His characters are by explicit

designation children of Whoever or Whatever it is that we fall back upon when we want to evoke the vastness and the mystery of this universe, and our comparative ignorance and uncertainty. His task is ambitious and enormously difficult—to tell his readers that we are not as knowing or in control of our lives as we assume. He cannot yet affirm with confidence life's possibilities. From the isolated highlands of Tennessee, he sends us original stories that show how mysterious or confusing the world is. Moreover, his mordant wit and his stubborn refusal to bend his writing to the literary and intellectual demands of our era conspire at times to make him seem mysterious and confusing—a writer whose fate is to be relatively unknown and often misinterpreted. But both Greek playwrights and Christian theologians have been aware that such may be the fate of anyone, of even the most talented and sensitive of human beings.

New Yorker, August 26, 1974

Second Coming

I have recently been reading, once again, a novel published in 1978. The novel's title is *Suttree*, its author Cormac McCarthy. At the beginning of this fourth, longest, and most ambitious of McCarthy's stories the reader receives a brief, grim notice. We are to visit an "encampment of the damned," McCarthy tells us. *Suttree*, like all his previous novels, is set in Knoxville, Tennessee, and points nearby. The city is abandoned, decaying. And not only this one city. "A curtain is rising on the Western World," we are told. Even those who compose "the audience" are sitting "webbed in dust." As for the man who is about to give us a story, "within the gutted sockets of the interlocutor's skull a spider sleeps and the jointed ruins of the hanged fool dangle from the flies, bone pendulum in motley." The world as we know it is inhabited by "four-footed shapes." In this world, only "ruder forms survive."

With that spiritual diagnosis (or prognosis) in mind, we are taken to a Knoxville that turns out to be a living hell—a place where the "righteous" live on one kind of turf and the lowly, the aberrant, the mad, and the derelict make do as best they can in their own precincts. The novel is meant to be a description of one person's time on earth. But the introductory letter informs us that something considerably larger is being constructed—an account, perhaps, of what might happen when the moment of Armageddon arrives.

The story proper begins with a man soon identified as "the fisherman" navigating his boat down a river, which is certainly the Tennessee and, by suggestion, also the Styx. As Suttree operates his skiff, he sees evidence everywhere of the decay of a so-called civilization—"gouts of sewage faintly working, gray clots of nameless waste." The pilot is running his lines, intent on catching a fish or two. But the natural world is by no means promising: "The grimy river littoral lay warped and shimmering in the heat and there was no sound in all this lonely summer forenoon." Soon the river offers not fish but a dead man—a suicide—brought to land by rescue workers. Suttree is neither surprised nor alarmed. He continues gathering his catch, which he distributes, we soon learn, to the lost ones, the outcasts, the scorned and rebuked, the black and white people who live near the river in shacks or on the river in flimsy boats.

Who is this Suttree, and what are we to make of him? We are given some of his background, but the author has no great interest in understanding the psychology of his principal character. His full name, we eventually learn, is Cornelius Suttree. He is of an educated, influential background (on his father's side) but has severed all connection with his family, including a young wife and their small son. Instead, he does his fishing and drinks a lot.

He seems to have virtually no acquisitive instincts. What money he gets he shares with others. If someone is hungry, Suttree is concerned that the person eat. Others take initiatives (with regard to liquor, sex, or plans to make quick fortunes) and he watches, listens, and responds, but he always seems detached—a wry if peculiarly vulnerable observer.

We learn that Suttree had a twin brother, who died at birth; that Suttree was born after a breach delivery; that he has another brother, who is rather conventional; that their father married "beneath" himself; and that this one son wants no part of his personal past. There are, in the first pages of the novel, traces of explicit social analysis and moral indignation. Suttree is not unaware of class and caste as they work within his own family and as elements in the world's scheme of things. Referring to his mother and father, and speaking to his uncle, he asks, "Can't you guess that he sees in her traces of the same sorriness he sees in you?" At another point, he rebukes the uncle this way: "You think my father and his kind are a race apart. You can laugh at their pretensions, but you never question their right to the way of life they maintain."

However, the author has no apparent interest in pursuing either the emotional or political implications of such observations. They may even have been offered to us as negative signposts: we are not here to explore yet another mind, yet another family crisis, or yet another instance of economic disparity or social intimidation. The storyteller closes the door to such contemporary temptations, in favor of a more impersonal approach to Suttree and, through him, to the world's inhabitants. It is as if the uncle's early departure from the novel marks the death of one Suttree. The city of Knoxville becomes dark, and a new Suttree emerges—a strangely dislocated but mostly quite even-tempered person whose fate it is to behold the world, to suffer it and suffer in it, rather than act to understand or change it.

That passivity of character stands in contrast to what happens in the natural world, whose restless, inscrutable momentum the writer approaches with a considerable power of pastoral description:

> Below here the river began to broaden into backwater. Mud-flats spiracled and bored like great slabs of flukey liver and a colony of treestumps like beached squid drying grayly in the sun. A dead selvedge traversed by crows who go sedately stiff and blinking and bright as black glass birds from ort to ort of stranded carrion.

And a few paragraphs further on:

> He went down a strand of mud and crusted stone strewn with spiderskeins of slender nylon fishline, tangled hooks, dried baitfish and small bones crushed among the rocks. Toeing tins from their molds in the loam where slugs recoiled and flexed mutely under the agony of the sun. The path climbed along a wall of purple sandstone above an embayment and in the sunlit shallows below him he could see the long cataphracted forms of gars lying in a kind of electric repose among the reeds. Bird shadows scuttled past but did not move them.

Suttree is forever shuttling back and forth from his houseboat to the river's shore, and thence to Knoxville's shabby tenements, stores, cafeterias, and bars. In the course of his expeditions he meets, watches, and goes on various ventures with an assortment of characters whose lively and truculent ways contrast with his own inclination to be disengaged from the world. We are given humorous, touching glimpses of a particular American city's mid-twentieth-century lowlife and, through the various characters, a sketch of vices by no means the property of any segment of any century's population.

Gene Harrogate is a Tennessee mountaineer whose naiveté and essential decency soon enough give way to a persisting, enormous greed. Abednago Jones is a giant of a black man, much feared and loved, who runs a gambling casino with a bar that is always open, it seems; he fights the police, whose violence is often no match for his own. There are, too, an American Indian living in a cave, surviving as best he can through his ability as a fisherman; some other river people, including a family Suttree takes up with for a while; a blind man, adept at using his fingers to read tombstones; a junkyard owner who collects all he is able to lay his hands on but doesn't know what to do with it; and an assortment of hermits, whores, drunks, panhandlers, and flea market operators. These lives are not rendered in the least pitiable, nor are they judged especially wrong or bad. The novelist is not intent on a satire, nor does he want to titillate the comfortable, normal reader with an account of the seamy and grotesque. Huddled in the various broken-down shacks are men and women who laugh and cry, calculate and manipulate, stand up for one another and betray one another—members of one marching company of the human parade Suttree seems ever willing to eye keenly. And if the parade is endless, so is the river Suttree also keeps observing closely:

> In the fluted gullies where the river backed or eddied spoondrift lay in a coffeecolored foam, a curd that draped the varied flotsam locked and turning there, the driftwood and bottles and floats and the white bellies of dead fish, all wheeling slowly in the river's suck and the river spooling past unpawled with a muted seething freighting seaward her silt and her chattel and her dead.

We are in the presence of a brilliantly resourceful writer, at home with the neglected subtleties of a particular language. He is also a gifted narrator, who knows how to move his characters along and provide humor, adventure, surprise—the incidents and accidents, the fluctuating circumstances that challenge us as we go about trying to live.

But exactly what aspect of life are we meant to comprehend? Although *Suttree* can be read as a picaresque novel (its pages are full of roguish exploits, bawdy scenes, and antic carrying on of all kinds), the author clearly has other purposes in mind. After his introductory letter to the readers of the novel, he abandons prolonged explanation, but he does provide us with hints. Suttree is a traveler, seemingly on a journey from one predicament to another. He moves in a "nether world." He crosses a river that is dark, reeking with dead matter. He meets his friend Gene Harrogate in prison ("By which also he went and preached unto the spirits in prison": I Peter 3 : 19). Gene's Adam-like innocence, unselfconsciousness, and idiosyncratic sexuality (a passion for watermelons) give way to a slow, carefully controlled deterioration—culminating in a man deep underground, clawing his knowing way toward the Mammon of Knoxville's banks. There are lush hillsides and a cleansing snow as well as a killing flood and icy waters: the beauty and pain of nature corresponding to man's ambiguous presence on this earth. A snake is mentioned and, repeatedly, the darkened sky. The landscape is clearest and most inviting when Suttree is farthest from everyone, farthest from the presence of sin—on a solitary trek up the high country of western North Carolina.

Eschewing cultural modernity in all its forms, as he has in his three previous novels, McCarthy continues to put his shrewd eye for the texture of a region's everyday life in the service of apocalyptic prophecy, a singular preoccupation for an American novelist of our time. It is as if he cannot forget that in two decades we will be two millennia past Christ's first appearance on this earth. It is as if he cannot get out of his mind the Revelation of St. John the Divine, that most severe and unyielding declaration in the Holy Book. In his message, St. John reminds us that satan was expelled from heaven, soon enough to find in Adam and Eve suitable instruments of evil. Since the snake glided triumphant in the Garden of Eden, evil has multiplied, and so have the possibilities of art. McCarthy has evidently taken a hard, appraising look at his country and decided that it needs (from him, at least) no further fictional mirror play, no acceptance of secular myths as a guiding point of view. When Copernicus told us that the sun and the stars did not pay circular homage to the planet Earth, he may not have done as much as we have been told to dethrone our pride, our self-centeredness. It was, after all, man the perceiver whose reputation was thereby enhanced—the creature on this planet whose central nervous system is able to figure out the secrets of the universe. Would Dante have written *The Divine Comedy* had Copernicus's discovery been made in 1300? Such a question is simple-minded, but the great poet was surely encouraged in his desire to mention "things difficult to think" by a wide vein of mysticism that was no longer present in the sixteenth century. Put differently, Copernicus replaced the earth with man's mind as the center of all things, and thereafter we have successively covered ourselves with the laurels of our discoveries and inventions. Our visionaries use microscopes and telescopes and come up with theories of human nature or society. They promise us longer and easier lives, better political systems. We grab at what is offered; we don't just anticipate and then rejoice in the arrival of various secular gifts—we believe in them as eternity's nods in our direction. All of interstellar space (even its black holes) revolves around us; so do the atoms and their particles, whose power we have snatched and now dangerously toy with. We possess a narcissism of infinite proportion, a messianic narcissism—and, it may turn out, a devilishly murderous narcissism.

Suttree navigates such a world as an exile or, perhaps, a visitor sent from on high to take yet another look at humanity. We meet him as a man—not old but no youth either. We know very little about his childhood, his years of growing up. He is there, a given for those around him. And what does he do? He keeps responding to his fellow human beings without deceit or conceit. There is a conspicuous absence of the self in this strange person who seems to have no great concern about how he looks or what he thinks or how others feel about him. He attends to his downtrodden neighbors in small, undramatic ways. He gives what he has, but not in return for allegiance or obedience, and not with any expectation of repentance. He does not require the μετάνοια, or change of mind, that philosophers and theologians long ago stressed as fundamental to the ministry of another, well-known stranger.

There is, of course, no way for us to know what a Second Coming would be like. In churches, which Suttree noticeably shuns, Christ's return is repeatedly portrayed as a déjà vu—what was will be again. But in this age of nuclear technology, the nations personified as Gog and Magog in the Book of Revelation seem impervious, so far, to ethical exhortation. The kinds of public ministry, parables, miracles, and demands that would characterize the opening struggle, in our time, for a New Jerusalem are naturally beyond anyone's ken. But a novelist, perhaps alone among us, has the capacity to make compelling guesses—to thread into a story a few notions about where we're going and what may be in store for us.

Knoxville's agents of law enforcement, its doctors and nurses and business people, its "principalities and powers," have no interest in Suttree; nor are they interested in those he chooses to spend time with, to know, and in his own way, to heal—though with a kind of attendance that is decidedly lacking in charisma. "I am here," he seems to be saying. "Come see me, but you are not an instrument of my ego, nor I a reflection of yours." Once or twice—at startling moments in the story—Suttree acknowledges the pain he feels, an inexplicable agony communicated, significantly, to no man or woman: "My life is ghastly, he told the grass." Usually he goes his way, handing out freely what money he gets, showing kindness in discreet, unaffected ways, claiming nothing for himself and asking nothing of anyone. Are we being presented with an Armageddon in which narcissism is Satan? Who has yet come among us prepared to wage a struggle with such an adversary? And how would it be waged, except by someone who goes unnoticed among his fellows, unremarked upon, and unheralded after his departure?

Suttree gets typhoid fever, a suitable disease for a man living an utterly humble, precarious life. Sick unto death, he dreams impersonal dreams: "Down the nightworld of his starved mind cool scarves of fishes went veering, winnowing the salt shot that rose columnar toward rifts in the ice overhead. Sinking in a cold jade sea where bubbles shuttled toward the polar sun." He leaves a place and its people, is believed dead by authorities, but is declared not dead by those who knew him. They are sure he has up and left and hear in his absence simply what the narrator calls "the departing steps of the fisherman." And then comes McCarthy's evocation for our time of a vision that St. John the Divine or Dante had their own ways of recording. Suttree at the roadside hot and perspiring. Suttree watching a construction gang at work. Suttree seeing "hands come up from below the rim of the pit in parched supplication." Suttree wanting water but not having it in him to ask, to demand, or to take care of himself (the one who ought to be—we are told today— "number one," and "OK," and his own best friend, and worthy of "actualization"). But a merciful moment arrives, with an east-Tennessee version of Beatrice: "He could see the pale gold hair that lay along the sunburned arms of the water-bearer like new wheat and he beheld himself in wells of smoking cobalt, twinned and dark and deep in child's eyes, blue eyes with no bottoms like the sea." And then a driver, unsolicited, offers a ride.

Behind him the city lay smoking, the sad purlieus of the
dead immured with the bones of friends and forebears. Off to
the right side the white concrete of the expressway gleamed in
the sun where the ramp curved out into empty air and hung
truncate with iron rods bristling among the vectors of nowhere.

The phrase "purlieus of the dead" brings to mind Dante's *"Per
questo visitai uscio dei morti."* A soulmate of that Florentine pilgrim
has followed suit and made another "visit," though in a different
time and place. Cormac McCarthy's thickly plotted and wondrously
spun *Suttree* also belongs in the spiritual company of Flannery
O'Connor's *Wise Blood*, another thinly disguised religious novel,
similarly full of sly, melancholy jest and similarly set among the
"primitives" of east Tennessee. Are we witness to the development of
one more literary school, or is it that, yet again, a message is emerging from the relatively obscure provinces of a mighty but seriously
troubled empire?

New Oxford Review, November 1984

Appalachia
The Human Landscape

John Fox, Jr., the author of *The Trail of the Lonesome Pine*, a classic of Appalachian literature recently reissued by the University Press of Kentucky, was himself born in Kentucky and spent his early years in the mountain part of that state. This novel was by no means his only stab at fiction, nor was the region known as Appalachia the only one he hoped to evoke in stories. Still, this novel, published in 1908, was his best-known literary effort, and it well deserves the new paperback life it now has. To be sure, the story itself is neither remarkably original nor free of a certain cloying sentiment that may well prompt discomfort in some of today's readers. But through this romance runs the social and political and economic drama of eastern Kentucky's mountain people as it is still being enacted—and so John Fox can help us, even now, to consider what Appalachia finally means to its people, never mind to the outsider who yet takes a strong interest in its ways and prospects.

The plot of this novel is as familiar in certain respects as the reality it is meant to mirror: an outsider comes to Kentucky's mountains to help mine their coal and meets a girl whom he will eventually marry, the daughter of one of the leaders of the region's feuding families. Through the eyes of John Hale, the engineer, the reader is given a glimpse not only of the powerful, forbidding, singular beauty of those mountains but also of their troubled, burdened human landscape. Through the eyes of June, the lovely daughter of "Devil" Judd Tolliver, whose clan feuds with the Falin family, the reader catches sight of the ferocity that lurks behind those apparently charming hills—the fratricidal vengeance, the grudges, and the rages that a long history of exploitation, disappointments, and betrayals have certainly helped nourish.

John Fox obviously struggled with what so many of us who have known Appalachia, as insiders or outsiders, have tried to settle in our minds—how to reconcile the decent and good side of these folk, descendants of America's first settlers, with the brutalities that persist up in certain hollows. Not that Appalachia has any monopoly on violence in the United States. But among our country's rural people, the family-centered spitefulness evoked in *The Trail of the Lonesome Pine*, and in song after song as well, is no wicked exaggeration foisted on an ignorant and gullible readership or listening public by entrepreneurial hucksters. This tradition of lawlessness (no longer what it once was) has been more than equaled by the violence prompted by so-called economic development—the fight of companies for money and more money and of workers for a share of that money. John Hale is himself a decent, thoughtful, idealistic man who is perplexed by the habits of hollow people but doesn't turn on them with disdain or contempt. He wants to improve their lot; he is the "good engineer" of the Progressive Era of American history. But others who entered the region were ready to tear it to pieces in search of the gold that coal would earn them—and then walk away fat and sassy, while caring not one whit about the consequences of their plundering ways: the land scarred and soiled, the people broken, deceived, injured, bereaved, or killed. No wonder bitterness persists, even now in this age of relatively civil labor negotiation.

Especially interesting in this novel is the fate of the heroine, June Tolliver. She is sent east to school by John Hale, and she returns a person of obvious thoughtfulness, discretion, and good judgment. The author has reminded us that coal is not the only important resource in eastern Kentucky, West Virginia, western North Carolina, or western Virginia: thousands of young people who live in those obscure, settled areas, up those somewhat inaccessible hollows, might well be very much like June Tolliver in potential. How convenient those celebrated feuds are for many of us outsiders—something to bedazzle us so that we don't worry too much about the human costs of "economic development." If we can convince ourselves that a people is somehow "slow" or "inbred" or impervious intellectually or emotionally to our purported meliorist aims, then we can relax morally and turn our attention elsewhere.

My experiences of Appalachian children kept coming to mind as I read this novel yet again. I have seen so many boys and girls who might also be "sent East," as June was, to good educational effects (these days, of course, there is no need for such a long and wrenching journey, because the region itself has a good number of strong centers of learning). Yet June Tolliver, upon her return, is not at all a complete stranger to her kin, to her personal past, to Appalachia's social history. Here is the eternal dilemma of the person who leaves home, learns so very much, becomes in many respects an altogether new person, and yet—contrary to Tom Wolfe—*does* return, though the pain Wolfe well knew keeps many from ever wanting (or being able psychologically) to do so.

In its rendering of this complex matter, the novel is quite shrewd and utterly contemporary in its lack of sentimentality. June, the returned person of education and culture, is not beyond sudden flashes of meanness and spite, irrational anger, or jealousy. Her emotional comprehension of her own family, despite her achievements as a student, as a person of knowledge and so-called culture, continues to be an important part of her, and it contrasts with the view of her family held by Jack Hale. We are reminded that any of us outsiders can go just so far in connecting with the passion we aim to fathom—hence the need to do our very best to learn from those in a position to teach us. The implicit but strong message of this novel, worked into its central plot, develops that argument continually: Jack Hale is June's initial educator, but in the long run, she is his teacher and the reader's as well.

Another important element in this novel that keeps it from the confines of easy and unedifying sentiment is the willingness of the author to link personal suffering to those larger events that constantly take place in our industrial world—the booms and busts, the fever of exploration and economic expansion, and the despair that goes with economic contraction. This is no social novel, no novel of protest; but in a quiet, subtle, knowing manner, John Fox has helped his readers understand the terrible costs the poor and vulnerable people of any country pay for what so many of us, all too abstractly, call "the economic cycle."

To read *The Trail of the Lonesome Pine* is to be entertained (any story's eternal purpose) but also to be instructed in the special way of the humanities. Those of us who do our social science research have our particular contributions to offer—the detailed observations of people and places that enable our various formulations, our generalizations, our assertive (and perhaps too eagerly heeded) commentary. But the humanities, specifically novels, offer something quite different—a moral and social inquiry that does not shun or try to conceal this life's paradoxes, inconsistencies, and contradictions. To read this "old" novel is to be put directly in touch with the continuing struggle of certain Americans today for dignity and self-respect in the face of exceedingly harsh circumstances. The author does not condescend to Appalachian people in the manner of so many outsiders, with their notions of why "they" are not like "us." The author's outsider, after all, *marries* the insider, the person he has sent outside for instruction but who isn't a clever social climber as she might have been in the hands of another novelist.

We ought be thankful for stories that help us think about what it means to be a human being, to struggle with bitterness and envy and meanness, or to feel within ourselves the generous and kindly affections and the idealistic strivings that also contend for our time and energy. For me to read this novel meant returning with pleasure and sadness to a region and to a people I grew to know—only somewhat—in the course of doing psychological research years ago. John Fox, however, needed no such research to create these portraits of the ancestors of the children I came to know in the 1960s. And if only it were possible for me and my ilk to approach in our writing the complexity rendered in this novel, and in so many novels that have aimed in their own way to increase our social knowledge.

Appalachia Journal, Spring 1985

Flannery O'Connor

Flannery O'Connor's Roots

There has been no shortage of critical response to Flannery O'Connor's all too brief but truly inspired writing life. She has prompted over a dozen critical books and many dozens of essays or reviews. Some of her readers are taken with her theological sophistication; they want to show how shrewdly she has worked it into her stories and novels. Others, more literary-minded, have found her one of the most compelling masters of fiction this country has produced in recent decades. And then there are those who connect her resolutely, and often enough with a touch or more of condescension, to the South; to them she is yet another strange writer with a strange name from that strange region.

She felt inclined to give the definitive back of her hand to that last breed in a wonderful essay, "Some Aspects of the Grotesque in Southern Fiction," and the words no doubt reflect a few moments of indignation on her part: "I have found that anything that comes out of the South is going to be called grotesque by the Northern reader, unless it is grotesque, in which case it is going to be called realistic."

Maybe Barbara McKenzie's book, *Flannery O'Connor's Georgia*, will also be called grotesque by some who leaf quickly through its pages. They contain, after all, pictures that stress God, fowl, a not especially populated landscape, oddly ornamental old homes, and people preoccupied with dousing their fellow human creatures in water or worrying about nothing less than the very end of this planet. As a Yankee college freshman I taught wrote in a paper a few years ago, "I don't understand those people in those stories." Later, in a conversation, he asked me this boldly: "Why do they have those funny names—Carson, Eudora, Harper, and Flannery?" Eager to be a psychological critic (no original direction, alas, these days), he had this connection in his mind: "Maybe their funny names make them want to imagine things."

I have seen even cruder and more fatuous psychohistorical explanations, though I must say I didn't dare probe the reasons such a link was made for fear, maybe, of meeting up with—well, the grotesque. It is so easy for any number of us to reserve for our own lives, our own physical and mental and moral landscape, the designations *normal* or *appropriate*, leaving for others various thinly disguised reprimands, expressions of patronization, or scorn. Flannery O'Connor, in fact, came from a distinguished and cultivated family. She lived in a state whose cultural traditions go back to the first days of this nation's history. She drew her personal strength from a broad range of the West's intellectual life. She lived in a country whose gently rolling hills, rich farmland, and complex, interesting village life are, in sum, a match for what can be found anywhere in the United States. And her neighbors, in Milledgeville proper or out Andalusia way, or anywhere else in Georgia, struggle with the same problems that confront those who live in New York's Manhattan or California's Marin County, not to mention Cambridge, Massachusetts: how ought one live this particular life we happen to have, and what does it mean, actually—if anything?

To be sure, there are regions in this large and diverse country. And this book shows an aspect of one of those regions—rural and small-town South, Georgia division. But Flannery O'Connor was no ordinary person; her mind was given the largest possible spiritual and creative leeway, it seems, by that fate we all puzzle over and try to figure out. She did belong, though, to the people she lived near; she belonged to them in the sense that they entered her everyday life, in one way or another, and also entered her fiction—dominated it, in fact. In story after story, and in her novels, she calls upon Georgia's yeomen, its small-town folk, its rural preachers and God-haunted believers, its citizens and workers and souls. They are not enough, of course, to account for the O'Connor fictional canon; she was a pure if not so simple genius. But no writer, however inspired by his or her visions and voices, lives apart from a given world. The task of a critic is to reflect upon and report the elements of the writer's particular achievement. This book's author-photographer, Barbara McKenzie, fulfills that responsibility wonderfully—with tact, intelligence, and originality. We'll never know what enabled a certain Milledgeville woman to give us those pieces of unforgettable fiction, but some of the nourishment, it can be said, that she called upon is presented in these pages. They form a modest but quite instructive contribution to many of us for whom Flannery O'Connor's presence in this century was a moment, all too brief, of grace.

Preface to *Flannery O'Connor's Georgia* by
Barbara McKenzie, 1980

Flannery O'Connor
A Southern Intellectual

The intellectual's version of pride is something Flannery O'Connor knew in herself. Her letters (published under the title *The Habit of Being*) are exceptional in their lack of self-centeredness. She had no big ego waiting for a vulnerable correspondent. She mocked her own work. She loved to write in plain, Southern country vernacular: no airs, ever. She looked deep into herself. Tactful, polite, able to laugh at anyone's pretensions, including a few quiet ones of her own (what writer is without them?), she was not inclined to settle for less than a thorough skepticism that included all humanity—even her fellow Catholics, even herself, as well as those she often took to task for their agnosticism or rootless sophistication. "Smugness is the Great Catholic Sin," she told one of her correspondents and then added this: "I find it in myself and don't dislike it any less." She could also acknowledge her "ego," and she once said, "So I wait for purgatory. . . ." But she wasn't excessively self-critical—a clever kind of pride. She knew where her soul was weak; she mentioned once that her "upbringing" had "smacked a little of Jansenism." Not her "convictions," she added; her stories, by indirection, refute Jansenism. Like the rest of us, however, she felt the tension between those two great mental forces in this life— what we learned to feel and think as boys and girls and what we came to think as we set out on our own grownup journey. Her letters show the influence of the Augustinian tradition, despite her affinity for Thomistic rationalism. She saw and wrote of that tension between the reasonable side of human beings and the constant temptation toward flights of fancy, with the attendant risk of self-indulgence.

Her portraits of Hulga in "Good Country People," of Julian in "Everything That Rises Must Converge," of Asbury in "The Enduring Chill," three intellectuals of sorts, are affecting if also comic and,

at moments, harshly sardonic. Without question these characters
are tough to take for any small-town, or even big-city, Southern man
or woman who has fought his or her way out of certain cultural constraints. Hulga may, in the end, reveal *her* smugness, her Jansenist
inability to connect her brain's life to the surrounding life of a
Southern rural scene. But she is also, quite clearly, a decent visionary who can't stand the crudities and stupid pieties that pass for daily
talk in her mother's home. Miss O'Connor is prepared, throughout
this extremely funny story "Good Country People," to let the blind
lead the blind—or maybe to finish one another off. The following
parody of intellectual reading (and of our twentieth-century attachment to logical positivism) is offered as a quote from a book of
Hulga's, opened by her prying mother, Mrs. Hopewell:

> Science, on the other hand, has to assert its soberness and
> seriousness afresh and declare that it is concerned solely with
> what is. Nothing—how can it be for science anything but a
> horror and a phantasm? If science is right, then one thing
> stands firm: science wishes to know nothing of nothing. Such
> is after all the strictly scientific approach to Nothing. We
> know it by wishing to know nothing of Nothing.

That was underlined, we are told by an author pushing us hard to
think of the dreary junk that ends up as impressive to "the girl [who]
had taken the Ph.D. in philosophy." But the foolish optimism of
Mrs. Hopewell (another O'Connor name meant to match a character's point of view) is no more appealing. And her daughter can be
attractively blunt and down-to-earth—her cynicism a balance to the
mother's fatuousness.

In the end, knowledge is no match for the workings of pride, a
familiar O'Connor theme. Mother and daughter alike are taken in
by a crafty Bible salesman whose triumph is not, however, achieved
through his own abilities as a confidence man. It is the sadness, the
loneliness, of a mother, a daughter, that sets them both up for various assaults. The author knows how quickly her readers will dismiss
Mrs. Hopewell and take an instinctive interest in the dour, shrewdly
observant Mrs. Freeman—who may well be the person meant to ex-
emplify a certain kind of intellectuality: coldly attentive to all that is
wrong in the world; pessimistic, if not sour and crabbed; willing, always, to feast off the failures, the disasters, the accidents, and the

tragedies of the world. Mrs. Freeman will be taken in by no one.
Mrs. Hopewell and her daughter are, in different respects, Mrs.
Freeman's prey. The salesman is a brief version of the longer-lasting
Mrs. Freeman—the darkness of the world, ever present. Though
some readers emphasize the harsh treatment given Hulga and,
through her, Mrs. Hopewell, Miss O'Connor can as well be showing us how difficult it is for such relatively decent (certainly naive,
all too corruptible, and hence, to a degree, innocent) people to survive—even in that very "country" part of the South mentioned with
such affection at times in *The Habit of Being* and in *Mystery and
Manners* (her collected essays).

In "Good Country People," an intellectual author's anti-
intellectualism is given controlled reign. She spoofs Hulga's braini-
ness, shows it wanting in a struggle with a devilishly intuitive country salesman, but in the end makes clear her conviction that there
are worse ones around than the Hulgas of the world. She has flirted
with nihilism, with the devil. Her visitor *is* the devil: "And I'll tell
you another thing, Hulga, you ain't so smart. I been believing in
nothing ever since I was born!" Before we come to that final moment
of ironic circularity, we experience its predecessor, Hulga's wrong-
headed condescension, as Miss O'Connor spoofs Kierkegaard's concept of the "teleological suspension of the ethical"—Abraham's surrender of his son Isaac to God, in the full knowledge that he may
take the son's life. Hulga realizes at one point that "for the first time
in her life she was face to face with real innocence." The boy wanted
to see her artificial leg. She refused him. He persisted. She asked
him why. He got to her with: "It's what makes you different. You
ain't like anybody else." Pride of a certain kind. When he told her of
her uniqueness she became his. "All right," she says; and the author
has her thinking to herself that "it was like surrendering to him completely," and further, "it was like losing her own life and finding it
again, miraculously in his." A kind of resignation. A kind of religious experience—a parodic version of what we are told in the New
Testament happens when one finds Christ. An intellectual's conversion. As such, a false turn—because not made with all her heart and
mind and soul.

There are signs along the good country roads of rural Georgia:
PRIDE KILLETH and PRIDE DECEIVETH. Satan is always waiting along
such roads, ready to take what we, as exiles from the Garden, are

prepared (by our *lack* of proper preparation) to give him. In this story of pride, an intellectual's pity becomes an instrument of her seduction, her psychological unmasking. The contempt she has had for others, the lower orders, soon enough turns into the rage of a person undone by an action of misplaced trust. Nor is brainy hauteur any match for a serpentine canniness that operates without the slightest tortuosity of thought. "Flattery will get you nowhere" is the kind of silly remark a girl pining for attention, if not flattery, makes to her suitor: an invitation masked as a refusal. How the self-styled mighty fall victim to the oldest and most humdrum of ploys, enacted in thousands and thousands of automobiles after untold numbers of high school proms! Doctoral candidates, doctors of philosophy, ought to know better, a Mrs. Hopewell might say. Mrs. Freeman would, alas, know better; and it is she who gets the last word in "Good Country People."

Miss O'Connor's treatment of Julian and Asbury, the two somewhat aimless and weak Southern liberal young men, is also connected to her complicated attitude toward intellectuals, many of whose ideas she shared. What she doesn't like about both those men is a certain snobbishness they can't help demonstrating—a wry insouciance toward the feelings of their own kin and, in contrast, a complete devotion to the values and feelings of certain others: the distant liberals of Yankeedom, the nearby blacks, or the South's own "progressive" people. Several critics have insisted that none of Miss O'Connor's characters beg the reader's "identification," but I wonder whether there aren't a few of us liberals, Southern or Northern vintage, who haven't found in ideas, in political argument, and alas, in the impatience we feel toward our old friends and members of our own family, a source of the very smugness Flannery O'Connor worried about in herself.

Julian and Asbury not only *have* those liberal, progressive, and, in the context of a time or a place, radical ideas; the two discreet rebels also *use* those ideas in various confrontations with their mothers and, really, with the black and white people they come into contact with. We've worked over "Everything That Rises Must Converge" fairly thoroughly in that regard. "The Enduring Chill" has the twist of a Southerner gone North, who is then compelled to come home, sick and (soon enough, we discover) sickened by what he sees and hears: the backwoods mentality of the rural South. But we become sickened with him—the author's intention, surely. Even the local and loyal blacks, whom he dramatically wants to favor (and become personally integrated with, in a manner of speaking), end up confused, impatient, anxious to be back in their own familiar world, segregated by race and class, rather than in the contrived presence of this ever so thoughtful, sensitive man who, nevertheless, is standing up for all the "right" things. Liberal humanism, yet again, gets a tough, sometimes scathing, going over. Yet we're not happy with the ignorant attitudes of Timberboro—*its* smugness, narrowness, and (one has to say it) the racism that is part of the life depicted there. It is important to realize that Miss O'Connor does do that depicting. Lest the sarcasm she pours upon the liberal-intellectual Asbury be allowed to overwhelm the reader, she can stop everything, including, maybe, her own satirical intentions, with this observation: "He had been writing a play about Negroes (why anybody would want to write a play about Negroes was beyond her) and he had said he wanted to work in the dairy with them and find out what their interests were."

At this point we are ready to conclude that an aesthete who won't end up writing any play at all is in a conflict with a bigot with social airs—hardly one to earn our sympathies. And when the author tells us, acidly, that "their [the Negroes'] interests were in doing as little as they could get by with, as she could have told him if anybody could have told him anything," we are not ready to gloat over this triumph of a maternal sensibility. Nor are we pleased when the authorial voice reminds us that blacks are made nervous by the likes of an Asbury. In her own indirect way, the author presents a devastating picture of segregationist swagger and intimidation—fought weakly, perhaps, and out of vanity, no doubt, and with a killing intellectual pride, but nevertheless fought. Haven't we the right to say, in retrospect, that in the 1950s, when this story was written, such an idiosyncratic, feeble white resistance to segregation was about all that there was to see in the small-town and rural South? And such resistance, Miss O'Connor makes clear, was quite often the intellectual's. A tortured stand—an inherently futile one, perhaps, with no money, no clout. But it is a stand the author chooses (by the telling of her stories) not to ignore, and not *only* to satirize.

Miss O'Connor's treatment of the somewhat intellectual figure, Rayber, in her second novel, *The Violent Bear It Away*, presents rather a different issue. The novel was a hard one for her to write. Several times in *The Habit of Being* she remarks upon her troubles with the plot and especially with the character Rayber. She knew the dangers of her own pride, her own prejudices. She could say that she had "a stomach full of liberal religion!" She could also refer, as mentioned earlier, to "all the stupid Yankee liberals." Why not caricature them through Rayber? And to be sure, some critics are convinced that she did just that. We are told by a friend of hers that the author knew, after the novel had been finished, that she had failed to do a good job with Rayber, making him something more than a liberal agnostic, all caught up with psychology and a few "humanistic perspectives," the title, these days, of courses in Southern as well as Yankee colleges. I doubt she ever would have, or could have, portrayed a godless intellectual in such a way that he or she triumphs over a person of the spirit, no matter how strange and apparently idiosyncratic that spirit happened to be. But I don't think she has been given enough credit for Rayber—who, in any case, isn't the main character of the novel. Certainly there are moments when satire gets overworked. I wish Miss O'Connor hadn't equipped him with a hearing aid. But I also think she worked a little too hard with Tarwater, who doesn't exactly come across as clean, pure, and holy.

Obviously the author wants us to consider Tarwater and Rayber together—and, in a way, she makes the outcome of the novel the result of their strong, tense, almost violent encounter. Tarwater's great uncle had wanted him to take up the mission of biblical prophesy: bury the old man; baptize an idiot cousin, Bishop, living with his father, Rayber, in the city; walk forward into the world as one of God's faithful preachers. Tarwater resists yet is also carried along. He goes to see Rayber and Bishop, and a good part of the novel has to do with their carryings-on: a man moving to accept, but at the same time fighting, the prophesy that he ought to and will preach the Holy Word meets a teacher all full of the tenets of educational psychology. It is not an unfamiliar O'Connor confrontation. Put differently, it is a battle between faith, as embodied in the old-time, evangelical Christian tradition, and secular modernity, with its strong intellectual bulwark of physics, experimental neurophysiology, and the social sciences—a thoroughly materialist viewpoint.

Caricature is applied on both sides; the author is (one can't repeat it too often) a humorist, among other things. She loves action in the service of a laugh. She also gives us liquor, a big fire, plenty of ranting and raving, a drowning, and a deftly handled and very funny roadside seduction scene. And she gives us those highways, leading to and from the city, with strangers ready to pick up strangers, all of them lonely and hungry for talk and for someone to listen. Christ, the onetime wayfarer—and all of today's interstates, full of people on the go, on the go. Where to, and with what purpose in mind? Rayber wants mental health, a well-adjusted personality, and a whole bunch of IQ points for his idiot son. Rayber wants an end to superstition. He wants teachers who have an eye out for "emotions." He wants visual aids; he wants audiovisual aids; he wants everyone to see through everything—the sham, the hocus-pocus of the benighted and those who play on their fears and trick them, best described as conjurers rather than prophets.

Still, these two men are not only emblematic figures in an author's personal and artistic struggle to make us, through her fiction, witnesses to a given century's version of the continuing struggle between those who recognize and fear God and those who have turned their backs on him in favor of themselves. Both men, after all, are of the same biblical stock. Both are descendants of a prophet, and each is strong willed and capable of frenzy, guile, and not least, despair, which is a version of pride. (We give up because we have less faith in God's purposes than in our own sense of what matters.) Neither man is without complexity, ambiguity. Tarwater doesn't seek out Rayber only to win over his pitiable son for Christ. Tarwater is not driven only by his "wise blood" (to use the title of one novel as help in explaining another) but also by a desire to test his ideas, to come to terms with them by coming to terms with someone who defines them through opposition. Rayber is, naturally, the logical choice— "wise blood" as against bad blood. He is the intellectual as the devil. And so they meet and come to grips and through their exchanges provide the reader with yet another sharply worded, though comic, debate: Faith as against Reason; Faith at all costs; Faith blindly stated against Reason not always undercut with sarcasm.

The reader can't help remembering, every once in a while, that the Tarwaters of this world don't write novels; the Raybers wish they could but lack the inspiration. It is a mixture of the two that many of us hope for, a faith that doesn't allow the intellect to become a victim of pride. I am not so sure that Miss O'Connor dares tell us exactly what a "right-thinking" (to use a rural expression not strange to Baldwin County, Georgia) prophet has in his mind or soul as he goes about his earthly journey. Paul's injunction is a hard one to spell out in prescriptive detail: "Not of the letter, but of the spirit; for the letter killeth, but the spirit giveth life." Tarwater is pulled by doubt as well as by a growing conviction that there are ordained (better, *fore*ordained) tasks for him to accomplish. Rayber is tormented by the disappointment life has sent his way—a son whose brain won't work right and is, thereby, a living mockery of all that seems so important to secular man, his head. These are not two neatly stereotypic foils for an author's prejudices.

One of the best scenes in Miss O'Connor's fiction is Rayber's pursuit of Tarwater, who ends up inside an evangelical "temple," where a child evangelist, aged "eleven or twelve," preaches a fiery fundamentalist sermon. Her message prompts a brief but powerful clash of faiths: the liberal humanist, who worries about hurt and suffering children, everywhere exploited by ignorance, poverty, and the manipulations of their craven elders, against the Christian, who knows that suffering is, inevitably, what life is about—suffering and mystery. Even before the child begins her passionate sermon, Rayber is more tempted by her than he has any way of knowing: "It was the thought of a child's mind warped, of a child led away from reality that always enraged him. . . ." A girl holding her arms up high, exhorting a crowd, with high-pitched intensity and considerable brilliance becomes for one listener (he is outside, peering through the window) a reminder of what he himself might have become.

The girl's message is brilliantly rendered. Miss O'Connor knows not to patronize Southern child evangelists. I've heard a number of them, and the inspired accuracy of this version carried me back in time. "Oh, ye unbelievers," I once heard a girl of thirteen say (right to me and no one else, I was then quite certain) in an open air meeting outside of West Point, Mississippi—1961, and all white. And she went on, lashing into the exalted sense of self that characterizes those she kept calling the "godless people." We can invent anything, she reminded us technocrats, think anything, she reminded us social scientists, but we "can't become what we aren't." A considerable pause. Surely, my wife and I thought, she won't spell *that* out! She'll pray for us, the lost ones. But she did: "You are all you've got—sinners leading sinners, the blind leading the blind. Yet you pray!" Another pause. A lapse of logic on her part? A mind hungry for such a lapse is ready to clap. Then she delivered her wallop: "You pray to yourselves. You are heathens in search of a god, and you always find one; you listen to your own words, and pray to yourselves for more and more of them."

A lot of words on *her* part, a defensive listener is quick to think. And then a version of Rayber the rescuer comes to life with *his* words: what is a *child* doing, coming up with all that talk? Does she go to school? Is she a pawn in an unscrupulous parental confidence game—the child used to bring in the dough? Interpretations such as those, at once social and psychological, come rather easily to a certain kind of mind, as Flannery O'Connor well knew. But occasionally a preacher penetrates the mind that comes up with those interpretations. One realizes oneself in the presence of a spectacle—in St. Paul's words: "For I think that God hath set forth us the apostles last, as it were appointed to death: for we are made a spectacle unto the world, and to angels, and to men."

The puritanism in Southern evangelicalism can suddenly disappear. A passion of exhortation reaches the listener, induces an excitement that is infectious, palpable, and quite threatening to a skeptical, cerebral onlooker. No, one thinks. No, one insists. No, one concludes, after summoning, as in a war, everything one's got: who *are* these people, and why do they shout so, and why do those who listen end up shouting so, and what is the *reason* for such goings-on, and that child, that mere child, that hollering, crying, over-excited, terribly wrought up child—what will happen to her in the future if *this* is her (determining) past? Only later does one remind oneself that these people have not divested themselves of clothes or calories or memories or sexual feelings, as others elsewhere do. These people, the listeners, quite simply, became awestruck. Their silence on that Mississippi summer night was uncanny. The stars seemed noisier than anything alive below them. A mosquito going about its business suddenly reminded one listening victim of what had been interrupted—a lull that seemed endless. And suddenly, the human voice again: "Thank you for praying to him, you sinners. I know some of you don't believe; but I heard your hush. You stopped listening to yourselves, even if you didn't start hearing him talk, our one and only Lord, Jesus Christ."

A reverie—brought back to mind while reading the account of

Rayber, crouching on the ground, his hungry eyes excited almost uncontrollably by a child evangelist's presence. The author uses the word *transfixed* to describe what happened to Rayber for a moment or two. He was not won over or converted; nor, in the other direction, was he alarmed or horrified. He was tempted by her: "Rayber's heart began to race. He felt some miraculous communication between them. The child alone in the world was meant to understand him." A moment of weakness? A moment of hysterical identification with a crowd, or with the overwrought speaker? The listener may not have been brought to Christ, but he was brought to himself, or at least, a hidden part of himself, as we learn when Rayber and Tarwater leave the tabernacle. For a few moments, Tarwater is approachable—is ready, almost, to turn his back on a prophetic calling, to turn toward Rayber with a willingness to hear, pay heed, follow. The tough, defiant young man becomes strangely gentle; he wants to talk with Rayber rather than to provoke him. But he meets a suddenly different companion—not the friendly, talkative, willingly open Rayber but a cold, shut-off man.

In an excellent article, the Southern literary critic Louis D. Rubin asks why the strange and pivotal transformation in both parties takes place, why Rayber is uninterested in Tarwater just at the moment when the latter has turned toward the former. Rubin's answer is helpful. Rayber had become taken with the child evangelist; the result was a reaction: "It is the schoolteacher's fear of the emotion of love that prevents him from being able to help Tarwater." The girl had almost, but not quite, broken through his shell of rationalism, intellectualism. As soon as he and Tarwater left her and her spellbound listeners, Rayber had to protect his newly vulnerable self in the face of Tarwater's newly conciliatory approaches.

I would make only one slight addition. Miss O'Connor nowhere does better with intellectuals than here. Is it that the child evangelist has threatened Rayber's "defenses" and so prompted a tightening up in him at just the point that he seems within grasp of what he has eagerly sought—*his* conversion of a young man's soul to the materialism of behavior psychology? Or is it that a shrewd novelist has moved us toward a revelation? Every evangelist I've heard has used that last word—often upon quoting from the gripping last book of the New Testament, the Revelation of St. John the Divine. Here is the ultimate in a Savior's prophesy, mediated by one of his followers. Here is everything an Old Tarwater could want for a younger version of himself: an unyielding distinction spelled out—a future apocalypse, whereupon the saved and the damned will go their separate ways. And what Southern revival religion wants in general, Rayber got: a revelation, a final statement of what is meant to be. Rayber has had a dream of conquest and has seen it slip through his fingers. For a few seconds the girl had become an object of his passionate interest; *he* would save *her*. But she turned from him, on him; she denounced him. Spurned, angered, his self-centeredness wounded, he pulls into himself. A preacher's vanity is exposed by another preacher. He not only fears that he will be undone enough to reveal his emotional side; he is also a disappointed, beaten man who reveals the behaviorist's cult of self that is mechanistic, coldly calculating, and psychologically reductionist. The apparent Rayber (an inviting rationalist who wants to explain, clarify, and offer the interpreter's handshake) gives way to the "real" Rayber—the prideful intellectual who, thwarted or crossed or let down, shows himself to be decisively cold, overbearing, and (emotionally) "violent." So it will go one day, when the quick and the dead get sorted out.

It may be that the above moment in her second novel is Flannery O'Connor's harshest judgment on our century's intellectuals. She caricatures them in her stories; she condemns them in her essays; she gives them the back of her hand, repeatedly, in her letters. But in this particular scene of her painfully wrought novel (seven years in the making) she placed them symbolically in hell—cold, cold people, unable to respond to others on any terms but their own: pedants in search of willing admirers. The child evangelist, Tarwater, young Bishop—all are the same: objects to be regarded with calculating, clinical circumspection by a man whose heart is a stone.

Not that Tarwater is recommended as an alternative. This is no book about personality, the mature kind and the immature kind. This is no either/or story; nor is it a duel that is won or lost, pure and simple, by A or by B. Bishop is baptized—but killed; Tarwater will pursue a Bible-haunted life. The author relentlessly documents the continuing violence that bears away our world: the decency in people loses time and again to various schemers, not the least of which are those who talk a good game about reform—social scientists of various kinds, with their endless plans meant to banish all the woes the world has ever known. But in the name of such ambitious virtuosity crawl dozens of serpents: prophets the match of old, demanding, relentless Tarwater; prophets smug and mannered and pretentious enough to make both the child evangelist and the younger Tarwater seem like pleasant innocents, like "fools for Christ."

Flannery O'Connor's intellectual life, rich and deep and complex and by her own choice decidedly restricted, is best approached with her regional roots in mind, as well as her strongly felt, binding religious commitment. She had no use for all the Confederate junk, physical and symbolic, that has continued to obsess certain Southerners. She was not especially worked up over the race issue, pro or con; she saw Dr. King to be doing what he had to do—and, in that regard, her resentment at those who wanted to push her to say more "liberal" things was not a reaction of the segregationist standing fast in the last ditch. She had a sharp eye for the faddism in our intellectual life—an aspect, she knew, of a rootlessness others like her have described with the same regret and, sometimes, foreboding. Simone Weil, in *The Need for Roots*, gives us aphoristic remarks such as "uprootedness breeds idolatry" or, with respect to the word *intellectuals*, the following description: "an awful name, but at present they scarcely deserve a better one." These two remarkably independent and gifted women, both of whom died young, had a similar religious sensibility and a common willingness to see in exceptional brilliance dangers as well as opportunities.

For Miss O'Connor, Simone Weil was an obvious source of fascination and, at times, inspiration. She read that French rationalist (and, ultimately, religious mystic) with considerable attentiveness. She comments upon her at great length in her letters. Even more interesting, there are remarks that suggest not only a profound intellectual engagement but an artistic response, which, alas, was never permitted by fate to materialize:

> Simone Weil's life is the most comical life I have ever read about and the most truly tragic and terrible. If I were to live long enough and develop as an artist to the proper extent, I would like to write a comic novel about a woman—and what is more comic and terrible than the angular intellectual proud woman approaching God inch by inch with ground teeth?

Lest we find in those words yet another snide put-down of an extremely significant life—in the interests of what gets called psychological realism or "psychohistory"—she has this to say: "By saying

Simone Weil's life was both comic and terrible, I am not trying to reduce it, but mean to be paying her the highest tribute I can, short of calling her a saint, which I don't believe she was." Then, in clarification to the friend addressed: "Possibly I have a higher opinion of the comic and terrible than you do. To my way of thinking it includes her great courage and to call her anything less would be to see her as merely ordinary. She was certainly not ordinary. Of course, I can only say, as you point out, this is what I see, not, this is what she is—which only God knows."

The intellectual renunciation in that last observation was, no doubt, difficult for a mind of such penetrating brilliance. Miss O'Connor knew that she required a bit more distance on herself if she was really to understand Simone Weil, let alone write a novel about a life such as hers. She was exceptionally candid about her own life when she wrote to a friend about that French intellectual, whom so many have described as saintlike. To the same person Miss O'Connor had been, off and on, sending comments about Simone Weil, the following was offered:

> My heroine already is, and is Hulga. Miss Weil's existence only parallels what I have in mind, and it strikes me especially hard because I had it in mind before I knew as much as I do now about Simone Weil. Hulga in this case would be a projection of myself into this kind of tragic-comic situation—presumably only a projection, because if I could not stop short of it myself, I could not write it. Stop short or go beyond it, I should say. You have to be able to dominate the existence that you characterize.

Those are reflections that come as close psychologically to what is called creativity as anyone in psychiatry has ever gotten or is ever apt to get. Those are reflections at once autobiographical and philosophical. The writer uses restraint when she alludes to herself yet indicates that she is willing to connect herself with one of her characters—provided she be permitted as much personal leeway in the matter as she would always insist on for her characters. Put differently, the intellectual who worried about the risks that go with abstract attitudes—the way they can confine the minds of readers, cut off imaginative possibilities, and cast shadows on one set of truths in the interest of emphasizing the presence of another aspect of reality—was not about to let herself be excluded from the caveats she had been uttering. She, too—any of us—is entitled to a little protection when it comes to someone else's effort to make a psychological characterization.

She knew, as mentioned earlier, her own kind of pride; and a devout Catholic, she no doubt waged a lifelong, prayerful struggle with herself—with her mind's self-importance, with a sinful yearning (pride) that goes back historically (or, some would say, mythologically) to the Garden of Eden. Her wonderfully knowing response to Simone Weil, that most idiosyncratic of twentieth-century religious pilgrims, is perhaps confessional in nature. And the offhand, indeed parenthetical, remark, "which only God knows," quoted earlier reveals yet again the deeply felt nature of her suspicion about intellectual activity.

Even though Flannery O'Connor loved St. Thomas Aquinas, read him again and again, and quoted from him; even though she took on the considerable, if rewarding, challenge of Pierre Teilhard de Chardin, whom she repeatedly mentions in her letters; and even though she read and understood Jacques Maritain, her Catholic intellectualism remained precisely that—always *sub specie aeternitatis*. She knew the (sinful) dangers of confusing the use of an intelligence (God-given) with the resort to ideas as a last court of appeals, as a fundamental act of self-definition. She had no psychological inhibition with respect to the intellect; it was hers to develop, call upon, and enjoy. But she had to keep in mind ownership, and yes, transcendence. For her, the intellect was a gift, and the donor was someone in particular—God become man in history. For her, the intellect was thereby a responsibility—something on loan, as it were. And for her, the intellect was always but one element in life, and by no means the essence of it. Even as she believed in a tripartite God, she believed as well in the tripartite nature of the human being—body, mind, and soul.

The soul for her had its own life, its own requirements. Anyone who confused it with the mind or tried to extend the word *mind* to include the word *soul* was for her badly confused, if not wicked. In an interesting letter to her friend Cecil Dawkins, she acknowledged "quite a respect for Freud when he isn't made into a philosopher." She was quite willing to put him alongside her beloved St. Thomas Aquinas: "They are rowing in the same boat." A high compliment indeed from her. "To religion," she added, "I think he [Freud] is much less dangerous than Jung." Flannery O'Connor, a Thomist, wasn't really interested in what Freud had to say about religion. He could call it an illusion a million times for all she cared. She knew that the illusion in question was *his*—the notion that psychological maneuvers explain what faith means or is.

She also knew what people have done with Freud in this century—and not completely without his acquiescence. He acknowledged his own political fantasies, his identification with the military leader Hannibal. He was not only a doctor, a thinker, a writer; he became the leader of a worldwide "movement," as it has been called all along. And he became, and for many still is, someone who has the answers for more than questions about the mind's everyday functional life. His ideas have become hardened into tablets of law. In the epilogue to *Childhood and Society*, Erik H. Erikson refers to "talmudic argument," "messianic zeal," and "punitive orthodoxy" as aspects of psychoanalytic life that must be looked at and admitted as distinctly possible dangers in the young psychiatrist's training experience, not to mention the nature of the older psychiatrist's teaching.

As for Jung, he was more dangerous, she realized, because he was attempting to meddle directly in religion. Freud, like everyone else, struggled with pride; and his followers, like many people, craved a godlike leader. But Jung felt he had an explicitly religious "answer"; his psychological knowledge had taken him, never mind his cohorts, into the realms of philosophy and religion. And he would draw from all religions—maybe in order, wittingly or no, to make one of his own. He would synthesize. He would interpret imagery. He would examine myths. He would call upon coins, the stars, legends, rituals from tribes and peoples all over. For Miss O'Connor, the plain materialism of Freudianism was at least that—agnostics doing the best they could to learn about their heads, and in excessive moments, revealing how much they inadvertently craved certain *religious* consolations. But Jung and his followers were addressing themselves to the spiritual and, really, telling one another (and others, through books and articles and lectures) that they had truths not only about the mind's life but the soul's—a psychology of the soul. For Miss O'Connor such an approach was a transgression, a misunderstanding of what the soul is, and an exceptionally dangerous kind of pride. We all at moments show how thoughtless or arrogant we are; but relatively few decide that they are in a position to challenge the various religious faiths—to weigh and sift and, in an ultimate sense of the word, *judge* (with respect to the transcendent). This presumptuousness of Jung's was matched only by the craven gullibility, Miss O'Connor knew, of his ardent followers, whose capacity to absorb and dote upon murkiness has to be remarked upon.

As one goes through the O'Connor correspondence, the philosophical sophistication of her mind becomes apparent. Once when I was in Milledgeville, I spent time looking at her books and examining some of her marginal notations. She had at her fingertips an impressive library—Aquinas and Maritain, Augustine and Teilhard de Chardin, Freud and Jung, but also Gilson, Bloy, Tillich, Romano Guardini, Eric Voegelin, and Gabriel Marcel. She had, too, the wisdom of novelists, Catholic and non-Catholic—Bernanos and Mauriac, Hawthorne and Melville, Tolstoy and Dostoevski, Dickens and Eliot and Hardy. The following excerpt from one of her letters, by no means atypical, reveals what went through the mind of a woman who could refer to intellectuals as "interleckchuls" and be scornful of much that has been taken to heart by important elements in contemporary American culture:

> I am currently reading Etienne Gilson's *History of Christian Philosophy in the Middle Ages* and I am surprised to come across various answers to Simone Weil's questions to Fr. Perrin. St. Justin Martyr anticipated her in the 2nd century on the question of the Logos enlightening every man who comes into the world. This is really one of her central questions and St. Justin answered it in what I am sure would have been her own way. Gilson is a vigorous writer, more so than Maritain; the other thing I have read of his is *The Unity of Philosophical Experience*, which I am an admirer of.

We have here no anxious lecturer choosing as a strategy of self-defense a vigorous offense: look what *I* know, or want you to think I know—lest any of you try to slip me up. Nor do we have an essayist doing likewise or parading her erudition immodestly before her all too awed readers: the sins of one soul finding congenial amplification elsewhere. Rather, a friend is unselfconsciously offering ideas, abstruse one time, quite connected to everyday living the next. As soon as that just-quoted portion of the letter ends, we read this: "My being on the crutches is not an accident or the energy-depriving ailment either but something that has been coming on in the top of the leg bone, a softening of it on acct. of a failure of circulation to the hip."

Hers was a mind able to move back and forth with a certain ease between matters transcendent and matters immanent. Hers was a mind inquiring, discerning, analytic, yet appreciative of the mysterious if not the mystical. She gave close attention to "local things," but she repeatedly entertained those larger conjectures about life in general. She was as delighted with a letter "from a West Virginia mountaineer whose favorite word is 'literature' which he spells 'litatur,'" as she was with letters from people she referred to as "scholars." In one letter she was referring to Santayana or Kafka, and in the next, she told a friend that she had "never read Kraft-Ebbing or *Memoirs of Hecate County.*" To which comment she added, tersely: "A little self-knowledge goes a long way."

She had strong preferences, a decided notion of what her own taste was and ought to be. She said a lot when she said, "I am a Catholic." She added a lot when she followed up those four words with the modification that she was "a Catholic peculiarly possessed by the modern consciousness." And she added a lot more when she noted this: "My audience are the people who think God is dead. At least these are the people I am conscious of writing for." And if anyone tried to update that God as a way of making him no longer "dead" for many of today's people, she could be contemptuously blunt: "As for Jesus' being a realist: if He was not God, He was no realist, only a liar, and the crucifixion an act of justice."

It is no small revelation to find her saying that Simone Weil and Edith Stein "are the two 20th century women who interest me most." They were, of course, two intellectual Jews who searched hard for God; one died coming closer, even closer, to the Catholic Church, and the other embraced it fully and ended up a nun. They were women who had to deal with strong intellects, tough and demanding wills; and they were women who moved an uncommon and unlikely distance—from sectarian intellectuality to a necessary surrender of the same to a higher authority, the person of God and, in one instance, the Church that claims to hold continuing custody of his flesh and blood. Such a surrender, Miss O'Connor knew, was enabled by grace. Born to Catholicism, she knew the believer's doubts. Despite her assertion that, for her, "dogma is only a gateway to contemplation and is an instrument of freedom and not of restriction," she could also, in the same letter, confess to a friend: "When I ask myself how I know I believe, I have no satisfactory answer at all, no assurance at all, no feeling at all. I can only say with Peter, Lord I believe, help my unbelief. And all I can say about my love of God is, Lord help me in my lack of it. I distrust pious phrases, particularly when they issue from my mouth."

Her freely admitted complicity ("human, all too human," as the saying goes) with her readers, with respect to the polarity of religious belief and doubt, may help us comprehend the vehemence of her occasional attacks on a group known for its skepticism, the intelligentsia. Add to that a Southerner's distrust of outsiders, especially preachy ones—as well as a sensitive Southerner's appreciation of the moral case those outsiders had, however a matter of history rather than something earned—and one can understand, perhaps, why a most learned woman could turn so sour when contemplating her own kind, many of whom, it has to be added, were also *not* her own kind in important respects. All she could do, she surely understood, was live out the contradictions within herself and note those within a number of other people. She pointedly affirmed, in a letter to an anonymous friend, this limited but significant connection to Hulga: "It's not said that she [Hulga] has never had any faith but it is implied that her fine education has got rid of it for her, that purity has been overridden by pride of intellect through her fine education."

Miss O'Connor knew that the poor, the uneducated, can also be thoroughly impure, as wretched spiritually as the rest of us who are by far luckier. Did Christ promise *every* poor person admission to heaven? A socioeconomic fact become an existential one! Each of us, rich or poor, holds on to the possibility of grace, holds on with one's teeth, if one is Flannery O'Connor. For her the loss of hope is a large sin, certainly. She had every intention as a writer of providing that hope, giving it the most palpable and suggestive form her wits as a storyteller enabled: "All my stories are about the action of grace on a character who is not very willing to support it, but most people think of these stories as hard, hopeless, brutal, etc." And to spell out what she meant about those "people," she said this: "Part of the difficulty of all this is that you write for an audience who doesn't know what grace is and don't recognize it when they see it." She was part of that audience, she knew. Who can assume for sure he or she is not? She wrote out of a "terrible need," a phrase she once used in connection with a religious hunger she felt evident in her friend Katherine Anne Porter. She wrote in fear too. It is hard for many intellectuals to understand this kind of intellectual, whose worries are indeed obsessive (in the nonpsychiatric and nonpejorative sense of the word); they are worries best indicated by an aphoristic phrase she once coined: "When there is nothing over the intellect it usually is tyrannical." She knew, Simone Weil knew, and Edith Stein knew the tyrannical side of a brilliantly aspiring philosophical mind, impatient with low-level discourse and outraged by the fake postures that others have no trouble calling upon for themselves. Tyrants lack charity—brilliant tyrants included. To feel charity is to have received grace. One senses Simone Weil, at the end, fighting hard against the imperial insistence of her own fiercely logical, perceptive, appraising mind. One senses Flannery O'Connor running to her Southern "country people," not because she saw them as saved—pure, righteous, and God-fearing. She was too wise, too knowing about that "Southern scene" for such an unqualified generalization. But she did find in that "scene" her particular refuge—a spiritual home as well as the place where she lived and died. Among people far less intellectual than herself she could, perhaps, keep the tyranny of her mind under greater control than would have been the case had she lived in places where that tyranny is rampant, even celebrated.

When she says that she believes "there is a fine grain of stupidity required in the fiction writer"; when she says that "the meaning in a story can't be paraphrased and if it's there it's there, almost more as a physical than an intellectual fact"; when she curtly declares that "subtlety is the curse of man"; when she talks of "sterile intellect"; when she announces that she's had "a stomach full of liberal religion"; when she talks of "a Unitarian or some pious liberal fraud," she is having a good time being scandalous, or she is being teasing and funny, or she is letting loose with a barb to friends who are, like her, themselves part of what is being criticized. But most of all she is fighting for her own respect. She knew how brilliant she was and how successful she had become. The word *celebrity* was used by her correspondents, and she could scarcely deny the fact that in a rather short writing career a great deal of attention had been given to her writing and, inevitably these days, to her as a person. Such a secular triumph was, for a person of her sensibility, a mixed blessing. "You will have found Christ," she told a friend, "when you are concerned with other people's sufferings and not your own."

At the time (1961), not all that far from death herself, and not unfamiliar with pain, she knew the extreme danger of what she once called a "swollen faith" in oneself: pride, self-centeredness, narcissism—the particular name or label mean little, the habit or attitude rather a lot. This continuing struggle with herself was the mark of her kind of intellectuality. I believe that it was a struggle enhanced both by her Catholicism and by her life as a Southerner. Anyone who has read Georges Bernanos, his polemical essays as well as his fiction, will recognize the struggle: he too was a sensitive and thoughtful writer, a man of ideas—many, many of them—who turned with outbursts of vehement denunciation on his own kind. Like her, he loved the poor and saw them as God's chosen people; and like her, he profoundly distrusted the intelligentsia, whom he regarded as pagan and self-centered. At the same time, their vanity was his lifelong temptation—as an essayist, a storyteller, a person anxious to tell others what they ought to think, like, dislike, and do. And like her, he gave geographical expression to this profound torment: Paris was the place of sin, the city where all those editors and publishers and writers and artists and academics lived. Eventually, after wandering through his beloved France, he imposed exile on himself. From far off Paraguay and Brazil he could be the *true* Frenchman and rail against those who had corrupted what he wanted—a nation-state merged with a Church into a pure community of believing, confessing Christians. The secular world constantly scandalized him and, unnervingly, reminded him of his own pride. In desperation, he clung to his fiction and hoped through it to redeem himself and to help a few others in their spiritual struggles.

It is not too hard, going through Flannery O'Connor's fiction and nonfiction, to find similar themes. Her cracks about New York, about Greenwich Village, about writers and publishers and magazines and colleges and, always, the intellectuals, are meant to show by their repetition and their adroit aim a sense of affiliation and a certain complicity with what is criticized—the former earned, the latter an inevitable consequence of the recognition she achieved. She could also direct her satire nearer home. "My mail for the last two weeks has been from rural Georgia," she told her good friend Maryat Lee in 1959; and after a recitation (which borders on the condescending) of the odd ones who wrote, she observes that "these letters are from people I might have made up. I don't want to get any nearer to them than in the imagination either." It is one of the least guarded comments to come from her in a voluminous and forthright correspondence. She was often quick to chide fellow Southerners, such as Maryat Lee, who had left the region. And God help any Yankee who tried to give her a secular sermon of any kind. But here she was, acknowledging the nonsense and stupidity and arrogance and pettiness that are to be found, she knew, in rural Georgia as well as in the Sodom and Gomorrah places up North. And here she was, keeping her distance from what she disliked and, inevitably, judged— through humor and scorn.

Southern Review, Winter 1980

Flannery O'Connor's Wise Blood

In the last years of her writing life, for all the pain, uncertainty, and physical frustration caused by the disease lupus erythematosus, Flannery O'Connor had quite obviously mastered the craft of constructing a tight yet powerfully suggestive short story. In "Parker's Back," for instance, her lifelong interest in religion, and specifically in the distinctions between Catholic and Protestant theology, got worked beautifully into a funny, sad plot. She never for a moment lost control of her characters. Every word is just right. Symbols are all over the place, yet one is not distracted by them. Things move along fast, as the medium requires, but a spell is soon upon the reader—who may, weeks later, find it hard to forget Parker and Sarah Ruth Cates Parker and her straight gospel talk and all that went on between them. O'Connor was an extremely able practitioner of what is called in hospitals "minor surgery": she had a keen eye for boils in need of lancing and she was well prepared to do the job. She wielded a quick, exact knife. The patient might not go home fully aware of why that boil got going in the first place, but plenty of hints were supplied, and there's just so much time a cutting doctor has, or an incisive storyteller.

The novel, however, lends itself to the more leisurely and speculative side of things; it is more like the internist's slow, painstaking diagnostic forays. O'Connor had a good deal of trouble with her two novels; they took a lot out of her before they were done, and she had serious doubts about the success of the second one, *The Violent Bear It Away*. The first one, *Wise Blood*, seems to have pleased her more; certainly it earned her a reputation as an exceedingly "different" writer, who could shrewdly draw upon regional life in the service of the most demanding, problematic kind of diagnosis—that of a particular civilization's spiritual malaise. She worked on the novel for years. (A movie has been made of *Wise Blood*, directed by John Huston.) Her letters in 1948 are full of talk about her struggles with it—what she hoped to do and what her own publisher, at the time, incorrectly believed her to be doing. "I am a very slow worker," she told her future agent, as she wrote of her plans for *Wise Blood*. When some of it was done and in the hands of her editor, she anticipated the worst—and got it:

> The criticism is vague and really tells me nothing except that they don't like it. I feel the objections they raise are connected with its virtues, and the thought of these lacks they mention is repulsive to me. The letter is addressed to a slightly dim-witted Camp Fire Girl, and I cannot look with composure on getting a life time of others like them.

A lot of Flannery in that, her friends might have said. She eventually found a spiritual home at Farrar, Straus and Giroux, which published *Wise Blood* in 1952. By then she had survived the terrible onslaught of the same disease that took her father's life when she was only fifteen and had gone home to Georgia to spend her remaining years in Milledgeville with a strong-minded and necessarily protective mother, to whom the novel is dedicated. It was the product, we were told by the author in 1962, a decade after publication and two years before her death at thirty-nine, of someone "congenitally innocent of theory, but one with certain preoccupations." We were also given this retrospective comment: "That belief in Christ is to some a matter of life and death has been a stumbling block for readers who would prefer to think it a matter of no great consequence."

More of Flannery. Hers was an intellectual's anti-intellectualism. In her letters, too, there were constant sideswipes at "theory," at social science, at the cosmopolitan Yankee world of literary and academic life. She had a strong religious appetite, apparent to the visitor who regards the books she once treasured, now located at Georgia State College, her alma mater. *Wise Blood* got plenty of negative reactions—comments that, ironically, indicated disbelief: obvious talent, but one of a weird bunch of people from that strangest of American locales, the South's Bible Belt. Perhaps the critical reaction to *Wise Blood* helped sharpen her own wonderful polemical writing: "Of course I have found that anything that comes out of the South is going to be called grotesque by the Northern reader, unless it is grotesque, in which case it is going to be called realistic"; and in the same vein, "Whenever I'm asked why Southern writers particularly have a penchant for writing about freaks, I say it is because we are still able to recognize one." A small, fragile person, she didn't mess around, and she had no trouble taking care of herself.

The principal character of *Wise Blood*, Hazel Motes, is a young war veteran who has come home to his parents' east Tennessee farm only to find it abandoned. He sets out on the train to Taulkinham, a city where people have lots to talk about. He's going to "do some things" there—a Southern country boy, the grandson of a preacher, on his way to find a destiny. But *Wise Blood* is hardly the conventional novel of youthful initiation. The author is for a while almost spoofing the genre—for example, with a hilarious encounter between Haze, as he gets called in the narration, and Mrs. Leora Watts, whose capabilities are publicly advertised in the men's room of the Taulkinham railroad station: "The friendliest bed in town!" On the way there in a cab, we get exchanges between the driver and Haze that tell us what is to come. "You look like a preacher," Haze is told. "Get this: I don't believe in anything," Haze soon enough insists. And shortly Mrs. Watts will hear an even more strenuous version: "I'm no goddam preacher."

Well, of course, he most certainly is one. It doesn't take him long to spot Asa Hawks, a supposedly blind martyr to Christ, who exhorts and begs the city folks on their way in and out of stores, to and from meetings. Beside him is his daughter, Sabbath Lily Hawks, whose comely features catch Haze's attention. And it doesn't take long for another country boy, Enoch Emery, to spot Haze. As for the reader who tries to make the acquaintance of these strangely driven and possessed people, it soon becomes apparent to him or to her that the blind are indeed leading the blind. Hawks is a fraud, we discover—a man on the make: he pretends helplessness to get money. Enoch is a lonely but delightfully enterprising youth, eager for someone or something to believe in. In the hands of a more sentimental writer (Carson McCullers, say) he'd steal the show from Haze as the appealing naif, anxious to form a relationship. For O'Connor, he is an occasion for humor and guile. She manages a few lessons of idolatry, without the slightest didacticism, and mostly gets us to laugh and laugh, as Enoch watches zoo monkeys carry on and takes Haze, who has the two Hawks on his mind, to meet a glass-encased mummy in a museum of sorts. Eventually Enoch joins a crowd of children, excited by the prospect of shaking hands with Gonga, a gorilla. It is a silly traveling show, but the youth is turned on. He becomes obsessed with the animal and is determined to follow in his footsteps—determined, that is, to seize the uniform from the man wearing it. The deed is done inside a truck, and soon thereafter a gorilla thoroughly scares a couple enjoying a roadside bench. Enoch is a reminder of our empty-headed gullible bestiality—our pitiable vulnerability to the various noises, pretenses, and dramatic tricks of this world. His carryings-on are also a particular novelist's occasion for having a little fun.

It becomes harder and harder as one turns the pages of *Wise Blood* to laugh with or at Haze. He announces himself as one who speaks on behalf of "The Church Without Christ." He elaborates:

> I'm a member and preacher to that church where the blind don't see and the lame don't walk and what's dead stays that way. Ask me about that church and I'll tell you it's the church that the blood of Jesus don't foul with redemption.

He goes further, with the cleverly worded testimony, redneck style, of the Anti-Christ. The author, in the topsy-turvy, caricatured world of Taulkinham, gives us ourselves: a country full of gadgetry, greed, calculation, phoniness, loud-mouthed claims and exaggerations, confidence men (and women), hucksters—all dressed up in pietistic avowals of various kinds. She is mercilessly sardonic as she introduces Hoover Shoats, another evangelical fraud, and Solace Layfield, his sidekick, who resembles Haze and gets run over by him. Haze's attempt to deny God is, of course, a measure of his moral seriousness, of the desperate nature of his religious search. He is, O'Connor would say long after *Wise Blood* appeared, "a Christian malgré-lui." He exposes the conceits and deceits, the plain foolishness or moral blindness of just about everyone he meets—all the while denying strenuously his own ethical superiority. His almost perverse modesty and lack of pretentiousness begin to grow on the reader. There is a freshness to his reversals of conventional (and badly tainted, if not wretchedly betrayed) Christian pieties:

> No truth behind all truths is what I and this church preach! Where you come from is gone, where you thought you were going to never was there, and where you are is no good unless you can get away from it. Where is there a place for you to be? No place.

But this down-home existentialism is not offered in the tones of fashionable twentieth-century despair. Haze is a prophet denouncing what prophecy has come to, hereabouts and now. And in the story, he is testing, always testing: is there any truth to what his eyes and ears find? In the end, his answer is no. He blinds himself. He ties barbed wire around his chest. He puts stones in his shoes. The pain of the world takes him over completely. He dies in a squad car, having been found in a ditch. His decent but self-centered and greedy landlady, Mrs. Flood, has not been able to comprehend him, try though she eventually does. The irony is powerful: a calculating woman tries hard to see what a blind man is up to, and can't do so. Haze has been touched by grace; she is "blocked" in her yearning to be part of what he has left to join.

Whatever O'Connor's theological interests, she does her work of character portrayal and narrative presentation well enough to avoid lectures. Her eye for the possibilities of satire is first-rate. She was politically somewhat conservative, and she never took to the swift social changes in the South that she only lived to see begin. But *Wise Blood* is a truly radical novel—full of scorn for the "principalities and powers" so many of us worship blindly: Mammon, Caesar, and not least, Satan set up in his digs as the local minister. The writing is lean, powerful, brilliantly suggestive. The humor is wild, yet terribly appropriate in its caustic attention to a range of our twentieth-century American obsessions. The landscapes are the familiar O'Connor ones: those ominous black skies, those stars that puzzle us so, the silver streaks of clouds, an occasional fiery sun, and the dark woods that loom in the distance of so many scenes—plain old Baldwin County, Georgia, all right, if not some indeterminate spot, halfway between heaven and hell.

New Republic, May 10, 1980

Letters Larger than Life

Astrong and necessary argument can be made for leaving the private lives of novelists alone, and I suspect Flannery O'Connor might have amassed her considerable powers of persuasion (including both a marvelous sense of humor and a sharply ironic, occasionally satirical eye) to the task of showing why that ought to be the case. She was wonderfully suspicious of the pompous, self-important strain that grows larger and larger in the psychologically oriented literary criticism of our time. For her a story had its own integrity (or, alas, lack of it). To see fiction as an interesting kind of psychiatric fall-out is to be a dreary and ignorant reader. And to use fiction as a means of discussing, teaching, or dramatizing psychopathology or the workings of the unconscious is to turn one of this life's honest pleasures into a sad waste of time and energy.

No one needs a story of Flannery O'Connor's to learn about the problems of those living in the Milledgeville State Hospital. By the same token, the alienists who work there—honorably one hopes and prays—have every reason to leave Miss O'Connor's stories alone. They are constructs of the imagination, honed down to proper size and shape by such psychological qualities as intelligence, good judgment, a keen ear, a quick eye, a good memory for what has been spoken, a lively sense of fun, and not least, a way with words. Since everyone has problems, since Freud decreed us all neurotics, what makes for a good storyteller is not his or her problems but gifts of mind and heart, gifts which impressed the founder of psychoanalysis enough to prompt in him a renunciation. He declared that his discipline had to "lay down its arms" (an interesting metaphor, indeed) so far as "the problem of the creative artist" goes, Dostoevski in that instance.

Once that surrender is made, psychology becomes what it ought to be so far as biography goes—a means of describing a particular person rather than an instrument in explaining a form of art. And why not go further? We might spend our time enjoying, discussing, and learning from that art, which is, after all, what really brings us to be interested in X or Y, in his or her capacity to use those words and phrases, that paint or marble. The combative answer to the rhetorical question is obvious: these individuals, these Faulkners and Weltys and O'Connors, for instance, are extraordinary human beings by virtue of what they can write—so why not, indeed, get to know them through the intercession of another kind of artist, the biographer?

In the letters she wrote, as in the essays that make up *Mystery and Manners*, Miss O'Connor shows no great enthusiasm for psychological or sociological abstractions; she had other ways of approaching human beings. But she never held herself back; she gave of herself generously, sharing her random ideas and temporary interests, her strong preferences and unyielding preoccupations. In her life she may have been (to strangers, at least) shy, formal, and reserved; she may have been for long stretches sick and a bit isolated; but she was emphatically not someone determined to preserve her privacy at all costs. She had no use for today's all too fashionable psychiatric reductionism as applied to biography (or, for that matter, to politics, social analysis, or of course, spiritual issues). But she was not on the run personally. One reads these letters and wants to know her. The letters are an important step in that direction—a biography of sorts.

Her strength of personality is constantly evident. This is one writer not haunted by whiskey or crazy voices or a quicksilver emotional life. This is one writer who felt no need to display herself anywhere. This is one writer whose opinions were strong but circumscribed. When she spoke of a social viewpoint or a political preference, she was being the particular person she was—in no way confusing her general body of ideas with her distinctive capacity to create stories of great power and complexity. She was neither arrogant nor falsely modest; to avoid either attribute of that polarity and be an exceptionally able storyteller and novelist is to demonstrate a marvelous immunity to an occupational hazard of the gifted.

Still, people of my ilk, psychiatrists and psychoanalysts, may well be among the more prominent of this century's fools. We seem ever ready to rush in anywhere with our heavy-handed, self-important, and frivolous or gratuitous interpretations. I wouldn't, therefore, count Flannery O'Connor safe; she's already received a few psychiatric punches, and she may be in for more. But these letters, so thoughtfully and tenderly assembled by Sally Fitzgerald, reveal such a warm, sensitive, responsive person; such a woman of give and take; such a sound and knowing overseer of herself and those she knew and loved; such a smiling yet serious servant of the Church, and through it of God Almighty, that one can only (thinking of that last attribute of hers) pray hard and long for those who want to use the so-called social sciences as a means of ultimate caricature.

What really matters about *The Habit of Being* is the nature of the correspondence it reveals, the important ideas it presents, the hints of what might have been—hence, the revelation of the tragedy that befell so many of us readers in August of 1964. In a sense, the letters argue silently for Flannery O'Connor as a character in a novel—a person whose apparently humdrum daily life, plainly more confined than most, is no match at all for the dramatic surges of her intellect and her soul both. What her body could not manage was more than balanced by the energies of her mind and heart. She possessed character, a quality of being that defies the rude approximations of modern psychology. And she was a character, someone not afraid to be herself and no one else. (Hasn't today's psychology, much of it, become insistently normative, intent on squelching the independent, the different, the idiosyncratic, in favor of an overwrought clinical consensus of sorts?)

She herself becomes gradually and ironically, in *The Habit of Being*, a part of a long, absorbing, entertaining, edifying story. Her correspondence forms a narrative one can't put down because one is learning, laughing, and experiencing the writer's pain or sadness or merriment as one's own. Her voice is at once familiar, down-home, and oracular—a twentieth-century Southern version of the wisdom George Eliot offered her readers. And that voice, one moment using the Georgia vernacular, the next as sophisticated as can be, is connected to a plot: a woman's struggle to master a craft, to gain a certain place in the world of letters, to find a means of doing justice to her considerable moral and philosophical concerns, and not least, to live a life in the face of an intimacy with illness most of us don't experience in our twenties and thirties.

Unintentionally—and without the slightest inclination of self-preoccupation or self-dramatization (quite the contrary)—a woman, a writer, an intense student of literature and religion, finds herself face to face with a disease that still today has its own "mystery" and requires of its adversaries (Miss O'Connor did not live as a victim) a certain fine yet sturdy adjustment of "manners." There was an unwanted and hardly sought-after drama in that coming home for good of the young Milledgeville story writer. The year was 1952; the home was, of course, a certain small city in Georgia. But Flannery O'Connor's mind wandered earnestly, respectfully, at times hungrily over all time and over the Christian world. There was a continuing tension in her entire life between the obvious connections she had and enjoyed having in a particular Southern community and the membership she held in the largest world imaginable—the conceptually layered universe of Teilhard de Chardin, not to mention that of God himself.

I have responded in my book, *Flannery O'Connor's South*, to *The Habit of Being*, but here I want to dwell a while on the intriguing spiritual relationship between Flannery O'Connor and Simone Weil—a relationship that these letters tell us a good deal about. I had noted books of Simone Weil in the O'Connor library at Georgia College and for years have thought about each in connection with the other. I have pictures of these two extraordinary pilgrims in my study, and strangely, they ended up side by side—one of those accidents my ilk perhaps makes too much of. One of my sons, in fact, asked me once if they were known to one another. I said no, confidently. But I was at least partially wrong. O'Connor knew Weil rather well.

Simone Weil struggled as hard as maybe anyone ever has with that special version of the sin of pride that befalls intellectuals. In the end, she was indeed "waiting for God," but she could never do that attending with any calm or confidence of his arrival. She wanted desperately to find him, but she had an enormous burden to come to terms with, an intellect that found Thomist reassurances unconvincing and Augustinian admonitions and self-criticism rather congenial. What does Flannery O'Connor mean when she describes Simone Weil as a "remarkable woman" who "intrigues" her, but one whose ideas ("much of what she writes") end up being "ridiculous" to her, "naturally"? That last innocent adverb may provide the necessary hint. No Christian believer can take for granted his or her faith—nor, of course, God's judgment of it: the final measure of this life. But a believing Catholic has by received or acquired faith learned to stop interposing himself or herself between Christ and his chosen intermediary, the Church. Simone Weil, in contrast, stood alone in the universe, scandalized by the corruptions and evils she saw everywhere and prepared to die in a personal and decisive encounter with Satan, whose strength and significance, it can be argued, she grossly exaggerated, reflecting the Manichaean heresy yet again with us. She also flirted dangerously with the Marcionate heresy, that effort of certain early Christians to remove Christ from his spiritual roots in the Israel of Isaiah, Jeremiah, and Amos, to separate him from a given people and place, and yes, religious tradition (they thus ignored Jesus the Rabbi and even Paul the saint, who struggled long and hard to keep Christians Jews).

Calling upon Dante's sense of "comedy," O'Connor had this to say about Weil: "Her life is almost a perfect blending of the Comic and the Terrible, which two things may be opposite sides of the same thing." In the same letter, to "A" in 1955, we learn that Simone Weil had indeed connected with a most significant side of O'Connor:

> Well Simone Weil's life is the most comical life I have ever read about and the most truly tragic and terrible. If I were to live long enough and develop as an artist to the proper extent, I would like to write a comic novel about a woman—and what is more comic and terrible than the angular intellectual proud woman approaching God inch by inch with ground teeth?

In her next letter to "A," O'Connor makes sure her correspondent does not mistake the content of the last letter she received: "By saying Simone Weil's life was both comic and terrible I am not trying to reduce it, but mean to be paying her the highest tribute I can, short of calling her a saint, which I don't believe she was." She was, O'Connor continues, a person of great courage. She was extraordinary in her serious struggle to understand the world and find an honorable way of living in it. "Of course," O'Connor insists to her anonymous friend, "I can only say, as you point out, this is what I see, not, this is what she is—which only God knows."

That last qualification of vision, that last demurrer, that last renunciation, actually, is for me one of the significant moments in *The Habit of Being*; it provides an utterly telltale insight into the essential nature of a writer who in her own way was as extraordinary and courageous as Simone Weil. In fact, I would venture to say that all her adult life Simone Weil wanted to be able to say what O'Connor did—to forget pride and yield to God. O'Connor would be the last one to claim herself virtuous for the capacity to do just that. She took pains to remind her friend "A" that for many devout believers Catholicism is an inheritance—the lucky, the mysteriously privileged. Still, not all of us hold on to what we have been fortunate enough to receive as an unrequested gift. And O'Connor had a strong, assertive, independent mind—a temptation at any time, and especially these days when the self-centeredness of intellectuals is welcome psychological news for many who claim no belief in God or in anything much except the various needs we are supposed to have.

In contrast, O'Connor took after intellectuals strenuously, mocking them, banishing them in her mind to the alien North of Manhattan, complaining of their humorless presumptuousness as critics of her work and the work of those she cherished. She knew how imperial anyone's eager mind can become without some saving self-criticism, modesty, and humility. She was saved—forever, she hoped and prayed—by the Church; but even on this earth, before God's summons came, one dares suggest she was saved (rather obviously, without claiming to be!) by her willingness, finally, to thwart that "unreflecting egoism" George Eliot spoke of.

What matters, O'Connor knew, was Simone Weil's achievements as a thinker, a writer, a person possessed of a soul and willing to fight for it more earnestly than for an intellectual's career. In the end, her moral obsessions won, and for that victory, Simone Weil has earned the vulture-like attention of various psychological reductionists, from whose company Flannery O'Connor knew deep in her bones she must dissociate herself. My own kind have words such as *anorexia nervosa* to diagnose Simone Weil—but they thereby miss the point: she deliberately kept her food intake down to that of her compatriots in occupied France. True, she had tuberculosis and needed a much higher caloric intake. But she was not pegging her food intake to her body's requirements or to the demands of her doctors; nor was she abstaining from food because neurotic voices or illusions or psychotic fantasies insisted that she do so. She had, ironically, attached herself to the concrete reality of millions of French men, women, and children.

The doctors who have speculated about her "reality-testing" have

put themselves in the strange position of ignoring the moral claims
of a woman who could not remove herself from the essence of her
nation's wartime suffering. Miss O'Connor was the last one to get
into that sort of psychiatric argument. Every instinct in her Catholic
spirit told her, in an instant, to reach out for the Simone Weil who
was seeking God. Who cares, really, what her problems were? Who
of us is without them? Who of us has, on the other hand, struggled
so hard to tame pride? Simone Weil was more of an intellectual than
many who lay claim to the word, yet she detested both the word
and the arrogance connected to some of its usage. In *The Need for
Roots* one suddenly comes across this: "A Condition of any Working-class culture is the mingling of what are called 'intellectuals'—
an awful name, but at present they scarcely deserve a better one—
with the workers." For somewhat different critical reasons, Flannery
O'Connor found the use, even the spelling, of that word *intellectuals*
similarly difficult and used instead her well-known "interleckchuls."

   All through Flannery O'Connor's correspondence one sees certain critical tensions being approached by an exceptionally vigorous
mind and by a soul attentive to the longer distance: *sub specie aeternitatis.* There is, for her, the South as sinner and the South as a
community of people no worse than others, and maybe, for all its
suffering and shame and wrongdoing, touched a bit by grace. There
is, for her, the North as a place of hypocrisy and self-righteousness
and the North of obvious culture and intellectual achievement.
There were, for her, the plain people of a rural region, whom she
closely watched, dearly appreciated, learned from, and not least,
drew from constantly in her writing. There were, for her, too, the
ignorance and prejudice that not only the South struggles with, but
which O'Connor never overlooked, no matter her sallies against the
Yankees. There were, for her, the other worlds of the saints, the philosophers, and the theologians—and how much of her time and
attention she gave to them. But there was also, for her, the mid-
twentieth-century secular American world, which for some strange
reason (a hunger it knew not how otherwise to acknowledge?) had
found itself drawn powerfully to her stories. She had a keen eye for
that last world, our world. She involved herself in its preoccupations
slyly and mordantly—through such hurt, confused, troubled characters as Hulga or Asbury or Rayber. And not least, there were, for
her, the ideas, the principles, the abstract speculations she savored,

rejected, or embraced; but always, contrapuntally, she insisted upon the particular, the concrete, the specific, the here-and-now. Like others of keen, scholarly instincts, but influenced always by the motions of the heart, she experienced the necessary vacillations between the transcendent and the immanent.

Finally, one honors her deep admiration and affection for that Yankee storyteller, who is spiritual kin of hers, Nathaniel Hawthorne. How severely that nineteenth-century, brooding, marvelously observant man took stock of the vanities, follies, and doomed ambitions of his day's intellectuals, the Concord and Cambridge men of ideas who lacked, he felt, a sense of proportion, men who couldn't see themselves as a mere handful in an infinite parade of sinners slouching toward Jerusalem or, alas, doomed all too surely for a journey of another kind. Hawthorne had contempt for the contentious, self-assured thinkers of his town and state because he distrusted not only their extreme pride but also his own sinful possibilities. The story saved him, as he admitted once: "'Come,' said I to my friend, starting from a deep reverie, 'let us hasten hence, or I shall be tempted to make a theory—after which, there is little hope for any man.'"

Can any of us read those lines (in *Mosses from an Old Manse*) and not think of Flannery O'Connor telling Granville Hicks in 1957, telling us in *The Habit of Being*, "I'm not an intellectual, and have a horror of making an idiot of myself with abstract statements and theories"? She never did, not once—not even when, in her letters and essays, she quietly made the effort to summon those "statements and theories." Always at hand was the smiling storyteller, Hawthorne's romancer, ready to "hasten hence" and thereby save not only herself but the rest of us too—if we would but understand our jeopardy.

Flannery O'Connor Bulletin, Autumn 1979

The Habit of Being
Flannery O'Connor's Illness
and Collected Letters

Milledgeville, Georgia, was the last capital of the Confederacy. Today it is a city of 12,000 people, with a mix of antebellum homes (still very much a presence and a continuing lure to tourists), an enormous mental hospital, and a growing number of light industries. Its real fame, however, is growing for other reasons.

Flannery O'Connor, the short story writer and novelist from Milledgeville, died in early August 1964. She was only thirty-nine years old and had had disseminated lupus erythematosus since her mid-twenties. The disease had claimed her father, Edwin O'Connor, who died in 1941 when she was fifteen. Her mother, Regina (Cline) O'Connor, survives. A descendant of an old prominent Southern family, she is now in her eighties.

When she died, Flannery left a legacy of short stories, essays, and novels. (One of the novels, *Wise Blood*, was developed into a film directed by John Huston.) Now, thanks to her friends Sally and Robert Fitzgerald, another legacy survives—her collected letters, which extend over the period from June 1948, when she was working on *Wise Blood*, to July 28, 1964, just six days before her death.

Flannery O'Connor grew up in Savannah, Georgia, and attended parochial schools there. She lived across the street from the city's cathedral. In 1941 after her father's death, she was taken to Milledgeville, where she finished high school and attended the Georgia State College for Women (now Georgia College). The Flannery O'Connor of the 1940s was a bright, independent person, not especially involved with any particular group or intellectual interest. In college she majored in the social sciences—something of an irony in view of her later severe distrust of them. She was adept at drawing cartoons, deftly executed sketches that reveal a keen, aloof, sardonic mind. Even at that relatively early point she was able to sense (and to summon in an art form) the continuing foolishness, hypocrisy, and pretense from which no era or region can claim immunity. After she finished college, she found herself stirred to give a verbal rather than a pictorial response to the world she saw around her. Her early writing efforts earned her admission to the writers' workshop Paul Engle ran at the University of Iowa. By the time she graduated from there in 1947, she had already begun to establish herself as a short story writer of considerable originality, power, and not least, humor. One by one her stories made their appearance in the literary quarterlies as well as in such magazines as *Mademoiselle* and *Harper's Bazaar.* She was accepted at Yaddo, an artist's foundation in Saratoga Springs, New York, and came to know the poet Robert Lowell, the novelist and critic Elizabeth Hardwick, and the poet and translator Robert Fitzgerald. She worked hard on a novel, *Wise Blood,* and in 1949 took up residence in Ridgefield, Connecticut, with Robert and Sally Fitzgerald and their young, growing family. She remained devoted to her mother and to her native South, but she seemed destined to live "up North," near, if not in close contact with, Manhattan's literati.

But in late 1950, illness intervened. Several nights after Sally and Robert Fitzgerald had sent their house guest south, homeward bound for Christmas, her mother called to tell them that "Flannery was dying of lupus." Sally Fitzgerald continues: "The doctor had minced no words. We were stunned. We communicated regularly with Mrs. O'Connor while she went through this terrible time and the days of uncertainty that followed during Dr. Arthur J. Merrill's tremendous effort to save Flannery's life." The writer was to have fourteen more years, but they were dramatically altered by her lupus.

No doubt about it, we owe to adrenocorticotropic hormone (ACTH) the striking harvest of those years: two novels, some thirty short stories, a collection of brilliant, idiosyncratic, penetrating critical essays, and not least, her recently published letters—*The Habit of Being.* Sally Fitzgerald, a devoted friend of the writer, has assembled a large correspondence that becomes, finally, a touching and instructive self-portrait of a novelist.

The physician's success was, of course, purchased at a price. Cortisone exacts its own progressive toll. Reading Flannery's letters, so full of shrewd asides and blunt wisdom, one realizes how much discomfort, pain, and weakness she had to experience as she nevertheless went about her work. It was a stretch of time devoted to approaching closer and closer the essentials of this life—hence the title *The Habit of Being*. (Flannery O'Connor read Maritain closely and knew well his use of the word *habit*. In *Art and Scholasticism* he observes that "habits are interior growths of spontaneous life"—a definition that is a far cry from the view that our behaviorist-oriented society would incline us to have of the efforts we make to bring discipline to our energies.)

Flannery O'Connor wrote stories that were meant to bring us to our senses, to help us sift and sort, to understand what matters truly and what is utterly inconsequential. She was a devout Catholic, although interested in biblical Christianity rather than compliant pietism. She was a Southerner, living in a rural part of the region, but a friend to a number of urban Yankee cosmopolitans. She was, finally, an ailing young woman, living longer and much closer to death than most of us do, whatever our age. But those aspects of her complex life never became an occasion for psychiatric indulgence. That is to say, she had no use for the religious uses to which many have put the social sciences, especially psychoanalytic psychology and psychiatry—the resort to behavioral interpretation or exploration that is meant to serve as a moral substitute for all too many of this age's secularists.

Her letters show her to be willing to say yes or no, willing to approve or condemn, willing to call on the Bible, on a particular moral philosopher or theologian, and yes, on God himself. Her letters, too, show her to be unashamed of tradition—a literary one and a regional one: "To my way of thinking, the only thing that keeps me from being a regional writer is being a Catholic and the only thing that keeps me from being a Catholic writer (in the narrow sense) is being a Southerner." She wrote in a time of unrest and social upheaval. She was repeatedly being urged to "get involved," to speak publicly about racial issues and the Civil Rights struggle, to sign various statements, petitions, and declarations. On the whole, she was guarded and reticent—but not from timidity. She considered herself part of a particular world, the inconsistencies, ironies, paradoxes, confusions, and downright evils that she never shirked evoking in her writing: "The traditional Protestant bodies of the

South are evaporating into secularism and respectability and are being replaced on the grass roots level by all sorts of strange sects that bear not much resemblance to traditional Protestantism—Jehovah's Witnesses, snake-handlers, Free Thinking Christians, Independent Prophets, the swindlers, the mad, and sometimes the genuinely inspired." But she was not one to be bullied by those whose self-righteousness or ignorance, however clothed in a moment of virtuous political activity, she could not help perceiving. She loved the South and wanted to see it change, but she knew, as did (in my experience) many of the region's black people, that in the long run it would be the local people themselves—Georgians, Carolinians, Alabamians, and so on—of both races, who would be left to come to better terms with each other. She was, I suppose it can be said, a radical conservative—deeply Christian and hence ever-mindful of Christ's ministry to the poor (most of her fictional characters are poor men and women) but responsive to (and anxious to defend) many aspects of a certain sectional heritage.

Her letters are also, and inadvertently, a chronicle of suffering endured with calm and a knowing dignity. She asks little of her correspondents in the way of sympathy and allows them precious few hints of the pain or physical restriction that is constantly her lot. Only at the very end of her life did she have this to say: "The wolf, I'm afraid, is inside tearing up the place. I've been in the hospital fifty days already this year. At present I'm just home from the hospital and have to stay in bed. I have an electric typewriter and I write a little every day but I'm not allowed to do much." She is, usually, the giver, the one who wants to teach, clarify, reassure, amuse, or offer hospitality. For an increasingly prominent and celebrated writer, she was exceptionally available—quick to reply when a letter or a telephoned or telegrammed request arrived. Guests were welcomed, too—persons from near and far who were drawn to this unusual woman, who may have been sick for years but who seemed a serene, wry, vastly amused observer of her fellow creatures.

At no point did Flannery O'Connor seem inclined to find psychological counsel for her medical predicament. She comes across as utterly uninterested in an examination of the way she was coping with her illness. She would have scorned the extreme self-consciousness of the "awareness movement"—the endless glorification of self that characterizes so much of our contemporary culture. And one can imagine what Flannery (as many of us feel comfortable in calling her, even now as we write of her) would have said about some recent excursions in thanatology. Tell people long enough that hope and prayer and a faith in—a passionate reliance on—God's grace, his promised Good News, are evidence of this or that psychological "mechanism of defense"; tell people they are "using denial" and resorting to "primitive" mental maneuvers; reduce the mind's struggles and yearnings, its long, slouching journey toward Jerusalem to a neurotic fix that needs to be categorized by "stages" and judged as "sick" or "mature"; speak about people and their real-life personal anguish with the stuff of cold, dreary psychiatric jargon—and of course there will be an ironic outcome. Those who once denied us "denial" now give us a denial (voices across the Styx!) that taxes everyone's credulity—in the name of science rather than religion.

No wonder Flannery celebrated mystery and embraced it in the workings of fiction and religion. (As did Hawthorne, she urged that "the task of the novelist is to deepen mystery.") When scientists (let alone social scientists) try to banish all mystery, the result, Flannery knew, would be a mere displacement: the inevitable assertion, as an aspect of our humanity, somehow and somewhere and sometime, of our sense of wonder and awe. Is it presumptuous to suggest *The Habit of Being* as a good text for medical students, physicians, and patients interested in a writer's effort to understand this life? As Flannery died slowly, and with clear comprehension, she wrote these stunning letters, and they certainly do offer us an example of a remarkable sensibility at work. However strenuous the medical strains provided by a still devastating, puzzling disease, she never yielded her good judgment, her courage, or her deep Christian faith. Her lupus became an occasion for moral reflection and spiritual growth. These letters remind us what novelists and poets yet have to offer us in medicine—a continuing evocation and celebration of this life's essential nature, not unlike the modest attention we ourselves give to that life, that nature, in the course of our daily medical work.

Journal of the American Medical Association,
September 26, 1980

Of Poets and Poetry

Psychoanalysis and the
Poetic Psyche

Freud warned others (and maybe himself preeminently) that psychoanalysts ought to be exceedingly wary of the "problem" of "creativity." In doing so he used the interesting (and by implication self-critical) imagery of military surrender: he said that one must "lay down" one's "arms" when scrutinizing, as he was trying to do in connection with Dostoevski, the mind of the writer, with all its stunning contradictions and triumphant achievements. He was clearly speaking about the futility, at least in that instance, of the psychoanalytic mode of inquiry; it is, of course, essentially reconstructive mental investigation, whereby present-day thoughts and fantasies, not to mention patterns of behavior, are traced back gradually and ever more distinctly (one hopes) to earlier experiences, to those "anlages" the German nineteenth-century scientists mentioned so often. Maybe that preoccupation with specific psychological antecedents, that *quest*, really, was destined to prove more frustrating and inadequate, even when undertaken with ordinary people of no artistic talent or pretensions, than Freud ever cared to imagine. He was, among other things, a romantic; he called himself openly a conquistador. For all his concern with theoretical formulation of a "scientific" kind (the only kind that would "take," he cannily realized as a social observer, cultural critic, and not least, a messianic, sectarian political leader of sorts), we find in his writing references to "meta-psychological" constructs; he probably knew that between the mind's actuality (in William James's wonderful phrase, "the blooming, buzzing, confusion" of ideas and feelings) and even the wisest, most patient, and most articulate psychoanalytic listener there are shadows—shadows of each person's particularity, of the diverse social, cultural, economic, and historical forces that variously impinge upon us, and of our ideas, beliefs, values, fears, or hopes. It is hard to generalize successfully (although some of us in the social sciences are all too willing to make the effort) in the face of the ironies, ambiguities, contradictions, and inconsistencies that are characteristic of all lives—not just those of artists like Dostoevski but those lived by millions of human beings, who defy as well as invite single-minded explanations of various kinds. Stories or myths help make sense of lives badly served by pretentious categorizations peddled as "scientific."

Nevertheless, it is in our nature to try to come up with answers; we are the thinking, speculative ones on this planet. We try to make sense of ourselves, of one another, of that banality "the human condition." We move (unless we are gifted and fortunate novelists) from the individual to the increasingly general, and often enough we pull back or give up in amusement, in despair, and maybe with a shudder or two; or we surrender out of the wisdom and modesty of old age, perhaps the case with Freud. Not that Freud ever meant to discourage speculation. He was ever anxious to make connections (see his book *Moses and Monotheism*, the last one published while he was alive), and he set no limits for that mixture of curiosity, psychological acuity, and shrewd social judgment he often demonstrated; he used jokes, for instance, to indicate something about the psychological and cultural situation of the teller and the listener. In rather unselfconscious achievements like that one (*Wit and Its Relationship to the Unconscious*), we find him a shrewd psychologist, as always, but anxious to leave his office and make a blend of aesthetic and cultural analyses, not forgetting history either: what is one to say about these people who amuse one another this way—about what have they gone through and what they still contend with?

Albert Gelpi's *The Tenth Muse: The Psyche of the American Poet* has prompted this perhaps too long windup. It is a strong, suggestive, and revealing book, exquisitely successful in the balance it offers of specific example, modest statement, and guarded psychological interpretation on the one hand and broad social history on the other hand. In a way, I ought to disqualify myself as a reviewer. Professor Gelpi acknowledges his continuing debt to the late Perry Miller ("he will always stand in my intellectual life as a Promethean Demiurge"); and I too fell under Miller's spell for a while. As I read Mr. Gelpi's finely wrought and extended readings of the Puritan poet Edward Taylor, and to a lesser extent, as I read the chapters on Ralph Waldo Emerson and Emily Dickinson, I kept on thinking of a class I once had with Perry Miller and of his insistent question, thrown at us, we sometimes thought, more than was proper or (that cool, slippery word) productive: "What kind of a *person* was he?"

Miller had in mind no raw, vulgar, presumptuous, reductionist statement. He wasn't necessarily being "psychological" at all when he asked the question of us; he wanted to make us fit the lines we were reading, written decades, maybe centuries ago, into a particular age's assumptions. He wanted us to speculate whether regions and classes and nations and ideologies don't somehow (how to know exactly?) winnow out voices and come up with their particular prophets. Some of those prophets, of course, go unrecognized during their lives, and not only because of their personal idiosyncrasies. But they have watched, listened, taken stock, and all important, put down convincingly and suggestively (not as polemicists or ideologues) what they have seen, heard, and come to think. Eventually they get paid attention.

In Edward Taylor we have, through Mr. Gelpi's interpretations, the Calvinist struggling mightily with his body's demands as well as with his mind's lofty effort to obtain God's grace. There would never be a resolution (another cool, slippery word of our time), but the achievements of an Edward Taylor show how agile, resourceful, and inspired a tormented mind can be, given that mysterious endowment that goes under the name of the writer's gift. Although Professor Gelpi avoids first causes or basic conflicts and refuses to emphasize the psychopathological in those psyches he wants to comprehend rather than categorically probe, he does end up ironically falling back, so to speak: the Puritan warfare of the soul, with antagonists fighting for high stakes, is the predecessor of later American cultural conflicts.

For Taylor, as for many Puritans cursed, they often believed, with the desire to write (and thus cursed with the pride, the self-centeredness that asks the regard of others), there are God's commandments to be obeyed without question and man's sinful desire to go off, be by himself, and make his own rules, his own world, thereby becoming to a degree satanic. Not a very promising scene for a writer, especially an ambitious philosophical one interested in making poetry out of Christ's message and one pilgrim's pursuit of it. Taylor's people left England, among other reasons, to be rid of a society increasingly tolerant of self-displaying, manipulative egotists—satans of an apparently disarming kind who use words as temptations, who seduce themselves and the rest of us with their idle tongues, however fancy, or with their cleverly put down words. Why, then, once in America, offer new embellishments, if not messages hidden between lines? Why give evil the life of poetry?

Somewhere in his tormented but not stultified or overcome soul (or psyche, and where are the boundaries to be drawn?), Edward Taylor knew what Edgar Allan Poe would say in reply—Poe, who for such a lamentably short time would speak up for the outcast, the misfit, the outrageous stylist, the connoisseur, the aesthetic and/or social critic, and the person who desires to ply his words, work up his images, and spin his web of "self and society," as the social science expression goes today. In every poet's life (and maybe the rest of us ought be mentioned too), there is the tension Gelpi elucidates first in its Puritan manifestation (Taylor), then in Emerson and Poe, and finally within the lives and poetic rhythms of Walt Whitman and Emily Dickinson. Emerson became a pillar all right; he became uncomfortably conformist, out of respectability (it can be maintained) rather than self-imposed poetic requirement. Thoreau's bluntness bothered as well as fascinated him. Whitman's personal exuberance and candor sent ripples of concern, and even a misgiving or two, down the Cambridge Turnpike to that splendid home near the village green—and not so far from its Unitarian Church, speaking of the devil or Satan.

But Emerson was no craven, calculating, self-promoting nineteenth-century matinee idol masquerading as a poet or, for that matter, as an essayist. He saw an industrial society beginning to run amok even in his time while others, Whitman, for example, were less grim and, arguably, less prescient. For Emerson man was an "object" as well as a "subject"; it was not for nothing that he used the word *transcendentalism*. He distrusted the self's orgies, even those of an inspired self. Professor Gelpi asks, quite wisely: "At what point does self-expression become self-indulgence and 'soul passion' become narcissism?" It is a question one feels on the mind of Edward Taylor (and, Lord knows, on that of Cotton Mather) rather often. It is a question Emerson, in his own fashion, asked of those he dearly loved (Thoreau) and strove hard out of admiration to help (Whitman). It is a question one can in good conscience direct at Poe, at Whitman—even at Emily Dickinson, who knew to ask herself every possible question to the point that her self-scrutiny, so unrelenting and merciless, becomes wicked in the Calvinist sense, or narcissistic, to call upon our contemporary demonology. In this book Professor Gelpi draws by acknowledgment on Jung, and deservedly so. Jung's notion of the unconscious includes territory other psychoanalysts have dismissed outright or declared (they too have a touch of the Calvinist in them) wicked—the notion of a "collective unconscious." But T. S. Eliot, with good reason, was moved to interpret Jung's admittedly obscure and sometimes easily abused or evilly usurped notion of what happens in our minds as we come to grips with more than a "family constellation" and (as a dash of salt and pepper) with those "socio-cultural factors" that are mentioned these days; he knew that when a people develops a culture, it works its way into the minds, hearts, and souls of poets (and of psychoanalysts, for that matter). Freud, skeptical always of Jung's seemingly romantic or murky ideas, nevertheless developed a seemingly irrational dislike of America on his only visit here in 1909. Or was it a premonition of what the future would hold: the marriage of his rationalist, materialist young science, with its mechanistic imagery, to elements of America's lapsed puritanism, now become lodged in a variety of sectarian, messianic movements, of which psychoanalysis has surely been one? (Needless to say, there is no reason to blame the discipline of psychoanalysis for the cultural immersion of sorts it experienced upon arrival in twentieth-century America.)

There is no definitive answer to the cultural paradoxes America's nineteenth-century poets or its twentieth-century ones (or indeed its contemporary psychoanalysts) have to live with. Whitman's wonderful and annoying openness and Dickinson's intense, uncompromising privatism are indeed, as the author shows, two sides of an American coin. In a letter to an English colleague in 1934, Freud observed that "psychoanalysts in America are constantly torn between their desire to work in privacy and the temptation to surrender themselves to the curiosity of the crowd." Then he added, lest his correspondent not take the observation seriously: "I am not exaggerating. I think we will end up knowing a lot about America before we are through with it, and it is through with us!" The latter development may be approaching, for our faddish preoccupation with psychoanalysis does indeed seem spent, at long last—so that analysts today are increasingly left to do their important work quietly. But poets have never been embraced by this nation's culture, not even faddishly. Yes, a particular poet has had a moment or two of acclaim (MacLeish, Frost); but even Emerson's position of honor was not to be confused (and he knew it) with a society's enthusiastic and pervasive nod of acceptance. One assumes that there is no imminent danger that to-day's American poets, or those of the twenty-first century, will be confronted by polarities or paradoxes much different from those Professor Gelpi discusses in his book. Whitman's combative or demonstrative heirs are among us, as are Emily Dickinson's quite retiring ones. The psyche of any American poet still has to place itself—no doubt both deliberately and unselfconsciously—in one or another position on the spectrum the author describes. It can be a demanding, even exhausting mandate, but it is apparently yet another occasion for the mind to glow and thereby afford the rest of us some of the vision we so badly need.

Studies in Romanticism, Spring 1976

How Sane Was Pound?

On the evening of Sunday, November 18, 1945, the poet Ezra Pound returned from Italy to the United States, of which he was a native and a citizen, after a long and exhausting flight from Rome. He had traveled on an Army C-54 that landed at Bolling Field, not far from downtown Washington. He was a federal prisoner and was taken immediately to jail to await arraignment on a charge of treason. During World War II, he had frequently participated in Italy's shortwave broadcasts to North America, making speeches that were not only full of praise for Mussolini and Hitler but outspokenly opposed to America's wartime purposes and its political leadership. The Constitution defines treason as "levying war" on the United States or "giving aid and comfort" to its enemies, and Pound certainly did the latter in his broadcasts, the government was preparing to argue in the courts.

We know the outcome: Pound never was put on trial because he was evaluated by a team of psychiatrists who unanimously concluded that he was insane and thus unable to be tried. The result was a prolonged hospitalization of the world-famous poet at a government facility, St. Elizabeths Hospital in Washington. (Pound was released in 1958 after twelve years of confinement, but he was never pardoned.) A federal judge was told by a prominent government psychiatrist that the potential defendant was "suffering from a paranoid state which has rendered and now renders him unfit to advise properly with counsel or to participate intelligently and reasonably in his own defense, and that he is, and has continuously been, insane and mentally unfit for trial." The doctor's affidavit even declared the patient "permanently and incurably insane."

Almost forty years later, E. Fuller Torrey, a Washington psychiatrist who has worked at St. Elizabeths Hospital and has a considerable interest in and knowledge of the complex and sometimes elusive phenomenon known as schizophrenia, offers us a chance to reconsider Pound's experience after he had been accused of treason. Dr. Torrey has been able to write about it, he tells us, because of a "recent release of files in the Department of Justice" through the Freedom of Information Act and because St. Elizabeths Hospital has lately been equally forthcoming with its psychiatric records. There were, of course, other reasons to prompt him: "My interest in Pound began when I noticed that I was following him around. I grew up in the town where he went to college, helped build a road through his grandmother's homestead [near Clinton, N.Y.] in Nine Mile Swamp, and as a student focused on the work of his protégé T. S. Eliot." Later this literary interest took a new shape: "I became intrigued with the myths Pound's friends had created, and I began playing hide-and-seek with him in the stacks of the Library of Congress."

The results of all that curiosity and research is *The Roots of Treason*, a book meant to remind us again of the many confusions prompted by the use of the insanity defense. When his research was done, Dr. Torrey felt confronted with "disturbing questions about the influence of the literati, the role of psychiatrists, and the performance of justice in our society." It is his contention that Pound was not insane, that the four psychiatrists who examined him in 1945 and 1946 knew that to be the case and that three of them were swayed by the powerful, if not manipulative, influence of the fourth to affirm a diagnosis sufficiently grave to preclude a trial.

The psychiatrist who engineered that outcome was the late Dr. Winfred Overholser, the superintendent of St. Elizabeths, who lived and worked for many years at the hospital. He was secretary-treasurer of the American Psychiatric Association and had a reputation as one of the nation's "foremost authorities on the legal aspects of psychiatry." Dr. Torrey has some astonishing statements to make about him. He says there is reason to believe that Dr. Overholser destroyed all records "of his meetings with Ezra Pound" and that "the destruction was deliberate, according to a psychiatrist who worked closely with him."

As one reads the comments of the other psychiatrists who talked with Pound, one surmises their perplexity. What to make of this sixty-year-old man who had been screaming for years against Wall Street bankers, American presidents, British prime ministers, magazine editors, book company executives, professors and university officials, fellow writers from many countries, and most of all Jews, always the Jews? How to comprehend his writer's mixture of sharply stated wisdom, marvelous irony, and penetrating imagery with hysterical exaggerations, obscene bigotry, and hateful distortion? Nor was it a matter, the doctors knew, of the poetry's being immune to the meanness and nastiness that characterized the infamous broadcasts and many personal letters. Some of Pound's cantos reveal the same moral sensibility that the poet displayed when he was paid by the Fascists to make speeches on Rome radio during the war.

Anti-Semitism was Pound's major obsession, a tenacious, virulent hatred that compelled him finally to fawn at the feet of genocidal Nazi power. Only in the last few years of his life did he renounce this idée fixe that had inspired decades of murderous invective that angered and disgusted some of his writing friends but only embarrassed others, who preferred a more genteel kind of prejudice. For the latter, Pound could at times demonstrate the contempt a true hater feels toward men and women who use a particular prejudice as a mere social convenience.

The doctors at St. Elizabeths quickly learned that psychological tests weren't going to be of much help. Dr. Torrey reports that "the Rorschach test was interpreted as suggesting 'a marked personality disorder of long standing.'" But we also learn that the psychologists could find "no evidence of psychosis." Nor was Pound unaware of the implications of his wartime behavior. In 1943, he had prepared a careful outline of how he would defend himself against a charge of treason after being warned in several ways that the Justice Department would not ignore a continuation of his broadcasts. Despite all his quirkiness and histrionics and all his bitter and even scatological outbursts, psychiatrists who examined Pound in late 1945 and a number of others who examined him during his twelve-year-long stay at St. Elizabeths found him sane in the legal sense of the word—that is, able to face a judge and jury, to understand the nature of the proceedings, and to defend himself vigorously and thoughtfully.

"We decided almost unanimously that he was neurotic," one psychiatrist who worked at St. Elizabeths told Dr. Torrey. (To make such a diagnosis, Freud told us, is to declare someone a human being.) But then there were second thoughts: "Out of loyalty to Win [Overholser] we had to respect Win's diagnosis. And since we had come to such a different conclusion we finally decided not to make any formal diagnosis at all. Then it wouldn't embarrass him." When the doctors told Dr. Overholser of their conclusions, he was "cordial." "He said he respected our diagnosis and that we had had more time to examine Pound than he had. However he said that we didn't need to disturb the practicalities of the situation by making it public and that we should just keep it to ourselves."

A marvelous phrase, "the practicalities of the situation"—one that surely would have amused the Confucian Pound of, say, Canto LIV. The not especially lyrical word *cover-up* might be used these days to describe what happened at St. Elizabeths. Dr. Torrey does not pull his punches:

> Overholser had exaggerated Pound's symptoms and disabilities; when exaggeration under oath crosses an indefinable line it can be perjury. Some of Dr. Overholser's colleagues think he may have crossed the line but say such perjury was carried out with the best of intentions. As one of them succinctly summarized it: "Of course Dr. Overholser committed perjury. Pound was a great artist, a national treasure. If necessary I would have committed perjury too—gladly."

Such remarks make this book memorable and quite instructive. One wonders at times whether Dr. Torrey's real subject, notwithstanding his long chapters on the poet's childhood, is Pound's mental life but rather the profession of psychiatry, its moral standards, and its continuing moral authority among the secular bourgeoisie, including those who make and administer our laws. Certainly the author is restrained and dispassionate in his presentation of a life by no means easy to comprehend or find admirable. There is in these pages an edifying refusal to account for Pound's literary achievements by recourse to psychological theory. At the end, Pound himself seems to have known how wacky some of his ideas were; they expressed an energetic social conscience (and a profound anti-capitalism) run amok, one suspects. Dr. Torrey emphasizes the truculent vanity of the man, the prickly pride that drove him to do and say such odd and self-damaging things, and, in the compact and felicitous phrase used by George Eliot before Pound was even born, his "unreflecting egoism."

With this book, as with others on Pound, we are once more reminded that psychiatry as a pontifical presence can serve the law poorly and that some of us will grant liberties to certain influential figures we certainly would deny to other men and women, who presumably are entitled to their fair share of this nation's "equal justice under the law." Not least, we are reminded that a human being can be intellectually accomplished, talented as a writer or artist, and also be a moral and political dimwit. That kind of ambiguous characterization was rendered by William Carlos Williams of his longtime friend:

> Ezra Pound is one of the most competent poets in our language, possessed of the most acute ear for metrical sequences, to the point of genius, that we have ever known. He is also, it must be confessed, the biggest damn fool and faker in the business. You can't allow yourself to be too serious about a person like that—and yet he is important. He knows all this and plays on it to perfection.

The saddest part of this book is the chronicle of willing, even eager seduction it documents: doctors, writers, and teachers allowing themselves to be demeaned, to be caught in a bewildered mind's mirror games, played, as Williams said, "to perfection." As a consequence, a well-known asylum became for years the location of an eerie literary salon, which was surrounded by special privileges and run by a man, alas, whose reported remarks about and behavior toward some of his fellow patients may be as damning as any of his published words. At the end of his life, during the years he spent in self-imposed exile in Italy, Pound took stock and repented this way: "Any good I've done has been spoiled by bad intentions—the preoccupation with irrelevant and stupid things." Dr. Torrey offers no evidence that similar self-criticism will be coming from the doctors and administrators at St. Elizabeths Hospital.

New York Times Book Review, October 23, 1983

James Wright
One of Those Messengers

s I went through James Wright's *Collected Poems* and his *Two Citizens*, I thought of the men, women, and children I have visited over the years in connection with my work. They are people who have lived on farms and worked them; or they have grown cotton and for doing so been called "field hands" by those who are proud to talk about their "plantations." As one Mississippi grower told me: "You have over a hundred acres and a few niggers working for you, and a Yankee comes along—well, you tell him it's a plantation. The other day I saw some dogs misbehaving right in front of my eyes, and I told them to mind their manners: this here's a plantation." Those "niggers" and those "rednecks" who work as tenant farmers in the rural South have never heard of James Wright or of all the rest that some of us take to be so important—the books and magazines and newspapers and universities, not to mention the great or small but captivating cities of Italy or France, which to a degree replace the Midwest as Wright's territory in his most recent volume of poetry. But I believe those men and women of the rural South or Appalachia would know Mr. Wright—one of "those fellahs," they might call him. Which "fellahs"? Three years ago I asked the question of a yeoman farmer, black it so happened, who lives in Tunica County, Mississippi, and he repeated himself and elaborated:

> Well, those fellahs—oh, I guess you don't know them. There are a couple of good school teachers; they taught my boys and my one girl—she's gone to her Maker, it's five years now. There was a man, he was the principal, and there was another man, a teacher; they taught my kids to read. They were always pointing something out to the children. They were always

saying: look over there; look over here; look right in front of
your nose; look up toward the sky; look over beyond the pines
there. My kids would come home and start getting me to look,
and I'd feel I'd been blind all my life after they'd finish their
pointing: the shape of those clouds, the nests in the trees, the
flowers all over, wild ones that I didn't know existed, and
those turtles that take you by surprise with the colors on the
shells, and then there were the egrets, don't you know. The
children would spot an egret, and watch her take off, and
they'd be so happy, so uncommon happy; and there I was,
taking every egret I'd seen these last twenty years for granted.
There was a time I used to notice a lot too; but I grew up and
lost my eyes—except for the bossman: he owns my eyes, and
they look where he wants.

Those fellahs, the teachers, there should be more of them;
they're the ones you have to depend upon for your children—
so they'll get some direction in life, some inspiration. I wish
every child of mine would be as intelligent as those fellahs.
Then I'd be sure my children would see more than most
people, and they'd hear more, too. Lord, they're after me
when they come home from school: Daddy, listen to that
sound, and *that* sound, and that *there* sound, and Daddy,
how could you not hear this, and *this*, and this *here!* I tell
them I can hear *them;* they're hurting my ears. I tell them to
wait; their daddy has to take orders. He hasn't time for birds
and the wind and the leaves and some dog way across the field
having a good time. But they say God is talking—through the
sounds he is—because one of those fellahs told them so.
Well, praise God in heaven for those fellahs; they're watching
and they're listening the way Jesus did when he was here. Not
a sight did he miss. Not a sound did he miss. There's God,
and there's those fellahs God has made his messengers: a good
minister—not all of them, but a good one; a doctor, if he's
honest, and some of them are no good, worse then the worst
bossman; and those fellahs who get my children all excited in
their minds. And when they're excited they act like Jesus himself; they're worrying about the animals getting hurt by the
tractors or the hunters, and they're paying attention to every-

thing, as though there's going to be another coming, the Second Coming, like the minister says there'll be: only it's going to happen any minute, and right in front of our cabin.

Once the bossman was here, and he heard them asking their mother all those questions and telling her she just had to come and see their frog, and there was the butterfly they'd caught but they let it go, and they never saw such happiness, the wings going and going. Well, how can you *see* happiness, the bossman asked me, and he was thinking my children weren't talking right. I told him he sure had a point there, and I scratched my head extra hard. He patted me on the back, and told me not to worry: it doesn't make any difference, the way kids talk, because they'll soon grow up and get these foolish ideas out of their heads. I told him yes, he sure was right. I came home and told my wife what the bossman said, and she said he didn't know what the word happiness means, and he was blind to everything but his cotton and his money in the bank and his whiskey, so how would *he* ever see happiness. And she knows him, because she cooks for them up in their house. But I know how he feels: I'm not the bossman, but I haven't time to see much myself—only what's ahead of me in my work. You have to be a special kind of person—one of those fellahs in the school—to be able to pay so much attention to this world we're in. That's why I say that God has his messengers, and they get put here to help our children along, and maybe some of the children will grow up and they'll be those messengers too—and it being pretty hard here, for most of us, you have to thank him, the Almighty, that he's kept a few people looking sharp and listening real close. Otherwise, there wouldn't even be the littlest bit of hope for us, and that would be real bad.

So it goes in Mississippi's Delta: where life and labor are cheap; where the blues are not an artform but an evening's moment of sadness and bewilderment; where stomachs regularly go unfilled or get pacified with Kool-Aid and french fries and more Kool-Aid and more french fries; and yes, where the most revolutionary kind of educational reform is to be found amid all the economic brutality, not to mention the continuing existence of a caste system. Children go hungry, suffer from malnutrition, feel confused or grim about their future, but often enough demonstrate an intense, almost visionary kind of responsiveness to the world around them (to the surprise of some of us observers, who are generous with pity but less inclined to admit that even the very poor and vulnerable can live complicated, ironic lives). If the confused child prompts confusion in his observer, perhaps one of "those fellahs," one of those strange, inspiring teachers, one of those astonishing messengers, will clarify matters:

I don't have much to say. I'm not a very good teacher, according to the state officials in Jackson; I don't have all the credits I should have. I probably fail the kids; hereabouts, anyway, the moment they are born they've lost, and maybe they know it, for all we know. All babies cry when they're born, but I've heard some long, low moans from our babies—born in the cabins and with no doctor around. They must know what's ahead. You'll hear the mothers apologizing too. You'll hear them saying: "I'm sorry, son, or it's too bad, daughter; I know you could have had a better life if you'd been born to someone else, but God has sent you right here, and everyone's life is his to decide on."

Well, I don't know. Who am I to have the answers? All I try to do is say: children, we're here for a few minutes, so let's have the best time we can. Let's use everything God has given us. Let's thank him for his sun and tell him we love that moon of his that comes and goes. Let's watch him put on his seasons and take them off, and say hello to his animals and goodbye, and call his birds away and send them back. And I don't have to sell the children too hard. They come to me wide awake, even if they're hungry and even if they're sick. Don't you know, if a person is headed for a coma, he's going to be all the more alive. Before you die, you're likely to take a last, good look around you.

I hope I am not being presumptuous when I call upon a Mississippi tenant farmer and his children and the child's teacher for help in a discussion of James Wright's poetry. Martins Ferry, Ohio, is not part of Tunica County, Mississippi, I know; but there are similarities enough. In both places the land is not yet covered with cement or asphalt, and so the eye and ear have their particular feast, if they are hungry enough to take notice. And so often it has come to that in Mississippi: terribly hungry children, and parents or teachers who have to live with the knowledge of what hunger can do to a boy or girl, together search everywhere for food—food for the stomach and yes, food for the mind, which wants to know with a special desperation *why, how come, what next,* and *when.* Sometimes I think all of America's comforts (and most of us by now find life inconceivable without them) systematically protect us not only from the world of hungry children but from that of hungry poets as well. A migrant farm worker once gave me a fantasy, a scenario of a future he very much wanted:

> If I had a house; if I had a car; if I had a refrigerator and a toaster and a washing machine; if I had the air conditioner those growers have—well, it would be a different life for me. I've been in a grower's house because I got to do some yard work for him, apart from picking, and I came back and told my wife: they don't have to pay attention to nothing, not the sky and not the wind or rain and not a single thing but their electricity. If there'd be no more electricity, they'd probably believe the Lord had come and it was Judgment Day.

We may be nearing gas rationing, and it seems "brownouts" are a threat to something called the continuity of urban living; but I'm not so sure Judgment Day is at hand, even given an extrapolation of our energy crisis and God knows what else. As for James Wright, he lives in the wilderness all the time; even when he is in Italy or France or Manhattan, he is wandering about, paying too close attention to efforts and signals and signs and movements and rhythms that are not controlled by buttons or computers or generators. Poor soul, he is like those children in Mississippi's Delta—cut off in a world most of us find archaic if not anarchic. In the pictures I have seen he looks well fed, and in the *American Poetry Review* he has recently told of eating a good deal of fish, but I fear the man is yet another hungry one and is, moreover, "alienated" and thoroughly "irrelevant" (as a million social scientists put it). After all, who can have much patience with those ants of his, and the caterpillars he mentions, and the birds coming and going—quail and sparrows and the rest, too much around, even lending their wings to people—and the dogs he notices, and the horses and ponies? Once a plantation owner in Tunica County, Mississippi, called the "bossman" by blacks, asked me with no show of petulance, merely impatience: "I hear there's a teacher over there telling the little niggers about the wind in the willows; and like my little girl, they're eating it up." That's the way it goes when over half the people in a county make less than a thousand dollars a year: wind becomes a rumored food. Has James Wright slipped south of Memphis every once in a while? Of course, he has in fact slipped into our national midst. He is as removed from many of us as is Tunica County, yet he is so close to just about every American that it hurts to read him: too much of our lives is there in those lives. Mirrors block every exit we try. He is in central Ohio, closer to ordinary working people (a son of his father) than quite a few who go under the name Simone Weil said they deserve—"intellectuals." He is in the Dakotas or Minnesota, near the Sioux and near the farm people. He is in Nevada, where gamblers cry out their own kind of hunger; and in the big cities, Chicago and New York; and finally, in Europe, where he can't stop looking back, leaping across the ocean, and where he is unable to free himself of himself, of us ("that brutal and savage place whom I still love"). One moment he is like Wright Morris, giving us stretches of Nebraska or Iowa as practically no one thinks to do these days—"Snow howls all around me, out of the abandoned prairies." Another moment he is another Walker Percy, drawing upon Dostoevski's underground man, wondering who we are—we make lists and draw distinctions and call others animals and ourselves human beings: words are our great possession. His political position is all the more powerfully and persuasively maintained because he does not grab us by the collar or shout what we, anyway, have been saying to ourselves. President Harding in Wright's hands becomes sad and a victim. Eisenhower's visit to Franco in 1959 becomes an occasion for an assault on political clichés. True, "the American hero must triumph over / The forces of darkness" is ironic if not sarcastic; but before that we have a line from Unamuno to temper our easy scorn: ". . . We die of cold, and not of darkness." He refused to care about so many people, so many things—that wide-smiling, genial general, beloved because he wasn't MacArthur, wasn't all those spit-and-polish master sergeants or eager to-do-and-die officers.

Meanwhile the White House and the Pentagon stand strong and firm—however jolting the words of a lyrical, shrewd, indignant, but controlled poet, who will not shirk putting his beliefs on the line but not either let a variety of bossmen get in the way of a man's songs and occasional hymns, his special language of amusement, surprise, and bewilderment. I suppose the price such a poet pays for going his own way is loneliness; it is the word Wright keeps using, and one is not at all tempted to doubt him or charge him with yet another variant of the boundless egoism so many writers feel compelled to display: see me lonely, hear me off by myself talking—and never forget how unique I have proven myself through my lines. In Wright's case the loneliness is casually remarked upon; often it comes across as natural, even a gift: "Men have a right to thank God for their loneliness." Or less portentously: "The wheat leans back toward its own darkness / And I lean toward mine."

His "darkness" comes across in every book. One smiles and one loves, but plunder and murder go on, and sometimes we can do nothing but settle for ourselves—in this case, a poet who would like a lot to be different but isn't inclined to preach to readers he suspects, anyway, are the converted. Still, however modest, worried, and realistically guarded about the future he is, there is the obligation to give the clearest emphasis possible to certain values. He chooses to translate César Vallejo's "Our Daily Bread," one stanza of which goes like this:

> I wish I could beat on all the doors,
> and ask for somebody; and then
> look at the poor, and while they wept softly,
> give bits of fresh bread to them.
> And plunder the rich of their vineyards
> with those two blessed hands
> which blasted the nails with one blow of light,
> and flew away from the Cross!

Christ himself, insofar as he was until his last breath human, could not accomplish what the Spanish poet and his American translator have set down as a wish of theirs. As for God, he seems to be infinitely patient; the New Jerusalem, we are told, is not of this earth. So we despair or we feel justifiable rage; or we turn away and for the rest of our limited time care about only our own door. A few dream, though. They keep on paying attention. They speak up and out. They even get heard by others—even if a poll hasn't been done and we don't know exactly how many others there are. Who are "they"? I would include in their number some children and teachers—"those messengers" in Tunica County—and too, James Wright, who might not mind being described the way I heard a father of Tunica County refer to his child:

> He comes home happy sometimes, singing; and I scratch my head and ask why. But who's to question a child's song? I tell his mother: the boy is up there, he's high, and not a drop of whiskey in him. He's no worse off than those butterflies he catches and brings home. He doesn't want them to suffocate, and he makes sure they don't. He's for them, and there'll be moments when I really do believe God is for him. So it all evens out. It isn't only the teachers and the ministers who bring you the Good News. No sir, a boy or girl of your very own can. A child can be a messenger, same as you or me or someone else—sometimes better than most of us. And if a man doesn't stop seeing what he did when he was a child, then he's got a special kind of luck going for him.

American Poetry Review, August/September 1973

William Stafford's Long Walk

The United States of America is William Stafford's country; it is Richard Nixon's country too, no doubt about that. Allen Ginsberg, from the Eastern Seaboard, is right: there is plenty of greed, envy, and murderous competitiveness abroad in the land. But there are also other sides to our people. The Nixons came from the Midwest, ended up near the Pacific, and soon enough confronted us with much of what we have become—and one has in mind not just the thirty-seventh president but his two ever so adroit and vigorous brothers. No arrangement is too complex for them, and if there is any sanction needed, there is always that marvelous, smiling, dynamic Billy Graham around, who doubtless appeases any anxieties he has with the utterly compelling truth: a minister must not flinch from a sinner, and we are all sinners.

But William Stafford also comes from the Midwest, and he too found his way to the Pacific. And though his eyes are as sharp as Ginsberg's and his ears as attentive, one meets quite another America in his poems. For ideologues the apparent contradiction is easily resolved—it is a matter of the superficial as against the deep. Everything is rotten in the state of Denmark, or else the nation is in fine shape, despite a few problems—and they, of course, are exaggerated for various reasons by various individuals. For Stafford, this is a land of compelling opposites, a nation that has indeed brutalized generations of Indians (toward whose habits, beliefs, and customs he is drawn) but a nation blessed with a marvelously varied natural landscape, at once subtle, striking, awesome, and for him, impossible to overlook. And too, a nation whose people can be generous, kind, and thoughtful; a nation of which his beloved parents and brother are citizens, and his son Kit, and the dying Bess, a librarian of tact and grace, and Althea, and the nameless girl whose boyfriend lied, and on and on. From those people, moments of whose lives Stafford evokes in his poems, one obtains a particular vision of

America—not Whitman's lyrical urging, really, but not a voice of despair either, and certainly no inclination to disgust or self-righteous condemnation.

Stafford is wondrously attentive to the land, sky, water, and foliage of our Midwest and West. He presents us with territory many of his readers will, perhaps, know not at all: "At the border of October / where Montana meets Alberta / that white grass that worshipped wind / climbed from summer to the sky, / which began to change." He presents us with "the firred mountains of Oregon," the "hay towns beyond Salt Lake." He presents us with "cornfield farms," with "a town by the track in Colorado," with a "prairie town," and the prairie dogs he used to gaze at for long stretches. Born in Kansas, he "lived in Indiana once," we learn, and while there "put these hands into those lakes / of counties near Fort Wayne." He knows a tornado—knows it the way someone watching the weather map on the *Today* show over coffee in Boston or New York cannot: "first the soul of our house left, up the chimney / and part of the front window went outward—pursued / whatever tore at the chest." There are people, he knows, connected to the land he wants to bring before us, and in his own quiet, indirect, unauthoritative, yet telling manner he introduces them to us. In a few lines he can offer more than a shelfful of sociological, anthropological, and psychological studies (with their "worldviews" and the "psychosocial" this or that of these or those):

> At the end of their ragged field
> a new field began:
> miles told the sunset that Kansas
> would hardly ever end,
> and that beyond the Cimarron crossing
> and after the row-crop land
> a lake would surprise the country
> and sag with a million birds.
>
> You couldn't analyze those people—
> a no-pattern had happened to them:
> their field opened and opened,
> level, and more, then forever,
> never crossed. Their world went everywhere.

So does his world it seems, in America at least—everywhere a lot of us tend to think of as nowhere. Who else brings us Elko, Nevada, or Sharon Springs, Kansas? More important, he has his very own way of bringing to bear nature on man, the willful and self-conscious one who threatens the planet with extinction. "At the Bomb Testing Site" goes like this:

> At noon in the desert a panting lizard
> waiting for history, its elbows tense,
> watching the curve of a particular road
> as if something might happen.
>
> It was looking for something farther off
> than people could see, an important scene
> acted in stone for little selves
> at the flute end of consequences.
>
> There was just a continent without much on it
> under a sky that never cared less.
> Ready for a change, the elbows waited.
> The hands gripped hard on the desert.

History interests Stafford, both the land's and our people's. He can't help noticing what people do and leave behind as they move about, fit into valleys, come close to rivers, trek the desert, and accommodate themselves to mountains, to the seasons, to the ocean's final no: not a step beyond. The Indians, more than any other Americans, know and treasure the Western land, and of course, they made a beginning of our history long before "we" were here, so full of ourselves and so determined to bend history to our purposes. A section of *Someday, Maybe* is titled "Wind World" and contains poems that in one way or another address themselves to Indians, to their experience on this continent and their way of looking at life. The poems turn out to be quite brief—"Indian Caves in the Dry Country": "These are some canyons / we might use again / sometime."— or only a little longer—"People of the South Wind" or "Origins." The latter offers a finely wrought piece of Indian lore every bit worthy of what one hears Indian parents telling their children in the Southwest. No boasting and vainglory; no effort to prove one's superiority; no ethnic pride; but rather an almost casual effort to link one's ancestors with the concreteness of life's "everydayness," to draw upon a word both Kierkegaard and Heidegger have used in an attempt to fight off the demons of the abstract, so tempting to those two men, among others. "So long ago that we weren't people then," one is told, "our hands came upon this warm place on a rack / inside a high cave in the North, in the wilderness." A Hopi mother recently told me that when her children ask her about where they all came from, she tells them: "It was too long ago for you or me or anyone to know. The stars know, though. They have watched, and they remember. They will not tell us, but that does not mean we have no history. In the world there is knowledge of us, even if we don't possess it." Such children may at first get restless: tell us more, make us more satisfied. So she goes on: "There must have been a moment when a man and a woman stopped and began to dig into the earth. They spent the night nearby, and in the morning they felt the wind upon their skin, and heard the wind's message: stay. They did, and now we are here."

At times Stafford emphasizes the rootlessness of some Americans; he himself knows what it is to drive, drive, drive on route 40, to enter and leave those towns, so many of them ghosts of their former selves yet by no means dead and gone—simply holding on proudly and bravely for dear life. But there is a sense of continuity, a faith in the ways of nature and at least a certain kind of man (themselves) that Indians unselfconsciously have as a psychological possession and as elements in their cultural tradition. These are not often to be taken for granted by the rest of us, even those Mr. Stafford knows, likes, and is moved to portray. Somehow we have lost touch with the world around us and ourselves, and the two developments surely go together, at least in Stafford's gentle but tough vision of America. "It is the time for all the heroes to go home," he begins the poem whose title, "Allegiances," he has given to his most recent volume of poems. Then he adds one of his elliptical asides ("if they have any") and goes on: "time for all of us common ones / to locate ourselves by the real things / we live by." The rest of the poem goes like this— and it is not at all a long-winded pronouncement or a self-important philosophical credo but simply a way of calling upon "heaven and earth," as those Palestinian nomads and prophets of several thousand years ago would put it:

Far to the north, or indeed in any direction,
strange mountains and creatures have always lurked—
elves, goblins, trolls, and spiders:—we
encounter them in dread and wonder.

But once we have tasted far streams, touched the gold,
found some limit beyond the waterfall,
a season changes, and we come back, changed
but safe, quiet, grateful.

Suppose an insane wind holds all the hills
while strange beliefs whine at the traveler's ears,
we ordinary beings can cling to the earth and love
where we are, sturdy for common things.

Stafford is just that, one of the "common" ones, and he is indeed "sturdy for common things":

The writer's home he salvages from little pieces
along the roads, from distinctions he remembers,
from what by chance he sees—his grabbed heritage;
and from people fading from his road, from history.
He reaches out far, being a desperate man;
he comprehends by fistfuls with both hands.

Stafford will not let up; he will not be, he knows not how to be, immodest. In such a confessional poem there is no hidden agenda— that ironic self-congratulatory line or stanza that will serve to punch any literal-minded doubter in the nose and let him know that pity is not what the poem really wants—but rather the kind of awe that may creep up but eventually obtains complete control. No, the next lines establish Stafford's knowing, touching, lyrical voice as utterly and convincingly diffident and unassuming: "But what can bring in enough to save the tame / or be home for them who even with roofs are shelterless?" It is, he is telling us, for others to criticize, berate, and condemn, "them," all those near and far away who are fellow citizens of this nation. He knows their sadness, the virtual hope- lessness they must sense if not recognize, even as he knows how it has gone for Sitting Bull and his descendants. And knowing, he still wants to sing—because as anyone who lives in a small town, however isolated, out West knows, you never can tell who will appear on the horizon, slowly work his way near, and reveal himself to have receptive ears and responsive eyes.

American Poetry Review, July/August 1975

Muriel Rukeyser's The Gates

Upon reading Muriel Rukeyser's latest volume of poems, upon going through *The Gates*, one feels silent, sad, instructed, grateful. No words of prose from a reviewer are needed to explain these poems; and to praise them is almost condescending. The woman who wrote them has been with us twentieth-century American readers almost half a century. She is a gifted observer of this world, a person who can sing to us and make our duller, less responsive minds come more alive, and not least, someone who has proven it possible to be a sensible human being, a woman inclined to give, to extend herself toward others, and also a first-rate poet. We all struggle with the sin of pride; Muriel Rukeyser has been blessed with less narcissism than most of us—especially remarkable in such an introspective, sensitive, and self-aware person, who has for so long been committed to telling others what crosses her mind. She is saved from self-centeredness by a compassionate concern for others, all over the world, and by a wonderful capacity for self-mocking irony: "Anne Sexton the poet saying / ten days ago to that receptive friend, / the friend of the hand-held camera: / 'Muriel is serene.' / Am I that in their sight?" And at another point: "I'd rather be Muriel / than be dead and be Ariel," an entire poem, and shorter than its title: "Not to be Printed / Not to be Said, / Not to be Thought."

Her poem "St. Roach" provides a beautiful lesson in the psychology and sociology of prejudice, a lesson worth dozens of social science articles or books. It is also an example of her capacity to distance herself from the self-serving demands of the ego. And as an additional bonus, we finally have a fitting rebuke to Kafka's *Metamorphosis*—Rukeyser's gentle, suggestive, wonderfully surprising moral lesson, which one suspects would have prompted an appreciative smile in the Prague philosophical storyteller: "For that I

never knew you, I only learned to dread you, / for that I never
touched you, they told me you are filth, / they showed me by every
action to despise your kind; / for that I saw my people making war
on you, / I could not tell you apart, one from another, / for that in
childhood I lived in places clear of you, / for that all the people
I knew met you by / crushing you, stamping you to death, they
poured boiling / water on you, they flushed you down, / for that I
could not tell one from another / only that you were dark, fast on
your feet, and slender. / Not like me."

She knows such a description is all too apt for other of God's creatures than the roach—especially so in this past decade of civil rights
struggles and war in far-off, "different" Vietnam. She reaches out for
all that is part of this earth—for the distant past and even for inani-
mate matter in the present. In "Painters" she reminds us of the pre-
historic men and women who etched animal forms on the walls of
caves—their effort to make sense of things, a desire to represent, to
show and tell. In "Artifact" she demonstrates an almost unnerving
capacity for calm detachment. "When this hand is gone to earth, /
this writing hand and the paper beneath it," she begins, and she
soon tells us what may be left, what may survive—tells us quietly,
with no sense of triumph or satisfaction—an artifact: "This pen.
Will it tell my? Will it tell our? / this thing made in bright metal by
thousands unknown to me . . ." She worries again, further on,
about those who worked on assembly lines, men and women both,
themselves rendered artifacts by the cold, manipulative, always pro-
fitable transactions of the entrepreneurs and those managerial lieu-
tenants who keep the factories in fit shape with high output, high
profits, and just enough wages to keep things "moving."

She has a visionary side to her: "There were poems all over Broadway that morning. / Blowing across traffic. Against the legs." In her
hands New York City becomes a series of brief images that remind
one of James Agee's short film "In the Street." She has a nagging,
important historical sense, a side of her that can jolt the reader. Simone Weil, who hated the Romans and saw them as early Fascists,
would have loved "The Lost Romans"—a stunning reversal of coin,
a reminder that we are all taught in school to think of Caesar and
Cicero, of legions and battles and conquests (all Gaul is divided into
three parts). Instead the poet asks us to think of other Romans:

". . . those young Romans / Who stood against the bitter imperial, their young / green life with its poems . . ." And the last line, a testimonial to a writer's broad-minded sense of kinship: "For we need you, sisters, far brothers, poems of our lost Rome."

A series of these poems is subsumed under a larger thematic effort, titled "Gates," the book's title. "The poet is in solitary," she tells us in a prose prologue: "the expectation is that he will be tried and summarily executed . . ." Then another person is introduced, "an American woman [who] is sent to make an appeal for the poet's life." This person "stands in the mud and rain at the prison gates— also the gates of perception, the gates of the body." Again Muriel Rukeyser modestly places herself as an onlooker, a compassionate, aroused, decent person who is not quite the other poet whose "stinging work—like that of Burns or Brecht" has managed to get "under the skin of the highest officials." She is no Brecht, nor was she meant to be. But she also shows her ideals through calls to brotherhood and sisterhood: "Through acts, through poems, / through our closenesses— / whatever links us in our variousness; / across worlds, love and poems and justices / wishing to be born."

Not that she blinks at the mean, ugly, corrupt, exploitive side of the world. In "New Friends" she makes clear her awareness of the terror many decent, morally honorable and outspoken individuals have to face, day after day. She is no friend to America's multinational corporations, but she is not deceived either by the repressive bureaucratic statism of eastern Europe. The word *liberation*, she tells us, has become a catchall slogan, thrown around by anyone and everyone in the interest, often, of crooks, thieves, and liars. But she is, again, not one for self-pity or for its larger more ideological version—social or political despair. She remembers the best messages of the Old and New Testaments. Her eye catches an infant, a "woman at vigil," a "woman seen as the fine tines of a pitchfork." She knows that if the "air fills with fear and the kinds of fear," there is also resistance: "Free our might free our lives free our poet." The massacres of this awful century haunt her: ". . . the butchered that across the fields of the world / lie screaming . . ." Still, there are friends, friends of the poet, friends of all that is decent and just in the world, friends who may be unknown to the poet and to all who suffer for their goodness and kindness and sensitivity but who nevertheless deserve recognition. Hence a book titled *Gates*, hence poems about the ordinary, the undramatic, hence a salute to those standing near the gates—no Brechts but comrades, indeed, and possessed of their own special, considerable, necessary virtue—Muriel Rukeyser, chief among them.

American Poetry Review, May/June 1978

Renaming the Streets
Poems by John Stone

O nce, in an interview with a student, the physician and poet
William Carlos Williams observed that "there is a natural
affinity between the practice of medicine and the writing
of poems." When pressed, inevitably, for an explanation,
he offered this one: "Doctors are right there, at life's critical moments; and poets try to be right there, too—capture such moments
in words." On the other hand, few physicians have those words
available, and thus John Stone's exemplary achievement is all the
more unusual. He sees patients in Atlanta, teaches medical students
at Emory University Medical School, and still finds the time to offer
us a steady output of truly affecting poems, which appear first in a
number of periodicals (both medical and literary) and are then collected in books. *Renaming the Streets* is his third.

Dr. Stone has a keen eye for what the novelist Thomas Hardy
called "life's little ironies"—the agility and soaring power of the
homely, lowly pigeon, for example, or the vulnerability that goes
with being the owner of that mighty machine, the automobile. He is
also on the watch for the small moments of affectionate concern
that, in their sum, turn the doctor's job into quite something else
and add largeness to a life that weds science to service.

Doctors know to turn coins over, to look for what lurks behind
appearance, and in that sense Dr. Stone is a physician writing
poems even when his subject matter is the world of the painter
Edward Hopper, the world of a cricket or a bird, the world of a
schoolteacher, or the world of a father on a fishing trip with his son.
In these poems the narrator helps the reader remember the surprising, the unexpected, the unpredictable side of this life, what physicians learn to accept as an everyday circumstance told them by pa-

tients—ongoing health interrupted suddenly by symptoms that seem to come from nowhere.

At several points in this book, the healer, the cardiologist, and the emergency-ward physician set poetry aside for prose, as Williams did, and I suspect for the same reason—a certain reluctance to tamper, through verbal play, with the particular dignity of another person's life as it has become part of one's own professional life. Even so, this poet works his enveloping magic as a terse teller of medical stories: a baby struggling futilely with a congenitally malformed heart; a doctor struggling unsuccessfully to revive a man who has had a coronary seizure; a young man finally dying of the consequences of what physician readers will recognize as Marfan's syndrome. These prose interludes offer dramatic medical moments highly condensed and suggestively told. But the stories are meant to be reflective as well: they reveal a busy, sometimes hard-pressed doctor struggling hard against the antagonist all doctors always have—death—and realizing, time and again, how lucky any of us is to live out that biblical three score and ten.

I have asked some of my medical students to read Dr. Stone's poems, and invariably they report their gratitude to him—for his lyrical gifts, his touching compassion, his sly humor, his wonderfully eye-opening manner of approaching "the things of this world." This new book offers further teaching opportunities; its rendering of loneliness, of love in its various and chancy and fleeting forms, of annoyance and frustration will help the rest of us yet again try to fathom those "motions of the heart." After all, in his compelling and touching poem "Rosemary" (about a man alone at breakfast with a waitress in a restaurant early one morning), Dr. Stone is all of us doctors. We get ever so close to our patients, yet soon enough we take leave of them.

New England Journal of Medicine, April 17, 1986

Teaching Old Folks
an Old Art

*I*n a letter to a young admirer, William Carlos Williams once had this to say: "I hear lines of poetry every day from my patients. They sometimes say what they see and feel in interesting ways. In my car, later in the day, I hear their words." Kenneth Koch has had the same willingness to pay close heed to the lyrical possibilities that many ordinary human beings possess and even demonstrate rather impressively, given any encouragement at all. One of his books, *Wishes, Lies, and Dreams*, tells of his work with children, who ache at times to use their imaginations and stretch the bounds of language, only to be put down repeatedly by various literal-minded, sadly restrictive adults. The boys and girls he came to know eventually produced strongly worded, suggestive, eye-opening poems. In *I Never Told Anybody: Teaching Poetry Writing in a Nursing Home*, Koch has taken his thoughtful, giving, resourceful, and patient spirit to quite elderly and often infirm men and women, in obvious hopes of finding among them a similar responsiveness of mind and heart. If anything, the result is a more poignant and dramatic victory, because many old people have learned only too well that even their prose statements, never mind any written poems they may come up with, are of scant interest to others.

The American Nursing Home (no less) is located on the Lower East Side of Manhattan, not far from the Catholic Workers' St. Joseph House. It was there, with about twenty-five men and women, that Koch tried to teach poetry. "The students were all incapacitated in some way, by illness or old age," he tells us. He is brief and matter-of-fact with specifics, his purpose being educational and literary rather than sociological: "Most were in their seventies, eighties and nineties. Most were from the working class and had a limited education. They had worked as dry cleaners, messengers, short-order cooks, domestic servants." To a significant degree they had given up on life; it was enough to stay alive, to be fed and cared for. Needless to say, they did not write poems. Yet one day Kenneth Koch and another poet, Kate Farrell, showed up and began to talk about poems, to read them, and to suggest that they were not only the creations (or property) of a lucky, privileged few. They showed that poems could begin to take shape in the thoughts of ordinary people and be acknowledged, shared, and enjoyed by them.

Koch had not romanticized his students. He knew that they were tired, hurt, and ailing. Some were blind or hard of hearing. They all had serious complaints, and a number were in constant pain. As he took the measure of his class, he observed the serious initial obstacles of memory loss and rambling speech among many men and women. But he was not there to dwell on negatives. He began by asking the people to think of a sentence or two. He had modest, concrete suggestions: choose a color, say something about it, then something else, then something else again, using the name of the color. He received gratifying responses. Mary Tkalek, for instance, offered this: "I like green; I used to see so many greens on the farm / I used to wear green, and sometimes my mother couldn't find me / Because I was green in the green."

The teacher became bolder. He asked his students to imagine themselves the ocean or to imagine holding a conversation with the moon, the stars. He suggested that they recall especially quiet moments, or make particular comparisons, or hark back to another time—the end of World War II, for instance. He read to them; he singled out, to start, the verse of Walt Whitman, D. H. Lawrence, and William Carlos Williams. He never looked down on his students; he regarded them as quite able to write poetry, given encouragement and provocative hints about what tack they might take. He did not want to blur the difference between the dead poets he cherished (and in a way was calling upon for assistance) and the members of the rather unusual writing class he had chosen to teach. He knew that, finally, he could only count on this from a given student: "The music of ordinary speech and the memories and feelings his long life had given him."

Over the weeks they learned to summon and repeat words joyfully, to exaggerate enthusiastically, to celebrate contrasts, to become immersed in nature, to imagine all sorts of places, to put themselves into many different kinds of shoes. Most of them were wheeled in, some arrived in walkers, and only a few came to class on their own—yet they reached out for the sky, crossed the seas, fashioned their own time-machines, and used them gladly, at times wantonly. And their teacher, clearly, loved what happened. He praised them, fed them more and more of his ideas, and received back increasingly intricate, dramatic, and subtle poems. "Poetry is like being in Inner Space," William Ross decided, early on. "Your leaves sound different," Nadya Catalfano told the season autumn one day: "I couldn't understand why / The leaves at that time of year / Had a rustle about them / And they would drop / At the least little thing / And I would listen / And pick up some of them."

The students were encouraged both to speak and to write their poems. They were treated to jazz, to readings of Keats and more contemporary poets, and as their blood stirred they were asked to talk about their past lives. Their teacher was not, however, interested in becoming yet another of America's flourishing breed of psychological counselors. He makes an important clarification: "I don't think I would like to adjust to a life without imagination or accomplishment, and I don't believe my students wanted to either. It is in that sense, perhaps, that it can best be understood why it is better to teach poetry writing as an art than to teach it—well, not really teach it but use it—as some form of distracting or consoling therapy." And a little later on, referring to one of his students: "We were never contemplating Mary L. Jackson, she and I, but the things she said and wrote." He never expected too little of her—that curious condescension that is masked as compassion: "One trouble with a kind of falsely therapeutic and always reassuring attitude that it is easy to fall into with old people is the tendency to be satisfied with too little."

And so those men and women, nearer death than most of us, worked hard and became in their spirits lively, attentive, and dedicated. "I'd like to write the book of my life / I've started it already," Mary L. Jackson observed. Their enthusiasm, their bursts of memory, reflection, and fantasy were matched by the evident satisfaction of their teacher. In this book he tells others how they too might work with elderly people. He shows us that in Iowa (he spent time at the Lutheran Old Age Home in Cedar Falls), as well as in New York, apparently apathetic, even dazed men and women can suddenly begin to sing with their own words. And with a sentence here and there, he gives us textbooks of psychology and sociology: "Many had spent most of their adult lives at jobs like housework, steam-pressing, being a short-order cook. They had unusual (for poetry) lives and were looking at them now in an unusual time." But he is not one to argue with others or to come up with pompous gener-alizations; he merely implies with a casual, personal thought the sig-nificant difference between his way of regarding people and that of others—with their talk of "cultural disadvantage" and whatever: "I did think sometimes, too, what a marvelous thing it was for some-one, for instance, to be writing poetry, and loving it, who had kept through decades of hard domestic work, a fine and delicate sen-sibility that she could now express with eloquence in words."

Mostly Koch encouraged in his students what he calls "unrhymed, nonmetrical, fairly unliterary poetry"; it was an easier kind for be-ginning students to approach. But they enjoyed hearing and occa-sionally trying to write a more formal and intricate language. They would, no doubt, recognize a familiar spirit at play in the pages of *The Duplications*, their teacher's long poem, somewhat arbitrarily divided in half by an autobiographical section. Using mostly rhymed octets, he sets out to abolish space, time, and historical experience in order to create exuberant images that entertain and occasionally (though with a light hand) instruct. The narrator is a rather sen-suous, symbol-prone itinerant, at once rhapsodic and skeptical. He clearly sympathizes with those "Students dreaming up some pure Havanas / Where love would govern all, not francs or dollars"; but he worries that new tyrannies, announced with messianic slogans, keep replacing their predecessors—one of the "duplications" in-tended by his title, which more broadly refers to the cyclic rhythms of life. He is, always, very much an individual—someone who might not bother Fidel Castro but who certainly would arouse the suspicions of his bureaucratic henchmen: "O Liberty, you are the only word at / Which the heart of man leaps automatically."

Koch has a delicious sense of ironic detachment running through his rather lyrical, if not ecstatic, celebrations of the flesh. On a Greek island, contemplating the serene beauty of the Aegean, he thinks of the life underneath: ". . . Fish are nice / In being, though we eat them, not revengeful / I think that we would probably be meaner / To those who washed us down with their retsina!" It is an observation utterly worthy of Pueblo or Hopi children, who, like Emerson or Thoreau—speaking of duplications—are not especially inclined to what in the nineteenth century was called "human vainglory." He is especially wry and touching when he tells of his struggles to write while living in Ireland. He had finished part of the poem, had put it aside for other interests (teaching children or the elderly how to write poetry?), and had come back to himself, his mind's (the writer's) selfcenteredness. Ought he to go on, "Continue my narration of the fallacy / We find by being born into this galaxy"? His answer is characteristically lacking in egoistic justifications or sly academic boasting. He simply wants to reach others, maybe to make them feel like singing or smiling in recognition of a particular vision, suggestion, or anecdote. Of course, he cannot resist occasionally tucking into his narrative a bit of philosophical speculation or moral concern.

His is a wanderer's unyielding struggle for life: ". . . Take that, you / Dull insect Death! . . ." His is a naturalist's pantheistic, humorous advocacy: "Now turtles have on Mount Olympus landed / With numerous troops, and pistols, flags, and bells / And hostile mottoes painted on their shells / DOWN WITH OLYMPUS! WHY SHOULD WE ENDURE / AN ALIEN RULE? LET TURTLES REIGN O'ER TURTLES! / AND GODS GO HOME! THE VERY AIR IS PURE / WE TURTLES BREATHE. WE DO NOT NEED MYRTLES, / THE OAK, THE BAY, THE SHINING SINECURE! / GIVE US OUR LIVES TO LIVE IN OUR HARD GIRDLES!" It is a point of view one can imagine the old ones in the American Nursing Home of New York's Lower East Side taking to rather heartily: their good, dear friend Kenneth Koch doing some of his marvelously entertaining and sometimes unnerving acrobatic stunts.

New York Times Book Review, April 10, 1977

William Carlos Williams

Thank You, Dr. Williams

Agreat privilege (and actually, turn of fate) befell me in the early 1950s. I was encouraged by a fine professor-friend of mine, under whose supervision I'd written my undergraduate thesis, to send a note to William Carlos Williams and ask him whether he'd mind reading a college student's effort to understand his poetry, especially the first book of *Paterson*. This inquiry was not thoroughly gratuitous or self-serving. Professor Perry Miller kept insisting in response to my fearful hesitancy, an attitude that surely (I now realize) protected me from realizing how much of my pride, if not narcissism (as today's psychiatrists call it), had been put into that research and writing effort. This particular poet, Mr. Miller reminded me several times, was hardly a favorite of many college professors and might well enjoy reading what a student writing in an ivy-covered dormitory library managed to say about *Paterson*, wherein no huge flowering of ivy is recorded.

Soon enough, I'd dispatched my essay and received a warm, friendly, and lively response to it, coupled with an invitation to drop by; and soon enough I did. For me, to know Dr. Williams, to hear him talk about his writing and his life of medical work among the poor and working people of northern New Jersey, was to change direction markedly. Once headed for teaching, I instead set my sights for medical school. The result was a fairly rough time both with the premedical courses, not easy for me, and with medical school itself, where I had a lot of trouble figuring out what kind of doctoring I'd be able to do with a modest amount of competence. During those years, ailing though Dr. Williams was, he found the time and energy to give me several much-needed boosts—as in this comment: "Look, you're not out on a four-year picnic at that medical school, so stop talking like a disappointed lover. You signed up for a spell of training and they're dishing it out to you, and all you can do is take everything they've got, everything they hand to you, and tell yourself how lucky you are to be on the receiving end—so you can be a doctor, and that's no bad price to pay for the worry, the exhaustion."

Anyone who knew him would recognize the familiar way of putting things, of approaching both another person and this life's hurdles: kind and understanding underneath, but bluntly practical and unsentimental. Not that Williams didn't have in him (and in his writing) a wonderful romanticism, an ardently subjective willingness to take big risks with his mind and heart. His greatest achievement, *Paterson*, is a lyrical examination of a given city's social history, from the early days of this country to the middle of the twentieth century, and the poet whose eyes and ears become the reader's is marvelously vibrant and daring. But there is also in that poem, and in other aspects of Williams' work, a sensible and skeptical voice—the side of Williams these stories reveal to us: a hard-working doctor whose flights of fancy are always being curbed by a sharp awareness of exactly what life demands as well as offers.

I will never forget an exchange I had with Williams when I was in my last year of medical school. He had been sick rather a lot by then, but his feisty spirit was still in evidence, and as well, his canny ability to appraise a situation—anyone or anything—quickly and accurately. I told him I wanted to take a residency in pediatrics. He said "fine," then looked right into my eyes and addressed me this way: "I know you'll like the kids. They'll keep your spirits high. But can you go after them—grab them and hold them down and stick needles in them and be deaf to their noise?" Oh yes, I could do that. Well, he wasn't so sure. Mind you, he wasn't being rudely personal with me. He was just talking as the old man he was, who had seen a lot of patients, and yes, a lot of doctors too. "Give yourself more time," he urged me, in conclusion. Then he regaled me with some (literally speaking) doctor stories, accounts of colleagues of his: how they did their various jobs; the joys some of them constantly experienced, or alas, the serious troubles a number of them had struggled to overcome; the satisfactions of x, y, and z specialties, and conversely, the limitations of those same specialties. It was a discourse, a grand tour of sorts, and I remember to this day the contours of that lively exchange. I told my advisor at medical school about the meeting, and I can still recall those words too: "You're lucky to know him."

We are all lucky to know him, to have him in our continuing

midst. Only in those last years of his life was William Carlos Williams
finally obtaining the recognition he'd failed to receive for many decades of a brilliantly original, productive literary life. But during that
early spell of relative critical neglect (or outright dismissal, or patronizing half-notice), this particular writer could rely upon other
sources of approval. Every day of a long medical life (and often
enough in the middle of the night too) he was called by the men,
women, and children of northern New Jersey—ordinary people,
plain people, who considered themselves lucky to hold a job, lucky
to be able to get by, barely, or not so lucky because jobless—families
who had one very important loyalty in common, no matter their
ethnically diverse backgrounds: a willingness, an eagerness, a downright determination to consider one Rutherford doctor their doctor,
W. C. Williams, M.D. We who think of poets often look wide and
far for their spiritual roots, their cultural moorings. William Carlos
Williams was one poet who made quite clear who his teachers were,
where they lived, how they affected him and helped shape his particular sensibility: "Yet there is / no return: rolling up out of chaos, / a
nine months' wonder, the city / the man, an identity—it can't
be / otherwise—an / interpenetration, both ways."

The city was, of course, Paterson, the Paterson of *Paterson*, the
Paterson of industrial strife, of smokestacks and foundries and assembly lines, the Paterson of foreign languages still native tongues,
of Italians and Jews and Poles and the Irish and the blacks, the Paterson of desperately poor people in the 1930s, part of that enormous
nation within a nation characterized by Franklin Delano Roosevelt
in 1933 as "ill-fed, ill-housed and ill-clothed." As the poet of Paterson declared, he had struggled himself in that city of hard-pressed
souls and so doing had become very much part of a given human
scene—not only the lyric observer or prophet, as in *Paterson* of five
epic volumes, but also the obstetrician and gynecologist, the school
doctor, the pediatrician, the general practitioner: the young doc and
the middle-aged doc and the old doc, who drove all over and walked
all over and climbed steps all over Paterson (and Rutherford and
other New Jersey towns), a family legend to hundreds and hundreds
rather than a literary giant (eventually) to hundreds and hundreds of
thousands.

"Outside / outside myself / there is a world," the poet of *Paterson*
declares himself to have "rumbled," and then he notes that such a

world was "subject" to his "incursions" and was one he made it his
business to "approach / concretely." No question he did, with all
the directness, earthiness, and urgent immediacy of a doctor who
knows life itself to be at stake—someone else's, and in a way (professional, moral) his own as well. I remember the doctor describing his
work, telling stories that were real events, wondering in retrospect
how he did it, how he kept going at such a pace—hauling himself so
many miles a day, getting himself up so many stairs, persisting so
long and hard with families who had trouble, often enough, using
English, never mind paying their bills. And as he knew and sometimes had to say out loud, and even mention in his writing, it wasn't
as if he was loaded with money or a writer who took in big royalties.
America's Depression was a disaster for Dr. Williams' patients,
and many of them never paid him much, if indeed anything at all.
America's Depression was also a time when a marvelously versatile,
knowing, and gifted writer who happened to be a full-time doctor
was not having any great success with critics, especially the powerful
ones who claimed for themselves the imprimatur of the academy.
No wonder this writing doctor was glad to go "outside" himself, to
greet and try to comprehend a world other than that of literary
people. No wonder, too, he shunned the possibility of a relatively
plush Manhattan practice as the doctor to well-known cultural figures. His patients may have been obscure, down and out, or even
illiterate by the formal testing standards of one or another school system, but they were, he had figured out early on, a splendidly vital
people—full of important experiences to tell, memories to recall,
and ideas to try on their most respected of visitors, the busy doc who
yet could be spellbound by what he chanced to hear and knew to
keep in mind at night, when the typewriter replaced the stethoscope
as his major professional instrument.

I remember asking Williams the usual, dreary question—one I
hadn't stopped to realize he'd been asked a million or so times before: how did he do it, manage two full-time careers so well and for
so long? His answer was quickly forthcoming and rendered with remarkable tact and patience, given the provocation: "It's no strain. In
fact, the one [medicine] nourishes the other [writing], even if at
times I've groaned to the contrary." If he had sometimes complained
that he felt drained, overworked, and denied the writing time he
craved and needed, he would not forget for long all the sustaining,

healing, inspiring moments a profession—a calling, maybe, it was in his life—had given him, moment upon moment in the course of more than four decades of medical work. Such moments are the stuff of these doctor stories—the best of their kind since Dr. Anton Chekhov did his late nineteenth-century storytelling. As one goes through Williams' evocation of a twentieth-century American medical practice, the sheer daring of the literary effort soon enough comes to mind—the nerve he had to say what he says. These are brief talks or accounts meant to register disappointment, frustration, confusion, perplexity—or, of course, enchantment, pleasure, excitement, strange or surprising or simple and not at all surprising satisfaction. These are stories that tell of mistakes, of errors of judgment, and as well, of one modest breakthrough, then another—not in research efforts of major clinical projects but in that most important of all situations, with the would-be healer face-to-face with the sufferer who half desires, half dreads the stranger's medical help. As I heard Dr. Williams once say: "Even when the patients knew me well, and trusted me a lot, I could sense their fear, their skepticism. And why not? I could sense my own worries, my own doubts!"

He has the courage to share in these stories such raw and usually unacknowledged turmoil with his readers—even as he took after himself in an almost Augustinian kind of self-scrutiny toward the end of the second book of *Paterson*. In almost every story the doctor is challenged not only by his old, familiar antagonist, disease, but by that other foe whose continuing power is a given for all of us—pride in all its forms, disguises, and assertions. It is this "unreflecting egoism," as George Eliot called it, that the doctor-narrator of these stories allows us to see, and so doing, naturally, we are nudged closer to ourselves. Narcissism, as we of this era have learned to call the sin of pride, knows no barriers of race or class, or of occupation or profession either. But as ministers and doctors occasionally realize, there is a sad, inevitable irony at work in their lives—the preacher is flawed in precisely the respect he denounces during his sermons, and the doctor is ailing even as he tries to heal others.

Williams knew the special weakness we all have for those who have a moral hold on us, for those who attend us in our life-and-death times. Williams knew, too, that such a vulnerability prompts gullibility, an abject surrender of one's personal authority—and the result is the jeopardy not only of the parishioner or the patient but also of the priest or the physician. Arrogance is the other side of eager acquiescence. Presumptuousness and self-importance are the wounds this life imposes upon those privy to the wounds of others. The busy, capable doctor, well aware of all the burdens to be carried, and not in the least inclined to shirk the duties, may stumble badly in those small moral moments that constantly press upon him or her—in the nature of a hello or good-bye, the tone of voice as a question is asked or answered, the private thoughts and their effect on the face, the hands as they do their work, the posture, the gait. "There's nothing like a difficult patient to show us ourselves," Williams once said to a medical student, and then he expanded the observation further: "I would learn so much on my rounds or making home visits. At times I felt like a thief because I heard words, lines, saw people and places—and used it all in my writing. I guess I've told people that, and no one's so surprised! There was something deeper going on, though—the *force* of all those encounters. I was put off guard again and again, and the result was—well, a descent into myself."

He laughed as he said that, and he worried about a comparison he nevertheless proceeded to make—with the achievement of "insight" in psychoanalysis. I say "worried" because he knew rather well that he had in mind a moral as well as a psychological or emotional confrontation, and he'd been hearing a lot in those last years of his life (to his amazement and chagrin) about a supposedly "value-free" psychoanalysis or social science. Not that he couldn't put aside his anger and disgust and simply laugh at his own pretensions and spells of blindness and at those of others. These stories abound with such self-mocking gestures—parody turned on the parodist, words used to take the stern but also compassionate measure of the doctor who dispensed words, among other things, and then went home to dish them out—well, "in the American grain." It is important to emphasize the humorous and tolerant side of this storytelling self-arraignment of a singular New Jersey doctor: even the terribly hurt, driven, melancholy "Old Doc Rivers" is not without his spirited decency— a dizzying mix of selfless honor, passionate concern, and alas, the unrestrained demonic constantly at work.

These stories are really frank confidences extended to the rest of us by one especially knowing, dedicated physician who was willing to use his magical gifts of storytelling in a gesture of—what? We all require forgiveness, and we all hope to redeem our own missteps; we all hope, through whatever grace is granted us, to make every possible reparation. Words were the instrument of grace given to this one doctor, and words are the instrument of grace, also, for the rest of us, the readers who have and will come upon these marvelously provocative tales. As Dr. Williams' beloved wife, Flossie (she appears now and then in these medical fictions), once said to me: "There's little in a doctor's life Bill didn't get at when he wrote." She'd been there with him, of course, all along. She knew the periods of irritability and impatience; the flashes of annoyance and resentment; the instances of greed or just plain bitterness that "they" can't, don't, or won't pay up; the surge of affection—even desire or lust; the assertion of power in a fierce wish to control, to tell in no uncertain terms, to win at all costs; and finally, the tiredness, the exhaustion, the despondency. She knew, as he did, the rush of it all, the fast-paced struggle, again and again, with all sorts of illnesses— and the victories over them, the defeats at their hands, and not least, the realization (the postmortem) of one's limitations, one's mistakes.

For years I have been teaching these doctor stories to medical students, and during each class we all seem newly awakened—encouraged to ask the important whys, to consider the perplexing ifs. The stories offer medical students and their teachers an opportunity to discuss the big things, so to speak, of the physician's life—the great unmentionables that yet are everyday aspects of doctoring: the prejudices we feel (and feel ashamed of), the moments of spite or malice we try to overlook, the ever-loaded question of money, a matter few of us like to discuss, yet one constantly stirring us to pleasure, to bedeviling disappointment in others and in ourselves. What, in fact, that is really important has Williams left out? Nothing, it seems. He gives us a chance to discuss the alcoholic doctor, the suicidal doctor. He prompts us to examine our ambitions, our motives, our aspirations, our purposes, our worrying lapses, our grave errors, our overall worth. He gives us permission to bare our souls, to be candidly introspective, but not least, to smile at ourselves, to be grateful for the continuing opportunity we have to make recompense for our failures of omission or commission.

He extends to us, really, moments of a doctor's self-recognition— rendered in such a way that the particular becomes the universal, the instantly recognizable: this is, after all, the function, the great advantage of all first-rate art. And not to be forgotten in this age of glib, overwrought formulations, of theories and more theories, of conceptualizations meant to explain (and explain away) anything and everything, he brings to us ironies, paradoxes, inconsistencies, and contradictions—in the small vignette that opens up a world of pleasurable, startling, or forbidden mystery. Doc Williams becomes William Carlos Williams the accomplished fabulist and anecdotist— and as well, the medical and social historian who takes the risks of autobiography. There were poems similarly harnessed and intended, and even journal entries, as in this wonderful statement found in the "little red notebook" Williams, the Rutherford School Physician, kept in 1914:

> I bless the muscles
> of their legs, their
> necks that are
> limber, their hair
> that is like new
> grass, their eyes
> that are not
> always dancing
> their postures
> so naive and
> graceful, their
> voices that are
> full of fright &
> other passions
> their transparent
> shams & their
> mimicry of adults
> —the softness of
> their bodies—

As I read through, once more, these medical stories, these medical poems, and the autobiographical account, "The Practice," all so touching and blunt, both, I kept returning to the words just quoted, to which I'd once heard him allude, and which I remember him trying to remember, to speak; and I remember the powerful, compelling, sensuousness of his mind, with its offering of a hymn of love to those children, those patients, those fellow human beings. On a few occasions physicians invited him to come speak at their conferences, their grand rounds, but he was shy, modest—afraid he had little to say directly to his colleagues, no matter how much he'd offered the world in general through his many and varied writings. But he was dead wrong; he had everything to say to us. He opens up the whole world, our world, to us—and so, once again, as many in New Jersey had occasion to say during the first half of this century, say and say again: thank you, Doctor Williams.

Introduction to *The Doctor Stories* by
William Carlos Williams, New Directions, 1984

William Carlos Williams
Paterson *and the Passaic*

merica obsessed and haunted William Carlos Williams; he could not stop regarding its contradictions and ambiguities, its quite apparent wealth and power, its episodic idealism, its strong appetites—and its mean, self-centered, exploitative side. He never felt satisfied that he had, once and for all, grasped his native country, figured it out and come up with the words that would help others do so. No wonder *Paterson* defies categorization, for all the careful and subtle efforts made by the best intentioned of friends and scholars. Everyone agrees that the poem is a long and ambitious one; but as one tries to estimate exactly where Williams stands and what, finally, he upholds (in the way of doctrine, dogma, faith, or moral beliefs), the imposing turmoil of the poem and the extraordinary stretch of its author's imagination stand in the way. Both the narrator and his subject matter—people, places, things, and not least, the social history of the United States—defy those whom, perhaps, Dr. Williams had in mind as he wrote: the "intellectual heads," as he once called them, who take evidence of inconsistency and confusion as a challenge, requiring yet another theoretical confrontation. The man who is Paterson brims with excitement, vitality, and hopefulness. The man who is Paterson also shows himself to be tired, sad, forlorn and soon enough ready for his last breath. The city that is Paterson grows, surges, and carves out a destiny for itself. The city that is Paterson seems hopelessly doomed almost from the start. Now you see it, now you don't, the poet seems to be saying to his readers; just try and get a "viewpoint" or a "position" out of me (or out of the people I try to evoke, or out of the various situations I address myself to) and you will soon enough be brought up short or left unwittingly high and dry, with a forefinger pointing frantically at but one segment of territory; and such is the fate of those who are or want to be all too sure of themselves.

The child who became William Carlos Williams, poet, novelist, playwright, painter, essayist, inveterate letter-writer, librettist, social historian, and not incidentally, a practicing physician for over half a century, was born to parents whose background was unusual and, no doubt, a source of occasional consternation for a growing boy. His father was English, his mother of Spanish, French, and Jewish ancestry. As if to balance such an inheritance, their son was born and died in Rutherford, New Jersey—these days in America a remarkable fact. But Dr. Williams in certain respects was simply another American; there are elements of fate and social circumstance in his family's past that millions of Americans share, even if they are never destined to live almost eight decades in one state, never mind one town. He had, for example, a grandmother orphaned as a child and desperately poor, who nevertheless made her way across the Atlantic and then up the social ladder, and other relatives scattered in various places outside or inside this country. Williams was not alone when he contemplated the mystery and magic of his existence—that a father and mother of such different origins should even have met.

If a case can be made for the psychological basis of Williams' never-ending interest in the social and cultural forces that decisively shape human character, there is no reason to make a case of his own life. Almost ravenously curious, never one to sit back and stop taking the measure of others (or himself), he nevertheless abstained from gestures or long-term commitments that, to a degree, would no doubt have appeased his quick and restless mind, so eager to travel so many roads. As a boy he was taken to Europe, even sent to school in Switzerland and France; and as a young man, and later the father of two sons, he was not averse to a return. But unlike Eliot and Pound, he mostly stayed home; more than that, he committed himself resolutely and unstintingly to the life of a small-town doctor. The demands upon him by his patients were constant, heavy, and hard ethically to rebuff—even when outrageous. He could never take even a modest night's sleep for granted; and like all general practitioners (hence their declining number), he had to contend with those explosively irrational moments that patients have in the course of their day-to-day lives. Yet this man who loved New York City and, especially in the 1920s, was drawn to the literary and artistic life of Greenwich Village, never forsook Rutherford—thereby, one can say, facing up to the almost exquisite tensions of his life: all-night vigils beside struggling men, women, and children, followed by a day of office hours and hospital rounds, and in between, a minute here, a minute there, notes to himself for poems, or the actual writing of them.

In *Paterson*, the reader is given precious few moments of abstraction—philosophical, theological, or literary. The contrast with Eliot's *Four Quartets* or Pound's *Cantos* is obvious, dramatic, and quite intentional. It is not simply a matter of case histories given, as in the fourth book: "M.N., a white woman aged thirty-five, a nurse in the pediatric ward, had no history of previous intestinal disturbance," and on and on. The section of the second book titled "Sunday in the Park," which might have been an occasion for broad social comment, turns out to be as concrete and vivid as the particular lives of patients must have been for a doctor who was, really, a general practitioner, willing to go, day or night, on house visits, one of a dying breed. "Voices!" the poet exclaims, with reference to the people in the park. But he does not try to submit those voices to psychological or sociological generalization; they are "multiple and inarticulate," and in case we are unsettled or made impatient or inquisitive, Williams confronts us with a pause, a stretch of empty space, as if to say: stop and don't breathe heavy in expectation of an author's cool, sly, analytic resolution of all this life he is trying to evoke. Then comes a period, and then a resumption: "voices / clattering loudly to the sun, to / the clouds. Voices! / assaulting the air gaily from all sides."

The doctor who admitted time and again how cheated he felt by his patients for the irreplaceable time lost was the doctor who depended upon them for more than grist for his storytelling mill. Like Simone Weil, he could refer to the "great beast"; but it is put in quotation marks, an allusion to Alexander Hamilton's contemptuous reference to the ordinary men and women who, in his time by the thousands and now by the millions, make up America. For Williams it is an occasion for irony; he knows that the history of the city Paterson's seamier, industrial side goes way back—in fact, to Hamilton, who, in 1791, as Secretary of the Treasury under George Washington, helped found the Society for Establishing Useful Manufacturers, which was located near present-day Paterson. From then on, New Jersey would be increasingly tied to the materialist, commercial ethic, though of course Hamilton had no trouble dissociating himself from such a development: let the lives of others make up the "beast," and let a happy and privileged few do the naming, the calling, and the judging, thereby keeping themselves at a safe remove from the bestial.

Much has been made of Williams' tirades against the academy and its various strictures or structures, but I do not think, Williams himself at times notwithstanding, that the issue was only T. S. Eliot's Anglophilia or his refusal to be bound by the localism that the author of *Paterson* or *Life Along the Passaic River* or the Stecher trilogy so consistently and ardently embraced. Nor is the issue a clearcut one of class and caste: the aristocratic interests of Eliot and his followers, whose references, images, and reflections direct one toward metaphysical ideas, or the psychological anxieties of the well-to-do that accompany the struggle to find meaning in life, as against Williams' plain, ordinary working people, who populate his Paterson and his fiction. Williams was not so loyal to America that he didn't ache for Europe. In a touching chapter of his autobiography he recalls how important it was on one occasion for him and his wife to leave New Jersey—to the point that they left their two young sons in this country for over half a year with relatives. Nor is Williams the proletarian poet and novelist who turns factory workers or yeomen farmers into larger than life heroes. Eliot's vision of the West's decline, his sense that many of us are virtually dead, spiritually, is not all that different from the portrait Williams sometimes offers in *Paterson*. At one point he refers to "a thousand automatons. Who because they / neither know their sources nor the sills of their / disappointments walk outside their bodies aimlessly for the most part, / locked and forgot in their desires—unroused."

Unlike Eliot, Williams feels a bond with his automatons and has by no means given up on them. Nor has he himself given up; *Paterson* was no preparation for an important religious conversion. But what really distinguishes Williams from Eliot—and from Ezra Pound—is his unrelenting insistence on balance: he portrays sadness, desolation, and evidence of decay everywhere, but he also gives us decent, kind, and honorable people, who are energetic, thoughtful, and impressive enough as human beings to warrant a good deal of attention from a man of letters who cares to witness and write down what there is to see and hear. Williams was too shrewd an observer to deny the validity of the *Four Quartets* as a major philosophical and historical judgment by an extraordinarily gifted poet. The point, he knew, was to look elsewhere, to look right around him. The "brown fog" Eliot refers to cannot be ignored. As those who travel on the New Jersey Turnpike know, Paterson often has plenty of fog, its eerie sulphurous quality perhaps worthy of the imagination of Eliot's hero, Dante. Yet there is more than bad air, violence, sexual hypocrisy, social discrimination, and economic injustice in northern New Jersey. Williams knew he could document the decline of the industrial West in one, as opposed to five, books. He believed, however, that in the midst of deceit, abandonment, and exploitation there is at least the possibility of love.

In the second book of *Paterson*, the poet relentlessly exposes the way an economic system gone berserk becomes for various individuals a life of degradation. No one is spared—neither the vulnerable and vulgar working people nor their rich, corrupt bosses, whose particular cheapness, however gaudy and expensive, does not go unnoticed. Still, even though "among / the working classes SOME sort / of breakdown / has occurred"; even though "semi-roused / they lie upon their blanket / face to face"; the poet feels inclined to turn on his own train of thought, maybe his own inclination as a social critic, and continue this way: "mottled by the shadows of the leaves / upon them, unannoyed, / at least here unchallenged. / Not undignified." He next asks us to pause, with two periods—and one does indeed wonder what more can be said about people once their dignity is acknowledged, even if a bit grudgingly through a double negative. Williams was never a miser; he simply knew how hard it is for any of us to claim "dignity," in view of what we are all asked to do again and again: compete, move on up, get ahead—and on Sunday between eleven and twelve pray for others left behind. He allows himself to become neither rhetorical nor pietistic; the dignity he has in mind is not the kind readily mentioned by politicians and ministers. He keeps his eyes wide open, declines an opportunity for sentiment, but tries to indicate how finally, at least for moments, a number of us, in Patersons all over the land, find a moment of affirmation: "talking, flagrant beyond all talk / in perfect domesticity— / And having bathed / and having eaten (a few / sandwiches) / their pitiful thoughts do meet / in the flesh—surrounded / by churring loves! Gay wings / to bear them (in sleep) / —their thoughts alight, / away / . . . among the grass."

The complexity of such a psychological and sociological appraisal of ordinary Americans is hard for many of us, raised on one or another ideology, to accept without confusion and maybe anger. And our anger can prompt us to attribute confusion to the poet: enough of his delicate tightrope walking; let's examine "the system" and take for granted (rather than point out as if a revelation) the unsymmetrical and even contrary nature of just about everyone's temperament. In the fourth book, of course, Williams does just that; he takes on Paterson's bankers, factory owners, and managers in a way that could only please his old friend Pound: "Money sequestered enriches avarice, makes / poverty: the direct cause of / disaster." Usury is his target: ". . . Let credit / out. Out from between the bars / before the bank windows." But unlike Pound he will not dwell on any single vice; and just as important, he is wary of specific political and economic solutions. He does permit himself this: ". . . Will you consider / a remedy of a lot: i.e. LOCAL control of local purchasing power. / ??" Today, as suspicion toward Washington, D.C., mounts and as measures like revenue sharing attract support even from liberals, such a suggestion must seem less fatuous than it might have when first published in June of 1951, when Harry Truman was doing his best to keep the remnants of the New Deal intact. Williams must have known why the owners of Texas oil wells or Alabama cotton plantations or North Carolina textile mills were anxious for the supremacy of a kind of local control. One has to assume that, fundamentally, he was asserting an anarchist position, for all its shortcomings: opposition to the inequities and dangers that are associated with the capitalist nation-state, that also go with Russia's state-capitalism, and that are associated, arguably, with all large-scale social and political structures.

He was modest, maybe shrewdly restrained, when he allowed himself economic analysis. Immediately after he has gone on a few pages about credit and usury, in the third section of the fourth book, he begins a new section with "Haven't you forgot your virgin purpose, / the language?" The question was obviously addressed to himself; his is primarily a search for new ways of regarding the American landscape and experience. But one wonders whether Ezra Pound was not also being reminded of something: he and Dr. Williams and others like them have always known best how to strip us of deceitful words, phrases, and images, thereby providing, one hopes, a measure of truth—the clarity of a poet's vision. If the children of Paterson, New Jersey, sing "America the Beautiful" when their stomachs are empty or their eyes tearing from sulphurous air or their bone marrow failing because of lead poisoning contracted in a rat-infested tenement building, then someone's "virgin purpose" ought to be a consideration of "the language"—the flotsam and jetsam that is not confined to the Patersons or Passaic rivers but spills into classrooms and churches and these days, every five minutes or so, television screens: "better living through chemistry," "executive privilege," or something called "the free world" (which includes Spain, South Africa, South Korea, and Brazil). The issue is words, phrases, and our response to them, our faith in them, as well as such "structural" matters as the control of "credit." Williams' much discussed localism was not only a matter of geography; he was no intellectual pygmy or political coward when he abstained from preoccupations that would take him far afield, such as metaphysical speculation or prescriptive (and moralistic) political sociology. He would stay on his particular territory and fight hard from there.

But he was capable of the bluntest social analysis. *Paterson* portrays, in Robert Lowell's words, a country "grown pathetic and tragic, brutalized by inequality, disorganized by industrial chaos, and faced with annihilation." Northern New Jersey does not lend itself to nature poetry; and one suspects that even if Dr. Williams lived in Kansas or the Pacific Northwest, he would not write poems like William Stafford's. What George Orwell, by accident almost, happened to see as a patient in a Paris hospital, and to record unforgettably in "How the Poor Die," Dr. Williams lived out every day as a protagonist, for he was a doctor whose patients often enough had no money and little if any prospect of success. If there is beauty in such lives, it is not readily apparent; moreover, as Williams kept insisting, it is not the kind of beauty our conventional language celebrates. Wider turnpikes, bigger airports, taller skyscrapers; they go to make up the urban or suburban beauty we are taught to appreciate as "renewal"—when in fact thousands of individuals and the homes they have tried to keep intact, against great odds, have been pushed aside by bulldozers. Our cameras, our wordy spokesmen or propagandists, don't seek and celebrate an old man's pride, an old woman's faith, a housewife's ingenuity and intelligence, her husband's almost desperate carpentry as it contends with urban blight, or a child's games or songs, whatever the ghetto or working-class neighborhood he calls home. Williams could not make up for the indifference of others, but he could approach "the roar, / the roar of the present" and try to indicate who was making what noise, who was trying to get across which messages. Williams makes clear in his autobiography the tension he kept feeling between his roles as the commentator and the participant, between the physician who attends people, and hence is all caught up in the rhythms of their life, and the poet who stands back and tries to condense, to make things more pointed and suggestive. In *Paterson* the poet, Noah Paterson, may have, for once, enabled his creator to free himself of that tension; Noah is free to walk, to hear and overhear, to wax lyrical occasionally, to sigh more often, but then to go ahead and practice a kind of medicine, the pathologist's, with an autopsy of twentieth-century, industrial America.

Williams could only be introspective or abstract in response to a concrete human situation or predicament. He was, again, the opposite of a metaphysical poet; he wondered about, worried over, sang of, and no doubt dreamed of the quite tangible things of this world, as it is put, among which human beings qualify. His father was a staunch Unitarian, and he himself never really strayed from the kind of attentiveness to the here and now that Emerson and Thoreau possessed. If there is to be transcendence, and one keeps hoping and working for it, then it will take place here on earth in the human mind, with a new ordering of reality, a different vision of what is possible.

Not until he was old and on the decline did he give up his practice; in the last years of his life, bedeviled by strokes, he himself became a patient. When he was, finally, free of the burden other ailing people placed on him, he still could not put aside his efforts to locate them, himself, all of us—man and woman in Paterson, in America, in this particular century. "In old age /" he pointed out at the beginning of *Paterson* V, "the mind / casts off / rebelliously / an eagle / from its crag . . ." At first one gets the impression this particular eagle would be different from the four that preceded it—

more preoccupied with the problems of art and the artist, with the creative struggle of generations of men and women who, like Henri Toulouse Lautrec (the poem is dedicated to him), had tried to witness faithfully the world and evoke it in a way that bestirs a viewer or reader to begin to see things differently. But midway in the poem—and significantly, in prose—we are told this: "It is no mortal sin to be poor—anything but this featureless tribe that has the money now—staring into the atom, completely blind—without grace or pity, as if they were so many shellfish." Midcentury America is living all too comfortably with the fake and the superficial; we have "come in our time to the age of shoddy." More specifically: ". . . the men are shoddy, driven by their bosses, inside and outside the job to be done, at a profit." In contrast, there is ". . . the Portuguese mason, his own boss 'in the new country' who is building a wall for me, moved by oldworld knowledge of what is 'virtuous.'" Then the mason is given his voice: ". . . that stuff they sell you in the stores nowadays, no good, break in your hands. That manufactured stuff, from the factory, break in your hands, no care what they turn out."

They had once again commanded his attention, the poor, humble people of northern New Jersey, and by extension America's working-class men and women. Despite the length and ambitiousness of *Paterson*, there had been no extensive way for the poet William Carlos Williams to come to terms with the people seen day after day by the physician W. C. Williams. It is one thing to scan a city or region, to highlight tersely its characteristics and, less sociologically, to weave the language of ordinary people into the extraordinary statement, *Paterson*. But if one wants to approach those people more closely in hopes of portraying the subtleties and intricacies of their lives, the development of their assumptions, the formation of their moral character, and the pattern of their actions, then fiction becomes a strong temptation. It is not only a question of narration; some poems are indeed epic. A novel permits the writer wider latitude with individuals; they can go on and on—in their speech, in the decisions they make, in the exertions they lend themselves to, and in the causes they may choose to pursue or oppose. Even a short story, for all its limitations, enables a more leisurely and detailed evocation of a particular segment of life—the examination of a given dramatic situation from a number of vantage points. The "Polock with his mouth open" or "the children with their dusty little minds and happiest *non sequiturs"* of *Paterson* can become carefully drawn individuals as opposed to occasions for intensely highlighted images. Williams worked on his fiction intermittently but with great care. It took him years to complete the stories that go to make up *Life Along the Passaic River* (1938), most of which are directly drawn from his medical practice; and he wrote the sadly neglected but terribly important trilogy of *White Mule, In the Money,* and *The Build-Up* over a span of three decades. Those stories and novels are not the inadequate but pretentious offspring of a poet who didn't always know where his genius lay, even as some writers of strong fiction persist in throwing off every once in a while a poem or two, ensured publication by their reputation. The trilogy, in particular, haunted him; it is in many respects a fictional counterpart to *Paterson*—long, wide-ranging, and closely connected to this nation's history, especially to the social forces unleashed by the industrialism of our Northeast. It can be said that fiction was for this particular writer a means of reconciliation. It was not in vain, the time spent in hospitals, in his office, on the road, going up the stairs of tenement houses to visit (so often) near-penniless immigrants who were in pain but often as not distrusted fiercely the doctor they also knew they required; rather, lives healed could become lives presented to others—and lives always, with Williams, made an occasion for moral instruction or ethical inquiry. The man who in 1925 published *In the American Grain*, with its brilliant evocations and interpretations of Cotton Mather, Abraham Lincoln, and the beginning of slavery in this country, was not one for distance from either his subjects or the implications their lives might have for those of us right now living ours.

Williams wrote about the working people who live near the Passaic River at a time when sociological studies had yet to gain the dominance they now have as the almost matter-of-fact way that readers choose to gain access to the lives of others. George Linhart published *Out of the Melting Pot*, a mixture of autobiography and fiction, in 1923, long before the appearance of *Beyond the Melting Pot*, the effort of Daniel P. Moynihan and Nathan Glazer to examine sociologically the immigrant experience of the Irish, the Italians, and the Jews, as well as that of the blacks and Puerto Ricans who have moved to our cities more recently. Before Linhart there were John Cournos' *Babel* (1922), Abraham Cohan's classic, *The Rise of*

David Levinsky (1912), Theodore Dreiser's *Jennie Gerhardt* (1911), Jack London's powerful *People of the Abyss* (1903), Isaac Friedman's *Poor People* (1900), and back into the nineteenth century, Stephen Crane's *The Open Boat and Other Tales of Adventure* (1899) and James Sullivan's *Tenement Tales of New York* (1895). There were the novels and stories of Edna Ferber and Fannie Hurst; there were also Upton Sinclair's attempts to show how immigrants, as well as native Americans, became hopelessly indentured to the needs of an expanding economy: *King Coal* and *Oil!* as well as his two-volume *Boston*. In 1917 a writer for the *New Republic* called such writing "sociological fiction"—unaware, of course, that quite soon, certainly from the time the Lynds' study *Middletown* appeared onward, such fiction would begin to diminish in impact, giving way, some would say, to the various fictions of sociology and other social sciences; the notion that with a questionnaire or a spell of fieldwork, followed by the extended resort to theoretical formulations, the various and complicated thoughts and experiences of many different kinds of people can be quite adequately presented.

In response, perhaps, novelists and even essayists began to pull back from "objective reality" and concentrate their energies on exaggeration, distortion, and escape, focusing on the weird, private fantasies of their chosen characters, bizarre plots and subplots, or the examination of the esoteric, the peculiar, or the so-called mythic. What was the point of writing about the poor or the recently immigrated when growing numbers of "experts," claiming a range of techniques and calling upon the almost unquestioned authority of the social sciences, were appearing here, there, and everywhere and coming up with something called "findings"? In contrast, each of the nineteen stories in the collection *Life Along the Passaic River* begins and ends without the slightest promise of handy generalizations: "I kept watching the Greek but he didn't look up, his face was like a board the whole time"; or, "Tried to get off her father's lap and fly at me while tears of defeat blinded her eyes." If there has to be a broader statement, Williams will occasionally oblige right off, as in this opening sentence: "He was one of those fresh Jewish types you want to kill at sight, the presuming poor whose looks change the minute cash is mentioned." In case the reader wants further elaboration about the type just characterized: "But they're insistent, trying to force attention, taking advantage of good nature at the first crack.

You come when I call you, that type." As for the requirement that the social observer maintain both detachment and neutrality, here is a storyteller's frank acknowledgment: "People like that belong in clinics, I thought to myself. I wasn't putting myself out for them, not that day anyhow. Just dumb oxen. Why the hell do they let them into the country. Half idiots at best. Look at them."

The story is "A Face of Stone," and with such a beginning one is hardly put in hopes of one of those humanistic perspectives today's college catalogues promise. (A little more tolerance, or at least discretion, can even be found in the autobiographies of Michael Pupin, Edward Bok, and Andrew Carnegie, all three so full of themselves as self-declared successes, the poor immigrants who made good and therefore have a right to give lectures to everyone else.) Williams is relentless in his description of the father and mother and makes no effort to conceal his own responses to what he saw: "He got me into a bad mood before he opened his mouth just by the half smiling, half insolent look in his eyes, a small stoutish individual in a greasy black suit, a man in his middle twenties I should imagine." His wife "looked Italian"; she had "a goaty slant to her eyes, a face often seen among Italian immigrants." She was clutching the baby to her; and the author easily could have set forth a scene worthy of Kaethe Kollowitz: the beleaguered, confused, but animated and proud mother holding a child who comes across as innocent, vulnerable, appealing. Instead we are told that the mother had "no expression at all on her pointed face, unless no expression is an expression. A face of stone. It was an animal distrust, not shyness." In the event anyone is still ready to romanticize or idealize the woman, the author tells us that there was a great deal of dirt under her nails, that "she smelled," and that the smell is the kind "you find among many people who habitually do not wash or bathe."

American Poetry Review, March/April 1975; originally in
William Carlos Williams: The Knack of Survival in America
by Robert Coles, 1975

A Writing Physician

I'm a doctor all day and into the night; I write on the run, or when it's plenty dark, before going to bed." That autobiographical fragment was sent to an inquiring Harvard undergraduate who wanted to make a clearer distinction between a particular person's vocation and avocation than the student was disposed to allow. I happened to be the lucky recipient of the message. I was writing a major paper on the American poet (and novelist, and writer of short stories, and essayist, and playwright) William Carlos Williams and felt emboldened to ask a few questions of him. He was more than forthright; he answered in strong, wry, bemused language. And he offered a bonus: If I ever wanted to accompany him on his medical rounds, I would be welcome. I quickly accepted and soon enough found myself utterly captivated by this brilliant, energetic, many-sided man from Rutherford, New Jersey, who was known to a whole world of working-class people from Paterson, New Jersey, as "Doc," and to another world of readers as a writer bravely, even fiercely, determined to develop and retain his own quite special voice and viewpoint.

When I was in medical school, I kept in touch with this unusual physician and got some idea of how inseparable his two careers were. He was constantly on the job, seeing patients in his office, seeing them in the hospital, and not least, making home visits. He needed no lecture on the importance of primary care; nor did he require instruction in the psychosomatic aspects of the physician's practice. Long before the phrase "holistic medicine" came upon us, and long before social scientists with their socioeconomic variables arrived in the corridors of our medical schools, Doc Williams was out there on the front line, connecting injuries and accidents and diseases, and consequent fear, sadness, worry, and pain, to the *lives* of those largely poor or working-class men, women, and children he attended, day in and day out. His doctor stories, collected under the title *Life Along the Passaic River,* reveal a sensibility open to the variousness of human experience. He saw each human as constantly responsive to the demands and constraints of culture and class, race and sex, occupation and age, history and regional tradition—all of those variables too many of us are inclined to acknowledge, summon, and study, yet in a way so strangely abstract that it does little for those millions who need not more interdisciplinary theory but a concrete series of connections made by a particular physician. Williams was such a physician—never inclined to turn a *person* into an excuse for a self-important display of jargon. "No ideas but in things," he kept reminding us in his long poem *Paterson.*

But W. C. Williams, M.D., was also a man haunted and possessed by words. He wanted to invoke them, arrange them, make them work—to bring them to us as light penetrating the shadows of our lives. I used to watch him, a man possessed, after a given housecall. He had heard a remark and caught sight of the muse in apparently unpromising circumstances. He was at pains to "get it down." On prescription pads, on pieces of newspaper, on scrap paper, he would scribble the lines. Later, in his office located in his home, he would type feverishly—and the product was, in sum, a literary contribution that made him a giant in American letters.

He was also an artist. For a while, in his early adult years, he thought of combining that kind of work with his medical commitments. One of his landscapes once served as a cover for the *Journal of the American Medical Association* (May 15, 1972). A friend of numerous painters, sculptors, and photographers, he wrote pieces of art criticism, sat for a portrait, and inspired through his presence, through his ideas and ideals and words, the responses of his kindred spirits, as in the cover of this issue of the *Journal* (January 2, 1981). Charles Demuth painted it, giving the composition the title of a line from a Williams poem, "The Great Figure." It is a brief one, as many were: "Among the rain / and lights / I saw the figure 5 / in gold / on a red / firetruck / moving / tense / unheeded / to gong clangs / siren howls / and wheels rumbling / through the dark city."

In his *Autobiography,* Dr. Williams tells how he happened to write that poem, and the account lets us know that he had left the Post Graduate Medical Center in New York City one warm July evening and was on his way to visit a good friend and painter, Marsden Hartley. "As I approached his number," the author tells us, "I heard a great clatter of bells and the roar of a fire engine passing the end of the street down Ninth Avenue. I turned just in time to see a golden figure 5 on a red background flash by. The impression was so sudden and forceful that I took a piece of paper out of my pocket and wrote a short poem about it."

Demuth's painting was, of course, meant to capture the sudden, brisk drama of a fleeting second of early twentieth-century New York City, a street scene with its rising and falling action. We are meant to see a world Dr. Williams saw: the abrupt, unexpected arrival of the red fire truck, No. 5, and then its gradual disappearance into the darkness of Manhattan. But this is a portrait, too, of "Bill," of a man the artist deems worthy of being a celebrity, his name lit up in the streets of Gotham; most of Dr. Williams' middle name is rendered in the painting. The vivid, alive, active, gripping representation on canvas is an artist's psychological as well as material tribute—a friend's spirit commemorated.

Williams was not reluctant to reciprocate; he registered in repeated essays and reviews a strong and continuing respect and affection for the work of certain painters and photographers, the homage his sensitive eyes impelled him to make. One published volume, *A Recognizable Image: William Carlos Williams on Art and Artists* (1978), indicates how strongly his artistic affinities exerted themselves. I can never forget those eyes: wide, open, at once skeptical and patiently trusting. A self-portrait, done in 1914, captures what they were like. He beheld so much—and not in a greedy, hoarding, smug, complacent, or self-centered manner. What he took in, he was ready to offer back, transmitted into the physician's healing, the poet's visionary speculations, the novelist's cautionary tales.

I know how privileged I was to stand now and then near this extraordinary person. And these days, I know that even though he died at eighty years in 1963, his work is as vital, compelling, and forceful as he had been. Each year I use his stories and poems in a medical humanities class I teach at Harvard Medical School, and as I find him (through those statements, songs, descriptions, and narratives) reaching, grabbing, addressing, reminding, remonstrating, begging, warning, and, always, deeply affecting his young readers on their way to joining a profession he deeply, continually, always loved, I think of that quick grin he had, that modest yet proud shrug he could give to his shoulders. "I try, I try," he once said, *very* quietly, rebuffing a compliment. Then he showed the young doctor how many patients he had seen that day. "I'm so tired," he continued, and added: "I think I'm tired enough to collect the lines I've been snatching all day, in between everything else, and hope they'll come out as a decent poem." The doctor as writer. The writer as ironic self-observer. The observer as, still, teacher to all of us—medical students and physicians and men and women everywhere, in each generation, who crave beauty: the sight of it, the sound of it.

Journal of the American Medical Association, January 2, 1981

Doctor and Poet

The William Carlos Williams bookshelf steadily widens. It holds an outpouring of articles and doctoral theses, at least a dozen book-length critical considerations, the valuable biannual *William Carlos Williams Review*, and now a second, solid biography, *William Carlos Williams: A New World Naked* by Paul Mariani. For much of his life, though, Williams went unnoticed. When, in his fifties, he did begin to attract attention, it was often of a negative kind—outraged or patronizing glances from critics who judged him crass, provincial. Nor did he work hard at ingratiating himself with important literary people. He shunned the academic centers, where more and more of those people, in this century, have found comfortable homes. He was quick, sometimes too quick, with the cranky or truculent broadside directed at a book reviewer, a professor, an editor, a particular poet. On the other hand, he could be wonderfully kind and generous to young writers, usually men and women who were going, as he put it, "against the grain," as he did. Hence his advocacy of them earned him only further disapproval in certain quarters. Like James Agee, he won the Pulitzer Prize posthumously—but he died half a year short of eighty, not at forty-five.

Williams lived a dramatic, hectic life, an ideal one for a conscientious biographer. Reed Whittemore's account (1975) offered a wry and wide-eyed poet commenting in a relaxed fashion on another poet. Whittemore obviously liked Williams, but as a biographer he wanted and achieved an ironic distance, a narrative calm that treats of a constant turbulence. In contrast, Paul Mariani's biography, larger and more detailed than Whittemore's, is the work of a teacher who acknowledges that he has come to his subject after long familiarity with the academic tradition Williams fought so long and hard. Yet Mariani seems to have forsaken some of the loyalty he once had to that tradition. His book is far less detached than Whittemore's, far closer in spirit to Williams the embattled partisan, fighting literary wars with poems and stories, and even fighting a few medical skirmishes on the side. (Unlike so many in his medical profession, he spoke up loud and clear when he came upon child abuse or malpractice among physicians.) Williams' son, William Eric Williams, also a doctor, referred to his father's "colossal, uphill solo battle"—a battle, Mariani tells us, "to remake American poetry for a wider audience." Whittemore was getting at the same point when he titled a chapter of his book "The Revolution (in a Still Place)." Williams sought images that would disturb the mind's sleepy compliance with the tireless conformity of everyday speech. He also was a morally earnest man, with deep attachment to the New Jersey working-class families he treated as a physician for about half a century. Their everyday speech inspired him, but true to his mother's intensely mystical nature, he fancied the resulting energy as a gift and himself as a medium of sorts, the beneficiary of a proletarian "them," which, however, was not a mere abstraction; as a general practitioner, Williams made a rather poor living because so many of his patients had no money to pay him for his good care. His obligation was to return the favor—to celebrate the largely unacknowledged beauty and dignity of a given world, while also taking note of its tawdry aspects.

Williams criticized no one more harshly than himself. "How strange you are, you idiot!" he says to himself in the first book of *Paterson*. And the long letter that terminates the second book of *Paterson* is in the Augustinian tradition of self-scrutiny: "You've never had to live, Dr. P—not in any of the by-ways and dark underground passages where life so often has to be tested. The very circumstances of your birth and social background provided you with an escape from life in the raw." Yet he was not daunted by such a fate. He forsook the possibility of a plush Manhattan practice for the tenements of northern New Jersey, and he was willing to take big risks with words and images:

A delirium of solutions, forthwith, forces
him into back streets, to begin again:
up hollow stairs amid acrid smells
to obscene rendezvous. And there he finds
a festering sweetness of red lollipops—

and a yelping dog:
Come YEAH, Chichi! Or a great belly
that no longer laughs but mourns
with its expressionless black navel love's
deceit.

Those lines in the first book of *Paterson* were part of an effort to save many of us from arid pedantry: "A reply to Greek and Latin with the bare hands." Again and again abstractions are denounced and particulars are stressed as redemptive, the famous "no ideas but in things." At times one imagines Williams quite drunk (by and large he drank very little, except when his wife and children were in Europe for a year, 1927–1928) and flailing at lots of hanging straw men. But at other times he is soberly acute in his judgment of the real world—the "clerks" he mentions in *Paterson*, who have "got out of hand forgetting for the most part / to whom they are beholden." He characterizes intellectuals as "spitted on fixed concepts like / roasting hogs, sputtering, their drip sizzling / in the fire." But his was not a self-serving combativeness—an embittered expression of rivalrous envy. An agnostic, really, he echoed Kierkegaard's pre-Freudian but utterly contemporary psychological self-penetration: "Who are these people (how complex / the mathematic) among whom I see myself / in the regularly ordered plateglass of / his thoughts, glimmering before shoes and bicycles?"

Such a devastating evocation of the calculating nature of literary narcissism was meant to be confessional in nature. Williams' powerful assault on his own egotism, on his greedy ambitiousness, was the stuff of a long life, as Mariani is determined to show. This is a biography of days and weeks and months and years carefully recited, but not in a way the writing doc would have minded, I suspect. I remember him in his old age, badly hurt by strokes and heart attacks and abdominal diseases, yet a fighter whose daily restlessness of spirit was still with him, one could see in it the eye muscles and the voice muscles, as well as those of his weakened but not resigned legs and arms. His activity was never random. The mind, he seemed to feel, is always prey to those ready to seize it, to paralyze it with toxins— the pieties so many of us get weary of questioning, let alone fighting. Mariani recognizes that Williams' life was itself one of those "things" he kept addressing. The insatiable curiosity of a Boswell is redeemed from pettiness or idolatry by the figure being pursued. Williams emerges heroic, able to stand tall and significant in a world he carefully circumscribed with daily medical rounds and regular stints at a typewriter in his Rutherford Victorian home. Mariani wisely reminds us that the tough warrior also knew when to seek peace. The story of Bill and Flossie Williams taking the train to Washington in order to hear T. S. Eliot read his poems and lecture is extremely touching. Eliot was a great poet, Williams knew in his heart; but he loathed his departure for England, his assumption of an aristocratic, highly mannered life. With the words "a local pride" he launched his answer to the Anglophiliac posture that he believed was something much larger than one great poet's idiosyncratic preferences. His outbursts against Eliot, one dares presume, were really directed at his own nation's university life; they could be construed in fact as a sign of deep respect toward, if unacknowledged awe of, the poet himself. And he stood by his old friend Pound, despite the latter's exiled aestheticism, not to mention his crazy political life; he stood by him as a great poet while denouncing all the while the obscene junk that the world heard, for instance, in the wartime radio broadcasts from Rome.

Also valuable in this biography is the appreciation of Williams the physician—*not* an alternative life a poet sought in order to make a living. In a chapter ("The Practice") of his autobiography, Williams eloquently described the spiritual nourishment that his profession offered him. To be sure, he was always an overworked, underpaid doctor and a writer on the run who worked at the end of a long day or in rare moments of leisure. But one wonders whether some of the astonishing energy that nature gave him didn't have to be taken away, each day, before he could write at any great length. His mind saw almost too much. Medicine tamed him and gave him a discipline—which, in turn, helped him with those words, those images.

He was an intensely private man, for all his ebullience and responsiveness to people, places, and things. There is a sexy loneliness to much of his poetry and his short stories, as in the art of John Sloan or Edward Hopper. Mariani's reading of the autobiographical story "Old Doc Rivers" is just right; it is a portrait of the mind's power to isolate even a naturally gregarious person. Williams' doctor stories (published as *Life Along the Passaic River*) reveal him caught up in a redemptive magic of sorts: the wounded, solitary seeker given a chance by the patient to be healed, to come out of himself, by attending someone with devotion—with an utter concentration Dr. Williams has described as befalling him by a nod of Grace. This is a definitive biography in certain respects. It contains all the details, and then some—high school report cards, for example, and medical school grades. Time haunted the busy doctor, the versatile writer, and time dominates this book, which is narrated with a strong chronological rather than interpretive emphasis, though Mariani does allow himself an occasional critical digression. His writing is energetic, fast-paced, a bit tough, not unlike the manner of the busy New Jersey writer and physician himself. This is a long book, and some will judge that parts of it ought to have been cut. But William Carlos Williams was *sui generis*, a citizen well worth inclusion in his own magnificent social history (good God, he did *that* brilliantly, too!) *In the American Grain*. It is a pleasure to have so much of his exceptional life run by one's eyes and reach one's mind and heart again.

New Republic, November 25, 1981

Dr. Williams at Harvard

The year 1983 marks the hundredth anniversary of the birth of William Carlos Williams, and surely a number of his friends, colleagues, and admirers will be recalling with affection, gratitude, and even on occasion a touch of awe the remarkable presence he was on the American literary scene for half a century. Even now, twenty years after his death, the exuberant power of his mind touches and persuades those who read his words; he had a contagious vitality and a shaping vision which still beckon. Still, during his lifetime recognition came exceedingly slow. (He was awarded the Pulitzer Prize and the Gold Medal for Poetry posthumously, and he died at almost eighty.) Not that he hadn't taken big risks, thereby offending all sorts of important critics. He once told a young friend that there were moments when he wondered whether much of his dignity didn't rest, finally, on the antagonisms he'd carefully nurtured over the years.

Nevertheless, in the last fifteen or so years of his life, the world of "principalities and powers" began to beckon him. In early 1951, for instance, the Alpha chapter of Phi Beta Kappa at Harvard announced that William Carlos Williams would be the guest poet at its annual commencement meeting in June. He said yes—a particularly significant honor for a writer who had been so constantly suspicious of the academic world. The first book of *Paterson*, published in 1946, was defiantly critical of the artistic directions taken by Eliot and Pound. Williams wanted "a local pride," one connected to the industrial working-class city of Paterson, New Jersey, of all places, where he practiced medicine so long and hard. At times he was considered and modest in his rejection of a traditionalism and aestheticism that made for (he believed) sterility, pomposity, or self-indulgence. More than occasionally, however, his line of argument became testy and overwrought.

For many weeks he wondered what he ought say in the poem

he intended to write for the Harvard occasion. By late March, however, he was an invalid, felled by a serious stroke. By May, miraculously, he was much better and had written his poem, "The Desert Music," which he did indeed deliver, no matter the weakened state of his health.

The poem was a bold and dramatic one. The Cambridge audience was summoned to the Southwest, "between Juarez and El Paso." The subject was the source of human dignity—given the inevitable dark side of our mental and spiritual life, not to mention the social and political tawdriness to be found in all countries. The poet chose a cloistered hall in the Northeast to sing of Texas and Mexico, of forlorn and betrayed Indians, or rowdy, bullying cowboys, of men and women twisted, hurt, debased. Yet his music rescued vitality and humor from the gutter: "What in the form of an old whore in / a cheap Mexican joint in Juarez, her bare / can wiggling crazily can be / so refreshing to me, raise to my ear / so sweet a tune, built of such slime?"

He asked his listeners to think of the whore's "customers," to contemplate how we find our various victims on this earth, how we cultivate a vigorous self-righteousness at the expense of others. Ailing, aware that future strokes were likely, and hence more and more deformity, Williams dared present himself as the old performer, warts and all, struggling, still struggling to find a halfway genuine act—a song and dance that would successfully affirm what he was meant to do: to make the effort, with words, to comprehend life's meaning.

The poem was a critical success. W. H. Auden, for example, no great admirer of Williams' work, was quite impressed. Williams himself drew strength from the dramatic irony of the occasion: his belated recognition as death approached; and his ability, still, and under such circumstances, to mobilize poetry in the battle against pietistic conformity. Williams' dancer in "The Desert Song" possessed a strange and arresting detachment; she knew full well that she was "part of another tune," as did the honored poet in Cambridge, as did, no doubt, many in the audience who heard him read.

Unfortunately, at his truculent, hectoring worst, Williams succumbed to his own kind of narrowness: the irregular, in meter and in social imagery, was permitted to distort a given reality. After he had returned from Harvard, he was making the old, worn distinctions in letters to friends describing Harvard as big and powerful and "semi-ecclesiastic" and himself as the feisty, lowly outsider. In the early 1950s, Harvard was, as a matter of fact, a place where W. C. Williams was not without avid enthusiasts. I remember, at the time, Perry Miller lavishing praise on *Paterson*. It was Miller who persuaded me as an undergraduate to try to interview the crusty, writing doc; and thereby I found a source of great personal inspiration, not to mention advice and more advice—free and firm and not rarely quite forceful. Now in my classes I try to carry the torch for "the old man," as Wallace Stevens, four years Williams' senior, referred to him in that spring of 1951.

The music still has its magic. *Paterson* does what its author intended when he devoted a long, epic poem to an examination of America's distinctive idiom, and as well, our complicated social origins. A good number of Harvard College undergraduates who read the lines find the mix of strenuous cultural criticism and relentless self-scrutiny altogether unnerving—precisely the response Williams desired. What, finally, is the author's point of view? With so much so mercilessly exposed or denounced, what is left to uphold, to stand by, to seek after? Nor does Williams' unremitting bias against the purely abstract fail to provoke students who have learned to master it—thereby getting into Harvard: "Say it! No ideas but in things." And this: "To make a start, / out of particulars / and make them general, rolling / up the sum, by defective means— / Sniffing the trees, / just another dog / among a lot of dogs. What / else is there? And to do?"

The poet is addressing the age-old inclination we all have to protect our elaborate, sometimes showy thinking, our highflown ideas and ideals, from the potential correctives or corrosions of concrete experience. What philosophers and theologians examine as a "polarity," transcendence as against immanence, Williams was anxious to regard as a matter of art's uncertain connection to conduct. How do we explore this world through words and images in such a way as to do justice to what actually obtains "out there"? How might we not only learn moral analysis but learn to use it in the course of our everyday lives? Williams, for all his suspicion of organized religion and of America's Puritan ancestors, was not averse to a scrupulous, Augustinian self-scrutiny. *Paterson* is filled with frank acknowledgments of the writer's desire to play god, to prescribe and proscribe, to use talent to gain glory—while condescending to let others deal with the ordinary, demanding, embarrassing requirements and routines this life presents.

He is not being a social scientist or a propagandist when he works into *Paterson* all sorts of details—the history of a region, the subjects of race and class, money and power—all matters that one immigrant group after another has had to confront. The rudeness and crudeness he dares evoke are not gratuitous. "The rest have run out— / after the rabbits," he reminds us, thereby divorcing the bardic life from everyone else's. He worried long and hard that too many of us use learning wrongly; in Walker Percy's recent phrase, we "get all A's and flunk life." It is a message that does not go unnoticed or unappreciated by Harvard students, who see ivy growing abundantly on lovely classroom buildings in an especially important yard, all at a certain remove from the nearby hurly-burly of a city's workaday imperatives.

Prose was also a compelling part of Williams' hectic, many-sided life. His novel *White Mule*, part of a trilogy, tells of the opportunities and hazards, the gains and their costs, that have accompanied social and economic ascent in America. Williams drew unashamedly upon the experiences of his wife, Flossie, and of her parents. His father-in-law was a worker, a union man, who became an exceedingly successful entrepreneur. *White Mule* is a novel, really, about consciousness—a child's, a woman's, a working man's, a nation's. Williams was interested, always, in what it means to be an American. To find out, he wrote his own kind of social history—portraits of mythic figures in our past, such as Columbus and DeSoto, Cotton Mather and Benjamin Franklin, Washington and Lincoln. But his Stecher trilogy (*The Build-Up* and *In the Money* are the second and third volumes) afforded him a chance to explore what Daniel Bell has aptly called the "cultural contradictions of capitalism" as they have become embodied in our children's upbringing, our occupational lives, our hobbies and sports, our sexual involvements, and our education—because what we learn and what we believe to be the purpose of that learning have to do with who we are and where and how we live or want to live.

Williams was, obviously, working American territory explored previously in *The Rise of Silas Lapham, The Rise of David Levinsky,* and *An American Tragedy* or sociologically, with respect to a number of countries, in *The Protestant Ethic and The Spirit of Capitalism.* But he was a shrewd obstetrician and pediatrician; he knew about the birth of hope in parents and their children, and too, its vicissitudes over the years. The result was a novel as complex and suggestive as the reality it meant to convey. It is, needless to say, a reality not unfamiliar in its bearing upon the lives of students attending a distinguished national university that has, for generations, offered a big lift to aspiring young people anxious to enjoy access to a particular nation's largesse.

The significance of the medical side of Williams' life was sometimes underestimated by critics, though not by Williams himself:

> As a writer I have never felt that medicine interfered with me, but rather that it was my very food and drink, the very thing which made it possible for me to write. Was I not interested in man? There the thing was, right in front of me. I could touch it, smell it. It was myself, naked, just as it was, without a lie telling itself to me on its own terms.

And elsewhere in his autobiography he wrote:

> It's the humdrum, day-in, day-out, everyday work that is the real satisfaction of the practice of medicine; the million and a half patients a man has seen on his daily visits over a forty-year period of weekdays and Sundays that make up his life. I have never had a money practice; it would have been impossible for me. But the actual calling on people, at all times and under all conditions, the coming to grips with the intimate conditions of their lives, when they were being born, when they were dying, watching them die, watching them get well when they were ill, has always absorbed me.

Williams was enormously responsive to human beings in their full and bewildering range. His medical life certainly did nourish his writing life, but there was also a reverse flow, so that his doctor stories, first collected and published as *Life Along the Passaic River* (1938), offer the general reader and certainly the members or prospective members of the medical profession a very special point of view. Such classics as "Jean Beicke" or "The Use of Force" or "The Girl With the Pimply Face" are unrivaled in the clarity they shed both on the work doctors do and on the emotions with which they must contend in the course of that work. It is unsettling, it is even scary, to read stories—in truth, thinly disguised personal accounts—that portray someone feeling lust, hate, vengefulness, disgust, prejudice, or morbid curiosity toward the men and women and children he sees as an old-fashioned general practitioner. In my experience, Williams' stories are themselves healing; they help my Harvard medical students bring up and understand the big unmentionables, the passions of the heart that naturally tug people privy to the secrets, both mental and physical, of others.

It is ironic that the present dean of Harvard Medical School once, years ago, tried to get Williams to come to talk to a group of doctors at a major medical center. No, the New Jersey loner said; he had nothing to offer, and he was in fact surprised at the mention of any such invitation. For all his spells of urgent egoism (so poignantly and candidly confessed and examined in *Paterson*), William Carlos Williams was in large measure a shy and humble physician whose way with words went relatively unappreciated for a long time indeed. His so-called betters in medicine awed him. Any number of poets and critics awed him—hence his occasional self-protective and accusatory outbursts. We know from his correspondence (and those of us privileged to talk with him remember from his strong-minded words) that Harvard awed him. But he need not have been so self-doubting. Now, at the time of the hundredth anniversary of his birth, his poems, his stories, and his novels command the eager, attentive interest of poets and critics, to be sure, but also of college students and medical students, including those at places such as Harvard.

American Poetry Review, May/June 1983

Instances of Modernist Anti-Intellectualism

Not rarely, modernist writers have appeared to lose their aim or perhaps (as they certainly felt) to widen their aim: an assault upon the supposedly sterile, self-important academy might, for instance, turn into a bitter denunciation of intellectuals in general, including the very writer making the accusation. William Carlos Williams' *Paterson* starts with such a mode of social analysis and interpretation. We are to be offered "a local pride," a pointed reference to those who leave America for places such as London or Paris—or who leave small towns within our country for cultural centers, either big cities or celebrated universities. Next comes "a reply to Greek and Latin with the bare hands." It is a not very obscure effort to make a claim for a proud, contemporary, intellectual excitement, worthy of attention and approval: one of W. C. Williams' several versions of modernism—in this case, a working-class machismo appeal to folk wisdom, to the polyglot ethnic intuitions that a Paterson, New Jersey, general practitioner had come to know so well.

But Williams was not only taking on an arid classicism. He used the word *daring* provocatively as a truculent response to Eliot's Prufrock, a tough challenge to enemies in the present, never mind those lost in the ancient world. He repeats his animus in these lines, meant to raise the eyebrows of those familiar with the fifth and last section of Eliot's "Little Gidding":

> For the beginning is assuredly
> the end—since we know nothing, pure
> and simple, beyond
> our own complexities.

Then he escalates his assault even further and takes on "ideas," the entire ambitious enterprise of Theory. He treats abstract formula-

331

tions as a means of removing oneself from countless human experiences, including those a poet ought to know and address in his or her writing:

> and the craft,
> subverted by thought, rolling up, let
> him beware lest he turn to no more than
> the writing of stale poems . . .
> Minds like beds always made up,
> (more stony than a shore)
> unwilling or unable.

A harsh broadside: Williams is the antagonist, who uses Paterson, New Jersey, as a base of operations in a fiercely ambitious military campaign. A few lines further the commanding general sounds his clarion call, to be repeated again and again: "Say it, no ideas but in things." Let others become swollen-headed with thoughts, interpretations, and extended reifications. This poet and, he hoped, his readers would, in the powerful intimacy of a particular American lyrical celebration, cling tenaciously to the infinite, exuberant reality of the concrete, the everyday, the tangible and visible and audible.

> Sniffing the trees,
> just another dog
> among a lot of dogs. What
> else is there? And to do?
> The rest have run out—
> after the rabbits.

With such lines as these Williams escalated his polemics even further, presenting the artist as a street dog. Not a prissy human being, locked in a library, removed from the flesh's vitality; and speaking of human beings, not an aesthete, chasing rabbits in some far removed, all too "pretty" field. A mongrel in a factory town, out to survive today, then tomorrow: find the food, have some sex if it's available, empty the bladder and the bowels—and no highfalutin pretenses or postures. Man is an animal, and if he forgets that or denies that, he is living a big lie, and soon enough other lies get going.

Nor is Williams himself, for all his daring criticism of others, immune to the skeptical poet's eye. He poses a question that contains a devastating self-indictment, rendered decades before the subject of narcissism became yet another (narcissistic?) preoccupation of the American intelligentsia:

> Who are these people (how complex
> the mathematic) among whom I see myself
> in the regularly ordered plateglass of
> his thoughts, glimmering before shoes and bicycles?

Literary smugness, the writer's preening egotism, the poet knew, cannot be banished by a few slaps at others. Modernism meant taking chances—not only with language, images, and forms but also with the range and depth of one's self-observation. Williams uses the word *divorce* as a signal of sorts in the first book of *Paterson*; and he knows that one form of uprootedness or alienation, those fashionable twentieth-century statements, is the divorce of the social critic from the objects of his criticism: so long as I tear into a "them" with my words and speculations and grim approximations (sometimes amounting to not so flimsily disguised denunciations), I am myself safe, protected, clean, and wholesome. No, a truly radical survey of a world and its language demands a lacerating introspection and an earthy return to origins:

> A delirium of solutions, forthwith, forces
> him into back streets, to begin again:
> up hollow stairs among acrid smells
> to obscene rendezvous. And there he finds
> a festering sweetness of red lollipops—
> and a yelping dog:
> Come YEAH, Chichi! Or a great belly
> that no longer laughs but mourns
> with its expressionless black navel love's
> deceit.

In the event that anyone should fail to notice the determined nature of such a return to the elementary, to the urgently physical (again, the dog!), Williams lifts his flag of battle again (a version of it), with "No ideas but / in the facts"; and a little further on, he lances yet again the boil of his own self-centeredness: "How strange you are, you idiot!" Then, a few pages on, he fires off this blast:

We go on living, we permit ourselves
to continue—but certainly
not for the university, what they publish

severally or as a group: clerks
got out of hand forgetting for the most part
to whom they are beholden.

spitted on fixed concepts like
roasting hogs, sputtering, their drip sizzling
in the fire

Some of us who got to know Dr. Williams, even across the distance of age and residence, remember that the above could be considered an understatement of his, if placed in the overall spectrum of sentiments professed during a lifetime—especially those uttered among friends. But for his poetry, this was one of the blunter moments; the imagery intensifies rather than mollifies an argumentative statement. Clerks, as in *trahison des clercs:* the intellectual is charged with arrogance, with bullying pushiness. Moreover, there is another bill of divorcement entered in the growing annals of *Paterson*—heady professors who are removed in heart and mind and soul from others in a given community or region or nation. Lest the reader (not to mention the first reader, who wrote the words) be troubled by the self-serving nature of such anti-intellectualism (yet another "them," which affords protection to an "I," a "we") a prose segment follows immediately—in sum, a devastating portrait of the self-preoccupied, if not selfish, practicing doctor. His own idle reveries take precedence over the specific, here-and-now complaints of a vulnerable, needy, ailing group of patients, whose number and condition get spelled out: "Twenty and more infants taking their turn from the outer office, their mothers tormented and jabbering."

This was an unflinching look inward, a spell of Augustinian self-scrutiny—part of an intellectual tradition, actually, that has both a religious and a secular aspect. Williams desires membership in that tradition. He jabs at his own kind, writers and thinkers; then for good measure, he gives himself a good kick in the pants—but quickly moves to the poor of New Jersey in the Depression years, to the dreary banalities of a general culture saturated with materialism, much of it crooked: commerce and its discontents. We begin to wonder whether he is simply flailing—a poet anxious to be a wise philosopher, a shrewd observer of his fellow human beings, but unable to summon the necessary, sustained cohesion, the required largeness of outlook. When, toward the end of the first book, a line "the knowledgeable idiots, the university" appears, we notice a dangerous repetition—and wonder why, given the careful ambitiousness of this major modernist statement.

Williams begins to redeem himself in that last section of the first book with a kind of candor that transcends the constraints of bitterness and invective. Here is Augustine improved upon—the way Pascal tersely, if not poetically, managed to do in some of his _Pensées:_

> Moveless
> he envies the men that ran
> and could run off
> toward the peripheries—
> to other centers, direct—
> for clarity (if
> they found it)
>   loveliness and
> authority in the world—

The references to Pound and Eliot are obvious—they both escaped, leaving the Doc to tend the patients he found stimulating and nourishing but also wearing, distracting. Anyway, he was himself unable to follow suit, able only to confront lyrically his envy—and in a startling reference a few lines further, to acknowledge the "ice bound" quality to his mind that kept him confined. Ice and glass—both are elements of a writer's imprisonment within himself: "vanity of vanities," as it is put in the famous passage of _Ecclesiastes._ Here is poignant release through scrupulous self-arraignment—the jail is an anteroom, where the glass will break, the ice melt, so that William Carlos Williams may begin to do his dancing and singing in unashamed earnest, free of the malignant self-consciousness a poet has been ascribing to everyone, it seems—as a way, of course, to acknowledge the eager intellectual who is himself.

But repeated self-accusation can be a coy form of the very egotism being condemned. After a while self-rebuke reveals its narcissistic origins, as does an overworked humility. True enough, Williams would no doubt have been the first to admit. Still, there _is_ a difference between a narcissism of self-importance and a narcissism of self-criticism as a corrective for (as well as an expression of) that self-importance. The only release from such endless psychological inquiry is in others, in the outside world—hence the admonition at the very start of the second book of *Paterson:*

> Outside
>
>   outside myself
>
>   there is a world,
>
> he rumbled, subject to my incursions ,
> —a world
>
>   (to me) at rest,
>
>   which I approach
>
> concretely—

That last word is no offhand adverb thrown in as the poet rushes along to his subject matter. Again he is at it: the "approach" of *Paterson* must be distinctively at odds with the kind of comprehension congenial to other writers, cultural observers, social theorists, and yes, political polemicists or activists; all those for whom the world is a means to one or another overriding purpose—an essay or treatise or poem or book, a big conclusion, a series of definitions, a plan or objective or program.

Williams was not without the above; he embraced his own, idiosyncratic American populism. He dipped into the Social Credit movement, so influential, for a while, with his old friend Ezra Pound. Nor was Williams unable to reach out *generally* to a given population. *Paterson* is full of his social indignation, his sense that injustice rules the day, and his compassionate yearning for more equity in America. The poor were his patients, after all; and plenty of times he worked for nothing. He could be, on their behalf, enthusiastically nonconcrete:

> Minds beaten thin
> by waste—among
>
> the working classes SOME sort
> of breakdown
> has occurred. Semi-roused
>
> they lie upon their blanket
> face to face,
> mottled by the shadows of the leaves

> upon them, unannoyed,
> at least here unchallenged.

That collective "they"—and, needless to say, "the working classes": Dr. Williams is distanced, as have been countless sociologists, reformist advocates, and revolutionary organizers. True, he is usually ironic, at the very least, when he generalizes. He moves from "picnickers" to "voices! / multiple and inarticulate," and then to this line: "The 'great beast' come to sun himself." He is taking on, politically, Alexander Hamilton and his class-conscious capitalism; but he is also struggling with his own situation as the Rutherford physician/writer who lived in a quite pleasant Victorian home on Ridge Road and who was educated, traveled, and in so many ways a lucky, privileged man. He was not Hamilton's kind of aristocrat with Hamilton's social views, and not (or not yet) Harvard's kind of poet; he was still not prized, still not covered with honorary doctorates, but nevertheless on his way—and aware that he had always been, from birth on, all things considered, a singularly blessed animal (socially and economically) rather than an anonymous cell of the "great beast."

Such awareness was not denied the author of *Paterson*; rather, such awareness fuels his intermittent rage, his episodic anti-intellectualism. He cannot escape himself and does not desire to do so. He wants a cleansing change in the way people get on—a shared vision that somehow enables a successful triumph over certain of his longstanding foes, and academic snobbery was only one of them. He detested materialism and the debasement of human affairs (language, sex, the environment, learning) at the hands of modern exploitive industrialism: the story of the city of Paterson's demise. Yet he had no confidence, really, in any of the proposed twentieth-century solutions other intellectuals have found attractive: statism (be it in the name of socialism or fascism), psychoanalysis, the withdrawal into art, religion, or personal adventurism and fulfillment of one kind or another. Even his much announced inclination to the particular, as opposed to the schematic or the theoretic, was by no means an unqualified source of solace or hope to him. When, in the first book of *Paterson*, he denounces "the whole din of fracturing thought," he quickly has to insist: "the particular / no less vague." There are few consolations offered *this* intellectual; hence, perhaps, his despair—based not only on a dislike for others but on a gnawing knowledge of his own inadequacies.

The second book of *Paterson* is full of a poet's frustration. The problem is utterly contemporary. Paterson is "debased by the divorce from learning, / its garbage on the curbs, its legislators / under the garbage, uninstructed, incapable of / self instruction." Again, the teacher is impotent: what language, what manner of education, what effort of will and analysis can turn around such an impossible state of affairs? Some of Williams' anti-intellectualism is an expression of his moody bafflement. His modesty, too, expresses his hesitancy, his doubt. He could on occasion mobilize the very impatient hauteur he criticized so strenuously in others, especially professors and critics. But in the second book, especially, he is down-and-out, skeptical, worried about everyone and everything, and not in the least able to see a way through the general impasse he has been documenting, line after line, in a lyrical social history spiraling downward without letup.

That second book ends with a long letter from a rejected correspondent of Dr. P; the correspondent is Williams himself, of course—sparing himself and his kind little. This resort to sustained prose, rendered in the form of the letter, brings to mind Pascal's *Provincial Letters* and the structure of Georges Bernanos' novel *The Diary of a Country Priest*. Both Pascal and Bernanos knew the dangers of prophetic insistence yet were sorely tempted, as all writers are. Pascal put limits on himself through an aphoristic style and through the medium of the letter, which lends itself to the pastoral and the reflective as opposed to the declamatory and the exhortative. Bernanos was rescued by the novel's demands—though he knew that other novelists had used stories as a means of collaring readers with this or that idea, and he also knew how strongly his mind was drawn to political journalism, the social essay, and religious controversy. In *The Diary of a Country Priest*, he finds a solution in the diary—a means by which grace can be given an incarnation without embarrassment. The priest's writing reveals him to be (like Dr. Williams in *Paterson*) troubled, confused, and self-critical. The priest lacks the fire in Williams' belly, but he shares with him a distrust of the high-and-mighty, in and out of the Church. There is, too, a streak of anti-intellectualism, easily recognized as that of Bernanos but worked tactfully into the ruminations of this somewhat desolate curé, a tragic figure indeed. And yet, he is a figure whose dignity and courage we gradually come to realize and admire. Even

his admitted mistakes and blunders and moments of excess somehow adorn him in our minds. His words are honest; they are meant
for no one else's eyes. We can be kind and generous to him—as
he cannot be to himself without the severe risks of manipulative self-
regard.

Similarly with *Paterson*, and in particular with the long, complaining letter that closes the second book: "You've never had to
live, Dr. P—not in any of the by-ways and dark underground passages where life so often has to be tested," she tells him. Then she
strikes at his vulnerable, writing self: "The very circumstances of
your birth and social background provided you with an escape from
life in the raw; and you confuse that protection from life with an
inability to live—and are thus able to regard literature as nothing
more than a desperate last extremity resulting from that illusionary
inability to live. (I've been looking at some of your autobiographical
works, as this indicates.)"

She spells out her differences with Dr. P further in a devastating
paragraph that gets to the very center of Williams' felt tension, in
Paterson, between art and conduct. Living, she stresses, is not something one plans, constructs, or *decides* to do. Life happens, "in a
small way, like measles; or in a big way, like a leaking boat or an
earthquake." He "brings to life," she charges, "purely literary sympathies and understandings, the insights and humanity of words on
paper *only*—and also, alas, the ego of the literary man." He is the
imposter who knows others of his own ilk, abandons their sinking
ship through angry verbal blasts at them, and tries to masquerade as
an enraged ordinary Paterson citizen—yet by his own admission, he
makes "incursions." Anti-intellectualism, she implies, is a form of
manipulation as well as an indication of self-loathing. The expression of anti-intellectualism is, at its best, confessional; at its worst, it
is an act of illusionary self-purification. The resort to "her" letter in
Paterson represents, it would seem, a penitential exercise; it is the
poet saying: I know the aforementioned, all of it, and can only use
words, once again, in the service of a self-critical truth about the
writer and those who read him devotedly.

Williams, we know, was constantly attracted to autobiography.
Little in his own life, including the life of his beloved Flossie's family (the Stecher trilogy), escaped the writer in him. But his anti-
intellectualism seemed also to be a constant attraction—and when

used, it was subject to his writer's censoring skills: intelligence, a sense of proportion, a respect for factuality, the desire to be clear, pointed, convincing. Modernism, so proximate historically with psychoanalysis and the devastating social satire of, say, Expressionist painters—never mind the probing of such political, intellectual, and literary figures as Kurt Weill, Gramsci, and Lukács—would naturally welcome Williams' socially conscious, morally earnest, emotionally relentless self-scrutiny. The intellectuals become, for Williams, a foil, a means of being all the tougher on himself. Without his vigorous explication of their sins, we would be tempted to dismiss his enunciation of his own failings, if not misdemeanors, as overwrought and unnecessary. Instead, we take him seriously with respect to himself, feel rather pained about ourselves, and are maybe even tempted to follow suit: to use that exclusively human disposition, language, as a weapon against someone, anyone, a bit like ourselves, who works in a library or a classroom.

One final function of anti-intellectualism in the modernist canon: it is a means of both connecting with and dispensing with a tradition. The Williams who assaults intellectuals is also the Williams who quotes them with evident interest and favor—as in the reference to John Addington Symonds' *Studies of the Greek Poets* given us at the end of the first book of *Paterson*. Williams did, after all, write *In the American Grain*, showing thereby that his writing makeup included the learned social historian. He was not barbarous; rather, he was a polemical enthusiast who wanted his intellectual allies to fight hard against their enemies. Modernism has been, in so many instances, a recourse to past invigorations, too brusquely and completely set aside by various "principalities and powers," so the particular, agitated modernist claims. Let the bullying interpretations be set aside, let the original voices be heard or new ones in this fresh linkage with those original ones: Williams, through Symonds, to Hipponax and his iambics, ending with a spondee or a trochee rather than the compulsory iambus.

Similarly with James Agee's agitated, exalted, burdensome, fuming, penetrating, vexing, and triumphant *Let Us Now Praise Famous Men*, a major tirade against all forms, all sorts and conditions of language; and curiously, at times, despite the dramatic, rebellious indulgences and discursive tirades, an effort that offers, finally, rather traditional lyrics—biblical not only in title, and Shakespearean not only by virtue of a significant, introductory reference to *King Lear*. This prose-poem, like *Paterson*, is fairly saturated with self-lacerating, titillating, provocative anti-intellectual passages—which feed grandly anyone's iconoclastic fires. *Let Us Now Praise Famous Men* is not only a young writer's piece of work, a masterpiece of the literary-documentary tradition (and perhaps, in it, the very last improvisation possible), but also a young reader's exercise. The energy is catching—an exhilaration to those starting out but wearying, one suspects, to many well along in this life. Agee himself aged considerably under the burden of this, his one major book. As for its anti-intellectualism, it is as brazen and unguarded and punishing as anything Williams has given us: "Most children prefer pleasure to boredom, lacking our intelligence to reverse this preference"; or, also in connection with children, "They are much too innocent to understand the profits of docility"; or with regard to academic people, "Disregarding the proved fact that few doctors of philosophy are literate, that is, that few of them have the remotest idea how to read, how to say what they mean, or what they mean in the first place . . ." These are some choice moments of but one, comparatively short section titled "Education"—wherein the author, as a sort of bonus, tells us this with regard to his subject, the Alabama sharecroppers of Hale County: "I could not wish of any one of them that they should have had the 'advantages' I have had: a Harvard education is by no means an unqualified advantage."

No need to dredge up more examples; they abound. They also uncannily resemble, in their sum, those of Dr. Williams, in the references to "vanity," in the surly self-denigration, rendered so trenchantly one cannot but be reminded that here is a first-rate writer whose self-imposed lashing is being done with great and singular panache. Agee's anger is directed at New York intellectuals; at the *Partisan Review* in its late 1930s, early 1940s heyday; at his beloved alma mater, Harvard; at Franklin D. Roosevelt, not exactly an enemy of America's Depression-era poor; at schoolteachers and college professors; at everyone, it seems, but his tenant farmer hosts, whose ignorance he acknowledges but then (almost a tic) contrasts favorably with the deadness and deceit that characterize—well, the life he lives, the kind of people he knows to call friends, colleagues, lovers. All in all a great performance: the privileged intellectual is a tormentor, a villainous spy, a phony, a pompous ass, an unknowing, pretentious fool—thereby springing James Agee, sending him into the company of the Alabama damned, the last who will one day be first.

And why not? James Agee did, indeed, belong spiritually with his Southern country people, the "famous" ones he tried so hard to love, warts and all (to repeat, there is a price for his modernist romanticism: the warts of Alabama folk go significantly unnoticed, or perhaps, unmentioned). His heart was large, even as his pride was (he knew) great and assertive. He wanted to conquer a certain world, and his "three families" were in bad need of someone who could help them fight, and with some chance of victory. On the other hand, words, even the brilliant, summoning juxtapositions of them in this extended oratorio, do not beat politicians and plantation owners and factory owners; not even foundation executives (the Guggenheim people also get it from Agee) or magazine editors can always be won over with language, however sublime. Anti-intellectualism becomes, therefore, a balm for the hurt frustration of basically gentle, giving souls, a kind of hate that seems therapeutic yet inconsequential (only the intellectuals will notice, and they can be counted on to understand, excuse, even to enjoy themselves). Of course, there is always a boiling point—not to mention a point of no return: Ezra Pound's references to American education as full of "syphilis," to American cultural life as full of "dry rot," were sad enough (and of a different order of animus than either that of Williams or Agee), but his sallies against American academics (and, as a matter of fact, against the same president, F. D. Roosevelt, to whom Williams and Agee were not always kind) eventually became unforgivably mean, wild, and in the end, as sadly incomprehensible as crazy talk can often be.

As Flannery O'Connor let us know in her letters (*The Habit of Being*), a writer's anti-intellectualism can be a variant of self-examination, self-parody—and an indirect call for mercy, an appeal for forgiveness in the Christian tradition. She lets us know that the Joy who turned into Hulga of "Good Country People" needs no gratuitous psychiatric interpretation from us. An author had done some sweating about herself and her kind. In story after story, as a matter of fact, O'Connor gives us pitiable, pretentious renderings of "interleckchuls"—the unpleasant spelling, used in her letters, is a sort of added boost. One thinks of poor Asbury in "The Enduring Chill" and poor Julian in "Everything That Rises Must Converge" and poor Sheppard in "The Lame Shall Enter First"—all the same character, really: heady (as in Mr. Head of "The Artificial Nigger") and so headed for comeuppance if not perdition. Modernism outside Dixie has given us grotesquerie in the short story, and so why not a few Southern oddball thinkers or pseudothinkers who try to read books and go to the North or become shrinky and reform-minded in their approach to life! There is, as always with O'Connor, a tough, astringent side to such portraits, but as one considers her own brave yet vulnerable life, one realizes that with her, too, as with W. C. Williams, as with James Agee, an anti-intellectualism is a cry of sorts, a cry of self-recognition and a cry of shame; it is also a promise that through the writer's craft there will be an attempt at transcendence, an attempt at healing through mocking self-disclosure—an example and a warning to the rest of us.

In *Modernism Reconsidered*, 1983

"Physician, heal thyself"

I well remember the interested skepticism William Carlos Williams brought to psychoanalysis. He had read Freud closely, intelligently, with admiration, and saw him (he once characteristically put it) as "a helluva doc—who let his imagination run loose, and then corralled it in with a writer's shrewd skill, and the next thing, of course, is the world watching with the greatest of interest, and there you have it, fame." Dr. Williams, with that summary, demonstrated his own "shrewd skill" at taking the measure of another writing doctor. But he went further, addressing readers of Freud (and surely himself and all other moralists disguised as doctors or as literary folk) with these remarks:

> The problems fame brings are big ones. The famous one can get a big head. He can get drunk on fame. He can swagger. He can end up believing his every word, and expecting everyone else to do the same—or else! And I'll tell you, often he's not disappointed enough! Too many of us are ready to crawl on our empty bellies before some big fellah who comes along and says he knows more than anyone else about something and he'll throw some crumbs our way, if we—well, *believe* him, rather than try to understand him, and say *right* here, but *maybe* there, and *wrong* here. When I read Freud, for instance, I'm told about "transference"—that if I'm his patient I load him up, in my head, with all the wrong-headed and crazy ideas I had about the people I knew as a kid, my folks (naturally!) and others, too, I guess. My psychoanalyst friends tell me "transference" is the biggest deal there is in treatment: you watch it develop, and you figure out when and how to take it on, show the patient what it's about. Then you're on your way to losing a patient—if you do it right. (If you do it

wrong, you also lose the patient—but that's another story, the
bad way to lose a patient!)

Of course, there's "counter-transference," too. Freud mentions it, and every once in a while (rare as can be!) a doc will
mention "counter-transference" to me, a psychoanalyst will.
That's the doctor loading up his pistol with his own mess of
a life and shooting it at the patient! Hell, I don't mean to be
nasty with my images—and anyway, I've noticed that "counter-
transference" isn't the big thing "transference" is. There's
much more talk—and writing—about "transference" than
"counter-transference." Why not? Doctors have the power
and patients are the ones you call "sick," not the docs! But the
real problem is the nature of this kind of criticism of others
and of yourself. I worry: those concepts of transference and
counter-transference don't deal with the reality of mistakes,
of errors—of a bastard who thinks and says the wrong thing
about another human being. You can't just hide behind your
childhood all your life—or someone else's! You're a doctor,
and you can make mistakes as a doctor, as a psychoanalyst—
apart from "transference" or "counter-transference!"

There's no point in taking such a conversational moment (tape-
recorded in 1960) and turning it into a biblical occasion; but that
moment has lingered in my mind over the years, as have other moments of that writing physician's self-awareness, if not self-scrutiny
and self-criticism—moments in Dr. Williams' great, lyrical examination of the American experience, *Paterson*. He was ever the blunt
observer of others, not interested in the sly condescensions of flattery
or effusive admiration. He distrusted his own ambitious competence
as a writer, his own ready capacity to find a few approximating words
for each and every person, place, or thing: slap those words on and
voilà—a great way of letting the world know not only about someone or something but about the wonderful one who offered the language, the appraisal, the judgment. Even as he could get to the
heart of the matter, with respect to the potential difficulties of moral
criticism (and self-criticism) in a culture overtaken with psychoanalytic imagery, he was not willing to exempt the poet or novelist from
a similar kind of tough regard.

The first two books of *Paterson*, as a matter of fact, find him repeatedly submitting himself to a direct, unflinching, even unnerving self-arraignment—credibly, convincingly, poignantly managed, lest the reader be conned into disbelief (and the writer be conveniently let off the hook). At the very beginning of *Paterson* the narrator emphasizes particularity and shuns general statements and esthetic self-importance: "The rest have run out— / after the rabbits." That line is often interpreted as a jab at T. S. Eliot and Ezra Pound, at their European sophistications (intellectual and social both) in contrast to his determination to stay in northern New Jersey and be a working doctor for those who lived in Paterson's tenements. But Williams knew that even such a commitment didn't protect him from his own moments of snobbish disdain for one or another of "them." His doctor stories, written in the 1930s before *Paterson*, reveal a physician openly struggling with his annoyance and irritation at the various habits or remarks of his patients, at the cultural distance between them and him.

His anger is often correctly attributed by literary critics to the drain that medical practice put on him—keeping him from what he felt to be so important, his writing. Moreover, he was not at all well paid for his extremely hardworking medical life; an all-around "general practitioner," he delivered babies and took care of them as well as their parents. The resentments he felt—natural even in a doctor of his sort who had no literary life—sought their expression. And sometimes his eager embrace of every coarse detail of New Jersey working-class life seems like an eminently civilized response to that dilemma, an effort to embrace what (at other moments) bothers the hell out of you. He calls himself "just another dog / among a lot of dogs"; but he knew that he wasn't one, in certain respects, or that he was of a highbred variety, with his vast learning that mingled easily (and noticeably) with the raw expressions of ordinary ethnic life he found so stimulating, so congenial, and which he used with such brilliant success.

Still, he knew he must observe himself as well as others. He kept insisting that a writer whose big ideas about life go unconnected to the workaday lives of individual people may be seduced into hermetic egoism. "Outside / outside myself / there is a world," he reminded himself in a powerful introductory moment at the very start of the second book of *Paterson*, and it is a world he sought to "approach / concretely"—again the implied remonstrance to himself as well as to those handy others. Through the immediately preceding words (taken from John Addington Symonds' *Studies of the Greek Poets*), Williams is telling the reader that there is an old and important tradition in poetry for the use of "common speech," as in Hipponax and others. Needless to say, the attempt of the poet to justify his pursuits is confessional; it is an aspect of his admitted membership in a particular smug and sometimes self-important world he also wants to leave, or at the very least, to see with the fresh eyes of an outsider.

Early in the first book of *Paterson* a prose section suddenly appears, out of nowhere it seems. A correspondent of the narrator/poet/physician tells him in a letter that she wants back the poems she sent him and that it was "the human situation and not the literary one" that prompted her to write to him. She declares herself concerned "less with the publishers of poetry than with . . . living." This is the beginning of what turns out to be a powerful prose self-arraignment, a lyric poet's running commentary meant to emphasize what he fears he may lack, as well as what he very much hopes to espouse—a commitment to this world's complex, demanding, often ironic or paradoxical or perplexing or frustrating but constantly invigorating everyday life. Ideas, he will say repeatedly in *Paterson*, have to be accompanied by action, lest the two become absurdly and dangerously polarized alternatives. The abstract requires a lifeline connection to the concrete. Theory must embrace practice and dare to be tested by it. Spoken ideals are high-sounding banalities, mere excuses for self-indulgence, self-promotion, and self-satisfaction, unless affirmed in the conduct of one's life. Similarly with "poetry" and "living"—an interesting and important distinction for a poet to make at the very beginning of his masterpiece.

I know from conversations with Williams, begun when I was a college student working on a study of his poems and continued through my medical studies and beyond, how much he worried that a major occupational hazard of being a writer, not to mention being a doctor, is self-importance, pomposity, or the sin of pride: "Twice a month Paterson receives / communications from the Pope and Jacques Barzun." Just a bit further on, the first book of *Paterson* offers this question: "Who are these people (how complex / the mathematic) among whom I see myself / in the regularly ordered plateglass of / his thoughts, glimmering before shoes and bicycles?" When George Eliot in *Middlemarch* wrote of "unreflecting egoism," she recognized the urgency of that question. For Williams it is a writer's plea, a doctor's plea, to himself that he somehow keep struggling to recognize the truths that exist—the reality that exists, the entire life that exists—beyond his own feverish mind, which he is frank to acknowledge as somewhat encased in glass, as with the narcissist whose reflection gets mirrored by water or, in this instance, by "plateglass."

The moral arithmetic of his life and his patients' lives ought to be reckoned; and he realized that their preoccupations with possessions, "shoes and bicycles" and on and on, are more than matched by his own. Poems, books, articles, bank balances, professional degrees, hospital affiliations—we all have our way of immersing ourselves in the distinctions and achievements that we crave and yet occasionally realize to be confining and maybe even spiritually killing. "They walk incommunicado," he goes on to observe, referring to the social isolation or loneliness many of his patients had reported to him. But he quickly reminds himself of the terrible dangers that await the one who has his own dangers to face, a person like himself who wants to be anything but "incommunicado," but who may nonetheless unwittingly be talking only to himself or to a very select few.

A bit further on he will note how "the language, the language / fails them." I remember, on the other hand, how strongly stimulated he was by the language of his working-class patients, whose blunt, earthy prose was free of the indirections, if not evasions, of a language he himself had learned to master. He found the talk of his poor and working-class patients stimulating and even necessary for his own survival as a poet, essayist, and novelist. A medical practice constantly fed a writer's appetite for experience. He was always turning to listen: "Voices! / multiple and inarticulate. Voices / clattering loudly to the sun, to / the clouds. Voices! / assaulting the air gaily from all sides." The contrast between their vigor and what he heard in colleges and universities troubled him—obsessed him, really: "the whole din of fracturing thought."

This anti-intellectual side of Williams is instructive. It links him with a number of other twentieth-century American writers (James Agee, Flannery O'Connor, and Walker Percy), and its roots lie in Emerson's distinction, in "The American Scholar," between "character" and "intellect." Emerson's *Journals* contain plenty of jibes at the academy and its members, but Williams worked that theme of intellectual aridity and arrogance—the scholar as snotty, dreary pedant—all too vigorously: "We go on living, we permit ourselves / to continue—but certainly / not for the university, what they publish / severally or as a group: clerks / got out of hand forgetting for the most part / to whom they are beholden. / spitted on fixed concepts like / roasting hogs, sputtering, their drip sizzling / in the fire." Yet just after that truculent outburst the language becomes prose, and a doctor confronts himself resolutely, unflinchingly: "He was more concerned, much more concerned with detaching the label from a discarded mayonnaise jar, the glass jar in which some patient had brought a specimen for examination, than to examine and treat the twenty and more infants taking their turn from the outer office, their mothers tormented and jabbering." There is more, and in its sum the doctor-poet levels at himself the same accusation he has directed elsewhere: his own self-centered pedantry risks excluding acts of considerate, responsive caring. If a few lines down there is another shrill assault on "the knowledgeable idiots, the university," the reader is prepared; he or she can recall the mayonnaise jar and the doctor preoccupied with labels, while his patients anxiously await him. Moreover, it is at this point that Williams comes clean on Eliot and Pound and other academically acclaimed poets he so often has insulted: "he envies the men that ran / and could run off / toward the peripheries." How many of us in medicine and psychiatry, or in literary criticism, how many who write poems and stories and plays, dare risk that kind of self-regard with a strong self-inflicted wound, a doctor's jab at his own solar plexus?

In the second book of *Paterson* the correspondent's prose appears at much greater length; and this woman who writes to Williams is, of course, himself addressing himself, sharply, devastatingly. He is accused of "ignoring the real contents" of her letters, of misunderstanding (in essence) himself, his intentions, and hopes, and of a kind of self-betrayal. He is accused of becoming an exile, as it were, from himself, the same "psychological injury" he has been at such pains to describe in all those impoverished, uneducated people who make up much of Paterson's population. One reads this and thinks of the social critics, the social theorists, the social scientists who carry on about our "mass-men," our "alienated" and "deracinated" ones: everyone but thee and me.

In further prose passages Williams continues with the most intense kind of self-scrutiny, a severe and unhesitating Augustinian self-confrontation. The correspondent becomes coy, arch, a bit long-winded (and at times medically pompous) in her self-protectiveness. Once more, that correspondent is really Williams, the doctor-writer who knows how to cover up his own doubts, mixed feelings, and confusions through all sorts of contrived postures, with psychological and literary language providing their eminent and debasing energy. The correspondent also becomes strenuously self-pitying: "I do not come easily to confidences . . . And so my having heaped these confidences upon you (however tiresome you may have found them and however far I may yet need to go in the attainment of *complete* self-honesty which is difficult for anyone) was enough in itself to have caused my failure with you to have so disastrous an effect upon me." These accusations (and not a few writers and doctors, no doubt, have experienced such from those who have written to them) are also, needless to say, self-directed. The struggle for a personal candor and decency is a long and hard one; there are so many mistakes, errors, lapses into deception or self-deception or both—and so, one inevitably feels sorry for oneself.

At the end of the second part of the second book of *Paterson*, the writing doctor's correspondent yet again appears, now berating him for his "indifferent evasion" of her letters and acknowledging the gap between her "true self" and "that which can make only mechanical gestures of living." She also dares to say that she has lost "faith in the reality" of her own thoughts and desperately wants to "recapture" a "sense" of her "own personal identity." The word "identity" has become a buzzword for many of us whose abiding secular faith is psychology. But Williams used "identity" long before Erik H. Erikson's *Childhood and Society* had appeared; he used the word as George Eliot had used it in *Middlemarch*, when she tackled those biblical, existentialist questions about one's ongoing life: what kind of person am I, and what kind of life am I pursuing, ought I pursue? Williams tells himself and his readers that if his poetry is affirming, soaring, absorbing, entrancing, or edifying and his life is sadly inadequate, pitiable, hypocritical, exploitative of others, or haughty and presumptuous (themes of "character" he addresses in his writing constantly), then such a disparity, at the very least, ought to be admitted as possible and emphasized as one more ironic element in life—as the mean and melancholy inadequacy of our actions, whatever our words. If the words speak louder than the actions—why then, we are lost utterly, says a writer who dares despair of himself in front of his reading public. Williams lays his condition bare, boldly examining his laurels, so that his readers might know whom it is they read, and in so doing, learn perhaps about their own moral and religious assumptions.

Williams' despair, fiery and self-lacerating but also boldly summoned to enable his searching examination of *Paterson*, of America, and of himself, reaches a culmination in a long prose passage concluding the third section of the second book. Our correspondent, being the woman she is, confronts the doctor in an extraordinary prefiguration of today's liberation struggle: it is one final reminder by Williams *to* Williams that he has not really dared do justice to his own artistic (feminine) underpinnings, nor has he made the morally requisite connection between his personal struggles as a sometimes neglected or rejected writer and the struggle of so many others, be they writers or ordinary people, who all the time experience the contempt of their so-called betters.

> You've never had to live, Dr. P—not in any of the by-ways and dark underground passages where life so often has to be tested. The very circumstances of your birth and social background provided you with an escape from life in the raw; and you confuse that protection from life with an *inability* to live— and are thus able to regard literature as nothing more than a desperate last extremity resulting from that illusionary inability to live. (I've been looking at some of your autobiographical works, as this indicates.)

She has a good deal more to say: an indictment of "the ego of the literary man," an accusation that the doctor-writer "brings to life . . . purely literary sympathies and understandings, the insights and humanity of words on paper *only.*"

So it went for him, that astonishingly open and humble man who dared take on his own pride and vanity in hopes that his readers might make a similar effort. Williams offers us good clean anger that never turns into sadism or masochism; it is used by the man with the stethoscope and the typewriter as a means of clinical, social, and literary observation, investigation, affirmation. Among his exemplary gifts to us, the audacious yielding to self-criticism is surely one of the most significant. It is a rare and earnestly meant declaration of solidarity with all of America's humble and hard-pressed people, who know how cruelly swollen with pride the world's influential and successful ones so often are, despite the biblical warning about who shall in the long run be first and who shall be last.

Times of Surrender

To Shawn Maher and Phillip Pulaski

Contents

Introduction

When I was a resident in child psychiatry at the Children's Hospital in Boston during the late 1950s, I was strenuously challenged and tested by a twelve-year-old boy who had all sorts of psychiatric labels attached to him—in the hospital chart and in my eagerly categorical mind. He was "impulsive." He had a "learning disability." Worse, he was "phobic" about school, reluctant to go and anxious while there. He had a "problem with authority." He had a "borderline personality"— a dire statement, indeed, with ominous implications for the future. All in all, this child, whom his parents called Junior for the usual, familial reason that he bore his father's name, seemed headed nowhere fast.

Junior was shy at first, and taciturn; but as we got to know each other better he became more forthcoming, and soon enough I began to realize how much sadness and disappointment and turmoil he had known already in the course of his brief life, as a consequence of the real events that had overtaken his family as well as his own mind's response to those events: his father's alcoholism and his mother's chronic and severe rheumatoid arthritis, with all the psychological as well as medical ramifications of both those diseases. The lad liked to play checkers a lot, and it was during those games, actually, that I learned the most about him. A sharp and careful player, he often trapped me, beat me—and as I would be stalled in some corner of the checkerboard, contemplating a seemingly inevitable disaster, he would talk about what had happened during the week or, for that matter, months or even years earlier. His remarks, of course, only distracted me further from the game at hand—and I began to realize that Junior had in his bright and observant way figured out my predicament: the earnest checkers player who was ever so anxious to hear more and more from a patient could be weakened by the patient's talking.

One day, as we were nearing the end of yet another game of checkers, Junior surveyed with tactful self-assurance my gloomy prospects. I was moving my black king back and forth in one of those corners of the board where losers are apt to take their last stand. "It's time to surrender," Junior announced. I can still remember the words, the look on his young face: eyes wide open and staring right at me rather than the board, the faintest of smiles, the front teeth showing, including the noticeable gap between two of his lower front ones. I didn't like the look, not that day. I said nothing. I kept moving back and forth, sending thereby my message: all right, fellow, come and get me. All right, he would. Rather as our navy gathers its boats from across the seas to one troubled spot, Junior marshaled his four crowned players. The closer he came to the coup de grace, the more annoyed I became—not only with him but myself: what was all this accomplishing? What would my supervisor, an experienced child psychoanalyst, think of these proceedings—of me as a novice, learning to work with children? Suddenly, Junior stopped short of finishing me off. He said he'd wait me out—and, of course, he put me on the spot: want to waste the entire "therapeutic hour"? I hesitated and made a gesture of continued resistance. He once more mentioned surrender as a suitable alternative, and I simply folded—whereupon he said, unforgettably: "Sometimes, if you surrender you're winning, because you're free of worrying about losing and you can find a better game for yourself!" There was a long pause—and then, as if to prove himself right, Junior for the first time mentioned some troubles he'd been having at home and asked for my sense of what they meant. Later, my supervisor would call that session "the start of therapy" for Junior.

Later that week, I found myself reading Freud's well-known essay "Dostoevski and Parricide," his effort to understand a great writer's personality and to indicate how a writer's fiction can be a response to his psychological difficulties. It is in this essay that Freud makes an interesting, edifying, and important renunciation of sorts: "*The Brothers Karamazov* is the most magnificent novel written; the episode of the Grand Inquisitor, one of the peaks in the literature of the world, can hardly be valued too highly. Before the problem of the creative artist, analysis must, alas, lay down its arms." In a sense, I began to realize, Junior had issued a similar warning to me. He had told me many times that I ought stop trying to "figure him out"—

and especially, he had been adamant about his checker-playing brilliance as a subject of my psychological inquiry: its purposes, its rationale in his overall emotional makeup. To be sure, he had his own "resistance" to a doctor's scrutiny, and it would not have been right for me to yield, in that respect, to his requests for an hour free of personal discussion. But he was, in his own manner, letting me know that my psychiatric and psychoanalytic intensity and eagerness ought to have limits—that at a certain point Freud's exemplary (though reluctant) modesty ought be remembered. I was all too full of youthful professional enthusiasm and no small measure, if not an excess, of ideological conviction—the heady faith of a mid-twentieth-century, agnostic upper bourgeois who was convinced that psychological analysis would provide answers to every one of life's problems, impasses, riddles. Such a naive Freudianism was, unfortunately, not only my particular idée fixe, as I think Junior knew when he cast his friendly, yet skeptical, glance at not only me but the clinic he entered once a week.

Gradually we got down to business, Junior and I; we worked at some of his troubles, and I learned to enjoy his capacity to play checkers and chess, too. This bright, sensitive, introspective boy helped me figure out not only some of *his* problems but some of mine, too—a lack of respect, at times, for the distinction between the intellect's realm, and yes, that of the spirit, too, as against the domain so often affected by our psychological burdens, if not demons. As Anna Freud once put it: "There are times when we can only be grateful for a child's mastery or talent—and at such times we ought not pause too long with our psychoanalytic questions." She knew so well how appropriate our questions are when connected to other times in a child's life. Her remarks, that is, were meant to be cautionary rather than an expression of fundamental skepticism or despair.

The foregoing is meant not to be discursive but rather to be a quite pointed prelude to the essays that follow. They form an account, really, of my struggle to find a point of view for myself that made sense, as I did my medical and psychiatric work but also tried to remember what Junior had taught me, not to mention the two Freuds and others in their tradition. Many of the essays that follow are witnesses of sorts to that struggle. All too often in recent decades, some of us in the social sciences have been unwilling to put suffi-

cient constraint upon ourselves, unwilling to accept times of surrender before life's thickness, its complexities, ironies, ambiguities,
and its chancy nature—meaning the ever-present possibilities (for
the good and bad, both) that arrive at our doorstep through luck,
fate, circumstance, or accident. One decides to make a turn, then—
a turn to our Dostoevskis, not with intrusive and all-encompassing
determinism but with respect and gratitude to our novelists and
poets and painters for their effort to understand the world, to do justice to its various aspects, to render it faithfully and suggestively and
compellingly. I think these essays, written during the past two decades or so, have that turn as a common theme—a turn to literature
as helpful, indeed, for one of my ilk.

I have let these essays stand as they were written. They address,
variously, my professional life, my work with children, my interest
in religion and politics. I have written books on those matters and
twice before collected essays on some of them—*A Farewell to the
South* (1972) and *The Mind's Fate* (1975). None of the essays that
appear here are to be found in those books, and many of the ones in
this book were written after those books appeared. In the past ten
years I have put a lot of energy into teaching medical students and
college students, and some of the writing that follows reflects that
commitment of time and effort. I have also tried to figure out how
to discuss moral questions with those students—in such a way that
they can connect what they learn to the way they live, no easy task
for any of us. In that regard, novels and short stories are a wonderful
resource, and some of the writing in the pages that follow has been
the result of my experience with such fiction in two ways, as the
solitary reader and as the teacher in a seminar or the lecturer before
a class.

Novelists such as Georges Bernanos or Dickens were no strangers
to their own kind of surrender. Like Freud, they respected the limits
a story demands, the requirements of plot and character portrayal.
Bernanos had no interest in using fiction to construct theology; nor
was Dickens taken with political science and psychology as disciplines—though, of course, both of those magicians of language
manage to convey experience wondrously: the nature of religious experience, or the nature of a kind of human experience we know all
too well today, the bureaucrat or political functionary or lawyer at
work. I rather suspect that it would not hurt some of us to become a

bit more intimate with writers such as Bernanos or Dickens, not only because they entertain us and keep us enthralled but because they have a very special way of instructing us—not through ambitious or pushy generalization and formulation but through relatively modest evocation of life in all its contrariness and with all its inconsistencies.

"Don't rush to clinical judgment," the psychoanalyst who supervised me as I worked with Junior repeatedly emphasized. That elderly and wise man worried about my nervous wish to tuck anything and everything under some broad theoretical rubric. Once, sensing those few words weren't enough, he went further and urged that I watch closely, listen hard, and "try to absorb the boy's story, as he lets you in on it." I was struck by his way of putting things—at such variance with the abstract, highly theoretical discussions I was having with any number of psychoanalytic teachers at that time in my life. I think I've held on to that bit of advice rather tenaciously over the years, and I think the essays in this book, in their various ways, reveal me still trying to do so. It would be a big boost for many of us if the world at large (America's late-twentieth-century culture) were more encouraging along those lines—less enamored of the conceits of theory. Still, there are plenty of encouragements around: the well-known writers of the past and present; or a wonderful gift that can be handed to us, out of nowhere, it seems—such as John Baskin's delightful and quite special *New Burlington*, a book that makes a whole library of sociology seem, somehow, not all that interesting.

I will not pursue the grinding of this particular ax any further here—only warn the reader of further attempts to come: a theme, a continuity, in the pages ahead. I conclude here with thanks to Paul Zimmer, Holly Carver, Brien Woods, and Wayne Arnold for their help with the emergence of this book, and especially to Shawn Maher and Phil Pulaski, who helped me in so many ways in that Harvard office during the past six years.

January 1988

Psychiatry, Psychology, and Literature

Unreflecting Egoism

We are not doing well at all, the historian Christopher Lasch tells us in his latest book, *The Culture of Narcissism*. He links his psychological title to a sociological subtitle: *American Life in an Age of Diminishing Expectations*. He wants to show us how the latter is connected to the development of the former. He is a strong-minded cultural theorist, eager to reveal us to ourselves—an ironic effort, he must know, because if many of us have turned into the narcissists he describes, then it is narcissism itself, and not the desire for psychological insight, that will prompt an excited rush on our part to glimpse even this severely disapproving picture of our mental habits. His argument draws its ammunition from a growing psychoanalytic literature, which itself is a response to the everyday clinical work of psychiatrists, who have for years recognized the usefulness and importance of the concept of narcissism. As early as 1914, Freud observed that certain patients, much hurt in various ways at an early age, had essentially given up as far as love for others was concerned.

A child who is often rebuffed or who has to face constant irrational shifts in the emotional behavior of a mother or a father may learn to be exceedingly guarded toward people. The child also feels sorely aggrieved, hence resentful. Since the outside world is so untrustworthy, so unreliable (seductively there one moment, achingly absent the next), the child falls back on himself or herself with a certain vengeance. Rather than take emotional risks and quite possibly end up losing, the mind concludes that it would do best to stick with itself, so to speak. The result is what George Eliot called "unreflecting egoism"—a driven kind of self-centeredness that dominates a person's mental life. Today's psychiatrists refer to "the narcissistic character disorder"—the affliction of one whose central, controlling ways of getting on give evidence of a strong avoidance of lasting attachments to other people, accompanied often by a hunger for just such human bonds and, in the realm of feeling, by an anger

3

(whose severity may not be recognized) at one's fate. There may be, too, a hard-to-shake sadness and a feeling of emptiness, of being lost, with no real hope of being found—by anyone.

Of course, we have all had our psychologically doubtful and threatening moments—in infancy, later childhood, youth, and beyond. Everyone has learned to fall back on his or her own resources, ideas, and daydreams. Few of us have failed to experience moments when just about no one seems worth counting on—except the self, as a body that needs care, a mind that needs its satisfactions. As is always the case in psychiatry, the issue is quantitative—the extent of a particular person's self-preoccupation and the effect it has on the way he or she lives. But Lasch insists that the issue today is also historical and cultural. He wants to make a connection between what he calls "the clinical aspects of the narcissistic syndrome" and "certain characteristic patterns of contemporary culture, such as the intense fear of old age and death, altered sense of time, fascination with celebrity, fear of competition, decline of the play spirit, deteriorating relations between men and women." His book is really a collection of essays meant to show that the so-called rugged individualism of the American past has given way to a collective narcissism, which suits the purposes of an economic system geared not simply to its own growth (as was the case in the past) but to a cultivated consumerism.

The first, and most devastating, critique is devoted to "the awareness movement." By now, we are rather accustomed to the dreary social stupidity generated by that movement, but the author is a historian, and he wants us to look back a little and be reminded of what went on recently in the name of "personal liberation." He goes directly to the sources—those who took part in the events of the last decade or so and decided to describe what they experienced. Here is Jerry Rubin talking about a stretch of twentieth-century time: "In five years, from 1971 to 1975, I directly experienced est, gestalt therapy, bioenergetics, rolfing, massage, jogging, health foods, tai chi, Esalen, hypnotism, modern dance, meditation, Silva Mind Control, Arica, acupuncture, sex therapy, Reichian therapy, and More House—a smorgasbord course in New Consciousness." I suppose such a list will make some laugh, and with good reason. But what kind of craziness, what kind of inner emptiness, what kind of blinded, rudderless personal condition has prompted many of us to join one, then another, then still another of these movements? They are, needless to say, quasi-religious in nature: an effort on the part of the lost to find something half-believable and at least a tiny bit transcendent. But the thrust of all those activities is eminently, if not obscenely, narcissistic—a glorification of the mind and body of the individual member or participant, for whom, most likely, God is dead and patriotism a joke. Once, most Americans committed themselves without qualification to religious passion; in some parts of the world people still do. In the early years of this century, the nation-state received the devotion formerly reserved for God. But in our time the flag, the military, and the political leadership of countries such as ours have excited the loyalty and enthusiasm of fewer and fewer citizens. What is left for them but themselves? Their narcissism, it can be argued, is a response to grim memories and terrible prospects. As Lasch puts it, "the Nazi holocaust, the threat of nuclear annihilation, the depletion of natural resources, well-founded predictions of ecological disaster have fulfilled poetic prophecy, giving concrete historical substance to the nightmare, or death wish, that avant-garde artists were the first to express."

Under such circumstances, why look back or think very far ahead? That is the question many men and women have asked; it represents a "waning of the sense of historical time," as the author calls this aspect of contemporary self-absorption. We want for the here and now "satisfying interpersonal relationships," "group skills." We want to own what is trendy to wear, to sit or sleep on; we aim to do what is chic or to go "where the action is." When a sense of the past or the future is either attenuated or lost, what is left but an endless series of fads? For every one of them, moreover, there seems to be a book that can command the dollars of thousands: *I'm OK—You're OK*, *Looking Out for #1*, *Your Erroneous Zones*, *Pulling Your Own Strings*, *Power!*, *Success!*, *How to Be Your Own Best Friend*, and many others. There are even some that are saturated with undisguised pornography or sadism. All are banal and are sold to the reader as an aid to his or her self-promotion and self-enhancement. The encouragement of greedy, combative self-assertion appeals, perhaps, to those who can no longer go to a frontier and explore it, conquer it, and plunder it, and who (after Vietnam and Watergate) can't work themselves up to nationalist truculence or self-righteousness. Why not learn how to win more limited victories over anyone who happens to come in sight or get in the way?

Psychoanalysts have wisely hesitated to make sweeping socio-logical statements on the basis of their direct observations in the doctor's office or in mental hospitals. But they do acknowledge that "changes in cultural patterns can affect family structure," and it is Lasch's chosen task to show how today's American culture does precisely that—intrudes upon the manner in which we act as parents, thereby decisively influencing the way our children grow up. In chapters on our schools, our sports, our treatment of the elderly, and our various secular "experts," he argues that we have been taught the importance of conformity—hence the importance of "adjust-ment" and the acquiescence that characterizes much of our educational and working lives. Once, there were families in which children saw their parents work and saw what that work meant—crops planted and harvested, or products made. But with industrialization, home life and work became separated, and the nature of the latter is such that few people get any real sense of achievement from it. Assembly lines and vast bureaucratic offices are often places of confinement, boredom, and despair—time clocked in. Meanwhile, children have to be taught that such is their future life. Parents who are not exactly sure what they dare to want for themselves or their children (besides the various objects incessantly paraded before them with wicked cleverness on the television screen or in newspapers and magazines) turn eagerly to psychologists and psychiatrists, members of the so-called helping professions, for advice; and they get it, in profusion. Even as parents have left the home to work in factories and offices, their children have had to come to quick terms with the outside world because of the significant surrender of parental authority over them.

The author refers at one point to "the evil of psychologizing," but he must be one of very few who have the detachment and moral self-assurance to use such a phrase. Millions of us are caught up in the pretentious jargon of child-rearing guides, manuals, and books. All that talk of "parenting." All those psychological explanations, not only naive and sometimes absurd but ephemeral as well—replaced by new guides or contradictory ones: psychology as an instance of consumerism. Is it the first five years that really count or the first three? And how you handle your child immediately after he or she is born? In one terse, sad quotation from a scholarly paper by Gilbert J. Rose, Lasch indicates what too many of us assume: "The naive idea that sickness accounts for badness and that badness necessarily results from being misunderstood is the prejudice of a therapeutic morality." We want to "analyze" everything, including our children's behavior, and at the same time we have convinced ourselves that we lack the authority to take a firm stand on much of anything—with respect to their lives or our own. A large crew of hustlers has gleefully moved into this moral vacuum talking "child development" and "human motivation." Why do parents rush toward these people, eager for their every pronouncement? What are the implicit promises made, if only one will obey all the rules handed down? As parents, we are obsessed with "techniques" in the home for the same reason that we turn to the counsel of industrial sociologists, practitioners of "personal management," and "guidance counselors." All these "experts" are disguised moralists who want to give us answers and more answers, to put us in our place: Do this, don't do that, lest you be judged "maladjusted," "sick," or "abnormal." The covert nature of their preaching (backed up by considerable political and economic authority) is a measure of how uncomfortable we have learned to be with an open acknowledgment of any moral—never mind spiritual—concerns we may yet have, despite the age and its culture.

A number of writers, Lasch points out, have referred to "the decline of the superego." But he wisely emphasizes that it is not enough to stop there or even to add, as he does, a cultural amplification—the obvious connection between psychological permissiveness and the hedonistic consumerism of advanced capitalist societies. To be sure, today's self-styled experts in "child care" don't encourage us to bring up thoroughly disciplined, proudly independent, morally concerned young men and women. ("Moral," for many, means "moralistic.") But Lasch goes on (backed, I would add, by plenty of evidence that has appeared in the literature of child psychiatry):

The parents' failure to serve as models of disciplined self-restraint or to restrain the child does not mean that the child grows up without a superego. On the contrary, it encourages the development of a harsh and punitive superego based largely on archaic images of the parents, fused with grandiose self-images.

Put differently, if children don't learn how to control themselves as they grow up they will forever be at the mercy of the worries, fears, angers, and desires that characterize early life. Hence the outbursts of wanton, senseless cruelty; the various binges of gratification (food, liquor, drugs, gadgets, travel); the spells of ferocious self-criticism that take the form of apathy, inertia, or the blues; a spurt of activity—motorcycles, cars—that is suicidal, and sometimes homicidal, in nature; the self-abasement that expresses itself not only in some of the cults we have recently had cause to notice but in the phenomenon of celebrity, which Lasch examines rather closely.

Who are these "stars" (not only, nowadays, entertainers but athletes, politicians, and even scholars, writers, and artists), and what does the adoring response of their followers tell us about ourselves? If the famous are caught up in the narcissism that this book analyzes, so are the various crowds that attend them with such abdication of personal responsibility and such apostolic fervor. Among those who regard religion as a joke, as inconsequential, or as a mere ritual, and who have come to view many institutions as corrupt or exploitative, there can be, ironically, a flight to individuals: a suspension of skepticism with regard to them, an outright worship of them. A mind deprived of one kind of discipline will somehow find another. We revert to a childlike narcissism; celebrities become the heroes that boys and girls dream of being, of knowing, of following in causes or cheering on various playing fields. We model ourselves desperately after other people because we haven't really been taught to accept the limitations of life—not when advertisers offer us the moon and one or two of us actually get there, whereupon we conclude that in no time at all the rest of us will be following suit. It is a grandiosity that serves the interests of those who have things to sell. But it is a grandiosity that finally becomes infectious and takes us all in—doctors who promise to "conquer" old age, engineers whose technology will supposedly subdue all of nature, and writers of futuristic stories, novels, screenplays, and essays who spin fantasies and more fantasies. Fantasies about what? About people sprung loose from themselves, on earth and in space—people who have become godlike. It is what Freud, in a paper ("On Narcissism"), once described with reference to the family:

> The child shall have a better time than his parents; he shall not be subject to the necessities which they have recognized as paramount in life. Illness, death, renunciation of enjoyment, restrictions on his own will, shall not touch him; the laws of nature and of society shall be abrogated in his favor; and he shall once more really be the centre and core of creation—"His Majesty the Baby," as we once fancied ourselves.

The trouble is, as this book convincingly demonstrates, such innocent and passing parental fantasies, as they once were, have become articles of faith for many of us. We possess no larger, compelling vision that is worth any commitment of energy and time. We are not inclined to settle for anything less than everything—all at once and at this very moment. What was once called "reality" has become for us a mere barrier, surely one day to be penetrated. We are good at getting things but unable to know where to start when it comes to facing the issues Freud referred to—the finite, complex nature of life itself. We shun the elderly, reminders of our own mortality. We worship superathletes, promoted by endless and sometimes corrupt schemes. We cultivate postures—ironic cynicism, skeptical distance—meant to keep us from the inevitable difficulties of human involvement. We play it cool, play it fast, and, in the clutch, place our faith in lotions and powders and soaps and dyes and surgical procedures so that we can stay—we hope, we pray—in the game as long as possible, playing at life, because from the outside (society) we have every encouragement to do so and from the inside (family life) we have also learned that such a way of getting along is desirable.

Christopher Lasch has given us a short jeremiad. Perhaps, in his urge to bring us to our senses, he has overstated his case and forgotten to mention some of the nonsense that *other* ages found congenial to their purposes. Certainly he has no answers for our situation. He distrusts many who have answers. His viewpoint is that of one who has looked back hard and looked around keenly. In a summary statement, he observes that "in its pathological form, narcissism originates as a defense against feelings of helpless dependency in early life, which it tries to counter with 'blind optimism' and grandiose illusions of personal self-sufficiency." He adds this:

> Since modern society prolongs the experience of dependence into adult life, it encourages milder forms of narcissism in people who might otherwise come to terms with the inescapable limits on their personal freedom and power—limits inherent in the human condition—by developing competence as workers and parents. But at the same time that our society makes it more and more difficult to find satisfaction in love and work, it surrounds the individual with manufactured fantasies of total gratification.

That is a serious bind to be caught in, and one wonders how we will ever get out of it—short of a drastic reshaping of our society and of ourselves as citizens of it. Meanwhile, our predicament would seem to resemble that of another civilization under extreme duress. When Aristophanes surveyed the Greek states caught up in the terrible destructiveness—personal, social, political—of the Peloponnesian War, he remarked, "Whirl is King, having driven out Zeus." It may give us some pleasure and yet be a blow to our narcissism as readers, writers, and social critics to know that in this "age of diminishing expectations" our doom is not as "different" as we like to think. The playwright's description still rings true, and the historical parallel is hardly reassuring. Even a widespread awareness of it would no doubt do nothing to lessen the narcissism among us.

New Yorker, August 27, 1979

Particular Memories

There are many dangers inherent in writing personal memoirs: inordinate self-display, self-flattery, a generally too narrow view of things. When these dangers are successfully skirted, however, the memoir can be a wonderfully educational and entertaining genre. It offers the writer a chance to share intimate moments with his readers, especially if he can put aside his egoism, or at least use it in the service of thoughtful detachment. Burrhus Frederic Skinner, the Harvard psychologist famous for his theories of behaviorism and his philosophical inclinations, has, in his seventy-third year, begun to look back upon his personal history; the result is the first installment of his memoirs, called *Particulars of My Life*. It is, on the whole, a successful job. Professor Skinner teaches us a lot about an earlier America, and about his family, his hometown, and his friends, neighbors, and teachers. He also speaks intently of the developing technology of the era—the telephone, the radio, the automobile, the airplane—whose imprint upon children, upon their assumptions and perceptions, has often been underestimated or overlooked by experts in child development.

In the first part of the book, Professor Skinner talks about his childhood. One might expect here the romanticized elaborations, the distortions, and the outright mystifications that adults often resort to when they talk about their early years, but Professor Skinner's astonishing power of recall takes him out of himself and helps him to avoid these pitfalls. "The first personal possession I remember was my Teddy Bear," he tells us early in the book. "Its imitation fur was light brown and it had a white knitted cap and jacket." This is obviously no vague recollection; Professor Skinner has a memory that penetrates decades of shadows with apparent ease. And he works into his detailed descriptions just enough social history and psychological comment to make his experience part of a past shared by many millions of his countrymen:

The Teddy Bear was a fairly recent innovation: a newspaper cartoon had shown Theodore Roosevelt sparing a bear cub during one of his big-game exploits, and copies of the cub came on the market as toys for children. It was the kind of doll a boy might respectably play with.

Professor Skinner summons up many other sights, sounds, smells, contours, and textures of the sort that most of us have long ago let slip into the darkness of the past. He recalls a jigsaw puzzle of a train, for example, that included advertising for the virtues of the Delaware, Lackawanna & Western Railroad; according to the puzzle, the company's trains used anthracite coal, not the bituminous variety, and were therefore said to be cleaner. The author tells us of "a beautiful girl named Phoebe Snow," who appeared in the puzzle clothed in white and standing at the rear of the train, and, miraculously, to this day he can picture "the polished brass railings" that enabled him to complete the puzzle. He remembers his toy trains in all their intricacy, and he can still call to mind a set of dominoes that he used over six decades ago; they were "made of thin slabs of ivory and ebony held together with brass pins turning green in the crevices."

This consuming attention to gadgets and other physical objects was not, apparently, a replacement for parental affection. Professor Skinner's mother was a kind and attentive person, and his father, an upright, conservative lawyer, treated him gently. Professor Skinner gives us, word for word, the "consoling" songs he heard as a child. He recounts the illnesses he suffered, the quarantines that accompanied them, and the earnest efforts of his parents to get him better. He recalls the old rituals of Christmas—the meals, the social arrangements and obligations, and, needless to say, the many rewards.

Professor Skinner's family was not rich, but it was comfortable, and the boy never lacked for material things. Just as important, he makes clear, was the assurance he came to feel as a result of his parents' reasonably secure social and economic position. Nevertheless, Skinner's childhood was not idyllic. There were tensions between his mother's family and his father's. His parents felt envies, rivalries, and apprehensions, and they were made nervous by anyone who was considerably better off than they were. His father never rose as high as he wished to, and his mother, who came from "better stock," sometimes adopted an aloof, condescending attitude toward him—the author describes her as "apparently frigid." Yet he also emphasizes how kind and helpful she could be to her husband as well as to his brother and himself.

Professor Skinner's memory for detail is also impressive when he describes the natural world of his childhood. He was born in Susquehanna, Pennsylvania, which is on the Susquehanna River, and his picture of the river—its twists and turns, its fierce struggle through stubborn, hilly countryside toward the ocean—seems flawless. He appears to have given an account of everything he saw growing around his house—"Our backyard offered black cherries, red cherries (shared with the robins), purple plums, green plums, Concord grapes, currants, raspberries, rhubarb, horseradish, and mustard"—and of the trees, plants, flowers, and animals that flourished nearby.

But when he comes to human beings, Professor Skinner is often guarded, tentative, and not nearly so thorough. After a long, touching, and quite precisely rendered description of a turn-of-the-century Pennsylvania landscape of meadows and forests, for instance, he observes that "there were people in that world, too, and some of them were interesting," but when he tells us about these people, it is only their work or their tools or their machines that seem to interest him. He mentions the blacksmith, the carpenter, a woman who ran a boarding house, and the owner of a candy store, and in each case he moves directly from the person's occupation or name to a depiction of something *done*: "The carpenter did cabinet work, and I was surprised to see how often he simply glued pieces of wood together, but the glue was hot and hence presumably stronger than the kind I used."

Even when Professor Skinner tries to be forthright about his parents and grandparents, he ends up giving more attention to their social origins than to their personal hopes and fears, which we are simply told were substantial. Concerning his relationship with Edward, his only brother, Professor Skinner is still more reticent—some might say naive. "Since my brother was two and a half years younger than I, there was little competition between us," he tells us, and we are also informed that there was "sibling affection" between them. True, we are told at one point that the brother became unaffectionate enough to write "Your a BOOB" on the flyleaf of the author's copy of *Alice in Wonderland*. But we might expect more from someone who can remember the most minute details about forests, rivers, and towns, and who can describe down to the last button the winter clothes he wore as a young child, and the complicated, comic procedures involved in his learning to drive a car fifty years ago. One feels obliged to mention these emotional blind spots in an otherwise thorough and compelling narrative because they seem so closely related to Professor Skinner's psychological theories. He has strongly maintained that our mental development consists simply of responses to an assortment of stimuli, which "condition" us and thus account for our behavior; his critics have wondered whether this theoretical system does not ignore the spiritual side of our mental life, whether the stimulus-response idea does not account for human feeling rather casually.

It so happens that a central event in Professor Skinner's life was Edward's sudden, tragic death, at the age of sixteen. The family had moved to Scranton, and the author, then a student at Hamilton College, was home for his Easter vacation. Just after eating a sundae, Edward fell inexplicably and gravely ill. He died within an hour or two. Skinner was present the whole time, except for a brief interval when he went to get his parents, who were in church. The father would never again be the same. The mother's grief was strong and lasting and is movingly conveyed in Professor Skinner's book. The author seems to realize that his own reaction was, to say the least, idiosyncratic, and, if we can judge from the contents of this book, it continues to be so. He tells us that he was very helpful to the doctors; he gave a careful and instructive account of what he had seen happening to his brother, what complaints were made, what symptoms set in. The doctors, later on, were grateful: "They told my father that my objectivity was helpful," Skinner writes. "With the same objectivity I had watched my parents as they reacted to the discovery that my brother was dead." He goes on to say that despite his objectivity he was "far from unmoved."

Perhaps we would not be disturbed by any of this if Skinner had let the matter of his brother's death drop there. After all, we would not want to read a self-serving outpouring of sadness, and we cannot ask for a description of the intensity of mourning experienced by this sensitive and observant man if he does not want to give it to us. But he does not let the matter drop. Instead, he insists once again that his brother and he "had never competed for the same things." They had different hobbies, involvements, and aspirations. Edward was, we are told, "closer" to their parents, and his death put Skinner "in a position" he had never wished for—one that would "become increasingly troublesome in the years ahead." But we don't learn any more about those difficulties, and Skinner's response to this crucial part of his life remains elusive and troubling.

We do learn a good deal, however, about what Professor Skinner calls his "selfishness" as a college student—his ability to develop a rather large, "self-centered microcosm." He is quite able to give us at substantial length a description of that microcosm, vintage young adulthood. He writes shrewdly and sardonically of the world he created for himself. He wrote poetry, stories, essays, and, even as a youth, reflective autobiography. Not content with an exceptional memory, he has obviously held on to every scrap of paper that contains his words—old diaries, class papers and themes, pieces written as entries in writing competitions, pieces published or meant to be published in various school magazines and other periodicals. He is excellent at evoking the college literary scene, with its mixture of sensitivity, earnestness, snobbery, faddishness, and, alas, keen envy and outright malice. He indicates from his own experience the price paid by those young writers who have not only some talent but also misgivings about it: they can't know what chance of success they have, and, worst of all, they don't know what to do about the warnings against writing as a career that they get from parents or other relatives. Skinner's father wrote him a long, forceful, and affecting letter when the young man announced that he would spend a year writing a novel after graduating from college. The letter was kept, and its reproduction, which takes up three pages, stands as one of this book's most luminous moments—a clear statement of the bourgeois reaction against "art," one that most satirists would find extremely tempting. Parental love, and the sincere worry that a father has for his son's future social and financial situation, can be all too easily caricatured or misrepresented.

The book also contains a letter from Robert Frost, who saw substantial promise in Skinner as a storyteller. The letter is dated April 7, 1926, and it was sent from Ann Arbor, Michigan. In it, Frost tells Skinner that he possesses "the touch of art." He goes on to say that as a writer Skinner is "worth twice anyone else I have seen in prose this year." But, in a brief postscript, Frost adds a note of warning: "Belief, belief. You've got to augment my belief in life and people mightily or cross it uglily. I'm awfully sure of this tonight." The great poet had made a positive judgment but had qualified it enough to become a rather accurate prophet with respect to Skinner's lifework. Soon enough, the young man abandoned his short-lived career as a writer. He does so right before the reader's eyes, reenacting in the book his growing disenchantment with his writing and eventually, it seems, with literature as a whole. He presents one specimen of his work after another, and comments testily, acidly, on what he once set down on paper. "This was dredging up the past, not writing anything new, and what was new was sorry stuff," he says about a published poem of his. "The truth was, I had no reason to write anything," he says at another point. Skinner's reservations about writers and their craft are perhaps most strongly set forth in a passage taken from one of his old notebooks. He had headed the passage "Desire to Write," and in it he offered a psychological analysis of sorts—one that he tried to apply to other callings:

> I am convinced that an essentially false desire-to-write is necessary to any author. Whether it be the desire to make money, the desire to be known as a genius, the desire to get one's name in the paper, or some mystical desire to "express oneself," it does not bear analysis without resolving itself into a mean satisfaction of a mean instinct. By "false" and "mean" I do not intend to condemn exactly. I mean simply that the same desires quite as often prod a man into big business or eccentricity or acrobatics or driving automobiles at excessive speeds or marriage. . . .
>
> The facile liar has a great deal in common with the artist who is expert in embroidering detail.

Not long after writing those words, Skinner was on his way to Harvard's graduate school to begin his career in psychology. The book ends at that point; the author is twenty-four and is looking forward to a new and exciting life—one we will no doubt read of someday in another volume.

The bitterness of the young diarist, alas, has not yielded to time. The man who presented an all too unqualified theory about why people want to become writers is not very different from the man who, at the age of seventy-two, offers us these comments:

I had apparently failed as a writer but was it not possible that literature had failed me as a method? One might enjoy Proust's reminiscences and share the emotional torment of Dostoevski's characters, but did Proust or Dostoevski really *understand?*

A little farther on, he adds this conclusion: "Literature as an art form was dead; I would turn to science."

So he did, and partly because he has been so successful in his chosen career we must take notice of his earliest memories. We admire his precision, but we have the unfortunate experience (a "disedifying" one, his rather proper maternal grandparents might have said) of being witness to another part of him as well—a part that has always been, one gathers, arrogant and condescending. Each reader will have to decide for himself or herself whether Professor Skinner has added something to what Frost in his postscript called "belief in life." Perhaps in this book he has indeed contributed to that vision "mightily," but he has also at some points managed to "cross it uglily."

New Yorker, July 26, 1976

Man's Pride

E very day psychiatrists struggle with the staying power that all sorts of illusions have over the minds of patients—and of their doctors, too. The neurotic Viennese burghers Freud listened to at the turn of the century were not simply mixed up and at odds with relatives and friends; they were also tenacious and imaginative individuals who had come to grief because under no circumstances, it seemed, would they give up certain fixed notions and wishes. Most of them had been going from one doctor to another in the hope that someone, at last, would stop collaring them, stop telling them first piously, then threateningly, to shape up and look at the world *this* way, not some other way they found irresistible. Finally one doctor let them be; anxious to learn rather than preach, enough of a rebel to be open-minded and maybe a little contemptuous of prevailing orthodoxies, Freud listened and questioned his own assumptions as much as those of his patients. Eventually he saw what they were up to—how they regarded others, how their minds made sense of the various signals this world presents to us. He saw, too, his own blind spots. Reared in a particular way, trained to have certain expectations, preferences, and values, he had found himself for a long time as puzzled as his colleagues by the bizarre and apparently witless thoughts and deeds of the people who consulted him. Nor did he unravel "their" mysteries in a sudden burst of genius; in fact, for a long time he unraveled nothing— except, ironically, the sources of his own worldview. That done (the twentieth century was about to begin), he was helpless as a traditional psychiatrist. How could he wave his arms, fiddle with electricity, shake his finger, ply pills, call upon conventional morality, and throw around labels of one kind or another when he had come to realize how much he himself shared with "them," the outcasts he had come to know so well?

At such a moment one begins to ask who is the doctor and who is the patient—a question Freud knew enough to ask, as his correspondence with Wilhelm Fliess demonstrates, and a question, of course, patients and their doctors still pose for themselves. The answer is not clear-cut—and Freud was indeed in trouble with his colleagues once he insisted that the doctor had to shed a good deal of his socially sanctioned moral authority, his immunity from criticism, and instead find in himself the sources of unrest others seemed (and sometimes *only* seemed) to manage less well. Such an attitude does not have to be *stated* to a troubled patient; it comes across in dozens of silent but important ways—a nod, a gesture, a look—and the result for a patient can be nothing short of redemptive: at last someone will listen almost as a comrade, certainly not as a self-righteous judge. So doing, Freud could glimpse and begin to fathom what others knew nothing about. So doing, he also felt godlike; and again, Freud's correspondence with Fliess shows how naturally and unashamedly a bold investigator can acknowledge just such temptations. Unfortunately, history has a way of giving those temptations a kind of sticky institutional reality that for a while seems almost unshakable—hence the conversion of suggestive formulations into dogma.

Yet, other things also happen in due time. In the case of institutionalized psychoanalysis, a man like Allen Wheelis appears not to differ with or attempt to modify theories that are merely a bit overwrought but rather to take up once again Freud's kind of lonely vigil, in the course of which firmly held beliefs are shown to be no longer so compelling and new ideas about man's situation are mentioned and explored. As one goes through Wheelis's first and very important book, *The Quest for Identity* (1958), one feels that with respect to background, temperament, and sensibility he has what it takes to achieve what he has set out to do: an original mind; the ability to stand apart from prevailing orthodoxies without at the same time becoming destructively resentful; and not least, the capacity to bear a degree of loneliness. Freud often attributed his own qualifications along those lines to his Jewishness; born an outsider, he had less of the status quo to defend. Allen Wheelis was born in Louisiana, reared in Texas. Like other white Southerners he was drawn to the cosmopolitan intellectual world of New York, and like many of them, he both joined in and remained aloof. *The Quest for Identity* is an effort of a psychoanalyst (only recently finished with one of the longest apprenticeships our society demands) to lift his head from the clinics and consulting offices and find his professional bearing anew. The book offers an intelligent, lucid analysis of American society, both rural and urban, and implicitly but forcefully asks psychoanalysts to consider the reasons for their modern prominence. The book also offers the first example of Wheelis's distinctive method of presentation—the use of parables and short stories as a means of first making vivid and suggestive what is then written about analytically.

Wheelis next turned to a full-length novel (*The Seeker*, 1960) and a series of extended parables (*The Illusionless Man*, 1966) in hopes, perhaps, of making certain points quietly and without resort to the thinly disguised rhetoric and the discouraging jargon that plague the social sciences today. On almost every page of those two books, and throughout *The Desert* (1970), another blend of essays and fiction, the reader has to come to terms with Wheelis's ironic detachment. He misses none of the banality and occasional malevolence some psychiatrists foist upon us; but more important, he wryly takes note of our widespread gullibility and vulnerability as middle-class Americans who live in a thoroughly secular society. Blessed with money and comfort and (more or less) something called "success," heirs to the wisdom ("applied" all over the place) of Einstein and Freud, not to mention Darwin, Descartes, Newton, and Galileo—back, back into time one can go—we apparently have everything and know everything, and yet we are persistently naive in our endless search for new sources of satisfaction or fulfillment. The divorce rate climbs. Suicides are by no means rare. One fad gives way to another. Things are bought, kept around for a while, go increasingly unnoticed, and get thrown out. Our rivers are streams of acid; no matter, there is an island in the Caribbean for us, handily available in a jet-propelled cloud of smoke. In case anyone gets a little nervous, there is alcohol (and an estimated five million alcoholics) and drugstores full of millions of pills, all of them a collective promise of serenity to millions of citizens of the world's richest, most powerful nation; and for those who want to push things even more, there are a host of illegal substances now called "drugs"—as if the biggest and most respectable of American businesses don't already profit handsomely from the drugs they push quite legally on anxious, apprehensive men and women. Finally, of course, there are psychiatrists, so many of whose hours are reserved for those with money and a certain kind of social and intellectual background, as Redlich and Hollingshead indicated convincingly in *Social Class and Mental Illness* (1958). One prominent psychiatrist, Ralph Greenson of Los Angeles, has called attention to the shift in symptoms he and his colleagues have witnessed in recent decades. Freud saw patients who tended to have specific complaints tied to (he discovered) identifiable experiences or patterns of behavior. Now a more general kind of malaise, a sense of aimlessness and uncertainty tinged with vague moodiness, prompts many to see psychiatrists—and by no means is it likely that such difficulties can be traced back to some moment of psychological injury or sorrow in early childhood and then exorcised. Not that doctors don't keep on trying, even as their patients keep on coming. Where else are the patients to go? Whom can one really trust anyway? What is to be believed for any length of time—a year, say, never mind a span called by the superstitious "eternity"? For Dr. Wheelis, those questions are not surprising; nor does he want to ignore them. In his latest book, *The End of the Modern Age*, he keeps putting forth such questions, and not in order to offer anyone some highly condensed and relatively inexpensive "help" or "guidance." Freud himself knew how to ask broad, contemplative questions, and after initially turning away from the excesses such questions can sometimes generate in favor of the clinician's realities, he was brought back to those questions, first by a terrible war and then in 1933 by the rise to power of the Nazi scum. In 1938, with scarcely a year of life left, the old psychoanalyst had to seek exile in England. No wonder a "death wish" became part of psychoanalytic metapsychology. No wonder Freud turned his attention more and more to religious and philosophical matters. Always one to correct his own mistakes first, he may have sensed that someone, someday, would have to give psychoanalysis a place in the larger tradition of the West's social and intellectual history. That is indeed what *The End of the Modern Age* manages to accomplish.

The book is short and possesses Wheelis's characteristic style—plain, understandable, strong prose harnessed to straightforward narrative presentation. The reader is meant to learn how many theories and pursuits are finally being seen for the illusions they have turned out to be, but the book is itself an illusion—so brief, unpretentious, deceptively easy to go through, yet in fact full of reflections about nothing less than the whole history of modern science. Though the title is dramatic, it is earned. The author goes back to the Middle Ages and shows how certain psychological assumptions began to be built up in the West as Copernicus and Kepler prepared the way for what, at last, became our age—in which humanity is known as an evolving part of the animal kingdom, the mind a deep mystery (but one that can be penetrated, if slowly and with difficulty), and the world made up of atoms (also now penetrated and somewhat under control). "The dream of mechanism," Wheelis says, is our conviction that everything in the universe, certainly including ourselves, "is nothing but a machine, and is thereby knowable as an object, as a machine can be known." Yes, we know now from theoretical physicists and cultural anthropologists how relative is the knowledge that for so long seemed to be fixed, simply waiting to be found. The mind boggles as "matter" is called "energy," as estimates are made about when and how the earth came into being, or about the number of light years that those stars we look at represent. Still, we hunger after certainty, and for many in the West certainty has to do with computers, statistics, and laboratories. Even among psychoanalysts, empathy and intuition can still be heard talked about as if one day they, too, will give way to an "objective," "value-free" study. (And, alas, there is the term *love-object*, which persists in the psychiatric literature.) In Wheelis's words: "So great has been the success of the scientific method that it has come to be identified with reason itself—as if there were no way of being reasonable with conjectures that lie beyond scientific reach. Such conjectures therefore are insidiously disparaged, ignored, as if to say, 'if it's not scientific, it's not important.'"

The point is not to mock the valuable things we have learned and continue to learn from natural and social scientists. Wheelis is no Luddite. Nor does he react against the excesses of this historical era by glorifying "natural man" or embracing a cult of craziness. He knows, out of his daily work he knows, how mean and brutish we can all be, and not *only* because a particular social or political system encourages such behavior. *The End of the Modern Age* was written simply to emphasize some of the distortions that have taken place in the course of the rise of the industrial West. There is, though, a passionate intensity that comes through in some sections of the book, no doubt a reflection of the author's sense of urgency as he looks back at what he, a man in his fifties, has already seen: the Nazi Holocaust; napalm bombs and atomic or hydrogen bombs; war efforts called "defoliation." So the book is many things: a sensitive and reflective essay on the West's intellectual history; an attempt to define the limits of words like "objective" and "subjective"; a look at what may be ahead of us as more and more people ask the kinds of questions Wheelis does: "What is important in life? What is worth struggling for, and how much? Should I love my neighbor, concern myself with his suffering? How far does neighborhood extend? To the coast? To North Vietnam?" Questions like those demand of us constant ethical concern. In Wheelis's words: "The computers are silent, the test tubes do not react to those queries, and he who concerns himself with them might do better in church than in a laboratory, and the church might better be a forest glade, if any such are left, than the temple of a tired sect."

I write this having just read that Werner Heisenberg believes "the ultimate has probably been reached in probing the innermost sanctum of matter." Indeed, as far back as the 1920s and 1930s Professor Heisenberg emphasized that there is a limit to what can be measured on the atomic scale because the process of measurement itself alters the situation. Our pride has brought us this far—for the good but also for the bad. Psychoanalysts, like physicists, can make the pursuit of knowledge a religion—and in so doing demonstrate how willfully blind even the best educated and most intelligent people can be. Allen Wheelis, in a sense, wants to help his colleagues come full circle around: Freud had a right to turn away from the temptations of moral philosophy and instead pursue the scientific imagery of his day, even if in so doing he fell prey at times to the pitfalls such imagery presents. But now, over seventy years since he made his great intellectual breakthrough, other challenges face us—challenges not unlike those that Schopenhauer and Nietzsche, the best of Germany's nineteenth-century philosophers, had the foresight to struggle with; and those challenges require from today's psychoanalysts the kind of ethical inquiry *The End of the Modern Age* at least begins to make.

Red Herring

I f psychiatrists are anything, they are historians; their job requires skill at preparing a case history—the record that enables a doctor to study the past of a particular individual. Yet psychiatrists and psychoanalysts rarely think about the past of their own profession, and the history of psychiatry (or, indeed, of medicine) is not taught in many medical schools, so young psychiatrists often come to regard contemporary theories of mental illness as the revealed truths that our era has miraculously unearthed rather than as the latest in a long series of speculations, each of which has a substantial connection with its predecessors. But there *are* some good books on the topic; for psychiatrists, one thinks of, for instance, *The History of Psychiatry* by Franz Alexander and Sheldon Selesnick. And now there is *George III and the Mad Business*, the product of years of research by two English psychiatrists, Ida Macalpine and Richard Hunter. The book is an ideal one for medical students and young doctors, not to mention for the general reader: it is clearly written and utterly without dismaying jargon; furthermore, it is about a particular person, a particular set of "complaints"—and therefore full of concrete descriptions in place of abstractions and polemical theories. Finally, it is a historical study that asks the reader to think about all sorts of contemporary social and political issues—which is to say that the situation in which an English monarch and his subjects found themselves 150 years ago is not unique but is potentially the problem of any ruler and his people.

In June of 1788, King George III of England suffered what was called a "bilious fever." The attack (termed "smart" in those days rather than "acute" or "sharp") persisted for a fortnight, and the King went to Cheltenham to take the brackish waters of a spring believed to help gouty patients. During the summer, he became well again, but in the middle of October he once more took sick. His stomach hurt. He had trouble breathing and cramps in one leg. He was given purgatives, but a fever developed, as well as a slight yellowing around the eyes, and his power of concentration began to fail. His speech became rambling, his spirits were low, and his behavior was erratic. William Pitt, who was his Prime Minister, and the other men in the Cabinet began to wonder what they should do if the King's condition worsened, which it did.

The King of England was not then a mere symbol of continuity; he shared power with Parliament and his ministers. His "mental illness," which is what we would call it, precipitated a constitutional crisis, and the nation's leading physicians fought one another madly (one is tempted to say) over the King's diagnosis, prognosis, and treatment. Was George truly out of his mind? Would he ever recover? Ought the Prince of Wales to take over? Should the King, increasingly wild and incomprehensible, be restrained and coerced like any "ordinary" madman? These questions suggest only some of the issues. Pitt and Edmund Burke were battling one another for political power. Pitt had good reason to hope for the King's recovery and to insist that he be given the benefit of the doubt during his illness; for Burke and his fellow Whigs, the accession to the throne of the Prince of Wales, who favored their views, was desirable indeed. The King's wife and many children and aides and servants and helpers were also willing to scheme and take sides and reveal themselves to be less than totally loyal to him. At stake was power, in jeopardy was a nation's government, and at odds were those at the top—men whose devotion to King and Country was matched by their devotion to their own ambitions and purposes.

The fifty-year-old George waged a tumultuous and poignant battle for his sanity. He knew, even before his doctors did, that he was losing control of his mind. He felt driven to talk, to keep on the move, however frivolous or absurd the activity. He became confused—at times silent and sullen, at times talkative and expansive. He seemed incurable, and in November of that year it was rumored that he was dead. The Prince of Wales was already allotting ministries to his friends and associates, and the fights between George's doctors were as severe as his condition, as malicious as the political intrigue. Each doctor, it seemed, had his particular medical theory, his particular political cause. And the need to confine the King (and thereby acknowledge his mental state) intensified the arguments between the physicians. Let us cite the authors:

The situation in which the royal physicians found themselves was not an enviable one. They were frightened by their unmanageable sovereign and his unpredictable behavior. They had to account for his condition and their measures to the ministers of the crown. They had to consider the feelings of the Queen and her family and to bear in mind that the King himself was likely to see their reports in the papers—if not at the time then surely if he recovered. They were also apprehensive that the future of the Government hung on what they said. They were shadowed by the Prince of Wales and the Chancellor, harassed by public opinion, and had newsmongers breathing down their necks. They had to think of their professional reputation, and above all else loomed the remorseless fact that they did not, as indeed they could not, know what was the matter with their patient.

The doctors unquestionably helped the King feel weaker, more confused, more frustrated, more frightened. They bled him. They blistered his skin. They made him vomit. They gave him cathartics and little to eat. They talked about the "fever," the "disorder," the "indisposition," the "restlessness." They knew he had lost his mind (once he "talked for nineteen hours without scarce any intermission"), and so they hovered over him, cowering before him in his rages but nevertheless playing tricks on him, lying to him, restraining him by keeping him "swaddled in fine linen." Finally, despite his "oaths" and "indecencies," they got him to Kew, where he would be nearer his London doctors than in Windsor and not so easily observed by the public. There they tied him to his bed and called in a Dr. Willis, "the keeper of a madhouse in Lincolnshire," a man "of peculiar skill and practice in intellectual maladies." His presence embarrassed not only the King but many in the royal entourage; "the poor Queen had most painfully concurred in a measure which seemed to fix the nature of the King's attack in the face of the world."

Dr. Willis came with his physician son and three keepers, called "physical assistants." He talked about "breaking in" patients, rather as horses are tamed. The battle between the doctors and the poor, beleaguered, self-doubting, but assertive and courageous King intensified: "No account of the illness from this point on can disregard the King's treatment, and to what extent the turbulence he displayed was provoked by the repressive and punitive methods by which he was ruled."

The King took an intense dislike to his new doctors, and was declared to have a delusional hatred of them. They began applying not only force to his body but another label to his state of mind—"consequential madness." They boasted of their experience with madness. They tied George in a chair and lectured him for hours. (The elder Dr. Willis had been a clergyman.) When he objected, he was gagged. Nevertheless, he gradually improved. ("Not always can nature be trusted to triumph against such odds," the authors of this book dryly observe.) He became more composed. He slept better. His appetite improved. Eventually, he was once again able to speak and write coherently. At the end of February of 1789, he ordered an end to his physicians' public reports on his condition.

For the next twelve years, during which he was in good health, doctors all over England kept speculating on what had happened to their King and how he should have been treated. One ascribed the illness to "nervous fevers," and chastised his medical colleagues for the cruel treatment of the King. Rather than starve, purge, and bleed him, efforts should have been made "to invigorate, by all possible means, the body, and to afford every consolation to the mind of their royal patient." There was talk of his "species of mania." The speculations heightened in February of 1801, when he lapsed into a "hurry of spirits." The Drs. Willis returned. Again the patient was berated, intimidated, brutalized, and his relatives and friends helplessly obeyed the arrogant commands of the doctors, versed as they were in "the mad business." Yet the King recovered in a month or two, only to fall sick in 1804 and once more in 1810. He had by then held the throne for fifty years, and this last attack in effect brought an end to his rule. He was growing senile, and he was put in the care of the Queen, a group of advisers, and the Prince of Wales, now the Prince Regent. He died in 1820 at the age of eighty-two, still under constraint:

What had placed George III at such a disadvantage as a patient were the exigencies of being King. Now these had ceased, and yet—however sad to say, he was treated worse than many of his subjects might have been—he was still kept prisoner in close solitary and silent confinement.

In these words, Dr. Macalpine and Dr. Hunter declare their great sympathy for George III. They have written a lucid account of a perplexing royal illness, and they offer a diagnosis that contradicts the King's doctors and all the speculations of their confreres—that the King was afflicted with porphyria, a disease known only since the 1930s. In every cell of the body there are purple-red pigments, or porphyrins, that give blood its color. Patients suffering from porphyria secrete abnormal amounts of pigments, and this can damage the nervous system. The disease, which is hereditary, is transmitted as a Mendelian dominant, which means that half the offspring of an affected parent can be afflicted. The exact nature of the biochemical disorder is not known, and no specific treatment exists. One sign of porphyria is discolored urine. King George's physicians mentioned "dark" or "bilious" or "bloody" urine in their reports, but porphyria is not the only disease that can cause such a development.

This diagnosis of King George would not be convincing unless Dr. Macalpine and Dr. Hunter could prove that the reports of the royal physicians accord with present-day knowledge of how porphyria manifests itself in the few patients who suffer from it. The two authors had also to adduce evidence that George's disorder plagued his ancestors and his descendants. Porphyria is, as I have said, an inherited disease, but it resembles a wide variety of infections, neurological diseases, and psychiatric disorders. The history of the Houses of Stuart, Tudor, and Hanover had to be scrutinized for evidence of similar seizures. And are any living descendants of George susceptible to porphyria? One can carry the disease but lack any symptoms. The excess pigment shows up in laboratory tests, but without these an afflicted person will be unaware that anything unusual has happened to him.

Our first task was to ascertain whether porphyria actually occurred in the family. We therefore searched for living descendants in whom its existence could be established in the laboratory. Although this meant a bold intrusion into privacy for which we still feel apologetic, we were fortunate to obtain the necessary coöperation which made it possible to diagnose it in four living family members. This provided the material evidence of necessity lacking in posthumous diagnosis.

After intensive search, the authors feel that they can demonstrate strong evidence of porphyria in a number of England's kings, dukes, and duchesses. No one will ever be able to establish whether Mary Queen of Scots, say, or George IV, the eldest son of George III, had porphyria, but they certainly had symptoms not unlike those of George III, though not as severe. Even today, doctors can fail to spot porphyria or mistake it for something else; even today, the diagnosis is not always clear-cut. The authors do not say that certain people in the seventeenth and eighteenth centuries could have suffered only from that disease; the tone of *George III and the Mad Business* is quiet, thoughtful, and undogmatic. "Facts have their limits, but theories seemingly none," say the authors. They have not forgotten their words. And they have added an account of how psychiatrists and certain historians have considered King George—as a neurotic, a manic-depressive, a victim of a psychosomatic disturbance, and so on. Every whim and fancy, every habit and decision has been abstracted to fit the needs of this or that psychiatric or psychoanalytic ideologue. The authors of this book speak of the "moralising and patronizing attitude" and the "strange lack of sympathy" in accounts of the King's difficulties. Other historical figures, too, have been posthumously "analyzed" in such a way that they become caricatures of themselves—and, indeed, of any human being—and thousands of other patients are still described in a degrading, insulting manner and treated like King George; that is, stripped of their dignity, locked up, and kept locked up. The two psychiatrists who have written about King George deserve thanks from the people of their own country for helping set straight a period of English history, from readers lucky enough to come across this book, and from those of us who have daily cause to know the injustices that thrive even in the best clinics and hospitals.

New Yorker, June 26, 1971

Us Unmistakably

Psychiatrists are, of course, physicians whose everyday work confronts them with troubled people and turbulent emotions. In twentieth-century America, psychiatrists have unwittingly (and occasionally, I fear, by conscious design) become something more—heirs to the religious devotion that middle-class agnostics still have, yet make a point of denying. I have in mind the "progressive" or "liberal" parent who has no interest in the Bible or prayer and no comprehension of what a church service can mean to someone, can *do*—yes, to an intelligent and well-educated person who is not at all "superstitious" or hung-up by some neurosis or, as Freud put it, some "illusion." As a matter of fact, if anyone's name has inspired awe and faith in the twentieth century, it has been Freud's. Did Freud say this or that? Do his ideas suggest we do one thing or another thing? Is Dr. X a true follower of Freud's, or is he a deviant, a revisionist, a man who is not recognized by the orthodox? The orthodox, in this case, call themselves psychoanalysts, scientists, observers of human behavior; but a wry observer from another planet could as easily confuse them with any number of dogmatic, punitive, narrow-minded sectarians who have their own special world, their own exclusive liturgy, their own spelled-out idea of what life offers in the way of purposes, possibilities, and evils.

Actually, there are signs that the most austere, distant, and self-righteous of psychoanalysts are worried. Some of them still act like a small band of misunderstood, persecuted souls, whose every word will naturally, inevitably (and gratifyingly) be misunderstood by the "lay public"—as I hear *anyone* outside called, however literate and honorable. On the other hand, one prominent organization of psychoanalysts has taken its case to a public relations firm—and an important psychoanalytic journal recently published a letter from some distinguished analysts who reminded their colleagues that if the Roman Catholic Church would respond to John XXIII, then perhaps it was time for some analytic institutes and associations to "open the window a bit," to let in a little fresh air.

What *can* psychiatrists do—besides help the relative handful who can afford their private care? And what can they do theoretically— besides toy and tinker with whatever gospel they choose to call their own? There does come a time when nervous, self-conscious parents will realize that no advice, no acquaintance with the unconscious, however profound and endlessly sought (and, as well, bought) can offer children immunity from anger and envy and hurt and disappointment and sadness—yes, and passions that are inconsistent or inappropriate or ill-considered or whatever. There does come a time when even the blindest followers begin to question or stray; a time when bold, curious, intelligent, and sensitive people begin to go elsewhere, think differently, and in general do exactly what Freud did between 1890 and 1900, when he looked for his own vision and came to his own conclusions.

We can find one example of the "fresh air" so needed by the psychiatric community in the work of Robert Jay Lifton. His recent book, *Death in Life: Survivors of Hiroshima*, is extremely important and valuable in its own right. In addition, as a thinker and an investigator the author offers us significant evidence that at least one young American psychiatrist can use psychoanalytic insight without worshiping psychoanalytic tenets; can observe the mind's life without turning all life into a subdivision of psychology; and, perhaps most important of all, can be both a doctor and a student of history and politics. Lifton's first book was *Thought Reform and the Psychology of Totalism*, published in 1961. The United States Air Force had taken him to Japan and Korea, and while there he became interested in Asia as well as in American military bases and the various tourist attractions that Westerners frequent. He also became interested in brainwashing, a particularly dramatic yet mysterious process that continues to puzzle and fascinate those of us in Europe and the United States.

What happened to those Western civilians who emerged from Mao's China in the 1950s full of praise for communism and full of criticism and scorn for themselves, their old ways and habits and beliefs? What happened to dozens of Chinese intellectuals who seemed to turn abruptly on their entire past, on all their ideals, for the sake of China's "new order"? How do revolutionary commissars go about indoctrinating a whole range of people, from Christian missionaries to Western intellectuals, from avowed anticommunists to vaguely sympathetic liberals?

Lifton tried to find the answers to questions like these by moving to Hong Kong and talking again and again with those who had gone through it all: the sequence of arrest, fearful interrogation, subtle and not so subtle intimidation, the trial, confession, "reeducation," and then, ironically, expulsion to countries like England, France, or America. Hong Kong was (and still is) the point of contact between two worlds, and there the youthful, curious, open-minded, hard-working psychiatrist could meet them one by one as they came from China—people who appeared tired, defeated, strangely exhilarated, confused, or anything but confused. What Lifton discovered cannot be easily summarized because he was, after all, a clinician. He saw all sorts of different people and in consequence wrote up a number of life stories, but he also extracted what he could from his observations and indicated how decisively we are all affected by political and historical events—particularly when men with power and cunning desire to *make* us be affected.

Nor did Lifton stop there. He was impressively willing to look at "totalism" as by no means a peculiarly Russian, Chinese, or "Oriental" phenomenon. In fact, he looked right here at home, at his own profession. We all learn to accept certain premises and values, to deny others as "wrong" or even "evil." Machines become gods, as do individuals and ideas. Particular theories are turned into catchall explanations for anything and everything. Tentative assumptions made by a man like Freud become for slavish followers the unassailable truth. Were Freud alive today he would be a different man struggling with different problems—but that makes no difference to dogmatic, partisan, arrogant psychoanalysts who claim his mantle, proclaim themselves his "heirs," build institutions around that kind of assertion, and proceed to demand of young aspirants compliance, devotion, and uncritical submission. Concepts like "resistance" or "transference" are used not only to explain what happens between a therapist and a patient but to stifle new ideas or disagreements with established doctrine. If I question the "libido theory" or something else that is "fundamental," I may be charged with "resisting," or with "acting-out" something in "the transference" that goes on in

my "training analysis." I can be called "borderline" or—in the
clutch—an "unsuitable candidate." In sum, Lifton did not shirk
pointing out the embarrassing parallels between psychoanalytic ideologies and others.

What does such a psychiatrist do next? He can, of course, return
to the fold, return not only to America but to all the blandishments
and restraints that a somewhat nervous, uncertain, but eminently
trusted and even adored profession can offer the eager and uncritical
practitioner. He can join the groups, the organizations, the societies—and dismiss whatever doubts or misgivings he once had,
not to mention any inconveniently unpopular or unusual views or
attitudes. He can write out a check or two for a social cause here, a
charity there—and remind himself that he has his job, his competence. Let the next guy do it—do whatever it is that *those people* do
when they get upset about wars, about atomic bombs, about forms
of violence that threaten to destroy the planet. And anyway, *those
people*, the ones who join demonstrations and protest against the
government—aren't they "neurotic" or "disturbed" or "sick" or
struggling with this or that "unconscious conflict" by "displacing" it,
by masking it with "nonpsychological" concerns, like the threat of
nuclear war, of our very extinction?

As a matter of fact, what about those two bombs we did choose to
let fall upon thousands and thousands of men, women, and children
back in 1945? What did the explosions do, not only to land and steel
and wood, not only to trees and water and fish and fowl, not only to
flesh and bones and blood, but to the minds of those who survived,
who were near but not fatally near, who barely escaped or were hurt
but not too much? Now how can *we* answer those questions? For
one thing, we are Americans, the ones whose deeds made the questions reasonable ones. We don't speak Japanese. We're here, not
there. And if we are psychiatrists, presumably interested in finding
out about such matters—oh, there are all too many barriers that face
us, like language, or "cross-cultural" differences, or the "limitations" of our professional competence.

Lifton somehow managed to overcome those barriers. Perhaps he
was "driven" to do so; and had he gone through that extra year of
analysis he might have become more "realistic," less involved with
the faraway, the morbid, the terrifying. Perhaps he is "rebellious":
while other American psychiatrists locate themselves by the hun-

dreds and hundreds near rich and disease-prone enclaves like Beverly Hills and Park Avenue, Lifton goes his own stubborn, defiant, unusual, original, and unsettling way. *Something* must be wrong; he *must* need "help."

In fact, Robert Lifton would probably be the first one to acknowledge that he and all the people he has observed in Hiroshima do indeed need our help. The survivors of the world's first atomic bombing need listeners, attentive listeners who will heed the grim and painful lessons that others have learned—and work to prevent the unlimited number of Hiroshimas now possible. Put differently, the survivors of Hiroshima need to be understood, not only as "others," as particularly wounded and unfortunate people, but very possibly, very easily, as *us;* indeed, at the push of a button, us unmistakably and us irremediably.

So, we can find out—those of us who want to know—what happened "back there" in 1945 when a plane, not an armada of planes, appeared over Hiroshima and dropped one small bomb, not a torrent of bombs. We can find out not so much what happened but what was set in motion and continues to exist: death in life. Lifton starts *Death in Life* by telling us honestly and directly about himself, his background, his interests, and his purposes. He wants to be a careful observer, but he knows that the cult of anonymity among psychiatrists can be as dangerous as the cult of personality is for a nation.

> In making arrangements for the interviews, I was aware of my delicate—even Kafkaesque—position as an American psychiatrist approaching people about their feelings concerning the bomb. From the beginning I relied heavily upon introductions—first from Tokyo and Hiroshima colleagues and friends to various individuals and groups (particularly at the University, the medical school, and the City Office), and then from the latter to actual research subjects. In the case of the randomly selected group, ordinary Japanese who would have been extremely dubious about a direct approach from a psychiatrist or an American, I first made a personal visit to the home together with a Japanese social worker from the Hiroshima University Research Institute for Nuclear Medicine and Biology. He and I, in fact, spent many exhausting hours that spring and summer

on the hot Hiroshima streets, tracking down these dwelling places.

He goes on to emphasize his "sense of the ethical as well as the scientific issues involved," and his hope that his work "might make some contribution to the mastery of these weapons and the avoidance of their use, as well as to our general knowledge of man." He also makes quite clear how flexible he wants to, indeed has to, keep his theoretical position. He was, after all, observing particular individuals, who nevertheless share a common social and cultural tradition. He was studying their responses to an overwhelming "moment"—a time in history. In a sense, then, he had to juggle all sorts of roles. He was delving into the minds of people; but he was also observing the way they respond as *Japanese* men and women; and in addition he was documenting certain universals—the way people respond to extremity, to the sight of widespread death, to the experience of lingering death, to the prospect of a deathlike life.

The heart of this book is its rich clinical material—pages and pages of words and feelings and ideas that give us a sense of what it was like when and after the Bomb fell on Hiroshima in the early morning of August 6, 1945. There had of course been the threat of bombings and, indeed, the likelihood that American planes would badly damage Hiroshima and many other Japanese cities. Yet no dread, no apprehension could prepare men and women for what happened:

I was a little ill . . . so I stayed home that day. . . . There had been an air-raid warning and then an all clear. I felt relieved and lay down on the bed with my younger brother . . . then it happened. It came very suddenly. . . . It felt something like an electric short—a bluish sparkling light. . . . There was a noise, and I felt great heat—even inside the house. When I came to, I was underneath the destroyed house. . . .

He was lucky. Thousands and thousands died instantly. A whole city was destroyed in a flash. A disaster not only occurred but persisted over time—with the deaths from "A-Bomb Disease," from the effects of radiation, from leukemia, occurring year after year.

Those who survived the immediate devastation became, for a while, dazed, broken in spirit, paralyzed, fearful, and "behaved like automatons." The world seemed at an end. Perhaps hell had finally arrived. But gradually the mind (so it seems) can deal with anything; and in chapter after chapter, Lifton shows us how various and particular men and women and children have done that—faced their unparalleled condition as *hibakusha*, "explosion-affected" people. The full play of human ingenuity was of course mobilized by such a disaster, and from year to year sick, anxious, desperately fearful people tried in all sorts of ways to keep their spirits up, to make do, to regain a sense of confidence and purpose.

Survival itself was a central issue for everyone who survived—and in much of this book we hear puzzled, grieving, lost souls wondering *why* and *when*: why it all happened, why they were still alive, when they would die. Lifton's portrayal of the scene makes one think of Dante's *Inferno*, with souls wandering about in terrible agony, guilt, remorse, pain, and terror. Everyone sought "trust, peace, mastery"—some sense that, after all and in spite of everything, the world was not beyond redemption. And everyone sought something else too: a conviction that life would somehow continue, no matter how imminent, inevitable, and specially triumphant death appeared to be.

I found it very hard to read this book. I found myself looking for diversions and distractions. If Hiroshima's *hibakusha* felt and continue to feel guilty even for being alive (as indeed do the relative few who survived the German concentration camps) then we, too, have every cause, every past and present cause, to shudder at what we did and continue to do as mighty, technological warriors who dominate the world yet also gravely threaten it (and ourselves). Lifton tells how the people of Hiroshima view America. We in America are perhaps less willing to think about Hiroshima—and, even more important, about what led up to it and what could yet again lead up to a total, annihilating war.

Still, toward the end of *Death in Life*, a certain measured but real and even inspiring sense of hope comes through to the reader. I do not speak of good cheer, or optimism, or a "cathartic" resolution of one or another "complex." I have in mind the kind of gloomy and severe and sharp but humorous sensibility that William Faulkner demonstrated again and again. The *world* is almost unbearably awful, but the *individual*, no matter how hard-pressed and death-bound, can endure and prevail *because* he or she is human—

vulnerable and sick and weary and abused and abusive; but also able to make, driven to make, the effort toward coherence, toward understanding. And so little Jewish children in the Terezin camp drew haunting pictures of the gas chambers, and little Japanese children wrote poems to celebrate, yes, celebrate, the "curse" their city suffered; yet this was also a celebration of their city's persistence, its lingering sadness, its protracted pain, its continuing rage. Death had a grip on Hiroshima, but at the same time its people could shake their fists at the world and try to live, live at whatever cost.

Despite the sensible and sensitive criticism that Lifton directs at rigid (and by now deathly boring) psychoanalytic doctrine, the formulation implied in the title *Death in Life* and developed throughout the book is essentially very similar to Freud's later view of humanity's central struggle—to stay alive and be nourishing in the face of the mind's destructive inclinations, the body's relentless decline, and the world's increasing threat to everyone and everything. In the latter part of the twentieth century, we have to pray not for a victory in that kind of struggle—by definition there can never be one—but for *time*, for the very time to continue to wage the daily struggle for life and against death.

Kenyon Review, Autumn 1968

Commentary on
Psychology and Literature

I don't think it is melodramatic to suggest that literary talent, in its inspired forms, has obsessed if not haunted psychoanalytic psychology. Freud's well-known remark on creativity, set down in an essay (1928) on Dostoevski ("Before the problem of the creative artist, analysis must, alas, lay down its arms"), indicates the frustrated combativeness of a man himself exceptionally talented. The psychoanalyst who thought of himself as a conquistador had a canny sense of when to abstain from a battle. Nevertheless, all of Freud's followers by no means followed his lead. In the 1930s Edmund Bergler, a New York City analyst, turned out a succession of books and articles meant to show how "sick," how "neurotic" writers are. (In that regard, the irony of his own writing campaign never seemed to strike him as odd or amusing.) When I got to know William Carlos Williams fairly well (I wrote my college "major paper" on his poetry), I was warned several times in letters about a trend he considered dangerous indeed: "I'm tired of seeing writers singled out for these blasts. If I read doctor Freud right, he's telling us that we're all full of conflicts—the way it goes for the human mind. So what's new! Oh, I pull back: what's new is that he's probed our mental affairs—whereas Sophocles or Shakespeare brought them to life. The probe is for doctors! When you leave the theatre and go to your office you need a probe! But some of these psycho-analytic literary critics have created a new medical specialty: the artist or writer as victim! You remember my dogs, 'sniffing' in *Paterson*? Some of the psychology I read, about writers and their writing, makes me think of 'sniffing'—that 'I smell shit look' people sometimes get."

In his paper on Heinz Kohut's interesting and important work, Dr. Ernest Wolf suggests early on that psychoanalysts have been wrongly charged with "besmirching and degrading" their various "betters," who have given us what gets called in the essay "sublime inspirations." Such a charge, we are told, is incorrect: "This distorted view of the psychoanalysis of literature surely does not fit Freud nor most psychoanalytic commentators." Yet later on the same author quotes Heinz Kohut himself as feeling it necessary to take issue with a good number of his colleagues: "He sharply criticizes the amateurishness and reductionism of some psychoanalytic critics." Needless to say, the issue is not percentages. Many, maybe most, psychoanalysts have all they can do to deal with the challenges of their everyday clinical work. But from those who have chosen to pursue "applied psychoanalysis," there have been plenty of logical lapses, not to mention abusive sprees, as Kohut seems to imply when he hesitates long and hard about the very point of using psychoanalytic ideas in a nonclinical intellectual setting.

Maybe Anna Freud had it right, so far as some psychoanalytic criticism of artists and writers goes, when she referred to "the universally envied gift of creative energy." Envy can take many forms, one of which is condescension—as in the astonishing acknowledgment in Marie-Louise von Franz's paper that "psychology . . . can even learn from it [literature]." Why the author felt it necessary to use the word "even" is, of course, her own business, but one is struck at the gratuitous presence of such an adverb. Nor is the following remark anything but a reminder of the kind of self-serving arrogance one not rarely encounters in supposedly "friendly" comments from analytic psychologists of the Jungian persuasion: "But more frequently the artist just simply has no idea himself of what has been said through him and is relieved and impressed if one can show it to him." A bit further on we are told that "all truly creative people know [this]: the woundedness of their soul through the creative impulse." No wonder Flannery O'Connor, in her letters (*The Habit of Being*, p. 491), observes that "to religion I think he [Freud] is much less dangerous than Jung." Maybe the same holds for literary criticism—because an apparent friendliness can mask a brutal hauteur. Nor do murky pieties about "archetypes" bring us all that closer to the contours of psychological reality, be it that of a patient or that offered us on a canvas or in the words of a poet, a novelist.

I refer to the above comments because I believe they indicate, yet again, some of the difficulties that plague a kind of psychological literary criticism. Nor is the issue only a matter of arrogance or single-minded (and self-serving) professional simplification of exceedingly complex issues. I wonder whether, finally, we are not confronted with a question of sensibility—that of the social scientist as against that of the humanist. "It is the business of fiction to embody mystery through manners," said Flannery O'Connor—and then she added this: "Mystery is a great embarrassment to the modern mind." For her, such mystery was not to be "resolved," that cool, slippery word that so many of us use today. If anything, stories and poems aim, unashamedly, to deepen mystery. To quote from another letter of Dr. Williams: "Some want to analyze the air—and tell us how much oxygen and hydrogen are around. Others want to enjoy the air, and mix things up—mist, fog, rain, blinding sun."

But even if we take social science logic on its own conceptual merits, we are in trouble when we come across a statement such as this: "An essay on Sylvia Plath by Weisblatt delineated the narcissistic elements in certain of her poems." Dr. Wolf admittedly has no time to tell us more about those "elements," but surely he ought to stop and remind us that there are "narcissistic elements" in *all* writing—all poems, all critiques of poems, and yes, all essays written on narcissism, or on other essays concerned with narcissism, not to mention comments such as these with respect to sentences that appear in that last-mentioned category. The issue is not narcissism—in Shakespeare's sonnets or the works of Yeats or Keats or, for that matter, in Heinz Kohut's writing. (The two leading theorists of narcissism, Kohut and Otto Kernberg, have proved their humanity by the way they have narcissistically argued with each other.) The issue is language—the uses to which it is put. There are "narcissistic elements" in all language, of course—that of the suicidally disturbed and that of the normal, that of smart critics and that of ordinary working people with no pretension to learned thinking, and not least, that of psychoanalysts and psychoanalysands, as well as that of men and women who write poems or who criticize the content of those poems and evaluate their words.

To tell us that Sylvia Plath shows to a reader "narcissistic elements in certain of her poems" is to tell us that Sylvia Plath was, finally, a human being. Sylvia Plath's narcissism was easily matched, if not exceeded, by the narcissism of thousands and thousands of other human beings. We remember her for her words and their arrangement. Her narcissism did not generate those words. What did? The mystery of the origins of language persists: neurophysiological and biochemical processes, speech centers in the brain—and on and on.

As for the cognitive gifts that enable a Sylvia Plath to see so much, understand so much—is biology to be denied a significant causative role? But geneticists and neurochemists or neuroanatomists or linguistic scholars or cognitive psychologists are not the ones who keep trying to "explain" talent or "delineate" this or that "element" in one or another poet's work.

Are we really helped to understand Shakespeare or Goethe, Tolstoy or Joyce (I disagree with, and resent, the characterization of *Ulysses* as a work flawed by "nihilistic bias" in the von Franz paper), by the statement of Freud's that "the creative writer does the same as the child at play"? The creative writer does quite something else. He doesn't "create a world of fantasy which he takes seriously." He creates a work of art. Sometimes, as we strain for resemblances (in pursuit of what—an explanation of someone else's enviable achievements?), we forget the most obvious distinctions in the world. Millions of children play; millions of adults create their worlds of fantasies and, God knows (as in mental hospital patients!), take their fantasies all too seriously. A few (James Joyce, for instance) come up with the astonishing subtleties and nuances of word and meaning, the triumph of scholarship and imagination, the bravura performance of a *Ulysses*.

What any number of us psychiatrists fail to perceive (and not only in connection with writers and artists) is that psychopathology and even normal emotional development are but one part of mental life. Language itself is, after all, what distinguishes us from all other creatures—the ability to gain distance on ourselves and our situation through words. We are the ones who ask why and how. We are the ones who come into consciousness through the strange phenomenon that still eludes us: the baby speaks—and thereafter, a new being, so to speak, has emerged. To paraphrase John of the New Testament: in the beginning, man's beginning, was the Word, and then "the Word became Flesh." For all Noam Chomsky's brilliance, or that of any other student of linguistics, semiotics, or whatever, we are yet left with cortical "areas," with inherited capacities, potentialities, and mechanisms. Granted, one day we'll know more about the mechanistic details of this most basic aspect of ourselves—but is there *any* reason why our emotional development need be so decisively and insistently brought into the matter? If both Chomsky and Piaget shrink from trying to explain to us the origins of literary accomplishment, if they refuse to tackle our Sylvia Plaths, whose cognitive and linguistic attainments are the reasons we attend them, then why are our experts in psychopathology so eager, on such scant evidence, to be so consistently interpretive, if not outright convinced of their speculative accuracy?

Why, moreover, these days, do literary critics, never mind historians, embrace so willingly these psychological ruminations? Is Jung doing religious thinking, not to mention ordinary, faithful worshipers of God Almighty, any favor when he tells us that we have a "religious need?" A noblesse oblige slap on the back, perhaps! A twentieth-century sanctioning nod to those who might otherwise worry all too much that they'll be considered naive, superstitious! Or a tautological banality: the observer who watches some of us praying quite hard, or struggling long and painfully to figure out the meaning of this life, and concludes thereafter that—we are doing, we are impelled to do, just that! Similarly with art and artists, literature and writers: they have graced us over and over again with their sketches and paintings, their statements, epic or epigrammatic, their chronicles, brief or ever so extended—and in this century some of us say yes, they are sick, this way or that, or yes, they would be sick, one way or another, if they weren't writing, or yes, it is a particular vulnerability, a certain reparative tendency, that accounts for *Middlemarch* and *War and Peace* and *Lear* and *Hamlet* and all the other plays, novels, stories, and poems. Maybe some of us are born (Nature's gift) with linguistic excellence. Maybe some of us have God-given visual or linguistic capacities—brains a touch more able to use words or to visualize and reproduce externally what is visualized. I don't know. No one does. Geneticists keep their silence and investigate. Neurobiologists do likewise. As do those psychologists who pursue the paths of our intellectual growth. I think that psychiatrists and psychoanalysts, some already struggling bravely to straighten out their own house, ought for a good while to stop poking into homes next door, if not those located on an entirely different street.

New Literary History, Autumn 1980

Medicine and Literature

Literature and Medicine

*I*n recent years an increasing number of medical schools have begun to offer medical students an opportunity to reflect upon the nature of their future work with the help of what I used to hear Dr. William Carlos Williams keep calling "the novelist's angle of vision." What did he mean when he used that phrase? He offered this explanation one day, in the last decade of his life, to a medical student who had crossed the Hudson river to visit him yet again:

> The abstract, categorical mind can be wonderful—the glory of the intellect at work, coming to its great big (and big-deal!) conclusions. But we've got to keep a close check on all that—the head running away with itself. The doctor treating a patient out there on the front line falls back on himself, his own manner of being with people—and he has to come to terms with not only a disease but a particular person: *this* patient, not patienthood, not lungs in general, or kidneys or hearts in general, but one guy, one gal, one kid who has some trouble and is handling it in a way that may be different than anyone else's way!

Vintage Williams, I'd learned by then—after years of hearing him whisper or quietly declare, but sometimes shout his head off. This was the writing doc who was always plain and unpretentious; who for years had been telling his readers "no ideas but in things"; who kept making the distinction between theory and conduct; who once exclaimed to his wife and a visitor that "smart ain't necessarily good." He was always doing that: slipping into the language of his working class and poor and immigrant patients of northern New Jersey—not to be affected, not to be a reverse snob, as I once thought, but to remind himself that language isn't important only to poets but to doctors who treat patients. He heard in the words of those he treated affirmations of strength, expressions of sadness, and not least, spells of great lyric power, no matter the grammar. "It's important," he once said, "to listen not only to the complaints of your patients but how they put them into words for you—how they choose to say (and regard!) what they want to tell you." Then he added this comment: "Of course, sometimes you're not only being told about your patients (by them) but told about yourself—even told off!"

I begin with those remembered moments because they address candidly and without affectation what the humanities have to offer us in medicine who want to pay them heed, whether teachers or students. Williams knew well the inherent affinity between medicine and the humanities—their shared interest in the concreteness of particular human experience. The poet sings of the seen, the heard, and puts in words, in images, what one mind has witnessed or imagined. The novelist spins yarns meant to evoke a specific situation or plot and specific characters. The doctor treats one person, then another, aware all the time (one hopes) that variation is a great constant of the work he or she does—those aspects of our individuality, those idiosyncrasies, those personal habits and beliefs and wishes and worries that distinguish each of us from the other, and that so often have a great bearing on the way a disease progresses (meaning how it affects a given life) and so, how a course of treatment will go.

Not that the humanities and (Lord knows) medicine are or ought to be unpreoccupied with principles, theories, and large-scale abstractions. The poet uses (or willfully chooses not to use) rhyme and meter; the novelist often has all sorts of ideas that get worked into stories; the doctor has that seeming infinity of factuality to tame, not to mention all sorts of formulations and rules. Yet, at a certain point there is, as Dr. Williams put it, "that awesome moment of application," when all the knowledge we have acquired, all the interpretations and theories, have to stand the test of—well, an *instance*: this poem or story, this patient here before me, who, yes, may have one disease, lupus, I have studied and know in general how to approach (which drugs, what "regimen") but who has a life and a mode of thinking and feeling and seeing and listening and responding that are no one else's and may well count for a lot in how that lupus proceeds. As Robert F. Loeb used to tell us medical students: "never say 'never,' and never say 'always'; and try to leave yourselves plenty of elbowroom when talking with a patient about what you've concluded and what you see ahead."

The linear mind and the categorical mind are an important part of ourselves. We all crave and need straight lines to connect the various points we envision, discover, or sometimes conjure up. We all rely upon generalizations, conceptualizations—abstract efforts meant to hold together "people, places, things." But life itself (so our poets and novelists remind us) and the practice of medicine (so we physicians discover after we've crammed all the data into our exhausted heads during the first year or two of medical school) have to do with the enormous range of possibilities our patients offer us. Life is not only cause and effect, not only "variables" with their inexorable and deterministic "symptomatology." Life is chance and circumstance and luck (good or bad). Life is surprises—irony, ambiguity, unpredictability, inconsistency. Life is strength coming out of weaknesses—even "diseases" prompting moral depth and intellectual growth, as Tolstoy knew when he gave us "The Death of Ivan Ilyich," in which a sick lawyer for the first time in his adult life (and at the very end of that life) recognizes the meaning of love. A medical or psychiatric "reductionism" does not quite explain how any given person comes to terms with his or her life, or illness, or final moments on this earth.

Novels and short stories or poems help us understand such matters: the patient confronting (and educating) the therapist or doctor in Tillie Olsen's "I Stand Here Ironing"; the decency and generosity of a particular alcoholic in her "Hey Sailor, What Ship?"—a contrast with the smug and self-serving "normal world"; the terrible irony of years and years of marriage, with no real knowledge of or trust for one another on the part of a husband and wife, as revealed by the onset of disease and the approach of death, evoked in her "Tell Me a Riddle." Also of obvious help are such old reliables of our literary tradition as George Eliot's *Middlemarch*, with its close examination of the moral and professional life of Dr. Lydgate; or Flannery O'Connor's stories—for instance, "The Lame Shall Enter First," with its hard look at a healer's pride and blindness, and yes, his need of a bit of the healing he offers others; and Dr. Walker Percy's serious yet comic "existential" analyses of our contemporary, late-twentieth-century American moral and spiritual lives (in his essays, collected as *The Message in the Bottle*, and his novels, such as *The Moviegoer* and *Love in the Ruins*).

All through Dr. Percy's writing, the reader is reminded of the spiritual "malaise" that afflicts so many of us, the boredom or mean-inglessness of our lives, the hectic pace we maintain—an effective deterrent to moral reflection. Like Tolstoy, Percy sees psychological and physical pain as potentially redemptive—a means by which the smugly self-sufficient are compelled to reach out, take note of others, and think about this life's purpose.

I would like to end where I began, by mentioning the wonderful storytelling and poetry of the physician William Carlos Williams. His *Doctor Stories* brings to life the everyday hurdles we face in medicine as we struggle not only with our diagnostic or therapeutic challenges but with ourselves, our inevitably flawed humanity, our times of bitterness or envy or frustration or greed, our passions and dreams, our sometimes extravagant hopes and eager expectations, and, of course (since our patients will one day die, and we as well), our moments of disappointment and melancholy. Still, we persist, as Dr. Williams did, through the efforts he made in his medical life and, too, through the stories he produced during his writing life, which render us and our patients in the round, so to speak: as whole, complex, and many-sided as we all are.

Journal of the American Medical Association, October 17, 1986

The Wry Dr. Chekhov

Many of us who attended Columbia's College of Physicians and Surgeons in the 1950s admired the clinical teaching of Dr. Yale Kneeland—his everyday tact, his civility, his able and alert diagnostic mind, his ready wit, and not least, the breadth and depth of his knowledge. In that last respect he was outstanding and unforgettable—for the novels and poetry he had read and was constantly offering his medical students as a gift; for his touting the humanities as the best possible way to comprehend this life we live, with all its inevitable worries, surprises, hurdles, disappointments, and losses. I had the special good luck of getting to know Dr. Kneeland rather well; he was my tutor in medicine, and because we both loved to talk about Dickens and George Eliot, about Dostoevski and Tolstoy, about William Carlos Williams and T. S. Eliot, we became good friends. Many times I'd get discouraged, go to see Dr. Kneeland, tell him I was a sorry medical student, indeed, and utterly ill-suited for the profession I was pursuing (out of motives I couldn't at all figure out). He would have none of my self-pity (or the egoism behind it). He approached his patients with a directness and candor, with an utter lack of condescension or guile, which we student onlookers found to be magical, refreshing, compelling; and several times I had occasion to feel rather as those patients must have felt—grateful for a particular doctor's blunt realism (all the more affecting for the charm and courtesy that characterized its presentation).

I especially remember a day of despair that ended in a visit to Dr. Kneeland's Presbyterian Hospital office. A third-year medical student, I had witnessed a young woman's death. She had been sick for several years with a chronic leukemia, and her lively intelligence and apparent physical beauty had made her an object of great concern and interest in the course of her repeated admissions to the hospital. She had taught school for a while before getting sick, and she rejoiced in making the doctors who attended her a bit more literate, if not literary, during the course of her (by then) increasingly frequent hospitalizations. They hovered around her, I noticed, and sick as she was, healthy as they were, the energy seemed invariably to emanate from her, with her medical caretakers becoming more and more animated, even radiant, as they heeded her observations, interpretations, and *explications de texte*. Finally, she would have given out all she had, and she seemed suddenly to turn pale, become mute. She would, invariably, punctuate the end of her discourse by letting her head fall back on the two pillows that had propped her.

I remember, one day, she went further. She took one of the pillows in her right hand and held it over the floor beside her bed for what seemed like the longest time—to the point that the doctor at the foot of her bed, not to mention me, began to worry: was she becoming a bit "strange"? We were grateful when the hand released the pillow, but then to our alarm we noticed that immediately thereafter the patient's eyes closed. But our questions ("are you all right?") were promptly and sensibly answered: "Yes, of course." Knowing her interrogators to be unsatisfied, she added: "I am as tired of hearing myself talk as that friend of mine, that pillow, is of bearing my shoulders up!" We laughed nervously. Never before had I thought of a pillow that way; never would I forget the soft noise of the pillow hitting the floor—a quiet yet dramatic resolution to a given moment of sadness, of outright despair, provided by a remarkable, dying lady of twenty-eight.

Unfortunately, I was on duty (four months and two hospitalizations later) one evening when that lady suddenly took very ill. I was drawing blood from a nearby patient when I heard these words: "This is the last night of my life." There was no great urgency or alarm in the speaker's voice; rather, she seemed resigned, wistful. She was, yet again, the knowing teller—the narrator anxious for any nearby listener to be informed. I recall looking not only at her but at the space around her bed: surely someone was there to whom she was addressing her remarks. But no one was near except the other patient, whose blood I'd just taken, and I. Yet her head was not turned toward us. I wondered whether she'd become agitated or disturbed, whether she might not be hallucinating. I wondered whether she was newly sick and might not need some late-night medical scrutiny—even though I'd been assured a few hours earlier that she was OK and might even be sent home once more the next day. Then, another statement: "I wish the world well." The same tone—matter-of-fact rather than strenuously insistent. She had been given some new medication, I seemed to recall: perhaps it—in conjunction with the chloral-hydrate pill she took, sometimes, to induce sleep—had gone to her head, had prompted a "reaction." The patient I had been working on came to the same conclusion. He had a serious disease himself, lupus erythematosis, and he knew what medication (cortisone) could do to the mind. He suggested that I go talk with her. His reason: "At night it's worse here: everyone is closer to death around midnight."

Lord, I thought to myself: I have an exam tomorrow, and it *is* midnight. This visit to her, across the hall, would be a brief one. No lectures from her on Willa Cather and Eudora Welty, on Tolstoy and Chekhov, their different ways of seeing the world, of being! I entered the room. Right away she looked at me. She smiled. I was already sure that she was all right. She seemed comfortable and calm. Her face had a quiet steadiness to it. I asked her if there was anything I could do before I left the floor—a way of speaking I'd learned from Dr. Kneeland: the low-key, general question that gave the patient a chance to declare something, to stress a conviction, to make a request. She said this to me: "You can do—well, you can try to be a good doctor." She was still being rather soft-spoken and cool in her way of speaking, but I was again having psychiatric thoughts, if not misgivings. This phrase came to my mind, a phrase I'd decided to suggest (at our next morning's rounds) be written in the chart: Psych consult. I saw from the corner of my eye a nurse walk down the corridor: she might be the one to implement that order by making a phone call. Should I tell her what was on my mind—take credit for being the first one to realize that something else was now wrong with this lady who had been having such a terrible, terrible time for several years, and who seemed uncannily in control of herself, we'd often noted, to the point we'd as much as arraigned her on *that* score: an excessive normality, as it were, which masked a deep and abiding fearfulness?

Suddenly, as I stood there, silently ruminating, I was asked this: "I hope we're not on Ward 6." No, I said, this is the seventh floor. I thought I saw a look of uncertainty cross this dying woman's face. I was sure that she was becoming confused—an aspect of her deteriorating medical condition or, perhaps, her mind's response to the treatment she'd been receiving. In fact, I was later to realize, she was perplexed about me: how to tell this young man that she was making a literary reference, but not to show off, not to be frivolous or provocatively skeptical? But at the time all I knew was the sudden terror that soon enough seized both of us in that room. The patient began to sit up, as if (I thought for a second) she wanted to tell me something. Then she lurched back in her bed and appeared to be struggling hard for her every breath. I rushed to her side, saw how very sick she was, ran to the nurses' station to page the doctors on duty, rushed back to the room in a state of helpless alarm—to find the patient unconscious. As I tried to feel a pulse, all I knew to do, a nurse arrived, took one experienced look, and told me that the young lady had died.

When I told Dr. Kneeland about this melancholy, late-night incident, he shook his head. He'd known the patient, known the prognosis, and was not surprised. I remember him leaning back in his chair, asking me what I "made" of the "reference to Ward 6." I recited my aspiring doctor's hunches and interpretations—the disorientation of the very sick I'd already begun to recognize as familiar. Dr. Kneeland said nothing when I'd finished my nervously detailed explanation; he reached over to a bookcase near his desk, took in his right hand a book, opened it, scrutinized the table of contents, turned to a page, put a slip of paper from his desk in the book to mark that page, then handed the book to me. I opened it and there it was: "Ward 6." I remember reading quickly the first words of the story: "There is a small annex in the hospital yard. . . ." I remember closing the book, my right thumb still on the page marked for me by Dr. Kneeland, noticing (a bit ashamed, by now) who had authored this "Ward 6." Before I had a chance to say anything (and I didn't know what to say), I heard this: "Take it with you. Chekhov should be every doctor's lifelong companion."

I'd read Chekhov's plays in an undergraduate course but none of his stories. Soon enough I would read "Ward 6," and then, one by one, all in that collection. A week or so later I returned the book to Dr. Kneeland, and we talked about Chekhov the doctor, Chekhov the social observer and storyteller, and of course, about the suffering patient, near death, who'd asked me that question. I thought I'd understood "Ward 6," and so was all the more puzzled as I tried to figure out what possible reason a patient had found to compare, even by indirection, the good and earnest care she was receiving at the Columbia-Presbyterian Medical Center in New York during the middle 1950s with the care the patients of an obscure, provincial psychiatric ward received in late-nineteenth-century Czarist Russia. Dr. Kneeland didn't even have to ask me what was troubling me; he saw rather clearly my mind at work and responded this way: "She was very sick for a long time. Death was closing in. She felt trapped and cheated by life. You were the nearest person at hand, a representative of 'life'; and so she told you what she felt was happening to her—with the help of Dr. Chekhov." For me that moment was a critical one—the single most important experience during the years of medical training I'd had and would have. A writer had been urged upon me, suggested as a lifelong companion. A patient's agony had been translated—explained to my uncomprehending ears. The considerable risks of a doctor's self-important and self-serving isolation from his patients had also been set forth—by an astute clinician who had shrewdly comprehended why a Chekhov story meant so much to a lady for whom death was an imminent visitor.

Now I teach Chekhov to certain medical students. We read "Ward 6" and discuss the visionary Dr. Chekhov's apprehension of the topsy-turvy psychiatric world, where "normality" is often enough to be found in the eye of the beholder, and where medical judgments merge all too commonly with moral ones—so that those called "sick" are treated as bothersome if not evil. But Chekhov did not only anticipate R. D. Laing or Thomas Szasz (psychiatric critics of psychiatry) by almost a century. In "Ward 6" and in "An Attack of Nerves," he had spotted something larger amiss than a self-righteousness that defends itself at all costs. Dr. Ragin of "Ward 6" has not only put himself at a remove from his patients; he is also lost to himself. He drifts. He is easily distracted. He reads but does not live. He is resigned to this life's considerable injustices, its mean and nasty sides—and his attitude, we begin to see, adds to the sum total of the very evil he presumably wants to ignore, if not resist passively. His protagonist, Gramov, is a patient whose canniness and directness do indeed make the reader question the concept of "insanity," not to mention a politics that allows a Dr. Ragin the control over others he has. But Gramov is as wildly self-centered in his own way as Dr. Ragin certainly comes across as being, and clearly Chekhov is reminding all doctors and all patients of their common susceptibilities, flaws, and moral failings. When Dr. Ragin becomes aroused to injustice, becomes more concerned with at least one patient, and surrenders his protective aloofness, he is exposed and soon enough himself becomes a victim, a suffering and hurt person—and a much more honorable one, we are persuaded to conclude. Who is healing whom on this planet—in any hospital, clinic, office, home? Chekhov knew how to pose an ironic question.

Even now, a quarter of a century later, I think of that very sick young lady, her intelligence so textured and lively, wondering with Chekhov's help whether any doctor would willingly stop for long to talk with someone like her about more than a procedure, a test, a medical diagnosis or prognosis. Maybe many of us doctors, with good reason, lack the time to have the long talks some of our patients crave and need. We are overwhelmed with necessary burdens. Those procedures and tests, as a matter of fact, can be critically important for our patients, even lifesaving. Still, Chekhov was a philosophical writer, a doctor who was himself sick for years and who died of tuberculosis at forty-four. (As with William Carlos Williams, his medical work was not an incidental biographical fact but rather an important element in a particular literary and moral sensibility.) He wondered what this existence meant as a person destined to die relatively young often does: he felt life's fatefulness and arbitrariness, its paradoxes, as (in their sum) a continual, vexing pressure but also as a challenge. That young woman of my early medical career no doubt had been making Chekhov's kind of powerful if understated ethical inquiries all during her prolonged, painful illness, and like him, she had wondered whether the time we spend here is not absurd, a spell of being in a "ward" in which the blind lead the blind.

"I am tired of theorizing about life," Chekhov once wrote. He hardly need have said so. His gifts to us lack the arrogance of so much conceptual thinking—its conquering self-centeredness. His gifts are the concrete particulars of those stories and plays; and in them doctors constantly appear, usually wry observers and searchers, spiritual diagnosticians (as in Dr. Walker Percy's novels and essays) of man's earthly malaise: the creature of consciousness. Dr. Astroff in *Uncle Vanya* is a provincial doctor who is overworked and thoroughly cynical. ("There's nothing I want, nothing I need, nobody I love.") Still, he does "want" and "need"; and he can love—and the degree of his bitterness tells us that early on. The medical student in

"An Attack of Nerves" has learned, sadly, to be annoyed by his lawyer friend's horror at a brothel's degradation. This lawyer will eventually be declared sick and treated with quieting drugs—while his
friend, a future doctor, consolidates even further an austere distance, a posture of iciness and smugness. At the other end of the
age spectrum, "A Boring Story," a particular favorite of Thomas
Mann's, offers a portrait of a distinguished medical scientist's old
age—the isolation produced by years of self-preoccupation. (Ingmar
Bergman's film *Wild Strawberries* uncannily pursues this same
theme.) Chekhov also shrewdly evokes in this tale the loneliness of
celebrity—the skepticism and suspicions generated by a person's
fame or his achieved power. If patients languish, cut off sadly from
others, so in their own way do big-deal doctors or others who have
climbed to the top of one or another ladder.

It is a central assertion of all Chekhov's writing that few of us
really escape one or another form of isolation—hence his constantly
wry vision of the writer's distance as a true measure of everyone else's
(if only they would know it) godforsaken apartness. Even those of us
who claim to be "happy" (that is, reasonably content with this life)
must rely upon the substantial reticence or tact or mute subservience
of others—as if happiness for some requires that others be out of
sight, out of hearing range. In "Gooseberries," a story recently
brought to my attention by a friend, Chekhov is quintessentially his
wry self: "I saw a happy man, one whose cherished dream had so
obviously come true, who had obtained his goal in life, who had got
what he wanted, who was satisfied with his lot and with himself. For
some reason an element of sadness had always mingled with my
thoughts of human happiness, and now at the sight of a happy man I
was assailed by an oppressive feeling bordering on despair."

Such "despair," though, is never a final destination for Chekhov,
it is rather an occasion for more wry probing, for philosophical (we
today would say "existential") analysis:

> I said to myself: how many contented, happy people there
> really are! What an overwhelming force they are! Look at life:
> the insolence and idleness of the strong, the ignorance and
> brutishness of the weak, horrible poverty everywhere, over-
> crowding, degeneration, drunkenness, hypocrisy, lying—Yet
> in all the houses and on all the streets there is peace and quiet;

of the fifty thousand people who live in our town there is not one who would cry out, who would vent his indignation aloud. We see the people who go to market, eat by day, sleep by night, who babble nonsense, marry, grow old, good-naturedly drag their dead to the cemetery, but we do not see or hear those who suffer, and what is terrible in life goes on somewhere behind the scenes. Everything is peaceful and quiet and only mute statistics protest: so many people gone out of their minds, so many gallons of vodka drunk, so many children dead from malnutrition—And such a state of things is evidently necessary; obviously the happy man is at ease only because the unhappy ones bear their burdens in silence, and if there were not this silence, happiness would be impossible. It is a general hypnosis. Behind the door of every contented, happy man there ought to be someone standing with a little hammer and continually reminding him with a knock that there are unhappy people, that however happy he may be, life will sooner or later show him its claws, and trouble will come to him—illness, poverty, losses, and then no one will see or hear him, just as now he neither sees nor hears others. But there is no man with a hammer. The happy man lives at his ease, faintly fluttered by small daily cares, like an aspen in the wind—and all is well.

Chekhov has sometimes been described as *too* wry—as the detached stoic he parodies in "A Boring Story," or the distant, sardonic physician who appears in story after story. But in the above moment he is wry in quite another way: the poignantly humane social visionary who holds himself at arm's length from any number of polemical commitments not out of indifference but a precious wisdom—the kind, I believe, my old teacher, Dr. Yale Kneeland, offered us medical students when he remarked one day that "this life defies all who want to pin it down exactly." He too was a doctor wary of absolutes—as was Chekhov, for whom the mind's exertions were themselves a drama to be wryly rendered rather than embraced as God's answer to all eternity's riddles.

Why Novels and Poems
in Our Medical Schools?

W hy novels and poems in our medical schools? I am hardly in a position to be objective about that question. I went into medicine, I think it fair to say, out of an enormous respect for and admiration of Dr. William Carlos Williams, poet, novelist, playwright, essayist, critic, and not least, physician. I wrote my college thesis on the first book of his long poem, *Paterson*, and thereby got to know him. Until then, I'd been a history and literature major, with a strong side interest in jazz. I went on house visits with Dr. Williams, came to know some of his patients, became utterly taken with the work he did, decided (quite belatedly) to take premedical courses—and had a devil of a time doing so. I managed the subject matter fairly well, but I had a lot of trouble with the fierce, relentless, truculent competitiveness that seemed inseparable from the study of biology, organic chemistry, and physics. And I regret to say that now, a quarter of a century later, I still see such an atmosphere at Harvard College—and no doubt other colleges have no immunity to the problem. Students come see me often, and their turmoil sends my head reeling with bad memories. How might we help intelligent, ambitious premedical students learn, yet resist the more unsavory aspects of premedical life? I do not think it an exaggeration to say that were it not for Dr. Williams' generous, personal support, I would not have lasted that first, college phase of scientific education, and maybe not the critical first two years of medical school—a continuation, then at least, of laboratory work, with virtually no chance to meet those ailing fellow human beings who get called patients.

What Dr. Williams did, over and over, was to suggest books I ought to read: Chekhov, Camus, Kafka, not to mention some of his own stories (collected as *Life along the Passaic*). He urged me to read *Arrowsmith* again—a book usually read in high school or early college, then forgotten by many of us who become physicians. He reminded me, repeatedly, how much Dostoevski and Tolstoy had to say about illness and its vicissitudes, and of course, Thomas Mann. As I responded, I found the pleasures a reader obtains from a good writer; but I was also prompted toward ethical reflection by novelists and poets who had a marvelous sense of life's continuing mystery, the ambiguities and ironies that never stop confronting us.

It is a privilege, therefore, to be able to urge some of those same books on others—on medical students who, of course, require a mastery of biological factuality but who also need (and in my experience, almost hungrily crave) a chance to ask those haunting moral and philosophical questions a George Eliot, for instance, in *Middlemarch*, keeps posing: what is the meaning of the life we doctors so constantly try to protect, and how ought that life to be lived—with what ideals and aspirations, with what accommodations, adjustments, and compromises in the face of this world's constantly pressing opportunities, frustrations, and obstacles?

Literature and Medicine, Autumn 1982

On Medicine and Literature
An Interview with Robert Coles

Interviewer: Much of the *Children of Crisis* volumes is made up of interviews. Do you generally use a tape recorder?

Coles: When I was in college, I got to know William Carlos Williams, and I used to follow him around and tape record his medical rounds in northern New Jersey. He was an old-fashioned, what we'd now call family practice, doctor—he was a pediatrician and an obstetrician, and basically a general practitioner. I'd visit him and he'd take me into the homes of his patients. He'd listen to them carefully, both as a writer and as a doctor, and then when he left each home, he'd sit in his car and write notes. I'd say, "What are you doing?" And he'd say he was writing down the wonderful expressions he heard from them. He would later use them in his poems. And some of the stories he heard from them he worked into those wonderful *Life along the Passaic* stories, which are doctor stories, really. He used to say, "The important thing is to hear." I've found that when I've used the tape recorder, at times it was because I thought I wasn't a scientist if I didn't have everything tape recorded. And then I'd remember what Dr. Williams said, and slowly I started weaning myself from it. But it's hard because you figure you get everything that way. And it has interfered at times, because I didn't listen as closely as when I didn't have it.

Interviewer: So when you didn't have it, you'd just write things down?

Coles: Afterwards. I'd write it all down. And I'd edit what I heard— you edit the tape anyway—I think I was editing in my mind as I was writing it down. You write down what you feel you really want to remember. It's a complicated thing, how you do this work.

Interviewer: I imagine you must have libraries full of tapes.

Coles: I do. I have a lot of tapes, and then more recently a lot of notes on my yellow pads. And often, even when I was using the tapes, I'd sit down in the evening and write an essay in which the important things that I heard were put together. Lately I've been working in Northern Ireland, in Belfast, with the Catholic and

Protestant children caught up in that struggle, and in South Africa with the black children in Soweto and Afrikaner children in Pretoria. I found myself not using the tape recorder.

Interviewer: Not at all?

Coles: Just occasionally. I'd use it so I could listen to the voices, for the use of language and dialect. I felt that I learned a lot just by listening and writing down afterwards what I had heard, rather than by trying to catch every word.

Interviewer: I carried several of your books home from the Cambridge library last week, a very thick stack of books—and I began to wonder how you are able to write so much. They had nearly twenty of your books: the *Children of Crisis* series, biographies, criticism, children's books, poetry. How do you manage to do all that?

Coles: I write on yellow lined legal pads. I write in the mornings, early, just after my children have gone to school. I think about what I'm going to write the night before. Then I sit down and by golly, I write. I write on a quota basis. I try to write three to four yellow pages a day, five days a week. And if you keep on doing that with some—almost a religious—dedication, the books mount up over the years. One of the reasons is some sort of a necessary feeling I have that I must do this fairly regularly. The only time I stop writing is when I'm out in the so-called field. That is, when I was in South Africa or Belfast I didn't write much, other than the notes I was taking. But when I'm at home either teaching or doing my work in this country, visiting families—usually I don't visit the families until the afternoons because the kids are in school all day—I will write in the mornings, and that writing mounts up. If you stop and think about it . . . also I have sort of a cramped hand, a cramped writing hand, so I would estimate that I probably write eight hundred to a thousand words a day.

Interviewer: Then do you revise a lot after that?

Coles: Yes. What I do is revise one time. All that is typed up. Then I approach the typed version with a whole new personality. I look at it as an editor—and I'm very tough with my own writing. Maybe some critics would say not tough enough. But there is a difference. If you saw the first draft, you'd see the difference. I cannot edit my own handwriting. It has to be typed. And then I just slash into it. As I say, maybe I should learn how to slash into it better.

There is that very important second stage of the writing, though—it's edited. And then it's done.

Interviewer: You mentioned your friendship with William Carlos Williams. How did you come to know him?

Coles: As an undergraduate at Harvard I majored in a combined English and history field, and I wrote my thesis on Dr. Williams and his poem *Paterson* and the novel *White Mule*, which enormously interested me. At that time, in 1950, Dr. Williams was not quite as celebrated as he later became in the sixties. He died in 1963, and when I was doing this writing he was a well-known poet but by no means well accepted in the academic circles, the university circles. The only reason I was able to work so well and congenially at Harvard on that subject, namely him, was because of Perry Miller, who was a professor of English and American literature at Harvard and was an enormous influence on me. He was an English professor, but I think it's also fair to call him a theologian. He was very much interested in the Puritan mind and in the moral issues the Puritans struggled with, and he was interested in the literature which that generated. And that was my major undergraduate preoccupation. But I had read Williams' poetry and wanted to write about him, and Miller encouraged me to do so and was my mentor. I envisioned myself going to graduate school and becoming a student of Miller's in American Literature. After I had written my paper on Williams, Miller encouraged me to send it to him. I got a reply from Dr. Williams, saying, "Any time you're here, come and say hello." And boy, I went down to New York fast. I then became a friend of his, a young friend of his. He was very, very helpful, as an older person. I talked a lot with him.

Interviewer: And he encouraged you to go into medicine?

Coles: Well, yes. I became so impressed with the dual life he lived as a physician and as a writer/social observer of sorts that I thought maybe I'd give it a try myself. So I started taking on premedical courses, and I applied to medical school. I was turned down by four or five of them, because they thought I was a little flaky, I think, although I did well in the premedical courses. They'd often ask me what kind of a doctor I'd want to be. I'd say that I wasn't sure but . . . and then I'd tell them what I'm telling you now. But at Physicians and Surgeons, at Columbia, I was interviewed by a

man named Philip Miller—the same surname but obviously no
relation to Perry Miller. He was a biochemist. He interviewed
me, and I told him how I'd come to that point in my life. He said,
"We ought to take someone like you, even if you're not sure you
want to finish medical school." So they did take me. I had to
struggle in medical school, because I wasn't really adequately prepared for the sciences, and I didn't do too well in them. But I
managed to get by. I would visit Dr. Williams, and I was very
much interested in religious matters through Perry Miller and
through my own life. I would go to Union Theological Seminary,
where I took a seminar which Reinhold Neibuhr gave before he
had his first stroke, which was in '52, I think. I guess I was trying
to combine my medical life as a student with these interests in
religion and in literature. That I think has been the struggle that
I've waged all my life.

When I finished medical school I interned at the University of
Chicago. And even then I remember, as an intern, with my white
uniform, dashing out of the hospital because Paul Tillich was
giving some lectures at the University of Chicago. Also during
that year, Dr. Williams came, even though he'd had a stroke and
was partially paralyzed. He came and read in the Rockefeller
Chapel there, read his poems. It was a very poignant meeting for
those of us who knew him, because it was hard for him to talk. Yet
there was something in him that wanted to take that poetry of his
and share it with others. When I finished up that year I came back
to Boston. The question came up: what was I going to do with my
medical training and internship? I guess by this time I realized I
couldn't go into pediatrics, which was my major interest, because
I wasn't tough enough. The kids would undo me. They'd start
crying and I'd almost want to join up—cry. And that's not good.
So Bill Williams suggested, "Why don't you try going into psychiatry, child psychiatry, and get to the kids that way." So I
did. I took a residency at the Massachusetts General Hospital, at
McLean Hospital, and then at Children's Hospital for a couple of
years in child psychiatry. And by this time I had become so immersed in child psychiatry that I tended to stop reading a lot of the
books in theology and even in literature that I'd been reading. But
then I was drafted into the Air Force under the doctors' draft, and
I went down to Mississippi where they put me in charge of an Air

Force neuropsychiatric unit. That was where my life really changed a second time, because the whole Civil Rights movement was getting going, and children were being marched into desegregated schools in New Orleans in the face of all the violence that was going on. I've described what happened to me in the first chapter of the first volume of *Children of Crisis*. This was kind of . . . This changed my life. I stayed there and got involved with these children, involved with the Civil Rights movement.

Interviewer: Were you particularly vulnerable then to getting involved in that conflict? You described in your book *Walker Percy: An American Search* that it was "a critical time" and you were "somewhat lost, confused, vulnerable, and it seemed, drifting badly."

Coles: I *was* drifting, I think. I guess I was trying to figure out how to combine this medical life that I had with my interests in literature and a kind of complicated religious background that I have. My mother comes from the Midwest, actually from Iowa. She is an Episcopalian. And my father comes from a Jewish and Catholic background, from England; they've lost their religion for a few hundred years. Some were Sephardic Jews who came from Spain, originally, and had been in England for several hundred years. Some were Catholic. He's an agnostic scientist.

Interviewer: So you had a religious and a scientific background.

Coles: Exactly.

Interviewer: Were you a religious child then?

Coles: Oh yes! My mother took us . . . We were brought up in Boston, my brother and I, with a good deal of religious, Christian, faith, I think it's fair to say. I struggle with that. At times I guess I'm an agnostic, and at times I'm very much connected to the Old *and* New Testaments. I love to read Jeremiah and Isaiah and Amos, and I love to read Mark and Luke and Matthew and John and St. Paul. The Bible means a lot to me, and theology means a lot to me. Williams, by the way, had no interest in religion. He was a wonderfully agnostic, exuberant, here-and-now person. And in a strange way that was a problem. Because I was drawn to T. S. Eliot's poetry, from college days on. And you know, Eliot and Williams had a rough time with one another.

Interviewer: *In the American Grain* by Williams is full of that.

Coles: Yeah, they really were antagonists. I couldn't figure out how it was that at the same time I was both an admirer of Eliot's and an admirer of Williams'. Once I talked to Williams about this. He said, "Well, you're not me. You can have this kind of distance. I'm in the middle of a fight, you're an observer." But you know, Williams was partly Jewish, too. And later I got involved with Erik Erikson, who is also partly Jewish. So this continuity in my life is strange, this involvement with people who have juggled religious issues. Erikson had been an artist before he went into psychoanalysis, and I think I identified with this struggle to go back and forth between the world of science—in his case psychoanalysis, in my case medicine—and the world of literature. And religion too, because of Erikson's involvement with Luther and Gandhi. *Moral* literature as well as novelistic literature.

Interviewer: So if you had it over again, would you have gone to medical school?

Coles: Definitely. It was a very important part of my life. I got to know patients as individuals, and I still remember many of them I treated as an intern. I went back and did a year of pediatrics just before I went into the Air Force, so I guess I managed to get that pediatric side of me well built up, as well as the psychiatric side. I think a doctor has a marvelous opportunity to get to know people in ways that perhaps no one else can.

Interviewer: Did your medical training make you a better writer?

Coles: Well in my particular case it did. My wife knew Flannery O'Connor when she was sick, in the hospital and very ill. She was in Georgia, and we were living in Georgia for several years, when I was working in the Civil Rights movement and with school desegregation in Atlanta. She had a long talk with her in the Emory Hospital. Obviously writers use their imaginations and don't need to have access to anyone, other than the richness of their own minds, which is more than enough for them. But because she had been involved with doctors in the struggle she waged against lupus, she said that she thought it would be a marvelous opportunity for a writer to be in these situations. And of course some writers have been doctors. One thinks of Chekhov and again Dr. Williams and Walker Percy. But clearly many writers have had no need for medical training to become the great writers that they've been. And obviously many doctors are not interested in writing. I think one thing that medical training offers, which is worthy of consideration by people with other interests, is that it's a really helpful antidote to social science. A person who has gone through the empirical training of medical school, and who understands the uniqueness of the individual which medical training reveals, does have an opportunity to do social science work in a way that I happen to think is very important, that is, with a respect for the humanities, for their concentration on individuality, their emphasis on irony and paradox and inconsistency and contrariness rather than the emphasis that social science training tends to place on theory and on abstraction and on trying to generalize almost at all costs. Sometimes the costs are very high.

Interviewer: Have you become more suspicious of abstraction and theory, of categorization into types and stages? It seemed to me, in going through your books, that there was a certain progression.

Coles: And you probably noticed a certain increasing animus against my own profession. Well, you're right. I started out as a psychiatrist, and I started getting psychoanalytic training in New Orleans at the New Orleans Psychoanalytic Training Center, which later became a full-fledged institute. I was . . . I think maybe I still am a smug, self-centered person. But if I am, I was even more so then. Boy, it's embarrassing when I stop to think of the psychiatric arrogance I was a victim of. It took me a few years to comprehend. This was what going into the homes of ordinary black and white people in the South tended to confront me with—my own narrowness and blindness and smugness and narcissism. Here I met people who were facing a tremendous social and historical crisis, and who were acquitting themselves with dignity, or showing the fear and anxiety of people who are threatened in ways that I had never been threatened. My whole way of thinking about them, with all the psychiatric terms and all the quickness to judge people indirectly through psychiatric categorizations—all of that was of little use in understanding the lives of these people. I had to begin to think of a way of looking at them that was different from that of psychiatry. Of course, what one realizes is that there are always George Eliot and Charles Dickens and Dostoevski—and all the writers who have helped one over the years to understand human beings—who are waiting in the wings to help you to get to know the people you're talking with in these homes. So I think I became somewhat disenchanted with my profession, and I think I began to lose interest in its way of thinking—and in its language, which is rather prolix and self-important.

Interviewer: Do you feel just that the *psychiatric* categorizations are useless, or that no system of thought can explain the various ways in which people, both children and adults, respond to crisis?

Coles: Flannery O'Connor put it beautifully. She said, "The task of the novelist is not to 'resolve' mystery but to deepen it!" The danger with social science, the danger for that matter with any kind of intellectual process, is that we take ourselves too seriously, and that we forget the difference between products of our own thinking and the world itself. We impose our notion of reality on the world and see only our notion of reality rather than the defiant complexity of the world—and of course the mystery of the world. Now, I'm caught in the middle, as you point out. On the one hand, I want to clarify and observe and point out and understand, and in a sense simplify in the nonpejorative sense of the word "simplify." But on the other hand, I'm constantly impressed with mystery, and maybe even feel that there are certain things that cannot be understood or clarified through generalizations, that resolve themselves into matters of individuality, and again, are part of the mystery of the world that one celebrates as a writer, rather than tries to solve and undo as a social scientist.

Interviewer: If you had it to do again, would you have not trained in psychiatry?

Coles: I think I would have gone into pediatrics and maybe family medicine, if I had it over again. I'd probably do primary care medicine is my hunch. At that time they didn't have it. And the kind of public health they had when I was a medical student was a matter of memorizing the charts of the life cycles of some species of worm in distant Africa, while at the same time there we were, just a few blocks from Harlem. And we never went there.

Interviewer: In reading *Still Hungry in America*, I was struck by the passages in which you talked about the diseases you'd seen—the malnutrition, skin ulcers, the parasitic infestations, the untreated serious kidney and heart diseases. Do you feel a special obligation since you're both a doctor and a writer? How can you leave those people after you've seen the very treatable conditions that are making their lives miserable?

Coles: That's a very important ethical point, and the only way I could answer that is to say that in the instances I have seen them I have done something. That's been a part of my work, to get them medical care. It's hard for me to write about that because it seems rather self-serving to say, "Look, I treated these people," which is what every doctor does. But the fact is that's what I have done. In every region of the country that I've worked, I've gotten involved with the existing medical situation. The kids and their families, I've come to know them over the period of a year or two, and pretty well. Visiting them I've come to know their medical problems, as well as trying to understand their feelings and their attitudes toward the world. And I have indeed gotten them connected to medical facilities when that's been necessary. Now the other side of one's contribution, at least one *hopes* it's a contribution, is that after all as a writer you can call attention to the larger issues that these people are struggling with. And in the case of hunger, my involvement in testimony before the United States Senate, and that very book which came as a result of that, was a part of the effort to get the Food Stamp program going, and to get this seen as a national problem rather than a series of individual cases.

Interviewer: So do you think your work has had a substantial effect?

Coles: Well I don't know. To tell you the truth I wish it had a *more* substantial effect. I've testified again and again before various congressional committees on migrant children, on the problem of hunger and malnutrition, on the problems of ghetto kids, on problems of school desegregation—a whole range of issues that have affected families and children. Sometimes I think some of that testimony has had some value, but at other times one despairs. But one tries. The problems of black lung disease among miners—I've testified again and again about that. And we have made some progress there. Black lung disease is now recognized as a medical entity that is connected to the occupational hazards of mining, and the miners who get black lung disease in recent years have been compensated for the disease. When I started this work in Appalachia, that wasn't the case, and I think part of the victory was due to medical and social testimony from people like me. And there've been a number of us who have offered that testimony—doctors and social observers who were involved with mountain families who had miners in the family, miners we got to know. Some of the legislation concerning migrant children drew upon the observations that some of us have made about how migrant children live and what their educational and medical problems are. I wish that migrant families were living much better than they are today. And as far as the occupational health legislation that affects black lung disease, and very importantly, *brown* lung disease among the textile workers of North and South Carolina, I wish that there were more and better laws. So on the one hand one works with these issues, but one is also pretty . . . at times discouraged. Certainly discouraged during the Nixon years, but even now, one wishes that this country could do more for the marginal social groups that are getting a pretty raw deal.

Interviewer: In *Irony in the Mind's Life,* you quote from George Eliot's *Middlemarch:* "Who can quit young lives after being long in company with them and not desire to know what befell them in their after-years?" I was wondering about the kids in the first volume of *Children of Crisis*—whether you'd ever be going back to them?

Coles: I have been. I go back once a year to the South and visit some of those families. I suppose I could call it follow-up work, but it's really just visits to people who were so wonderful to us, who taught us so much, and offered us so much hospitality. That's a beautiful quote from *Middlemarch.* We have done that, my wife and I. And some of those kids of course we've followed so long they are obviously no longer children but are themselves in their twenties or thirties and parents.

Interviewer: Have you written about it?

Coles: A bit in *Farewell to the South,* a collection of essays. There's a long introduction in which I offer some follow-ups. But you know, when you've travelled as much as I have, and lived in so many different parts of the United States—I've been in every American state, including Alaska obviously, and Hawaii, all fifty states, and worked in every region of the country, North, South, East and West—there comes a point when you can't follow up all the people you've met, unless you're in a state of constant manic ascension, with no sleep and moving around endlessly from airport to airport. But there always have been one or two families with whom we've been especially involved, and those are the families we've kept up with, just making a visit every year or so to say hello. I'm haunted though by that question of George Eliot . . . oh well, I'm haunted by George Eliot.

Interviewer: So you have seen changes when you've gone back to visit the people you first wrote about?

Coles: Some changes. I see some changes, and Lord knows, having been involved with SNCC and the whole Civil Rights movement, I've seen wonderful changes with respect to segregation and school desegregation, to the point that school desegregation by and large is more a reality in the South than in my own hometown of Boston, and if that isn't an irony, what is? I've seen a lot of social and racial changes in the South, and I've seen some changes for the better among the people in Appalachia, but there are also things that haven't changed much. For instance, we lived in New Mexico for several years, and I worked on the reservations of the Southwest, and the problems of the Indian people are very severe and *not* getting better. I worked in Alaska with Eskimo families, and the problems that Eskimos face are now getting *worse* rather than better, due to the pipeline, the refineries, the influx suddenly of a combination welfare economy and a one-time glut of cash. They've suddenly been yanked out of a subsistence economy in which, nevertheless, they have a certain amount of dignity and personal sense of themselves as hunters and fishermen—and now what are they? So you see alcoholism, and you see a kind of passivity and dependence on the visit of the airplane once a week to the village with pizzas. You go into the villages and you hear Linda Ronstadt blaring forth on hi-fi and you see skimobiles and kids drinking Cokes and eating pizzas and potato chips, and you say, here's modern America in these Eskimo villages. And though there are advantages to this, there are also severe moral and psychological losses. It's a real problem, how the Eskimos are coming to terms with the sudden presence of technology and money and so-called Lower Forty-Eight civilization. The risk is that one gets condescending. The Eskimos themselves, some of them, will say, "Hey, listen, this is what we want, just like you people have wanted it." But there's a good deal of evidence that, in addition to what they have gotten out of this, that is in the way of cash, they've experienced a substantial loss in morale and in their own self-respect. They weren't prepared for contemporary American life as most of us were, because it crept up on us gradually over a generation or two. Our ancestors came here and were part of building up whatever this country is—and Eskimos suddenly had it thrown at them. So it's a mixed answer I'd have to give you.

Interviewer: In the past twenty or thirty years, medicine has become more institutionalized and technically oriented; and relatively little interest is placed in the kinds of social issues you're so involved in. And very little interest in what one might call the medical humanities. Do you as a result feel estranged from the medical profession?

Coles: I don't know, I don't know. You'd have to ask other doctors. One student here was interviewed for medical schools and mentioned that he'd taken a course with me—this in conjunction with his own interest in writing. He was told by the people on the admissions committee that they didn't think he ought to go to medical school if he wanted to be a writer, and that if I happened to have pulled this off that was fine, but they didn't want people announcing before they even get to medical school that they were interested in going to medical school because of an interest in writing and the help this would give them as writers. And I can understand that; I mean, there's such a need for doctors, and I think they felt this was a little frivolous. Also, I didn't go to medical school to get a medical education from which I would then draw upon as a writer. I went to medical school out of a real desire to become a doctor and live the doctor's life that I'd seen Dr. Williams living, and also that I'd seen an uncle of mine living, my mother's brother. And somehow, later in life, I connected these interests.

I've written articles for the *New England Journal of Medicine*, for the *Journal of the American Medical Association*, on writers— I've written on Flannery O'Connor and Dr. Williams for the *JAMA*, and I've even written about *Middlemarch* for the *New England Journal of Medicine*. And I've written for the *American Journal of Psychiatry* and for psychoanalytic journals—and I've done book reviews for many of them. So somehow, again, it's a tightrope. I've balanced this life in some way. I love . . . I still read the *New England Journal of Medicine* and I read the medical articles in it, not just the social comment. And I do think of myself as a physician, very much so. One reviewer said I'm a writing doctor. And that was very well put. If I had more ability, I'd write novels like Walker Percy or I'd write poetry such as Dr. Williams did—but I don't have that ability, I just don't have the ability to do that. So I . . . if you don't have the ability you don't have the ability.

Interviewer: Haven't you published a book of poetry?

Coles: I have written poetry, and I've listened to children and pulled their words together in a form that I guess one would consider a kind of poetry. It's not the best kind, but . . . but I have written poetry and some of it has been published, and there is the book of poems drawing on the work with children.

Interviewer: Are you teaching now?

Coles: Yes. I teach a course in the medical humanities at Harvard Medical School, and I teach undergraduates two things. I teach an undergraduate course called "Moral and Social Inquiry." We start with James Agee's *Let Us Now Praise Famous Men*. We read George Orwell's *The Road to Wigan Pier*. We go on to read Flannery O'Connor and Walker Percy, Ralph Ellison, Tillie Olsen, Dorothy Day's autobiography called *The Long Loneliness*, about the Catholic Worker movement. And we end up with *Jude the Obscure* of Thomas Hardy, and *Middlemarch* of George Eliot. So it's a mixture of novels and social documentary writing and autobiography and moral essays. And we see some movies that connect with the reading we've done. We read *The Diary of a Country Priest* by Bernanos, and we see the movie that Bresson did. And then last fall I taught a seminar called "Religion and Twentieth-Century Intellectuals." So I teach on both sides. And at the Medical School what we read is William Carlos Williams' doctor stories, *Life along the Passaic River*, Walker Percy's novels *The Moviegoer* and *The Last Gentleman* and *Love in the Ruins*— all of which have a doctor in them. The first one is a future medical student, and in both *The Last Gentleman* and *Love in the Ruins* a physician is a central part of the narrative. We read *Middlemarch*, which has Dr. Lydgate, and we read *Arrowsmith*, the old favorite, that unfortunately is read by too many medical students when they've been in high school or college. Anyway, we use novels to approach medical issues.

Interviewer: Do you read different kinds of doctors' writing—Céline or William Burroughs?

Coles: Céline is especially important, and I haven't used him yet, but I'm going to next year. I think he's a very interesting physician—that's for sure. Obviously it would be hard for some medical students, as he has been hard for a lot of readers, to take. But I don't regard Céline's fascism as the central issue in his life. I think the issue in his life is that of his disgust for the hypocrisy of the world, a world that he saw from the point of view of a doctor as well as a political person. He's an interesting writer, a very gifted writer. He would be a valuable addition to that course, you're absolutely right.

Interviewer: And Burroughs?

Coles: Burroughs I have trouble with. The trouble I have with him is that while politically I'm fairly liberal—quite liberal, I guess—culturally I'm more conservative. I used to have discussions with Williams about this. I guess I can go as far as Williams, not too much further. There's obviously a stodgy part of me culturally. I tend to want to assign nineteenth-century writers like George Eliot and Dickens and Hardy to my students—because I think they were wonderful moral observers. Someday I would love to teach a course, maybe at a law school, on Dickens and the law, because the various kinds of lawyers that he portrayed and the way he looked at a profession are, I think, still of great interest today. The moral insights he offers us about professional life are very shrewd. You go from *Bleak House* to *Great Expectations* to the lawyer in *Tale of Two Cities*. And of course, George Eliot, with Dr. Lydgate—you can teach a whole course around *Middlemarch* to medical students or undergraduates. The issue of what makes for the moral decisions of professional life, centered around Lydgate and what happens to him . . .

Interviewer: Have you become more interested in moral issues in recent years?

Coles: No question. I am increasingly interested in moral issues, and the ways that writers, that is novelists and poets, have come to terms with these moral issues. And I'm interested in what these people have to say to people like me, doctors and psychiatrists and intellectuals, though I don't like that last word—to people who are psychologically trained.

Interviewer: You say in the introduction to the first volume of *Children of Crisis* that "there seems no end to crisis in this world." Is that the case?

Coles: (Laughs.) Or whether I've manufactured crises in order to . . . to justify my writing . . .

Interviewer: Let me rephrase that. How many volumes of *Children of Crisis* will there be?

Coles: Well, there have been five dealing with twenty years of work in America. It is important to point out—I want to make an editorial point here, maybe a self-justifying point—I didn't publish my first book until 1967. And the work started in 1959. So for eight years there were no books. I think if you were to talk with my editor, Peter Davison, who is editor at the Atlantic Monthly Press, he'd tell you that he really had a devil of a time getting me to write that first book. Hard to believe it may be right now, but I was very reluctant about writing at first, because I was so overwhelmed by the complexity of what I'd seen, and the enormous difficulty I had in doing justice to that complexity as a writer. Now maybe I was overly ambitious in wanting to do justice to that complexity. I suppose I could have carved out some area of it and written psychiatric articles about that area. But I had and still have, over my shoulder, the shadow of someone like George Eliot. Now I'll never be able to do justice to that complexity, the way she did in *Middlemarch*. But by golly, those are the models. She and Tolstoy and Dostoevski and Henry James, and one at least remembers them as writers. Finally I did write those portraits, and the first volume went to press. Since then I've done those other volumes, dealing with the various parts of the country where I've worked. I've been working recently in Northern Ireland, where I think any observer would feel there's "crisis" going on in the children's lives. And I've been working in South Africa, also critically caught up in a racial struggle. And I must say, though I've just turned fifty and feel myself entitled to stop this fieldwork, I can't do it. I love going into a new part of the world and getting to know children, getting to know their parents and their teachers, and just *seeing* that world, the way maybe Orwell did when he used to do the kind of travelling he finally wrote up in *Down and Out in London and Paris* or in the *Wigan Pier* book. I can't write, again, as well as he; I don't have the gift for narrative presentation that he had. But I do just love to look at the world and try to do justice to some of its rhythms, especially through the eyes of its children. The other thing I would mention is the considerable interest I have in the art of children and in interpreting that art, which goes back to my mother's interest in art. My brother is very much interested in art and teaches courses at the University of Michigan that connect literature and art. I think that if I've done nothing else in those volumes of *Children of Crisis* and in my other writing about children, I've tried to point out what children's drawings and paintings can teach us about their moral and psychological perceptions. This has been an interest now for over two decades. I've interpreted drawings and connected them to the lives of various children, whether they be black or white or Appalachian or Eskimo or Indian or Chicano children. I think some of that writing has been valuable both for my profession and for other interested persons. And I'd like to continue doing that in connection with children abroad, in Ireland and South Africa, because I think it teaches us something about the relationship between a political or historical crisis and the ways that children grow up; more abstractly, call it child development or human development.

Interviewer: We've talked about your mistrust of psychiatric categories and language. Yet with the children's drawings you do make interpretations; you do make generalizations in a psychiatric framework.

Coles: But you'll also notice that I'm always taking one step forward and at least a half a step backward, or at least sideways, by making the observations and trying to put them in other contexts, and maybe even qualifying them or maybe even pointing out that they apply to these children but might not apply to other children— and that in any case they may be overwrought. And that my own writings may be guilty—probably are guilty—of the various sins that I criticize in other writings. And I use the word sin because I think the issue is moral. How presumptuous is the observer becoming? How godlike does he feel himself to be? And the best people in my profession—people like Erik Erikson and Allen Wheelis, who are my two heroes, of sorts, within psychoanalysis—they pointed out again and again the limitations of this work, and the need we have for understanding the dangers we get into in connection with our own arrogance, and in connection with gullible or hurt people who want to elevate us into positions we have no right to be put in, or to allow ourselves to be put in. Allen Wheelis points this out in a marvelous essay, "On the Vocational Hazards of Psychoanalysis," which is part of his really fine book called *The Quest for Identity.* He points out that we are put in a godlike position and become intoxicated with our own self-importance.

Interviewer: After your work with children in South Africa and Northern Ireland is done, what next? Are you working on other biographies or criticism?

Coles: The work in Ireland and South Africa and one or two other countries will take a number of years. I have a book on Flannery O'Connor coming out this spring. And I'm working, in a more intellectual vein, on the life of Simone Weil. She's a source of great interest to me as a moral philosopher, and her life as well as her writing can offer a lot for us to think about. There are certain people whose moral and intellectual example has meant a lot to me. I suppose I'm hoping that I'm given the life to do it, and in one way or another I'll come to terms with their lives. Not necessarily with long biographies, because I'm not really very interested in doing that. But in either intellectual biographies or essays or whatever. Erikson was one, I've done a book on him. I wrote a long paper on Anna Freud because she's meant a lot to me, her work with children. I've written a book in conjunction with a photographer about the Catholic Worker movement and especially Dorothy Day. I've written some about James Agee, and I think I'll probably end up writing some more about him. Same goes for Orwell. Dr. Percy, I've written a book about him, and a book about Dr. Williams. And Georges Bernanos, the French Catholic novelist, has meant a lot to me. *The Diary of a Country Priest* is one of my favorite novels, and I'd be surprised if in some way I don't come to terms with that. And that just about exhausts the list. (Laughs.) And probably will exhaust my life.

Interviewer: What do all these people who are your heroes have in common?

Coles: What they have in common, I guess, is that they've struggled with moral and religious issues. They have had their literary sides, too—more than sides in some cases. And more than that, there is the issue of service. Orwell struggled with this in a certain way, and Agee, and hence the anguish in *Let Us Now Praise Famous Men,* the issue of how much do you exploit as a writer, and what do you offer in return to the people you're writing about? This comes up if, as a writer, you are dealing with external reality, if

your writing is not made up only of the internal, or fictional, subjective experiences which you mold into characters and narration.
And since I've been so involved with the world outside of me, this
issue comes up: what does one owe the world? You brought this
up very appropriately in connection with the hunger issue in the
late 1960s. The hope is, if you're caught up in the Civil Rights
movement or in the struggle migrants are waging for both personal dignity and a larger share of the economic world that they
manage to hold up through their labor, that the writing and the
testimony and some of the medical work at least pay back some of
the debts that you've rung up from going place to place and asking
people to tell you things which you then write up and tell to
the world at large. It's a haunting question, though: what does
one owe?

Interview by David Hellerstein, *North American Review,*
June 1980

Medicine and the Humanities

In previous centuries, the humanities were concerned with grammar and rhetoric, with the classics, with moral and philosophical inquiry through the essay, casual or systematic, or through the writer's imagination: the novel, the short story, the drama. Such "polite learning," as the humanities were once described, all too readily became connected to notions of class, privilege, and social position. In *Jude the Obscure*, Thomas Hardy dared broach such matters with a late-nineteenth-century Victorian audience. His central character, a sensitive, intelligent, idealistic member of the working class, watches all too closely the privileged students of a university community, which is thinly disguised but apparent to everyone as an Oxford, a Cambridge. The earnest affection for the humanities felt by the relatively uneducated artisan is made to contrast with the smug self-importance, the arid pietism, the callous arrogance of a community of much-honored scholars—whom Hardy knew to be as vulnerable to meanness of spirit and even, ironically, downright prejudicial ignorance as any other group of successful mortals. Of course, Matthew Arnold had already stirred things up among nineteenth-century England's custodians of high culture with a sweeping insistence that the literary sensibility, the informed intelligence of novelists, poets, and critics, be brought to bear on vexing contemporary issues—rather than be held in all too lofty and disdainful reserve as the property of a self-selected few.

Yet those writers were not everywhere heeded; nor were Dickens and George Eliot in England, Balzac and Zola in France—all proponents of a vigorous examination, through the novel, of the nineteenth century's social problems. In our time, the kind of social and psychological analysis Matthew Arnold urged upon his Oxford colleagues (to their considerable protest), the kind done so literately and circumspectly during the 1840s in America by Alexis de Tocqueville, has become the property of the social sciences. As for the natural sciences, they have become an adversary culture, of sorts, to the humanities—a characterization C. P. Snow chose for dramatic emphasis but not without appropriate recourse to the way many of us tend to think: the hard facts, as against the mushy, anecdotal, impressionistic forays of "art." As for the sociologists and psychologists, no one is going to find most of them anywhere but in the camp of explicit, insistent "science"—arguably, as in the expression "more Catholic than the Pope," making up for any still-pressing element of professional uncertainty or confusion with nervous avowals of faith.

Of course, C. P. Snow knew how sad and wrong-headed the split between the "two cultures" has ended up being for all of us. There is no inherent conflict between a chemist or physicist at work in a laboratory and a novelist busy constructing a plot and a number of characters. A biologist may go full speed ahead, developing ideas and doing experiments without in any way casting doubt upon the worth of an artist, a sculptor, or a scholar anxious to figure out poetic imagery or the nature of the connections that bind a particular school of painters. The issue is not the antagonisms generated by different intellectual initiatives; the issue is, at heart, religious and philosophical—the ideological uses to which various disciplines have been put. In the nineteenth century, as science was growing in leaps and bounds, the German philosopher Hegel decided to become a "scientific" philosopher; he would banish mystery, ambiguity, and uncertainty, replacing them with the precise formulations that men who worked in laboratories felt able to offer. The Danish theologian (and wonderfully astute psychologist) Soren Kierkegaard read Hegel's treatises carefully, appreciated their unquestionable ambitiousness, and acknowledged that they explained virtually everything (how history itself had worked, was working, would until the end of time work) except for one small matter: what it means to be a particular human being, living in the world and aware of oneself, one's situation, one's unavoidable future—death.

It is possible, the cranky hunchback from Copenhagen was insisting, to know an enormous amount, to do research and more research, and yet miss the essential point of things. One need not, for example, in any way take issue with the honorable efforts of behavioral psychologists to connect human actions to the conditioned responses of rats who have learned to negotiate their way through various mazes. But when one hears those same "hard" social scientists referring to our "superstitious" anthropomorphic tendencies—

the inclination some of us have to attribute human characteristics to the natural world—one is tempted to remind these colleagues of an inclination of their own, perhaps best described as "ratomorphic": a tendency to attribute without necessary qualification to one kind of life on this planet—humankind—the qualities of the rat.

We all have our reflexes, but it is men and women who use language, know what their fate is, and struggle with the pleasures and disappointments of awareness. One says that not in self-congratulation but in order to point out one of the hazards of a kind of quantitative or experimental work: an overall context is lost sight of; a rather obvious qualitative distinction is too strenuously minimized. My own field, psychiatry, has had its problems in that regard. I draw from a distinguished psychoanalyst, Leslie Farber: "For while the creatures described [in psychiatry] may bear some resemblance to animals, or to steam engines or robots or electronic brains, they do not sound like people. They are in fact constructs of theory, more humanoid than human; and whether they are based on the libido theory or on one of the new interpersonal theories of relationship, it is just those qualities most distinctively human which seem to have been omitted. It is a matter of some irony, if one turns from psychology to one of Dostoevski's novels, to find that no matter how wretched, how puerile, or how dilapidated his characters may be, they all possess more humanity than the ideal man who lives on the pages of psychiatry."[1]

Does medicine have all that much to learn from such a way of looking at people—the psychological reductionism, so banal and pompous, that Dr. Farber is at such pains to deplore because he knows how influential it has been in this century? More broadly, has medicine become involved in the cultural crisis C. P. Snow referred to a while back—yet another ally of "science" in the increasingly explicit contest for mastery of a century's mind? One historian of medicine, Stanley Reiser, who teaches at this medical school, has recently sounded an important warning:[2] all too many of us physicians have confused science with technology and, so doing, have indeed become caught up in a polemical, and at times farcical, position. We shower our patients with tests, run them through a gauntlet

1. Leslie Farber, "Martin Buber and Psychiatry," *Psychiatry* 19 (1957): 110.
2. Stanley Reiser, *Medicine and the Reign of Technology* (New York: Cambridge University Press, 1978).

of machines, talk to them less and less, and ask them fewer and fewer questions about how they as individual men, women, and children are getting on with their lives. We are "scientists," so it is insistently said, and our aim is to go after patients with instruments, gadgets, and procedures in pursuit of "findings," the more the better.

Who in his right mind would want to ridicule those modern modes of medical inquiry in and of themselves? As one who lived and worked in the South for years, I know the risks of nostalgia—the foolishness, the outright mischief it can come to. The agrarian tradition, in the hands of many, became a clever apologia for the good old days of segregation, extreme poverty, and rampant, murderous racism. On the other hand, writers such as Robert Penn Warren and Ralph Ellison have known that both black and white people lost a lot when they came North and exchanged one flawed way of life for another in its own ways seriously deficient. Similarly, the point is not that medical technology is, in itself, anything but valuable. Rather, one wonders, as Dr. Reiser does in his book, whether today's doctors haven't been first captivated and then captured by that technology; it becomes *the answer*, a central, controlling preoccupation. Meanwhile, we rely less and less on our eyes, our ears, our ability to have a reasonable and revealing conversation with our patients— one in which they tell us about their complaints, the story of their aches and pains, and thereby let us know a good deal about themselves: human beings who have come seeking help from doctors, who are presumably fellow human beings rather than conduits for laboratory centrifuges, X-ray machines, computers, and yes, the overwrought theoretical classifications of psychopathology.

In 1964, while working in the Mississippi Project, an effort of American youth, black and white, to challenge once and for all the heartland of segregationist power, I came across an extraordinary young black man who had just finished the eleventh grade at a consolidated high school that served his community of Midnight, Mississippi, a sleepy Delta hamlet that for generations had been part of the South's sharecropper-based cotton economy and recently has been suffering the pain generated by a rapidly collapsing rural life. Machines have replaced people, who have the alternative of staying put and living a wretched life of extreme poverty or trekking North to increasingly inhospitable and dreary ghettos. This black youth had caught the attention of several black teachers in the all-black school he attended, and after a talk with him I could easily see why. He was a wonderfully thoughtful person, open to speculation, honest as could be, deeply religious but with no accompanying, cloying sentimentality. He hadn't received the best education, of course, but he also hadn't learned to be glib, jaded, all too sure of himself—or conventional in his way of responding to the world. He had none of the liberal agnosticism so many of us wear proudly, if discreetly, on our sleeves. He was a hard-praying Baptist, yet he could read J. D. Salinger's *Catcher in the Rye* with exquisite respect and comprehension; and even if he misspelled a lot of words in his themes, they were full of what Tolstoy or Dostoevski, without the least condescension, knew to appreciate as "uncorrupted peasant wisdom," the latter's polemical phrase meant to be a slap at the arrogance of Russia's nineteenth-century intelligentsia, and maybe at all of us who become overly impressed with ourselves as intellectuals.

A number of teachers knew that the black youth deserved better, in the way of higher education, than he would get at the time in his home state, and no doubt in the entire South. They wanted him in the North, in a "good school." He wanted to be a physician, they kept telling me, and after a number of weeks their student confirmed that impression of theirs: "I've wanted to be a doctor for a long time, but I fear to mention it. Christ healed the sick; he worried about 'the lame, the halt, the blind,' and he tried to do something good for them. He worried about the poor. He worried about the 'rebuked and the scorned'—the folks all the uppity ones looked down on. You mustn't *decide* to be a doctor. It's a *calling*, our minister says. If you're hoping to walk down Christ's path and be a healer to your neighbors, then you've got to have his blessings. So, no sir, I can't say I *want* to be a doctor, or I'm *going* to be a doctor; I can only say that in my prayers to God Almighty I tell him that I'd like his blessings, and then I might try to be one."

At the same time this humble person could be assertively knowing; he thought that "the trouble with Holden Caulfield is this: he has everything but he doesn't know what the purpose of his life is, so he doesn't have everything, after all." As for Walker Percy's *The Moviegoer*, which I had strongly recommended, the young reader was not in the least daunted by the barriers of class and race that separated him from the novel's main character, Binx Bolling: "That guy in the story is trying to find out how you should live your life—

how *he* should live *his* life. He knows a lot. He's figured out that you can be real smart, but that's just the beginning. He's figured out that you can be on top but feel real low, because you're looking around and you're seeing how bad things are, instead of fooling yourself by painting a pretty picture of the world. A lot of people, they spend half their lives trying to kid themselves, and the other half they're sick, because they're in pain, their soul is, and they don't know how to cure themselves of the trouble. They've gotten themselves an illness, but they don't know it, and they don't know who to go see—for a diagnosis and some treatment."

Not a bad analysis of a notable American existentialist novel. In the youth's senior year, we all set to work on our errand, liberating from the Delta a bright and studious black person, the son of grievously poor tenant farmers who had precious little schooling to their name (we had not yet, in the middle 1960s, come upon all those fancy, self-important phrases—"culturally deprived," or "culturally disadvantaged"). For my part, I wrote to the then president of Amherst, a physician who had taught me medicine, and he was anxious to help. Eventually, this young, black Southerner came to Cambridge, Massachusetts, where he tried hard for four years to learn—to find a direction for his life. He told his freshman adviser of his *hope*, medicine—not his "goal," and not his "plans" for his "future career." The adviser wasn't quite able to comprehend the young man's tentativeness; one either wants to be a doctor, or one has doubts, or one doesn't have in mind medicine as an occupation. As for the "waiting" the student mentioned, the "waiting for God's judgment" on the matter—it has for a long time been the function of universities such as Harvard to replace naiveté and superstition with "enlightenment." Time, and four courses a semester, would work miracles (of a decidedly unreligious kind) on the student's way of thinking about himself and his possibilities—or so it was thought.

And so it seemed to happen. In his sophomore year the student, as a matter of course, and with no mental scrupulosity or religious anguish, became a "premed." He took biology and inorganic chemistry. He was, though, still a reader of novels, short stories and poems; so he chose to become an English major, and as such did not forget to heed Ralph Ellison's advice (and warning) that blacks ought to hold on, for dear life, to their regional roots. He studied Flannery O'Connor's short stories, Faulkner's novels, Eudora Welty's tales,

Walker Percy's fictional exercises in soul-searching, and Reynolds Price's efforts to harness the genre of family romance to the requirements of plot and character portrayal. By the time junior year came around, the student was heavily involved in organic chemistry and physics, while at the same time taking English and history courses. He seemed on top of everything, an example of a broadly educated student on his way, soon enough, to being accepted at a first-rate medical school. But something happened in the middle of that fateful year, and I had best let the young man himself do the remembering: "I was doing fine, I guess, until one day in the lab, the organic chem lab, I saw a kid take out something from a bag, and wink to his partner at the next bench; and then seeing me looking at them, they turned their backs on me. Suddenly I woke up from a long sleep. This wasn't the first time I'd seen kids cheating, but I guess I hadn't wanted to notice, not *really* notice. Now I remembered other things—slips of paper I saw kids sneak in and use on the tests, and the yields made bigger with sugar or salt, or other stuff. I used to think the things I heard were funny; I used to think that no one *really* cheated on those tests or in the lab. But I had conned myself and I know the reason now; I didn't know what to think, what to do. Once I saw some bad cheating on a chem hour exam, and I was going to report the kid, but I couldn't bring myself to do it.

"After I saw the lab cheating, I went to see the minister in the church I attended, and talked to him. He said you can't always be your brother's keeper; you have to try to be good yourself, and leave the rest up to God. I told him it was fine to say that, but what if a lot of cheaters became doctors later on? He said that maybe I was exaggerating what was happening in school. I said that, to tell the truth, I was doing just the opposite. And besides, there were plenty of kids who were killing each other for grades. You can't get them to tell you anything, to share anything, to help you in lab. All they say is that it's dog-eat-dog, and we're all enemies, fighting for our place on the curve. Then you go back to the Houses, and you hear these people planning, all day long they're planning: what to do for 'activities,' and what kind of voluntary work to sign up for, so it'll look good on their records. It's 'murder,' that's what they all say, and that's what I began to realize—that I was becoming a lousy, mean, selfish 'murderer,' like the rest of them. And I didn't want that to happen."

In his senior year this young man was in anguish. He had obtained good marks in all subjects, including the sciences, mostly B's and some A's. Yet, he did not like the premed students he had spent so much time with, and he began to have second thoughts about a career in medicine. He told his adviser of his misgivings and was encouraged to think of other occupational choices. Still unsettled and increasingly apprehensive in the late autumn of that year, and now a member of this century's American intelligentsia, he sought psychiatric "help." After three "sessions," he had even more to worry over: "The doctor said I am afraid of competition. He said I'm letting other people—what they do, and how they act—determine my behavior. He kept on asking me how I get along with my brothers and my sisters. I told him fine, but I don't think he believed me. The more I told him about the premed people, the more he told me the 'problem' was mine. Then I got angry and asked him what he thought of people who bragged about cutting each other's throats. He said that was '*their* problem,' and we should look at '*my* problem.' He's just like the minister up here.

"No minister back home would talk like that. No one in my family would, either. Up here, the ministers (a lot of them) don't really believe in God, not like they do where I grew up. Up here the ministers try to talk like psychiatrists, and the psychiatrists talk to you like some of the ministers do back home—as if they have a direct line to Heaven! I guess I'll do without any of their 'help.' I guess I'll try to get a job teaching. I may go to the graduate school of education. I'd like to be able to go back to Mississippi and get a job in a school, somewhere near home, helping people—introduce good books to kids and get their minds going. The only thing that bothers me is this: some of the kids will end up in my boots—up here, wondering what's right to do, and what's wrong, and being told they're 'depressed' because they shouldn't wonder, shouldn't ask questions; they should just go ahead and get ahead, and if people get pushed to the left and to the right or in back, then that's *their* problem!"

He graduated *magna cum laude* in English, went on to get a master's degree in education, did indeed go back to Mississippi, to a job as a high school teacher in the town of Greenville. He still wonders whether he made a mistake, whether he ought to have gone to medical school. Sometimes, with undue bitterness perhaps, he turns on those of his classmates who did pursue his original dream and are now young physicians. At other times, he is more self-critical, more resigned, more humble, and, I think, more challenging: "I wasn't made to be a doctor. I wasn't determined enough, tough enough. There are so many people who really want to go to medical school. They've dreamed all their lives of going. They'd do anything to go. The medical schools haven't got any time to waste on people like me. I'm too shy; I get absorbed in a novel I'm reading, and it becomes my life for a while. If I can help some of the black kids I teach, through these novels, to think about what life is all about, and what's important, and what's not important, then I'll be glad. Doctors are too busy to worry about life the way a good novelist does. But I'll never forget *Middlemarch*—the doctor in it, Lydgate. I think of him a lot when I think of my years in college."

A young teacher, highly ethical and reflective, a decent and compassionate man, makes mention of George Eliot's great nineteenth-century novel, and in it, the doctor who as a young practitioner wanted to help change a sadly ignorant and corrupt profession. The idealistic doctor who comes to naught, to ruin, is hardly a stranger to literature. F. Scott Fitzgerald, in *Tender Is the Night*, has shown a twentieth-century audience what George Eliot offered the Victorians—a portrait of hopes and dreams badly undercut by the flaws of character that all too promising individuals manage to conceal from themselves, never mind others. Perhaps the young black man had seen not only his own severe limitations but a few warts, and more, in those of his classmates who were not afflicted with his fateful inclination toward a loss of nerve. In any event, we need not be haunted only by his example. Lord knows, there are others who stayed the course, who are right in this profession of ours, and who also wonder quite earnestly what is happening to it, given the fierce competition, the sometimes sleazy manipulations that are connected to undergraduate premed life and later to admissions procedures; given the unqualified emphasis, in some quarters, on grades or scores; given the obsession many of us have for technological procedures, tests, and routines; given the continuing coziness, in at least some parts of this country, between physicians and the quite well-to-do, whereas the poor, the socially or economically or culturally marginal, must often make do without us.

I recommend strongly the recent advice of one of this nation's wisest and most literate physicians, Lewis Thomas. In the *New En-*

gland Journal of Medicine of May 25, 1978, he strenuously criticizes
the premedical curricula, as all too often given sanction by our
medical schools. He is not calling, in remediation, for the nervously
bloated, pseudoscientific language one finds in too many psychological, sociological and psychiatric conferences—the blah-blah that is
part of the problem rather than an answer to it. He makes clear that
he is calling for a recognition of the importance the humanities have
for us—not as pieties to be conveniently summoned, then easily
shoved aside, and not as a bit of slick polish to be worn with self-
congratulation, but as a terribly important part of our lives when we
are college students, medical students, and well beyond, too.

Perhaps the time has come for a careful look at the relationship
of the humanities to undergraduate premedical training, medical
school curricula, and our postgraduate education. I remember two
of my favorite medical school teachers, Robert F. Loeb and Yale
Kneeland, Jr., referring to the novels of Dostoevski, which they as
busy, full-fledged professors were reading in a "study group." One
day, as a matter of fact, Dr. Loeb reprimanded us for knowing a
given patient's lab scores better than the details of her life: "You
don't have to *be* a Dostoevski, but you ought to read him, because
he had an eye and an ear for people, and that's what you'll need as
much as knowledge of what the normal values are in the blood tests
you're ordering."

No one would fault that great Russian novelist the "eye and ear"
mentioned, but he had something else, as did George Eliot, as does
an important, contemporary American novelist who also happens to
be a physician, Walker Percy: an abiding interest in human complexity and a determination not to see it "resolved" (that cool, slippery word of our time) by any scheme of classification, by any in-
ventory of traits or symptoms. What these storytellers have wanted to
examine is the nature of human *character*, an old-fashioned word
badly in need of revival—in our national life, and in connection
with medical school admissions, medical school education. Character is not to be confused with "personality" or "mental health," or
with an "attitude" or two. Psychiatrists talk a lot about "character
disorders," but what do they tell us about character? The young
black mentioned earlier would be the last one to push himself upon
us with applause, but in fact he did have "character," a good deal of
it—maybe too much for his own good, things being as they are.

Character is connected to a philosophical search—a person's struggle to understand what is right, what matters, what in eternity's scheme of things is worth pursuing in the second or two, relatively speaking, we have on this earth. We each engage in that pursuit in our own way. If there is one central conviction of the humanities, it is that of human variousness, individuality. As physicians we also know, or ought to know, that each person is different, each patient reacts in his or her special way to any illness, indeed to life itself. A sense of the complexity of human affairs, a respect for human particularity, an interest in the ethical, the just and unjust sides of the social order, an awareness of life's unremitting contingencies, an awe of the mystery that clings to us "world without end"—these are the stuff of the humanities at their best, and ought to be, too, of the doctor's education, the doctor's everyday, practicing life. The knowledge that one gets in college and in medical school may no doubt have its uses—but it is, finally, worth little if not part of a morally sensitive and reflecting tradition, one to which each generation of physicians has to add its particular contribution.

Graduation address to the Harvard Medical School Class of 1978,
Harvard Medical Alumni Bulletin, July/August 1978

Medical Ethics and
Living a Life

Ablack woman in Mississippi's Delta told me this in 1969, as I went from home to home with other doctors trying to understand how it went for extremely poor and hard-pressed people:

We don't have it good here. It's no good at all. I turn and ask the Lord, a lot of times, why it's so—the unfairness in this world. But I'll never get an answer. My daddy told me: "Don't expect answers to the really big questions—not from anyone. We're put here, and we don't know why, and we try to figure out why while we're here, and we fight to stay around as long as we can, and the next thing we know, it's slipping away from us, and we're wondering where we're going, if we're going any place." If I was a doctor, I guess I'd wonder every day what it's all about, this life. A lot of times my children ask me these questions, ask me why people behave so bad toward other people, and why there's so much greed in the world, and when will God get angry and stop all the people who don't care about anything but themselves. I have to say I don't have the answers. Does anyone? If you go to college, my oldest girl said, you learn the answers. She's twelve. She thinks that the more education you get, the more you know about how to be good and live a good life. But I'll tell you, I'm not so sure. I think you can have a lot of diplomas to your credit and not be the best person in the world. You can be a fool, actually, and have a lot of people calling you professor, lawyer, even doctor.

That "even"—a measure of hesitation, of lingering awe, of qualified respect. She had experienced her "rough times" with doctors—not only segregated facilities but poor care and more insults than she cared to remember. A self-described "uppity nigger," she had finally spoken up to a doctor, had an argument with him. She remembered the critical essence of their confrontation this way:

I heard him saying bad, bad words about my people on the phone, and then he came into the waiting room and he gave me the nod. He never is polite to us, the way he can be with his white patients, and the more money they have, the bigger the smile they get out of him, and he's as eager to please as he can be. But with us, it's different; we get one sour look after the other. That day he told me to "shake a leg." I guess I wasn't walking into his office fast enough. Then he started talking about all "the welfare people," and saying, "Why didn't they go get themselves work?" Then, as he poked my belly, he gave me a lecture on eating and my diabetes—how I should "shape up and eat better."

That's when I forgot myself. I told him he should look to himself sometimes and stop making cracks at others. I told him he wasn't being much of a credit to his people and his profession, the way he was making these wisecracks about us poor folks. I told him he should know better, that there wasn't the jobs, and only now are we getting the right to vote, and the schools we've had weren't like the ones he could go to. I told him I expected more of him. Isn't he a doctor? If he can lord it over people, being a doctor, then he ought to remember how our Lord, Jesus Christ, behaved. He was the Son of God, but did he go around showing how big and important he was, and calling people bad names, and making wisecracks, and sidling up to the rich and looking down his nose at the poor? Jesus was a doctor; he healed the sick, and he tended after the lame, the halt and the blind, like our minister says. I told our doctor he ought to read the Bible more. I told him that instead of saying bad things about the poor people and us colored people, he should take a hard look at himself and see if he's living the best life he can—the kind of life a doctor should live—if he's going to preach to the rest of us, and be looked up to as if he's the best of the best.

She didn't get very far with such words, although, to his credit, the doctor not only heard her out but smiled and thanked her for the obvious courage (in the year 1967) that she had displayed. And it may be all too easy now, as it has surely been in past years, to call upon such an incident, the South being once again a convenient scapegoat for the rest of us. In fact, there aren't too many places in America, one suspects, where such a candid encounter could take place. How many of us in medicine have been asked by anyone—patient, friend, relative, student, or colleague—to connect our professional position with the kind of life we live, the way we get on with those we attend in an office, clinic, or ward? That woman, who today would be categorized as "culturally deprived" or "culturally disadvantaged" (the dreary banality of such language!), had managed to put her finger on an important issue, indeed—one that philosophers, theologians, and novelists have struggled for a long time to comprehend: How does one live a decent and honorable life, and is it right to separate, in that regard, a person's private life from his or her working life?

In a sense, too, that woman was struggling with the issue of medical ethics: How broad and deep ought such a subject cut—to the bone of the doctor's life? Without question, we need to examine the ethical matters that press on us every day in the course of our work. Recently, such matters have gained increasing attention and have been worked into the curricula of our medical schools. The traditions and resources of analytic philosophy have been extremely helpful, as we wonder when life ends or contemplate priorities so far as scarce (or experimental) technology and medicine go. It is utterly necessary for us to confront our values (or lack of them) as, for example, we work with patients too young or too old or too sick to be able to speak for themselves. And the dying patient has, of course, by and large benefited from the recent attention given that final stretch of earthly time, though one hastens to wonder whether a certain kind of psychological self-consciousness has not had its own dangers: all those "stages" and the prescriptive arrogance that can accompany "reform." Aren't there some people who have a right to "denial," not to mention to a belief in the Good News? When does psychological analysis become a kind of normative judgment, if not smug self-righteousness? Sometimes, as I read the literature on "death and dying," I get the feeling that agnostic psychological moralists have the complete run of the field, with all too many ministers worrying all too much about something called "pastoral counseling," when a few old-fashioned prayers might be in order for the sake of the patient, the attending clergyman, and the rest of us as well.

Be that as it may, the woman just quoted from the outer precincts of Clarksdale, Mississippi, was aware in her own way that there have been, all along, two philosophical traditions—the analytic and the existential. The former allows us to ponder a host of variables and to make a specific (for the doctor, a medical) decision. But the latter tradition urges us to go along with Kierkegaard, who surveyed Hegel's analytic abstractions with a certain awe but managed to remind himself and his readers that a man who had scrutinized all history and come up with a comprehensive theoretical explanation of anything and everything that had happened or would take place nevertheless had not much to tell us about how we ought to live our lives—we, that is, who ask such a question and know that we have only so much time to find an answer. The existentialists (I don't like the glib, trendy use of the word, but what can one do these days with any word?) have stressed the particulars of everyday life—hence their interest (Buber, Marcel, Camus, Sartre, and the father of them all, that at once high-spirited and gloomy Dane, Kierkegaard) in short stories, novels, plays, and essays concerned with specific, concrete matters, as opposed to large-scale theoretical formulations meant to explain whatever comes in sight and then some.

It is the everyday life that clinicians also contend with—the unique nature of each human being. Since no patient is quite like any other, the doctor has to step from well-learned abstractions to the individual person at hand—an important move, indeed. Novelists as well are wedded to the specific, the everyday; their job is to conjure up details for us, examples for us—the magic of art. And, as our black woman friend pointed out, everyday life has its own ethical conflicts. No wonder novelists do so well examining the trials and temptations that intervene, say, in a doctor's life. The point of a medical humanities course devoted to literature is ethical reflection, not a bit of culture polish here, a touch of story enjoyment there. There is an utter methodologic precision to the aim taken by George Eliot in *Middlemarch*, F. Scott Fitzgerald in *Tender Is the Night*, Sinclair Lewis in *Arrowsmith*, and Walker Percy in *Love in the Ruins*. They are interested in exploring a kind of medical ethics that has to do with the quality of a lived life.

In *Middlemarch*, Dr. Lydgate, a young doctor with high ideals, gradually must contend with a world of money and power. His marriage, his friendships, and his everyday attitudes and commitments are revealed to weigh heavily, in the end, on the nature of his work. When he leaves Middlemarch for his excellent practice "between London and a Continental bathing place," he is not only abandoning a promising research career; he has changed so imperceptibly that he has no notion of real change. The ethical implications of his change of career are rendered with great subtlety. This greatest of English novelists knew better than to indulge in melodrama—the high-minded doctor come to naught through bad luck or a bad marriage or the bad faith of a particular banker. She makes it clear that to the outer world Lydgate is never a failure; he becomes, rather, more and more successful, as judged by the (corrupt and ignorant, we now know) standards of his time and place. The measure of his failure is his own early and well-muscled ethical resolve. He had wanted to combat typhus and cholera—aware of the social as well as personal devastation those diseases wrought. He had wanted to take issue with the "principalities and powers" in his own profession. He ends up writing a treatise on gout. No doubt, gout, too, imposes suffering on people. And who is to decide what each of us ought to do—in any profession? But Lydgate had, indeed, made a series of decisions for himself and had hoped to see certain hopes and ambitions realized. *Middlemarch* provides a chronicle of disenchantment. A steady series of minor accommodations, rationalizations, and mistakes of judgment contribute to a change of purpose, if not of heart. A doctor's character is proved wanting, and the result is his professional success by the standards of the time. Such a devastating irony leaves the reader in hopes, no doubt, that a bit of contemplation will take place: a person's work is part of a person's life, and the two combined as lifework must be seen as constantly responsive to the moral decisions that we never stop making, day in and day out. What George Eliot probed was character, a quality of mind and heart sadly ignored in today's all too numerous psychological analyses.

Similarly in *Arrowsmith*, a novel that many of us, arguably, read and take seriously at the wrong time in our lives—as high-schoolers, rather than during medical school and the years of hospital training. Sinclair Lewis was no George Eliot; he had a ruder, more polemical nature as a writer, and he lacked her gifts of narration. But he knew how professional lives become threatened, cheapened, and betrayed. And he knew that such developments take place gradually, almost innocently—the small moments in the long haul, or the seemingly irrelevant big moments, such as a decision to live with one or another person and in this or that setting. His novel offered a powerful indictment of the larger society (always Lewis's intent) that exerts its sway on medicine, even research medicine, which is supposedly insulated from the vulgar world of cash and politics. But, of course, nothing is completely removed from that world—not doctors and not writers and not church people either. *Arrowsmith* is a novel that confronts the reader with a doctor's repeated ethical choices, a novel that makes it clear that such choices not only have to do with procedures (to do or not to do) or plugs (to pull or not to pull) but with the fateful decisions of everyday life that we are constantly making.

Such decisions are the stuff of each person's life. Once made, such decisions shadow us to the last breath. That is why Dick Diver haunts us in *Tender Is the Night*, and that is why Thomas More of Walker Percy's sad, funny, and compelling novel, *Love in the Ruins*, makes us so uneasy with his shrewd, satirical observations about himself and his fellow human beings. Those two physicians, the reader knows, have asked important questions about life—how to live it honorably, decently. They have also stumbled badly, and their "fall" troubles us. We want to know why. But the reasons, the explanations, are not the categorical ones of modern psychology— some emotional hang-up. Those two principal characters speak for novelists who know how seamless a web life is, how significantly each physician's career connects with his or her moral values. It is a truism that one takes a risk by isolating the various moments of one's time on earth; yet we commonly strain to do so, and we are even allowed, if not taught, to do so in our colleges and graduate schools and postgraduate training.

Every day, for instance, I see undergraduates not only working fiercely in courses such as organic chemistry but showing evidence of malevolent, destructive competitiveness. I have talked with some of those who teach such courses—heard the horror stories, the accounts of spite and meanness and outright dishonesty. Yet, again and again one listens to the same question: What can we do? And the students tell themselves and we tell ourselves—we, who have gone through the maze ourselves—that it is something inevitable and, once over, forgotten. But these bothersome novelists tell us that we don't forget, and Lord knows Freud managed to make that point rather tellingly during his lifetime. We may appear to forget; we may convince ourselves that we do, but the small compromises, evasions, and surrenderings of principle have their place in the unconscious, an element of geography yet to be done justice to by psychological theorists—the way we repress our moral sensibility, accommodate to various situations, and die in the way George Eliot indicates.

Each year I receive respectful letters from ministers, bishops, and church officials of one kind or another; I am asked to pass judgment psychologically on candidates for the ministry. Once my wife, in a moment of mischief and perhaps common sense, wondered what would have happened to all of us, historically, had Rorschach tests, Thematic Apperception Tests, or, yes, psychiatric interviews, been given to St. Francis of Assisi, St. Teresa of Avila, Martin Luther, or Gandhi, not to mention the Old Testament prophets or Jesus Christ. Would they have "passed" those psychiatric interviews—they with their anger at the injustices of this world and their extraordinary willingness to suffer on behalf of all of us? One shudders at the psychiatric words that might have been sent their way. For that matter, she also wondered: Would Freud be given a grant from the National Institute of Mental Health today, and would he even be willing to fill out those idiotic forms, one after the other? But setting that detour of my wife's aside, one is still left with the "spectacle" (to use a word that St. Paul favored at a critical moment in the affirmation of his faith) of religious authorities relying rather eagerly on the judgment of my ilk regarding the selection of candidates—as if psychiatrists were especially successful in finding for themselves, never mind others, how it is possible to live a principled life.

In psychiatry and medicine, as in other walks of life, we might ask for a few letters ourselves—not only appraisals of mental function but judgments about the ethical qualities of our various candidates. Do we often enough ask for such judgments? Do we ask ourselves and our students the kind of questions that George Eliot had in mind when she gave us (forever, one hopes) Dr. Lydgate, who would soon enough realize that there are prices to be paid for not asking certain questions? Dr. Lydgate forgot to inquire about what it would mean to him to become financially dependent on the philanthropist Bulstrode. Dr. Arrowsmith saw again and again the way doctors, like others, fall in line, knuckle under to various authorities who curb and confine independent thinking, never mind research. What those novelists move us to pursue is moral inquiry of a wide-ranging kind, in the tradition of Socrates or the Augustinian *Confessions* or Pascal's *Pensées*, or again, the best of our novelists: intense scrutiny of one's assumptions, one's expectations, one's values, and one's life as it is being lived or as one hopes to live it. The pivotal questions are, of course, obvious. How much money is too much money? Who commands one's time, and who does not? What balance is there to one's commitment of energy? And, from another standpoint, when do reformers start succumbing to the very arrogance or cruelty that they claim to fight? How ought we to resist various intrusions on our freedom, on our privacy as persons and as doctors—the bureaucratic statism that no one, however anxious for various governmental programs, should dismiss as being of little consequence, not after this century's testimony? And so on. Is there room to teach that kind of medical ethics, that kind of program of medical humanities in our medical schools? Is there any better way to do so than through the important stories and character portrayals of novelists who have moved close to the heart of the matter—the continuing tension between idealism and so-called practicality in all our lives?

New England Journal of Medicine, August 23, 1979

Religion and Religious Writers

The New Being

For years, Paul Tillich struggled to bring the Protestant theology he knew so well into a forthright and necessarily unsettling encounter with modern scientific thinking. A restless man with a powerful and hungry mind, he allowed himself again and again to be brought up short by what physicists and anthropologists have discovered in recent times, or by what psychologists and sociologists have claimed to be important. He also did not shirk looking skeptically at his own training as a minister and theologian. Will traditional Protestantism, however numerous and influential its avowed adherents, ever recognize its crusty, dogmatic, self-centered side? Will the rich and powerful nations of the West, so proudly "advanced" politically and economically, ever realize how enslaved they are by outworn traditions, senseless antagonisms, and constricting loyalties? Tillich was not sure how those questions would be answered in the immediate future, but because he was a hopeful man he did envision an eventual, decisively changed set of historical circumstances—perhaps akin to St. Paul's "the new creation." For Tillich, the Christian message is the message of "the New Being," a phrase he uses repeatedly in volume 1 of his *Systematic Theology* to describe a "reality" this beleaguered planet will (one can only pray) finally witness—a reality whose power will overcome "the demonic cleavages of the 'old reality' in soul, society, and universe."

Tillich never expected to see "the New Being" become a fully realized "fact" of life. He was writing about matters insubstantial and spiritual—matters no one can record on a chart or measure with a ruler or experiment with in a laboratory. Yet he may have been onto something that future social historians will record—something that others also sense and are moved to write about. Recently, for example, three short books have appeared whose titles Tillich would find engrossing. And it can be said that "soul, society, and universe" describes accurately what these books concern themselves with as they examine "the demonic cleavages" in our contemporary world.

Ivan D. Illich is a Roman Catholic priest and theologian, and his *Celebration of Awareness* takes up issues of the soul; Robert Jay Lifton is a psychiatrist, whose *Boundaries* is concerned with the way our society is changing, thus making us in certain respects different human beings; Loren Eiseley is an anthropologist, archeologist, and naturalist, whose *The Invisible Pyramid* tries to comprehend the universe, from the bewildering vastness of the skies to the equally puzzling more immediate world we call the "mind" or the "self." It is not an accident that the titles of these books contain words or implied concepts Tillich came back to constantly during his long and productive life. Awareness haunted him—awareness, which can be so fickle and which churches ought to encourage but often stifle. Boundaries were to him a paradox—at once a stimulating challenge and an outright enemy if they are not questioned or transcended. ("The man who stands on many boundaries experiences the unrest, insecurity, and inner limitation of existence in many forms.") As for the invisible, a theologian of Tillich's stature could not for long whistle in the dark to the tune of religious pieties, not when there is so much for humanity to find out about our own mysterious origins, not when we will either learn the secret of self-mastery or perhaps disappear—one more dead end of inscrutable nature.

I think the religious and social activist in Tillich would especially respond to Illich's book, which is just what its subtitle says: *A call for institutional revolution.* To Illich, Christ was a passionate and uncompromising rebel who preferred to die rather than modify his positions so that they threatened no one and could appeal to everyone. But even Christ would not be spared the second death, so to speak, that institutions visit upon the ideas of those lonely people who inspire and arouse (and thus frighten) others. Tillich could never forget how blasphemous some of today's ministers have become as they mouth chauvinistic platitudes and self-aggrandizing slogans in the name of a man who challenged with every word the religious and political and economic power of his day. Now, in the early 1970s, Illich, who once served in one of New York's Puerto Rican parishes and later became vice-rector of Puerto Rico's Catholic University, proclaims openly and forcefully his disgust at the way his own Church and others offer us "pharisaic legalism" and endless justifications of unjust (un-Christian, one can say) social and economic institutions.

Illich is now in Mexico. He has for years observed the way his Church gets along in Latin America. He has tried upon more than one occasion to keep quiet when he felt there was reason to speak out. Indeed, he stayed within the Church's conventional structure long enough to become a monsignor, and an intelligent, eloquent, charming, even charismatic one at that. But enough was enough; eventually he spoke out, and this collection of short articles and speeches of his recent years shows how dismayed and aroused he is, and how unequivocally he condemns the Church's present jeopardy: "A large proportion of Latin American Church personnel are presently employed in private institutions that serve the middle and upper classes and frequently produce highly respectable profits; this on a continent where there is a desperate need for teachers, nurses, and social workers in public institutions that serve the poor. A large part of the clergy are engaged in bureaucratic functions, usually related to peddling sacraments, sacramentals, and superstitious 'blessings.' . . . Theology is used to justify this system, canon law to administer it, and foreign clergy to create a worldwide consensus on the necessity of its continuation."

He describes the manner in which this country has extracted oil, metals, bananas, and coffee from its poor and vulnerable neighbors to the south while aligning itself with military dictators who use American guns and tanks and planes to defend the interests of a handful of families. He wonders why a nation that fights dictatorships in Europe and Asia supports them in Central America. He wonders why the Vatican ignores the role of its missions in Brazil and Costa Rica and Paraguay and Colombia. "We must acknowledge that missioners can be pawns in a world ideological struggle, and that it is blasphemous to use the Gospel to prop up any social or political system." He struggles with the dilemma St. Paul posed to the Corinthians: "Do we begin again to commend ourselves? Or need we, as some others, epistles of commendation to you, or letters of commendation from you?" No, said Paul, with an emphasis only a tempted man could summon. The point is to seek a living truth rather than "tables of stone." The point is that "the letter killeth but the Spirit giveth life." Illich knows that it is hard to follow Paul's advice. Powerful institutions protect men from the uncertainties of life, give them their niche, and take away a million worries and fears. Still, if we are to grow, we have to realize that pain and suffering and doubt and nightmare are ahead. It is this kind of uneasy and troublesome growth that Illich celebrates. He seems to be saying that not only the Catholic Church but many of our schools, universities, corporations, and legislatures are losing their moral authority over us because they are now out of touch with their own purposes and values or because they are no longer interested in the rock-bottom psychological and spiritual needs of human beings. We may submit to the power of those institutions, but they do not inspire us, and the stage is set for unrest, skepticism, and social violence.

Such a social and religious crisis is also described by a scholarly Yale psychiatrist who has extended the boundaries of his profession and in so doing learned things about those "inner" boundaries that both help us clarify life and at times constrict our vision and possibilities. Dr. Lifton, in his *Boundaries*, never forgets how complicated the mind is and how hard it is to free ourselves not only from the tug of earlier experiences but from the powerful pull of the times in which we live. It is his thesis that today's world places on us severe demands of a very special sort: we can for the first time destroy all life in an instant; we are at the mercy of machines and industrial "processes" we hardly can fathom, let alone control; we are multiplying too rapidly—on an earth with diminishing resources. But we continue to display an ability to be mean and thoughtless and hateful to one another, not just as individuals but as collections of people who set ourselves off by class, race, neighborhood, region, nation, religion, and then—from those vantage points—feel self-righteous or distinctive in a way that requires the humiliation or weakness or vulnerability of others. To a psychiatrist like Lifton or a theologian like Illich, the existence of sinful and destructive qualities (one takes one's choice with the descriptive words) in human beings is not surprising. What makes our waywardness so urgent a matter is the world's economic and technological situation: never before has it been so important that our leaders get along rather than go after each other with those followers who always do the dying in the name of jingoist or ideological slogans.

In response to such a state of affairs, we as individuals are going through private changes, says Dr. Lifton. Some of us are pulling the shades down and cursing anything new or controversial; others (and not just the young, who can produce their share of submissive, conformist, and narrow people) are in the best sense unnerved, puzzled, questioning. We see how blind we have been to the needs and aspirations of others. We recognize that something is not only wrong but mad about an industrial empire whose rivers are foul, whose air is dirty, whose land is ravaged, whose wildlife is being killed off, whose machines are dangerous, and whose food is contaminated. And because we trouble ourselves about such things we become broader, more alert, more responsive, less complacent and self-satisfied. In Lifton's terms, we are on the way to becoming "Protean man"—not free of flaws and limitations but alive to the disasters that threaten us: "The Protean style of self-process . . . is characterized by an interminable series of experiments and explorations, some shallow, some profound, each of which can readily be abandoned in favor of still new psychological quests." And if the quests fail or become dangerously single-minded or bizarre, that is not cause to deplore the efforts. "I want," Lifton adds, "to stress that this Protean style is by no means pathological as such, and in fact may be one of the functional patterns necessary to life in our times. I would emphasize that it extends to all areas of human experience—to political as well as to sexual behavior, to the holding and promulgating of ideas, and to the general organization of lives. To grasp this style, then, we must alter our judgments concerning what is psychologically disturbed or pathological, as opposed to adaptive or even innovative."

It is no accident that both Illich and Lifton use "revolution" in the subtitles of their books. Illich is making "a call for institutional revolution" and Lifton is attempting to assess "psychological man in revolution." Illich finds arrogance and thoughtlessness in various religious organizations (among others), and Lifton scolds his psychiatric colleagues for being self-aggrandizing, limited in vision, and moralistic in a way that helps out those who uphold the status quo; men and women, he says, who question our various norms too closely and take action to show their disapproval are called "psychologically disturbed" or "pathological."

In contrast, Loren Eiseley seems untroubled by such problems, though he does not conceal his judgment that there is a great deal wrong with our institutions and how we get on with each other. What distinguishes him from Illich and Lifton is not his profession but his philosophical viewpoint and the way he conveys it. He is not concerned solely with the last half of the twentieth century, nor does he write with any special program or appeal or critique in mind. For him, our contemporary ailments have origins we will never know in full and a destiny that is beyond any era's (let alone generation's) comprehension. His range of reflections makes the broadest of our historians seem a trifle parochial. He has been looking at the stars farthest away from us as well as at the earth, which still holds on to a large number of apparently inaccessible secrets. He feels a lonely awe at the hugeness of the universe. In a touching beginning to his speculative journey, he brings us back to his childhood and to the childhood of the human race, whose ancestors must have had the same sense of doubt and mystery and passionate curiosity the author had when he was a boy, and still has. He assembles thoughts and speculations he has struggled with over the decades. They are questions, really, that perhaps can be asked only as Gauguin did when in 1897 he wrote on one of his canvases, "From where do we come? What are we? Where are we going?," or as Richard Strauss did when he tried to make music respond to Nietzsche's philosophy in the tone poem *Also Sprach Zarathustra*. The mysteries that command Eiseley's attention defy any particular art form, and he himself harnesses lyric metaphors and allegories to the task of scientific exposition.

Who, indeed, can possibly fathom the riddles of the universe in phrases alone—even the rich and suggestive ones a good poet constructs? As Eiseley cannot stop reminding himself and us, we are here for a fraction of a second, and all our vanities and conceits and proud achievements and noble dreams amount to little—once the archeologist and the astronomer in us stop us in our tracks and get us to think a little. Not that an active, energetic, effective man like Loren Eiseley wants us to become paralyzed by useless ruminations. He realizes that we are entitled to a certain amount of self-centeredness. He recognizes how significantly modern technological civilization has confronted at least some of the universe's inscrutability. We will never know what we are blessed and cursed with the desire to know, but we do have the ability to find out so very much, and we are on our way to places in the sky as well as deep within ourselves.

For Eiseley, those inner, essentially ethical explorations (and they are explorations people like Illich and Lifton continually make) may be more important and decisive than any landing on a distant planet. Eiseley is a moral philosopher and a passionate naturalist. He is worried: "In the endless pursuit of the future we have ended by engaging to destroy the present. We are the greatest producers of nondegradable garbage on the planet. In the cities a winter snowfall quickly turns black from the pollutants we have loosed in the atmosphere. This is not to denigrate the many achievements and benefits of modern science. On a huge industrial scale, however, we have unconsciously introduced a mechanism which threatens to run out of control. We are tracking ourselves into the future—a future whose 'progress' is as dubious as that which we experience today. Once the juggernaut is set in motion, to slow it down or divert its course is extremely difficult because it involves the livelihood and social prestige of millions of workers. The future becomes a shibboleth which chokes our lungs, threatens our ears with sonic booms, and sets up a population mobility which is destructive in its impact on social institutions."

So it goes in America, a great and confident world power whose well-to-do people (never mind our poor) feel uncertain, frightened, and at the mercy of forces hard to understand, let alone control. Eiseley is a scientist, but he fears that we are beguiled by our scientists (and engineers and doctors and planners), whom we turn into prophets and magicians, and upon whom we project "questions involving the destiny of man over prospective millions of years." He is also a blunt and uncompromising essayist. Like Tillich, he feels that we are driven from within by demonic forces one can call greed, selfishness, or arrogance. (The list is a long one.) Eiseley has little hope we will ever be rid of this inheritance. In a sense, tragedy is our birthright: "Suppose, my thought persisted, there is still another answer to the ruins in the rain forests of Yucatán, or to the incised brick tablets baking under the Mesopotamian sun. Suppose that greater than all these, vaster and more impressive, an invisible pyramid lies at the heart of every civilization man has created, that for every visible brick or corbelled vault or upthrust skyscraper or giant rocket we bear a burden in the mind to excess, that we have a biological urge to complete what is actually uncompletable."   .

And yet we have to go on, lucky to have among us the sensibilities a person like Eiseley demonstrates. Driven, wild, thoughtless, and hurtful we are—and maybe doomed—but because we are human we have a chance to show the tact and intelligence and decency

Eiseley has achieved. If his words that evoke images and suggest a universe of their very own make the reader more thoughtful and considerate, more a part of "the New Being," that is enough for any explorer before he ends the journey all of us make and try to comprehend and struggle to shape and know must end but hope in some small way to make significant.

New Yorker, November 6, 1971

The World and the Devil

Theologians can easily acquire lack of interest in the world's condition. They seek after knowledge of God and formulate the nature of religious belief. Since the supernatural offers ample leeway for the theoretical mind, as well as enough problems to keep it busy, a sensible division of labor seems in order: let other scholars try to make sense of "the things which are Caesar's." Even if Christ himself made a distinction between political authority and God's realm (though not with any intention of telling theologians what are or are not their proper objectives), he more than once became immersed in secular matters. While promising those who would follow him another world, he took after moneylenders, rebuked the rich and powerful, and linked God's grace to a social ethic he not only preached but tried to practice. By the time he was on the cross, he had managed to alarm all sorts of influential people, and the representatives of a powerful empire felt they had to do away with him. No wonder some of the best philosophers and theologians (from Augustine, Aquinas, John Calvin, and Martin Luther to Paul Tillich, Karl Barth, and Reinhold Niebuhr) have not been able to keep their minds from concerns that sociologists, historians, and political scientists (not to mention politicians) might well consider theirs and no one else's. No wonder kings and emperors were told by Christian students of the Bible not only what they should do to save their souls but how they should rule: by which avowed authority and set of principles, which hierarchical and administrative apparatus. No wonder, in our time, Reinhold Niebuhr found himself writing *The Structure of Nations and Empires*, becoming a founding member of Americans for Democratic Action, serving as an adviser to George Kennan's policy planning staff in the State Department, and, toward the end of his life, receiving visits and letters from the scholar Ronald Stone (he teaches social ethics at Pittsburgh Theological Seminary), who was working on the book now published by Abingdon as *Reinhold Niebuhr: Prophet to Politicians*.

Professor Stone has concentrated on Niebuhr's political attitudes and activities and on his enormous influence on a significant number of this nation's policymakers and politically active intellectuals. To deal more comprehensively with his wide-ranging social and historical essays (even without an analysis of his more conventionally theological writing) would require a much longer book, perhaps a biography. Niebuhr has made it clear, in *The Nature and Destiny of Man*, that he regards irony and ambiguity as the essence of what all people must understand and live with, and as one goes through his work the ironies and ambiguities mount to a point at which, for the sake of comprehension, they are best fitted into an account of a vigorously productive life of seventy-nine years or organized around a specific theme. An avowed pessimist and skeptic, Niebuhr worked tirelessly to bring about social and political change, no matter how gloomy he felt about the prospects of the human race, at least on earth. A thinker called upon for counsel by architects of this nation's Cold War posture, he revealed a strong if qualified Marxist streak. A contemporary intellectual who insisted upon the usefulness of a concept like original sin (as a metaphor that suggests the limits and problems every mind has, however cultivated and probed), he was widely read in psychoanalysis and drew upon that discipline with intelligence, discrimination, and restraint—no easy achievement in the 1930s. A man of deep feeling, a powerful and unashamedly emotional preacher, an activist far too responsive (for his health's sake) to the demands upon him, he could be severely logical, given to precise abstractions, and detached to the point of resignation, of *che sarà sarà*.

Such qualities will give Dr. Niebuhr's eventual biographer a deal of work; meanwhile, Professor Stone shows how a gifted, unconventional, and energetic Christian theologian could immerse himself in the political struggles of his time, occasionally feel hopeless about their outcome, hesitate one moment and plunge ahead the next, remain consistent here but contradict himself there, sign dozens of statements, urge many kinds of programs, stand up for a succession of causes and candidates, and, despite all that commitment of time and effort, develop a carefully reasoned and persuasively argued political philosophy set down in scholarly and by no means out-of-date books—as opposed to his incessant political journalism, much of which was casually written in response to one crisis after another.

Professor Stone wrestles briefly with biographical enigmas. Why did a man of German Lutheran ancestry, born in Wright City, Missouri, brought up with the values of the American heartland (optimism, patriotism, the virtues of hard work and good works), a graduate of a theological seminary, become in his forties the deliverer, at the University of Edinburgh, of the Gifford Lectures, in which so many of the West's pieties, to say nothing of those of his native American Midwest, are challenged or, as in his treatment of the doctrine of original sin, given a new and startling meaning? As the author indicates, young Niebuhr was brilliant, strong-willed, and possessed of a creative mind. The book starts where his childhood and youth ended—with the developing thought of a grown man who in 1915 became a pastor at Detroit's Bethel Evangelical Church and soon showed himself willing to take risks (in the way he thought as well as acted) others found unacceptable.

Even in the early years of this century, Detroit meant automobiles, and the city Niebuhr lived in for thirteen years was the germ plasm of America's highly developed industrial society: a plasm to be found first in the factories and stores and homes Niebuhr came to know so well and wrote about in *Leaves from the Notebook of a Tamed Cynic.* The title is misleading, because one is asked to believe that a young cynic was brought under control. The fact is that Dr. Niebuhr came to his parish a somewhat naive but resourceful man who only in time sensed how effectively he and his kind were used; the high rhetoric of Protestant idealism, he finally realized, concealed the ugliness and exploitation of an expanding but morally regressive economic system. In the author's words, "Ford became a symbol to Niebuhr of America's technical genius and social ineptitude." He began to think about questions many of us don't want to. Who owns what, who works for whom, and at what wage, in contrast to what level of profit? In the 1920s, there was no United Auto Workers union, and few ministers were advocating one, let alone advocating, as Reinhold Niebuhr did, a guaranteed annual wage. Thus, a somewhat innocent and well-intentioned person became familiar with the seamier aspects of this country's social order, began to speak out against injustice (on account of which efforts were made to strip him of his position) and to change the way he thought about his responsibilities as a Christian. Christ said that whoever wants to change the world must have the qualities of a serpent as well as those of a dove, and such a balance, as Niebuhr spent a lifetime learning, is not easily obtained.

From the late twenties until the early sixties, when, under the threat of a long and exhausting struggle with illness, he gave up everything except writing, Niebuhr taught at Union Theological Seminary. However developed and intricate his philosophical ideas, he never could forget the experience in Detroit, and in essence Professor Stone's book shows how a man grandly preoccupied with nothing less than "creation as revelation" (to draw upon the title of one section of *The Nature and Destiny of Man*) could also be obsessed by the everyday dilemmas that confront us as liberals or conservatives, Americans or Russians, workers or owners. Perhaps that obsession became a distraction; perhaps Niebuhr never fully realized himself as a theologian and philosopher because he spent so much time struggling on behalf of the poor, trying (in the thirties) to alert this nation to the menace of fascism, wrestling with the problems Stalin's Russia presented to the Western democracies, agonizing over the domestic and international crises we have lived through in these recent decades. Yet Niebuhr's "Christian interpretation" of humanity's role, as offered in the Gifford Lectures, called for the kind of life he lived, and a man who railed against hypocrisy and the arrogant self-righteousness of the intellectuals could not stand aloof, sending down from his academic study a few prescriptions and ex post facto reprimands. He preferred to test the validity of his ideas by fighting for them—and was self-critical enough, when he found himself wrong, to admit publicly his errors and use them to encourage his readers to ponder whether they, too, have blind spots, whether they justify in the name of God or a moral code something that is flagrantly self-serving.

Niebuhr's career as (in Professor Stone's words) a "prophet to politicians" took a series of dramatic turns, each of which involved a renunciation of held positions. In the 1930s, he renounced his liberal views and insisted that men never can be assumed to be without greed and self-serving ambitiousness, despite their generosity and kindness to others; liberals, he felt, emphasize too strongly these last two qualities while ignoring the first two or attributing them to "environmental factors"—poverty, for example, or the effect that an economic system or educational philosophy has on a growing child's character. It was in this context that Niebuhr began to formulate his bold ideas about human "nature"; the best of us are sinners, he told his secular, optimistic, liberal friends, and no matter how much money we are guaranteed by the state, or how satisfying our work, or what dignity we achieve, or how well we know ourselves or express ourselves, we will still covet, be envious and smug, self-pitying, and so on and on. He told them that no mixture of Marx and Freud would turn men and women into angels. If all that seems not especially original, one need only recall, in our recent history, how many utopian promises have been offered to us under many auspices, and how many messianic creeds persist today, *if only* we enact this law, live this way, or get rid of those ideas (or people). Niebuhr was aware of the fallacy of such reasoning and, too, the pride involved, though there were sins that, in his particular hierarchy of them, were much more serious: a skepticism that leads to indifference; an awareness that leads to a paralytic self-consciousness; a faith in the next world that numbs any sense of outrage (and any political activity) that might be mobilized in this world.

In the middle 1930s, Niebuhr added some Marxist thinking to his Christian philosophy and—essay by essay and book by book—tried to find a position both radical and solidly grounded in the realities of life. It is possible to become so wildly hopeful that one whistles in the dark as a Stalin crops up out of nowhere. It is also possible to be so realistic that one unwittingly speaks for those who plan to seize whatever social and political power they can. Niebuhr came to admire certain British Socialists, envied their political closeness to a powerful trade-union movement, and wondered why American liberals and progressives of the middle class have such a hard time getting along with the working people whose cause seems to be at the heart of our reform movements. Professor Stone shows how the activist theologian tried to make sense of that irony, and finally managed it, in the interpretation of our society he called "the irony of American history." Indeed, Niebuhr spent much of his later life insisting that irony, ambiguity, paradox, and mystery are inescapable in the life we lead, no matter what the achievements of the natural sciences and the social sciences; thus there is need for what Professor Stone names "Christian realism." He quotes from Niebuhr:

> Yet the Christian faith tends to make the ironic view of human evil in history the normative one. Its conception of redemption

from evil carries it beyond the limits of irony, but its interpretation of the nature of evil in human history is consistently ironic. This consistency is achieved on the basis of the belief that the whole drama of human history is under the scrutiny of a divine judge who laughs at human pretensions without being hostile to human aspirations. . . .

The Biblical interpretation of the human situation is ironic, rather than tragic or pathetic, because of its unique formulation of the problem of human freedom.

An honest man, Niebuhr acknowledged his inclination toward the kind of sin this passage obliquely refers to; he could be grim and scornful, haunted by the abundant tragedies of this century, sure that nothing really would work out well. He could become preoccupied with involvements and issues that were petty and passing. Professor Stone's book reveals how a farseeing philosopher could be trapped by the confines of his era, especially when he moved close to those "powers and principalities, those political leaders and government agencies," that his Biblical self should have told him to avoid. Still, a kind of grace came upon him toward the end, or perhaps was always at his side. If, in middle age, he dared unmask the pretensions of his own liberalism, at the end of his life he was issuing Isaiahlike denunciations of the folly of those who adhered so literally to the political realism he had advocated and even, at times, thrown in the teeth of his idealistic friends who talked of "One World" and "man's basic goodness." Early on, he saw what we were doing in Vietnam under cover of that "realism," and at home he saw "realism" called upon to defend vested interests, to keep black people in their place, to deny the working people a larger share of the wealth they produce. Ailing and old, he spoke out, sparing nobody, including himself. So the end was like the beginning and the middle; a social thinker's agile mind, able to shift from theme to theme, and to weave criticism and self-criticism into a coherent, Christian view of life, remained steadfast, whatever the challenges. One is left with that final irony of a career: none of the historical discontinuities the theologian Reinhold Niebuhr sought to understand could break up the continuity of his own life.

New Yorker, October 7, 1972

Bringing Words out
of Silence

In early October, 1948, the firm of Harcourt, Brace in New York published the autobiography of a man who was then only thirty-three years old and living in rural Kentucky at a Trappist monastery. The book's title was *The Seven Storey Mountain* (in Dante's *Divine Comedy* Mount Purgatory has seven stories), and the original printing order was for 5,000 copies. But a young editor, Robert Giroux, a contemporary of the book's author at Columbia University during the late 1930s, had sent galleys to Evelyn Waugh, Graham Greene, and Clare Boothe Luce, and soon enough their enthusiastic praise would alert those who worked in the publishing house that, with luck, they might have a modest success on their hands. Instead, they had the enviable task of keeping up with an apparently insatiable (and continuing, and international) demand for a book whose cover, today, announces "over one million copies sold."

Not that *The Seven Storey Mountain* was the only book the young Cistercian monk Thomas Merton (known in his monastery as Father Louis) would publish in 1948. The purely religious books, *A Guide to Cistercian Life* and *Cistercian Contemplatives*, were published without his name. A good and caring friend, James Laughlin of New Directions, published a collection of Merton's poems. A Catholic publishing house issued *Exile Ends in Glory: The Life of a Trappestine, Mother M. Berchmans*, and a Catholic college (St. Mary's, Notre Dame) brought out *What Is Contemplation?* All this—and so much more to come in the years that followed, forty books, hundreds of articles, and thousands of letters addressed to men and women the world over—from someone who had chosen to live a cloistered, predominantly silent life.

In retrospect, it is not hard to figure out why *The Seven Storey Mountain* caught on so astonishingly well that year, the same one in which readers were offered Orwell's *1984*. For the second time in less than half a century, the so-called civilized nations of the world had resorted to prolonged war, with millions of soldiers and civilians killed. All the faiths, religious and secular, had not prevented those wars. The nation of Goethe and Beethoven, and of Luther and a strong Catholic tradition as well, had built genocidal crematoriums. Science had enabled nuclear bombs to be built. A poet of Ezra Pound's vast knowledge and powerful literary gifts had ended up mouthing fascist doggerel for Mussolini. High communist and socialist ideals had become Stalin's monumental perversities; they were comprehended quickly for what they were in the 1930s by Orwell, Ignazio Silone, and Simone Weil, and in the late 1940s they were being seen by more and more people as, in their sum, one of the worst tragedies in recent centuries. Meanwhile, millions of men who had fought in obscure Pacific islands or yet again in France's bloody northern territory, had returned home, all too familiar with pain and suffering and death, with the workings of fate and chance and luck, good or bad—the old familiars of storytelling.

No wonder that, at such a time, a young man's struggle to find meaning and purpose in this often cruel and always unpredictable life attracted the attention of so many readers. Still, as Waugh realized instantly (and before the book was even published), the compelling power of *The Seven Storey Mountain* had to do with more than its poignant personal and spiritual story: a boy of relatively good fortune, both social and economic, loses his mother at the age of four, his father at fifteen, watches the world go murderously crazy as he grows into manhood, becomes a bit of a rake, drinks a lot, flirts with Freud and Marx, turns relentlessly to Catholicism, and chooses to be a priest, one willing to accept the stern discipline and the demanding isolation of the Trappist order. Waugh spotted the emergent lyric writer in Merton; he understood that a poet of some considerable skill had found in the personal memoir a congenial means of gaining the attention of others and eventually captivating them. Skeptical of the all too numerous sentimental or melodramatic conversion stories he'd heard or read, he yielded nevertheless to Merton's charm, passion, and adroitness as a writer.

This still haunting and influential autobiography (marred only occasionally by moments of religious triumphalism) would not be the last of Merton's self-presentations. He had started a journal of sorts when he was eight and kept one all during his adult life, persisting even as a Trappist monk. He shaped his ideas and worries, the thoughts that came to him as he lived his life, into one book after another. He also dispatched a stream of letters to friends near and far; and those letters, too, were instruments of spiritual discussion—with himself, often enough, as much as with his particular correspondent. In the end there were 1,800 separate folders, many containing scores of exchanges with the famous and distinguished (Boris Pasternak, Czeslaw Milosz, Walker Percy, and Dorothy Day). On the other hand, Merton responded warmly to certain unknown individuals who occasionally more than held their own with him—such as the sixteen-year-old California girl who posed this startling question to a monk she had taken to calling "Tom" in her letters: "Do you know that I looked you up in the *Guide to Catholic Periodicals* at school and GOOD GRIEF, why do you write so much?"

No doubt Michael Mott, himself a fairly active poet and novelist, must have asked himself that question as he studied Merton's papers. Mr. Mott's *Seven Mountains of Thomas Merton* is the authorized biography, which was to have been done by Merton's longtime friend, the writer and photographer John Howard Griffin, who died before he could accomplish the requisite research and writing. The girl in California would surely have been even more in awe of Merton's prolific pen had she been given access, as Mr. Mott was, to Merton's journals, only parts of which (edited, of course) saw the public light of inclusion in his various books.

An important evaluative moment in the biography offers this explanation of the meaning a torrent of confessional prose had for a particular Christian: "The journals were a method of sabotaging the ideal Merton. If they preserved the spontaneity, they preserved the scandal, the whole man (whole, sometimes, to the point of exhaustion). The pages on God, on prayer, on humility, would distress some; the pages of criticism of the Church would worry many; the praise of the Church, others; references to drinking, to dreams, to periods of depression—references to his own evasions, to his capacity for kidding himself, to his being less than an honest lover, to costly mistakes of fact and judgment. When he was used, or used up, the journals would speak of him without editing, crossings-out, polishing—a place where the narrow-minded, or those who had made a cult of him, would flounder and where the seekers of truth without pretense would find him."

He was, in a sense, one of those "seekers"—anxious and determined, throughout his life, to face himself down honorably, an Augustinian task made progressively more difficult, he realized, by the very attempt to do so, insofar as it was shared (through his articles and books) with hundreds of thousands of complete strangers, who yearned to see and worship his every word, even when he was being self-indulgent or wrongheaded or presumptuous—as he knew he, like the rest of us, could occasionally end up being. Again and again he takes himself to task for being prideful, for being too self-conscious, for letting egoism cloud his vision or affect his various involvements. At one point he refers to the "old narcissism," rather as George Eliot used to make mention of the "old Adam."

His biographer refers to "crises of solipsism," after which he attempted "to adapt and identify himself with others." Those "others" for over half of his life were his fellow monks, and much of this book offers a running account of his complex relationship with Dom James, the abbot of the monastery of Gethsemani, who in an earlier life "had graduated from the Harvard Business School at the age of twenty-one," and for whom "the ideal monk was one who lived in anonymity and who died known only to God and to a few of his fellow monks."

In his own way, Merton agreed—hence his solitary side, his wish to live as a hermit within the confines of Gethsemani, his hope at the end of his life to find someplace (he was considering Alaska) where he could once and for all be rid of the press of outside attention. Still, an active, successful literary life made it certain that he would be always tempted: "Merton told them [visiting friends] Don Ameche had telephoned the monastery at Easter asking if anyone had bought the film rights to *The Seven Storey Mountain*. If not, Ameche would like to make the film, presumably playing the part of Thomas Merton himself (Merton had been thinking more of Gary Cooper). Dom James had said no to the film and gone right on to ask if Ameche had made his Easter duty. Don Ameche said he had been to communion that morning."

This amusing anecdote, Mr. Mott knows, is more generally edifying with respect to Merton's Cistercian life than many readers are likely to realize until the end of the book. Merton was much attracted to a secular culture he also fled from; and his biographer does well to give us, in clear and unpretentious and vigorous prose, the many details of that ambivalence. The author also is wise to resist the temptation, surely substantial in this case, to hagiography—

though, if one were to choose a psychological patron saint for Merton, the much-tempted St. Anthony would be more fitting than, say, the austere St. Benedict.

The first chapters offer slow reading because Merton's family and his early life, his youth, too, are presented as they were—a good deal of foolishness and self-indulgence. The reader's attention becomes completely fixed once a somewhat dissolute man has begun to wrestle in earnest with the devils in him. But this is no work of cynical skepticism. The author obviously admires his subject and wants to evoke with compassionate understanding his sometimes heartbreaking difficulties—not only of the child who lost his artist mother, the youth who lost his artist father, the man excited and tormented by his writing gifts, but also of the monk who fell in love with a beautiful nurse who cared for him when he was sick in the hospital, the political activist who had grave doubts about the manner in which various protests were being enacted, and finally, the Roman Catholic ever more strongly drawn, toward the end of his life, to the significance of Eastern religions.

That last interest might have been further pursued had Merton not been accidentally electrocuted on December 10, 1968, while he was attending a conference on monasticism in Thailand. He was fifty-three. His death, of course, attracted much notice, and the depth of sorrow felt by so many people, of such varied backgrounds, is powerfully rendered in *Merton, By Those Who Knew Him Best,* a thin volume of memoirs assembled by Paul Wilkes, who directed a recent public television program devoted to Merton's life. In no way, one begins to sense, has Merton left his friends; they talk of him as if he will always be near at hand, smiling broadly, roaring his infectious laugh, sharing with them his thickly textured knowledge, his penetrating wisdom, and his urgent idealism. (He was an early supporter of the Civil Rights movement, a tough critic of our Vietnam involvement, and an eloquent opponent of the development of nuclear weaponry here and abroad.)

In his final year, Mr. Mott tells us in the biography, Merton declared himself taken with "the idea of starting out into something unknown, demanding and expecting nothing very special, and hoping only to do what God asks . . . whatever it may be." By now, one hopes and prays, he has found the answer to that implied question, the all-important one for him. Meanwhile, on the occasion of this long, detailed, affectionately knowing but stoically unsentimental biography, a good number of readers will reach a conclusion about an aspect of God's design for his eager, ardent servant, Thomas Merton—that his words and deeds were meant to touch many of us deeply, instruct us significantly, and reveal to us in various ways a divine grace as it came, wonderfully and mysteriously, to inform a singular, memorable life.

New York Times Book Review, December 23, 1984

Gravity and Grace in the Novel
A Confederacy of Dunces

Simone Weil was a brief, visionary presence whose gifts to us of the twentieth century are still being sorted out and estimated with a certain surprised awe by her various critics and admirers. She combined, in a life of only thirty-four years, a radical social and cultural disaffection with an intense, conservative yearning for certain elements of the past that she hoped to see given new life in a world whose moral contours she tried to imagine and describe in various essays—while all the while (it can be said) dying the death of someone who had a profound skepticism of what the future offered this terribly endangered planet. She ached for the poor, the humble, the hurt, the ailing, the vulnerable; she scorned what in the Bible gets called derisively "principalities and powers"— those who earned the outspoken contempt of Jeremiah and Isaiah and Amos in the Old Testament and, of course, of Jesus Christ himself in the New Testament—the smug, pompous, and self-important ones whose merciless and vain extortions are done at the expense of the rest of us.

On the other hand, she saw precisely, and early on (she was, indeed, a prophet), how mean, vicious, and dangerous some of this world's so-called reformers are—full of pride and its consequences: the ruthless, arrogant failure to consider anyone's point of view, unless it serves the purpose of a particular (ideological) cause. Simone Weil needed no reminder that original sin is far from a quaint term, entertained gullibly and in ignorance by those who lived in earlier times. She looked relentlessly, candidly into her own mind and heart. She observed others closely. She concluded that no political or economic changes, no matter how well intentioned, will take from us our humanity, our moments of doubt and disappointment, envy and truculence—aspects of our very condition. We are, as Lord knows our novelists and philosophers have been telling us over the generations, the many-sided creature who (through words and ideas) looks at the stars but who rivals—arguably, outdistances—any and all so-called animals or beasts when it comes to such behavior as rage, rapacity, and even wanton murderousness.

Her torment, then, resided in her intellectual, if not spiritual, breadth—a stubborn, idiosyncratic, original-minded, personally devastating capacity for, even insistence upon, living marginally, and thereby embracing ambiguities and inconsistencies others shun as intolerable. Through her marvelous, hard-won spirituality (a gift to her as she became physically sicker and sicker), she managed to find, ironically, a strong interest in the concrete, particular world, the day-to-day routines and objects of involvement that, she knew, tell so much about us. "No ideas but in things," William Carlos Williams has reminded twentieth-century urban Americans in his poem *Paterson*. Simone Weil knew how dangerous it can be for a Christian pilgrim to ignore one or another version of that injunction. The penalty turns out to be the Gnostic heresy, a direct challenge to a God who willingly, if not ardently, assumed "the flesh." And gnosticism is related to other fatal splits—that, for instance, of ideologues who assume they can spend hours, days, a lifetime with the seductive, self-serving pleasures of theory, while putting aside as unworthy or of lesser significance the countless pressing details of this life. I remember, for example, when Harvard's buildings were seized in the early 1970s, I stood watching the assault with Erik Erikson, who wondered this out loud: "When they leave the building, will they help some old person trying to cross the street and in danger of being hurt? For that matter, will you and I do so—as we do our arguing or meditating or analyzing?"

As I read John Kennedy Toole's *A Confederacy of Dunces*, I found the above train of thought gripping my mind constantly. Simone Weil gave us an unforgettable polarity: "gravity and grace." By gravity she meant the ever-present "weight" of our minds and our bodies. (She was a great one for seeing the poetry of physics and mathematics.) We are, inescapably, acted upon by the atoms and molecules, the muscles and hormones, the synapses that make up, in sum, ourselves. And, too, we are constantly acting upon one another: asking, taking, beseeching, demanding, telling truth and telling half-truths, and lying, and manipulating, and exhorting, and imploring, and loving, and demonstrating fearful possessiveness, angry petulance, sly displeasure, open resentment—as the expression I keep hearing in church puts it, "world without end." But there are moments also of transcendence, strange moments, unexpected moments, even unearned ones—unless one will have God to be a Puritan, a vigorous bourgeois. "Grace is everywhere," Georges Bernanos has his curé saying at the end of *Diary of a Country Priest*, and surely Jesus Christ, as he walked through Galilee and as he suffered in Judea, taught that lesson to "all sorts and conditions" of human beings—if I may again, and conservatively, call upon the "old" Book of Common Prayer I remember so fondly. As Dorothy Day used to put it, for "the lame, the halt, the blind," not to mention the skeptical, the loony, the extremely vulnerable, even the strenuously condemned and the exiled—grace becomes theirs, and not through the laws of state, and not, either, through the arbitrary, rigid classification of the Church, but through an unexpected, a mysterious, an utterly providential arrival: Him. Dunces and doubters, men and women demeaned by political and religious doctrine—grace lifted them all, gravity having been decisively defied.

In New Orleans, the novelist Toole is determined to show us the unyielding pull of gravity. We are all dunces, of course, and that certainly includes any would-be prophet who happens to know how to spin a yarn. But what, exactly, is a "dunce," or indeed, a collection or "confederacy" of them? All of Toole's characters are dim-witted, driven, distended by their maker's insistence upon satire. They are true to the biblical moment of Mark: the Gadarene swine, repositories of the madness of a legion (and, alas, waiting in the wings, historically, have been thousands of other legions). They are the blind leading the blind, or conniving or manipulating, or ruining altogether. It is Toole's contention that Freud missed not a trick about our silliness, our pretentiousness, our hell-bound lustiness, and our feverish, egoistic possessiveness with respect to one another. It is Toole's contention, further, that a "walk on the wild side," as the saying goes, will give us, finally, ourselves—all of us who seem remarkably *un*like Mr. Toole's various comically exaggerated men and women, until, of course, we stop and look closely at those warts and more that we have learned to conceal from others, not to mention ourselves.

New Orleans has long been a cosmopolitan city, so it provides a natural and splendid setting for Mr. Toole's moral and spiritual purposes. He knows that no high-minded critique of humankind of any value can do without the devil, under whatever name, and needless to say, Freud's "death instinct" was one such name. "The devil has slippery shoes," I often heard black people in Mississippi's Delta say as they contemplated, in the early 1960s, the workings of our nation's political life, and Mr. Toole has his particular black friend, Jones, tell us that again and again. Jones's running commentary is, actually, a strangely sane, earthy, shrewd, and knowing one, a valuable and activist counterpart of Astor and Sulk, those two "handymen" Flannery O'Connor gave us in "The Displaced Person." Faulkner started it, I suppose, with Dilsey, the most powerfully developed, noble, and sustaining of all the characters offered us by white Southern novelists. The Compsons fall apart in *The Sound and the Fury;* Dilsey retains her dignity and offers what little she has, which turns out to be rather a lot. I detect a similar irony in *A Confederacy of Dunces.* The whites, all of them so much better off, supposedly, than Jones, by virtue of their skin color, turn out to be collectively out of their minds and especially incapable of sensible, pointed, and appropriate social and psychological judgments. But he is down-to-earth, clear-headed, and above all, attentive. He has, in Simone Weil's theological way of seeing things, devoted himself to seeing the gravity of his, of everyone's situation. (She obviously uses that word "gravity" in both its scientific and moral senses.) The result is a curious and winning grace, that of the observer who is not by any means as weighted down by the grave apprehensions that afflict all those other New Orleaneans. The meek one is certainly not going to inherit a patch of the earth known as "the city that care forgot," but he rises above others whose burdens manage to put the South's racial crisis into the largest possible perspective: *sub specie aeternitatis.*

I began my postpsychiatric residency working life in New Orleans and also had my head examined there—psychoanalysis on Prytania Street. I was a Yankee alienist (if I may revert to that older medical designation for ironic purposes) and felt that there were certain advantages to being such at the time—the outsider who can glimpse a serious crisis (the Civil Rights struggle) with a bit of detachment. But I was a mere novice in that regard, I eventually learned. It was a group of black children who began to teach me that perceptual acuity with regard to individuals or the social scene is not necessarily nourished by education or absent in those who have received *their* education on the streets, in the alley, on the factory floors, or out in the fields, up the hollows, across a reservation or two. Here, for example, is a six-year-old New Orleans girl giving a not insignificant lecture to a Boston doctor not exactly trained to be humble: "The white folks say all these terrible things to us. My momma says they have bad tongues, and I should feel sorry for them. One woman tells me she hopes I die. It's not even nine o'clock in the morning, and she's there, every day, telling me I won't live much longer! I decided to get even with her. I stopped and told her I hoped she lived for another hundred years! She got all red, and she didn't say another word. The next day she was gone! The [federal] marshal I like best says I really 'got' to her. He asked me who told me to say what I did. I answered him: no one. If you're black and you go downtown, and you listen to the white people talking, a lot of things come to your mind, but you can't say them. White people say anything they want. Not us, we listen more than we talk, until we're alone!"

I considered myself privileged to be hearing those words. Soon enough, though, I was told in no uncertain terms not to be so proud of myself: "If you came from here, you wouldn't be visiting us." Then, a significant pause, followed by a canny and candid speculation: "My mother said you wouldn't be in that mob." Again, I felt touched, complimented. But this mere child, just beginning to read and write, knew to add a certain pointed explanation, a qualification: "My uncle works at the Touro; he's there at night, cleaning the floors. He says the doctors live nearby, a lot of them. It's way far from here."

One of those "free associations" Freud told us to heed. Here was an "outsider" who knew how to put another "outsider" right in his place—as Toole's character Jones does in A Confederacy of Dunces with just about all the white people he gets to meet and watch and know. And who are they? A particular city's splendid variety: the rich and the poor; the apparently comfortable and secure as against the quite desperate; the old and the young; the quite proper and the rather unseemly; the all too educated and the untutored, the innocent. They all are seen, rather obviously, through the unifying presence of Ignatius Reilly—a series of refractions emanating from a rather large diamond indeed. He is not quite the narrator, but his sprawling, at times unwieldy, other-worldly thoughts and actions make us wonder, in the existentialist tradition, where he came from,

who he is, and whither he goes. Am I stretching things too intoler-
ably when I think of Ignatius as a representation of the Catholic
Church itself, struggling in the midst of a crooked and unjust and
often enough quite crazy world, struggling through the lives of its
members, clergy and laity alike, with all their cravings, conventional and irregular, with all their failings, evident and barely concealed and deeply rooted in this and that kind of past, struggling to
survive, to make sense of this world, to live for some purpose larger
than the self and its demanding requirements? The Catholic Church
Mr. Toole tried to comprehend was the Church of the 1950s, the
Church that still yearned, as Mr. Toole keeps putting it, for "theology and geometry." How Simone Weil, with her love for the Greek
mathematicians and for the Church of plainsong and troubadours,
not to mention an adamant theology, might have loved that phrase
with its message of order, hierarchy, structure, and interdepen-
dence—all under Heaven's exceedingly alert eyes!

But Mr. Toole knew that the clock was running out, the clock of
D. H. Holmes on Canal Street and the clock of the hundreds of
Catholic churches in countless American towns and cities, where a
commercial ethic belonging to an agnostic, secular age rules supreme. He does not try to foist Ignatius Reilly upon us; we are to be
entertained and slyly brought up short rather than preached at or
converted. There was, there is, Toole knew, a lot of foolish nonsense
in the Catholic Church, among other institutions. If Christ was betrayed by one of his handpicked followers, his earthly representatives
over the centuries have shown themselves more than able to keep
alive the tradition of Judas. But the Church, like Ignatius, had to
keep trying, keep reaching out to the entire arc of humanity, keep
hoping in various ways to become a spiritual instrument in the lives
of every possible kind of person, as Ignatius, for all his absurdities
and tics and postures and excesses, manages to be for the characters
in *A Confederacy of Dunces.*

Maybe the word with regard to Ignatius's behavior is follies, as in
"fools for Christ," a phrase Dorothy Day used all the time, helped
by her beloved Dostoevski, who knew that the "politic, cautious,
meticulous" ones, the utterly circumspect and unnervingly "rational" ones, have not ever been, by and large, the ones who live
minute by minute with Christ's example in their hearts, minds, and
souls. Ignatius is an odd one, if not the biggest of all the "dunces."

He is sexually irregular, to say the least. He is an occupational misfit. He belongs, it seems, to no community whatsoever. His life seems a messy, hapless one, a dead end. He needs, we have a right to think, treatment—lots and lots of it. Is he schizophrenic or just plain loony? As for Jesus Christ and all the saints who have struggled and died, one after the other, for him and his cause, they too have made us who are blessed (are we really?) with today's wisdom wonder about our mental health, our problems, our peculiar if not absolutely scandalous acts, our expressed ideas, hopes, beliefs, values (what these days one gets used to calling "behavior" or "attitude").

Needless to say, Ignatius is sprung, but where is he headed? Does grace appear, of all ironies, in the person of Myra? Is the Holy Roman Catholic Church rescued from some of its corruptions, blind spots, hopeless impasses, and contradictions by the avowed enemy, secular humanism (to use a contemporary phrase!) militantly espoused? Or is Mr. Toole making a less decisive judgment, simply telling us that the Church of the 1960s had, quite clearly, lurched in the direction of the Myras of this world, with the outcome of such a development (the Vatican of John XXIII and early Paul VI) uncertain at best? The author, remember, is a dialectician in the Augustinian tradition, able to envision the devil as a prodding if not provocative ally. A second novel, sadly denied us, might have given us Ignatius (or an equivalent) in Manhattan on Myra's home territory, where, believe me, the reservoir of madness, banality, and stupidity—sometimes called by the designations of "high culture," or "progress," or "contemporary living," or "modernity"—is no less wide and deep than that of the New Orleans given us by the talented, short-lived, wonderfully astute John Kennedy Toole.

University of Southwestern Louisiana Journal, 1983

Bernanos
The Writer as Child

I do not imagine that Georges Bernanos expected to gain a wide audience for the novels and articles he wrote from about 1925 to 1948. He was French, proudly French, and peasant French at that; he was also a fervent Christian pilgrim. He had no interest in transcending such "limitations," certainly not in order to cross the Atlantic Ocean and become yet another American fad. For that matter, as a person, a novelist, and a political journalist, he challenges not only the secular stranger from abroad but the people of his own country, to the extent that they are inescapably loyal to this century.

Bernanos was born in the Paris of 1888, when the memory of an emperor was still fresh and a republic was in its adolescence. He was educated by Jesuits and later studied law and literature—particularly Balzac and Zola. He became interested in politics and eventually associated himself with Léon Daudet, the novelist's son, who had joined with Charles Maurras to make *Action Française* an all-out nationalist and royalist newspaper. For a while he lived in Rouen and edited a monarchist weekly, but by the autumn of 1914 the war drew him to the battlefield, where he was wounded and decorated. In the midst of the awful futility of trench warfare, he met up with the melancholy, furious, apocalyptic message of Léon Bloy, who so decisively influenced Jacques and Raïssa Maritain. Bloy had little use for the hypocritical, deceitful politicians of the Third Republic, but his outrage was nonpartisan and certainly fell hard upon the manufacturers of the day, who worked children mercilessly, as well as upon the decadent counts and dukes, who never seemed to be done with pretending. Though by temperament he was not as fierce and stern as Bloy, Bernanos sensed in him a kindred spirit. They both were Catholic by precarious faith rather than ritual or inheritance; they both were emotional; and each of them by nature was tied concretely to the poor—in contrast, that is, to being wordy, theoretical advocates of the proletariat, advocates who preach "humanity" but cut down anyone in sight with highly refined thoughts. After the war, Bernanos found himself increasingly at odds with the purposes and tactics of *Action Française*. He became inspector for an insurance company and in that capacity roamed France. He had married in 1917 and by 1933 was the father of six children. To all outward appearances, he was exactly the kind of humdrum, petit bourgeois person who applauded conservatives like Daudet, though something in him seemed to say no and, more significantly, to drive him to write out his own position.

He wrote and wrote, in hotels, railroad stations, and cafés, wherever there was a table for paper and pen, so that by 1930 he had published three novels (*Sous le Soleil de Satan, L'Imposture,* and *La Joie*). They were not overwhelming successes, though they revealed a sensual, poetic, and religious mind in search of a congenial literary form that would enable coherence and control. To some extent, Bernanos had already made that discovery as a journalist. By 1932, he was contributing one emotional but pointed article after another to *Le Figaro,* which allowed him considerable freedom to say what he wanted about politics and literature.

Money was still scarce though, and in 1933 he was badly injured in a motorcycle accident. He wrote a detective novel (*Un Crime*) to become solvent and all the while kept traveling, unhappy with this place, dissatisfied there, sick and in need of rest, outraged at what he saw, and so compelled to move on. By the midthirties, he had long ceased to be anything but a writer—a novelist, a critic, a journalist, and a pamphleteer, whose output was steady and incredibly diverse in character.

In 1934, he left France for Majorca, the first of repeated exiles he would undertake. For three years he stayed there, and they were the three most productive years of his life. We owe to them *The Diary of a Country Priest* and *Mouchette,* which has just now been translated into English. The two are companion pieces, and together they are an almost unbearable experience for any reader even remotely susceptible to the vision of this world that drives Bernanos to such agonized expression. In a sense, they are one book; in different ways they treat of pride and innocence, those two states of mind and soul that struggle within us for command of whatever destiny we may have in this universe. In both books, the reader is taken to the same world—bleak, isolated villages, whose air is always damp and land always mud-soft and covered with leaves. The rain comes down thin and steady, or it pours so hard that the author has it lashing away at people who, anyway, are beaten through and through. They are poor. They are ignorant. They are cruel to one another. They hate and lust without the decorative guile and pretense that money and clever ideas enable. They are no better than kind and sensitive aristocrats and no worse than the pompous, self-sufficient owners of a galaxy of electrical gadgets and some bank books that—you can be sure—will never get wet in *any* rain. For Bernanos, they are like all people, the occasion for God's presence and absence on this earth.

In *The Diary of a Country Priest* Bernanos found the perfect form for his digressive way of handling a few very pointed themes. The young, ailing priest can write down his thoughts openly and naturally without feeling any need to tailor them to the particular demands of conversation. The novelist is not so tied to his scenes and characters and is less tempted to use them gratuitously as his own mouthpieces, so that by no means are we confronted with a thinly disguised personal journal, another version of the various letters and private notebooks Bernanos published—or others did for him after his death. The priest is an unforgettable person, and so is his encounter with a grieving countess, whose dead child has provided her with the excuse she needed for that peculiarly disarming kind of pride that clothes itself in tragedy and uses self-pity as a bludgeon. The author's desperate and fierce religious struggle, lived out on three continents, against a background of revolution, war and death camps, submerges itself almost miraculously in the novel's discouraging, inauspicious countryside—with its raw weather everyone's fate at one time or another, and its peasants, clergy, and nobility as mean and driving, as ordinary and self-congratulatory, or as vulnerable and decent as their equivalents in other places.

To Bernanos, Christ's Sermon on the Mount contained so much irony and paradox, so much pitiless contempt for the vanity of our institutional life, that no one can feel safely Christian, though a case can be made for some more easily than others. That is the writer's challenge, as he saw it, to allow each of his characters to make his case. In *The Diary of a Country Priest*, and even more tersely in *Mouchette*, he sets out to create them, supplicants all, and give them their circumstances, in the sure knowledge that whatever they do he will be there—observant, surprised, and horrified. Like Mauriac, he both entreats and abandons the reader. The novels are suffused with spiritual concerns, but the mystery of Christianity, of salvation and damnation, remains almost austerely beyond analysis or even speculation. By the same token, human motives are not fixed upon and scrutinized as ends in themselves; to do so would be sacrilegious. What matters is how we act, and specifically how we act toward one another—always against the background of a perplexing Sermon that seems particularly foreboding to people of authority or apparent success, among whom can be found successful novelists.

Bernanos cannot forget Christ as the child and the passion of the cross. Childhood and death are the themes that came up again and again in his writing, and they are inevitably joined together. The priest is a child, not one of our successful, competent (those are indeed the words) nursery school children, whose parents are cramming the whole world into his brain for the sake of *their* salvation, but a defenseless child, who is nevertheless capable of hurting both himself and other people. Bernanos has no interest in what Rousseau or Wordsworth saw in childhood—a sort of *tabula rasa*, or a shelter where only lambs and doves live. Nor is he interested in the psychoanalyst's idea of what makes a boy nervous or a girl worried. He assumes all along that one can be vulnerable and hurtful, patient and capricious, forgiving and predatory—and be a child. More radically (and here I think he is very much with Freud, whether he likes it or not), he assumes that childhood is a continuing state of mind, a terribly important one that is never outgrown or left behind—but murdered, yes, by being thwarted, stifled, or terrorized.

The priest, like a child, tries to do what he is told but feels within himself all kinds of confusing, urgent wishes. Like a child, he embraces, then pulls back; like a child, he can walk perfectly well one minute and then stumble, without marking that fact down in a ledger and making it part of some overall count or "evaluation." In fact, Bernanos ingeniously splits the reader, the writer, and the priest from one another. The priest's reactions are not ours. If he could see himself and write about himself as we see him and read of him, through his own words, he would be damned not saved, just another self-consciously "aware" man. Through the use of a diary, Bernanos can bring out the child in the curé, his fantasies and doubts, the flow of fear and desire he experiences, the impromptu conversations with himself that in later life we come to call daydreams or reveries, or in a doctor's office, free associations. The lesson seems clear: self-knowledge and reflection are obligatory for anyone who seeks God (hence the effort of a diary), but a certain kind of "distance" on oneself (and others) can lead to arrogance and pride, to the kind of mind found in mature, "grownup," and educated people who make guns and order them used. If the reader feels himself judging the priest, and thus uncomfortably close to acting like God, Bernanos can only smile wryly. He distrusted intellectuals, himself included. Eventually he fled them, himself included, by leaving France.

In Spain he saw Franco's work. The man who started as a follower of the right-wing Maurras was on his way to being claimed by the leftist readers of *Esprit* as a Catholic humanist, a radical fighter for the rights of the poor. One day in Majorca, he saw trucks moving up a road and in them "miserable human beings, their hands on their knees, their faces covered with dust, but sitting up straight, very straight, holding their heads high with the dignity Spaniards have in the most atrocious situations." What he saw—the men were republican hostages being driven to their execution—had the following consequences: "Naturally I did not deliberately decide to make a novel out of this. I did not say: I am going to transpose what I saw into the story of a little girl tracked down by misfortune and injustice. But what is true is that if I had not seen these things, I should not have written the *Nouvelle Histoire de Mouchette*."

We are fortunate to have this particular translation of the novel, done by J. C. Whitehouse. Bernanos loved the French language and took advantage of all its subtleties. His words are simple and plain, like so many of the people he describes. He sets phrase upon phrase, again all done very directly but in the interests of achieving his intricate design. His prose is lyric and open, not densely metaphorical, and would have been damaged by even a capable translation. Whitehouse has done a lovely job: "The dark west wind, the sea wind, was already scattering the voices in the darkness. It toyed with them a moment and then lifted them all together, dispersing them with an angry roar. The voice which Mouchette had just heard hovered in the air a long time, like a dead leaf floating interminably."

Mouchette is fourteen years old, and so solitary that she has never felt lonely. She has a sharp, cutting eye for the insincerity and intrigue in her classmates and for the nervous self-importance of her teacher. She has been ignored or beaten by her drunken father and her tired and sick mother. There are many children in this peasant family, and they all are part of a village whose life seems timeless. The story is deceptively brief: the girl, both timid and proud, walks home alone from school in what turns out to be an unusually severe storm. She meets Arsène, a poacher and braggart, who has been hurt in what he claims to have been an encounter with an enemy of his, the forest policeman. He is running from the law, she from a world never really entered. The confession she hears from a murderer is ironically the first act of trust, the first intimacy she has ever known. Rather than find Arsène frightening, she is drawn to him. They have taken shelter together, and she admires the way he forthrightly cauterizes his wound with a burning brand. She reaches out for him, and suddenly finds herself able to sing. For only a second can he return her gentle trust; drunk, basically a coward, he rapes her. She goes home to find her mother dying, and in a heartbreaking scene tries to tell her secret. The mother dies. Mouchette learns of Arsène's deception, and even worse she realizes that her family and the town can offer her nothing—except the spectacle of death, which slowly seizes the girl's imagination as something to be achieved in the absence of love. She leaves a village that forced her to close in on herself, that made a mockery of her effort to be generous, and she drowns herself.

Bernanos was obsessed with the betrayal of one person by another. It is not stretching things to connect Mouchette's death with the crucifixion. In Spain he saw where the twentieth century was headed, with its "realism" and its "progress," its Chamberlains, Hitlers, and Stalins. In a letter to him, Simone Weil wrote: "Having been in Spain, I now continually listen to and read all sorts of observations about Spain, but I could not point to a single person, except you alone, who has been exposed to the atmosphere of the Civil War and has resisted it. What do I care that you are a royalist. . . ."

He had long since stopped being a royalist when those words were written in 1938. He had just returned to Paris, only to leave that same year for Paraguay. From there he went to Brazil. He tried farming. He supported de Gaulle and the resistance, attacked the

Vichy government in a torrent of articles, and returned to Paris in 1945. Two years later he was in Tunisia, disappointed with the Fourth Republic—and a year later he was dead.

A restless, turbulent man, drawn to politics but impatient really for Armageddon, where he would fight to the death, Bernanos has very little to offer today's world. Like Péguy, he can be "summed-up," labeled as reactionary, naive, impractical. He had no "workable" political or economic vision; he knew little about any "existential crisis," and he didn't seem to care about the workings of the unconscious, though he did say this once: "As soon as I take up my pen, what comes back to me immediately is my childhood, my quite commonplace childhood, so like everybody else's and from which I draw all that I write, as from an inexhaustible source of dreams."

When he died, he was quite lucid and anxious to admit that he had enjoyed his life on this earth more than he ever dared acknowledge. Like any honest but shy child, he had complained only about what he loved, and now the time had come to say thank you, say good-bye, and hurry home.

New Republic, April 15, 1967

Bernanos's Diary

A *Country Priest* as Everyman

No book has meant more to me than Georges Bernanos's *The Diary of a Country Priest*. I have read it and reread it, and I keep it in front of me on my desk. At times I do Bernanos a sacrilegious injustice; something particularly provocative or troubling has taken place, in my own life or in the larger world that we all share, and I am drawn to *The Diary*, drawn to a number of well-marked passages, which, I suppose, have a scriptural significance for me.

I first read the book while in college, but at a friend's suggestion rather than any professor's. At the time, I was hungry for answers, the more clear-cut the better, and to my frustration I found precious few in *The Diary*. Years later, though, while taking my training in psychiatry, I went back to the novel—after hearing Paul Tillich refer to it in a lecture sharply critical of secular America's almost religious interest in the human mind. Anyway, the second reading marked a turning point in my life. Tillich's message came across all the more strongly—so that thereafter I could manage a smile when I heard yet another bit of psychiatric theory proclaimed as the way to the New Jerusalem.

Bernanos was a French novelist and essayist who died in 1948. He told powerful, haunting stories in a lean, self-possessed style that carries over very well in translation. He is unfortunately not well known here, probably because his struggles as a passionate Christian pilgrim simply do not interest most Americans, even those who nominally call themselves believers. Perhaps that is why several of his eight novels and almost all of his forceful, brilliantly argued religious or political essays are not even available in English. But *The Diary of a Country Priest* is very much available, and the film of it, done by Robert Bresson, is occasionally shown in a film series—though each year I find that most of the students I teach have not heard of, let alone come across, either the book or the movie.

The Diary was written in the mid thirties while Bernanos lived in

Majorca, an island he loved. There, as well as on the Spanish mainland, a civil war was already under way, and the sensitive novelist felt personally and philosophically challenged by the terrible injustices he witnessed. He also felt driven to words, to an effort that would give a life to his doubts and anguish and make them subject to the scrutiny of others.

His essays burned with indignation that human beings could make other human beings suffer so; that politicians and generals could be as wretchedly cynical and corrupt as they were in Spain and in his native France; and, worst of all, that the Church, the Roman Catholic Church he loved with all his heart, could betray Christ and stand beside a collection of decadent, greedy nobles and landlords. In his novel, *The Diary of a Country Priest*, the same sense of disgust and shame appears again and again but far more unforgettably—because the priest and others are carefully developed characters in an almost unbearably delicate and touching story.

Bernanos made a crucial and inspired decision when he chose to put the novel in the form of a diary. The priest can say what he pleases, openly and honestly and directly and unashamedly. In a sense he is given complete freedom—from the presence of the author. As a gentle, troubled, inward man, the priest has a right to think about all sorts of things: the value of prayer; the nature of childhood; the effects of poverty on the mind and spirit; the only too apparent flaws in the Church, and, indeed, in every single institution—whether social, political, or religious. But he can also act, abruptly and spontaneously; and, above all, he can act unselfconsciously. We as readers can judge him, and later he can judge himself.

Almost miraculously, though, Bernanos has removed himself from the novelist's great temptation to cheat on his characters by not taking care that their speech, their ideas and ideals have been earned—that is to say, that they must emerge as naturally the property of the person portrayed. Not once does Bernanos call attention to himself as the author. When *The Diary* is over and its author dead, we feel we have met him: an ordinary priest whose parish is "like all the rest"; a tempted priest, who inevitably succumbs repeatedly to the sin of pride; a sad and confused priest, who drinks and almost stumbles his way through a short and apparently unremarkable life; and finally, a man of God, perhaps a saint, whose faith we can appreciate, even as he doubts it until the very end.

Obviously, *The Diary* has no formal or coherent plot—any more than a real-life diary would. But lives have their particular trends, and in the long run what seems aimless, haphazard, or accidental can figure as all of a piece. In this case, the curé from the beginning is old beyond his years, in almost constant physical pain, and alive in a town that itself seems stagnant if not damned outright. The rain beats the land incessantly. Constant fog makes it hard to see beyond one's feet. The village seems like a hasty afterthought, something that was never meant to be. As for the parishioners, they are tired and lonely and bored. Yes, they go through the motions, even work up appetites, preferences, hates; but their priest hears something else: the fears, the misgivings, the self-lacerations, and worst of all, the pride that masks itself in fake piety and in a slyly boastful resignation to "things as they are."

The curé knows how awful it is for everyone, and he himself has little to offer—to them or himself. He can only find himself wanting, lacking, doomed perhaps to the exquisitely poignant but inert wisdom he writes down in his diary. In one crucial episode, he confronts the town's leading citizen, a countess, with her pride. Her son died as a child, and she still wears a medallion that contains a lock of his hair. Her husband seeks the company of other women, and she is desperately unhappy, but no matter: what seems like a stubborn inner strength enables her to appear always correct, always dignified, always able to endure her fate. All of which the curé slowly exposes for the pride it is. A kind of stern, moralistic stoicism is not quite what Christ had in mind as redemptive; and certainly he did not die so that others would continue to nail themselves to a succession of private (hence idolatrous) crosses.

Not that the curé is some cool, carefully trained technician who knows how to pace himself and make his "interpretations" (always authoritative and correct, of course) at just the right moment. One moment he can be rude, tactless, himself insufferably priggish. Then he turns, catches himself, and speaks in an honest, strong, and clear way that can only be called revelatory—and particularly so because the diary, which tells us what happens, is full of exactly the mixture of self-doubt, genuine humility, and blindness that even inspired saints necessarily demonstrate. In fact, it can be argued that the curé is meant to be a saint, meant to be a man whose holiness is unknown to himself but instructive beyond all words for those of us who read the diary.

Though a writer, Bernanos profoundly distrusted words, which he knew to be the money that intellectual confidence-men put to a million corrupt and murderous purposes. In *The Diary of a Country Priest*, the words are plain and strong, the talk almost unbelievably pure, down-to-earth, unadorned. Quietly but relentlessly, the curé goes about his struggle, and eventually—so Bernanos must have believed—all who read *The Diary* must choose, must find that struggle either compelling or trivial, since from the very beginning Christ insisted upon making *choice* humanity's inescapable right and burden.

But beyond esthetics, beyond *any* choice, the self-serving ones of everyday life or the literary ones or the exalted and agonized religious ones, a kind of peace can come after the choice has been made: "True grace is to forget oneself. Yet if pride could die in us the supreme grace would be to love oneself in all simplicity—as one would love any of those who have loved and suffered in Christ."

A saint and the grace he or she somehow receives are presumably everywhere to be found, though in *The Diary* one does get the impression that some places and some roads are better than others. More than anything else, Bernanos fought the temptation to ignore life's uncertainties and ambiguities, its built-in mysteries, its setbacks that can mean so much and its victories that are nothing, nothing really. For years he succumbed to sin and raged against those he believed to be his enemies—the clever, self-serving intellectuals who have a name, a label for everyone and anything, and who kill one another every day with words sharper than any knife could ever be.

But the author of *The Diary of a Country Priest*, like the curé in it, may have at last and unwittingly achieved his particular moment of grace, of sanctity. "Does it matter?" the priest asked as he neared the end. One can almost hear Georges Bernanos asking the same thing: Do they matter, all the shrill and confident ideologues around? No, the curé would say, and wryly smile; and no, Bernanos at last could say to himself.

New York Times Book Review, November 3, 1968

The Pilgrimage of Georges Bernanos

Among French novelists of the twentieth century, Georges Bernanos is one of the least known and least appreciated by English-speaking readers. Even the relatively sophisticated ones who are likely to have read many of the novels or essays of Camus or Sartre or Gide and who may know Mauriac by reputation draw a blank on mention of Bernanos. In France and, indeed, throughout the Continent, it has been otherwise—Bernanos's novels and his social or political essays were widely appreciated during his lifetime (1888 to 1948), and they still command the strong interest of a literate public, especially that segment of it with religious and philosophical interests. As for his *Diary of a Country Priest*, it was a great success among both general readers and critics when it was published fifty years ago, and it has been, unquestionably, the Bernanos novel that has earned the most lasting interest of readers, no matter what their background or nationality.

Bernanos was born in Paris and brought up in a middle-class, devoutly Roman Catholic home. He came of age at a time when France was deeply divided culturally and spiritually—a division that the Dreyfus Affair only served to accentuate. On the one hand, Paris was a cosmopolitan city of international renown—a home for early twentieth-century secular thinkers, artists, and writers. On the other hand, millions of French citizens (those living in rural areas, especially, but also the social elites of Paris) were still very conservative—devoutly religious and, significantly, monarchist in sympathy. In the early years of this century, that split threatened the stability of the nation. Demonstrations and street fights were by no means rare, with the Dreyfusards and anti-Dreyfusards at each other's throats, republicans taking on monarchists and agnostics challenging Catholics. The young Bernanos was then a fiercely conservative Catholic royalist, deeply suspicious of those so-called progressive forces that claimed to speak for a new century and way of regarding this life, forces that were man-centered, optimistic, and wedded to social change, political reform, and cultural experimentation.

As he grew older, Bernanos tried to figure out what to do with his life. He had been educated by the Jesuits and had taken courses in law and literature. He had joined the notoriously conservative, if not reactionary, Action Française movement headed by Charles Maurras and Léon Daudet. Indeed, just before World War I he was editing the royalist weekly *L'Avant-Garde de Normandie*. During the war, he fought in the French army and was wounded and decorated. In 1917, he married Jeanne Talbert d'Arc, a collateral descendant of Joan of Arc; they would eventually be the parents of six children. After the war, he began a gradual reconsideration of his social and political views that culminated in a decisive break with Action Française. He did so in response to his craving for ideas, fiction, and moral reflection. In the 1920s, when he was in his thirties, he found himself noticing the poor, the humble, the scorned, and wondering why his beloved Catholic Church was so deeply connected to the powerful and wealthy people of France.

At the time, he was working for an insurance company. He was always on the move, from train to train, hotel to hotel. As he moved, he looked carefully and took notes, and he felt a strong and continuing desire to write—stories, novels, literary essays, political jeremiads. By the early 1930s his early novels—*L'Imposture*, *La Joie*, and a detective story, *Un Crime*—had earned him modest recognition. By 1935, when the last of those three had appeared, Bernanos was a frequent contributor to *Le Figaro*—a thoughtful conservative writer with a strong Christian conscience who wavered between his respect for established religious and political institutions and his fiery individualism and anarchic contempt for those earthly powers that both the Hebrew prophets and Jesus had so roundly condemned.

He was a loner, too, utterly contemptuous of the literary salons so many other writers delighted in frequenting. A motorcycle accident in 1933 only made him more reclusive. He was partially crippled for the rest of his life, and by the middle 1930s he had become a full-time writer, though by no means financially self-sufficient.

In 1934, Bernanos had moved with his family to Majorca, and soon enough two more novels, *Un Mauvais Rêve* and *Monsieur Quine*, appeared. He was a witness to the human consequences of the Spanish Civil War and eventually went through yet another personal and political transformation. Even as Simone Weil and George Orwell were horrified and disgusted by what they saw in Spain on the left—the betrayals, deceptions, lies, and cruelties of various Communist leaders and organizations—Bernanos had come to realize how murderously vicious Franco and his henchmen were turning out to be. He did not hesitate to speak out and thus risk the condemnation of his fellow Catholic conservatives.

It was at this point that Weil addressed her famous letter to him. In 1938, Bernanos published *Les Grandes Cimetières Sous la Lune*, and the Vatican itself was shaken by his searing, powerfully rendered account of the terror Franco's legions were inflicting on innocent men, women, and children, all in the name of Catholic nationalism. "I recognized the smell of civil war, the smell of blood and terror, which exhales from your book; I have breathed it, too," Weil wrote. But she recognized that in Bernanos's literary hands a new clarity, honesty, and decency had been reached, an exceptionally edifying and inspiring level of political writing: "I must admit that I neither saw nor heard of anything which quite equalled the ignominy of certain facts you relate, such as the murders of elderly peasants or the Ballillas [an Italian Fascist cadre] chasing old people and beating them with truncheons."

In that same letter, Weil praised *Journal d'un Curé de Campagne*, which had been published in 1936. Bernanos wrote that book too in Majorca, and it would turn out to be his most celebrated one, justly so—a masterpiece, really, whose wisdom will never become outdated. *The Diary*, as many have learned to call this singularly affecting novel, is the simple story of an obscure, rural French priest who seems virtually overwhelmed by what he judges to be his own inadequacies, not to mention the isolated, woebegone nature of his parish, which he describes in one of his entries as "bored stiff." This humble curé tries hard against such odds to minister unto his obscure, lowly flock.

It is a stroke of genius, of course, for Bernanos to give him to us through his journal, because the priest is not apologizing or boasting, scolding or excusing. All through Bernanos's writing life he tried to comprehend saintliness, holiness, and it is in *The Diary* that he most nearly approaches that complex and forbidding subject with evident success. Saints, he knew, do not give discourses on saintliness, and authors who attempt to do so risk rhetoric and sentimental bombast. But the literary device of a diary permits a candor, a lack of self-consciousness and self-importance, so that gradually this ailing, seemingly confused, melancholic young priest becomes to the reader a virtual incarnation of divine grace. His unpretentious, stumbling, honestly earnest manner, his mixture of knowing sadness and naiveté, his moments (and longer) of self-doubt, followed by quiet spells of prayerful trust in the Lord's intentions for him and for everyone, all are evidence for the reader of what a true *homo religiosus* is like inwardly.

As the curé goes from home to home, from situation to situation, we witness his brief, painful, unimportant life, so full of conflict and uncertainty, and finally we begin to realize how spiritually triumphant this life has been, no matter the opinion of the one who lived it. Not that there are any obvious victories in the conventional sense. This young priest dies of cancer, having felt himself to have failed both his church and his own personal ideals. We know otherwise, however, we who have been exposed to this diary, this account of one soul's arduous ascent toward its Maker. What we read, of course, is Bernanos at his most brilliant, daring to assert in this century of agnostic, materialistic skepticism a fervent plea for religious faith and also for a humane social ethics that is worthy of the lives Isaiah and Jeremiah and Amos lived, the life that Jesus lived.

"How little we know what a human life really is—even our own," the curé writes. Then he makes this declaration: "To judge us by what we call our actions is probably as futile as to judge us by our dreams. God's justice chooses from this dark conglomeration of thought and act, and that which is raised toward the Father shines with a sudden burst of light, displayed in glory like the sun." A little further on, the curé notes that "the wish to pray is a prayer in itself," and he even dares to remark that "God can ask no more than that of us." Later, the temptation to prideful self-righteousness is acknowledged: "He who condemns sin becomes part of it, espouses it." Then, toward the end, the disillusioned Georges Bernanos (who would wander through Brazil and Paraguay in the late 1930s and, after fighting Hitler as a friend of de Gaulle's, would leave for North Africa and die at the age of sixty as much a loner as ever) merges with the curé in this fashion: "The Pagan State: the state which knows no law but that of its own well-being—the merciless countries full of greed and pride!"

Nonetheless, despite a few such harsh and grim asides, this novel, with its account of various meetings, incidents, and chance encounters, with its small victories and defeats, is steadily true to the essentially forgiving and redemptive message offered the world some two thousand years ago in the incarnation of Christ. The curé exclaims at the end: "How easy it is to hate oneself!" Then he turns himself around: "True grace is to forget. Yet if pride could die in us, the supreme grace would be to love ourselves in all simplicity—as one would love any of those who themselves have suffered and loved in Christ." This is no cult of contemporary narcissism or of salvation on the cheap. By the time we have read that last entry in the diary, we have ourselves made a pilgrimage of sorts—with our guide and mentor, of course, a particular novelist who was himself an ever-seeking pilgrim and who, one suspects, died rather as his curé did, glad at last to be headed home.

New York Times Book Review, June 8, 1986

Minorities, Art, and Literature

Human Nature Is Finer

Seven years ago, I was taken to a tenant farmer's cabin in Clarke County, Alabama. I was taken by a young Civil Rights worker who was born in the cabin. Though his parents had died, his grandmother and an aunt and uncle still lived "on the place," and he wanted me to get to know them somewhat, which I did—somewhat. We talked. We didn't talk. We tried to make talk. We were at our most comfortable when talk wasn't expected or necessary—in church or out in the fields or walking through the woods, where I could, the grandmother said, "take in the scenery" or "sit myself down in God's house," and see and hear and not feel constrained to think up things to say or get others to say something.

At the end of a weekend, the young man and I went on to Mississippi, where he was working to get his people the right to vote and I was talking with relatives of several black children I knew. (They were the first black children to enter white schools in New Orleans, amid something less than "law and order.") As we drove, we talked about the circumstances under which blacks live in the rural South and the road ahead if changes were to take place. I had seen extremely poor people living hard and brutish lives. I had seen the illnesses, the fearfulness, the weariness. And my friend, on leave from a small, all-black college in Alabama, at twenty embittered because in the early sixties his people couldn't even vote in this richest and strongest of the world's democracies, had only one retort to my expressions of sympathy; he wanted to let me know a thing or two: "I don't recognize myself or any of the people I grew up with in those articles people write. I decided to major in sociology because I thought I'd really learn about my people that way. But you read and you read and you say to the author: Listen, man, you're lost. You're looking at the trees, and a lot of them are in bad shape, but there's a whole forest, too, and it's still around, after all the fires we've had, and all the trees they've cut down, and the drought, and everything

else bad. We're standing, and we're going to keep on standing.
People should come around and see *that* and explain *that* and write
about *that*—just for a change."

For a change, his wishes have been realized. He probably would
not agree with everything Albert Murray has written in *The Omni-
Americans*, but the book's argument will be welcome to the many
black and white political activists who know how cleverly a government intent on foot-dragging can utilize all the reports and findings,
all the data from all the research projects—so many of them supported by federal money people could use for food or clothes. Mr.
Murray is not primarily a political person. He commands no cadres,
no followers. He speaks for himself, and he speaks as a literary critic,
an essayist, and a short-story writer. But he also speaks as a man who
is proud of his people and their considerable achievements. In *The
Omni-Americans*, his purpose is to set forth those achievements and
to warn against America's "experts," especially what he calls "social-
science survey technicians"—people who ask a lot of questions and
tabulate the responses and proclaim without modesty or qualification lots of conclusions and prescriptions. They do not, says Mr.
Murray, see the richness, the complexity of the black experience in
America (or, for that matter, any group's experience); they merely
contribute to the caricatures that so many of us cannot get out of our
heads. Mr. Murray says that social scientists are most comfortable
seeing the problems people have, not the people: the fears, the tensions and hates they feel compelled to reveal, the hesitations and
infirmities, the exhaustion and despair. He does not deny that millions of blacks have had the worst possible life. He was born near
Mobile, has taught literature at Tuskegee Institute, and has lived in
Chicago and New York as well as the rural South, so he has seen
how political discrimination and economic hardship produce the
mean lives that some men and women live—and then hand on as
an awful inheritance to their children. Nevertheless, he insists that
black people have never been as used up and shattered as some of
their more hysterical observers have maintained. He sees and hears
in Alabama and in Harlem things quite different from what most of
us are accustomed to read in newspapers and magazines and books.
He sees people who have shrewdness and toughness and style and a
liveliness that three centuries of American history have been unable

to destroy. He sees children who can run and sing and dance and laugh. He sees youths who are thoroughly in tune with concrete realities. He sees men and women who have "soul," who do indeed have rhythm, who swing, who throb with a vitality, a responsiveness, a spirituality that will not be denied. He hears jazz and the blues and work songs and spirituals and gospel songs. He hears people who have no trouble testifying and signifying, who have no "communication block," who have long known about "dialogue" and "group support" and "emotional catharsis" and "interpersonal relationships." And from all he has seen and heard, he has decided that his people can demonstrate an elegance of taste, can live intense, glowing lives, can have a gusto that certain observers and social scientists naturally *would* miss—given their limited, dreary outlook, their pretensions, their insistence upon submitting everything to a theory or a conceptual system. Mr. Murray simply wants to balance things out:

> *The Omni-Americans* is based in large measure on the assumption that since the negative aspects of black experience are constantly being overpublicized (and to little purpose except to obscure the positive), justice to U.S. Negroes, not only as American citizens but also as the fascinating human beings that they so obviously are, is best served by suggesting some of the affirmative implications of their history and culture.

Those implications are spelled out forcefully. The heritage that enabled a Bessie Smith, a Coleman Hawkins, and a Duke Ellington is not an "adaptation to stress" but the distillation of a particular human experience—one that has inspired people as well as discouraged them, for black people have never been as far removed from America's "higher" world as they have seemed to be. Neither Mark Twain nor Melville nor Faulkner could escape black people, any more than the blacks could escape the whites' religion, habits, values, and language. Anyone who has spent much time on a plantation manor sees (or struggles not to see) how much rich Southern whites have learned from their "help." A decade ago, when I lived in Mississippi, I was told by a lawyer in Pass Christian that his daughter was "as sassy as a nigger." Mr. Murray would have wanted me to notice that the lovely belle in question was brought up by a black woman, liked her way of preparing food, used a lot of her words, even walked a little like her, and was "sassy" like her, which means that she had the same intense and unyielding spirit. Mr. Murray would wish all of us to remember that those thousands of young white people came to the Woodstock festival so that they could talk in a certain way, sing in a certain way, respond to a particular kind of music, and that the songs and words and responses showed how close we can be to each other, how black in spirit and culture many white-skinned Americans are.

This book contests "the systematic oversimplification of black tribulations" to be found in the press and in the journals and books social scientists fill up with their special prose—a prose that certainly lacks the direct, strong, lucid words "disadvantaged" children use every day. In the eagerness to examine black parents, black youths, and black families, the serious problems and flaws of white people are nearly ignored. To Albert Murray, it is as if white hypocrisy, duplicity, boredom, crime, and family instability were off-limits for those interested in "pathology" and "deprivation." Sometimes Mr. Murray states his complaints against social scientists so sweepingly and angrily that he undermines his own important argument. Blacks who live in either Alabama or Harlem *do* have serious difficulties, as do whites in the fanciest of our suburbs. Sensitive psychologists and historians like Kenneth Clark and C. Vann Woodward have to dwell upon the sad and bitter and painful moments (in the life of both individuals and a nation) even as they pay respect to the fact that, after all and through everything, those people and this country are still very much alive. The best of our social scientists— such as Oscar Lewis and Elliot Liebow and Allison Davis—know that the people they work with (and, incidentally, feel very close to) are not the absurd caricatures that come out of many "studies." All the same, *every* American reporter and critic and social scientist could profit from this book. If Mr. Murray can get too outraged, too fussy, too insistent, he can also grin and enjoy himself and write provocative, intelligent, original prose. This is how he talks about the "new" effort by certain blacks to achieve "self-esteem," which is one of many questionable abstractions that this book mocks:

> If U.S. Negroes don't already have self-pride and didn't know black . . . is beautiful, why do they always sound so good, so

warm, and even cuss better than everybody else? Why do they dress so jivy and look so foxy, standing like you better know it in spite of yourself? If black people haven't always known how beautiful black is, why have they always been walking, prancing like they'd rather be dancing, and dancing like everybody else is a wall-flower or something? If Louis Armstrong doesn't know he has black beauty to spare how come he can create more beauty while clowning than them other people can giving all they got? How come a hard-boiled cat like Johnny Hodges got so much tenderness and elegance left over? And what's Coleman Hawkins doing turning the blues into such finespun glass, and what were Dizzy Gillespie and Yardbird Parker doing all them acrobatic curlicue lyrics about? How come Count Basie and Lionel Hampton think they can make a hillbilly jump, stomp, and rock—and almost do it? Why does everybody take it for granted that Duke Ellington can wipe out anybody anywhere, anytime he wants to?

Though everybody acknowledges Duke Ellington's abilities, many of us are less willing to give him and Ralph Ellison and Langston Hughes and Alain Locke and Arna Bontemps and W. E. B. Du Bois and James Weldon Johnson and John Hope Franklin their place in a particular culture, which is black and yet which draws widely upon this nation's traditions and customs, its folklore, its idiosyncrasies and ceremonies and values—thus the title of the book. Albert Murray thinks that we should be mindful of that culture: built up and tested and strengthened in the rural South, then brought into the cities, where "Walkin' the Ground Hog" and "Fishing in the Dark" and "See That My Grave Is Kept Clean" gave way to "Harlem Air Shaft" and "Concerto for Cootie" and "Sepia Panorama." Himself a Southerner, Mr. Murray knows his people's muscles and nerves, knows how attentively they can listen, how closely they can look, how artfully they go about their business, how keenly they judge their blustery "betters"—who are so sure of themselves and of everything around them and yet so unaware of a whole world of sharp eyes and ears and intelligent minds and hearts, torn and saddened but capable of generosity and hope and devotion. "Scenery is fine, but human nature is finer," wrote young John Keats to a friend. Albert Murray, whose love for the poet's language, the novelist's sensibility, the essayist's clarity, the jazzman's imagination, and the gospel singer's depth of feeling is so apparent, would no doubt agree with that nineteenth-century white man's strange suggestion that no matter what distracts us from each other or about each other, *we* are what really matters—each of us and all of us.

New Yorker, October 17, 1970

More Exiles

The exile is no stranger to history, and certainly not to our time. The story of the Jews is so familiar that it is difficult for anyone to try to tell it again. The exile of the Negro in America is just beginning to be known by the society that once allowed him little travel and no entrance to its social or cultural life. Whether the exile is enforced or claimed, its very definition is its detachment, and from this condition arises both the yearning and the anger.

Blues People is a book of large ambitions. LeRoi Jones, poet, essayist, story writer, and jazz critic, will not confine himself to the history of the development of the blues as music. He will not simply talk about blues people, how they felt in their double exile—as Negroes and as artists—from a country they never left. He subtitles his book *Negro Music in White America*, and from the first page we are informed of his larger sociological and anthropological interests and of his intention to show us the roots of blues in a people and their fate.

Yet the book is at its best when Jones is less concerned with these large questions and traces the history of early blues and their relationship to early jazz, to purely instrumental blues, then to the more classic blues, sung as formal entertainment rather than as an expression of a person's private life or a people's social tragedy, and finally, to the emergence of boogie-woogie, ragtime, and dixieland. We are next led through what the author calls "the modern scene." We see big-band jazz marching to its death in the "watered-down slick 'white' commercializations" of swing. We hear about the *separation* (the author italicizes words like this) of the Negro musician from both white and Negro middle-class culture. Beboppers restore jazz, but their *antiassimilationist* sounds antagonize white America; and the middle-class Negro emulates his white "bossman" again, "trapped in the sinister vapidity of mainline American culture." Finally, in the origin and development of progressive and cool jazz, the white musician comes into his own—and jazz, of all things, is split into two mutually segregated forms. Thus, the progressive jazz of Stan Kenton comes from a white, upper-middle-class cerebral tradition, and cool jazz is most suitable for "white musicians who favored a 'purity of sound' . . . rather than the rawer materials of dramatic expression." But the bebop of Charlie Parker "re-established blues as the most important Afro-American form in Negro music."

Mr. Jones falters when he leaves this study of Negro music and its various forms for extensive forays into history, sociology, psychology, and ethical judgment of class values. For instance, he tells us that narcotics users, and particularly heroin addicts, are really a rather self-assured and aristocratic group. His incredible words are: "Heroin is the most popular addictive drug used by Negroes because . . . the drug itself tranforms the Negro's normal separation from the mainstream of the society into an advantage (which I have been saying I think it is anyway). It is one-upmanship of the highest order." Such talk is nonsense of the highest order. The medical and psychiatric agonies, the sickness and desperation of the addict, whether he is high, low, or withdrawing, do not deserve such ill-informed sentimentality.

It is ironic that this gifted young poet, bent on fighting middle-class American culture in all its shabby superficiality, yields so willingly to that very culture's most vulgar jargon, its narrowest, pseudosociological mode of thinking. A writer who has written fine poetry to honor Charlie Parker tells us in this book that "the verticality of the city began to create two separate secularities, and the blues had to be divided among them if it was going to survive at all." Scattered through the book are phrases like "pseudo-autonomous existence" or sentences like "the lateral exchange of cultural reference between black and white produced an intercultural fluency."

If Mr. Jones plans to persist with such talk, and if he really wants to pursue his lay sociology and psychology, he should be more careful about the tone of some of his descriptions. I am not recommending that he follow the model of those heartless social scientists whose work so often panders to those who want abstractions about people rather than the truth of their actual lives. But the sociologists, the psychologists, and the anthropologists whom he so much admires have a serious job to do, gathering information about people and their societies and trying to make sense out of it. Their concern must be strong, their values real, their work passionate, but none of these to the detriment of their curiosity and good sense as observers. They may not like what they see, but surely they cannot confuse their hopes with their study. At times one finds in this book less concern with information than polemical writing disguised in the latest jargon of the social sciences. And often this jargon is not even used to communicate or describe but to condemn.

The book is most effective in its simple, direct information about blues music and its people and in its willingness to relate the suffering of generations of Negroes to the tenaciously redemptive power of their music. What was one kind of hell, the author says, now turns into another as Negroes succumb to the blandishments of the white middle-class world. The blues and their successors in the several forms of jazz are thereby threatened. No less so, however, than the writer—living in that same world—who tries to do them justice.

Dan Jacobson clearly felt himself enough threatened by *his* world to leave it. The longest essay in his *Time of Arrival and other Essays* tells of the author's arrival in London. His childhood as a South African Jew weighed heavily upon him. His youth and its choice of loyalty to this past or departure from it was very much his challenge. The possibilities of his manhood as a writer, as a person with friends, family, and a place to live cropped into his mind at almost every turn in the great city of London, a city movingly appreciated by the young emigré. He comes to it like a cook, an artist, a musician—savoring it, noticing its bulk and its more subtle shapes and forms, responding to its light and shadows, hearing its various sounds.

Jacobson obviously enjoys travel. The book has four parts, three of which are given the names of countries: England, South Africa, and Israel. These three nations in their customs and traditions are closely involved in the writer's life and identity. He writes about each with a special intimacy, and where there is desolation or agony to describe it is done clearly and with compassion. We are taken to the Jewish ghetto in London, dying yet twitching still with life and with memories for the susceptible visitor. In four essays, we are exposed to South Africa's uniquely tragic and disastrous racial situation, and in two more we hear about Israel from one of *its* exiles. The author is at his very best in dealing with ironic situations, as in the resemblance of a crowd lunging after visiting royalty to a racist mob; the reactions of whites as they watch a native African festival; the strange twist of history that makes Israel no solution for the problems of the Diaspora, making in certain ways Jewish identity—in the continuing "abroad" that is the world outside Israel—more emphatic, even less defined, still puzzling. All through these three parts, the essays are both simple and tightly organized, the decency and charity of the writer always present, and his essential good sense and lucidity of mind a pleasure to encounter.

Of *Uncle Tom's Cabin* Jacobson says: "I am not sure whether we can learn more from the book's faults than from its merits; but I am sure at least that we can learn something from our own misguided insistance, over these many years, that the book has no merit at all." He goes on to wonder whether "our revulsion from Tom doesn't spring in part from an uneasy fear that his way of asserting his humanity might be as effective as any other way open to him—or to us." He goes on to make his critical judgment: "Stowe never fully imagined that the day would come when Negroes would read her novel and comment upon it . . . [and] this failure of imagination is a crucial one; and one for which she is less and less likely to be forgiven in the future." Yet, he concludes wryly with these words: "We can trust her sufficiently to say that she would not have minded this at all."

These are the words of one who understands the relationship between the individual and the historical moment. We act out of our lives and make history; but we act *in* history, too. To denounce from the perfections of a later period the "failure" of a book that was itself striving toward that period, to see its malicious "influence" retrospectively rather than its contextual meaning, its still partial relevance, and certainly its integrity, is to abandon, Jacobson feels, one's vision and one's humanity.

Jacobson's feeling for the humane comes through again in his treatment of Mark Twain and *The Adventures of Huckleberry Finn.* The dismaying misapplication of psychiatric theory and nomenclature to literature has hardly left the relationship of Huck and Jim untouched. Who can ignore the provocations of a jazzy, doctrinaire criticism, plucked from psychoanalysis, and thrown foolishly, accusingly, sometimes with unbridled sanctimony at the lives of writers or the characters of their books? Here is Mr. Jacobson on Huck and Jim:

By any definition of the word, the relationship between Huck and Jim on the river is considerably more "civilized" than any relationship which they can enjoy with anyone else or with each other, on the shore. The relationship between the two on the raft demands from them both the sacrifices which civilization demands from us all, and which we frequently find most burdensome to make: it demands mutual responsibility, self-abnegation, and moral choice. . . . The tragedy of the book is that the fineness of Huck's relationship with Jim is impermanent; it cannot survive on shore, as the last chapters dismally demonstrate. Though he did not realize it, this is the saddest and fullest judgment that Twain was ever to make of "the damned human race."

The essays are very much like Orwell's in their clarity and warmth. And their author's mind is both sensitive and sensible, an unusual combination these days.

Partisan Review, Winter 1964

To Try Men's Souls

We all know that America's cities are in trouble, especially because blacks have fled to them in mixed hope and fear. We know, because we are constantly told, that the whites don't understand the needs of the blacks, that we will go from bad to worse, that it is too late because another apocalypse is at hand. But almost no one has tried to tell us about the early lives, the *inner* early lives, of black people, the particular ways that black children in a rural setting grow, only to leave and become the urban poor, the "social dynamite" we hear abstractly described again and again. The tragedy had to be documented, yet social documentation and political prescription can be static and flat and self-defeating when the men, women, and children involved become merely part of something called "a history of exploitation and oppression." And books and thinking that carry on in this fashion will not, unfortunately, really be counterbalanced by Alice Walker's *The Third Life of Grange Copeland*. Novelists and poets (Miss Walker is a published poet, too) are not the people we look to for help about ghetto children and racial violence in our cities. Moreover, Miss Walker was born in and has spent most of her life in the Southern countryside, and she is now a writer-in-residence at Tougaloo College, a black Mississippi school that is not in a city. What can she know of the crime and violence, the drug addiction and alcoholism and despair we have been told exist so significantly in our urban ghettos? What can she volunteer about the attitudes of black children or their problems?

In her own way, she has supplied some answers, but she has not written a social novel or a protest novel. Miss Walker is a storyteller. A black woman from the farmlands of Georgia, she knows her countryside well—so warm and fertile and unspoiled, so bleak and isolated and blood-soaked—and especially she knows the cabins, far out of just about everyone's sight, where one encounters the habits of diet, the idioms of speech, the styles of clothing, and the ways of prayer that contrast so strikingly with the customs of the rest of us. Fearful and vulnerable, rural blacks (and whites, too) can at the same time be exuberant, passionate, quick-witted, and as smartly self-displaying as the well-dressed and the well-educated. She knows, beyond that, what bounty sharecroppers must hand over to "bossmen," and how tenant farmers struggle with their landlords, and how subsistence farmers barely get by. But she does not exhort. In *The Third Life of Grange Copeland*, the centuries of black life in America are virtually engraved on one's consciousness. Equally vivid is Grange Copeland, who is more than a representative of Georgia's black field hands, more than someone scarred by what has been called "the mark of oppression." In him Miss Walker has turned dry sociological facts into a whole and alive particular person rather than a bundle of problems and attitudes. Character portrayal is what she has accomplished, and character portrayal is not to be confused with "motivational analysis."

Grange Copeland is a proud, sturdy black yeoman who has the white man on his back. He picks cotton, lowers his head when "they" appear, goes through the required postures a segregationist society demands—the evasions, duplicities, and pretenses that degrade black people and make moral cowards out of white people. Underneath, he is strong enough to hate, and without rage a person like him might well become the ingratiating lackey he has to pretend to be. His anger is not really political or ideological. He sulks, lashes out at his wife, his young son Brownfield, and her illegitimate infant. He sees too much, feels too much, dreams too much; he is like an actor who has long ago stopped trying to estimate where he begins and his roles end. He works backbreaking days in the field and then comes home saddened and hungry for sleep but tense and truculent. ("By Thursday, Grange's gloominess reached its peak and he grimaced respectfully, with veiled eyes, at the jokes told by the man who drove the truck. On Thursday nights he stalked the house from room to room and pulled himself up and swung from the rafters of the porch.") He is nearly consumed by his contempt for the white landowners, the bossmen, but he and his wife struggle tenaciously for the little integrity and self-respect they can find. Eventually they conclude that they are losers and take to drink and promiscuity, followed by hysterical efforts at atonement on Sunday mornings. Then Grange abandons his wife, and she poisons herself and her illegitimate infant. Brownfield, the child of their hope and love, is left to wander across the land, left to learn how much a child has to pay for the hurt and pain his parents live with and convey.

I suppose it can be said that *The Third Life of Grange Copeland* is concerned with the directions a suffering people can take. His first life ends in flight, and his wandering son takes flight, too, becoming in time a ruined and thus ruinous man, bent on undermining everyone who feels worthwhile and has a sense of pride and dignity. For a while, the lives of father and son converge on the establishment run by Josie, a sensual, canny, generous, possessive madam whose café and "rooms" full of women feed off the frustrations men like Grange and Brownfield try to subdue. There are complications, accidents, sudden and surprising developments. And always there is the unpredictable and potentially violent atmosphere of the small Georgia towns and the dusty, rutted roads that lead from them into the countryside.

Grange's second life, in Harlem, is equally disastrous. He becomes slick, manipulative, unfeeling—the thief and confidence-man our respectable world (which has its own deceptions and cruelties) is shocked to find and quick to condemn, yet not wholly unfeeling: he tries to help a white woman in distress and is rebuffed. His hatred of whites presses more relentlessly, and so he goes South to find escape from them at any cost. Josie is waiting for him. Brownfield has married her niece, a charming girl, "above" her husband in intelligence and education and sensitivity, but step by step he goes down, systematically destroying his wife and daughters. Yet Grange finds at last—in his third life, as an exile returned home—the freedom he has asked for. The whites are everywhere still powerful, so it is not political and economic freedom he achieves. But he does take care of his son's youngest daughter after her mother is killed by her drunken husband, and, finally, he can say to his beloved granddaughter, "I know the danger of putting all the blame on somebody else for the mess you make out of your life. I fell into the trap myself. And I'm bound to believe that that's the way the white folks can corrupt you even when you done held up before. 'Cause when they got you thinking that they're to blame for *every*thing they have you thinking they's some kind of gods!"

Brownfield tries to get his daughter back, and to prevent that Grange kills him. What goes on between that daughter, that growing child, and her grandfather is told with particular grace; it is as if one were reading a long and touching poem. But Alice Walker is a fighter as well as a meditative poet and a lyrical novelist. She has taken part in the struggles her people have waged, and she knows the struggles they must yet face in this greatest of the world's democracies. She also knows that not even ample bread and wine or power and applause can give anyone the calm, the freedom that comes with a mind's acceptance of its own worth. Toward the end of his third life, Grange Copeland can at last stop being hard on himself and look with kindness upon himself—and one wonders whether any achievement can be more revolutionary.

New Yorker, February 27, 1971

A Dream Deferred

No one who was involved with SNCC and CORE in the 1960s will read *The River of No Return* without a good deal of nostalgia, sorrow, and bitterness—not a very pleasant mixture of emotions, but things haven't turned out so well, either. The author, Cleveland Sellers, is a longtime Civil Rights activist. He comes from a small town in South Carolina, and is of a middle-class family. He needn't have worked so long and hard on behalf of his people. He might easily have become yet another member of E. Franklin Frazier's "black bourgeoisie." Instead, he joined up with SNCC in the early 1960s and to this day is working as an organizer and political activist. As he himself says, "I don't have a personal life anymore."

Much of this book is appropriately impersonal. We are told less about the author's life than about the life of the Civil Rights struggle in the South. Especially evocative, haunting at times, are the recollections of the "old days," when it was "black and white together"; when it was "we shall overcome"; when a relative handful of students could think of taking on the whole segregationist state of Mississippi—and do so with more success than they dreamed possible. (They never underestimated the dangers, the lives that would be lost, the beatings that would take place.) Success, of course, meant the vote for previously disenfranchised people—along with a seat in a Howard Johnson's or a movie house, if one had the money. Yet by no means have the region's Eastlands given up their economic power. By no means, either, have the rural poor Mr. Sellers knows so well had any reason to give up their heritage: fear, extreme poverty, constant anxiety, and a sense of vulnerability that no SNCC or CORE can remove—not when a Voting Rights Bill or a Public Accommodations Bill is followed by an administration such as we have now. So Mr. Sellers expresses his rage and confusion. He persists, tries to do what he can, feels hopeless one minute but on the whole determined—and utterly selfless about his dedication. What matters is his people, still at the bottom of the ladder, still at the mercy of sheriffs and landowners, and yes, high government officials, who right now are cutting the heart out of valuable domestic programs (ones that *do* work but have been denied proper funds, and now will lose all funds) but making sure that all those military bases in states like Mississippi and Alabama stay well supplied with a "cash flow." Mr. Sellers is not surprised at all that, but then why should he be? He has written his book, presumably, to tell the rest of us that our surprise and chagrin are matched by his people's daily pound of flesh—and more.

New Republic, March 17, 1973

Through Conrad's Eyes

I remember going to our nation's capital during the late 1960s to testify before various congressional committees. I had been working in the South, and in Appalachia, and in our Northern ghettos, and presumably I knew something about matters then of significance to the country as a whole and to the men and women who represent us in Washington, D.C. I went before one Senate committee and talked about what I'd seen in some of the worst urban areas of the Northeast. To another committee I described what I'd seen of the life migratory farm workers must live. To yet another committee I reported on the findings a group of us physicians had made while touring the Mississippi Delta—widespread, severe hunger and malnutrition in children. I was becoming, I suppose, one more American expert, called to make his definitive statements, to come up with his appraisal of what has been, is, and ought be—a heady but not altogether rare experience for people in my profession, to whom so many in our contemporary world turn for suggestions and advice, if not a dose of consolation.

In the course of such journeys, I came to know one person fairly well; he was the junior senator from New York, Robert F. Kennedy. I first met him in 1965, when I testified before a committee whose concerns (ghetto problems) were very much his. He relentlessly questioned us witnesses about those problems, and so doing, he seemed to be getting away from the usual facts-and-figures approach. The senator was wondering about how people who are extremely vulnerable regard not only themselves and their neighbors but this life—its purposes, its ethical underpinnings, if any. Later, he took us to lunch, and as we talked I could again feel the moral intensity of the man, a certain thirst and hunger in him as he probed and probed, those blue eyes always staring directly at one's face, and the ears never missing a single word, and for that matter, hearing the silences, too, the remarks not made, whether out of ignorance or stupidity, or arrogance, or shortsightedness. Toward the end of the meal, he suddenly turned to me and asked me what I'd recommend that he read if he had the time for one book, only one—with respect to the racial question in this country. I paused and seemed unable to answer. I remember the blank in my head, his stare continuing, my sense that I was once more going to flunk a course, and then my mind's desperate summons of my wife's views, her often expressed opinions, her way of looking at things, her sensibility. She is a school teacher, and I suppose a pupil in bad trouble was calling for whatever assistance he could find. I heard her say, in my head, *Invisible Man*, and then I heard myself say it: *"Invisible Man."*

Right off, the academic arrogance, the condescension of my kind asserted itself: better tell him the author's name and say something about the book. But say what? Why had I, anyway, passed over dozens of sociological and psychological studies in favor of a particular story? This man opposite me was a busy, tough, shrewd, demanding, hardheaded, and practical man, who needed concrete, specific answers to concrete, specific problems. What would *Invisible Man* offer him? In any event, as that line of thinking crossed my intimidated, awestruck, ingratiating head—the eager social scientist-hustler glad to be within sight of a mighty empire's world-famous legislative and executive buildings—the senator did an end run around me. I remember my sense of frustration as he told me how much he admired that novel. Did I have any idea whether Ralph Ellison was working on a second one? I readily reported that I was sure Ellison was, then quickly added the obvious, that Ellison was taking his time. I'll never forget the comment that followed, which I can offer almost word for word: "There was *so* much in that novel; it'd be hard to know what more to say."

Well, *we* had no more to say on that subject, at least then. An aide of the Senator's approached the table, there were some whispered exchanges, and soon enough he was on his way and the rest of us on ours. When I got home (we'd just moved back North to Massachusetts, after living in Louisiana and Georgia for five years), I told my wife of that moment, and she wondered at *my* problem, never mind the problem (racial turmoil) we had discussed at that lunch. I could only say that I didn't think, at the time, that *Invisible Man* was quite the kind of book the senator had in mind for me to suggest. He was clearly upset terribly by what he'd been seeing in his visits to various American cities, and he very much wanted to figure out how to change this nation's social and economic direction so that our poor and so-called working-class families would be getting a better deal. He had a razor-sharp mind, I'd discovered, and was vigorously pragmatic in his nature—qualities I'd not only observed but had occasion to feel as I tried to respond to his thoroughly alert, conscientious, and independent-minded manner of posing questions and discussion. I was glad when our preliminary discussion of *Invisible Man* and its author had been interrupted. What would I have said, I kept wondering, had the question (which single book to read?) been put to me yet again? Surely the asker had not been seeking the kind of answer I'd offered.

My wife said she certainly hoped he *had* been seeking the very answer I supplied. I became annoyed; one doesn't seek an answer to something if one already has the answer, unless one is being rhetorical, and that was not the case then. Not necessarily, my wife persisted. We may have our own ideas, but we do want to know what others think. True, I realized, but this was an extremely busy man, who wasn't summoning experts to Washington or talking with them at lunch in order to have a "great books" or "important ideas" discussion. No Senate committee needed me (or anyone else) to come and tell them that Ralph Ellison had written an extraordinary novel, which in its own way said as much as (well, quite a bit more than) the honorable legislators were likely to hear from the collection of social scientists then testifying and (given this nation's culture, its values, and habits) likely to continue testifying.

My wife knew that even anyone as sure of himself and willful and well-read (and versed in Sophocles, Shakespeare, the nineteenth-century romantic poets, all of whom Robert Kennedy often quoted) as the senator was not about to declare war on such objects of secular idolatry as psychology and psychiatry, sociology, anthropology, economics, and political science. She knew, too, that such disciplines had their own particular truths to offer, and the point was not to blame them without qualification for what all too commonly happens—the overestimation of their usefulness, these days, by so many of us. Still, she was not going to relent on her central point— that there is a crying need in this country for a persuasive moral vision and that it is a pity people such as Ralph Ellison aren't the ones testifying before congressional committees, in as much as they seem far more knowing, far more eloquent and savvy with respect to what ails us, what we have been and are and might be, than those who constantly arrive in Washington, D.C., with their "data" and their theories and their "policy proposals." Soon enough, she added another novelist's name as the sort of person she'd like to see talking with our nation's legislators, and she reminded me of a book of his, published a few years earlier, which had meant a lot to us: *Who Speaks for The Negro?* by Robert Penn Warren.

Today the use of the word *Negro* is unwelcome to many—though not to Ralph Ellison, as a matter of fact, who for his own stoutly maintained reasons, keeps using that word. Back then the word *black* had (almost overnight) become a powerful claimant upon the (ever-anxious) white liberal vocabulary, even as black radicals were just that, suddenly—*black*. But at the time it was not the word *Negro* in Robert Penn Warren's book that had bothered many readers. It was a certain point of view, perhaps best explained by one of the (white) Civil Rights activists we knew who had read the book and turned against it, as had happened with *Segregation*, an earlier book of Robert Penn Warren's I'd also once recommended to him and others: "You like these literary folks! They look around, talk with people, then say this is a very confusing world, and it's complicated (they're *always* saying that!), and no one really knows the answers to a lot of these troubles, and so all we can do is try to see as much as we can and write as honestly as we can about what we do manage to see. Right?"

I could hardly say "wrong"; but I did try to amplify his own remarks by asking him whether there wasn't, actually, room for (and need of) precisely that kind of tenaciously reflective and aspiringly evenhanded manner of inquiry. Maybe there was for such as me, he agreed reluctantly and with some accusation (I felt) in his voice, but not for those who were in the middle of a serious social struggle to end, at last, the South's segregationist power. Why need such a struggle preclude paying attention to the helpful observations of a Robert Penn Warren, not to mention Ralph Ellison? *He* took on Robert Penn Warren, and a black friend of ours, sitting nearby, took on Ellison, and together their argument went like this: Listen, buddy (if such you are!), we are involved in a big fight, and we want to win, and we have a clear idea of what we're fighting for (the vote, access to everyone else's schools, moviehouses, restaurants, and so on), and why we're waging that fight, and how we plan to achieve

our victory. Along you come, preaching at us through these novelists who (we'll acknowledge) have strong social interests, a strong desire to help change things for the better, racially—but who also
come up with nothing to say that will help us in this war of sorts
we're waging, and who even come up with a lot that makes it damn
hard at times to go out and take the risks of being a soldier, because
when you keep getting told that life is almost infinitely complex, and
that ambiguities are everywhere, and ironies, and troubling inconsistencies (namely, in you and your comrades as well as in the
enemy's camp), then by God, you're in danger of becoming so
"weighed down" (they both used those words) you just feel like
surrendering.

This summarizes a long, long series of conversations—of the
kind, I knew at the time, Mr. Warren himself would have wanted
(talking about irony!) to put into his book, which did, indeed, show
how *various* the views of black people were, hence how utterly human their situation: not a herd, a "them" for racists (or supposed
friends who had endless amounts of advice to give, aid to offer, and
in the clutch, with disagreement, that same aid to withdraw) to hate
but the almost infinitely diverse human beings we all are, no matter
our racial, religious, ethnic, social, or cultural background, once one
pays attention to the words and deeds of particular men, women, and
children. I must say that I wasn't inclined to argue too strenuously
with those two friends. As in my meeting with a given senator, I
knew how important a struggle those two youths were waging, how
tough the odds were at times, and how precarious the victories
achieved. Is it not under such circumstances a luxury (of certain
writers, and the college students or comfortable members of the
bourgeoisie who make up their major audience) to take the long and
reflective view of the humanities?

Of course, soon enough, the Civil Rights movement, once a band
of brothers and sisters, no matter the skin color of anyone, had become torn apart, with all sorts of voices in exhortation and condemnation directed at all sorts of targets. Who *does* speak for "the Negro,"
everyone was beginning to ask—and who, for that matter, speaks for
the white people, whether those who belonged to, say, SNCC and
CORE and SCLC (abbreviations for the three major Southern activist groups: the Student Nonviolent Coordinating Committee, the
Congress of Racial Equality, and the Southern Christian Leader-

ship Conference), or those who were, simply and not so simply, ordinary Americans? The country was seriously splintered, and we needed all the perspective we could find, each of us, if we were to be able to figure out why that division had happened and in what direction we might turn. Moreover, Ellison's story had turned out to be uncannily accurate—the way, for instance, people long persecuted learn to imitate their persecutors, even to the point of visiting upon themselves the old, familiar responses learned from "the man."

I remember, by 1967, thinking that Ralph Ellison and Robert Penn Warren not only knew "everything" (as poets or novelists at their best seem to) but had reserved for themselves some special gifts of prophecy. They'd both made extraordinary judgments about the manner in which white and black people get caught in blindness even as they struggle to catch sight of what is true and significant and valuable, and not least, worth upholding, worth fighting for—no matter the temptations of envy, rivalry, greed, ambition, and egotism, those qualities none of us ever manages to shed; no matter our skin color, our success, the number of years we've undergone psychoanalysis, the articles and books we've written, and yes, as both Mr. Ellison and Mr. Warren would remind us, even the fine poems and novels we may have by the grace of things managed to compose.

By late 1967 and early 1968, I was having the chance to see Robert Kennedy talk with people I knew in the Mississippi Delta, in the hollows of Appalachia, as he made his restless trek through America, fueled by his burning desire to help others far less fortunate than himself. I remember another talk, similarly brief, about books. Now we were in the rural South and had just seen some extremely hard-pressed tenant farmer families struggling to get by. They were black people, and they possessed within themselves a mix of desperation and dignity that a privileged outsider could find awesome, intimidating, accusing, and unnerving. Suddenly the busy senator started talking about the hurt and ailing people we'd met and about the strange effect they'd had on him, on us. He was searching for words, for a way of putting what he saw and felt. He was searching in vain, it seemed, for a while. He had such moments, one knew—when he stopped talking altogether, or his stream of talk sputtered, and came in fits, starting and stopping and starting and stopping. All of a sudden he mentioned Joseph Conrad, how much it had meant to him, back in college, to read *Heart of Darkness* and

The Nigger of the Narcissus. We talked about the novels, about Conrad's personal life—and I had in my distressingly single-minded way concluded that we were now diverting ourselves, trying to find relief in intellectual talk, in the life and work of a man long dead who lived far from the state of Mississippi and had no great interest during his life in America's racial difficulties. The senator kept talking about Conrad, though; and soon enough those two stories were under surveillance once more by both of us—the greed and despair, the nihilism of the imperialist West, its "darkness," and the effect that James Wait, the dying black man, had on the crew of the freighter the *Narcissus*.

This United States senator (thank God) was no pedant or psychiatrist. He had no interest in pushing his interpretations on anybody, himself included—no interest in dressing them up in fancy, portentous language, the better to dazzle and, eventually, command the obedience of the listener. At one moment in our talk, though, he did say this: "You look around you here, and you can see the point of seeing the place and the people through Conrad's eyes." I was now able to think again of that black man in *The Nigger of the Narcissus*, of the fear and the hate he inspired in others, of the "weight" of James Wait as he waited for death, and of the "weight" we all can be to one another, even as we can inspire and uplift one another, too—as Conrad did with his story. Now, fifteen years later, I hear my sons discuss those stories, and not rarely my mind goes back to that late afternoon of a warm and humid Delta early autumn day: the car speeding to the airport, the press of politics exerting a toll, the presence of suffering nearby; and suddenly Conrad's eyes, his heart and soul, his mind and spirit, upon us in their mighty power to instruct morally—world without end, one hopes and prays.

American Poetry Review, January/February 1984

James Baldwin Back Home

James Baldwin will turn fifty-three on August 2. He was born and grew up in Harlem. He left this country when he was twenty-four for France, where he has, mostly, lived ever since. This summer he returned to New York City but not on yet another brief visit—the expatriate dipping into the forsaken land for a draught of outrage or disgust. He is coming home to live and glad to be back. But if one presses him a bit on the virtues of this country, he is quick to spell out his particular point of view: "I left America because I had to. It was a personal decision. I wanted to write, and it was the 1940s, and it was no big picnic for blacks. I grew up on the streets of Harlem, and I remember President Roosevelt, the liberal, having a lot of trouble with an antilynching bill he wanted to get through the Congress—never mind the vote, never mind restaurants, never mind schools, never mind a fair employment policy. I had to leave; I needed to be in a place where I could breathe and not feel someone's hand on my throat. A lot of young Americans, white or black, rich or poor, have wanted to get away as a means of getting closer to themselves. For me, France was the beginning of a writing life; I wrote *Go Tell It on the Mountain* there. It was there I began the struggle with words."

He is not at all sure, however, that he would go to Paris now if he were a young, black, would-be writer: "I think I'd probably go to Africa, to some part of Asia—the Third World. I love France; I know it well, have good friends there. But it is a *hermetic* place, in certain respects—plenty of arrogance and smugness among its intellectuals and upper bourgeoisie. History brings changes to countries and continents. Exiles, wanderers, refugees find different havens, from generation to generation. I still love France; I do not want to repudiate a former mistress. But Europe has changed. I went there to get enough away from the American Negro Problem—the everyday insults and humiliation, the continual sadness and the rage—so that I could sit down and write with a half-clear head. Now many of the former slaves of the Western colonial empires have come to Europe: blacks, Mohammedans, Pakistanis, Moluccans. A Harlem is rising in Paris."

He talks some more about his life in Europe and again resists, partially at least, an opportunity to clothe himself in the garb of the repentant critic who has finally come around and is effusive with praise for what he once had only scorn: "This country has experienced important changes. When I've returned on visits, over the years, I've gone South and seen how different it's become there. It's still no paradise for blacks in Alabama or Mississippi. Let's not start sounding like chamber of commerce boys in Montgomery. I've seen the same wretchedness in the rural areas—broken-down shacks, and fear in the eyes of people who have to watch out every minute for the bossman and the sheriff, the whites who run the show. And there are urban black slums in Atlanta—the same high unemployment and poverty that millions have to accept as 'life' in Harlem or Chicago's Southside. But in the South, the black man and the white man still get on personally—haven't yet become strangers. I think there's more hope in the South, right now, for the people of both races. It's too early to know whether that hope will turn out to be justified. I don't wish, at this point in my life, to turn into a Southern romantic. The region has been badly served by its apologists—and there's always an interesting market up North for such people. There's little hope in Northern slums, where nearly half the black young people can find no work. Would America's white people stand for that—unemployment figures like those in the ghetto?"

He is somewhat drawn to Jimmy Carter. In an open letter to him Baldwin said that "you, in my lifetime, are the only President I would have written." He sees Carter and Andrew Young as products of a similar regional experience. He is not at all surprised that during the election year blacks turned so quickly and overwhelmingly to Carter. He does not expect the statements of either the president or his roving black ambassador to change very much the concrete realities of power as it affects the lives of millions of malnourished, virtually starving people in the underdeveloped countries, or for that matter, the victimized people of Eastern Europe. Still, he is a writer and not completely down on the value of words, though not, also, without his moments of doubt: "Words can be disguises for inaction—a smokescreen. But words can open up possibilities too. I think Andy Young knows what he can and cannot do. He's sending out signals. The people meant to hear them are listening. They are no fools, don't expect miracles. But they are waiting too. What will come next? How committed is the United States to the poorer countries? We sent billions abroad to rebuild Germany, twice our enemy. Is there an interest of that order in countries who have never fought us and whose resources we have taken when we have needed them, at no great profit for 'the natives'? I think Andy Young is giving it a try; he's waiting to see what will happen, as a writer does when he pours out the truth as he sees it and wonders if some people will sit down and read, and read, and then say: Yes, by God, *yes*."

He hopes the president will be able to live up to the populist side of his instincts, but he points out repeatedly that the presidency is but one part of a given political and economic system. And besides, there is a history we all have to contend with: "For a long while, liberty was a privilege in this country. Blacks had to learn, growing up, a severe interior rigor—to the point that they didn't need the state's police on patrol to keep them in line. In Eastern Europe there is austerity for the masses and the constant presence of the police, the military. Here it is different—if you're doing well, you can say a lot and get away with it. If you're poor, you can shout to your heart's content, provided no one starts listening to you and your message doesn't threaten too many people. I think blacks have to say to themselves something like this: We will act as if this is a free country, until the white people tell us it's not by jailing us or killing us. And a lot of us have been locked up or murdered over the centuries we've been here. It's a hard thing to talk about, the Iron Curtain and its significance. I know that my books have been very popular in the Soviet Union. But *Giovanni's Room* cannot be published there. And why have the Russians been so eager to read and praise me? On the other hand, it's no credit to this enormously rich country that there are more oppressive, less decent governments elsewhere. We claim the superiority of our institutions. We ought to live up to our own standards, not use misery elsewhere as an endless source of self-gratification and justification. Of course, people tell me all the time in the West that they are trying, they are trying hard. Some have tears in their eyes and let me know how awful they feel about the way our poor live, our blacks, or those in dozens of other countries. People can cry much easier than they can change, a rule of psychology people like me picked up as kids on the street."

In France, or elsewhere abroad, he hasn't been able to stay away from the events in this country. The Patty Hearst case prompted him to think of the Weathermen and others like them, the enraged products of privileged homes who turned so bitterly and violently on America, and finally on one another. He would like, one day, to write about such matters, the disenchantment of people who have so much and yet, it seems, so little. He has been reading *The Possessed* again. He has been thinking of the nineteenth-century Russian intelligentsia, among them the political activists who became so fiercely against the status quo and at such a high cost to their personal lives: "It's ironic—some black kids know that their fathers are criminals, have been arrested, have been in jail again and again. But what to think of a Patty Hearst, or others like her—though they never went as far as she did—who begin to think that *their* fathers may be a bit 'criminal' too? Whites and blacks have met at that point—an awakened sense of the subtleties of injustice. Each time I come back to this country, I travel-lecture on several campuses. The races are less obsessed with each other than was the case in the 1960s. Many black students tell me they pay no attention to whites—though indifference may conceal many other emotions. We hear that whites have gone on to other concerns—themselves and their careers. But I have met many white students and hear by mail from others, and they seem bewildered, troubled, at a loss to know what to do, where to go. I'm not sure they're as passive and inert as some social observers say, or wish. Maybe some of them have learned a lot, as a result of the Civil Rights movement, the Vietnam War, Watergate, the assassination of beloved leaders, and so on. Maybe those young people are trying to figure out what's right, what ought to be done, now that they've seen before their eyes what's wrong. Inertia, even despair, can be a stage in one's growth, a way of coming to terms with what one has gone through and learned."

He is insistently the "native son" essayist, full of strong-minded, if not polemical, comments of a social or political nature. But he is a novelist, and when asked about that important side of his life he becomes more guarded, more tentative, less inclined to speak in a forceful, even provocative, manner. A book of his meant for young readers, and already published in England, will come out in September: *Little Man, Little Man*. It tells of a short time in the New York City lives of a seven-year-old boy and another boy and a girl. He has for some time been working on a novel, one that means a lot to him. It will actually take up where *Go Tell It on the Mountain* left off. He has, he thinks, been skirting the subject all his writing years—the life and death of a gospel singer, a man: "I have a few more months of work on the novel. I'm going back to France in a few days, because that's where I can best finish the novel. Then, I guess, I'll be able to come home. People stop me and say: 'Coming home, Jimmie?' I say yes, soon, but I've got to go back and finish something. Maybe it'll be the end of more than the novel—a long apprenticeship, I sometimes think. It was in France that I could start a career of writing English because there I was not able to speak French and so I was driven to recognize myself as an outsider *that way*: not as a black man, but as an English-speaking person. In Harlem, as a boy going to school, I also felt myself an outsider. I knew a language different from the ones teachers were trying to make me learn—the language of jazz, spirituals, the blues; the language of testifying and signifying; and the language of cool black cats, street kids, holding on to life by their fingernails while they heard their parents screaming up to their God in heaven, asking him what's going on, and what's going to happen, and when, oh Jesus, when?"

He is asked to tell more but pulls back into a writer's self-protective nervousness. He hopes, but cannot be sure, that he will do justice to a subject that has haunted him: his people's struggle, through the passion of religious faith, for some understanding of what life means, if anything. His hands, ordinarily on the move rather constantly—grasping for words, slicing up sentences, swinging at enemies, reaching for agreement or pushing strenuously in the face of disagreement—become strangely still. As he talks about the character of the gospel singer he is trying to evoke, as he talks about the preachers he has known, the messages they have handed down, as he remembers the Holy Rollers, remembers Billie Holiday in a green dress sustaining one evening a mixture of irony, detachment, sadness, and terrible, mocking amusement at the spectacle of her own celebrity, he loses the physical intensity he has had and willingly spent. The hands knock gently on the table's wood. He doesn't want to talk about the novel he is trying to achieve; he wants to leave the country, finish it, and come back to live in America, a country he insists he has never really left, only crossed the ocean to look at more intently. He hopes he can capture sharply and suggestively the "pacing" of a certain kind of desperate spiritual life: "I remember in those Pentecostal churches when I was young, the tension, the drama, the struggle for a handle on life. I hope I can remember *well*. A person would get up and he'd say, she'd say, to begin with: 'I'm going to step out on the promise.' I guess that's what I'm trying to do. I look at Andy Young on the screen and see the frustration and hurt in his eyes—all the pain he's seen here and now sees abroad, but there's a glow in his eyes too—a smile that says he's going to keep taking a chance, one more and then one more after that. And some of the black kids I see in Harlem or elsewhere, the same goes for them— they're stepping out on the promise, and that's about all I guess they can do, each one of them."

New York Times Book Review, July 31, 1977

Behind the Beyond

We are removed from many people on this planet by more than distance, and we are apt to judge them by our standards. Neither planes nor television nor any other technological achievements have turned the world's population into understanding friends and neighbors. One can go everywhere without losing a self-centered view of the world; one can watch a thousand travelogues or *cinéma vérité* documentaries and still distrust people who look or act "different." The tug of our own lives often is too much for us, and if anyone tries to pull us toward "them"—Asians or Africans, or our own Indians or Eskimos—we are quick to react: our informant is merely an anthropologist, who has made a career out of tribal observation, or a polemicist. Occasionally, an observer who has ventured into regions unknown to nearly all of us can educate us in the most disarming way—informally and patiently, without any academic or ideological agenda. One thinks of James Agee among Alabama's sharecroppers in the 1930s, of George Orwell doggedly pursuing the "lower depths" of Paris or London. They bring fellow human beings so close to us that we can recognize them as brothers and sisters under the skin, no matter how unlike us they seem; a hard-driven Alabama field hand comes across clearly, a man on skid row whom Orwell happened to meet is conveyed to us in a compelling manner.

Sheila Burnford's *One Woman's Arctic* is in that tradition. She tells what she has observed in strong, straightforward prose, and she organizes her ideas and observations so that the reader learns more than he or she may realize; she avoids didactic insistence: the people I studied have certain traits and can be categorized in a certain way. She has spent years in the out-of-doors of her native Britain and in Canada's sparsely settled north woods. In her fifties, she is still active, adventurous. During the Second World War, she drove an ambulance. She hunts and fishes; she sails; she has a pilot's license; she wanders far and wide taking note of the natural world. Her first book, *The Incredible Journey*, is at initial glance a tale for youthful readers—the trek of a young Labrador retriever, an ancient bull terrier, and a Siamese cat through the Canadian wilderness. What distinguishes the book is the author's special understanding of animals and the terrain these ones traveled. In *The Fields of Noon*, she presents the reader with tender, knowing sketches of dogs, of a canary, of open countryside, and deep woods—in Scotland, in Spain, and in Canada. More recently (1969), Mrs. Burnford turned her attention to human beings—the Cree and Ojibwa Indians of Ontario, whom she describes with empathy and shrewdness in *Without Reserve*. Now she tells us of people in the Northwest Territories well above the Arctic Circle, where she spent two summers with the Innuit Eskimos, mostly in Pond Inlet on remote Baffin Island. With her was Susan Ross, an equally hardy older woman.

Mrs. Burnford was there, she says, not to preach to the Eskimos, teach them her values, convey her kind of knowledge, buy anything from them, or enlist them as hunting guides: "I was there 'just to be there.'" She acknowledges "mild amateur interests in birds and wild flowers, animals, and artifacts." And she is sure that the Eskimos were puzzled by her: "We were two Kabloonahs, white women *d'un certain âge*, as the French so happily put it, with grownup families." It took a while to get used to the twenty-four-hour days of the Arctic summer. A visitor loses a sense of time: it is for others, far away, to look at watches and clocks. Not that the life of Pond Inlet is static or uneventful. The day has its rhythms—all related in the mind of the Eskimo to the movement of the sun across the sky, but not fitted into a strict chronology. One responds to Nature's moods with no notion of schedules or quotas to be met within a given time frame. For the Eskimo, the world is awesome, people small and vulnerable; one tries to survive and to stay in touch with the environment rather than subdue it.

Mrs. Burnford is quite aware of the subtleties of the changing landscape:

> Now the strait was ice-locked to silence and there were no birds; soon there would be the sound of open water and shifting, groaning, creaking ice floes, the air filled with the music of dozens of different gulls and waterfowl. Now the rocky hillside was covered in snow; in a few days it would spring into brilliant

life, carpeted with myriad wild flowers. One moment the glaciers opposite would seem remote as another continent; next time I looked it would seem that I only had to walk a mile or so across the ice to be at the end of their thousands-of-years-old road. Or the mountains would be cloud-wreathed, the sun striking in silver shafts across the ice below; then a pure white peak from the ice cap would rear through the clouds, catch the sun, and so change light and color again.

As for the Eskimos, "like a piece of blotting paper I simply absorbed whatever came my way, content to be given bits of information, not to question or inquire, more interested in the land, and in the people as villagers and friendly faces, than in their relationships, or in the workings and economy of the settlement." Yet we have an excellent account of how a community overcomes a vast range of obstacles. We are brought close to that community. "It was impossible to feel shy or a stranger for long." The Eskimos of Pond Inlet, like Eskimos elsewhere, are generous, hospitable, helpful to outsiders in whatever way, and no questions asked. Perhaps people constantly reminded of their extreme vulnerability are not carried away with themselves, or perhaps they are simply by nature gentle and easygoing. It is as if they regarded themselves as brief guests on this earth, with an obligation to help one another and to be prepared at any moment to leave. In the vastness of the Arctic, the entirely white mountains that appear so near seem to recede as one approaches. A strange and haunting medley pervades—the wind sweeping across the land, the ice moving, groaning, "the cries of gulls and long-tailed jaegers overhead; the excited, rushing patter of a flock of a hundred guillemots' feet on the water; the high-pitched scream of terns; sometimes geese calling far out, snows and white-fronts, or the amazingly melodic gossip of old squaws drifting across the water." Then the clouds that have been threatening vanish, the noise abates, the silence becomes a noticeable presence. "I felt suddenly overcome with the magnitude of it all compared with the infinitesimal dot that was me standing in the middle of a frozen sea; so infinitesimal that it seemed ludicrous that anything so nearly invisible could have cold hands or feel hungry—could do anything in fact except just *be* and no more. I have seldom felt so utterly content. I was often to experience this most peaceful acceptance of my microscopic unimportance. I think I began to understand then how this land binds so strongly, and is bound up with, its people. The two are one."

From Mrs. Burnford we learn who settled in the Arctic and what befell them, what it is like now, as more explorers, surveyors, engineers, and officials arrive. She raises a vexing issue that is a constant presence in every one of her books: How is one to regard the Eskimos or the Indian tribes who live to the south of them? Are they our moral superiors? Are they hopelessly isolated and primitive people who barely hold on to life? Are they ill suited to another life situation? Only by implication do we learn that her attitude is essentially admiration and practicality: live and let live. The Eskimos have never wanted to move south, acquire land that is somebody else's, or insist that others conform to their way of life. They have received all visitors and have been patient listeners and observers, if not the most willing and compliant of hosts. Whalers and hunters have come to the Arctic, and adventurers, gold-hungry explorers, missionaries, misfits, geologists looking for oil, and surveyors to plan wells, roads, and pipelines. And the reward for the willingness to extend a helping hand is the shantytowns of Alaska and northern Canada—inhabited by a demoralized people who have lost touch, who no longer have a purpose, who spend their time in bars or in the lineup in front of government agencies. Mrs. Burnford acknowledges that the white culture can bring the Eskimo a longer life, a more comfortable and secure existence. But she speaks, too, of "laziness and greed, loss of skills, and eventually loss of racial pride."

This has not yet happened in Pond Inlet. There the author saw a people of enormous vitality and resourcefulness go about their chores. To stay alive is a constant achievement: today's supply of food, or bearable weather may be followed by near-starvation, wind, snow, and cold of an intensity we of the Temperate Zone cannot comprehend. The Eskimo is clever, alert, ingenious, quick of reflex. Mrs. Burnford, mother of three children, notes that the Eskimos do not make the child an object of veneration; children are allies, successors who need to learn quickly how to survive, even though by trial and error. A child perpetually protected cannot survive.

"Thirty years ago Rasmussen observed," says Mrs. Burnford, "that he had learned from an old Eskimo 'It is generally believed that white men have quite the same minds as small children. Therefore one should always give way to them. They are easily angered, and when they cannot get their will they are moody, and, like children, have the strangest ideas and fancies'—a somewhat sobering estimate, and one that time does not seem to have modified." But what the famous Arctic explorer said then can apply to the Eskimos as well; they, too, can be "small children," susceptible to blandishment. Six hundred miles from Pond Inlet lies an enormous base built by the United States Strategic Air Command. The base has been closed, but the city that arose around it remains, and so do many of the Eskimos who worked there before the airmen departed:

> "Difficult to judge how many millions of dollars thrown away when they left," I wrote in my journal after wandering the site, still surrounded by its towering fence, the catwalks on stilts in case of "whiteouts" still intact, the Operations Room with tiered seats just like the movies. All electrical radio, radar, etc., equipment burned or hacked to pieces, shed after shed of twisted, broken remains. The cars and trucks were put into gear and sent over the hill to the gravel pit below, then bulldozed over, so that no one could possibly benefit from them. Yet they left canteen furniture, bunks, etc. With such an example of white wastefulness to a people accustomed to making something out of nothing, everything out of something, perhaps it's small wonder that the Eskimos exposed to it were never the same again. . . . Small children asking for "pennies," tarty-looking teenage girls emerging from the Palace Theatre, one memorable character with the shortest of sawn-off shorts, purple fishnet leotards, and a small dirty baby in a filthy *amouti* on her back—puffy-eyed, flabby-faced boys shouting uninhibitedly Anglo-Saxon badinage after them.

So it goes: a great nation moves to defend itself, and a scattered, defenseless, but brave and sensitive people become, in a way, casualties of a war they never saw or understood. Perhaps some Arctic travelers would, instead, emphasize the marginal nature of Eskimo living, the many infants who die because no medical care is available or grow up to live needlessly risky lives. Mrs. Burnford, it is true, sought out a particularly sturdy and self-reliant community of people and became a comrade and a partisan. She was a guest in their cabins, a welcome friend who ate their raw fish, their seal meat, their muktuk (the skin of narwhal), and traveled with them behind a dog team. Her Arctic is a place where genial people come to respectful terms with a splendid stretch of unspoiled land; and for all its challenges of weather, it is a safe land—no robbers, no assault, no pollution (at least in Pond Inlet) of air or water.

As one reads Mrs. Burnford's books, a question comes up that she has anticipated: What did the Eskimos or the Indians with whom she spent so much time think of this not so young woman, the mother of grown children, who wanted to see and photograph and tape-record birds of the Arctic? But the Eskimos, reticent and polite as they are, do not question other people; people are entitled to privacy. Perhaps Sheila Burnford was one of the more pleasant surprises for Pond Inlet. However isolated, however resigned to "fate" or accepting of "Nature," they have learned to live with a modicum of white visitors and no doubt to expect lectures, sermons, questions, instructions, even commands. Instead, two women arrived, stayed some months, demonstrated the most intense affection and concern, even a bit of envy, and then left in obvious sadness. One wishes that this book could be read by those whose land, character, and spirit the author conveys so well. But surely her Arctic friends know how much she hopes, for the sake of all of them, that there will be a middle ground between the precarious, brief, but dignified life of the hunter or fisherman of Pond Inlet and the life of the Eskimos she saw near that Air Force base only a few hundred miles away.

New Yorker, September 23, 1974

Outsiders

As Martin Luther King kept reminding his black compatriots at a time when simply going to hear him was a risky business, there were people all over the nation who shared their social and economic condition. To my knowledge, he never included Asian-Americans, the subject matter of a book, assembled as an "anthology of Asian-American writers" under the unusual title of *Aiiieeeee!*, by four anthologists—Frank Chin, Jeffery Paul Chan, Lawson Fusao Inada, and Shawn Hsu Wong. These men are all Asian-Americans—a term they apply mostly to those who were born in America to parents of Asian ancestry, those "who got their China and Japan from the radio, off the silver screen, from television, out of comic books, from the pushers of white American culture that pictured the yellow man as something that when wounded, sad, or angry, or swearing, or wondering whined, shouted, or screamed 'aiiieeeee!'" They are, as we all must be well aware, a substantial and hurt and troubled group, deprived of their rights and liberties by both law and prejudice and by a process of exclusion that has brought about poverty, unemployment, inadequate education, and a high incidence of preventable diseases. These people cannot easily turn back to China, Japan, or the Philippines; they are, after all, the children, the grandchildren, even the great-grandchildren of American citizens. Their ancestors helped build this country, especially the West—doing menial jobs others considered beneath them but that had to be done if the nation was to carry on. There has, it is true, been some movement back and forth across the Pacific, especially by the somewhat better-off Asian-Americans, whose small businesses have enabled a modest accumulation of cash. Then, there are some in this country who were born in China and came here, just as there are Asian-Americans who have spent a lot of time in Asia. And there has been assimilation, too: the *Pacific Citizen*, a newspaper put out by the Japanese-American Citizens League, reported in 1972 that about half the Japanese-American women and

Chinese-American women are now marrying men of other races.
(We are not given any statistics about what the Japanese-American
and Chinese-American men are doing.) That also troubles these
editors: Will their people slowly disappear, become absorbed?

The editors of this anthology struggle, besides, with the problem
of deciding what is genuinely "Asian-American" literature. For
seven generations now there have been Asian-Americans, yet to
many of us, we are told in the introduction, an Asian-American still
means a laundryman or someone who lives near or works in a restaurant in an area called Chinatown. And to most of us, the term
"Asian-American literature" brings up memories of Fu Manchu or
of Charlie Chan, who, said his creator, walks with "the light dainty
step of a woman." The editors of the anthology see him as the literary figure who represents to millions of us the "best" of the Asian-
Americans. They also regard him as the precursor of a whole literary
genre—the *Chinatown Book, Father and Glorious Descendant, A
Chinatown Family*, and volumes with titles like *Inside Chinatown*
and *Chinatown, U.S.A.* The editors deplore all this, and most especially Charlie Chan, "the fat, inscrutable, flowery but flub-tongued
effeminate little detective"; if some white people regarded him as intelligent, observant, and inventive, these Asian-American editors
consider him to be emasculated and passive, one of the all too familiar Chinese men who are pictured as "worshiping white women and
being afraid to touch them." For a long while, many of us never
distinguished among Japanese, Chinese, and Filipinos; they were all
"Asiatics," as in "Keep the Asiatics out." (There is something of that
sentiment today, as the South Vietnamese refugees wait in their encampments.) And keep them out we did—after the hard work of
opening up the West was completed, so much of it by "coolie labor." For a while, too, "Japan and China, as well as Japanese America and Chinese America, were one in exotica." During the Second
World War, when thousands of American citizens of Japanese ancestry were interned in camps in denial of their constitutional rights,
a distinction was at last made: "Chinese-Americans became Americans' pets, were kept and groomed in kennels, while Japanese-
Americans were the mad dogs who had to be locked up in pounds."

That opinion may seem a brutal way of confronting what can indeed be brutal in American life, but the stories, the excerpts from
novels and plays, and the autobiographical essays in this book have

quite another tone—not the dreaded passive attitude but a wry, thoughtful detachment, even in the face of hardship and misery. One of the most touching of the lot is the work of the Filipino-Amerian poet and short-story writer Carlos Bulosan, who died in 1956, at the age of forty-one. For years, in California and elsewhere, he was a migrant fruit picker, riding freight trains between jobs. Eventually he became a labor leader, but, worn down by many years of bad food, unsanitary living conditions, and lack of medical care, he succumbed to tuberculosis just as, after several books of his had been published, he was becoming a political and literary spokesman for his people. "I tried hard to remain aloof from the destruction and decay around me," he wrote in *America Is in the Heart*. He did not always succeed. Despair and a desire for vengeance sometimes overcame him. But his descriptions of the farm workers in California, of the subtle differences among his own people, the Chinese, and the Koreans, are sensitively rendered. He summons up humor when he happens upon adversity, and he resists self-pity. He wishes to evoke the world he has seen, not to deliver polemics. The Japanese-American novelist John Okada, who also died young (in 1971, at the age of forty-seven), likewise manages placidity under difficult circumstances; in his *No-No Boy*, part of which appears in this anthology, a youth, Ichiro, is trying to understand the behavior of his strange, remote mother, who dreams of a triumphant return to Japan, and of his father, good-humored, tolerant, willing to come to terms at any cost with the demands made by America on its outsiders. To the mother, Japan is a beautiful, strong, proud country; its people are noble, refined, honorable. She has ignored Pearl Harbor, the imperialism that prompted it, and the postwar industrial resurgence of capitalist Japan. In her Japan, people are more concerned with how they behave toward one another and with the state of grace they may one day obtain for themselves through a life of devotion to others. The real Japan arrives in a letter from her sister, and her husband tries to impress the facts it contains upon his wife, but she moves even deeper into fantasy, and he pulls back, gently begins to help her maintain her illusions. The son becomes enraged at his father, at his mother, at having to live a life quite different from the one his parents, in their separate ways, have contended with.

The younger writers who appear in this book are more interested in the relationships between their own experiences and the experiences of other Americans. The Chinese-American novelist Jeffery Paul Chan, thirty-two years old, offers a tense, unsettling story, "The Chinese in Haifa," that tells us how "integrated" Chinese-Americans can be when they become part of America's suburban professional class, with its drinking, its pot, its nicely furnished homes, its divorce rate, and its mixed feelings about having children. There are brilliant exchanges between a recently divorced Chinese-American schoolteacher and his Jewish neighbors, one of whom observes that since "there are Jews in China, there must be Chinese in Haifa." The dialogue between the Chinese-American and his neighbors is sharp, ironic, painfully revealing. None of these people is hungry or jobless, and yet there is so much suspicion, so much prickly self-consciousness. An outsider, aware of the raw nerves and the vibrant perceptions of these Chinese-Americans (and, for that matter, of their Jewish neighbors), might wish he could enter the scene, offer comfort, reassurance, affection, and suggest that the past be forgotten so that we all can join in a common effort to make do on this increasingly endangered planet. But the past does not yield so easily to the demands and the realities of the present. The past, with all its class tensions, racial animosities, and ethnic antagonisms, remains part of the present, as this book poignantly reminds us.

New Yorker, June 2, 1975

Children and Literature

Lost Generation

For years Ned O'Gorman, a white man, a poet, an essayist, has been working with Harlem's young black children in a storefront nursery and children's library he founded. He has already written two books about the nursery: *The Wilderness and the Laurel Tree* and *The Storefront*. This latest book, *The Children Are Dying*, with its grim, admonitory title, is not meant to describe the further educational observations of an especially dedicated and honorable man. He is at this point in his life desperate, sad, enraged. He believes that isolated efforts such as his mean little in a world he comes close to writing off as a living hell, populated by an American *lumpenproletariat*:

> The children who come to me are children who exist in a colonial "outpost" of the American empire. I have been eleven years in Harlem, *eleven full years*: I have watched a place on this earth decay while the nation in which that place exists grows in power and wealth. It is as if Harlem, like Biafra or the gutters of Calcutta, had become a dispensable part of the fabric of national life. Nothing has happened in eleven years to make one jot of difference in the lives of the children conceived during that time or in the lives of the children who came to my nursery since 1966.

At another moment he is even more drastic and unqualified: "The wreckage in Harlem is almost total, and the possibility for change now, as I write, is almost nil. I think that the generation I teach in my little school is lost, and I think their children will be lost, too."

The beginning of O'Gorman's book is less gloomy. He sounds like the James Agee who wrote the scripts for *The Quiet One* and *In the Street*, earlier views by a white poet of Harlem. A thirteen-year-old black boy, already a liar, a would-be rapist, and God knows what else, prompts in the author rage but also words like these: "But I

187

thought, too, of his beauty, of his childhood and of those years that had come to him since birth with all the human plagues. I wondered what he was like when he was a year old, when he lay in someone's arms, watching the light and dark hover over him, bringing the seasons and music but bringing, too, the attendant swells and hammerings of death. . . ."

Such soaring, touching words soon yield to plain autobiographical detail, followed by brief narrative accounts of young lives in the process of rapid, fatal deterioration. The author tells us that he does not live in Harlem, that he can come and go as he pleases; he was born lucky and has "lived always in the midst of beauty." He also tells us that he knows that he will stir many to anger and scorn: yet another white man, some may say, peddling his noblesse oblige, his clever generalizations, and his self-dramatizing stories, meant to alarm but in a curious way reassure liberals—because bad as things are, and modest as the author appears, surely he is living proof that one decent, kind-hearted soul can make a difference, even in Harlem. Moreover, in the book's early pages the author may seem a familiar young existentialist, a source of inspiration to those troubled bourgeois souls in the throes of an "identity crisis":

> I came to Harlem because I simply had to decide what to do with my life. The task I was ready for was teaching in a college, but I did not want to traipse about forever clutching English literature anthologies in my arms. I did not want to rot away in academia, and the two years I spent in it were sure signs that if I did teach, I would rot. Harlem drew me.

No doubt some blacks will be offended by such vulnerable self-description and even more put off by the evidence of psychological abuse and degradation so relentlessly presented in this book. The author has no interest in protecting himself. His work is dangerous; on upper Madison Avenue he daily has to face down threats in a neighborhood where knives or guns are used all the time. This book will earn him additional enemies. He attacks those who "romanticize Harlem, a task some black intellectuals have taken on as their special mission." He also attacks a "cruel power elite" that (in the case of New York) he does not flinch from spelling out: "Catholic, Jewish, Black, Protestant, Religious, Judicial, Educational." Like many truly religious people, he abhors the pretensions of priests and ministers who, calling upon the name of God constantly, hold hands with the prevailing powers. Harlem is full of people claiming to be God-possessed yet willing to turn their backs on their down-and-out neighbors.

Ned O'Gorman's "problem," apparently incurable, is that he can't act in that way. He detests what he calls "abstract calm": that of intellectuals, all too ready to mull, sift, sort—and have it both ways by advocating political changes while living high on the hog; and that of various bureaucrats, church authorities, and school officials who offer pieties and banalities by the bushel to a people dazed and broken. He wants for the spiritual life of Harlem's children what he calls "the fury and the passion of revolution."

The author is not without his own fury, which he tries hard to control as he tells us of suffering. Child after child appears in this book as wounded, in deep pain, ready to give up emotionally and spiritually. After a while, the reader wants to say *basta*—enough of all this. And no doubt many of us will resort to the old rationalizations, the pain-saving psychological deceptions we have learned to use. We may remind ourselves that there is equal or worse suffering elsewhere in the world. Surely one could find hurt, betrayed children in other neighborhoods (white and better off), if one was of a mind to do so. Surely one must recognize that some racial progress has been made in recent years. Meanwhile, nations spend billions so they can blow up the planet, whereas Harlem's thousands of children waste away daily and the pleas of Ned O'Gorman go unattended. Those who talk of complexity, the long haul of history, and comparative economic or social analysis are dealt with as harshly in this book as are O'Gorman's liberal friends, from whom he has come to expect much sympathy but no action.

Sometimes the author comes close, maybe closer than he really intends, to saying that Harlem is hopelessly mired in "a culture of poverty":

> You see, I think the cycle of poverty becomes almost a physical occurrence in the oppressed people. It establishes in the blood a weakness and a tendency to capitulate, just as in some families, mine for one, liquor lurks in the shadows to grab up the best of our minds and destroy them.

He hastens to add that he is not embracing a "genetic weakness" but rather "a psychic-imaginative one." But a few pages later he returns to the same theme, however cautiously: "I tread carefully here because I must ask if the children of the oppressed—black, poor white, North African, Indian—generation after generation do not inherit a *faiblesse* toward failure, toward despair, toward annihilation."

Do they "inherit" such a weakness—a fatal tendency "toward" the destiny the author mentions? In fact, the blacks of Harlem are predominantly recent comers North who inherited the workings of centuries of painful experience: abrupt, enforced removal from one continent; an awful passage to another; generations of slavery, in which explicit, socially acknowledged family life was legally forbidden, and in which children were often treated as chattel; additional generations of vigorously enforced segregation, accompanied by extreme deprivation, exploitation, lynchings, and a virtual denial of education; and starting in the second decade of this century, the trek toward Detroit, Chicago, and New York, there to be the last hired, the first fired.

Of course such a chronicle is known to the author, known to those who (unlike him) peddle far more ambitious and categorical notions of how blacks are culturally, even biologically, "impaired"—an impairment, so it is claimed, "responsible" for the apathy and cynicism and bitterness and disintegration of spirit to be found in places such as Harlem. But those same places also suffer from unemployment rates of fifty percent for young people. They have received people systematically beaten, confined, despised—for a long time defined by the glorious Constitution of the United States as property.

In any case, the author is no theorist bent on making a point at all costs. He sometimes comments on the strength and vitality he has also seen in Harlem, especially among black women, the mothers and grandmothers of the children he correctly describes as in extreme danger of losing their mental and spiritual lives. And he does, here and there, give us specific instances of lives being saved—almost always the result of intelligent action: a child was taken from one unpromising or sordid situation and placed in an environment that gradually exerted a redemptive influence. The boy or girl in question, he believes, must have to begin with at least some valuable sides to his or her psychological "inheritance," qualities often lacking even in well-to-do white families where childhood psychiatric disorders may prove intractable to changed circumstances and concentrated psychiatric care. "I have seen the loveliest of children turn into animals," the author declares. And he adds: "I have seen beautiful, caring women turn into passive mothers who transmit to their children the malignant despair that had bent their own lives out of shape." The strength and dignity have been passed on—but still they are overwhelmed by what happens in the wretched streets of one of the world's richest cities.

A man working against such awful odds, and doing so voluntarily out of his persisting decency, will not forever keep cool and retain in the forefront of his mind the long-range political perspectives that others manage to summon up so handily. At times this gentle and giving man, this Harlem poet, becomes bitter and scornful. He turns on almost everyone in sight—even the families of the children he loves and works with, not to mention those of us who proclaim good intentions but are not able to live the life in Harlem he has chosen for himself. There are lapses of logic and overstatements: "Harlem, as is true of all the cities of the dispossessed, is a completely unpolitical, nonpoliticized community." *Completely?* "An open classroom always praises the genius of a child's imagination." *Always?* And there are passages that seem to suggest the writer's premature intimations of death, as if he has caught the disease he set out to conquer. He tells us he may well be in mortal danger himself, and he warns of the possibility of future collective violence. Reading these premonitions of large-scale disaster, we may remember the slogan "Burn, baby, burn," heard when the accumulated grudges of a people erupted into a death cry—aimless, futile jabs of vengeance. Soon enough an obituary appeared: there was a flurry of sympathy mixed with reprimands and disgust from those cross-town whites who were on television cameras or wrote newspaper or magazine columns.

Now and then this book turns guardedly encouraging. We are told what we might do if we were a different society—more democratic-socialist and less democratic-capitalist. Resources would move toward what amounts to an underdeveloped nation within a nation. Instead of celebrating the personal life of a singular man, Ned O'Gorman, and instead of feeling pleased when we learn from him that a boy here, a girl there, has been "snatched totally" from a decaying, foul tenement and an aching, dazed family, we would as a country take active notice. The author refers to a needed "corps of field-workers," who would work with entire families on their many problems. He talks of a "community of healing." He dreams of local "twenty-four hour clinics," with not only medical concerns but larger social and economic interests. But he recognizes that there is no likelihood that the kind of drastic political change he has in mind will take place in the foreseeable future. He falls back, instead, without much hope, on the prospect of a "whole new body of laws" that might take a given "oppressed child *away from* the forces of oppression."

He gives such laws impersonal, Orwellian names: what seems needed is the imposition of "the surrogate will" and "the monitoring intelligence." He acknowledges the dangers such concepts pose—"an alien notion to this democracy." He is being both ironic and furiously rash. No doubt he has heard of those in the past who felt the awful risks of dictatorship preferable to certain death from hunger for many people. In the late 1930s, my mother's uncle, a politically conservative American missionary in China, became "disturbed" one day after hearing the illustrious Madame Chiang Kai-shek speak about the threat that communism presented to the "tradition of liberty" in China. He is reported to have lost all sense of decorum, to have raised his voice and asked the beguiling Wellesley graduate: liberty for whom? An old and vexing issue for the morally upright who go out to save others, hopelessly damned, in the name of Christ or of simple human equity. There are occupational hazards to such endeavors, a price to pay emotionally. But from them, perhaps, one obtains an occasional flash of revelatory insight, no doubt quickly cut short, lest yet another person become a "revolutionary."

The last word in this book is given to Edna Driver, a pseudonym for a Harlem mother overwhelmed, driven to near madness, but eloquent and knowing in her capacity to look both inward and outward Harlem's dreary streets. "Life is a strange thing to live with," says this thirty-five-year-old woman who is haunted by mysteries, obsessed by complexities no less worthy of attention than those that are debated in universities: the terrible psychological importance of fate and circumstance; the enigma of God's, of nature's purposes, if any; the question of whether or not to struggle for bare, mute survival in the face of frightful daily burdens. Is this woman "hopeless," by virtue of a "culture of poverty," or does our country, by virtue of what it permits, still, in such places as Harlem, have a morally impoverished culture?

Ned O'Gorman, surveying Harlem, does not dwell upon its twentieth-century cultural renaissance—the achievements of Langston

Hughes, Zora Neale Hurston, Countee Cullen, or Claude McKay. Still, his point of view is not unlike McKay's, whose *Home to Harlem* gave us a vivid glimpse into a city's black "lower-life." McKay was a teller of sensual and erotic stories. Ned O'Gorman is a poet who has for the most part lost hope and is attending to the world he sees rather than the one he can conjure up with a pen put to paper. When he talks about the Harlem he works in every day, about the "fortresslike aloofness" of its buildings, he brings to mind Ralph Ellison's "Harlem Is Nowhere," written to plead for the harassed minds of a community whose "blues," whose fiercely assertive jazz, like Ned O'Gorman's book, become, finally, voices of resignation or torment that are heeded aesthetically by us fortunate outsiders—the only response possible, we tell ourselves, as we think about our own constraints and frustrations.

New York Review of Books, September 28, 1978

The Holocaust and
Today's Kids

Forty years ago, the murderous Nazis were well on their way to achieving what would later be known as "the Holocaust," a genocidal assault on European Jewry, as well as on other men, women, and children whose background, interests, views, or activities made them enemies of the German state of the early 1940s. Since the end of the Second World War, the entire world, in one way or another, has lived in the shadow of that unspeakable tragedy. No longer would Europe's cultural and scientific advances hold the promise they once did: signs of civilization's advancing possibilities. The Germany of the 1930s had no group that we might have called "culturally disadvantaged" or "culturally deprived." Nor did that Germany have illiteracy as a burden. The Gestapo and the concentration camps emerged in the nation of Goethe and Schiller, Beethoven and Brahms; in a nation whose people, in impressive numbers, had a thorough mastery of science, philosophy, art, psychology, and sociology. Moreover, in no time Hitler and his henchmen were quite able to count on the support of professors, doctors, lawyers, journalists, architects, and, I regret to say, many of my kind—psychiatrists and psychologists—who submitted with no protest to the dictates of those who ran the Third Reich.

We will, one hopes, never stop contemplating that set of events— the rapid accommodation of a once exquisitely civilized nation to a political regime whose explicit purposes, from the very start, were declared to be viciously hateful.

John Milton, the seventeenth-century poet, once told us that the power of truth would make men free. Yet there was no absence of truth in Weimar Germany. Freud's truths were available, as were Einstein's and Thomas Mann's. And in art, expressionists were much concerned with the nature of German social reality. In engineering, in the social sciences, and even in the contemplation of religious and moral issues, Germans excelled mightily. Still, the devilish fascist thugs took power quickly in January 1933 and consolidated their rule without great turmoil. Within five years, a nation went through an enormous transformation—a descent into hell; and nothing at home (or even, alas, abroad) seemed likely to change that state of affairs.

How are we to comprehend such a turn of events? One hastens to insist that such a question not only be turned into abstract speculation but also be grounded in real, human situations—parents informing their children, teachers doing likewise with their students. There is, in any case, no series of sociological or psychological abstractions that explains, definitively, the emergence of Nazi power, the hypnotic spell Hitler exerted over so many people, the murderous behavior his followers demonstrated openly by 1938.

In *retrospect*, we see everything: the trickery, the lies, the bluffs that, tragically, German politicians, church leaders and, ultimately, the political leaders of other countries failed to call. In *retrospect*, we know that the Hitler who became Germany's chancellor in January 1933 became a mass killer, conquered much of Europe, presided over the utter destruction of his own nation—and, all the while, commanded a fierce loyalty from thousands of followers.

As one goes through the newspapers of the 1930s, the magazines, the news documentaries made for the movie houses, and yes, the personal letters and diaries of all sorts of people—Jews and Gentiles, the rich and the poor, the educated and the less educated—one finds no such clear, collective awareness of what awaited the people of this planet: an unparalleled spectacle of our capacity for bestiality. Rather, even among the vulnerable Jews who lived under Hitler in the mid 1930s—or maybe *especially* among them, given their desperate situation—there never ceased to be hope.

In *Never To Forget: The Jews and the Holocaust*, an excellent historical account of Jewry's fate under Hitler (an account that was written for children and that draws heavily on recorded memories, firsthand observations, and fragments of letters, diaries, songs and poems), Milton Meltzer asks: "How could anyone have overlooked the signs [of the coming Holocaust]?" He hastens to answer his own question in this instructive way:

> With the advantage of hindsight, it is not hard to ask that question. But the Jews living through the experience could behave only on the basis of what they knew then. The German Jews,

the first in Europe to fall victim to Hitler, could reach no real
agreement on the nature and extent of the danger threatening
them. Nor could they agree on what to do about it. We must
realize that there was no historical precedent for the Holocaust.
It was a *new* event in world history; the mechanical mass-
murder system of an Auschwitz had never happened before.
Like any person anywhere, each Jew thought and acted on the
basis of his own level of understanding, his own degree of courage, his own moral judgment.

Those last two words, of course, challenge all of us: What capacity does each of us have for "moral judgment"? How might we react
in the face of political evil and madness such as that which came to
prevail in Germany during the 1930s? And that latter question, of
course, cuts both ways: How might we have acted had we been Jews,
or had we been so-called Aryan Germans? Meltzer does not shirk
asking such questions even as he conveys for his young readers the
enormous outrages, the bloodthirsty excesses of the Nazis—who, by
the late 1930s, were acting like craven animals of the lowest kind,
yet also like mischievous and canny human beings, able to play on
the inevitable mix of optimism and despair we all have as our psychological inheritance. Meltzer is at pains, in that regard, "to indicate how hard it is for anyone to resist a ruthless totalitarian power
which commands modern weapons and employs elaborate means to
crush opposition."

I have read a fair number of books written for young readers, and
among such books, Meltzer's is especially edifying. He has no interest in brushing the complex truth of his subject matter under this or
that ideological carpet. The Jews of central Europe had to face a
devil hitherto unknown to humankind: the modern, technologically
buttressed state as an instrument of wholesale terror and murder.
Under such circumstances, the resistance of even a handful becomes a major miracle.

Given the singularity and atrocity of the events, one appreciates
the challenge to any historian, any writer. Several storytellers, nevertheless, have aimed to convey to children what it was like—for, say,
boys and girls their age—to witness hell itself unfold. Similarly,
those who were actually there, Jews and non-Jews, have used autobiography as a means to reach youngsters today. Finally, some essay-

ists have aimed at prompting reflection in young people through narrative exposition, accompanied in some instances by questions meant to provoke moral self-scrutiny.

In *The Holocaust: A History of Courage and Resistance*, Bea Stadtler takes her youthful readers, step by step, through the rise of Hitler and the subsequent horrors visited upon the Jews. The narration is strong, lucid, compelling, and it is interrupted by powerful personal accounts—remembrances of men and women of what they saw, heard and not least, experienced. On the evening of November 9, 1938, for instance, the Nazis struck at Germany's Jewish people. Synagogues were destroyed; the Jewish sacred books were burned; thousands were arrested, hurt, and killed. It was called *Kristallnacht* (Night of the Broken Glass), because glass was smashed all night long, the glass of Jewish homes and businesses and places of worship.

Sentence after sentence confronts today's schoolchildren with one of the worst nightmares mankind has ever experienced. Then "things to think about" are presented, and surely to good effect. The "things" are a mix of statements and questions, as in these two examples:

> Many Jewish homes were robbed, looted, or destroyed; and many Jewish men were hauled to concentration camps during the night and morning of *Kristallnacht*. Do you think it was possible that the Nazis alone were responsible for such a terrible event?

> We have heard of people in large apartment buildings watching a person being robbed and murdered in the courtyard and not even calling the police for help. Is this any different from the attitude of Germans who watched their Jewish neighbors being taken away, or beaten, or robbed, without saying a word? Would you be able to sleep through a *"Kristallnacht"*?

Given what takes place in all too many of our schools, one can only be grateful for such a line of moral inquiry. How many of our schoolchildren, one wonders, have been asked to read about and ponder the significance of the Holocaust—or for that matter, of some recent events in our own nation's history: the Civil Rights struggle of the 1960s, for instance? How many of *us*, young or old, know how to answer the question of responsibility? We realize that the Nazis somehow had to enlist the active complicity or passive acquiescence of millions of fellow citizens to accomplish the Holocaust. Might we have been among those citizens, had we been Germans? Might we even have been one of the many neighbors who watched silently as Jews were threatened, attacked, and forcibly removed to camps? We know that in any society a criminal assault upon one is, in effect, a criminal assault upon all; and we know that the person who does nothing to interfere with such a collapse of the legal and moral structure of a democratic nation is himself or herself made a criminal. Still, each of us wonders how we might have acted, had we been living, say, in Berlin during the 1930s, as neighbors to Jewish people. The Nazis were quite shrewd on that score, understanding our self-protective and self-enhancing instincts. They comprehended brilliantly the workings of fear and greed and guilt: how we lose self-respect as we clutch at what little privileges we have and then turn on those less fortunate, on victims of all sorts, with scorn, because they remind us of our flawed and corrupted morality.

One wants with all one's heart and soul to say, confidently: "No, I'd not sleep a wink though *Kristallnacht*. Never! Nor would I merely stay awake. I'd run into the streets, try to save my neighbors, help them in any way possible. If necessary, I'd fight the Nazis to the death." I have, in fact, asked children I know about such hypothetical situations: What would you do if you saw a Klan mob attacking a black child, say, or a grownup? How would you sleep if you heard the police on a rampage outside against people you believed to be innocent—a family, perhaps, condemned by virtue of their background, their skin color, their accent, their religious avowals? Almost invariably, the children respond as I would hope they might: they declare their (hypothetical) willingness to fight directly and hard in the cause of justice. I put that word in parentheses not out of cynicism but rather out of a sad doubt about all of us, for each and every one of us must travel a considerable distance between moral reasoning and the achievement of a moral life that is grounded in particular actions.

To be sure, it helps us, helps our schoolchildren, to read these historical accounts and to reflect upon questions that connect the lives, for example, of Jewish boys and girls living under the Nazis in the 1930s and 1940s to our own lives as we attempt to live them in America in the 1980s. The brief but stirring book *Joseph and Me: In The Days of the Holocaust* is explicitly written for such purposes. The author, Judy Hoffman, lived through the terrible darkness of the Nazi reign—in Germany and in Holland. She understands only too well what it means to be separated from one's parents, to live in daily terror, to be snatched and sent to a concentration camp. She tells her story in such a modest, straightforward, and touching way that one can only sit back and wonder what significance this life can possibly have, given that it is a tale of tragedy but also, ironically, a tale of good luck, when compared to the sagas of millions of others who never lived to tell of their experiences. At the end, in anguish and sorrow, the author addresses the young reader this way:

> There is more, but you don't have to know the rest. What is important is that I have shared my story. It was not an easy story to tell. As I told it, many sad thoughts came back to me, and I felt much of my pain again. But pain is a small price to pay when I think that perhaps you will see to it that such a horrible thing as the Holocaust never happens again. No one believed it could happen, but it did. Please, *please* try with all your might to see that it doesn't happen again. Please!

The book is accompanied by a pamphlet, A *Guide for Teachers*, which offers questions and topics for written and oral discussion. Readers are asked: "What would it take to survive in these [concentration] camps?" And: "How can the people of the world prevent future Holocausts?" I have no doubt that such questions prompt—at least in some sensitive youths—all sorts of honorable responses. Yet surely, we all must wonder, in considerable humility, what we would do *if*—and what we can truly do, *now*, about this or that political and human tragedy. And so wondering, we may join hands, maybe, with a young black child, whom I met in Mississippi in 1965, and heard speak in this fashion about her experience:

> I have a cousin, and she had to go by a mob, and they were standing in front of the school, and they told her they'd kill her, and she was scared to death, and she wanted to run away, but she knew if she did, they'd catch her, and when she came over to see me, she asked me if I wouldn't just take her place, and I said I'd do it, I'd be scared, but I'd try, and she said I can't, and I knew I couldn't because she's she and I'm me; and she said if she was me, she'd say what I said, she'd volunteer, but because she's she, she knows she wouldn't volunteer, not if she was me!

Then, she said what the minister said, that no one can be someone else; God makes each of us different, and there's only so
much *we* can do, and *we* can know, and no one can take our
place, because it's *us* we are, and someone else is walking down
a different road, and there are as many roads as people.

Such explorations into the nature of selfhood are the task of philosophers, teachers, doctors and, of course, all of us, including children. How will we ever know our moral worth—until we are tested
by this life's events? Yes, we must indeed pose questions to ourselves
constantly, ask ourselves what we believe, what we hold dear, how
we would respond under any number of circumstances. But the
question for teachers, always, is one of method: how to prompt such
inquiry in a manner that truly engages a child's imagination, intelligence, and thoughtfulness. I have no easy answers to such a question—especially when it is asked in connection with the Holocaust
as a subject for schoolchildren to contemplate. All I can do is recall
how Anne Frank's moving personal story stuck with me for months
and longer; how a recent story by Jana Oberski, *Childhood*, also
pulled at me, stayed with me; how the autobiographical account of
what it meant to grow up as a sensitive Aryan in Nazi Germany,
Howl Like the Wolves by Max Von der Grün, kept reminding me
that Hitler betrayed thousands and thousands of Germans whose affirmed Christianity was, for *der Führer* and his Gestapo cohorts, the
worst possible sign; how Ilse Koehn's *Mischling, Second Degree*,
which describes what a "mixed" child (part Jewish, part Gentile) endured under the Nazis, kept stirring memories in me of people,
places, incidents; and very important, how a brilliant novel by James
Forman, *Horses of Anger*, managed to evoke, better than anything
I've read, what happened to young people during the Nazi period.

Not that a novel such as *Horses of Anger* gives the reader any specific categorical answers. It is a story about four of the Hitler Youth
and how they respond to a dictator's leadership and the horrible consequences this had for Germany. The Holocaust is not specifically
explored for the reader who goes through Forman's story. Yet the
author works hard to illuminate a world black with evil; he tries,
really, to push us, in mind and heart, closer to the German situation
of a half-century ago—in the hope, surely, that we will thereby be

able to gain some sense of what *we* are, what *we* might be, what we can only beg God that *we* never become. Whether or not we live a decent life depends upon what our moral imagination makes of us. As that black child told some of us nearly twenty years ago, it is all too easy to *say* what one ought do, what one would do, or even to know, confidently, what one should or should not do; it is quite something else to *learn*, in the course of a given life, what chance and circumstance, fate and luck (good or bad) have encouraged or enabled us to do, and discouraged or prevented us from doing. We ought, forever, all of us, to be haunted by the Holocaust. Without question, its lessons ought be taught, with factual recitations and thorough, intelligent discussions. Toward this end, the good novel is an invaluable moral resource. Through it, the texture of experience can be rendered so truly and forcefully that we are, for a while, transported into quite another world and thereby challenged by its messy (but quite realistic and terribly scary) ethical choices.

Forman has a Nazi youth emerge as morally tortured, confused and, in the end, aghast at where (and with whom) he's found himself—even as Jewish children have wondered, understandably, what kind of meaning or purpose this life can possibly have, given this century's history. To evoke moral conflict convincingly when it is present in the belly of the beast, so to speak, is, needless to say, no easy job—and yet, one is strangely grateful for the effort. Why? For reasons known to those who formulated the explicit questions in the books mentioned earlier. Hitler knew that he not only had to win a political office but that he had to convert the people of a nation. In due time, it came down to "the neighbors" of Germany's Jews; and it comes down to those "neighbors" for us, too. Will "they" help us in one or another clutch? And most important, since all of us are "neighbors" to others, what will we do when tested by fate collaring us and forcing us to choose?

Those who write for children about the Holocaust have embarked upon a bold, often fierce effort at moral analysis. Their point, again and again, is this: you who read must have the following ultimate question in mind: How could "they" have done what "they" did? I fear Forman and others give us the answer in their moral fables: once the devil obtains power, he bewitches many (oh, so many!) he approaches, exposing a vulnerability none of us can presume to be absent in ourselves. One can, then, pray not only for the strength to resist one or another devil but for the luck to be ineligible (as a matter of fate) for his beckon. One can, too, keep reading about others who stood up to the devil, who lost faith in him after being bewitched, who died innocently in the wake of his wretched visitation. One can pray and pray, and read and read, and as that black child implied, hold one's breath in hushed and worried awe.

Learning, November 1983

Children's Stories
The Link to a Past

I n November of 1960, amid the terrible strife of school desegregation in New Orleans, I found myself talking with a black child, six years of age—a pioneer of her race, and every day coming close to being a martyr, because she had to face mobs and threats of violence, all to enter a school boycotted by whites. I worried about her. I wondered how long she could endure the constant harassment; the severe threats, repeated daily; and not least, the spectacle of a crowd of mean-spirited people denouncing not only her but her people in the vilest of terms. But she proved strong, astonishingly so; and she proved resourceful. Her parents, her kinfolk, her neighbors, her teachers, her friends, all would at one time or another wonder about her. How did this child, the daughter of former sharecroppers, manage to do so well, over the long weeks and months of a particular social and racial crisis? It would take me some time—weeks turned to months, then years—before I would begin to sense a few answers to that question. Yet I now realize that the young lady, at six and seven, was more anxious to help me than I was able to realize at the time.

She told me stories at the age of six. And when she was able to read fairly well, at eight or so, she read me stories given her by a black minister friend of the family's. They were stories of black rural people, Mississippi sharecroppers, stories handed down through the generations and carried ultimately from the Delta (Greenwood) to the eastern, industrial section of a cosmopolitan Southern city. They were stories of canniness and grit, of cleverness used against an adversary powerful and unpredictable. They were stories of victories and defeats, of miscegenation and lynching and racial hate and frustrated populism, and, always, of a Christianity that would not die and that is, I believe, considerably misunderstood by both Marxists and those psychiatrists who place too much stock in Freud's *The Future of an Illusion*.

I recall one of those stories—an account of a near lynching in the

1920s. The child had no specific dates, but she knew it was in her grandfather's time and after the First World War. He'd come home from the army, and a white man was sure he had a rifle he should have left behind in some military camp. Her grandfather was an "uppity nigger." So the child emphasized to me—as she explained what that expression meant and what happened to the man who was the occasion for such usage of the language: "My momma's daddy was tall, and it made the white ones jittery. He was light, as the colored people go, and *that* made the white ones even more jittery. And now he'd been out of the South and in the army—no telling what he'd come home and do!"

That was as far as the girl could go for a start. She paused and seemed a bit lost. She had an Oreo. She washed its crumbs down with a Coke. Her listener, once more, started worrying about her sugar intake, her teeth, her general nutritional intake. She smiled, seemed withdrawn. Was she "anxious"? Was she then, on a Sunday, anticipating tomorrow's street bedlam? There is a "story" in *that*, too: the cultivated psychological "awareness" that can't let anything or anyone just *be*, and what such a frame of mind does to others— say, a girl of six trying to be a narrator. In any event, Ruby Bridges of New Orleans, Louisiana, resumed her account after a few moments: "My grand-daddy had a bad habit. He didn't move off the sidewalk and onto the road—the dirt road, it was—when a white one came along. They'd been telling him to do that before he went into the army, all the Negroes who knew him. When he came back, they told him again, only they were really worried. And you know why? [No pause for anyone's answer.] Because they'd heard what the white ones were saying."

Then she paused, shrewdly. Her guest had all sorts of guesses as to what those "white ones" might have been saying. However, her guest was being given a calculated rest: end of chapter; settle yourself and turn the page, please. Another Oreo, another sip of that bad, bad sugar-saturated, dark, fizzy drink, and a resumption: "The white ones said there was one of them who was protecting my grand-daddy, and he was the most important person, the bossman of all the bossmans. He was a good man. But there was a bad man, and he came into town in a truck and he had a gun, and he said he was going to 'get' my grand-daddy, no matter what."

She stopped, looked me right in the eye, made sure she'd got out of me exactly the response she'd hoped for; and when she was sure that she had, indeed, obtained my complete interest—to the point of rather elaborate, lurid fantasies—she continued her story, now briskly: "He shot my grand-daddy. He hit him, but it wasn't a bad hit. He drove off. My grand-daddy fell on the sidewalk. The white ones stood there, and the colored came and they were going to drag him to the road and put him on a wagon, but he was wide awake, and he said they mustn't. They had to come over and talk with him, and when they did, he said they should never stand aside for *anyone* on that sidewalk, ever more; and the white ones heard him, and a couple of them said amen. And my grand-daddy became the one who went and talked to all the bossmans, from that day on."

The end—she indicated by a knowing look. She was her grand-father's granddaughter, she told me, through another look. Did I want an Oreo? Had I ever been to Greenwood, Mississippi? How old was I? Those were questions meant to tell me that she was, indeed, through with her story—and so now *I* could eat, rather than sit transfixed, listening, watching her replenish her narrating body with food and drink; and tell me, as well, and rather tactfully, that I probably didn't know the Delta all that well, and in any case, couldn't (given my age) have possibly known the Delta her grand-daddy lived in and tried to come to terms with, as best he could. As for her, she was following suit, and she was also letting a rather inquisitive (and terribly naive and all too self-assured) doctor know that if he would only stop asking her his constant questions about how her appetite was holding up and how she was sleeping and what she was *feeling*—well, then, she would do what any child, in the course of time, would do: tell him something, perhaps, through one or another kind of story.

Later on, Ruby would read stories as well as relate ones she'd been told. We've heard, many of us, of the oral tradition among certain "primitive" or outlying people; and it is true, among rural folk, or urban people newly arrived in the city, that there is a strong tradition of talking, of storytelling—and yes, of tall talk. But education is not necessarily a damper to that inclination. I know Indian children, Appalachian children, Eskimo children, Chicano children, and yes, white middle-class suburban children who have all sorts of stories to tell (family stories, tribal stories, personal experiences) and who *also* have learned in school to read and thereby gain possession of even *more* incidents to relate: quite often to others of their age, and without the knowledge or applause or intervention of their parents. The truth is that many of us (certainly many in my field of child psychiatry) don't give enough credit to the natural, normal, everyday development of narrative interest, narrative sense, narrative response, narrative competence in boys and girls of all backgrounds—and all that not out of any mental pathology, or to solve some emotional conflict or problem, but as part of the mind's developing capacity to comprehend what is taking place in the world. To be sure, stories heard or read, and told and told again, often help children to resolve in their minds worries or fears or anxieties—to come closer to a difficulty through a story of which that difficulty is the subject matter. But the mind is not only fueled by traumas or turmoil. We are a perceiving creature: we want to know, to understand; and not least, we are, distinctively, a talking creature. We are the ones (as little Ruby was letting me know back then in a city seized by near insurrection) whose nature it is to use words, and more words in the course of our lives—in good moments and bad, and be we rich or poor, black or white or brown or red or whatever.

Eventually I would begin to realize how important a clue I'd been given then, at the start of my fieldwork with children. Years later, in a small coastal Eskimo village of Alaska, I would hear this from a nine-year-old boy I'd come to know fairly well: "My father took me fishing, and while we stood there and waited for the fish to bite, he told me the story of our people. He said we were going to be put here to fish, and the spirits asked us where we'd like to be. We could have our choice. We chose here, near the ocean and the Kobuk river, because we'd *have* to fish. In the Lower Forty-eight, the teacher says, you fish when you want to fish. A long time ago our people thought of moving south. They got together and decided they'd leave here. They started out, but they got hungry, so they stopped and began fishing. They ate the fish. Then an Eskimo said: What if we walk and walk, and it gets warmer and warmer, and we decide to stop and make houses for ourselves, and we are happy, but we look for a place to fish, and there isn't a place? What will we do then? We'll stop being Eskimos then. We'll be like the white man. So, they never left; and here we are. I told the story to our teacher, and she said it's a 'nice story.' I told her it's what our people decided. She said it's a 'nice story.' I told my father what the teacher said. He said, 'She's a nice teacher.'"

So much for irony, wry humor, and the difficulties of Eskimo life, Eskimo education. But that Eskimo boy had noticed something important: a white teacher's lack of understanding, her failure to see that when she dismissed an earnestly told account of a people's collective experiences, apocryphal or not, as a "nice story" she was not doing justice to the intent of a people—to clarify their condition with a good deal of ingenuity, detachment, implied humor, resignation, pride, and, yes, regret. They are people who, after all, must pay dearly for that decision to stay and fish rather than flee to a less circumscribed environment. They haven't explained their fate in order to hear themselves say "nice" things—or be told by others that such is their way of storytelling. It is a matter of some importance for them that they know what they live by and, also, what they live for. Put differently, they are no less inclined than Gauguin was in the far warmer world of Tahiti (the same ocean, though!) to ask those unforgettable and universal questions: Where do we come from? What are we? Where are we going? Those are not only the questions of artists in exile, or of philosophers, or of this century's knowing analysands. Nor are they questions that necessarily bespeak an Oedipal complex or some other evidence of neurosis. They are the eminently reasonable questions that it is in our nature as human creatures to ask. Call them cognitive or existential questions; the point is not wordy, showy characterizations but a recognition on our part that each one of us is so equipped that we use language to ask, to try to contrive an explanation, an important one indeed—on a matter of life and death to us: the whys and wheres of our destiny.

It is to such a purpose that the story lends itself, in my experience, at a very early age and to all children in America, no matter their racial, social, cultural, or geographic situation. Children don't only crave information; they don't only seek facts. They have every intention of pulling together what they see and hear and wonder about and what others have seen, heard, wondered about, and passed on. They do so by putting words and ideas and speculations and incidents and worries and hearsay and sayings and jokes and admonitions into a series of stories, some ever so brief, others a bit longer, still others rather long indeed. They can be heard all over the country passing on received wisdom as Hopi tales, Eskimo legends, Southern country stories, ghetto jokes; and they can be heard passing on news of what happened in a suburban school, in a small town neighborhood, not just yesterday, but *there* and *then*—the amplified incident that has become the shared story of boys and girls on a yellow bus or at play in a backyard, a street, a pleasant grassy knoll. For some of those children there will be, soon enough, the encounter with other, more experienced and ambitious storytellers, ones who get called writers; but I doubt any child has ever heard a story read, or come to read one himself or herself, who hasn't already heard various unwritten stories and also told more than a few of them. Stories connect children to the past of their parents, their people; stories also enable children to connect themselves to something even more fundamental, their very essence as talking, listening, thinking creatures, who are anxious to fit together, as best they are able, whatever they learn about human experience. Soon enough they will begin to sense the limits of such knowledge. Soon enough they will appreciate the mysteries of the world—the stuff of another level of storytelling.

In *Children's Literature*, 1980

The Poetry of Childhood

They're hungry. / So hungry, they bark the pain. / They would eat me / Down to the last meat / On the last bone. / But they'd still run and growl / So, it's lucky the police have a chain on them / The mad white dogs!" Those were the statements of Ruby Bridges, a black girl of six in 1961; she faced viciously threatening segregationist mobs every day for months as she desegregated (all by herself) a totally boycotted elementary school in New Orleans. Many Americans may well remember her—escorted by federal marshals past the howling men and women. She knew they wanted her blood. Yet she smiled at her tormentors. She even told me she prayed for them. Why? Because her grandmother told her that "they were to be pitied—as Christ pitied his assailants." But Ruby was not one to bury her fears in the sands of nightly appeals to God. She was plain scared. She was also plain smart; she took careful, daily estimate of the dangerous world around her. She tried to understand what was happening and why. No student of history, no political scientist, and bless her, no psychologist or psychiatrist, she yet was able to come to a conclusion or two and assert her humanity by putting her sense of things into the instruments of a particular language: words.

I have taken some remarks made to me in February of 1961, in the course of a few minutes of innocent afternoon talk, and put marks between the various sentences that followed one another, just as they do above. Ruby intended no poem: yet she was calling upon a sustained image, and her brief, pungent sentences, punctuated by occasional moments of silence—pauses that possessed great power— were not easily forgotten by my wife or me. Nor by one of the federal marshals, a big, burly, somewhat morose fellow, who only gradually overcame some of his strenous white, Alabama prejudices enough to take an obvious, if reluctant fancy to "the kid," as he always called Ruby. One day the marshal, often ravenously hungry himself, had a comment for my wife and me: "She's right, the kid. They're crazy, those people on the street; and they're hungry—for her. They *would* eat her up alive if we weren't there to protect her! She's a smart one. She's like a poet; she says these things, and you don't forget them. I tell my wife what I've heard the kid say, and my wife asks how come our daughter doesn't talk like that, and she's nine, three years older. Maybe our daughter *does*, though; maybe we don't hear her."

I got to know his daughter, eventually, and a number of other ordinary white Southern children, who, like Ruby, had to go through the confusions of historical change—which had become for them everyday life. A white girl, a year older than Ruby, and a member of a family that lived on the same street as the federal marshal just mentioned, had this to tell me one day in 1962: "It's over, the storm. / The black clouds came / The white clouds came / Then, lightning and thunder, a bad rain / We almost drowned / Fire and noise and water / Now the sky is clear / The sun shines on both races / Like the Bible says / The rain falls on the just / The unjust, too—some of us white folks / I pray for all people / In this city, not God's: New Orleans."

She spoke those words in May of 1962, already a hot and humid day in that old, cosmopolitan port city. I've not pulled sentences out of context. I've not really left out much—a few stray words, a few oh's and ah's. She was telling my wife and me a story of sorts. She was remembering. She was trying to make sense of what she'd gone through. As she talked, she used her hands, her arms. She used her voice: ups and downs of excitement, sadness, fear, bewilderment, all those emotions my kind talks and talks about. But she had no interest in going from personal experience to the abstractions of the social sciences. She had been through a lot of difficult, perplexing moments, and she wanted to evoke them, to do justice to their continuing, collective significance in her life—and not only hers. She called upon abstractions all right, but they were the kind a novelist or a poet rather than a psychologist or psychiatrist would likely summon.

I am not anxious to call her a poet or to insist that she had a rare and beautiful mind, as yet unspoiled by the incursions of our wicked (adult) world. There is no point figuring out one more way to romanticize children, to make them the chaste repositories of all that is clean and uncluttered and clairvoyant in this otherwise earthly hell (save for a few grown-up poets!). In fact, the girl quoted immediately above was, often enough, a cranky, demanding child, all too willingly able to say mean and nasty things about—yes, the girl quoted at the start of this essay. By this time, one hopes, we have learned that one can be a child who is sensitive and thoughtful and unspoiled by various social ills but also be a child who is willful or self-centered or indifferent to the pain of others—or quick, even, to add some of one's own malice or mischief to the total supply around. So with the rest of us—including poets, whose marvelous perceptions, given strong and touching expression, do not preclude narrowness of vision, spite, arrogance (and on and on) when it comes to this life's everyday behavior.

A white girl saw her world changing, and out of her humanity, her mind's struggle to figure things out and put the result into words, came a few vivid, earnestly felt remarks. Because my wife has taught English composition (prose and poetry) to children, she had a particularly responsive way of listening to such statements made by the boys and girls we were getting to know. She heard them all, really heard them. I was too busy, alas, studying them—trying to estimate what was happening in their heads. As we'd play our tapes later, my wife would stop the machine, reverse it, listen again, and then say: "another poem!" I would smile: oh, the well-meaning efforts of school teachers to find a spoonful of honey somewhere, anywhere.

The years of our work would eventually humble me a little. Gradually I learned to stop categorizing "psychological defense mechanisms"—which all of us have, no matter who we are and where we live—and instead pay heed to the particular life I was privileged to see, day after day: children caught up in a moment of significant political crisis and terribly anxious, therefore, to comprehend what fate had put before their eyes and within hearing distance of their ears. I began to listen again and again to what we'd been collecting—those tapes that prove one a scientist! On them, not to mention in our daily life and work, we found ourselves in the cumulative presence of—well—the poetry of childhood, I'll try calling it. That is to say, we heard boys and girls, America's young, singing or crying—through words, images, and symbols, telling us what they had come to understand was happening around them.

Of course, there were not only intellectual, so-called cognitive issues at stake for these children. They were struggling with their moral perceptions as well. I am sick and tired of those theorists in psychology and psychiatry who have the moral life of children all figured out—on the basis, mind you, of their theories or some experiments they've done: questionnaires handed out or observations made in "human development" laboratories. It is curious, indeed, the way this century has treated children, I keep saying to myself as I try coming to terms with observations in South Africa and, in retrospect, with remarks such as those offered above. On the one hand, we insist that children are astonishingly knowing—all taken up with clever psychological surmises. But those same children, sensitive (it seems, or is claimed) to just about every emotional nuance imaginable, are declared moral idiots of sorts. They are described as incapable of being anything but compulsively obedient or fearfully obliging—with provocative interruptions of hedonism, selfishness, truculence, and so on: a collective evidence of the "developmental stage" into which they are locked, ever so firmly and conclusively, by (of course!) the various social scientists who have done their studies.

There certainly are limitations to this life, and surely we experience them in different ways at different times. But there are all sorts of exceptions, leeways, possibilities for each of us. We are not necessarily bound to be, at every moment, what some psychologist says we are or tend to be. We may well be a lot of things that one or another psychologist has not thought to inquire about—even to think possible. Ruby Bridges was, I suppose, what I rather drearily called her when I was first getting to know her—a poor child of black parents, "culturally deprived" and "culturally disadvantaged." (No poetry to those labels!) But she was also a caring, plucky child— "one of God's children," her doting grandmother called her; a girl who was driven as all of us human beings are to make moral sense of what takes place in this world and to do so through language—a habit, it seems, for our particular kind of creature. And so, she gave my wife and me (and herself) various words and images, her comprehension of what had happened and almost (God forbid!) did happen; her hope, too, of what might happen. "There are days / really sunny days / when I look at the sky / and God is there, I know. / I don't see him / I see the blue / I make him up / The wind might be his voice / A cloud, a small puffy one / All alone, his smile. / Thank God for you / I say to him / And please, I ask, remember my grandmother."

She did indeed "ask"; she wondered all the time: why do people act as they do to one another, and why do they act as they do to her as she goes to school, and when would all that grim and pitiable adult activity stop, and when would the dear Lord, whom she had been taught to love so very much, come and stop such behavior, make New Orleans better, make America better, bring us "the new heaven" and "the new earth" she heard mentioned, time and again, in church? Such a line of curiosity, of apprehensive concern, would become, through statement after statement, a kind of continuing moral inquiry rendered—it can be said, vividly enough, dramatically enough, persuasively and compellingly enough, metaphorically enough, pointedly and suggestively enough, to warrant (from us, the keepers of the keys!) the acknowledgement, I hope not reluctant or begrudging, of poetry. A black child's lyrical utterances, a white child's similar movement of the mind and heart: two girls growing up in New Orleans during a bad spell were finding through words and more words a touch of grace—for themselves, for the rest of us.

The Lion and the Unicorn, 1981

The Vision of the Humanities for the Young

The humanities ought to offer young people in school a means of fitting various pieces of knowledge into a larger view of things—to draw upon a Latin phrase: *sub specie aeternitatis*. The humanities have to do with perspective—the long haul of time; and they have to do also with values, with a sense of what ought to be as well as what is. The humanities begin with language—the distinctive attribute of human beings. We are the ones who become self-conscious, through words; who begin to ask questions as well as respond to reflexes; who gaze and wonder, then put into talk what crosses our minds. With language comes distance, a capacity to draw back and render an account of what is and has been taking place: history. Language is the means by which we keep trying for answers, not only to specific, factual matters but to the mysteries of this universe. The big questions, those asked by Gauguin and written on his famous Tahitian triptych, are the essence of what the humanities try to fathom for us, through poems and stories and plays and essays and factual narratives: where do we come from, and what are we, and where are we going? Such questions have to do with "the meaning of life," a phrase once summoned commonly, but these days all too sadly left unused. The humanities bring us closest to our essential nature, as the ones who speculate: what, if anything, is the meaning of our existence?

Needless to say, a teacher's point of view becomes a student's experience through the mediation of certain texts. Nor did those who wrote, say, the novels or poems many high school students read spend a lot of time constructing theories of education, or guides to accompany one or another collection of stories. A *Tale of Two Cities*, for example, is just that, a tale given us by a nineteenth-century story-teller. Each student who reads Dickens makes him his or her own companion—brings to Sydney Carton, let us say, a particular kind of sympathy, or indeed, lack thereof. Put differently, the humanities do not begin in a student's reading experience but in our lives—the moral preparation we bring to school, to our reading time. Still, there *is* the teacher who uses those books as a means of conversation, speculation, edification, exhortation, and occasionally, imprecation. What goes for the reader, of course, goes for the reader who is called a teacher—a lifetime's preparation for Mr. Dickens. But one need not surrender, yet again, to twentieth-century determinism. *Part* of that lifetime, an important part, takes place in the daily activity of a given classroom, where a teacher can hope for the same transcendence Sydney Carton sought, even as that teacher hopes to spring a few students, each year, from the moral as well as intellectual constraints of their lives.

I feel myself, already, a bit too abstract; and I am not sure that the humanities ought be under such a tether. The humanities have to do with the moral and spiritual concreteness of our everyday lives, as a number of American youths have reminded me in no uncertain terms. Here, for example, is a New Orleans high school student, lecturing a doctor on the significance of another doctor's life—the latter a character in *A Tale of Two Cities*:

> They gave us the book to read and said we had two weeks, and we'd better settle down and read fast because we had to finish, and if we didn't, they'd find out, because we'd be tested, and they'd use "spot identifications." "They" were the two of them: the regular (older) teacher and the younger one, helping out— and learning, I guess. They kept on saying Dickens was a tough writer, and we should pay close attention or we'd get lost in the novel, and we'd lose interest, and it'd be a real disaster for us.
>
> When I first picked up the novel, I was really annoyed: so big, so long! I had a lot else to do! What did they mean, by assigning that book for us to read, and in the spring! I was on the baseball team! I had a job! I had a lot of trouble at home: my dad was sick, and I was the one who took over some of his chores, and I was the one who tried to keep my younger brothers and sisters in line, while my mother was out working, or home cooking. Besides, who can go back into the past that far? They wrote different English back then. Even the teacher admitted that it's hard to understand a writer if you're alive a hundred or more years after he wrote his novel.
>
> I got into *A Tale of Two Cities* fairly fast! I was surprised! I

just picked it up, and I got interested. I now realize that the first sentences are famous, and a lot of people who haven't read the book know those lines: "It was the best of times, it was the worst of times. . . ." But when I first read them, I thought to myself: yes, that's how it is, right now, for me and my family! We're having trouble, but we're fighting this segregation, and we're beginning to win a few battles, so there's trouble, but there's hope, and it more than balances the trouble.

I got involved with that Sydney Carton, and it was he who carried me through the book. If it hadn't been for him, I never would have finished; I would have skimmed, maybe! Also, Dr. Manette interested me: all the suffering he experienced, and yet he managed to stay alive, and when the right moment came, he got better, or mostly better. I kept trying to figure out how he kept his sanity while in prison; and how he recovered his sanity, once his daughter took him away from Paris. He seems to have lost his sanity in between—while he stayed with the DeFarges. Do you have an explanation? If they'd sent him to a psychiatrist in Paris after he was released from jail, would it have helped? What good can a psychiatrist do when a person is being mistreated very badly and there's no way of stopping his punishment, even if it's cruel and unfair? The psychiatrist would have to *rescue* the person, not *treat* him!

Among other reasons, novelists obviously write to give others a glimpse of a particular vision. Here in the twentieth-century American South, Dickens had found a spiritual kinsman of sorts—a fellow human being whose mind was utterly responsive to A *Tale of Two Cities*, and more, to the moral struggles Dickens had deemed to be so important. In fact, one wonders whether the young man's English teacher was similarly responsive to Dickens. Are novels meant to be studied as if they are bodies of factuality, to be taken apart, limb by limb, and identified? I fear I went through—in college, never mind high school—an experience not unlike that described above: a course titled "Dostoevski and Tolstoy," in which we had endless multiple-choice tests, all meant to prove we had read the books, remembered the names of the characters, principal or minor, and, as well, the various deeds they accomplished. Irony is a favorite device of novelists; but life, as we all know, cannot only prompt art but follow it—when, for instance, one reads stories whose purpose is to help the reader (not to mention the writer) go beyond the narrowness and pettiness of everyday life but ends up once more constrained, now by a narrow and petty didactic method. The transcendence of both Sydney Carton and Dr. Manette in *A Tale of Two Cities* is not necessarily available to many of us, who face no revolution or imprisonment as our fate.

The youth quoted above was, however, not only a critic of a given classroom. He had taken pains to question the very nature of the humanities—their significance to us, their peculiar way of addressing the broadest, yet also deepest, aspects of our human experience. Of course, we teachers have a right to demand that our students do, indeed, pay heed—read the books we assign and remember their contents. But such activity is a prelude to reflection, and not only the kind that has to do with textual criticism. *A Tale of Two Cities*, one young reader dared notice, is a story brimful of mystery. Not so much the conventional kind—cloak-and-dagger intrigue—but rather the mystery we all know as we contemplate this life (even elementary school children, one hastens to add). Here, for example, is a white child who lived in New Orleans during the early 1960s and who (at nine) had never heard of Charles Dickens or Fyodor Dostoevski or Leo Tolstoy:

> I see that colored kid walking past the people, and they're all grown up, and they're telling her they're going to kill her, and I wonder why God put her here, to go through such trouble. In our church, the minister is always telling us that God was very unpopular with the important people because he had his own ideas of what was right and wrong, and He didn't agree with the big shots. On television, I heard that colored girl's daddy say he hoped and prayed the white people would think of Jesus when they saw his daughter trying to get into the school. So, I did think of Jesus! Then, I thought of the colored kid. Then I had this terrible thought that she'd die, like Jesus did, only we don't have crosses to nail people on, I don't think.
>
> I asked my mother what she thought would happen, and she said the colored kid is a pawn, and it's the fault of the Supreme Court. I asked my mother about Jesus, and she said Jesus felt sorry for everyone and that includes all the colored, but you

can't live your life like he did, Jesus, because he was God and we're just people—and besides, he was killed, and he didn't mean for everyone to go get killed, and if we all did, there'd be no one to worship him! Then, I asked my mother if God had a plan when he made some people one way and some people another way. I mean, some people are always having pain, or they're in trouble, and some people are always hurting other people, and the ones who do the hurting say they're Christians, and the ones who get hurt say they're Christians, too, and you get confused when you hear the minister talk, and your momma, and your daddy, and the teachers; and they all *are* confused, I guess, and even Jesus couldn't convince everyone so they didn't feel confused, and I guess all you can do is be glad if someone gets you to do some "good asking," that's what my grandma says: "always try to be true to the Lord, and always ask yourself questions, the way the Lord did." So, I try!

So do we all—try to figure out this world, its endless puzzles, paradoxes, and inconsistencies. The essence of the humanities has to do with moral inquiry, done, of course, with grace, dignity, and aesthetic distinction. When I was a boy, my mother took me to the Boston Museum of Fine Arts rather often. (She was an artist.) There, she would not only comment on certain pictures she found appealing, even compelling, but also ask me to let my mind wonder and wander both, prompted by the artists, and yes, by her as their interpreter, my teacher. Her favorite in the entire museum was the powerful triptych (1897) of Paul Gauguin, mentioned earlier—done in Tahiti as he struggled with suicidal despair. The canvas evokes the entire span of this life—infancy to old age. The canvas also evokes questions, not the least three supplied directly by the artist—one of those rare occasions when words are to be found in such a "place." Those three questions, rendered in French and mentioned earlier in this essay, were translated for me, again and again, by my mother until (finally!) I knew them in English by heart—and gladly repeat them here: Where do we come from? What are we? Where are we going? I also remember only too well this pointed observation of hers: "We're the ones on this earth who ask those questions!"

A mother's meditative side! A Boston woman's philosophical affinity with the existentialist tradition. A teacher's insistence that

Gauguin's genius be saluted intently, seriously, with continuing respect. And yes, a teacher's desire that Gauguin not be confined (by a
given pupil) to Tahiti, to the late nineteenth century, even to a particular profession or branch of the humanities. Even as he was
driven by his anguish—by his talent, as well—to ask the hardest
questions in the most enduring manner, a teacher was anxious to
pay homage not only to him but to her own humanity, and her student's, by embracing the responsibility that goes with attentive regard, with personal appreciation. Put differently, my mother was
doing as that New Orleans child (a mere fourth grader!) was wont to
do, as teachers of all levels aim to do; she was aiming to exert her
intelligence, her imagination, in the direction of a scrutiny directed
inward and outward both.

This life is full of questions—the general kind Gauguin posed and
the specific kind generated by the circumstances of one or another
life. The humanities are meant to help us *try*, as the child quoted
put it, to find useful, decent, appropriate, sensible answers. Not that
there ever will be complete, definite, thoroughly clear answers. The
humanities are not, at heart, preoccupied with factuality. One turns
to George Eliot not for data in its modern sense—the unequivocal information we all learn when we take arithmetic, or science courses, or
for that matter, spelling. "The task of the novelist," said Flannery
O'Connor, "is to deepen mystery"; and if ever there was both an implied definition of what the humanities are about and a rebuke to a
predominant contemporary sensibility, it is contained in that critical
observation—one of many shrewd, pointed, often caustic comments that marvelous and all too short-lived, twentieth-century storyteller from Milledgeville, Georgia, gave to the rest of us who continue to make our way toward the year 2000.

Miss O'Connor added that "mystery is a great embarrassment to
the modern mind," and with that aside she got to the very heart of
what ails so much of the teaching done today in the name of the
humanities. Rather more of us in the humanities than we care to
acknowledge are all too awed not by this world's mysteries but by
those who claim to have banished them rather thoroughly—the
confident technicians, the strutting social scientists, the men and
women who know how to punch machines, manipulate materials,
and come up with a yes, a no, a true, a false, a solution, definitive
and final. Our "embarrassment" bespeaks our loss of self-respect,

our shame, our sense of frustration, our feeling of incompetence: others manipulate things and prove themselves "practical," whereas we "merely" watch, listen, muse, and acknowledge the strangeness of things. Why, we even cultivate a many-sided, uncertain, perplexed posture with respect to the world's events!

It is, of course, absurd to expect those of us who teach the humanities (in schools, in colleges, wherever) to ignore the powerful thrust of a culture, a historical moment. The issue, surely, is not our "embarrassment" before the power of technology but what we do with that "embarrassment": ignore it, pretend it is of little import, make it of consuming import, pity ourselves on its account—or use it, wryly, to further our own purposes, as the ones who hope, always, to reflect upon the nature of things when confronted with this life's numerous moments of trial or error. One of the first humanists, Socrates, asked us to regard ourselves with exceeding care, not with a self-centered orgy of reductionist psychology, as too often is the case these days, but with the conviction that honest self-scrutiny can reveal much about *others*. In that tradition, O'Connor's "embarrassment" tells us not only about the predicament of the humanities but also about the situation of all this world's people. We are, so many of us, embarrassed by the seemingly endless evidence that we are finite, flawed, and all too clearly fumbling—no matter the computers at hand or the ponderous phrases committed (if I may call upon W. H. Auden's delicious use of that verb) in the name of sociology or psychiatry. ("Do not commit a social science!")

Moreover, embarrassment has many faces, as Dickens or Eliot, Dostoevski or Tolstoy, always knew: arrogance, preciosity, smugness, self-importance, pedantry, narrowness of mind, smallness of vision, coldness of heart. Have I, with that list, suggested a few traps faced by us who want to teach the humanities—the maneuvers we summon in fear and trembling because we dare not come out and say, with O'Connor's candor, how hard it can be to press upon others, press upon ourselves, the vexing, alarming, saddening exhilarations of our visionary writers and artists? I remember a hero of my youth, whom I was lucky to know, William Carlos Williams, putting the above this way: "On a good day I see enough to say enough to scare myself. If a reader tells me how *pleasing* a line I've written is, or a story, I always wonder whether I've failed. I want 'them' to be pleased—oh sure!—but I want to dig below the surface, and there's lots of pain in digging, or in becoming a digger, by sympathy, yourself."

I suppose I'd better not *recommend* pain in our classrooms—not in an age devoted to countless utopian dreams and repeated romances with prophylaxis of one kind or another. These days, we want not only penetrations to all of nature's secrets but protection from all of its hazards and hurdles. Not for us the willing assumption of vulnerability—as in the Christ mentioned by the two children I have brought into this essay, or as in our own nation's forebears, when they eagerly chose jeopardy in order to obtain a greater measure of freedom. For so many of us the point is security, certainty— the eradication of all ambiguity. No wonder we veer strongly to multiple-choice tests, to summaries and more summaries—of plots, of positions, of policies. "I haven't time to read *Middlemarch*," a not so stupid or ignorant Harvard undergraduate once let me know, without O'Connor's "embarrassment," and indeed, almost casually rather than worriedly or apologetically. Where did he learn such an "attitude"? Not, I presume, in the course of going through the "oedipal" stage of his "psychological development." Not in a fancy suburban home or in a ghetto, either. He learned it in a succession of classrooms. The time has come for all of us to stop hiding behind psychology or sociology; to stop throwing our hands up as we contemplate the erosion of literacy in consequence of television, or the "culture of narcissism," or God knows what else.

The black youth quoted above, whom I regarded as his own kind of Dickensian scholar, could have been quickly assigned to some convenient and faddish sociological ashpile—"culturally disadvantaged," say, or "culturally deprived." Instead, a diligent and thoroughly demanding (without "embarrassment!") teacher had grabbed him (literally, sometimes!), collared him (not literally!), and pressed upon him a novel. She read it aloud to him and his classmates. She pointed out what its pages meant. She virtually sang it, as well as singing its praises. She indicated her belief in it, and she persuaded a number of her students to give their assent—to her, to Charles Dickens, to O'Connor's "mystery and manners," which is what, in sum, our novelists, all of them, try to set down for us to contemplate. It is my hunch that the particular teacher in question and her students, too, require neither exhortation nor analysis from the rest of us—what to do or how to do it. They would like, to be sure, our company as delighted, convinced readers—sharers of a burden of work they have assumed and would gladly have us assume. In the absence of our commitment to their kind of journey, they would probably shrug their shoulders, as Sydney Carton sometimes did— not too hopeful about the prospects of all humanity but willing to stand up for its worth by standing up for themselves as readers and, thereby, unembarrassed dreamers.

In Benjamin Ladner, ed., *The Humanities in Precollegiate Education*, 1984

Politics, People, and Literature

Notes from Underground

Some questions are never old: How could the nation of Bach and Beethoven and Brahms, of Goethe and Schiller, of Thomas Mann and Rilke, of Gropius and Käthe Kollwitz turn to the Nazis? How could a gang of brutal thugs take over a modern nation, its citizens able to read and write, its industry advanced, its technology unsurpassed, its physicians and chemists and physicists and philosophers among the world's finest? Why did a people loyal to Luther's Protestantism and the Holy Catholic Church suddenly accept feverishly and uncritically the pagan and murderous leadership of men like Göring, Goebbels, and Himmler? These questions have been asked ever since the National Socialists (as they cleverly called themselves) began to demonstrate that murderers could assume the guise of Germany's institutionalized political authority and then lie and cheat and blackmail and kill on a scale only a "civilized" nation could sustain. This irony haunted Friedrich Percyval Reck-Malleczewen, whose *Diary of a Man in Despair*, now published by Macmillan in a translation by Paul Rubens, offers future generations a chance to learn what Western twentieth-century men were capable of doing. His descriptions of Nazi Germany are not those of the scholar bent on documentation or of the victim who has been tortured by sadists. Instead, we are offered a diarist's observations, set down with passion, outrage, and almost unbearable sadness—and set down (among other reasons) to show how easy it would have been for him to be a part of what he came to detest. Like confidence-men and cutthroat social climbers, the Nazis had an unerring eye for the weaknesses of those they intended to use and flatter and extoll, then intimidate and rob and kill.

In May of 1936, when this diary starts, Hitler and his men were not the objects of near-universal condemnation they eventually became. They had taken control with the support of powerful industrial, military, and even religious leaders. Outside Germany, the Nazis were considered important allies by many who believed themselves honorable human beings. Particularly among those Europeans whom the left would have called "conservative" or "monarchist" or "landed gentry" or "aristocrat," there was a tendency to look upon fascist governments as bulwarks against the plague of bolshevism. In the midthirties, few leftists would have recognized a man of Reck-Malleczewen's class and background as a likely anti-Nazi. He was, after all, an avowed royalist, born to a distinguished East Prussian family in 1884, who served in the German army in the First World War and finally settled on an estate in Bavaria. It was there that he saw, at first hand, the rise to power of a group of men who must have seemed laughable and harmless to many other well-educated and well-off Bavarians. In the twenties and thirties, while the implausible was becoming the all too real, Reck-Malleczewen immersed himself in literature, philosophy, and religious history. He traveled. He read. And he worried, not for himself but for the whole world, which he felt was caught up in a collective madness of long duration—a madness in which the Nazis were but one of the many kinds of crooks, liars, and cheats who had over the centuries betrayed both humanity and God.

The diary begins with "Oswald Spengler is dead." Reck-Malleczewen admired Spengler but knew his limitations as a philosopher and a man. We are told that Spengler had seen the rot in Western life but had been fatally compromised by the money that businessmen make available for sharp social critics who have a taste for good food, comfortable surroundings, and the applause and favors powerful hosts and elegant hostesses can offer. For Reck-Malleczewen, Spengler's *Decline of the West* was undercut in this fashion: "Halfway through his work, he let himself become dependent on the industrialists, and began to think less well. How else can one possibly reconcile that really magnificent piece of writing he did in 1922, in which he prophesied the coming of a new, Dostoevskian Christendom, with that technocracy-nonsense in his later work?"

Remarks like that are the heart of *Diary of a Man in Despair*, and they make up a conservative political and religious philosophy that I believe a lot of us today in America will find nearly incomprehensible. Nor is the cultivated Prussian ex-soldier and country gentleman any spiritual kin of the many citizens of the United States who call themselves conservatives. He rails against not only Hitler and the corrupt Western governments that were so easily fooled and pushed

about by him, but the ordinary, reasonably well-to-do burgher of the
West, who pays lip service to God and country yet devotes himself
to the appeasement of his own appetites. In this diary, the Germans
who shouted "*Sieg Heil!*" so long and loud are declared to be not
unlike the French, English, and Americans who in the clutch are
capable of stampeding down blind alleys. And it is interesting to
note that thirty years ago this strange, eccentric, lonely, brilliant
man saw the dangerous, even fatal traps that await us, Hitler or no
Hitler: "I tremble for each tree and each woods that disappears, for
each silent valley that is devastated, for each stream that these pirates
of industry, the real masters of our land, threaten." As Germany's
land is virtually smothered by its newly made bombers on parade,
the proud airplanes of a great world power, he comments, "Now,
still, overhead, these white savages steer their moronic automatons,
flying toward brutality and crime, drowning out the peaceful stillness of this spring day." And as National Socialism is steadily ascen-
dant, as Germans see their land covered with more highways, their
factories pour out more products, their Army and Navy and Air
Force become the envy of less "developed" nations, the author turns
more despairing (and maybe prophetic): "Gasoline, as the basis for
all motorized happiness, has contributed more to the inner decay
of mankind than alcohol." He does not see how "technology and
mechanization can escape being relegated to the dust heap, or at
least to the periphery of life." He denounces "superfluous bureaucrats" and "totally useless questionnaires." He warns against the
dangers of "rabbitlike reproduction." He says that "only the 'New
Adam,' a savage who by an accident has a white skin; who today uses
all this equipment with an unconcern bordering on impudence; to
whom it never occurs that one must replenish the thought-world
from which all this technology derives; only mass man can doubt its
destructibility."

For Reck-Malleczewen, Hitler was merely the latest one to assume leadership over mass man and to do it in the name of aggressive military preparedness and expansion—buttressed, as always, by
nationalist self-righteousness, an ethic of political pragmatism, and
the rhetoric of seemingly harmless pieties. Reck-Malleczewen insists
that "Hitlerism is only a symptom." For centuries, we had been
moving toward all that goes with Hitler (and Stalin and Mussolini
and Chamberlain and Daladier and Franco). Before those men were

even born, Bismarck and his equivalents elsewhere were setting
the stage for the wars this century still endures. Proud, greedy, self-
justifying leaders have betrayed one generation after another, leaving
us "the bankruptcy of the last five centuries."

It is hard to come to grips with the author of this astonishing,
compelling, and unnerving diary. Early in the thirties, he foresaw a
terrible Second World War. He was a moralist, a man of candor, a
cynic like the Greek philosophers who criticized the social customs
and beliefs of their day, and, finally, a German who easily could
have prospered under the Nazis but who chose to write against them
with devastating scorn and to show his hatred in small but direct gestures and remarks. Eventually, the Third Reich began to burn up—
a victim of not only English and American bombs but its own desperate craziness. Reck-Malleczewen was denounced, jailed, sent to
Dachau, and shot. His last entry, in 1944, shows him unafraid, devoutly Christian, contemptuous of the riffraff his people were still
calling their legal political leaders. It is noteworthy that he did not
take part in the plot to kill Hitler, that he never joined any resistance, never fled Germany in order to take up the struggle elsewhere. Perhaps he felt he had nowhere to go; Spengler was right, the
diary says: the West is doomed. Reck-Malleczewen calls English
culture worthless, no better than Germany's—"with the exception
of the old aristocracy." He indicates that his aristocracy includes yeoman farmers, artisans, and the dukes or princes they once looked up
to and in turn drew support from (or so he believed). To him, the
Nazi seizure of power is additional evidence that an orderly, rational, decently hierarchical world, a world dominated by his kind
of aristocrats, is no longer possible: "I am a conservative. In Germany, naturally, this is an almost extinct political species. I derive
from monarchical patterns of thinking, I was brought up as a monarchist, and the continued existence of the monarchy is one of the
foundation stones of my physical well-being."

Yet he attacks Germany's last Kaiser and the nineteenth-century
Prussian military leaders. His own sort of monarchy—valuable and
worth believing in—may never have existed. What is to be done
when a monarchy like eighteenth-century France or nineteenth-
century Germany becomes corrupt? What is to be done when Hitler
takes over everything? Like Edmund Burke, the author of this diary
has a passion for order and justice. In the tradition of Burke, his de-

spair over the world's evils—the vulgarities and banalities as well as the gross inequalities—turns into a volley of sarcasm and ridicule against phony and pretentious politicians, double-dealing industrialists, and crooks who masquerade as professional men and business leaders. Burke was a patriot, a ruthless enemy of crooks and tyrants, an upright and thoughtful legislator who wanted order and stability and continuity—not to keep the entrenched power of a few inviolable but to prevent one form of violence and corruption from being supplanted by another, world without end. The French Revolution did away with the Bastille and the royal court—only to demonstrate its own viciousness, its own arbitrary, murderous will. And the czar gave way to Stalin and his gigantic excesses. When is a government so bad and unjust and corrupt and tyrannical that revolution is justified? In 1789, Burke said no to the French Revolution. In our time, Reck-Malleczewen, despite his hatred for Hitler, never really suggests sabotage, organized resistance, or a revolution to end the Third Reich. The issue is not whether such activity was "realistic" or "practical" or even "possible." (Some Germans kept trying to thwart or even kill Hitler.) Reck-Malleczewen may have confined his political opposition to a diary because history seemed implacable, because he believed that he could not forestall an apocalypse so imminent.

This lonely diarist refers to his house as "a very isolated place more than six hundred years old, which has long been regarded as haunted." He mentions Knut Hamsun, the brooding, aloof, austere Norwegian novelist, who had no real knowledge of or taste for politics but did have a clear notion of the corruptions and duplicities in the liberal democracies Hitler attacked, one after another. Dostoevski is mentioned with admiration. And, no doubt about it, the "man in despair" who wrote this diary hated violence and cheapness and meanness. Like his house, he was rooted in a distant past; like Hamsun, he had an artist's sensitivity, which in a flash could spot hypocrisy; like Dostoevski (and his character who speaks so boldly and devastatingly in *Notes from the Underground*), he struggled to make sense of his religious mysticism, his political idealism, his deep and reverential love for the earth, for his nation's history and traditions, for the "soul" of his people—while hating what the Church and German politics had come to, what had happened to the land and water and air, and what his countrymen were doing. All *he* could do

was write down the ambiguities he felt with fierce intensity and dedication—and wait for the death he knew he would experience at the
hands of the Gestapo. His immediate objects of hate are gone, but
his mind had other enemies, and they are still with us. How Reck-
Malleczewen would disdain those American "conservatives" who
ally themselves with the oil companies that deface our shores, the
coal companies that desecrate our land with strip mines, and how he
would disdain the rhetoric of those who justify slander and murder
in the name of political slogans, however "egalitarian" their message. Still, though he knew exquisitely and unbearably what he was
against, he had very little idea of what he was for—and still less of
what he might work to achieve. So he simply sat back and put into
words his thoughts—as a member of a spiritual underground that
the highly industrialized, well-armed, agnostic West has little reason
to fear.

New Yorker, January 3, 1971

An American Prophet

As we march through history, our direction so much influenced by the past, our time and energy consumed by the demands of the present, there always seem to be, thank God, a few visionaries around; they seek the high land and try to tell us, after finding out for themselves, where we seem headed. Not that everyone who talks about the future of this or any other nation is worth listening to. Each century has produced its fair share of moral monsters, third-rate hucksters, or political confidence-men, all masquerading as far-sighted statesmen. Yet, men of wisdom and courage have also been around from the very beginning, though by no means have they had the clout to do much more than speak out or set down in words what in their judgment is going on, and just as important, what ought to be going on, come a better day. And maybe, through some dialectical twist that Hegel and Karl Marx alike could not possibly foresee (neither of them pretended to paint in the details of the huge canvas whose outline both men claimed knowledge of), there is something about a highly developed capitalist society that not only makes for material abundance but a surfeit of prophets, if not idiot-savants; certainly we in today's America have no shortage of social critics and self-appointed oracles; and book publishing being what it is, not to mention television with its talk shows, they have wide access to readers and listeners—us, the hungry and confused and, upon occasion, the thoroughly gullible. So, when a book like Michael Harrington's *Socialism* comes out one wonders not only about the intrinsic value of what has been written but its larger significance. A sign of the times, that such a man and his ideas seem to be reaching more and more people? An eccentric outburst, doomed to change, *really* change, no one and nothing? A brave effort, all right, but one rather quickly destined to be undercut by the apparently limitless capacity of this society to stop a second and savor things, acclaim to high heaven what has come along, then go on to the next moment's opportunities?

Harrington himself must wonder what possibilities might someday appear for America's Socialist Party, of which he now has become a leader, Norman Thomas's successor—if anyone, however
gifted and forceful, can quite become that. Michael Harrington may
even have a wry sense of detachment about his book: perhaps he
hopes it will persuade many who call themselves liberals or progressives, not to mention some who bandy around the word *radical* to
suit their own purposes (self-enhancement, self-righteous assault on
others, gratuitous and faddish posturing), that the time has come for
those who analyze this nation's economic and political life to do so
thoroughly and pointedly. For the fact is, as Harrington points out in
his book, that the word *socialism* has become an oddly ignored or
feared one in the United States; many shun it without even knowing
what it stands for, and many know in their bones rather than their
heads what it stands for. A mine owner I once talked with in eastern
Kentucky gave a good working definition: "It means I'll lose my
money and power, and so will the other stockholders, and instead
everything that comes out of this place will go into one big common
pool, and I'll be a nobody, just another citizen, I guess."

Unlike him, a number of people secretly think socialism is a fine
idea, a great thing to dream about—but let's be *practical*, they say,
which means reminding oneself that no one can get away with calling himself a socialist and hope to accomplish anything, hence the
need for evasive substitute words and the insistence on piecemeal
programs, undertaken with the silent and pious conviction that in
the end it will somehow come about, the redistribution of money
and power people like Harrington have dreamed of and fought for
and foretold as a future reality. On the other hand, many who call
themselves liberals sincerely struggle for social and political change
but just as sincerely shrink back from the implications of socialism,
even the democratic kind, which in this book is held to be the only
true kind. If only, they insist, a greater degree of control might be
exerted on the erring, self-satisfied corporations. If only the military
were curbed, the FBI (and now, the Supreme Court) rendered more
responsive to the spirit of Tom Paine rather than that of the merchants and landowners who also (for their own purposes) fought
against England in the eighteenth century. If only, to draw upon a
contemporary way of putting the matter, the populist tradition (the
better side of that tradition, one quickly adds) were to be revived, this

time successfully, so that the White House and Congress would fall under its spell.

Harrington would naturally welcome such developments; he is no ideologue, no arrogant and self-centered theoretician who scorns the immediate, the concrete, the less-than-perfect encounter with the present that those who work for (rather than dream and write about) a utopian future have to take for granted. He is active in a political party and active also as an ally of America's labor unions. Still, there is in him the historian and the philosopher, and maybe, too, the theologian—and in *Socialism* it is those sides he has drawn upon. The result is a powerful and convincing statement, broad in its command of facts, deep in its examination of various economic and political systems, and tempting in its analysis of our psychological capabilities, as they emerge, given favoring circumstances, in the larger world we refer to collectively as "the society"; and finally, it is a statement that can sometimes become unnerving to many of us— because of the implied questions that come across repeatedly in the author's narrative, though he is too kind and tactful to force them upon us. (Maybe he is also resigned in a way Kierkegaard as well as Karl Marx knew how to be: when the time comes for those questions to assert themselves persuasively, they will; any attempt to push them on people or, more grandly, to push up that time is at the least presumptuous.)

The questions have to do with fundamentals, of course, nothing less than the economic and moral basis of the nation's institutions: the profit motive, the nature of capitalism and its connection with imperialism—the old-fashioned kind but also the more sophisticated kind, wherein corporations rather than armies enter those foreign lands. By the same token, the questions are personal. What kind of children *can* we bring up, however enlightened and decent our schools, however knowing and helpful our child psychiatrists and educational psychologists, and on and on, if in the clutch every boy and girl eventually gets to learn that he or she either controls or is controlled, either works day in, day out for wages others set at their convenience or takes in profits as they accumulate, with no obligation to do anything in particular for anyone, including those whose work in the first place made the whole thing possible? Socialists answer that a transformation of capitalist society is necessary. They say that individualistic economic forces have to be brought under social control, and until that happens slaves working on plantations will give way to cannery workers or migrant farmers employed by agribusinesses; and unorganized men and women crowded into sweatshops for twelve hours a day and up will give way to a labor force strengthened by the power of unions, at work eight hours a day in bigger, less dangerous factories—but still, the basic nature of the society will persist: a relative handful owns a lot, whereas the large majority of people have a kind of "enough" that never even remotely approximates, either politically or economically, what those few on top and near the top claim as a right.

For Harrington, as for Karl Marx, whom he so very much admires, the point is not to shout and scream at the "bosses" and their ever-ready lackeys. There is a certain grandeur to Marxist historical reasoning, and it comes across strikingly, refreshingly perhaps, in these rancorous times, as the author writes about the history of socialism, which he does in great detail. Human history is seen as the outcome of never-ending struggles for power engaged in by various classes. The cause of these struggles is the "powers of production"—the issue of who gains command over all that man has learned to take from nature and build up into something valuable and productive. As that struggle goes on, social forces develop and become institutionalized, property rights become consolidated, class relationships get arranged and rearranged; and all of that (since Marx knew full well, despite what some critics say, that men do not live by bread alone) is sustained and given sanction by various political and ideological systems, some rather explicitly tied to the "powers and principalities" involved, some vaguer and more philosophical, perhaps in recognition of a changing and uncertain moment in history, when new "interests" are set to take over.

At such moments, definite discontinuities arise in particular societies; social and political structures reflecting a given stage in the relationship between classes become obsolete. A struggle ensues, and new structures appear. The struggles can be slow or dramatically brief, and again, can involve ideas and values as well as votes or arms. In fact the struggles, one is to believe, *are* history; they are what decisively move things along. "Man always makes his own history," Marx said—but he then insisted that man can do so at any particular moment only to a limited extent, that is, in keeping with the material realities then present.

Much of Harrington's book is taken up with a thoughtful and conscientious analysis of all that—how a number of socialists, especially Marx, have regarded the world, with its various and unequal
continents, nation-states, and within them, classes. There is no
doubt that Harrington has his own point of view, his own belief that
certain thinkers were right and others were wrong and sometimes
evil. The evil ones transformed Marxist thinking and potentially socialist political efforts into repressive political leviathans of the worst
kind, and that outcome clearly haunts the author. That is why he
constantly writes of *democratic* socialism. That is why he spends so
many pages trying to show that Marx was no cold, aloof, morally
neutral observer anxious to spin abstractions that proclaim a love for
humanity but also contain ample justification for quite another tack.
In particular, he wants us to know that Marx's use of the phrase "dictatorship of the proletariat" had a specific historical context: "The
problem is Marx did not mean dictatorship when he said dictatorship.
Even in his *Class Struggles in France* which was written during the
bitter months in early 1850, the term is used so as to be compatible,
even identified, with democracy. '*The constitutional republic,*' Marx
wrote of the peasants, 'is the dictatorship of their united exploiters;
the *social democratic* red republic is the dictatorship of their allies.
In each case, it is possible to have a republic, and in the latter instance, a social democratic republic, which is also a dictatorship."

Well, I don't know. I rather suspect that anyone, no matter how
decent and kind, has his moments of impatience and anger, which
in turn prompt some wish for the urgent if not the drastic confrontation that once and for all will change things for the better. In any
event, Harrington takes pains to emphasize the moral and activist
side of Marx, which better than any intellectual and logical pre-
cocity made for a kind of analysis rich in its capacity for irony and
ambiguity. If, as he puts it, the "talmudic reading" of Marx that
Lenin and others have made such a prominent part of the twentieth
century has done the man's ideas a gross injustice, several chapters
in this book at least set things straight for the record. But there is
more to this book than that. The author is not yet another sectarian
polemicist. He is at once a serious scholar, an impassioned social
critic, and a man right in the middle of a struggle now being waged
in America—between those who want to hold on to what is (and
what they have) and those who believe this nation's wealth and

power ought to be used and shared by its working people in a thoroughly different way than is now the case. In that sense he is a prophet, not unlike Isaiah in his attitude toward social injustice but, too, not unlike Jeremiah in his willingness to be guarded about human nature—"the stubbornness of the heart" that Old Testament writer refers to. At the end of *Socialism*, we are reminded (in a somewhat startling aside, since so much of the book is devoted to projecting a moderately contented socialist utopia) that "it may even be possible that mankind cannot bear too much happiness."

I suppose with such a remark Harrington weakens his argument— or perhaps reveals some of the spirit or background which years ago caused him to work alongside Dorothy Day in the Catholic Worker movement. He is unlike her in many respects; not for him the kind of strongly emotional and biblical "communitarianism" she and Peter Maurin have advocated, drawing on Christ's life and teachings, with boosts from Tolstoy and Gandhi. More intellectual, more drawn, I suppose it can be said, to the rational and analytic tradition lapsed Jews and Protestants built up in the nineteenth and twentieth centuries, he nevertheless is at home with some of those riddles theologians never stop considering, and not with any intent of "resolution." For him, socialism is over there, way up history's road—to be sought and fought for. Let others decide to stay put where they are or wander from place to place with little worry about tomorrow; Michael Harrington believes he knows what is fair and honorable for his fellow human beings, has spelled it out in more than one book, and no doubt every day of his life will make sure his considerable intelligence and energy go toward achieving not a New Jerusalem but a society so set up that more people than ever before live in reasonable security and dignity, live free of want or the threat of want.

For Better or for Worse

*I*n the seventeenth century, England went through a political crisis: the monarchy fell and then was restored, though it was never again to be quite so powerful because a rising middle class had secured a measure of freedom for itself. Two great political philosophers, Thomas Hobbes and John Locke, were at hand to comment upon the changes in a nation's assumptions about itself. Though the two did not agree about human nature, or what the social and political order should be, they shared certain values, and they could presume an audience of rational readers, willing to be educated. When Hobbes's *Leviathan* appeared (1651), it was read by the young Locke, and he had to contend with it as he set down his own ideas in essays like *Two Treatises on Government* (1690). In both these books we are asked to imagine a "state of nature," wherein man has not yet become a member of society and lives on his own. Hobbes saw this "natural man" as someone constantly trying to solidify his situation, often at the expense of everyone else, and spoke of the fear that induced men to resort to trickery, deceit, and cunning lest they be conned or killed. Hobbes was a thoughtful, learned, and gentle person, upset by the disorder and threat of chaos around him; he simply presented his "state of nature" as a means of analysis, a step in an argument, to show that men need to be free of their vulnerability, to be protected from their capacity to become almost infinitely exploited. Locke was more convinced of our inherent decency and rationality; in his version of the "state of nature," he emphasized the spirit of equality that obtained. Men basically respected one another, he said, though, like Hobbes, he felt that they were driven by the instinct of "self-preservation." For Hobbes, the fulfillment of that instinct would unleash havoc unless it could be restrained by a strong and universally sanctioned political authority. For Locke, the same instinct caused men to be considerate. Nevertheless, he made note of possible "inconveniences" in the "state of nature": lawbreakers might appear and might be punished without due process—hence the risk that a certain kind of aggressive self-righteousness would be mistaken for justice. To remedy those "inconveniences," which historically have become real and common, Locke advocated a social and political order respectful of each man's integrity, his right to express his ideas, to petition for redress of felt grievances, and to be granted at least a measure of privacy. Freedom means not only the right to do all this but a degree of protection from the officious, the overly expansive and self-important, who want to curb or deny completely the "unalienable rights" that were to become a part of the Declaration of Independence, which was written by men much influenced by Locke.

In the eighteenth century, the scene of political struggle shifted to the Continent, in particular to France, and there was an accompanying increase in speculation about the rights and responsibilities both of citizens and of those who govern them. The Bourbon dynasty would not yield. When the French Revolution came, over a century after England's "Glorious Revolution" of 1688, there were plenty of philosophical "voices" to call upon in support, justifiably or not, even as Hobbes was cited in defense of Stuart absolutism (better that than the lawlessness he feared) and Locke in defense of a strict limitation of royal power. These were voices of the "Enlightenment"—Voltaire's and Montesquieu's, Diderot's and Rousseau's. Critical and unorthodox though such men were, they were respected by the very kings whose mentality and manner of rule are satirized or scorned in *Candide* and *The Spirit of the Laws* and the *Encyclopedia* and *The Social Contract*. Salons celebrated these men, and a few reforms came about but not enough for the needs of the burghers, to say nothing of the working people. The excesses, the awful dangers of the Revolution itself were given thoughtful scrutiny by political philosophers like Edmund Burke and Joseph de Maistre, who, from the comfortable distance of England and Switzerland, looked on in dismay.

This century has had its upheavals, but our philosophers often seem less interested in political theory or what used to be called social ethics than in the nature of "communication" or in analyzing the structure of matter or in developing an "existentialist" viewpoint. They do indeed take political positions, even quite polemical ones, but they do not argue them convincingly. A notable exception is Barrington Moore, whose *Reflections on the Causes of Human Mis-*

ery and Upon Certain Proposals to Eliminate Them, along with
ideas and studies he has already presented, should—but, given the
temper of our times, probably will not—earn him the highest respect and renown. One has to doubt the likelihood of such recognition because his stubbornly honest and analytic mind refuses to consider any conventional wisdom sacred, even that which appeals to
his own political thinking. He doubts and he questions, though his
stand may offend those whose cause he very much favors as a citizen, a voter, a thinker and a dreamer. And he does dream—of a
world without the misery we seem helpless to eliminate, even here
at home, for all our wealth and power. The misery he has in mind is
not the subjective kind; he is concerned not with mental distress but
with the malnutrition and outright starvation that afflict millions of
the world's people. He is concerned with nations whose people are
overwhelmingly illiterate—where children die because doctors are
almost unheard of, where there is rarely sanitation of any kind,
where families huddle in crowded shacks or tenements under intolerable conditions. And he wonders whether all this will ever end,
given the governments that prevail—given, that is, the social and
political order these governments impose, be they in South and
Central America or in Asia and Africa.

Mr. Moore says he has "for some time held that the radical indictment of American society constituted a reasonably accurate description" of it. His classes at Harvard have attracted students who have
become active in the social struggles we have recently witnessed—as
antagonists of the status quo, intent upon changing it. In this book,
he is once more skeptical of doctrine, insistent upon questions that
embarrass friends as well as enemies. He wants his students to feel
just as free, and so he opposes any abridgment of civil liberties,
whatever the excuse for the abridgment. He does not try to rational-
ize all the misery that revolutions have produced in the name of
doing away with injustice. He is not another Edmund Burke, aghast
at the thought of a spreading anarchy, though he writes as intelligently and lucidly and argues as persuasively and eloquently. (The
title of his book is one that Burke—or, indeed, any other seven-
teenth- or eighteenth-century philosopher—might have used.) Nor
is he among the timid gradualists who offer sops to the needy when
pressures build up but in the clutch join ranks with those on top.

What Professor Moore wants, really, is a "democratic and humane socialism," but he considers the obstacles great indeed. On the political right are those who do not want to let go of the money they have or of the laws that protect their money in ways denied other people's money. On the political left are those who refuse to recognize the important social achievements that Western democracies, such as England and the United States, have managed, despite the persistent assaults and, in this country, the more subtle erosion these achievements appear to be suffering at the present time. Eager for the maintenance of "conditions for free intellectual inquiry," he rejects "any implication to the effect that radical movements ought to try to prohibit or prevent the advocacy of the views they are attacking." He is a friend of Marcuse, but he cannot accept his notion of "repressive tolerance"—part of an elaborate argument for radicals' taking and keeping power. The dilemma, as Professor Moore points out, is "*Quis custodiet?*" Exactly who is to make decisions, watch over the course of a nation, hold the keys? A self-appointed politburo? A military junta? A collection of warlords who have stashed away millions in Swiss banks? Or the "vested interests" whom Harry Truman railed against and Dwight Eisenhower called "the military-industrial complex"? Eisenhower's epithet is now a commonplace, yet the military-industrial complex persists, and so does the disparity between the wealthy and the poor. Professor Moore is convinced that a society that hopes to eliminate misery and to guarantee the freedoms of our Bill of Rights must be one in which people like him constantly annoy political activists of all kinds with bothersome essays. So he asks questions:

> The radical can and does reply that pleas for discussion and dialogue are often a smokescreen for delays and evasions, during which time people are dying and suffering. How many napalmed children do American liberals have the right to demand as the price for continuing peaceful dissent through orderly channels? How many twisted lives in the black ghettos? To such questions all possible answers are agonizing. The replies come down to highly uncertain estimates about the future and to counterquestions. How likely is it that the radicals in the present situation may produce even greater suffering and disaster, both in their efforts to gain power and in their efforts to put through their policies? The ultimate test of violence is, after all,

results too. And which radicals? And what policies? What is the appropriate time-span in passing judgments of this kind?

Such questions will not earn applause from the political left. Nor will his charge that the word *fascism* is used too freely by critics of this country, carried away by hysteria and perhaps by spite. Nor will his corollary criticism of those who in the name of activism and radical politics assail us with outbursts that "constitute no more than a form of moral self-indulgence." But defenders of our economic system fare no better. Professor Moore calls us a "predatory democracy," and to some extent he sides with those who decry the manipulative and sometimes coercive role our military might has played all over the world—not without attendant advantage to our economic system. So it is, he points out, that we are allied with dictators and despots while we preach freedom. So it is that our politicians rarely make a frank appraisal of the relationship between America's commercial interests and its military involvements. So it is that the press, certainly less controlled here than in most other countries, largely refrains from analysis of our entanglements with other nations. Yes, we are occasionally told about a government in Greece that spies on and tortures people, a government that denies its citizens even a semblance of democracy; or we hear that Brazil's prisons are full of men and women, among them priests and nuns, who dared criticize the military leadership. We denounce dictators in some countries and embrace them as our allies in others, but the overall pattern is often ignored or else presented in euphemisms. What, precisely, has our "good-neighbor policy" toward Latin America amounted to? What interests prompted Wilson to send troops to Mexico and Johnson to send them to the Dominican Republic? Why did the Central Intelligence Agency conspire to overthrow a government in Guatemala? Professor Moore believes such questions to be part of larger ones, candid answers to which may so threaten important people that the risks of asking them are great indeed.

It can be argued that the critical problem Professor Moore poses for himself and fails to resolve (he is not, after all, writing a platform) has to do with the "little man" he speaks of, by which he really means all of us who vote, and thereby *might* alter the structure of our society. To this author, "the weakness of the demand for change, or its lack of political effect, begins to look like a key aspect of the

whole problem of predatory democracy. Certainly it is a puzzling
one, about which severe critics of American society disagree sharply
among themselves. . . . The lack of effective demand for change
may be the key to our whole problem." For some of us, he concludes, it is a matter of indifference or a simple desire to go about
our daily lives untroubled by the "inconveniences," or worse, that
we think might be generated by social change: we are not evil or
mean-spirited; we have but one life to live, and we do not want it
threatened—perhaps to no good purpose. After all, we may have to
"pay the freight for well-meant efforts at improvement" that do not
achieve their aims. Among other citizens, less well-off and so still
more wary because more vulnerable, there is, Professor Moore says,
a feeling of confusion and outrage. Both psychologically and sociologically, these people are influenced, or even bound, by "the connection between frustrated effort and rage," he notes. "In the present
American context, for many little men it is the radical, and especially the romantic and cultural radical, who is the apparent source
of frustration." No one will find it easy to take issue with that observation. Professor Moore's unsurprising explanation of the situation is
that blue-collar and white-collar workers try to hold on to what they
have and that they are envious of people who are better-off. Envy is
mixed with rage when these workers are told directly, or by implication (through their critics' choice of language, appearance, manner
of living), that they are uninformed, stupid, even dangerous. He
notes the "hatred" of the French peasants for urban radicals, the
German "white-collar support for the Nazis," the "conservative
trends" in our own labor movement. The difficulty may be "that
human beings value what they must work for, *not* that they work for
what they value," so a factory or office worker goes along with his
social and economic situation, however precarious.

But does Professor Moore do justice to America's share of the
"little men"? If one is to believe historians like C. Vann Woodward,
the populist tradition in this country has been enduring and substantial, if not triumphant. If one is to believe sociologists like Herbert
Gans and Andrew Greeley and Richard Sennett and Jonathan Cobb,
the motivations and feelings of working-class Americans are as complicated and contradictory as those of our well-educated liberals and
radicals. Professor Moore writes about the two latter groups, it seems
to me, more sensitively and compassionately—or perhaps it is know-

ingly—than he does about the others. He has an eye for the foibles of political activists, and for their dangerous blind spots, but also a certain respect for their possibilities as human beings; that eye and that respect are not brought to bear on our labor movement. This brief and honest book cannot be casually recommended; it is a somber book, intended not to appease our anxieties but to document their sources and what these anxieties may lead to. The continuing capacity of human beings for cruelty to one another—exacting from workers labor at low wages and under unfair, unhealthy conditions; submitting people to peonage; dropping bombs—is a sad and familiar litany, one that makes Thomas Hobbes naively optimistic when he speaks about the "brutish" quality of those who lived in a "state of nature" but speaks with so much hope for those who come later in history. Still, Barrington Moore, patient, intelligent, of kind disposition, is not without hope; as he says, the true pessimist has lost faith in the responsiveness of others and their capacity for growth, and so doesn't even bother writing a book.

If any book can make us think hard about where we are going, this is the one. It is preoccupied with what Hobbes and Locke might have called "woe and weal"—the relationship between our afflictions and the political order that sets so much of the tone and rhythm of our daily behavior. One suspects, though, that Professor Moore wants more from us than hard thinking; he wants us to act in such a way that at least a significant dent is made in the problems whose size and complexity he has made plain to us.

New Yorker, March 3, 1973

"Are you now or have you ever been . . ."

lthough her writing is quiet, reflective, at times touchingly limpid, and always straightforward, Lillian Hellman makes clear in the title of her latest autobiographical memoir, *Scoundrel Time*, that both her mind and heart have struggled for a quarter of a century with an unremitting moral outrage, which this book explains and justifies once and for all. Throughout her life, she has been an outsider of sorts, no one's safe bet. She is a Southerner; her roots are in rural Alabama and the rather special, even exotic cosmopolitanism of New Orleans.

She came to the theater and the movies, to the influential, sometimes nervously insecure, and not always generous or farsighted intellectual world of the Northeast, a strong-minded, fiercely independent woman, a person inclined to be self-observing, even self-critical, and not least, an artist never willing to set aside a highly developed moral sensibility. Her early plays earned her fame and success in a world (Broadway and Hollywood) she had many reasons to question severely, if not hold in contempt. They are plays of subtle psychological observation, not far removed in theme from the playwright's personal knowledge and experience—the workings of the comfortable but inwardly torn, saddened, worried American bourgeoisie.

In the late 1930s and early 1940s, both as a writer and a citizen, she became more explicitly involved with the broader social and political problems that pressed hard, she knew, even upon those very assured and well-off people she gave us in *Watch on the Rhine*. She has never been an ideologue, but neither has she been a fussy and arrogant loner or, certainly, an opportunistic joiner quick to discern where to place her signature in order to gain the approval of a particular clique or age. She saw, early on, the relationship between art and politics; she felt an obligation to characterize and respond to the exploitative cruelties that have passed for everyday events these past decades in the Western capitalist countries. She went to Spain during the Civil War to give her energies to the Loyalist side. She pointed out the dangers and rotten evils of fascism at a time when many of her countrymen were loath to pay heed. A woman brilliantly in touch with Freud's unsparing vision of the mind's deviousness and self-enhancing capacity for illusion, she could not shirk noticing how greedy businessmen and servile, corrupt, or monstrously evil politicians have collaborated to lie, cheat, steal, and ultimately, it turned out, be parties (in one way or another, actively or out of indifference) to the deaths of millions of defenseless human beings.

After World War II, Miss Hellman was as outraged by what she saw happening here as by the continuing horrors of totalitarianism abroad. She refused to join the self-congratulatory chorus of former Communists, now converted to well-paid, confessional red-baiting, or the various cliques of self-described liberals and intellectuals ready in an instant to come up with the most intricate of rationalizations for the "practical," the "necessary." Soon enough our high and mighty evangelists of the Cold War (not a few of them personally quite suspect in one way or another) were after her and others like her—prominent and even revered individuals whose intimidated, groveling, expiative presence, so the McCarthys and J. Parnell Thomases hoped, would not only provide an example but also, and very important, distract the working people of this country from thinking about who owns and gets what out of our economic system.

The inquisitors hauled more and more citizens to Washington for "questioning" in the late 1940s, as Gary Wills tells us in his sharp and uncompromising introduction to this book. The witnesses came willingly, a lot of them—or with fear that quickly gave way to eager ingratiation. Yesuh, yesuh, we'll agree, we'll affirm, we'll tell all— or in the case of some professors or writers, we'll do what we can (a lot, that's for sure) to give a cheap, rotten, phony witchhunt the high gloss of historical necessity and urgency.

Unfortunately for Miss Hellman, she is stubbornly discerning and ethically sensitive. The poor, benighted creature can't stop asking herself what is right. Nor could she stop seeing, in McCarthyism, the distracting—and intimidating—function of political melodrama. She was summoned before a body that, in its exquisite modesty, had declared itself to be the Committee on Un-American Activities of the House of Representatives. She would tell everything she knew—

or else, as the congressmen and their manipulative, calculating aides and lawyers had the power to warn. The result was an honorable but hurtful scene within a larger and disgusting act in which the nation of Jefferson and Lincoln became the property of political Snopeses, one of whom would eventually sully the White House itself.

As Miss Hellman makes painfully evident, and the reader must never forget, a lot of important people in her world were falling all over themselves trying to apologize, atone, beg for forgiveness—and for the chance to make a lot more bucks. Nor are a good number of them rushing into print now to examine their motives or express some of the self-doubts Miss Hellman, still eschewing the blandishments of self-righteousness, comes forth with. She was then, maybe still is, a lonely figure—brave precisely because she was afraid and knew the power and cunning of her accusers. She saw them at lunch in the Mayflower, the illustrious J. Edgar Hoover and his sidekick Clyde Tolson; she read about them every day in the newspapers and magazines—the saviors of "the American way." What would she say before them? What would she do? What could have been a quick and rewarding hour or two became something else for her: a moment of self-appraisal, a time of explicit, unhedged moral decisiveness at whatever cost (and, in money and property, the cost was great).

This book tells how her mind worked as she decided to stand up and say no to the prevailing principalities and powers. It is a personal statement and a strong moral document. Kierkegaard would have loved *Scoundrel Time* for its fine, sardonic humor, its unsparing social observation, and not least, the skill of its narration. He had contempt for the smug and phony intellectuals of his day—always anxious to preach to others but ever so protective of themselves. He longed for companions who would summon personal memory, among other modes of expression, to the task of making concrete and specific ethical analyses—as opposed to cleverly worded abstractions that conceal as much as they tell. In Lillian Hellman he has a kindred spirit, and we a voice making itself heard in what still is, alas, a wilderness of bluff, guile, and deceit.

Washington Post, May 9, 1976

Stories and Voices

I n the early 1970s, the United States Army Corps of Engineers
set about constructing yet another of its dams to restrain Caesars
Creek, a tributary of the Little Miami River. This project required the sacrifice of the two-century-old Ohio farming village
of New Burlington, which was south of Dayton and just north of
Cincinnati; the town occupied the site of the reservoir that would be
created by the dam's construction. During the sad and final year in
the life of this Midwestern rural community, John Baskin, a young
writer and woodcutter, lived in it, in an abandoned farmhouse, and
came to know its inhabitants. Mr. Baskin, who had recently graduated from Mars Hill College, in North Carolina's western mountain
country, is himself the son of farming people. He has turned the
experience he had in New Burlington into an excellent book—*New
Burlington: The Life and Death of an American Village*—which is
hard to classify. It is certainly not a study by a social scientist; the
author has no interest in conducting interviews, accumulating data,
and coming forth with findings. In fact, in his brief but lively introduction Mr. Baskin refers to the "bleak treatises" of sociologists and
says that he wants no part of them.

Instead, he simply wants to describe a scene that he has witnessed.
He wants to set down the words he has heard—to tell us what the
people of New Burlington have to say about themselves and their
lives. He realizes that these people have managed to gain access to
us only through him—the wanderer, the listener, the visitor—so he
begins the book with an account of the "accidents" of his life that led
to his encounter with the dying town. Soon after he arrived, he
learned from the villagers that before long they would be gone.
Their children and grandchildren would be water-skiing over their
cornfields, some of which were nearly as old as the nation itself.
"Full of complaint," the author says, describing his reaction to the
news he heard, "I thought . . . I would *restore* New Burlington." He
would do so, he hoped, by writing something that breathed life into

the statistics and the abstract reports on the village that the Corps of Engineers had relied upon in making its decision about the dam. He would try to write what he calls at one point the town's "obituary." Before "the world (engineers) crashes in to obliterate the past (the village)," Mr. Baskin tells us, he wanted to take notice, to give us "a book of stories and voices in which the characters ponder some of their time on earth." In this respect, he says, he "perceived New Burlington as a *gift*." The book, too, is a gift: it is an excellent social history, strong on personal statement and deliberately weak on what the author calls "noise" and "messages."

A prologue tells us, on a rather broad temporal scale, about the town's origins:

> New Burlington, Ohio, in the Paleozoic Era was very largely limestone, at the bottom of the sea. Later the ice came, so heavy it depressed the spine of the continent and after the ice, cranberry bogs prepared the ground for the great hardwood forests.

Some fifteen thousand years ago, the Indians found their way to this land. After the arrival of white people, it became known first as the Northwest Territory and then, in 1803, as the State of Ohio. The whites made their way west in increasing numbers. The Indians retired farther west. Settlements like New Burlington grew. A decade or so after the Civil War, Mr. Baskin tells us, the town consisted of "one sawmill, two churches, one school, one hotel, three groceries, one wagon shop, two dry goods stores, two doctors, one carpenter, one cobbler, one undertaker, three blacksmiths, and one chicken thief. Population: 275. Real estate: $16,281."

Nearly a century later, in 1973, just before the moment of extinction, the town had not grown very much. Its single street offered farmers a brief, intimate, tidy stretch of stores and churches. These farmers, along with the people who healed them, ministered to them, and taught their children, were those in whom Mr. Baskin was most interested. Their lives unfold in all their strangeness, banality, drama, and dreariness. One family, the Haydocks, originally came to New Burlington from Yorkshire, England. Their very name connects them to farm life. Sarah Haydock Shidaker, now in her eighties, obviously reminisced with Mr. Baskin a good deal, and from what she told him he has reconstructed old conversations and events:

At the school commencement in 1913, Sarah meets Edwin Shidaker. They have known each other forever but this time they regard each other differently. Edwin drives Sarah home in his buggy. She invites him in but he says no. "My horse is rather fractious and I should get him home," he says.

Throughout the book, in an extraordinary and compelling manner of presentation and evocation, Mr. Baskin has thus woven the past and present together, mixing in old photographs and new photographs, quoting letters written a long time ago, using excerpts from diaries and church records and notebooks, and reproducing fragments of remembered songs, poems, and sayings. The author often uses the present tense to bring the reader closer to the particular person, situation, or kind of existence that is being described. It is obvious that Mr. Baskin collected more than enough material to sustain this novelistic-factual mode of presentation: at various places in the text, Sarah and others are allowed to speak at considerable length without interruption. When the author takes the liberty of acting as commentator or chronicler of events, he does so with a directness, immediacy, and verve that are impressive and touching. He begins a section called "Light" this way:

> In the late Twenties electricity comes to New Burlington. A traveling man comes to do the wiring and boards on a nearby farm where he milks a cow to pay his keep. His work goes slowly because the cow kicks him and breaks his leg. Finally curious neighbors gather outside a lower New Burlington home and watch a porch light switched on. The bare bulb hangs from the porch ceiling on a long cord. When the light goes on the people think they see the darkness shaken as if it were dust settling.

The paragraph immediately following that one indicates how skilled Mr. Baskin is at connecting the general to the specific, the historical to the personal:

> Lights in the village make Sarah happy. Light dispels mystery and she too would have it. An old villager explains to her how it works: "You pull a cord," he says. "On and off, you see." For the Christmas of 1939 electricity lights the Shidaker Yule tree. Sarah buys lights for the tree, the table, the ceiling, a floor

lamp, and a radio. When Edwin turns on the radio a voice is singing.

There are marvelous moments on page after page of the book. Sometimes Sarah and her fellow-townspeople seem informative and dignified—tough, hardworking men and women who have endured. At other times, they show eloquence and wit. "The fall of the year is my favorite time by far," Sarah says at the beginning of a section titled "October." Then she adds a simple "O Yes." A bit farther on, she tells us, "I have always liked the stars. I was born under Libra. Justice, you know, is blind. And erasers are on lead pencils to take care of the wrong we do. The signs have an effect upon our dispositions. If the moon can change tides why not dispositions?" She provides no answer and moves quickly away from metaphysical speculation: "My but I am old. This was once a dimple. Now it's a crack. I have trouble with my feet and my conscience. First one pains me then the other." Then, continuing her almost contrapuntal expression of the straightforward and the slightly rhetorical, she gives this general account of her habits and her thoughts:

> "I do not smoke, drink, or drive an automobile. There's nothing left for me to do but play the piano. Lay not up your treasures on earth where moth and rust corrupt. But if I married an old man I would want him to have $90,000 and a very bad cough. . . . I am the last leaf on the tree and I believe I am outliving everyone else. My love for my people has been very strong. I am root and branch New Burlington."

Near the conclusion of the section about Sarah, Mr. Baskin adds an ironic word or two of his own:

> The old villagers are mostly gone now and Sarah's grandchildren study science in distant universities. A young man lives in the upstairs which she rents out. He is training to be a psychologist. Sarah listens carefully to his definitions. An interstate highway slices in front of the old Shidaker homeplace and she is the last of the family to own any of Preserved Fish's land. New Burlington itself is mostly gone. The rest waits for the waters of the new reservoir.

There are others besides Sarah—from somber Quakers to lively Methodists. They have memories of their own, and they remember their parents and grandparents remembering, and we are thus carried back almost to the earliest days of the Republic. One man, John Harlan Pickin, recalls hearing about the Spanish-American War and about Grover Cleveland's election, when his great-aunt exclaimed, "The country is finished!" (A Democrat had not been elected president in twenty-eight years.) John's mother was a grown woman before she laid eyes on a Catholic, and she knew only one Jew in her lifetime. John offers us particularly vivid descriptions of farm life, which, he tells us, was "hard on everyone":

> "There were horrible stories of people going through manure spreaders, of tractors rearing up and crushing the driver, ragged cuts that led to lockjaw. My aunt felt sorry for the women because they had no one to talk to. They spent their lives looking at the backside of a cow."

We learn that Charles Dickens passed through New Burlington and that it was a stop on the Underground Railroad. We learn that men and women left the town, year after year, to go farther west. They sometimes wrote back home, sometimes lost touch. And they sometimes came back. We learn that drink was a "secret passion" in the village, that it was considered "more shameful than illegitimacy." At Quaker meetings, drinkers were prayed for, long and hard. The man who speaks of these matters—the secret lusts and shames of his neighbors—is one Joshua Scroggy, who, at ninety-two, can still recall the essence of H. L. Mencken's definition of Puritanism: "The suspicion that somewhere someone might be having a good time." There were also what Joshua refers to as "mental problems" in New Burlington—illnesses that used to be regarded as a "curse." And there were suicides. "We had all these things," Joshua says in summary, "all manner of pride and gluttony, and sins real and imagined, but the village life caused a tolerance among us. It had to. Everyone came face to face each day."

Nevertheless, no one in the town comes across as a sage from whom Mr. Baskin seeks "answers." On the contrary, the people of New Burlington for the most part tether their comments about life to the shared, familiar experiences or occasions of everyday life. "Never saw a family tree that didn't need spraying," one old-timer remembers hearing. "A good hot egg is a small miracle," another person declares. Speaking of the Great Depression, Mary Robinson, a woman of seventy-five, recalls, "After the commotion on Wall Street, a farmer down the road came home and said, 'The stock market has crashed!' His little boy heard him and asked, 'Was any cows hurt?' That's all the stock market meant to any of us."

Still, New Burlington did suffer during the Depression—for a long time and badly. Many proud families were reduced to a barter economy. But they never went hungry, as did many who lived in crowded, and thus more vulnerable, cities. "We grew what we ate during the Depression," Mary says, "and husked corn in the flat land for six cents a shock." For all that, the people of New Burlington did not take very kindly to the New Deal or to President Roosevelt; Mr. Baskin gives us a limerick that was current in New Burlington during the Depression:

> There once was a lady of fashion
> Who had a very fine passion.
> To her boy friend she said
> As they jumped into bed,
> "Here's one thing Roosevelt can't ration."

The people of New Burlington watched the seasons come and go with special care and were prepared to take advantage of any generosity that Nature offered. The author is keen and lyrical in a section called "Syrup." He learned from his friends all about the technique of syrup-making, and he also tells us about the patience they brought to this enterprise. The style that Mr. Baskin uses in this section makes one hope for a second book from him in this genre, and a third:

> When the trees are scratches against the surly February sky Charles McIntire goes into the woods where his breath hangs in balloons as if momentarily the balloons might fill with language. He drills small holes in the maples which he recognizes by the dignified bark which looks like marbled slate. And waits for the precarious succession of freezing nights and warm days which makes the sap rise in the irresolute veins of the maple. There is no clue that inwardly the maple seethes in the breaking up of winter. The world seems still and vague. It is as though

color and motion have never existed except in the imagination. For Charles to come here is an act of faith in a dead season. The woods could be etchings.

These men and women may have experienced many hard times, but they were, by and large, stoic, and they maintained a robust sense of humor. The Quakers among them, Mr. Baskin tells us, knew that "human equilibrium is poor and the fall from grace constantly imminent." Severely tested people—even austere people—can manage a smile, or at least develop a certain wry, amused perspective on themselves. Mr. Baskin cites a man named Carl Smith, who at the age of eighty-six acknowledges his luck in having lived a long life and waits patiently, expectantly, for the end: "A long life is partly care, more mystery. Providence watches over fools and children. And I'm no kid." In a grimmer vein of humor, the author tells us about the man who went mad during one of the floods that have periodically devastated or threatened the countryside. He was found splashing in the kitchen sink by the rescuers who entered his house. "You'll all drown," he warned them. "Only I am safe. When the water rises up to me, I'll pull the plug." A time was when there were five-party and ten-party telephone lines. Ten different rings in each house! "Farm houses sounded like fire stations," Della Wilson recalls, and she is only forty-six.

The older people cling tenaciously to their past but stumble during the slow wait of the present; a good number of them are in their eighties—survivors, who did without antibiotics and all sorts of medical technology, and who never dieted or took vitamin pills or had their cholesterol measured or their emotions analyzed. Elizabeth Beam, at eighty-five, acknowledges that she knows "more people underfoot than above." She goes on as best she can, even though her faculties are failing: "With fading eyesight she puts Jell-O in the skillet thinking it is liver." The widow Jemima Boots goes to sleep easily and stays asleep, but she has her secret worries and keeps a cowbell under her pillow, just in case. Her neighbor Ellen Jenkins, also a widow of advanced age, "puts on her best dress when expecting the telephone to ring."

The town of New Burlington is gone now, but in a way it will never be gone. Its landscape, its people, and their traditions and customs, their experiences, victories, and defeats, and their abiding memories have been given new life in this rare moral document, written by a young and imaginative observer. John Baskin now lives on a farm in Wilmington, Ohio, not far from where many of his New Burlington friends, whose ideals and manner of endurance he obviously admires and wants to uphold, settled after their town died. Mr. Baskin's book—which resembles James Agee's *Let Us Now Praise Famous Men* in spirit and in grace of writing as well as in subject matter—demonstrates that he is also not far from what Agee called "human actuality."

New Yorker, June 6, 1976

Plain People

Recently, the word *populist* has appeared once more on the American scene. Many modern politicians refer to themselves as populists, and even our new president has connected himself, both in his autobiography and in his spoken statements, with populism—the tradition of political protest, economic analysis, and social criticism that started in the late nineteenth century. As Lawrence Goodwyn makes clear in his book *Democratic Promise: The Populist Moment in America*, it is a tradition often misunderstood and often misrepresented or wrongly appropriated by various essayists, not to mention political activists of one sort or another. Goodwyn is a historian who teaches at Duke University. He is also one of the directors of an ambitious oral-history project, sponsored by the history department at Duke, that is aimed at rescuing from obscurity the memories and impressions of ordinary Southern working people who have been involved in that region's recent episode of painful and important social change, and for years he was a journalist at the *Texas Observer*, a muckraking periodical that has been challenging vested interests for more than two decades.

Today, Professor Goodwyn points out, populism is a vaguely appealing word, partly because it is without clear-cut ideological significance. Clearly it has some connection with "the people," and few of us would ever want to be against them. Those who don't care to be known as liberals, perhaps because they reject some of the assumptions common to many so described, may call themselves populists with the hope that they are thereby expressing a more strenuous dissatisfaction with the prevailing social order. To be sure, the label has also taken on negative connotations. In this century, it has been used by some Southern politicians in the cause of racism and extreme economic conservatism as well as by Midwestern isolationists. Sometimes "the people" become a mob, angry and ill-informed and mean-spirited, and a demagogue is literally a "leader of the people"—a shrewd manipulator of unrest, animosity, and dissatisfaction. But for the most part these days, populism is used in a positive, though unclear, way by those who speak for the small farmer, by political reformers anxious to break up large corporations and strengthen the economic position of the poor and the working-class people of the country, by activists eager to get away from politics as usual and set up what they call alternative institutions, and by conventional politicians—the kind who cite Harry Truman as a true populist, as if to say that a populist has never been more than someone of humble origins who makes good but still has a blunt, unpretentious manner, who favors helping those not so successful, and who proudly says of himself that he is "an ordinary human being."

Although Professor Goodwyn takes pains in the first section of his book to let the reader know that such usages have little to do with the historical movement called Populism, he is not fussy and pedantic when he describes the true sources and philosophical premises of the Populist moment. He simply wants to do justice to a particular effort, serious and honorable, on the part of many thousands to make a significant critique of American capitalism just as it was entering its maturity, in the last years of the nineteenth century. Populism did eventually become the basis of a specific political movement, even of a third party, but in essence it was a general vision of the world, a means by which plain people—mostly farmers and those better-off but in sympathy with them—began to organize their thoughts into a coherent set of social, economic, and political objectives. In the author's words, "populism is the story of how a large number of people, through a gradual process of self-education that grew out of their cooperative efforts, developed a new interpretation of their society and new political institutions to give expression to these interpretations."

The process Professor Goodwyn mentions began in the late 1870s. The Civil War was over, and a ravaged nation had renewed its expansionist growth both territorily and economically. Railroads were probing the frontier. More and more factories were being built in or near the major cities. The United States was not yet a world power, but it was rich in its resources, in its increasing and willing work force, and in its accelerating agricultural capacity. Certain individuals were becoming not merely well-off and influential but enormously wealthy. They were determined to stay that way, to receive special treatment, and to make their presence felt on the national scene. At the same time, the country was plagued by recurrent, seemingly inescapable economic collapses. These disasters raised questions about the very meaning and nature of money: What was it, and who had a right to make it, and with what as a guarantee of its worth—gold, silver, or nothing save the government's promises? These questions, in turn, raised other, larger ones: How was the nation, now intact after a terrible bloodletting, going to be run? More precisely, what would be the attitude of the government—particularly the Treasury Department and the Interior Department—toward commerce and industry, toward agricultural interests, toward the growing number of mine owners, and toward the oil wells and refineries that would soon be a major source of American wealth? Were the president and the congress to maintain a hands-off policy—to let increasingly successful, self-confident, and aggressive businesses have full rein so that they could conspire and combine or squabble and fight among themselves as they pleased? Would Washington become a mediator, an arbitrator? Would it become an ally of the most successful and importunate commercial interests? How would it approach the foreign countries with which American businesses traded and from which they wanted raw materials? And the land, the American land—once the Indians' land—rich with various treasures: how would it be apportioned and developed? For a moment—the "populist moment" that Professor Goodwyn refers to—the nation held its breath and tried to figure out what kind of nation it would be, what kind of assumptions and values would prevail politically and economically.

America of the 1880s and 1890s was made up mostly of farmers. There was a smaller number of factory and shopworkers, and a still smaller, luckier group who belonged to the so-called commercial class. But each group was fragmented by affiliations that prevented clear-cut social, political, or even regional confrontations. The Republican Party contained not only wealthy Northern and Western conservatives but also white- and blue-collar Yankee Protestants and impoverished blacks (those who could and did vote). The Democratic Party contained Southern whites—rich and poor—and Northern immigrants. The Civil War had continued to divide voters along nostalgic and emotional lines that were, we now realize, irrational and often against their own best interests. Men voted "as they shot," thereby denying themselves a chance for redress of legitimate grievances through the ballot. The author speaks of this fragmented and emotional political situation as "a non-ideological milieu." (To a degree, our two major parties still cover a very wide spectrum of opinion, in that both are divided into liberal and conservative wings.) Voters of the post-Civil War period were sentimental and inattentive to the specific positions politicians held with respect to wealth, the rights of industrial workers, and, especially, the needs of farmers— credit, cheap railroad rates, and so on.

The Populists were at the beginning people from the agricultural South and the frontier West—Texas, in particular—who began to take a hard look at who owned what and at who was profiting from the rules, regulations, arrangements, and laws. Under the "crop lien" system in the South, thousands of hardworking farmers were in constant bondage to "the furnishing man," otherwise known as "the advancing man" or—to blacks, who had a way of linguistically stripping things to their bare essentials—"the Man." The South had become, in the words of one historian quoted by Professor Goodwyn, a "giant pawn shop." Interest rates were "frequently well in excess of 100 per cent annually, sometimes over 200 per cent," the author tells us, and, once hooked, the farmer rarely got free. No wonder people went West, left peonage in order to start a new life—even one with new and grave risks—in Texas and beyond. But toward the end of the nineteenth century there was, increasingly, no real escape: "A Tennessean fleeing worn-out land, interest, and the freight rates of the Louisville and Nashville Railroad would arrive in the Cross Timbers of Texas to find that the Texas and Pacific Railroad owned much of the most promising land."

Still they trekked westward, impoverished and bitter and hopeful and determined—the South's white yeomen and not a few black tenant farmers. Every year during the 1870s about a hundred thousand of them went to Texas alone—initially to the warm, wet "piney-woods" section abutting Louisiana, then westward to the open, inviting prairie land. And out there, in east and central Texas, those farmers did more than scratch hard for a living. They began to talk about their fate, their needs, their beliefs. For the first time, they did not feel beholden to creditors or to distracting sectional pieties. In Lampasas County, Palo Pinto County, and Cook County, on the Red River, they formed "alliances"—the basis of the National Farmers Alliance. By the end of the 1880s, more than a quarter of a million American "men of the soil" would be members of the NFA. Rather than pay outrageously high prices for fertilizer and equipment, the farmers joined hands and formed buying committees. Rather than deal individually with buyers who underweighed cotton or overcharged for their services as middlemen, the farmers formed cooperatives and took action that they could not have taken without being organized.

Needless to say, there was opposition. "Town merchants opposed cooperative schemes, as did manufacturers and cotton buyers," Professor Goodwyn tells us. But the movement had its weapons and strengths. Hardy and eloquent NFA organizers wandered from county to county, explaining, arguing, and exhorting. (A number of these organizers and their beliefs, their personal ways, and their travels are presented in this book.) There were, moreover, obvious and tangible financial benefits from the cooperative efforts. Perhaps most important, the rural South and West were still quite removed from the intimidating social and cultural controls—newspapers and established social hierarchies, with their conventions and orthodoxies—that so often persuaded individuals to ignore their own interests, and sometimes even frightened them into positions that worked against those interests. When the farmers of Texas railed against the distant exploiters (the railroads, the banks, the cotton brokers), they were not quickly denounced and isolated as "Socialists." Rather, for hundreds of thousands, they were other kinds of radicals: believing Christians, for instance, who remembered Christ's triumph over "powers and principalities" and his egalitarian Sermon on the Mount.

Populism gradually became more than a shared sensibility or even a series of local cooperative initatives loosely bound into an alliance. By 1892, the word itself had been attached to a full-fledged and vital political movement based on a radical analysis of the fast-growing industrialism of the day. What started as an agrarian revolt spread to the cities. The NFA became affiliated with the Knights of Labor—an early effort of urban working people to fight collectively for better wages. A more explicitly class-conscious ideology gradually appeared in the language of Populist speakers and writers. The wretchedness of the urban proletariat was spelled out. Attention was drawn repeatedly to the corrupt or toadying politicians catering to the small number of fortunate men who owned so much of the nation's wealth. As

W. E. Farmer, a Knights of Labor leader, put it, "We have an over-production of poverty, barefooted women, political thieves and many liars. There is no difference between legalized robbery and highway robbery."

It was a time when children as well as grownups worked from dawn to dusk for a pittance; when factory and mill conditions were, by our standards, unspeakably grim; when the local police—or, if necessary, the state militia or federal troops—almost invariably came down on the side of the employer in labor disputes; when labor unions as we know them were nonexistent; and, as the author keeps emphasizing, when farmers were constantly being manipulated, or cheated outright, by land companies and livestock commission agencies and cotton buyers and owners of wholesale houses. It was, without exaggeration, a time of constant misery and suffering—even starvation. It was also a time of significant "capital-formation"—a cool phrase from economic theory that fails to convey the Dickensian horrors that millions of men, women, and children sustained as a matter of course.

Populists had their own response to such horrors, which was, Professor Goodwyn tells us, a distinctively American one:

> Populists were not capitalist reformers, as we understand that phrase in modern political language; neither were they socialists. Though their mass movement literally grew out of their belief in the power of man as a coöperative being, they also accepted man as a competitive being. They cannot conveniently be compressed into the narrow (theoretically competitive) categories of political description sanctioned in the capitalist creed, nor can they be compressed into the (theoretically cooperative) categories of political description sanctioned in socialist thought.

The movement Professor Goodwyn describes was thus made up of American citizens who cherished the Jeffersonian tradition of political democracy but also, in the spirit of Tom Paine, wanted to achieve true social and economic democracy. Populists feared centralized, concentrated power—that of the corporations, that of the government. Their movement bore no resemblance to this century's state-run, bureaucratized socialism. They were proudly devoted to localism, cooperativism, and not least, democratic principles.

In its brief decade or so of existence, Populism generated a lively and stubbornly idiosyncratic literary and rhetorical tradition in newspapers, magazines, pamphlets, and meetings. Men like Henry Demarest Lloyd and Clarence Darrow were vocal Populist reformers. Journals like the *American Non-conformist*, the *Appeal to Reason*, and the *Progressive Farmer* were forums for the morally fervid and unflinchingly outspoken Populist ideals. All over the country—but especially in the South and the West—people met, listened, talked, argued, changed one another's minds, and agreed enthusiastically. There were prolonged encampments, lectures, and town meetings, in which no one set the rules. Everyone was encouraged to have a say concerning what values children should possess and how the thunderous call to justice of Isaiah and Jeremiah and Amos, or the gentle but unyielding social vision of Jesus, could become an American reality.

Those questions may have been satisfactorily answered in the abstract, but real economic change was quite another matter. Certainly hundreds of thousands of farmers and industrial workers came to know, and to express rather pointedly, what they believed in, and they even managed, through the People's Party, to elect governors, congressmen, and a few senators. With the election of William McKinley in 1896, however, it became apparent that corporate money in enormous quantities, a press owned by the self-serving rich, and the clever manipulations of men like Mark Hanna (a predecessor of many twentieth-century campaign managers) were too much for the poor and the nearly poor, no matter their number. A third party could not make enough inroads, and neither of the two major parties offered much hope. The Populists and their supporters—Tom Watson and Eugene Debs and the nameless, faceless "agrarian rebels" and Knights of Labor—wanted to do more than fight over gold or silver, as McKinley and Bryan did, or arrange for some slight modification of tariffs or a shift in foreign-policy rhetoric: with their parades, rallies, demonstrations, assemblies, and homespun journalism, they looked toward a second American Revolution of sorts. But they soon enough realized the futility of their dream.

The Populist moment was a complicated one, and Professor Goodwyn has done a first-rate job of describing it. His tone is at once detached and sympathetic. He wishes, no doubt, that the Populists had prevailed, but he understands why they didn't. He is very helpful in showing why Populism should not be confused with liberal reformist politics or Theodore Roosevelt's "progressive" policies. And he also makes a clear and very important distinction between Populism and the racism and parochialism that eventually developed in some areas of the country and in some embittered Populist leaders, like Tom Watson, who had at least one election taken from him by corrupt wealth. As our own century has shown, when money and power make justice unobtainable, a resentful narrowness and meanness can set in. If one cannot have the assurance of work and a measure of dignity, one turns to the sinister satisfactions of spite and hate. But Populism is not to be blamed for what happened after its failure.

The proudly radical activists of Populism did succeed in making some helpful changes in America. Industrialists and their political allies and lackeys, who were indeed frightened by the widespread appeal of the Populist indictment of corporate America, began to make adjustments—a gesture toward the conservative guild-unionism of Samuel Gompers, restrained antitrust legislation under the Roosevelt and Wilson Administrations, a gradual end to the more flagrant sweatshop abuses. Then the Depression produced millions of new victims—victims of a system that continued to seem reckless, arbitrary, and anarchic. The New Deal struggled valiantly but with no decisive success. It took a world war to make things economically better, and a Cold War and two "local" wars to keep them better. We could do worse now than to reflect on the Populists and to call upon their candid and eloquent mode of social and economic analysis.

Lawrence Goodwyn has done justice to a much-neglected and clouded segment of our history. He has also given us a potential boost toward collective self-examination at a time when we need just that. His book is scholarly yet accessible to the general reader. Maybe the man who has just moved into the rather large and imposing white mansion in Washington—a man who has called himself a Populist—will cast a glance or two at this book and help move us along toward political reconsideration.

New Yorker, February 7, 1977

The Humanities and Human Dignity

The humanities were once regarded as "polite learning": the study of grammar, rhetoric, and especially the classics. We could do worse than encourage such study among our young— so many of whom badly need to know how to write clearly, logically, and coherently as well as to understand what Socrates kept reminding his students: that the truly wise person knows, among other things, how little he or she knows, how much remains to be learned. It is a sad day, our day, in which many school children exhibit a declining adequacy in the use of the English language; exposure to the crudities of certain television programs is constant; and an idiotic and pretentious social science jargon has worked its way into various curricula.

Our lives in twentieth-century America are dominated by the natural sciences. Every time we flick a light switch, get into a car, or receive penicillin, we silently acknowledge the influence of engineers, physicists, and chemists on our everyday assumptions. The so-called social sciences have tried to follow suit, on occasion prematurely, to tell us that they also have begun to master some realms of the universe: psychological and sociological riddles, rather than those posed by organic and inorganic matter or the distant constellations of stars. Still, it has not been altogether a blessing for America's sectarian culture—this technological mastery enabled by the natural sciences, coupled with the increasing conviction of social scientists that our habits and thoughts will soon enough yield to one or another interpretive scheme. Kierkegaard's nineteenth-century grievance—that the increased knowledge of his time enabled people to understand, or think they would soon understand, just about everything except how to live a life—might well be our complaint too. We have at our fingertips the energy of the atom; we have dozens of notions of why people do things as they do; but many of us have forgotten to ask what we really believe in, what we ought to *be* in contrast to *do*.

The natural sciences offer us much-needed answers and solutions. The social sciences, now and then, offer us helpful explanations—along with, occasionally, a good deal of dreary, pompous, overwrought language. The humanities, in the hands of some, can also be reduced to precious, bloated, and murky prose. But the humanities at their best give testimony to the continuing effort to make moral, philosophical, and spiritual sense of this world—to evoke its complexity, its ironies, inconsistencies, contradictions, and ambiguities. The humanities begin for a scientist when he or she starts asking what a particular fact or discovery will mean for those who want to comprehend the obligations, the responsibilities of citizenship, the possibilities and limitations a given society presents. The humanities come into play for a social scientist when he or she starts wondering what some observation or theoretical construct or piece of data tells us about himself or herself—the person who has made a discovery, who lives with and by some larger vision of things.

To make a point, I would like to call upon the voice of an American factory worker I've come to know these past years. The physician in me has tried to contend with the illnesses that have afflicted him and his wife and children. The social scientist in me, a psychiatrist doing so-called fieldwork, has tried to comprehend how a man manages the various stresses imposed by a tough, demanding, exhausting assembly-line job. But there is in this person the stuff of the humanities, and I only hope I am sufficiently responsive to, respectful of, what he has to say: "I feel good on the way to work. I leave the house early. It's the best time of the day. I see the sun come up. I do some thinking. Once I'm on the job, I have no time to think of anything; it's go, go, go—until I punch that card and leave. But on the road to my job I stop and ask myself questions. I mean, you want to have something to aim for; you want to believe in something. My oldest boy, he's starting college this September, the first one in our family to get that far. I told him—I said: Get the best education you can, and it'll help you live better, and you'll get the respect of people; but don't forget to keep your common sense, and don't forget what life is all about.

"Sometimes, I think there's nothing to believe in, except the almighty dollar—and a little influence, that always helps. Sometimes, I see people behaving real rotten to other people, and I remember the wars in my lifetime, and I think of the troubles all over the world, and I think back to my father and how he couldn't find a job when we were kids, and my mother being upset for him, and for us, and I remind myself of what a lousy life it still is for most of the people on this earth—well, I can get real low. But for all the trouble my family has had, and the world has had, I guess I'm lucky, because I don't stay down there in the dumps too long. I stop and say to myself that life may be a big mystery, like they tell you in church, but there's your family to hold on to, and the future your kids will have.

"My little girl, she's eight years old; she asked me the other day if God pays attention to every person, and if He does, where does He get the time, and does He have the patience, or does He get tired? I told her it's not for me to know how God does His job, but I'll bet God thinks each grown-up person should have a job and should look after a few people and try to pitch in—to help people who are in trouble.

"My wife and I have always tried to teach our children to be good and kind. I don't believe in church on Sunday and let the Devil run the show the rest of the week. I don't believe in talking to your children about God and then teaching them to be cutthroat artists. I tell my children to stop themselves every few days and look up at the sky and listen to their conscience and remember what they should believe in: Give out as good as you want to get.

"That was my father's philosophy of life. He didn't have a lot of material things to give, but he had himself—a big person he was; and he was always there to make us think twice before we stayed mean too long, and he was always there to make us realize the world doesn't circle around us. My wife says it's a real stroke of luck to be alive and living in this country and not a lot of other places; and I'll tell you, people ought to stop and say yes, that's right, and yes, I'm here, and I'm going to give of myself, the best I know how—and maybe tomorrow I'll find a way of being a better person. You try to think about this life and what you owe it, and you try to get your kids to think about this life, too, and what they owe it."

His reflectiveness, his effort at detachment and introspection in the midst of the press of everyday life, his struggle for decency and integrity and generosity in the face of inevitable self-centeredness (the sin of pride) with all its attendant psychological mischief, ought to qualify him, as much as anyone else in this land, as a humanist—

a person who draws upon and contributes to the tradition of the humanities. The humanities do not belong to one kind of person; they are part of the lives of ordinary people who have their own ways of struggling for coherence, for a compelling faith, for social vision, for an ethical position, for a sense of historical perspective.

Over a century ago, in Oxford, England, no less, Matthew Arnold urged novelists, poets, and critics to become actively engaged in social, economic, and political affairs—to bring their kind of sensibility to bear upon "the things of this world." He didn't have to send such a message to his contemporaries Charles Dickens or George Eliot; they kept their eyes carefully focused on the world and through their fiction held up a mirror to an entire nation. George Eliot, as a young woman, was constantly letting herself learn from the rural English people she would later write about so knowingly. Here at home, William Faulkner made it his business to spend long hours with his fellow townspeople of Oxford, Mississippi—watching their habits and customs, hearing their stories, learning from them as well as sharing their news and their bourbon. Where does the "real" Oxford end and the "made-up" Yoknapatawpha begin? Of course, Faulkner was an imaginative artist, a man who made brilliant use of his mind's dreams and fantasies. But he came home every day, from what could be called his field trips, a rich man. He had been willing to be taught by his neighbors and as a result had a lot to draw on as he sat at his desk writing.

The humanities demand that we heed the individual—each person worthy of respect, and no person unworthy of careful, patient regard. The humanities are blues and jazz; gospel songs and working songs; string quartets and opera librettos; folk art and abstract impressionist art; the rich literary legacy of nineteenth-century Concord, or of the twentieth-century South; the sayings and memories and rituals of countless millions of working people; the blunt, earthy self-justifications and avowals of desperate but determined migrant mothers; the wry, detached stories handed down on Indian reservations, in Eskimo villages, generation after generation; the cries of struggle and hope of Appalachia's people of the hollows, put into traditional ballads and bluegrass music; the photographs of Lewis Hine and Walker Evans and Russell Lee—ourselves presented to ourselves; the confident, qualified assertions of scholars; the frustrated, embittered social statements of ghetto teachers or children who at all costs want to get a grip on this puzzling, not-always-decent or fair world.

The humanities are Ralph Ellison's essays and the novel *Invisible Man*, so full of a writer's determination that race and poverty, still cruelly significant to a person's destiny, nevertheless are but partial statements—never enough to rob a person of his or her particularity. And the humanities are the essays and novels of Walker Percy, so full of wit and wisdom and shrewd moments of social analysis. The humanities are also the remarks of the New Orleans suburban people, the Louisiana bayou people Percy knows and learns from—whose remarks are indeed worthy of being recorded, transcribed, and added to an oral literature. And, too, the humanities are the musical sounds and the strong, spoken vernacular Ellison has taken pains in his writings to remind us of.

The humanities should strive to do justice to the richness and diversity of cultural life in a nation whose people are not, many of them, afraid to say what is on their minds as well as sing or draw or paint or write what is on their minds. They thereby cast penetrating, knowing, critical judgments on what is happening in the world—judgments that ought to be put on the record and acknowledged as part of America's cultural tradition.

Address at the installation of Joseph Duffey as director of the National Endowment for the Humanities, *Change,* February 1978

Character and Intellect

Before he was shot and especially when he was running for president (in 1968), George Wallace used to give himself much pleasure by poking fun at the smugness and arrogance of intellectuals. Sometimes he'd say that "all of them" are "snobs"; sometimes he'd become a bit discriminating: "a lot of them put on high and mighty airs." I have those quotes on paper—from a talk I had with him in the early part of 1968, before Dr. King and Robert Kennedy had been killed. When the governor was feeling expansive, generous, and unthreatened, he'd back off a bit, play the bemused, reflective Southern stoic: "I don't think college professors are all bad—just the noisy ones who forget what they don't know and grab everyone in sight to tell them what they do know."

He was not himself averse, of course, to grabbing a few listeners to hear his particular words of wisdom. In my experience, following him north on the campaign trail and watching him in action among his fellow Alabamians, he was especially successful with those listeners when he came up with one or another version of this question: "Have you ever heard one of those professors tell you what's right and what's wrong—they've got an opinion on everything—and then seen him get on a bike and fall all over himself or knock down ten people while taking himself for a ride?"

Not all that funny as one reads it in one's old notes or, surely, on this page. Still, many who heard him were not merely being mean or bitter when they applauded vigorously and gave him the familiar, encouraging salutations: "Atta boy, George," or "You said it," or "Amen." Nor will vaguely sociological epithets such as "redneck" or "cracker," or fancy psychological attributions such as "paranoid" quite do justice to the complexity of things—the shrewd observations, say, an unemployed Alabama steelworker could make in retrospect (1981):

You don't notice old George hitting away at college professors any more. Here in Birmingham the University [of Alabama] is our biggest employer. When I started out no one ever thought that would happen. Back then it was coal and it was steel, and I don't even think there was any university here; it was over in Tuscaloosa, and none of them branches. George knows where the votes are: he'll be slapping those professors on the back now, and calling them our best "natural resource"!

I wouldn't mind being a professor myself! My son went to college, and it's done him a lot of good. He has a job. Not like his old man! You ask me, we laugh at professors because they're an easy target. They don't have the money and power that bankers do, or the people who own U.S. Steel and Ford Motor Company, and like that, our corporations here in Birmingham and elsewhere in the country. So, you get your laughs off some guy—like our George used to say—who's all full of big thoughts, but he don't know how to tie his shoes or cross the street without causing a traffic jam; or he talks a big line in his classroom or his books but he's a sonofabitch to his own family or the lady who does the cleaning in his office or the one who answers his phone—and the students who want a second of his time, but he's out in space thinking, or he only associates with people like himself, or those who have something to offer him: a favor, some money, you know. . . .

I must say that those last two words, innocently added, it seemed— a sentence trailing off—managed to catch my attention and hold it fast. I looked sharply at the speaker, but he did not at all appear to be looking sharply at me! Nor had he spoken, I concluded, with a touch of irony, never mind with any portentous design. His "you know" was said in a matter-of-fact manner—was, in fact, one of his speaking tics, which ordinarily I edit with no qualms or apprehension. On this occasion, however, my nervousness was all too significantly persistent, even though we did go on and pursued other matters unselfconsciously. I *do* "know," I fear—as do so many of us who try to reconcile the studies we do (the intellectual life we pursue) with the demands (let us hope they are real and pressing!) made by our consciences—the moral life we also live. In that regard, we

sometimes try to make splits or divisions or distinctions that are
meant to help us (to continue with my Alabama friend's language)
not know—stop noticing ironic inconsistencies and paradoxical
contradictions. Yeats was, of course, more candid with himself,
pointedly if not brutally so: "The intellect of man is forced to choose/
Perfection of the life, or of the work,/And if it take the second must
refuse/A heavenly mansion, raging in the dark."

Needless to say, there are those who don't feel that the dramatic
alternatives posed by Yeats (a secular version of the theological either-
or Kierkegaard presented to us) quite do justice to the way this life
bears down upon people—and very important, the way some of us
respond to the various temptations or possibilities that appear, often
out of nowhere, it seems. Surely not a few of us with strong intellectual inclinations, convictions, and attainments have also managed
to attend the responsibilities of a home, a family, a membership in
a particular community—involvements with friends, colleagues,
neighbors. Nor does one want to ignore a contemporary possibility,
a consequence of a given culture, its preoccupations if not obsessions: a person who is so attentive to the creature comforts of his or
her life, and of course, its emotional aspects, that there is nothing
left of any importance—not even, say, "perfection of the work,"
never mind moral issues to confront or sacrifices to make on behalf
of others in distant communities or nations. (Talking about "raging
in the dark"—in this case the domain of the self!)

Put differently, Yeats may not have realized what some members
of the upper bourgeoisie might have to say about the duality he
evokes in the lines quoted above—as in this young man, just about
to graduate from one of our country's best-known law schools:

> I wanted to go to graduate school—in English and American
> Literature. I wrote my thesis in college on Melville. I was all
> excited. I had great hopes. But there's no future in graduate
> work—no jobs, no money. I switched to law, like many others.
> I don't like the law; I've been bored for three years. I'm sure I
> won't ever really like what I'm doing. I'll just go to a big firm in
> New York and stick it out. Why? Look, I want to live a certain
> kind of life, that's what matters to me: I want to enjoy myself; I
> want to have a good, comfortable home in the country; I want
> to travel; I want to understand myself—probably go into analy-

sis. I've had two years of therapy, and so has my girlfriend. Let's be blunt: we're from modest backgrounds, she and I, but we've learned all the tastes of the well-to-do Ivy League types! And those tastes cost! I wouldn't be comfortable on the small salaries teachers get, even college professors. I want to be able to live well, and I want my wife and kids to live well, and if I have to be bored at work for that to happen, then it's a small price to pay.

Besides, boredom is something you get bored with—eventually, I mean, you start forgetting to be bored! You remember, as soon as you're bored, that you've just bought a house, or you need a new Brooks Brothers suit, or your wife likes to go to Bonwit Teller's, or your shrink costs a lot and it's money well spent because it'll help your kids be a little less screwed up than you are! So, you start enjoying yourself—just like you have to do when you're studying in college. Well, not really *enjoying* yourself! But I've found education a pain, and yet I'm really glad I've gone through it, and I've enjoyed the success, the getting into the best schools, and I'm sure I'll enjoy my law work in the same way and for the same reasons—the results, what the work means, so far as the kind of life you live.

There is more, much more. At times I have sensed rather more self-assurance and nonchalance and intrepid certainty than the particular speaker may have actually felt. But he is, as he has often reminded me, not alone in his determination to have a certain kind of life—even if the work he does has, on its own merit, no great charm or satisfaction for him. The home he has in mind is, of course, no "heavenly mansion"; and I am sure his psychiatrist will help him, on the quick, if he feels himself "raging in the dark." Yet one wonders about the moral dimension of such a life, and, I suppose, one craves a contemporary poetic analysis of "this side of paradise": that American mix of consumerism, self-advancement, and self-cultivation, which is enabled by intellectual achievement of sorts. F. Scott Fitzgerald, too, one fears, along with Yeats, needs a successor: some of our particular high livers (or more mordantly, budding Gatsbys) belong to another breed.

Indeed, that young lawyer cannot be dismissed as frivolous—or as remarkably, noticeably uncouth. He has, I have to add, taken courses as an undergraduate in philosophy, even in moral reasoning. In law school he studied legal ethics. He has read widely, deeply; he majored in history and graduated summa cum laude with a thesis that examined an aspect of twentieth-century American politics. We have, then, a well-muscled intellect, and as we put it these days, a "stable personality." We even have a somewhat reflective young man, who has done his fair share of reading in Spinoza, Locke, Hume, Santayana, Whitehead. (I mention the philosophers he has mentioned seriously to me—not name-dropped—in the course of our conversations.) We have, too, someone in possession of that almost sacred present-day characteristic: "insight." ("My doctor has really helped me sort all these things out. I've been open with him, and I know where I'm ambivalent and where I'm not. I've thought out what my options are, and I think I know enough about my problems to keep them from dragging me down, or pushing me into a dead-end street.")

As the worn saying goes, someone who appears on the verge of "a long and happy life"! Intellect, he has often reminded me, brought such a fate to his doorstep: those A's in high school, those high test scores, the brilliant work at college, continued at law school. Among his A's were two in "moral reasoning." Moreover, I'm sure his psychiatrist is pleased with what gets called these days "progress." Is he not good, oh so good, at "reality-testing," as we put it? Hasn't he developed a variety of "coping skills"? Certainly he has proved himself "mature," able to handle "stress." His "psycho-sexual development" appears to be in good shape. He appears to have solved without undue difficulty his "identity crisis"; and I suspect that if yet another American tester or American researcher presented him with a number of moral scenarios of sorts—hypothetical situations to which he'd be asked to respond with what he judged to be the ethically "right" attitude or reaction or recommendation—he'd score very well indeed, as he has elsewhere in his triumphant educational career.

In his "American Scholar" address, Ralph Waldo Emerson insisted to his audience that "character is higher than intellect"; and in our time, the novelist Walker Percy has reminded us that one can "get all A's and flunk life." I keep mentioning these two writers and their just-quoted remarks to my students—to myself. I keep hoping that they (and I with them) can manage somehow to bridge the two worlds (it seems) Yeats constructs in those lines summoned here earlier: two worlds supposedly with two different kinds of inhabitants, their destinies quite distinctively separate. I keep wondering whether the law student I just brought in witness might not—with more or better therapy, with a different curriculum, with better, finer, more powerfully engaging and committed teachers—become in future years (well, even right now) a person of broader and deeper moral sensibility. I keep asking myself, as I read Emerson or Kierkegaard, Percy, Dickens, or Dostoevski, how to learn from them in such a way that my intellect grows, the intellects of my students grow—*but also* we become personally more decent and honorable human beings, meaning of higher character than was the case before.

How to do so—to enlarge our store of facts, our "creativity," our originality of perception, of performance—and not end up, as Yeats warned, well on the way to hell? How to redeem our lives—become morally more energetic and forthcoming? One ends with such rhetorical questions—in the hope against hope that the next moment's, the next day's hurdles will provide a chance to live out the start of some answers. But in this regard there is, perhaps, less we can take for granted (including those of us with walls covered by big-deal diplomas) than we may sometimes think.

American Poetry Review, September/October 1983

Life's Big Ironies

Novelists and poets try hard to appreciate and evoke the ironic strains of this life—the incongruities between appearance and reality always besetting us, if we care to attend closely. Social scientists, taking their cue from the natural scientists who are valued so highly in our Western industrial world, insist upon banishing ironies with all possible dispatch, if such can be done. The point is exploration: if the cobbler's son has no shoes, or the doctor's daughter seems chronically and inexplicably ill, then let's get on with it—find out why, and having done so, change the set of circumstances. Irony thus regarded becomes a kind of fanciful illusion of a decidedly reactionary character. I remember noticing in a certain Georgia city how odd it was, the repeated fires that plagued the homes of firefighters, one of whom I knew well. A friend of mine objected (correctly, I guess) to a certain heightened aestheticism he must have sensed: the delicious symmetry of those incidents. I was not, I hope, sadistically flushed, but I had commented on the peculiarly ironic nature of this particular series of news stories, and my friend wished I'd reserved my energy for his kind of inquiry: the underlying reason for a suspected collection of crimes—a vendetta perhaps, launched by criminals against a group of municipal employees who had insisted on doing their job all too well, thereby endangering some hitherto "protected" property-owning arsonists, anxious to keep collecting money from insurance companies.

Still, an appreciation of irony need not deteriorate into an abstract, self-centered, frivolous, or uncaring posture. Nor need irony become an end in itself, or an obstacle toward further exploration of this life's nature, this world's evils. Often enough, the presence of irony provides a reminder or a signal, if not an important warning. Irony may offer us the best hint we may get of vulnerability or jeopardy. "I'm always fighting violent people," a police officer told me when I was doing one of those research projects my ilk favors, "and I guess one day the enemy will infiltrate my home." He knew, by then, that more than a few of his son's friends had been caught speeding in cars, while tanked up on beer. He also knew the burden and temptation his work placed on his sons, especially: "My daughters seem to be law-abiding; my sons want to test the law, or break it—minor delinquency, so far, and I hope it will all end soon. It's hard having a cop for a father, just like it's hard being a cop—I mean, a clean cop."

He stopped then, to muse—and so did I: a *second* irony, with those last two words! He'd told me weeks earlier stories that chilled me—about crooked cops, and yes, firefighters who helped dishonest, crafty real estate owners collect mounds of money on the fire insurance they'd bought on already broken down tenement houses, which mysteriously caught fire. I remember, at the time, thinking of that old canard—or is there some substantial truth to it?—namely, the noticeable number of psychiatrists whose children seem wayward, or who themselves seem dour and grumpy, or nervously difficult, or plain nuts. In fact, my police officer friend allowed irony to help him collect his senses—and maybe, help someone else do likewise: "I guess you're always most sensitive to the things that matter to you," he observed. Then he broadened his remarks: "If you spend your life fighting crime, you'll be a set-up for one of your kids who wants to fight you! He'll flirt with what's your soft spot! It's like a kid of yours [a doctor's] pretending to be sick, or making himself sick, to catch the old man's attention or shame him. By the same token, when a cop gets cozy with thieves, or a fireman sets a fire—that's turning everything upside down. It's like a lawyer becoming a robber—breaking the law, not upholding it—and it's like a doctor trying to do in a patient, not heal him, maybe for some money from a relative!"

All of the above is not, alas, mere anecdotal reportage. On the grandest scale, in this century, we have witnessed ironies that have (one hopes) given us pause, at the very least. A revolution presumably meant not only to oust a czar but to achieve bread, work, freedom, and justice for the poor and humble of Russia soon enough ended up offering the obscene and vile spectacle of Stalin and his murderous henchmen. Lenin saw, in the last months of his life, a glimmer of a terrible, forthcoming evil; Trotsky died at its hands. Both of these ideologues, like Marx before them, had proclaimed the necessity, the historical virtue of a "dictatorship of the proletariat," and if that dictatorship has made the czar seem like an exceptionally kind and generous and thoughtful leader—well, so much for the irony of history's "dialectic." As for the *scientific* basis of Marxism-Leninism and its well-known and loudly proclaimed aversion to an "opiate" such as religion, the Lenin Mausoleum and those placards of Karl Marx paraded here, there, and everywhere are twentieth-century artifacts of sorts—ironic lessons for us: those who scorn the beliefs of others do not, thereby, prove themselves without their own tenacious articles of faith.

As for my own profession, the psychoanalytic speculation that gave the world *The Future of an Illusion* has not proved adequate as a warning against idolatry, some of it as mean-spirited and arrogant and condescending as the Crusades at their worst proved to be. In the name of clear-headed science, many of us in psychiatry have become pushy advocates of one or another point of view—and have not hesitated to insult if not villify those who disagree with us. Our chief weapon, alas, in these sectarian struggles has been the old exclusionary one of character assassination—a kind of *ad hominem* (and *ad feminam*) truculence lent enormous power by a general culture obsessed by psychology and all too willing to heed it if not fall in prayer before its tenets, some of them rank speculation if not assertive propositions (as in so many disciplines) of those on the professional make. No wonder, long ago, Clara Thompson left a meeting of the New York Psychoanalytic Institute with the hymn "Go Down Moses" on her lips—a terribly sad moment, and a reminder that we can "repress" not only our sexuality and our aggressive inclinations but our hunger for faith, for membership in a community of believers.

When I see my kind (after years and years of clinical training and supervision and personal analysis) torn by angry disagreements and splits; when I see grown men and women, well educated and supposedly well aware of the reasons for their conflicts, nevertheless demonstrating nasty, envious, rude behavior towards others, be they colleagues, students, or fellow citizens, then I realize, yet again, that "aggression" is not only something postulated by eager theorists but is part of everyone's life, including theirs—no matter the education, the accumulation of credentials, the recognition accorded by universities, hospitals, and training institutes. Whether we have, indeed, gained all that much by abandoning "the sin of pride" in favor of "the aggressive drive" or "narcissism" is, perhaps, a matter for earnest (and not, one prays, haughty and self-important) discussion. As for the concept of "narcissism," it has recently provided quite a special source of irony for all of us—the example of exponents of one or another notion of "narcissism" engaging in strong and often bitter enough confrontations, yes, narcissistic ones, occasioned by those old familiars of human experience: rivalry, envy, ambition.

Nor have the world's political and military and ideological struggles been without their unhappy, even tragic, ironies. In Vietnam, those who fought European colonialism have shown themselves quite able to subdue their neighbors, quite able to be brutally self-serving, fiercely opportunistic, corruptly insensitive to their own stated historical and social purposes. In Nicaragua, those who fought tyrants have not been without their own tyrannical lapses, as a number of that nation's hurt and vulnerable Indian people have had cause to observe, and too, some of the decent and honorable people who fought long and hard on the Sandinista side. In Africa, too, black despots, cruel and murderous, have replaced, all too often, their white colonialist predecessors. One need not be an apologist for South Africa's government to observe that thousands and thousands of blacks have been murdered by their fellow black oppressors, and not only in the well-known instance of Uganda but in countries such as Rwanda and Burundi, right near South Africa's borders. We who are white and who are concerned with racism anywhere and everywhere are justifiably quick to be alarmed and enraged by news that arrives from Johannesburg or Cape Town but instructively silent, not rarely, when we learn of massacres in, say, Zaire, or yes, drastic infringements on the civil and political rights of the people of such "socialist" countries as Tanzania or Zambia. Sometimes it is not only our silence that proves ironic; we mobilize strange justifications or apologies or excuses—maybe even racist ones: as if black people aren't entitled to the same sympathy, in the face of viciously implacable statism, that the people of, say, Poland or Czechoslovakia have quite justifiably obtained from us.

When Thomas Hardy gave us the phrase "life's little ironies," he had in mind, of course, the continuing distance, in all of us, between intention and actuality—between our stated intentions about how this life should be lived and the manner in which fate and circumstance, chance and accident and incident, end up shaping the particular destiny that is ours. It never occurred to him, one suspects, that he was summoning (God save us!) what some of today's social scientists, in their heavy-handed and dreary fashion, might call "a methodological tool of historical analysis"—irony as a mode of social reflection. Yet, a century that has witnessed so much violence, so much self-righteousness, so much intellectual presumptuousness—while all the while laying claim to more and more progress in the name of science, in the name of technology, in the name of mental exploration and political analysis and sociological investigation—such a century, surely, can begin to give us all some little pause. Did Hardy, after all, know something that some of "our" giants overlooked—Marx and Freud and all sorts of other social and political visionaries: that life's little ironies offer, in their sum, a big lesson for us about ourselves, our limited possibilities, and the ever-present danger that faces us as the creature who has never yet been rid of a capacity for self-deception and polemical nastiness, though also able occasionally (please God) to demonstrate generosity, moral courage, and fair-minded compassion?

American Poetry Review, January/February 1983